ADVANCED ACCOUNTING
Student Manual

Richard Bozec Ph.D., CPA, CGA

Advanced Accounting: Student Manual
2ᵉ Edition

Richard Bozec Ph.D., CPA, CGA

Editor: Parmitech
Interior and Cover Design: Parmitech

Copyright © 2020, Parmitech, Ottawa.
Parmitech. All rights reserved.

This publication is protected by copyright, and permission should be obtained from the publisher prior to any prohibited reproduction, storage in a retrieval system, or transmission in any form or by any means, electronic, mechanical, photocopying, recording, or otherwise.

Printed in Canada

ISBN 978-0-9739225-8-5

PREFACE

About the Manual

The objective of this manual is to satisfy the need of today's accounting students by providing relevant, contemporary, and engaging material in advanced accounting. In contrast to available textbooks, the building-block approach and user-friendly style privileged by the author make the material much easier for students to comprehend and apply. The manual presents an overview of the basics of intercorporate investments, business combinations, consolidation of financial statements, and foreign currency transactions under IFRS. For each module, the fundamental concepts are introduced prior to advancing to the procedures. The content of the manual is logically organized and integrated so as to provide a quick and easy to follow review of current advanced accounting topics. The manual includes comprehensive illustrations, end-of-module review questions, quizzes and exercises.

The building-block approach used in this manual to illustrate the consolidation of financial statements is summarized below.

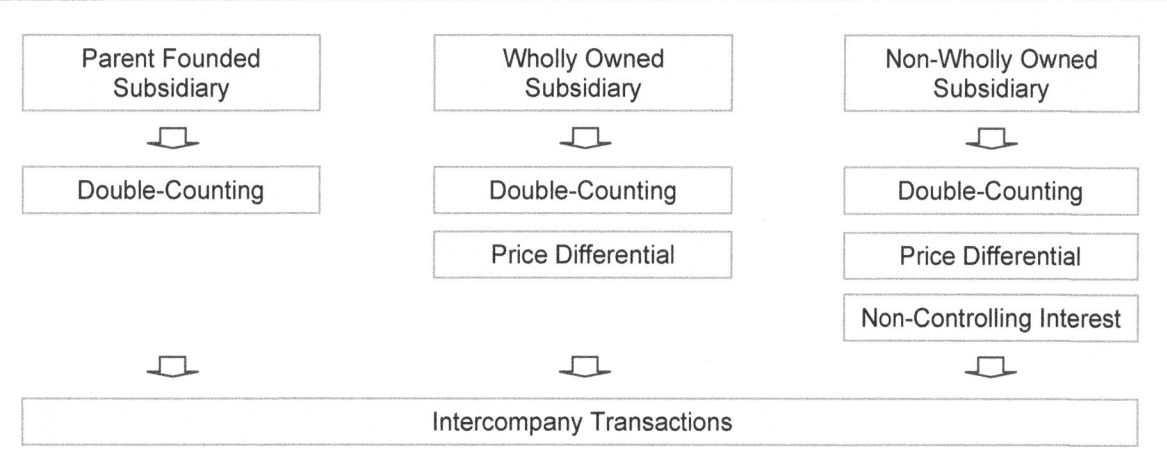

About the Author

Richard Bozec Ph.D, CPA, CGA, is Full Professor of Accounting at the Telfer School of Management, University of Ottawa. He teaches financial accounting at the undergraduate and graduate levels (Ph.D.) in both French and English. His main research interests are in the field of Corporate Governance.

Supplemental Material

This manual provides supplemental material for users of *Consolidation of Financial Statements Under IFRS: A Visual Approach* (2016) from the same author.

For more information, please visit the editor's website, Parmitech, at: www.parmitech.com

CONTENTS

Module 1 — Accounting for Control Relationships: Introduction

1. SHARE INVESTMENTS: TYPOLOGY
2. CONTROL RELATIONSHIPS: DEFINITION
3. CONSOLIDATION OF F/S: OBJECTIVES, PROCESS AND BENEFITS
4. ALTERNATIVE ACCOUNTING METHODS FOR PRIVATE ENTITIES

APPENDIX A: NON-STRATEGIC INVESTMENTS: FV METHODS
APPENDIX B: INVESTMENTS IN ASSOCIATES: EQUITY METHOD

Exercises and Solutions

Module 2 — Consolidation of Parent Founded Subsidiaries

1. CONSOLIDATION OF PARENT FOUNDED SUBSIDIARIES AT THE DATE OF CREATION : THE DOUBLE-COUNTING ISSUE
2. INTERCOMPANY TRANSACTIONS: INTRODUCTION
3. CONSOLIDATION OF PARENT FOUNDED SUBSIDIARIES IN PERIODS SUBSEQUENT TO THE DATE OF CREATION
4. EQUITY METHOD

Exercises and Solutions

Module 3 — Business Combinations

1. INTRODUCTION TO BUSINESS COMBINATIONS
2. ACCOUNTING FOR BUSINESS COMBINATIONS
3. PURCHASE OF NET ASSETS: ILLUSTRATION
4. CONSOLIDATION OF WHOLLY OWNED SUBSIDIARIES AT THE DATE OF ACQUISITION: ILLUSTRATION
5. MERGER

Exercises and Solutions

Module 4 — Consolidation of Wholly Owned Subsidiaries: Reporting Subsequent to Acquisition

1. CONSOLIDATION OF WHOLLY OWNED SUBSIDIARIES IN PERIODS SUBSEQUENT TO THE DATE OF ACQUISITION
2. EQUITY METHOD
3. PRICE DIFFERENTIAL: ADDITIONAL CONSIDERATIONS

Exercises and Solutions

Module 5 Intercompany Transactions

1. INTERCOMPANY TRANSACTIONS: BASIC PRINCIPLES
2. INTERCOMPANY SALES OF NON-DEPRECIABLE ASSETS
3. INTERCOMPANY SALES OF INVENTORY
4. INTERCOMPANY SALES OF DEPRECIABLE ASSETS
5. INTERCOMPANY LOSSES

Exercises and Solutions

Module 6 Consolidation of Wholly Owned Subsidiaries Subsequent to Acquisition: Comprehensive Illustration

Exercises and Solutions

Module 7 Consolidation of Non-Wholly Owned Subsidiaries

1. CONSOLIDATION THEORIES
2. CONSOLIDATION OF NON-WHOLLY OWNED SUBSIDIARIES AT THE DATE OF ACQUISITION
3. CONSOLIDATION OF NON-WHOLLY OWNED SUBSIDIARIES SUBSEQUENT TO THE DATE OF ACQUISITION
4. EQUITY METHOD

APPENDIX:
CONSOLIDATION OF NON-WHOLLY OWNED SUBSIDIARIES UNDER THE BV APPROACH

Exercises and Solutions

Module 8 Other Consolidation Issues

1. JOINT VENTURES
2. CHANGES IN OWNERSHIP INTERESTS
3. MULTIPLE INVESTMENTS SITUATIONS
4. INCOME TAX ALLOCATION
5. PUSH-DOWN ACCOUNTING
6. CONTINGENT CONSIDERATION
7. INTERIM ACQUISITIONS
8. SUBSIDIARY WITH PREFERRED SHARES

Module 9 — Foreign Currency Transactions and Hedging Activities

1. ACCOUNTING FOR FOREIGN CURRENCY TRANSACTIONS
2. HEDGING ACTIVITIES USING A FORWARD CONTRACT
3. HEDGE ACCOUNTING

Exercises and Solutions

Module 10 — Reporting Foreign Operations

1. FUNCTIONAL CURRENCY versus PRESENTATION CURRENCY
2. TRANSLATION OF FINANCIAL STATEMENTS OF PARENT FOUNDED FOREIGN SUBSIDIARIES
3. TRANSLATION OF FINANCIAL STATEMENTS OF ACQUIRED FOREIGN SUBSIDIARIES
4. RECAP

Exercises and Solutions

EXERCISES

Module 1

1.1	Cost versus Equity Reporting
1.2	Acquisition Price
1.3	Investment Income
1.4	Journal Entries under the Equity Method

Module 2

2.1	Transfer of Net Assets at the Establishment of a New Subsidiary
2.2	Data from Consolidated Income Statement of Newly Established Subsidiary
2.3	Investment Account in a Newly Established Subsidiary
2.4	Accounting for a Newly Established Subsidiary
2.5	Consolidation One Year Post-Creation
2.6	Newly Established Subsidiary and Equity Method

Module 3

3.1	Stock Acquisition with Cash
3.2	Stock Acquisition with Bonds
3.3	Purchase of Net Assets with Cash
3.4	Consolidation at Date of Acquisition (no Goodwill)
3.5	Purchase of Net Assets: Post-Acquisition SFPs
3.6	Negative Goodwill
3.7	Stock Acquisition versus Purchase of Net Assets
3.8	From Case 3: Global Inc.
3.9	Consolidation at Date of Acquisition (with Goodwill)

Module 4

4.1	Consolidated versus Separate-Entity Statements
4.2	Equity Method Subsequent to Acquisition (with no intercompany transactions)
4.3	Equity Method and Net Adjusted Value Subsequent to Acquisition (with no intercompany transactions)
4.4	Worksheet Approach and Equity Method Subsequent to Acquisition (with no intercompany transactions)

Module 5

5.1	Downstream Sale of Truck
5.2	Upstream Sale of Land
5.3	Downstream Sale of Equipment (1)
5.4	Downstream Sale of Equipment (2)
5.5	Upstream Sale of Equipment & Consolidated Comprehensive Income
5.6	Downstream Sale of Land & Consolidated Comprehensive Income
5.7	Downstream Sale of Inventory
5.8	Upstream Sale of Inventory
5.9	Consolidated versus Separate-Entity Statements
5.10	Intercompany Transactions and Worksheet Adjustments (1)
5.11	Intercompany Transactions and Worksheet Adjustments (2)
5.12	Intragroup Transactions & Consolidated Comprehensive Income

EXERCISES
(Continued)

Module 6

6.1	Multiple-Choice Questions
6.2	Consolidation Subsequent to Acquisition: Direct Approach and Equity Method
6.3	Consolidation Subsequent to Acquisition: Direct Approach
6.4	Consolidation Subsequent to Acquisition: Worksheet Approach
6.5	Continuation of Plus Inc. (Case 7) in Year X8
6.6	Continuation of Plus Inc. (Case 7) in Year X9
6.7	Consolidated Retained Earnings
6.8	Consolidation Subsequent to Acquisition and Negative Goodwill

Module 7

7.1	Partial Control: Direct Approach and Worksheet Approach
7.2	Valuation of NCI at Date of Acquisition
7.3	Consolidation Subsequent to Acquisition: NCI, Profit and Retained Earnings
7.4	Consolidation Subsequent to Acquisition with NCI: Worksheet Approach
7.5	Consolidated F/S, NCI, Profit and Retained Earnings
7.6	Partial Control: Consolidation and Equity Method
7.7	Partial Control: Worksheet/Direct Approach and Equity Method (Year 5)
7.8	Partial Control: Worksheet/Direct Approach and Equity Method (Year 6)
7.9	Partial Control: Worksheet/Direct Approach and Equity Method (Year 7)
7.10	Partial Control: Direct Approach and Equity Method

Module 9

9.1	Loan in US Dollar
9.2	Receivables in Pounds Sterling
9.3	Receivables in Pesos
9.4	Monetary Balances in Euros
9.5	Forward Contract to Hedge a Liability
9.6	Forward Contract to Hedge a Receivable

Module 10

10.1	Translation - Statement of Financial Position
10.2	Translation - Income Statement
10.3	Translation of Financial Statements and Translation Gain/Loss
10.4	Translation of Financial Statements

Accounting for Control Relationships : Introduction

Module 1

What you will find in this section

- How to Walk Through Module 1
- Slides
- Exercises and Solutions

Module 1
Accounting for Control Relationships: Introduction

How to Walk Through Module 1

◇ <u>Readings</u>

1- <u>Book</u> "Consolidation of Financial Statements": Introduction
2- <u>Student Manual</u> "Advanced Accounting": Module 1
   PART 1: SHARE INVESTMENTS: TYPOLOGY
   PART 2: CONTROL RELATIONSHIPS: DEFINITION
   PART 3: CONSOLIDATION OF F/S: OBJECTIVES, PROCESS AND BENEFITS
   PART 4: ALTERNATIVE ACCOUNTING METHODS FOR PRIVATE ENTITIES

APPENDIX A
NON-STRATEGIC INVESTMENTS: FV METHODS
APPENDIX B
INVESTMENTS IN ASSOCIATES: EQUITY METHOD

◇ <u>Assignments</u>

3- <u>Student Manual</u>: End-of module review questions
4- <u>Student Manual</u>: Exercises 1 to 4

◇ <u>Additional readings</u>

5- <u>IAS</u> 28; <u>IFRS</u> 10, 12

When you have successfully completed this module, you will be able to do the following:

- Describe the conditions for the use of consolidation;

- Identify the proper accounting treatment for intercorporate share investments including the Cost method, the Equity method, and Fair value methods.

ACCOUNTING FOR CONTROL RELATIONSHIPS: INTRODUCTION
Module 1

Copyright © 2020 Parmitech

Advanced Accounting: Student Manual

Copyrighted Material

Editor: Parmitech

This publication is protected by copyright, and permission should be obtained from the publisher prior to any prohibited reproduction, storage in a retrieval system, or transmission in any form or by any means, electronic, mechanical, photocopying, recording, or otherwise.

Corresponding Author

Richard Bozec Ph.D., CPA, CGA
bozec@telfer.uottawa.ca

Copyright © Parmitech

TEACHING MATERIAL
Electronic Sources

IFRS

IFRS 10   Consolidated Financial Statements

IAS 28   Investments in Associates

IFRS 12   Disclosure of Interests in Other Entities

TEACHING MATERIAL
Exercises

Module 1

- **1.1**   Cost versus Equity Reporting
- **1.2**   Acquisition Price
- **1.3**   Investment Income
- **1.4**   Journal Entries under the Equity Method

OUTLINE OF THE PRESENTATION

1. SHARE INVESTMENTS: TYPOLOGY
2. CONTROL RELATIONSHIPS: DEFINITION
3. CONSOLIDATION OF F/S: OBJECTIVES, PROCESS, BENEFITS
4. ALTERNATIVE ACCOUNTING METHODS FOR PRIVATE ENTITIES

---------- *APPENDIXES* ----------

A. NON-STRATEGIC INVESTMENTS: FV METHODS
B. INVESTMENTS IN ASSOCIATES: EQUITY METHOD

Introduction ---------- Module 1 ---------- 5

RECAP

5. REVIEW QUESTIONS
6. QUIZ QUESTIONS
7. KEY TERMS INTRODUCED IN THIS MODULE
8. RECAP ON THE OBJECTIVES OF THIS MODULE

Introduction ---------- Module 1 ---------- 6

PART 1
Share Investments: Typology

Objectives of this section

Present the different types of share investments, including non-strategic and strategic investments.

Introduce the proper accounting treatment for both passive and strategic investments.

Key concepts

- Strategic vs. Non-strategic investments
- Portfolio investments
- Investments in Associates
- Controlled Entities

INTERCORPORATE SHARE INVESTMENTS
Typology

Investments

NON-STRATEGIC
(Passive Investments)
- Fair Value Through Profit or Loss (**FVTPL**)
- Fair Value Through OCI (**FVTOCI**)

STRATEGIC
- Associates
- Controlled Entities:
  - Subsidiaries
  - Structured Entities
  - Joint Ventures

Financial Assets - IFRS 9   Non-Financial Assets

Part 1

INTERCORPORATE SHARE INVESTMENTS
Non-Strategic Investments

FVTPL

Trading in securities is what financial institutions do. Brokers, banks, pension funds, and other financial institutions make some of their money by actively trading securities on the open market. Trading securities are classified as **FVTPL** investments and reported at market value. If such a value is not available, it has to be estimated. In such a case, we could use the current market value of a similar security or a valuation technique like the option pricing model. Changes in value (realized and unrealized) are reported in the statement of comprehensive income.

The vast majority of other corporations (non-financial corporations) do not have trading securities. Instead, they hold **available-for-sale securities**.

Introduction ---------- Module 1 ---------- 9

Part 1

INTERCORPORATE SHARE INVESTMENTS
Objectives

Investments

NON-STRATEGIC
Earn dividends and/or profits by actively trading the shares for short-term profits.

STRATEGIC
Control or significantly influence the operations of the investee corporation.

Short-term   Long-term

Introduction ---------- Module 1 ---------- 10

Part 1

CONTROLLED ENTITIES
Typology

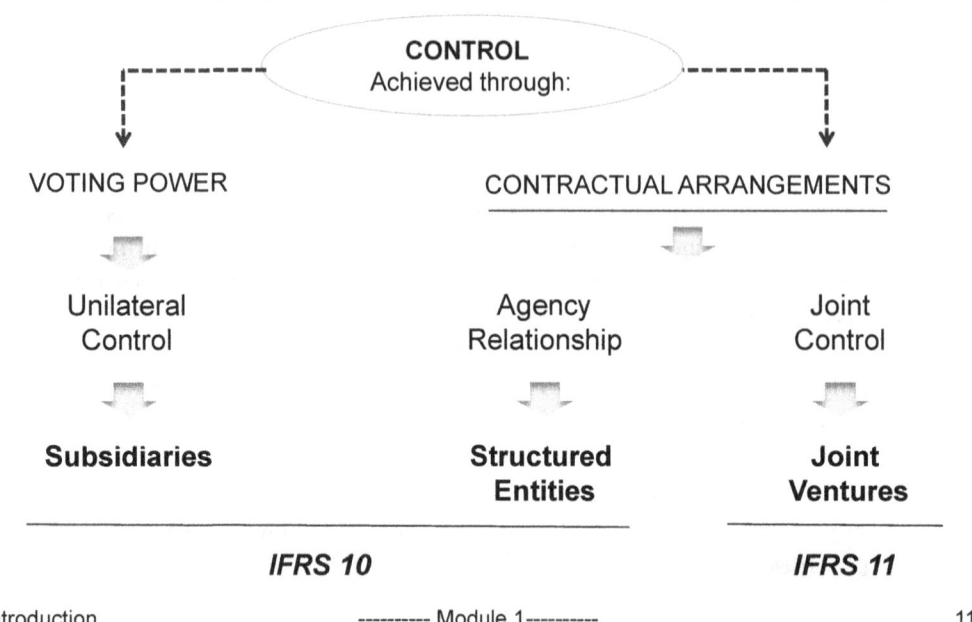

CONTROL Achieved through:

- VOTING POWER
  - Unilateral Control
    - **Subsidiaries**
- CONTRACTUAL ARRANGEMENTS
  - Agency Relationship
    - **Structured Entities**
  - Joint Control
    - **Joint Ventures**

IFRS 10 (Subsidiaries, Structured Entities) — *IFRS 11* (Joint Ventures)

Introduction ---------- Module 1 ---------- 11

Part 1

CONTROLLED ENTITIES via VOTING POWER
Contexts

SUBSIDIARIES

- **CREATED**
  - Legal Process
  - **Module 2**
- **ACQUIRED**
  - Business Combination
  - **Module 3**

A parent-subsidiary relationship is created between two companies when one holds a controlling interest in the other (as defined in this module). One parent company can establish several subsidiaries, all under its control. Companies with multiple subsidiaries and no primary business activities of their own are also known as holding companies. A parent company can create a new subsidiary from within (Parent founded subsidiary) or take over a controlling interest in an existing company (Acquired subsidiary).

Introduction ---------- Module 1 ---------- 12

Part 1

INTERCORPORATE SHARE INVESTMENTS
Conceptual Basis for Classification Based on Voting Power

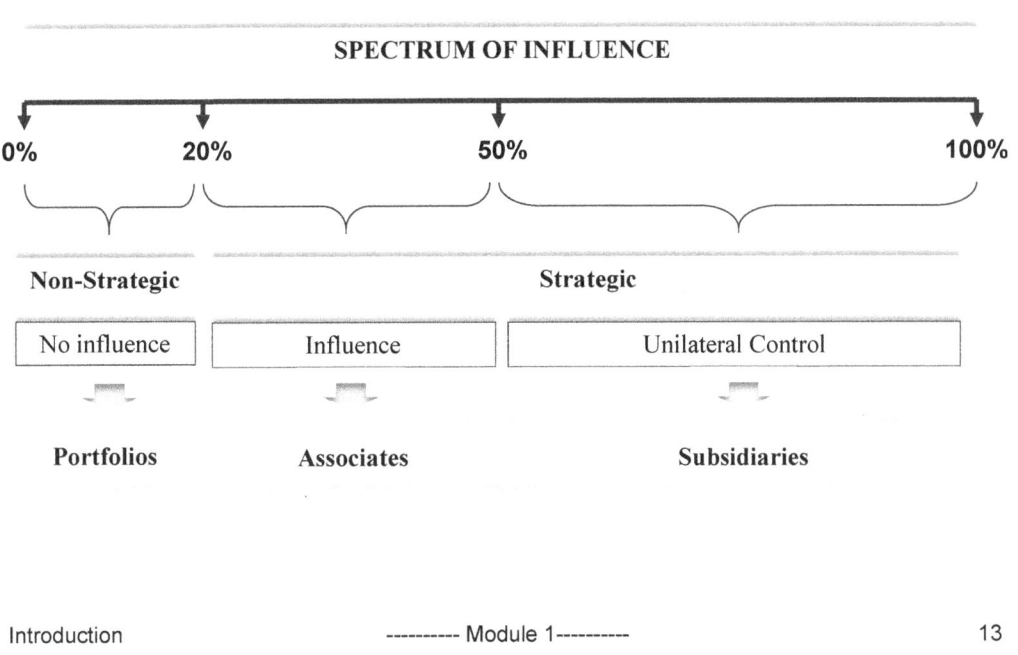

Part 1

INTERCORPORATE SHARE INVESTMENTS
How to Compute Ownership Interest

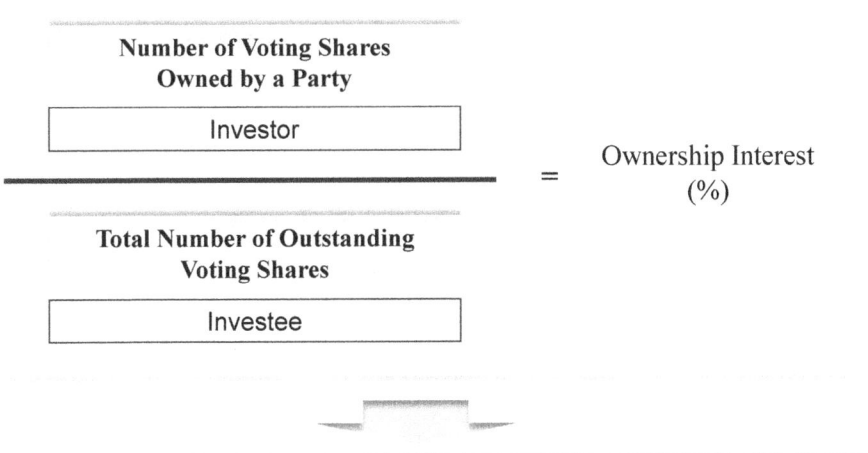

Use the number of voting rights instead of voting shares if the investee holds dual-class shares.

Part 1

ACCOUNTING FOR INTERCORPORATE SHARE INVESTMENTS
Accounting Methods

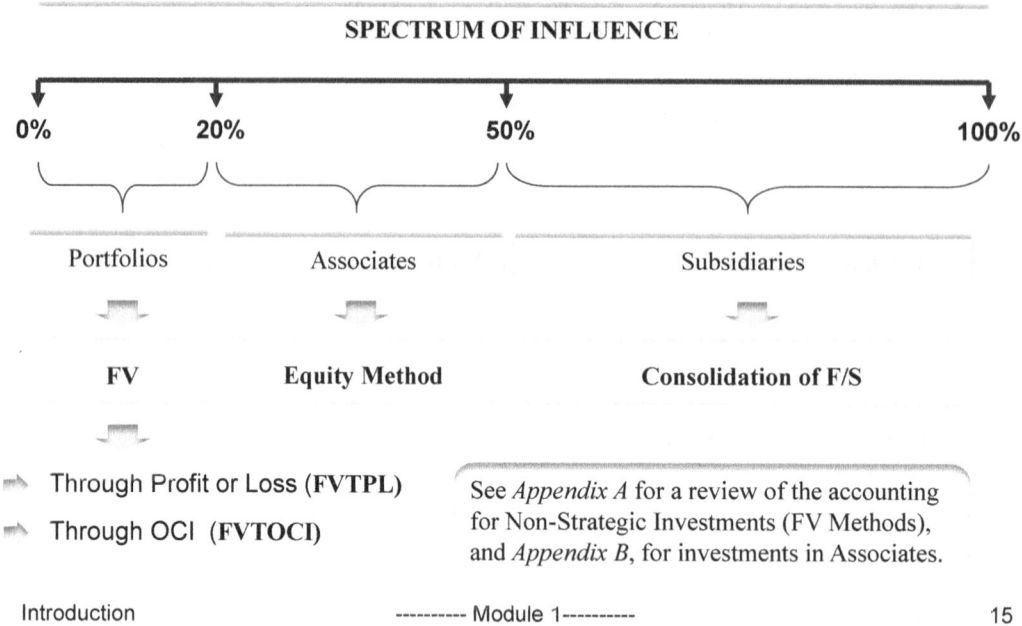

See *Appendix A* for a review of the accounting for Non-Strategic Investments (FV Methods), and *Appendix B*, for investments in Associates.

Part 1

CONTROLLED ENTITIES via CONTRACTUAL RIGHTS
Structured Entities or Special Purpose Entities (SPE)

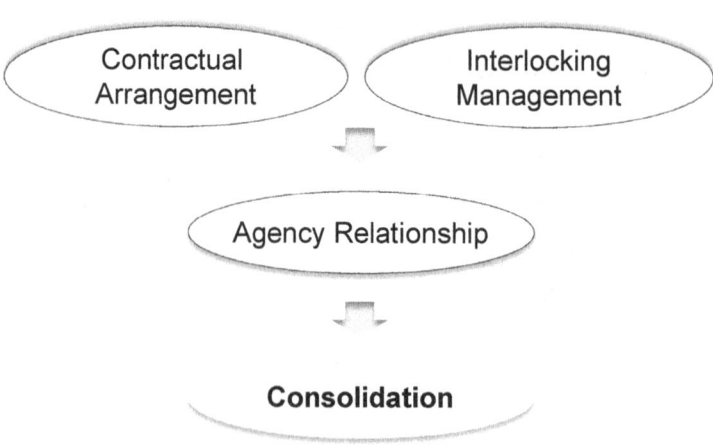

Part 1

CONTROLLED ENTITIES via CONTRACTUAL RIGHTS
Joint Ventures - IFRS 11 - Module 8

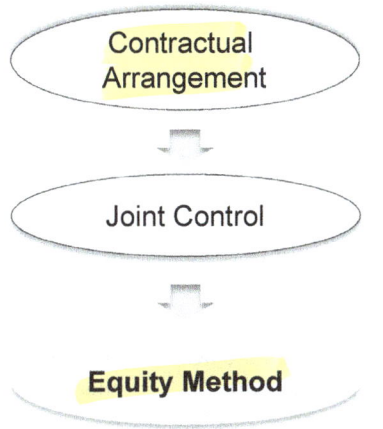

A jointly controlled entity operates in the same way as other entities, except that a contractual arrangement between the venturers establishes joint control over the economic activity of the entity.

No co-venturer controls the joint venture. Instead, major decisions require the consent of all of the co-venturers, no consideration given to their ownership.

Part 1

FLOWCHART OF KEY INTERNATIONAL STANDARDS

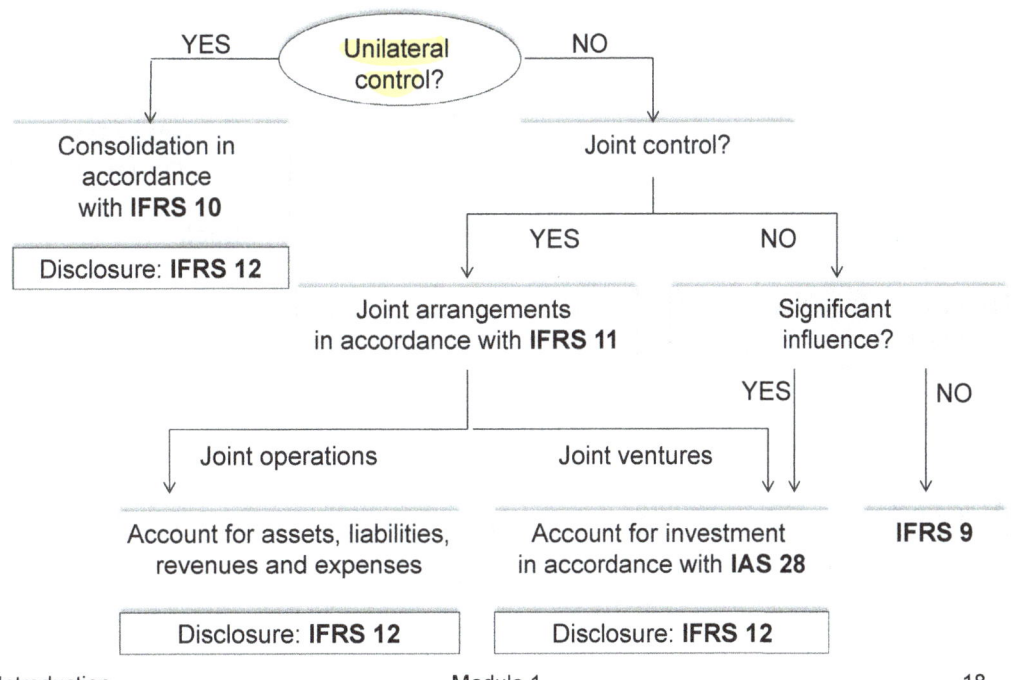

SHARE INVESTMENTS
Key International Standards

Part 1

- IAS 28 Investments in Associates
- IFRS 3 Business Combinations
- IFRS 9 Financial Instruments
- IFRS 10 Consolidated Financial Statements
- IFRS 11 Joint Arrangements
- IFRS 12 Disclosure of Interests in Other Entities

IFRS 10 Consolidated Financial Statements outlines the requirements for the preparation and presentation of consolidated financial statements, requiring entities to consolidate entities under their control.

Introduction ---------- Module 1 ---------- 19

TEACHING MATERIAL
Main Objective

Part 1

Objective
Illustrate the basics of consolidation in the context of a Parent – Subsidiary relationship using a building-block approach.
Modules 2 – 7

Specific consolidation issues are covered in **Module 8.**

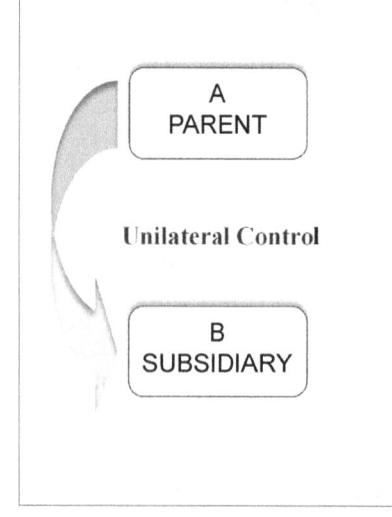

Student Manual
Advanced Accounting

Book
Consolidation of Financial Statements Under IFRS

From Richard Bozec, PhD.

Introduction ---------- Module 1 ---------- 20

Part 1

TEACHING MATERIAL
Building-Block Approach

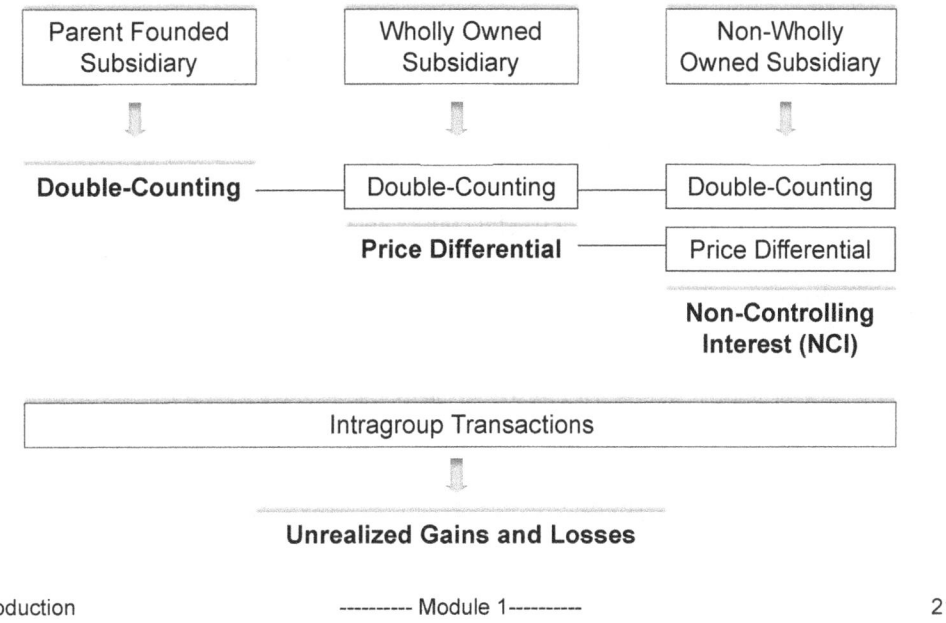

Introduction ---------- Module 1---------- 21

Part 1

TEACHING MATERIAL
About the Cases in the Textbook

Cases	Parent Founded	Full Control	Partial Control	Intragroup Transactions
1	X			X
2	X			X
3		X		
4		X		
5		X		X
6		X		X
7		X		X
8			X	
9			X	X
10			X	X

Introduction ---------- Module 1---------- 22

OUTLINE OF THE PRESENTATION

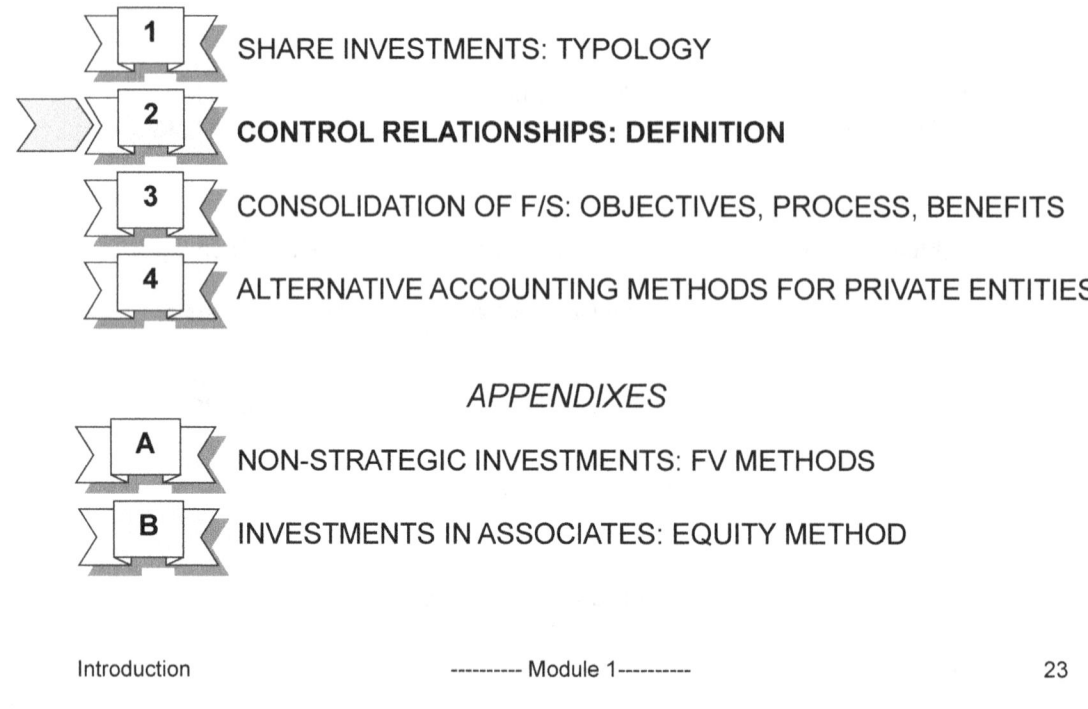

1. SHARE INVESTMENTS: TYPOLOGY
2. **CONTROL RELATIONSHIPS: DEFINITION**
3. CONSOLIDATION OF F/S: OBJECTIVES, PROCESS, BENEFITS
4. ALTERNATIVE ACCOUNTING METHODS FOR PRIVATE ENTITIES

APPENDIXES

A. NON-STRATEGIC INVESTMENTS: FV METHODS

B. INVESTMENTS IN ASSOCIATES: EQUITY METHOD

PART 2
Control Relationship: Definition

Objectives of this section

Define *control*.

Key concepts

- Control, direct, indirect, absolute, de facto
- Subsidiary
- Parent company
- Special Purpose Entity (SPE) or Structured Entity

Part 2

DEFINITION OF CONTROL
Single Model since 2013 (IFRS 10)

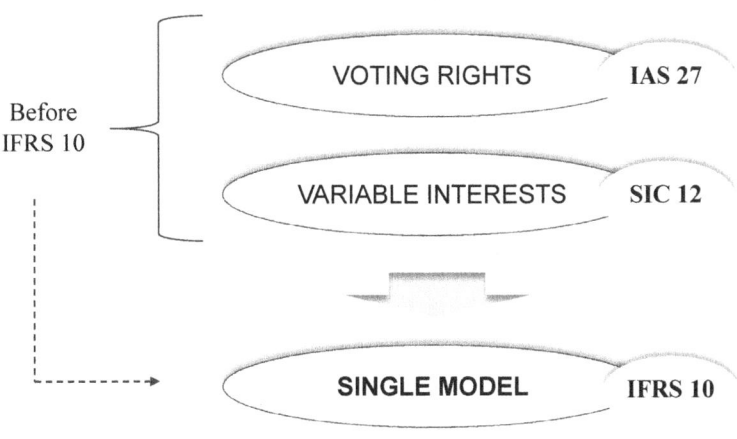

Since 2013, IFRS 10 provides a single consolidation model that identifies control as the basis for consolidation for all types of entities. IFRS 10 & 12 replaced IAS 27 and SIC-12.

Introduction ---------- Module 1 ---------- 25

Part 2

CLASSICAL DEFINITION OF CONTROL
Voting Interest Model

IAS 27

A **parent** is an entity that controls one or more entities.

A **subsidiary** is an entity that is controlled by another entity (ie the parent).

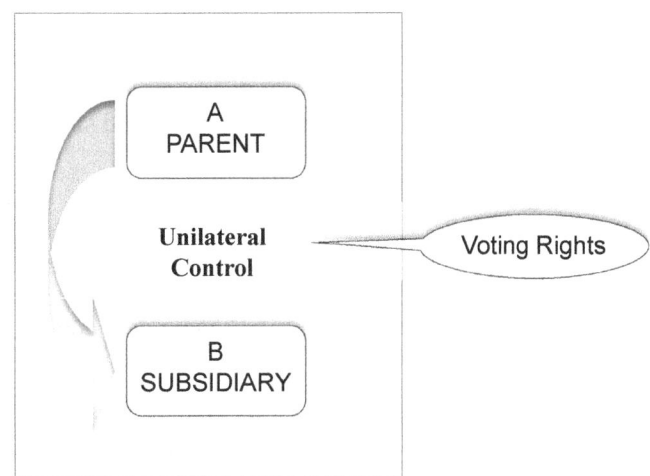

Firm A, the **Parent**, controls Firm B, the **Subsidiary**.

Introduction ---------- Module 1 ---------- 26

Part 2

IAS 27

CONTROL WITH VOTING RIGHTS
Corporations

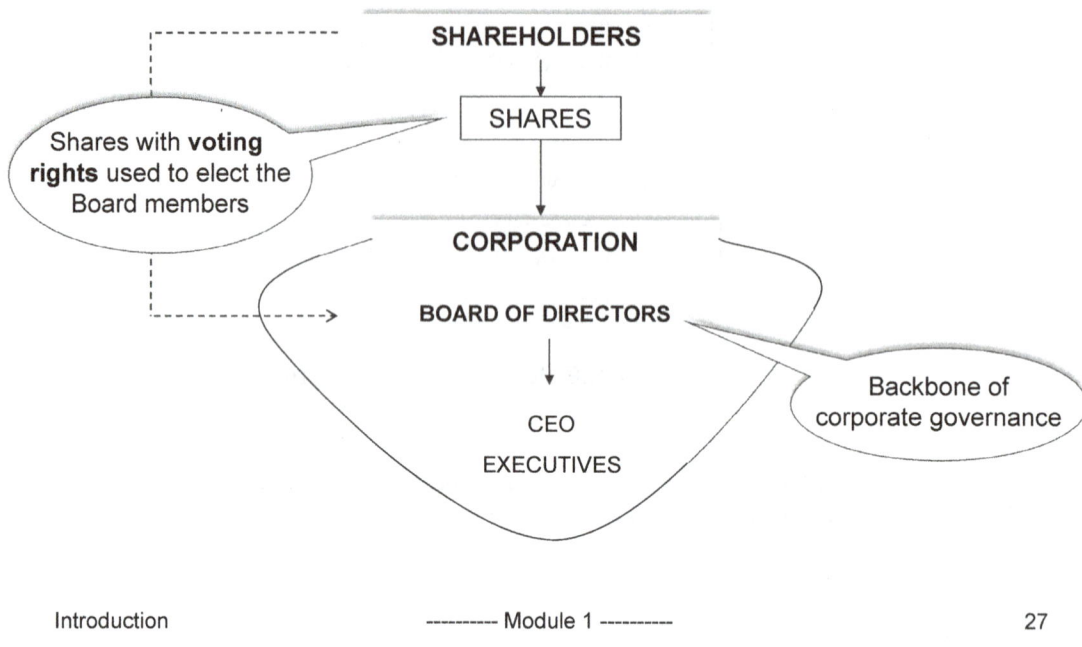

Introduction ---------- Module 1 ---------- 27

Part 2

IAS 27

CONTROL WITH VOTING RIGHTS
Key Role of the Board of Directors

The **board of directors** is the backbone of corporate governance.

The board determines a corporation's strategic, operating, and financing policies. More precisely, the board should be focusing on four key areas:

- Establishing vision, mission and values;
- Setting strategy and structure;
- Delegating to management;
- Exercising accountability to shareholders and being responsible to relevant stakeholders.

The board hires the CEO. The CEO then hires all of the other employees and oversees the day-to-day operations of the business.

The parent corporation can control the corporation's decision making process through its power to elect the subsidiary's board.

Introduction ---------- Module 1---------- 28

IAS 27

CONTROL WITH VOTING RIGHTS
Voting Interest Model
Operational Definition

Part 2

- **LEGAL DIMENSION**

    VOTING SHARES > 50%

- **SUBSTANCE OF THE RELATIONSHIP**

    ⇒ PARENT CORPORATION HOLDS CONVERTIBLE SECURITIES OR STOCK OPTIONS THAT, IF CONVERTED OR EXERCISED, WOULD GIVE THE PARENT A MAJORITY OF THE SEATS ON THE BOARD OF DIRECTORS

    ⇒ IRREVOCABLE AGREEMENT WITH OTHER OWNERS TO EXERCICE VOTING RIGHTS

    ⇒ DE FACTO CONTROL

De facto control is given more attention under IFRS 10. We will return to this issue later.

IAS 27

CONTROL WITH VOTING RIGHTS
Dual-Class Shares

Part 2

The use of a **dual-class shares** structure is quite common among public companies controlled by families. It allows continued founder control over a company to keep it growing while injecting new equity capital instead of debt.

For instance, in Canada, Magna International holds both Class A and Class B shares. However, Class B shares carry 500 votes for every one Class A share vote giving Magna's founder and Chairman full control over the company with only 3.4% of the company's equity.

The use of dual-class shares has been very controversial, especially when this device translates into legal control, giving the controlling shareholder more incentive and more power to extract private benefits from the company.

CONTROL WITHOUT VOTING RIGHTS
Variable Interest Model

SIC 12 — Part 2

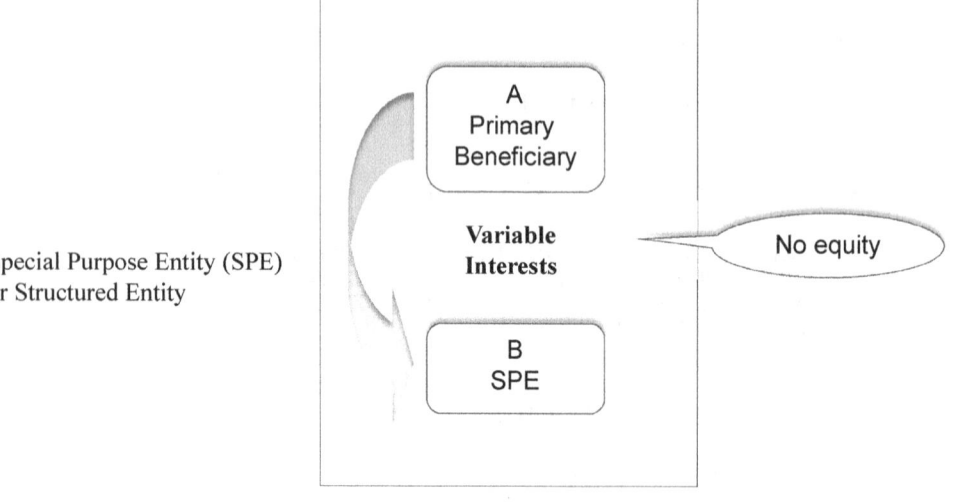

Special Purpose Entity (SPE) or Structured Entity

Firm A, the **Primary Beneficiary**, controls Firm B, the **SPE**.

SPECIAL PURPOSE ENTITIES (SPEs)
Context

SIC 12 — Part 2

The **Variable Interest Model** originated largely to close the loopholes that had previously allowed such companies as Enron to keep partnerships or other entities under the company's control off its consolidated financial statements.

Transactions involving SPEs have become increasingly common. Some reporting entities have entered into arrangements using SPEs that appear to be designed to avoid reporting assets and liabilities for which they are responsible, to delay reporting losses that have already been incurred, or to report gains that are illusory.

SPEs
Illustration 1

SIC 12 — Part 2

Business enterprises (or their financial institutions) often create SPEs to help the business convert large amounts of credit card receivables more quickly into cash. The SPE first buys a block of receivables from an enterprise in exchange for a short-term note payable. The SPE then issues debt securities for cash, which it transfers back to the enterprise. Interests and principle payments on the debt are then paid as the SPE collects the receivables.

As long as the SPE is independent, the sponsoring firm effectively transfers the risk of collecting the receivables to the owners of the SPE who, in exchange, obtain a discount on the value of the receivables.

SPEs
Illustration 2

SIC 12 — Part 2

Low-cost financing of asset purchases is another main benefit available through SPEs. Rather than engaging in the transaction directly, the business may sponsor an SPE to purchase and finance an asset acquisition. The SPE then leases the asset to the sponsor.

This strategy saves the business money because the SPE is often eligible for a lower interest rate. In fact, by isolating an asset in an SPE, the risk of the asset is isolated from the overall risk of the sponsoring firm.

Moreover, the business activities of an SPE can be strictly limited by its governing documents. These limits further protect lenders by preventing the SPE from engaging in any activities not specified in its agreements.

SPEs
Illustration 3

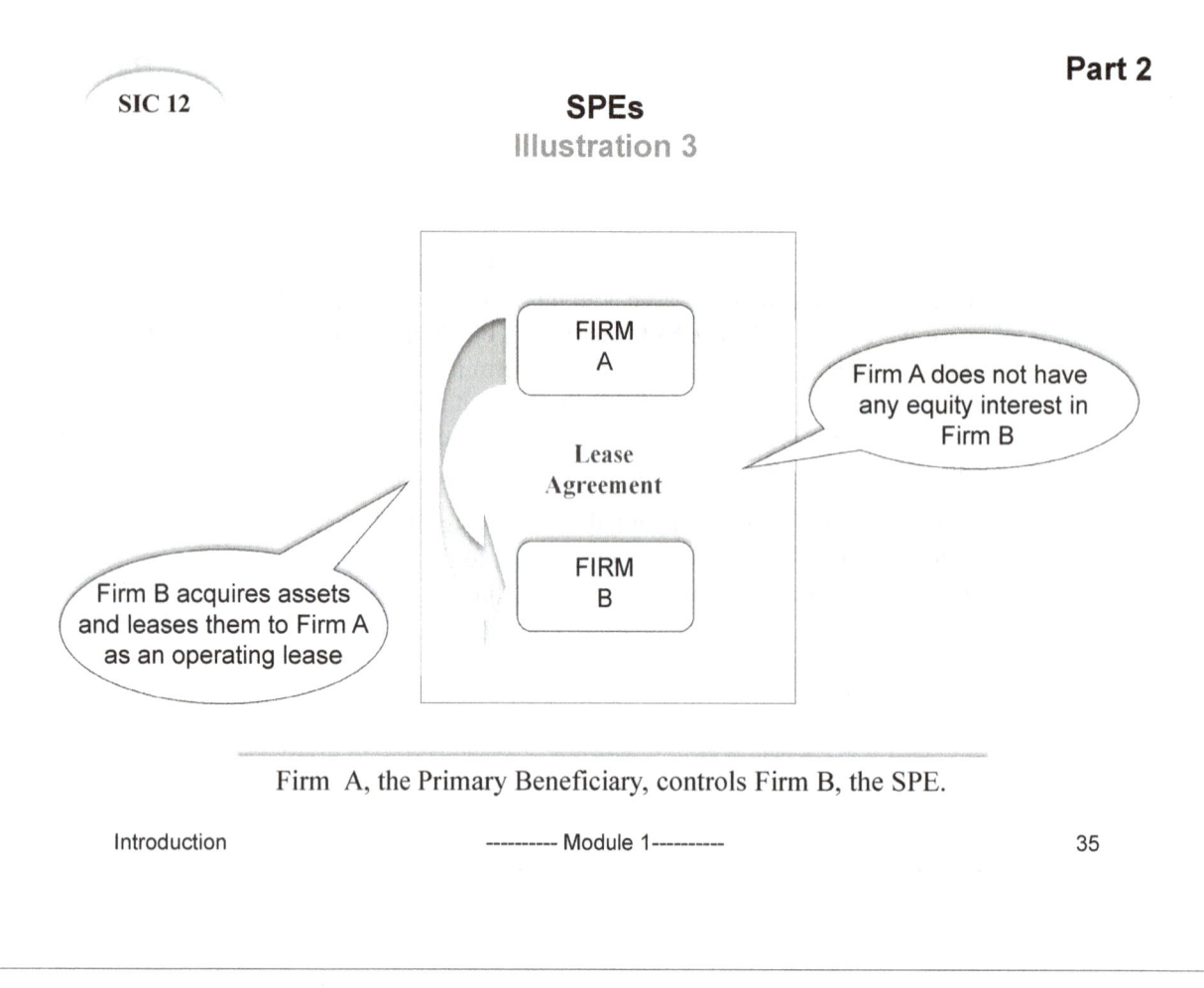

Firm A, the Primary Beneficiary, controls Firm B, the SPE.

PRIMARY BENEFICIARY OF AN SPE
Characteristics

THE FOLLOWING CHARACTERISTICS ARE INDICATIVE OF AN ENTERPRISE QUALIFIYING AS A PRIMARY BENEFICIARY OF AN SPE:

- THE DIRECT OR INDIRECT ABILITY TO MAKE DECISIONS ABOUT THE ENTITY'S ACTIVITIES
- THE OBLIGATION TO ABSORB THE EXPECTED LOSSES OF THE ENTITY IF THEY OCCUR, OR
- THE RIGHT TO RECEIVE THE EXPECTED RESIDUAL RETURNS OF THE ENTITY IF THEY OCCUR.

NO EQUITY INVESTMENT

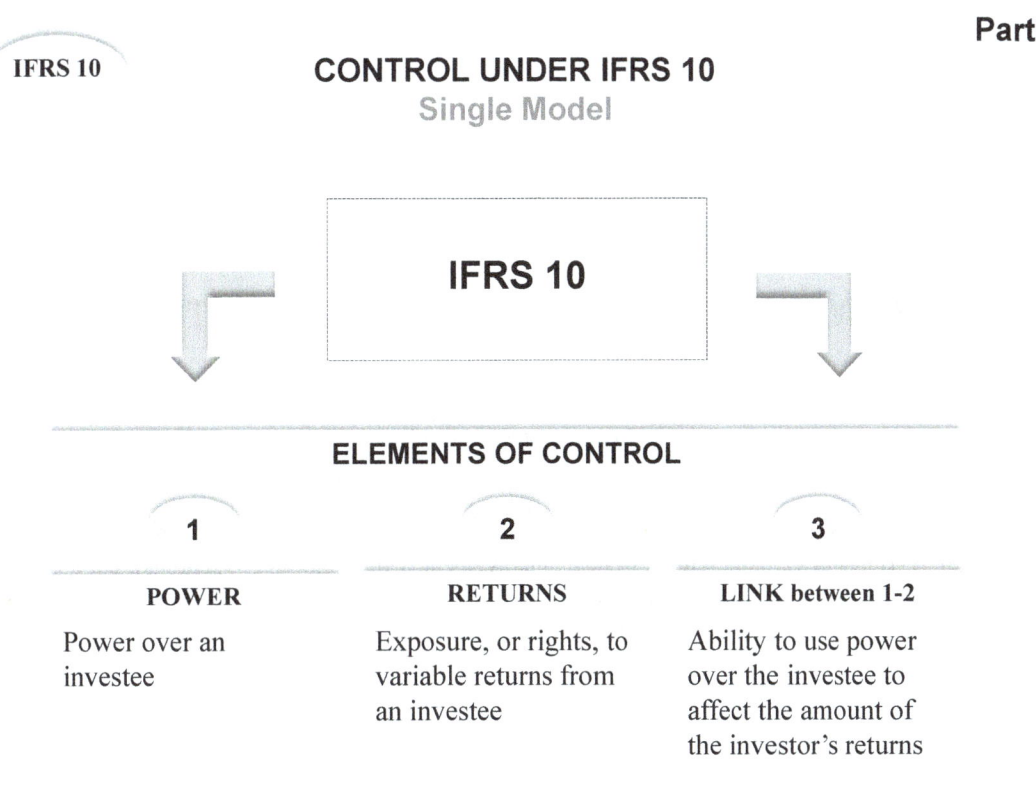

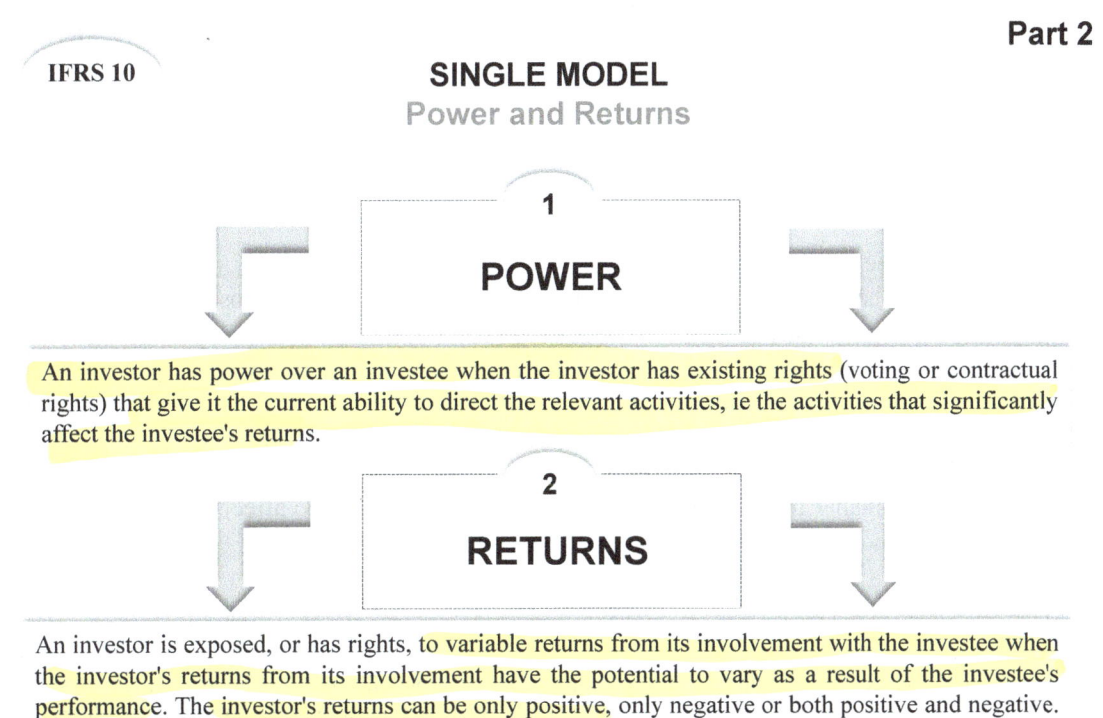

IFRS 10 — Part 2

SINGLE MODEL
Link Between Power and Returns

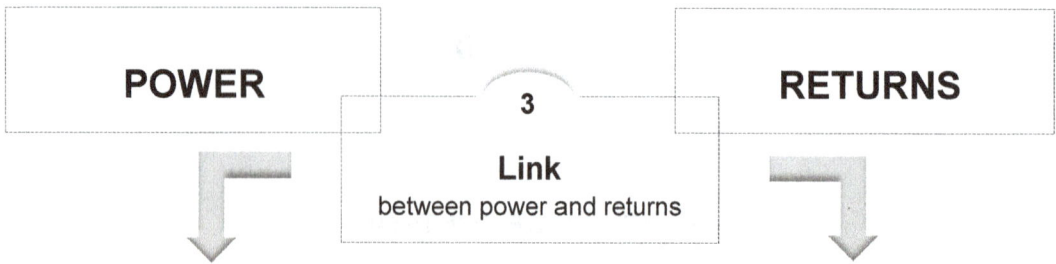

An investor controls an investee if the investor not only has power over the investee (**power**) and exposure or rights to variable returns from its involvement with the investee (**returns**), but also has the ability to use its power to affect the investor's returns from its involvement with the investee (**link between power and returns**). These three conditions must be met in order to support the existence of a control relationship.

Introduction ---------- Module 1 ---------- 39

IFRS 10 — Part 2

SINGLE MODEL
Factors to Consider when Defining Control

1. The purpose and design of the investee;
2. What the relevant activities are and how decisions about those activities are made;
3. Whether the rights of the investor give it the current ability to direct the relevant activities;
4. Whether the investor is exposed, or has rights, to variable returns from its involvement;
5. Whether the investor has the ability to use its power to affect the amount of the investor's returns.

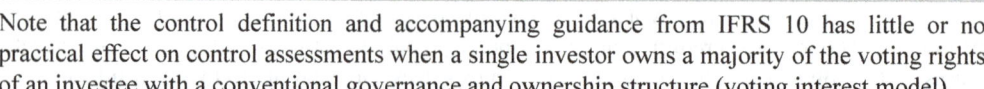

Note that the control definition and accompanying guidance from IFRS 10 has little or no practical effect on control assessments when a single investor owns a majority of the voting rights of an investee with a conventional governance and ownership structure (voting interest model).

Introduction ---------- Module 1 ---------- 40

IFRS 10 — **Part 2**

IFRS 10
Other Key Elements

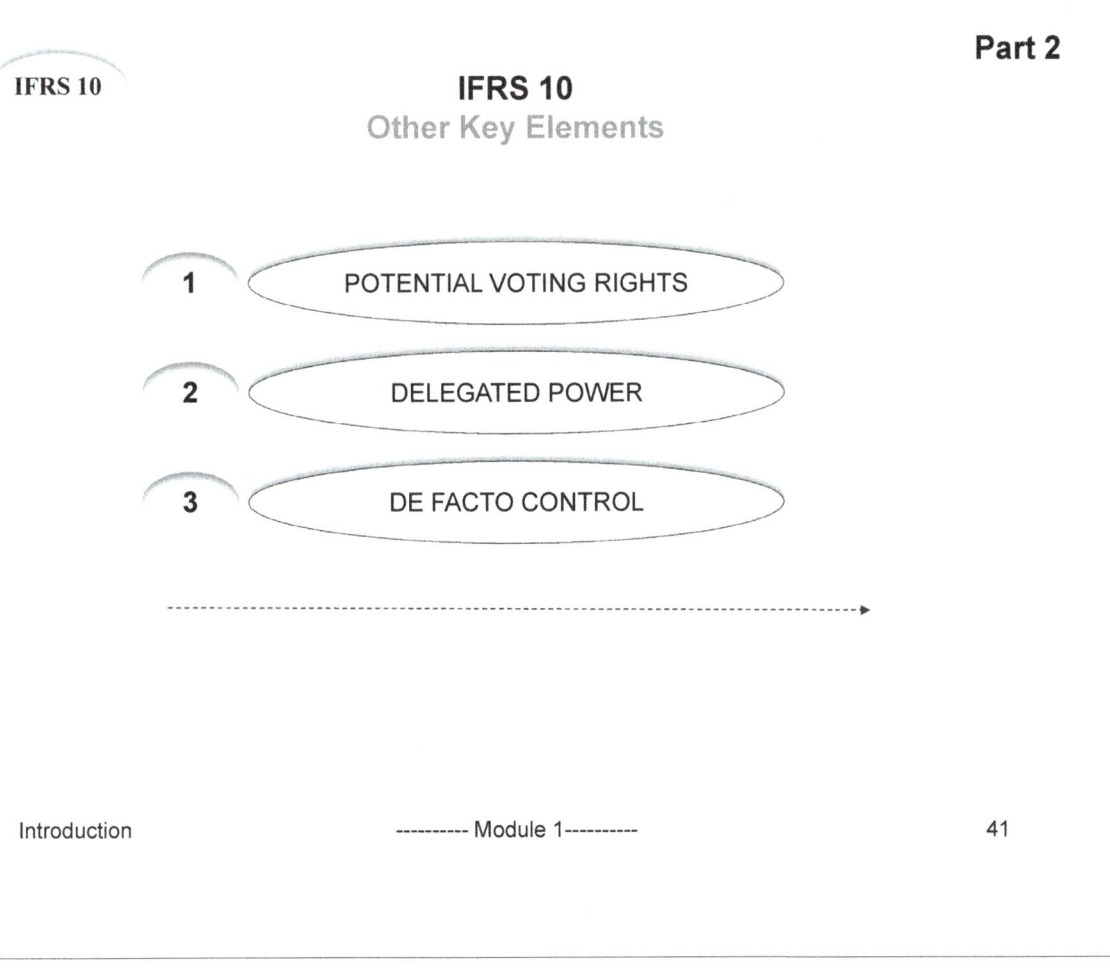

1. POTENTIAL VOTING RIGHTS
2. DELEGATED POWER
3. DE FACTO CONTROL

Introduction ---------- Module 1 ---------- 41

IFRS 10 — **Part 2**

OTHER KEY ELEMENTS
Potential Voting Rights

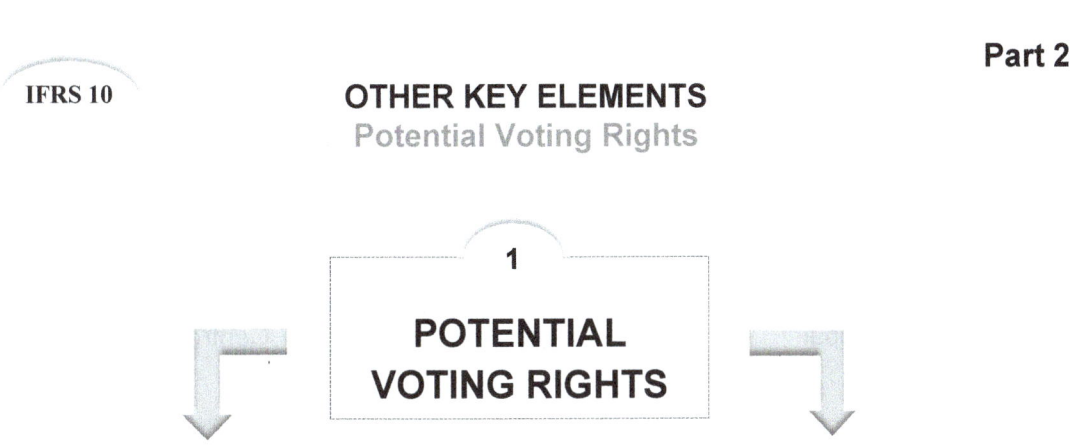

1

POTENTIAL VOTING RIGHTS

An investor **may hold instruments** that (if exercised or converted), **give the investor power to direct the relevant activities**. These are called **potential voting rights** and may be held through ownership of the following types:

- Share options and warrants;
- Convertible bonds;
- Convertible preference shares.

Under IFRS 10, potential voting rights may convey or contribute to control if **substantive**. For a right to be substantive, the holder must have the practical ability to exercise that right.

Introduction ---------- Module 1 ---------- 42

OTHER KEY ELEMENTS
Delegated Power

2 DELEGATED POWER

IFRS 10 includes extensive guidance on whether an investor is a principal or an agent.

An investor engaged primarily to act on behalf of other parties (ie agent) does not control the investee.

DELEGATED POWER
Illustration

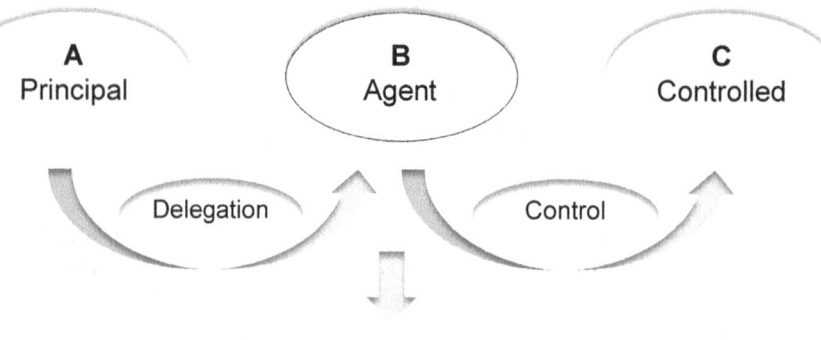

In this scenario, control over C resides in A, not in B.

OTHER KEY ELEMENTS
De Facto Control

3

DE FACTO CONTROL

De facto control is demonstrated, for example, when other shareholdings are widely dispersed, or when a sufficient number of other shareholders regularly fail to exercise their rights as shareholders (like voting at general meetings) so that the non-controlling shareholder wields the majority of votes actually cast. IFRS 10 includes explicit guidance that a large minority holding may confer control where other shareholdings are widely dispersed. While control assessments involving majority ownership are relatively straightforward, IFRS 10 requires more focus on investees in which the investor holds a significant minority of voting rights.

DE FACTO CONTROL
Voting Power of the Dominant Shareholder

ASSESSING THE SIZE OF THE INVESTOR'S VOTING RIGHTS

1	2	3
Number of voting rights held by investor	Size of investor's holding of voting rights relative to other vote-holders	Number of other parties that would have to act together to outvote the investor
The more voting rights an investor holds, the more likely the investor is to have power.	The more voting rights an investor holds relative to other vote holders, the more likely it is to have power.	The greater the number of other parties that would need to act together to outvote the investor, the greater the likelihood the investor has power.

IFRS 10

DE FACTO CONTROL
Illustration 1

Part 2

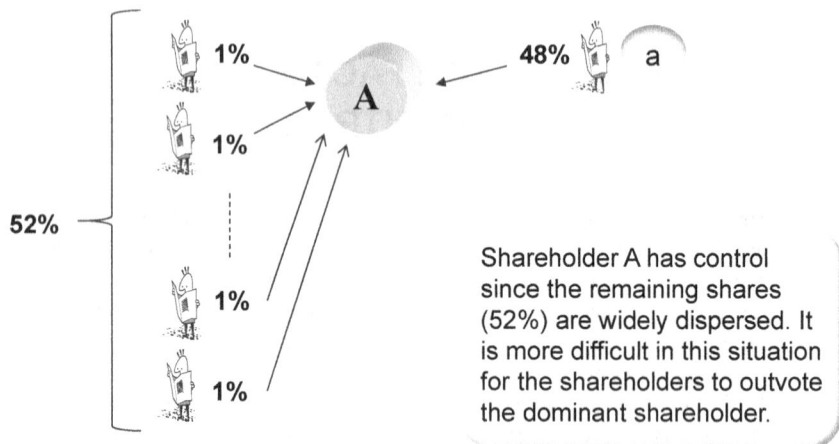

Shareholder A has control since the remaining shares (52%) are widely dispersed. It is more difficult in this situation for the shareholders to outvote the dominant shareholder.

Introduction ---------- Module 1---------- 47

IFRS 10

DE FACTO CONTROL
Illustration 2

Part 2

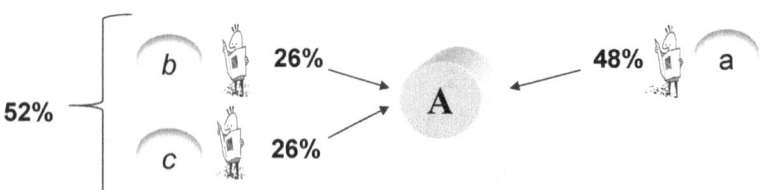

Shareholder A does not have control since shareholders B and C could easily get together to outvote shareholder A.

Introduction ---------- Module 1---------- 48

IFRS 10

DE FACTO CONTROL
Illustration 3

Part 2

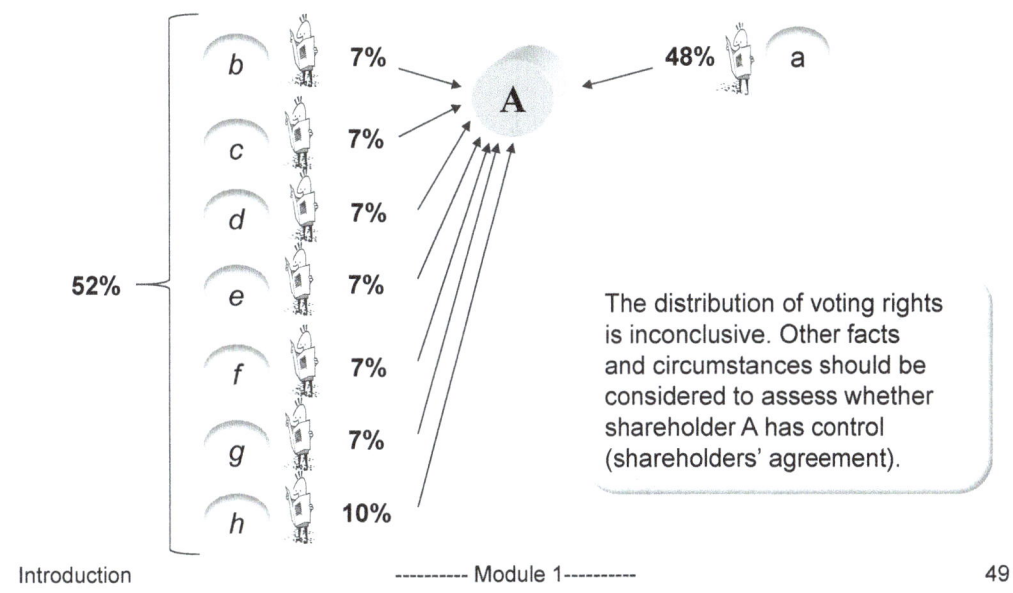

The distribution of voting rights is inconclusive. Other facts and circumstances should be considered to assess whether shareholder A has control (shareholders' agreement).

OTHER DIMENSIONS OF CONTROL
Direct, Indirect, and Absolute Control

Part 2

1   DIRECT CONTROL

Exists when a subsidiary is controlled directly by the parent company.

Parent ----> Subsidiary A

2   INDIRECT CONTROL

Exists when a subsidiary is controlled by another subsidiary rather than by the parent company.

Parent ----> Subsidiary A ----> Subsidiary B

3   ABSOLUTE CONTROL

Control of at least two-thirds of voting shares necessary to approve special resolutions, including proposals to change the corporation's charter or bylaws.

Part 2

INDIRECT CONTROL
Scope of Consolidation - Illustration 1

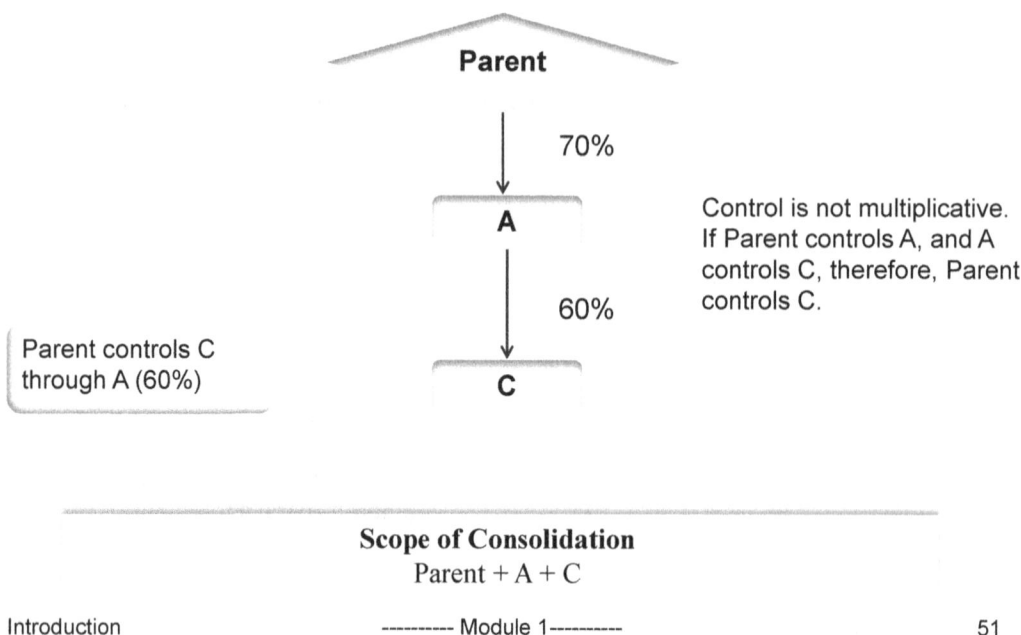

Control is not multiplicative. If Parent controls A, and A controls C, therefore, Parent controls C.

Parent controls C through A (60%)

Scope of Consolidation
Parent + A + C

Part 2

INDIRECT CONTROL
Scope of Consolidation - Illustration 2

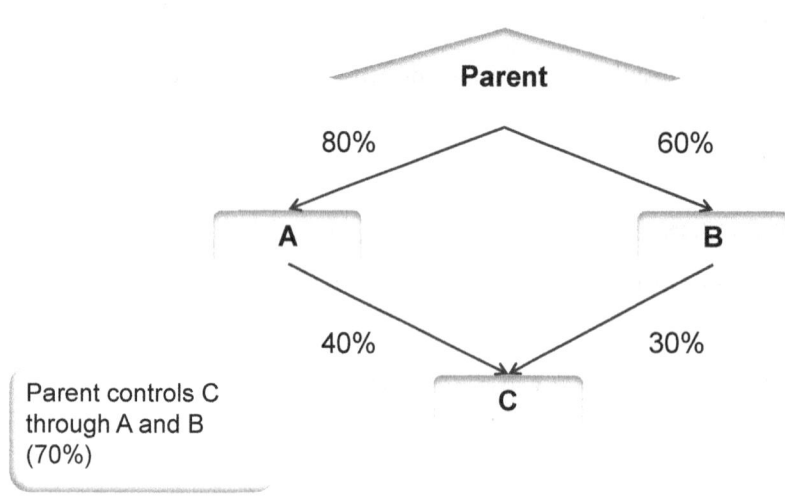

Parent controls C through A and B (70%)

Scope of Consolidation
Parent + A + B + C

Part 2

INDIRECT CONTROL
Scope of Consolidation - Illustration 3

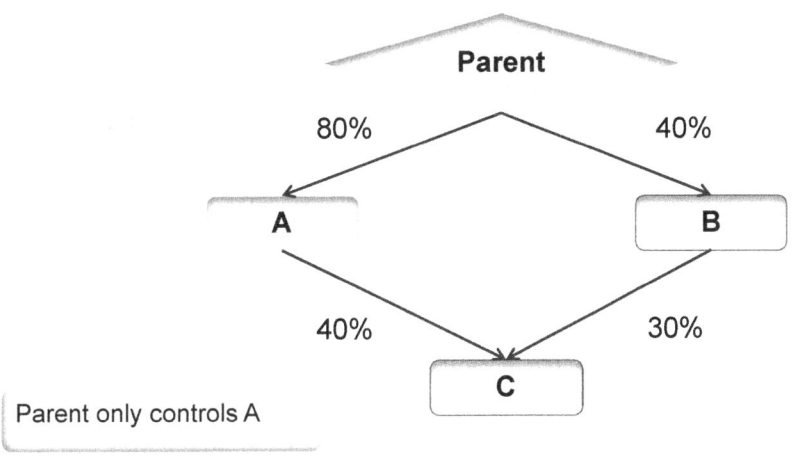

Parent only controls A

Scope of Consolidation
Parent + A

Part 2

INDIRECT CONTROL
Scope of Consolidation - Illustration 4

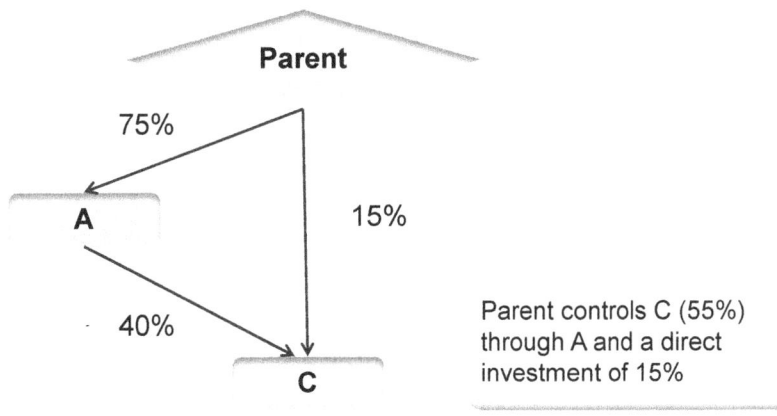

Parent controls C (55%) through A and a direct investment of 15%

Scope of Consolidation
Parent + A + C

Part 2

CONTROL
From Bombardier - 2016 Annual Report, page 141

The Corporation consolidates investees, including structured entities when, based on the evaluation of the substance of the relationship with the Corporation, it concludes that it controls the investees. The Corporation controls an investee when it is exposed, or has rights, to variable returns from its involvement with the investee and has the ability to affect those returns through its power over the investee.

The Corporation's principal subsidiaries, whose revenues or assets represent more than 10% of total revenues or more than 10% of total assets of Aerospace or Transportation segments, are as follows:

- Subsidiary Location C Series Aircraft Limited Partnership (Canada)
- Bombardier Transportation GmbH (Germany)
- Bombardier Transportation (Holdings) UK Ltd (U.K.)
- Bombardier Transport France S.A.S. (France)
- Learjet Inc. (U.S.)

OUTLINE OF THE PRESENTATION

1. SHARE INVESTMENTS: TYPOLOGY
2. CONTROL RELATIONSHIPS: DEFINITION
3. **CONSOLIDATION OF F/S: OBJECTIVES, PROCESS, BENEFITS**
4. ALTERNATIVE ACCOUNTING METHODS FOR PRIVATE ENTITIES

APPENDIXES

A. NON-STRATEGIC INVESTMENTS: FV METHODS
B. INVESTMENTS IN ASSOCIATES: EQUITY METHOD

PART 3
Consolidation of F/S: Objectives, Process, Benefits

Objectives of this section

Define *consolidation of financial statements*, the objectives, the process, and the benefits.

Review the conditions for the use of consolidation.

Key concepts

- Consolidation of financial statements
- Economic entity
- Worksheet Approach
- Direct Approach

CONSOLIDATION OF FINANCIAL STATEMENTS
Definition

CONSOLIDATION REFERS TO THE MECHANICAL PROCESS OF BRINGING TOGETHER THE FINANCIAL RECORDS OF TWO (OR MORE) COMPANIES TO FORM A SINGLE SET OF FINANCIAL STATEMENTS

CONTROL
relationships

Part 3

CONSOLIDATION OF FINANCIAL STATEMENTS
Main Objective

THE PURPOSE OF CONSOLIDATED STATEMENTS IS TO PRESENT THE OPERATING RESULTS AND THE FINANCIAL POSITION OF A PARENT AND ALL ITS SUBSIDIARIES AS IF THEY ARE ONE ECONOMIC ENTITY.

Viewpoint of the
ECONOMIC ENTITY

Introduction ---------- Module 1 ---------- 59

Part 3

CONSOLIDATION OF FINANCIAL STATEMENTS
Economic Entity

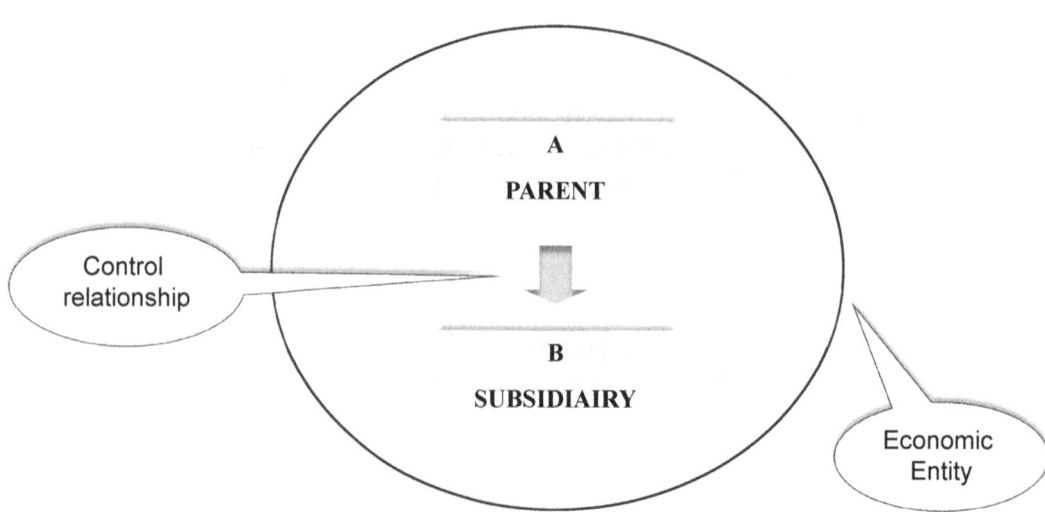

Introduction ---------- Module 1 ---------- 60

Part 3

ECONOMIC ENTITY
Key Concept

- **ABSTRACT ENTITY**: THERE IS NO LEGAL ENTITY THAT CORRESPONDS WITH A CONSOLIDATED ECONOMIC ENTITY.
- PARENT AND SUBSIDIARY CONTINUE TO EXIST AS TWO **SEPARATE LEGAL ENTITIES**.
- AFFILIATED COMPANIES ARE VIEWED AS A SINGLE ENTITY FOR REPORTING PURPOSES.
- CONSOLIDATED STATEMENTS ARE SOMETIMES REFERRED TO **AS ACCOUNTING FICTION**.

SUBSTANCE OVER FORM

Part 3

CONSOLIDATION OF FINANCIAL STATEMENTS
Process

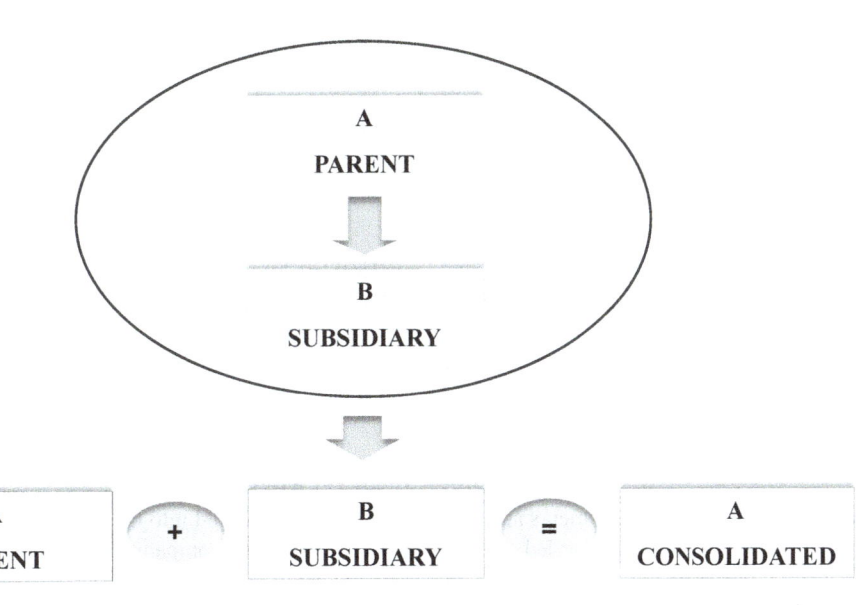

Part 3

CONSOLIDATION OF FINANCIAL STATEMENTS
Approaches

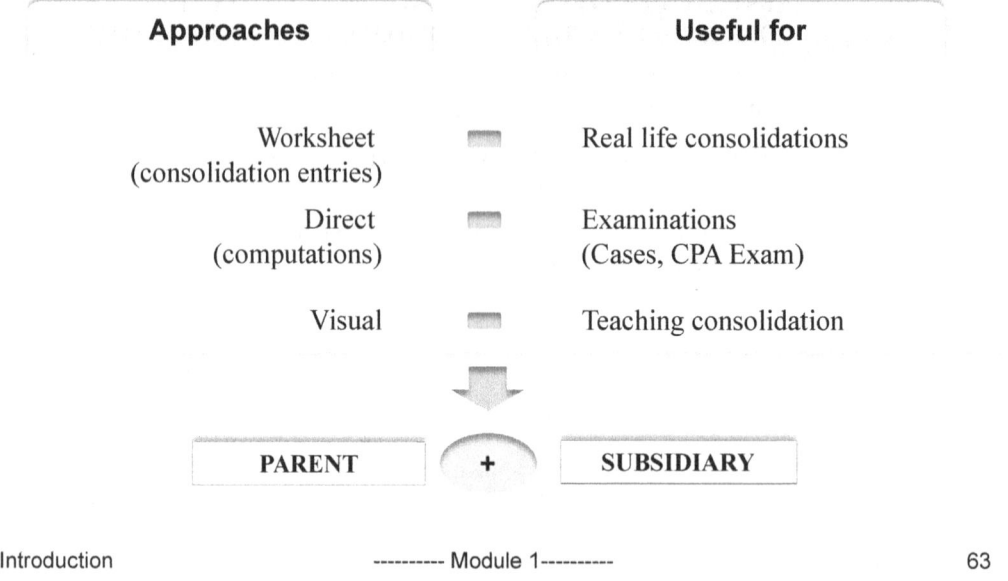

Introduction — Module 1

Part 3

CONSOLIDATION OF FINANCIAL STATEMENTS
On Worksheet

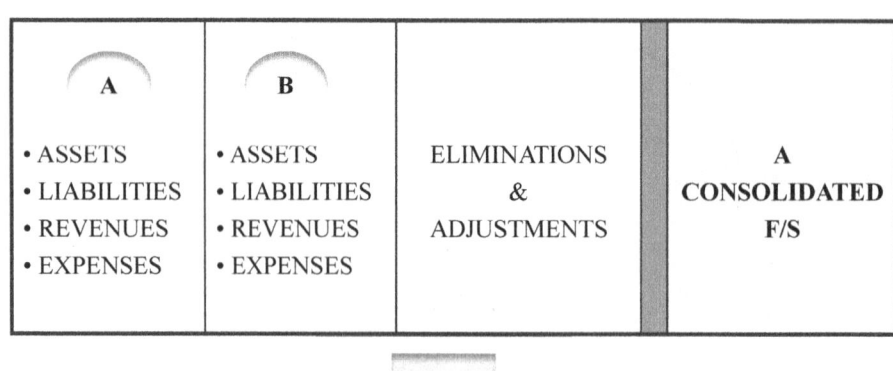

Consolidation is made on **working paper**
Consolidation adjustments and eliminations that are entered into the consolidation worksheet are not recorded on the books of the affiliated companies. This explains the recurring nature of the work involved in consolidation.

Introduction — Module 1

Part 3

CONSOLIDATION PROCESS
Worksheet versus Direct

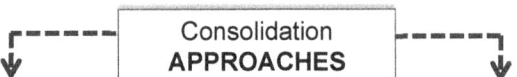

Consolidation **APPROACHES**

WORKSHEET
Uses a multi-columnar worksheet to enter the trial balances of the parent and each subsidiary. Then eliminations and adjustments are entered onto the worksheet, and the accounts are cross-added to determine the consolidated figures.

DIRECT
Prepares the consolidated statements by computing each balance directly.

Introduction ---------- Module 1---------- 65

Part 3

CONSOLIDATION OF FINANCIAL STATEMENTS
Why Consolidation Entries are Required

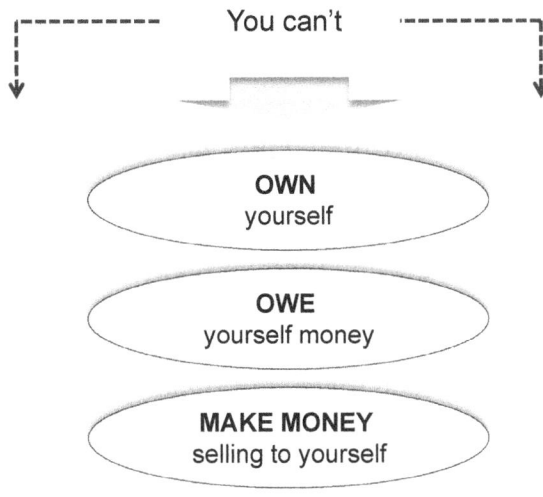

You can't

OWN yourself

OWE yourself money

MAKE MONEY selling to yourself

Introduction ---------- Module 1---------- 66

Part 3

CONSOLIDATION OF FINANCIAL STATEMENTS

Consolidation Entries

```
                    Consolidation
          ┌ ─ ─ ─     ENTRIES    ─ ─ ─ ┐
          ▼                             ▼
    ELIMINATIONS                  ADJUSTMENTS
```

ELIMINATIONS
Changes that prevent certain amounts on the separate-entity statements from appearing on the consolidated statements.

ADJUSTMENTS
Made to alter reported amounts to reflect the economic substance of transactions rather than their nominal amount.

WORKING PAPER ENTRIES

Introduction ---------- Module 1 ---------- 67

Part 3

CONSOLIDATION OF FINANCIAL STATEMENTS

Benefits

1. Provide **Relevant** Information

2. Provide **Comparable** Information

3. Ensure **Accountability**

4. Report **Risks and Benefits**

Introduction ---------- Module 1 ---------- 68

Part 3

BENEFITS OF CONSOLIDATED FINANCIAL STATEMENTS
Relevance

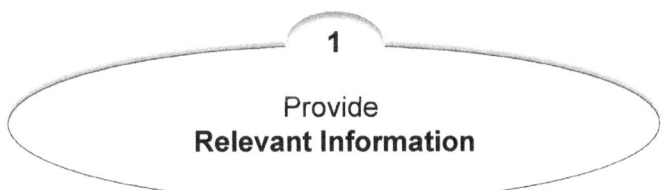

The information obtained from the consolidated financial statements is relevant to investors in the parent entity. These investors have an interest in the group as a whole. They have interest not just in the parent entity only but in subsidiaries also. To ensure these investors obtain their required information from the financial statements, consolidation is made. The entities comprising the group would place a large cost burden on the investors. See next slide.

Part 3

BENEFITS OF CONSOLIDATED FINANCIAL STATEMENTS
Cost Burden of Non Consolidated Information to Investors

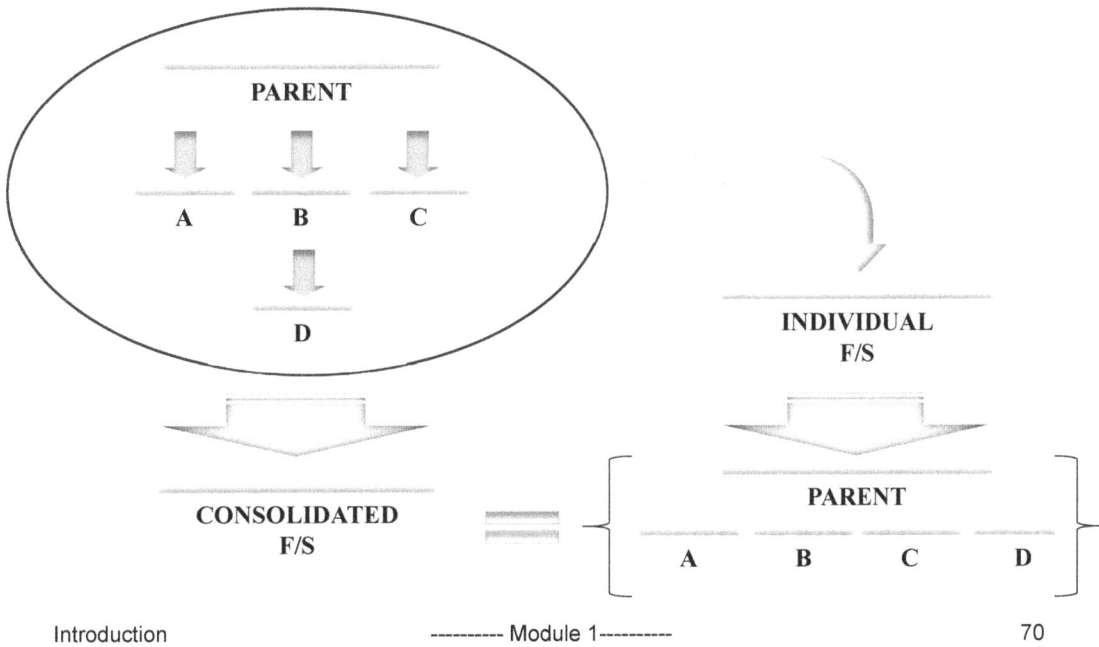

BENEFITS OF CONSOLIDATED FINANCIAL STATEMENTS
Comparability

Part 3

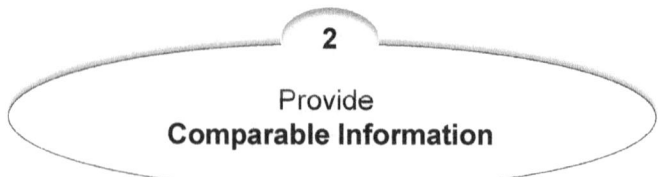

Some entities are organized into a group structure such that different activities are undertaken by separate members of the group. We will present the strategic motivations for this type of structures in Module 2. Other entities are organized differently, with some having all activities conducted within the one single entity. Consolidated financial statements make the comparative analysis an easier task for an investor who wants to make useful comparisons between entities. See next slide.

BENEFITS OF CONSOLIDATED FINANCIAL STATEMENTS
Group Structure or Single Entity

Part 3

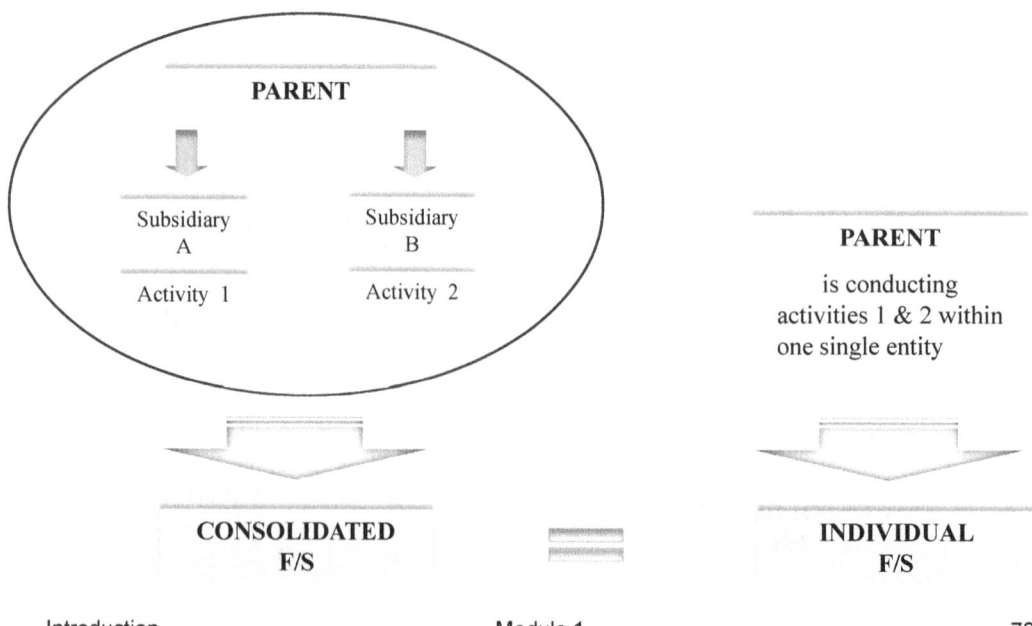

Part 3

BENEFITS OF CONSOLIDATED FINANCIAL STATEMENTS
Accountability

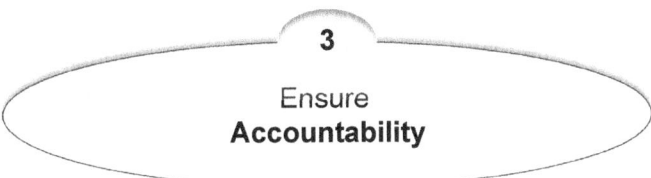

The management of the parent entity is not just responsible for the management of the assets of the parent itself. As the parent controls the assets of all subsidiaries, the assets under the control of the parent entity's management are the assets of the group. The consolidated financial statements report the assets under the control of the group management as well as the claims on those assets.

Part 3

BENEFITS OF CONSOLIDATED FINANCIAL STATEMENTS
Risks and Benefits

There are risks allied with managing an entity, and an entity rarely obtains control of another entity without obtaining significant opportunities to benefit from that control. The consolidated financial statements allow an assessment of these risks and benefits.

INDIVIDUAL FINANCIAL STATEMENTS
Stakeholders

Consolidated financial statements are not substitute for the statements prepared by the subsidiary and the parent company. In fact, individual financial statements are useful for **creditors**, including **bondholders**, in assessing, for instance, the degree of protection related to their claims. Individual financial statements are also useful to **regulatory agencies**. Subsidiary-company-only statements may be needed for **minority shareholders** (or **non-controlling interest**), if any.

In individual financial statements of the parent company, the investment account in subsidiary (ies) must be accounted for using the **cost method** or in accordance with **IAS 39** (Financial Instruments). The investment could also be accounted for using the **equity method** (less likely scenario).

INVESTMENTS IN SUBSIDIARIES
Accounting Methods for Internal Recording versus External Reporting

INTERNAL RECORDING

For internal record-keeping, the investment in subsidiary can be accounted for using the **cost method** or the **equity method**.

The method used has no impact on the consolidated financial information since the investment account is eliminated as part of every recurring consolidation.

EXTERNAL REPORTING

For external reporting purposes, **consolidation** is required.

CONDITIONS FOR NOT PRESENTING CONSOLIDATED FINANCIAL STATEMENTS

A PARENT NEED NOT PRESENT CONSOLIDATED FINANCIAL STATEMENTS IF AND ONLY IF:

- THE PARENT IS ITSELF A WHOLLY OWNED SUBSIDIARY;
- THE PARENT'S DEBT OR EQUITY INSTRUMENTS ARE NOT TRADED IN A PUBLIC MARKET;
- THE PARENT DID NOT FILE, NOR IS IT IN THE PROCESS OF FILING, ITS FINANCIAL STATEMENTS TO A SECURITIES COMMISSION; AND
- THE ULTIMATE OR ANY INTERMEDIATE PARENT OF THE PARENT PRODUCES CONSOLIDATED FINANCIAL STATEMENTS.

INVESTMENT ENTITIES
Exception to the Consolidation Requirements in IFRS 10

DEFINITION

An investment entity is an entity whose business purpose is to invest funds solely for returns from capital appreciation, investment income or both (includes venture capital organization, pension funds, and investment funds).

EXCEPTION

Investment entities are required to report entities that they control as **FVTPL investments**.

PART 3
Recap

- UNILATERAL CONTROL
- ECONOMIC ENTITY
- CONSOLIDATION

PART 3
Concept Check

Explain how the accounting principle "substance over form" applies to the consolidation of financial statements.

OUTLINE OF THE PRESENTATION

1. SHARE INVESTMENTS: TYPOLOGY
2. CONTROL RELATIONSHIPS: DEFINITION
3. CONSOLIDATION OF F/S: OBJECTIVES, PROCESS, BENEFITS
4. **ALTERNATIVE ACCOUNTING METHODS FOR PRIVATE ENTITIES**

APPENDIXES

A. NON-STRATEGIC INVESTMENTS: FV METHODS
B. INVESTMENTS IN ASSOCIATES: EQUITY METHOD

PART 4
Alternative Accounting Methods for Private Entities

Objectives of this section

Present the accounting methods for share investments in the context of private enterprises (ASPE), including investments in:
- Associates
- Subsidiaries and,
- Joint Ventures.

Part 4

PRIVATE ENTERPRISES
Definition

A private enterprise is a profit-oriented entity that is not a publicly accountable enterprise, that is :

1. an entity that has not issued, or is in the process of issuing, debt or equity instruments that are, or will be, outstanding and traded in a public market; and

2. an entity that does not hold assets in a fiduciary capacity like banks, insurance companies, securities brokers/ dealers, mutual funds

ACCOUNTING STANDARDS FOR PRIVATE ENTERPRISES (ASPE)

Introduction ---------- Module 1---------- 83

Part 4

INVESTMENTS IN ASSOCIATES
Private Enterprises

A private enterprise shall make an accounting policy choice to either use the:

1. The equity method; or

2. The cost method.

When an associate's equity securities are quoted in an active market, the investment shall not be accounted for using the cost method. Under such circumstances the investment may be accounted for at its quoted amount, with changes recorded in net income.

Introduction ---------- Module 1---------- 84

Part 4

INVESTMENTS IN SUBSIDIARIES
Private Enterprises

A private enterprise shall make an accounting policy choice to either:

1. Consolidate its subsidiaries; or

2. Account for its subsidiaries using:
   - the equity method; or
   - the cost method.

When a subsidiary's equity securities are quoted in an active market, the investment shall not be accounted for using the cost method. Under such circumstances the investment may be accounted for at its quoted amount, with changes recorded in net income.

Part 4

INVESTMENTS IN JOINT VENTURES
Private Enterprises

A private enterprise shall make an accounting policy choice to either use the:

1. The equity method; or

2. Proportionate consolidation.

ACCOUNTING FOR CONTROL RELATIONSHIPS: INTRODUCTION
Module 1 - Recap

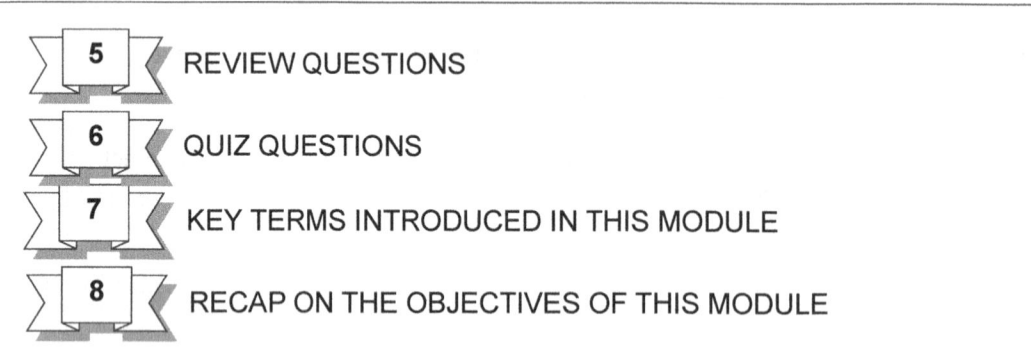

PART 5
Review Questions

1. Define or explain the following terms:

- Consolidation of financial statements
- Control
- Economic entity
- Subsidiary and parent company
- Special Purpose Entities (SPEs)
- Non-strategic vs strategic investments
- Cost method
- Equity method
- Significant influence
- Associates

2. What criteria would be used to determine whether the equity method should be used to account for a particular investment?

3. The equity method records dividends as a reduction in the investment account. Explain why.

Part 5

REVIEW QUESTIONS
(continued...)

4. The extent of share ownership does not necessarily coincide with the extent of control exercised. Explain.

5. What are the two main types of non-strategic investments? What is the appropriate method of accounting for each of them?

6. What are the two main types of strategic investments? What is the appropriate method of accounting for each of them?

7. Name two circunstances for which the cost method can be used for strategic investments?

8. What is the objective of preparing consolidated financial statements?

9. What are the conditions that a corporation must meet for not presenting consolidated financial statements?

Part 6

PART 6
Quiz Questions

On January 1, X0, Parent buys 500 outstanding voting shares of Subsidiary for $1.20 per share. On September 1, X2, Parent buys an additional 1,000 shares of Subsidiary for $1.50 per share. Finally, on July 1, X3, Parent buys all the remaining shares of Subsidiary for $7,000. Relevant information regarding Subsidiary:

Year	Comprehensive income	Dividends	Market value-Shares
X0	$10,000	$1,000	$1.40
X1	8,000	1,000	1.45
X2	15,000	1,000	1.80
X3	10,000	1,000	2.50

Parent uses the FV through profit and loss method for its non-strategic investments and the cost method for its investment in subsidiaries (for internal reporting).

Dividends are declared and paid at the end of each year. Profit is earned evenly over the year. Finally, note that Subsidiary has 5,000 outstanding voting shares from X0 to X3.

Part 6

PART 6
Quiz Questions - Investment in Subsidiary from X0 to X3

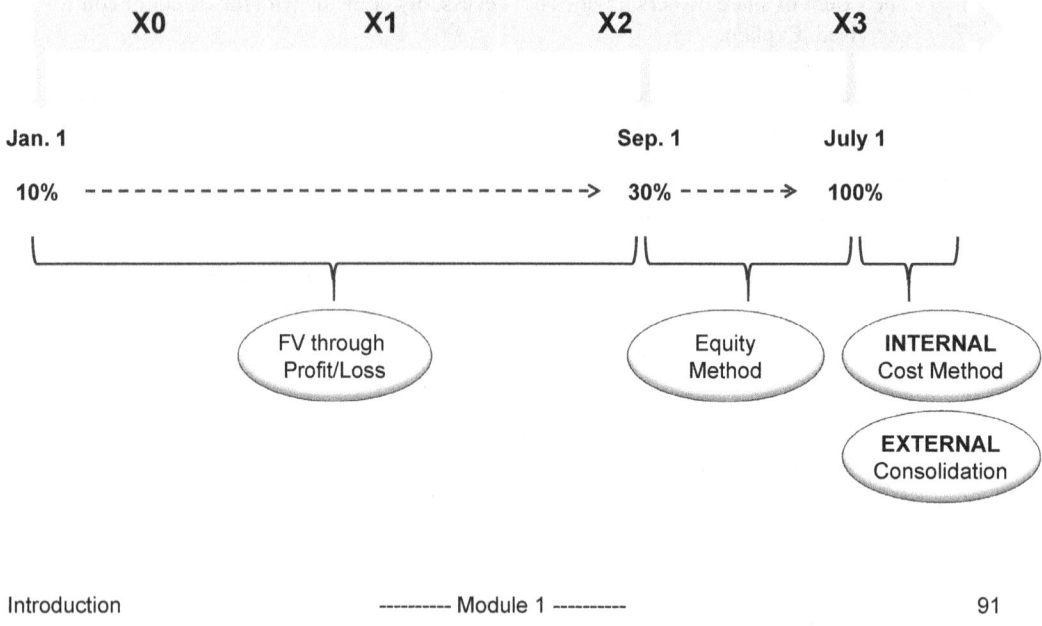

Introduction ---------- Module 1 ---------- 91

Part 6

QUIZ QUESTIONS

1

Provide all the journal entries for the investment of Parent in Subsidiary for X0.

January 1, X0

December 31, X0

Introduction ---------- Module 1 ---------- 92

Part 6

QUIZ QUESTIONS

2

Provide all the journal entries for the investment of Parent in Subsidiary for X2.

September 1, X2

↳

↳

Introduction ---------- Module 1 ---------- 93

Part 6

QUIZ QUESTIONS

3

Provide all the journal entries for the investment of Parent in Subsidiary for X2.

Continued…

December 31, X2

↳

↳

Introduction ---------- Module 1 ---------- 94

Part 6

QUIZ QUESTIONS

4

Provide all the journal entries for the investment of Parent in Subsidiary for X3.

July 1, X3

December 31, X3

Introduction ---------- Module 1 ---------- 95

Part 7

KEY TERMS INTRODUCED IN THIS MODULE

• Strategic vs. Non-strategic investments • Portfolio investments • Investments in Associates, Controlled Entities	**Part 1**

• Control, direct, indirect, absolute, de facto • Subsidiary, Parent company • Special Purpose Entity (SPE) or Structured Entity	**Part 2**

• Consolidation of financial statements • Economic entity • Worksheet Approach • Direct Approach	**Part 3**

Introduction ---------- Module 1---------- 96

Part 8
RECAP ON THE OBJECTIVES OF THIS MODULE

Part 1
Present the different types of share investments, including non-strategic and strategic investments.

Introduce the proper accounting treatment for both passive and strategic investments.

Part 2
Define *control*.

Part 3
Define *consolidation of financial statements*, the objectives, the process, and the benefits.

Review the conditions for the use of consolidation.

Part 4
Present the accounting methods for share investments in the context of private enterprises (ASPE), including investments in:
- Associates.
- Subsidiaries and,
- Joint Ventures.

Appendix A
Non-Strategic Investment: FV Methods

This publication is protected by copyright, and permission should be obtained from the publisher prior to any prohibited reproduction, storage in a retrieval system, or transmission in any form or by any means, electronic, mechanical, photocopying, recording, or otherwise.

Copyright © 2020 Parmitech

APPENDIX A
Non-Strategic Investments: FV Methods

Objective of this appendix

Review the accounting for non-strategic investments including:
- Fair value methods
- Cost method

Key concepts

- Investments at fair value through profit or loss (**FVTPL**)
- Investments at fair value through other comprehensive income (**FVTOCI**)
- Cost method
- IFRS 9

Appendix A

IFRS 9 - EQUITY INSTRUMENTS
Fair Value Methods

1. Fair Value Through Profit or Loss (**FVTPL**)
   - Market value
   - Realized and unrealized gains and losses
     → Profit for the year

2. Fair Value Through Other Comprehensive Income (**FVTOCI**)
   - Market value
   - Realized and unrealized gains and losses
     → Other Comprehensive Income (OCI)

   No recycling

Trading securities will be classified as FVTPL. Trading in securities is what financial institutions do (banks, pension funds, brokers, …).

Introduction ---------- Module 1 ---------- 3

Appendix A

IFRS 9 - DEBT INSTRUMENTS
Fair Value Methods

1. Fair Value Through Profit or Loss (**FVTPL**)
   - Market value
   - Realized and unrealized gains and losses
     → Profit for the year

2. Fair Value Through Other Comprehensive Income (**FVTOCI**)
   - Market value
   - Realized gains and losses
     → Profit for the year
   - Unrealized gains and losses
     → Other Comprehensive Income (OCI)

   With recycling

Introduction ---------- Module 1 ---------- 4

NON-STRATEGIC INVESTMENTS
Fair Value Method for FVTOCI Equity Investments

Appendix A

No Recycling

IFRS 9 no longer allows recycling of gains/losses from OCI to net income when FVTOCI equity investments are sold (no recycling).

This may prevent any manipulation of earnings from managers by selling FVTOCI equity investments that have appreciated/depreciated so as to report gains/losses in the net income as and when needed to hit earnings targets (or reduce earnings volatility)

USE OF THE COST METHOD
Exceptions

Appendix A

Type of investments		Conditions
Available-for-sale investments	+	No quoted market prices
Strategic investments	+	Presentation of separate financial statements
Investments in subsidiaries	+	Internal recording

Appendix A

THE COST METHOD
Overview

- **STATEMENT OF FINANCIAL POSITION**
  - INVESTMENT SHOWN AT HISTORICAL COST

- **INCOME STATEMENT**
  - DIVIDENDS AS REVENUE WHEN DECLARED BY THE INVESTEE

- **REDUCTION OF VALUE**
  - MARKET VALUE DROPS BELOW THE HISTORICAL COST (LONG-TERM DECLINE)
  - LIQUIDATING DIVIDENDS

Introduction ---------- Module 1---------- 7

Appendix A

ACCOUNTING FOR NON-STRATEGIC SHARE INVESTMENTS
Illustration

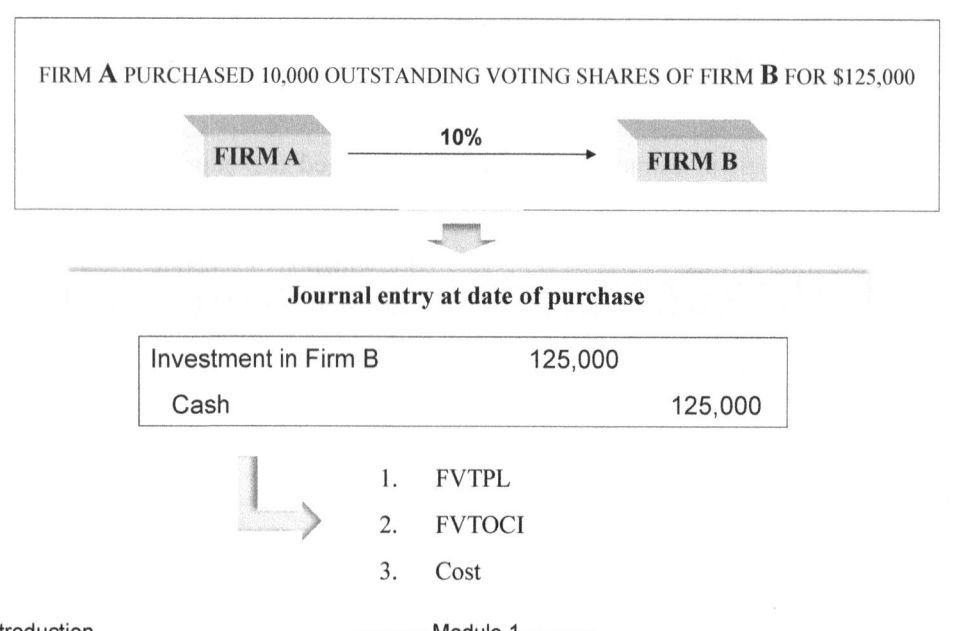

FIRM **A** PURCHASED 10,000 OUTSTANDING VOTING SHARES OF FIRM **B** FOR $125,000

FIRM A —10%→ FIRM B

Journal entry at date of purchase

Investment in Firm B	125,000	
Cash		125,000

1. FVTPL
2. FVTOCI
3. Cost

Introduction ---------- Module 1---------- 8

Appendix A
ACCOUNTING FOR NON-STRATEGIC SHARE INVESTMENTS
The Investment is Designated at Fair Value Through Profit or Loss
Year-End

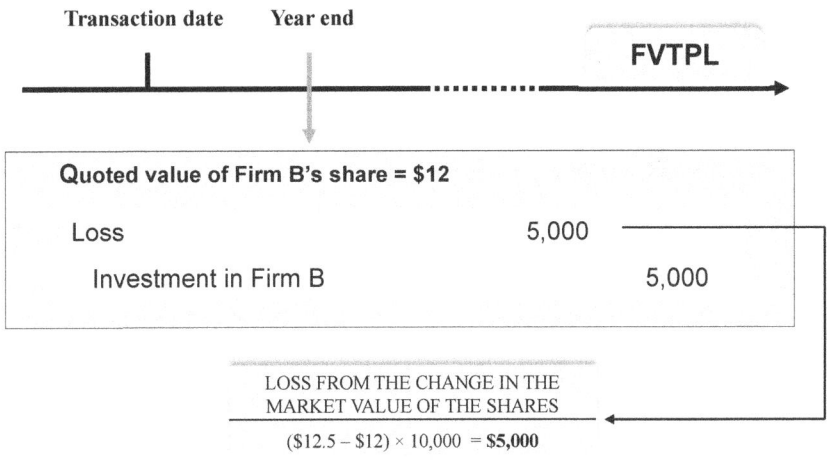

Appendix A
ACCOUNTING FOR NON-STRATEGIC SHARE INVESTMENTS
The Investment is Designated at Fair Value Through Profit or Loss
Date of Sale

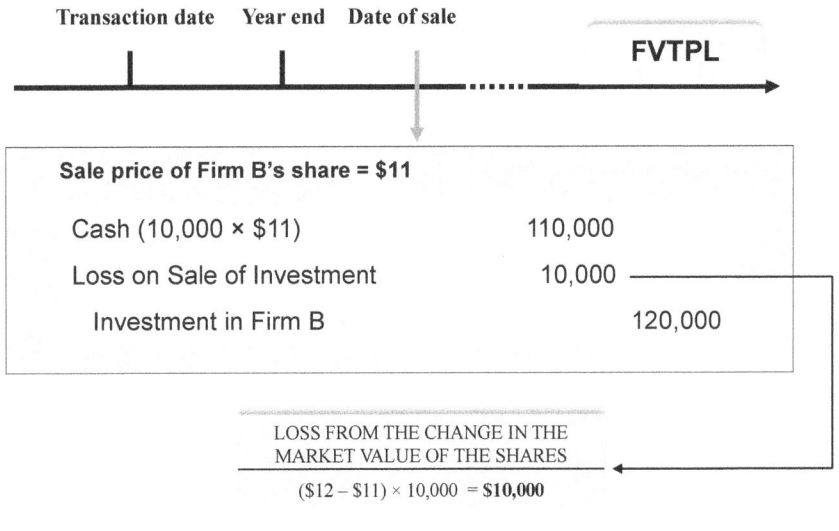

Appendix A
ACCOUNTING FOR NON-STRATEGIC SHARE INVESTMENTS
The Investment is Designated at Fair Value Through OCI
Year-End

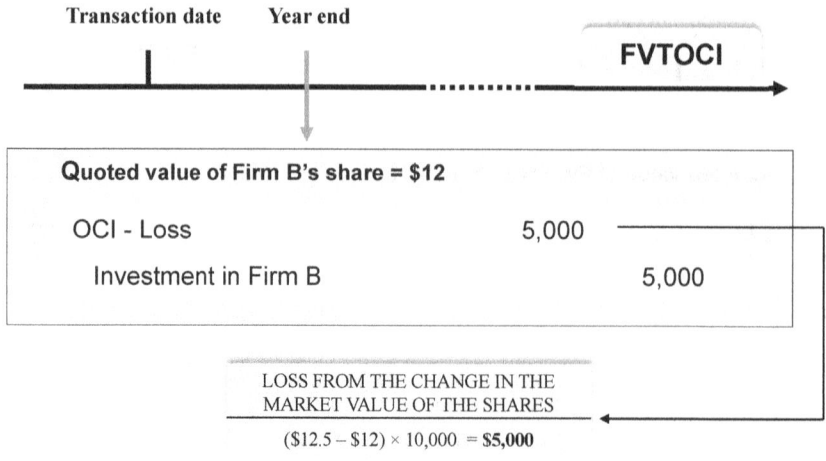

Appendix A
ACCOUNTING FOR NON-STRATEGIC SHARE INVESTMENTS
The Investment is Designated at Fair Value Through OCI
Date of Sale

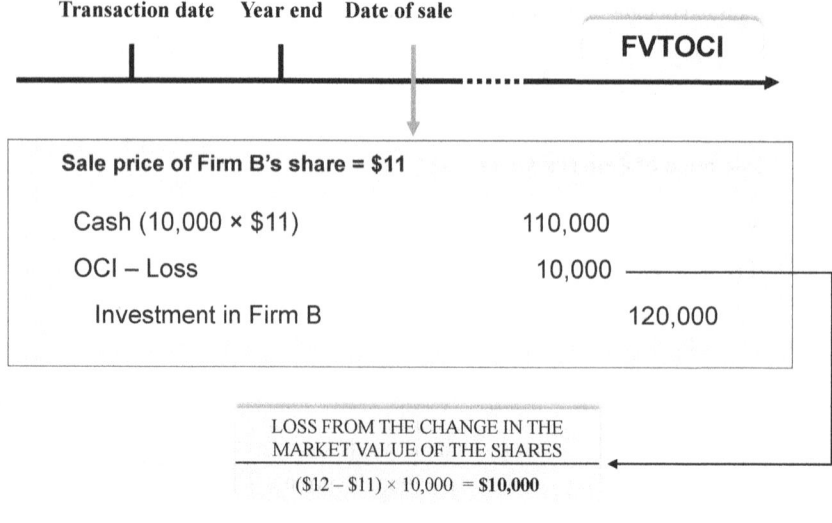

Appendix A
ACCOUNTING FOR NON-STRATEGIC SHARE INVESTMENTS
Under the Cost Method
Year-End

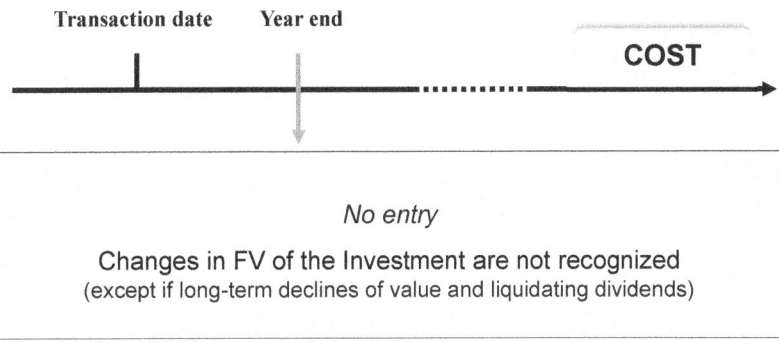

No entry

Changes in FV of the Investment are not recognized
(except if long-term declines of value and liquidating dividends)

Appendix A
ACCOUNTING FOR NON-STRATEGIC SHARE INVESTMENTS
Under the Cost Method
Date of Sale

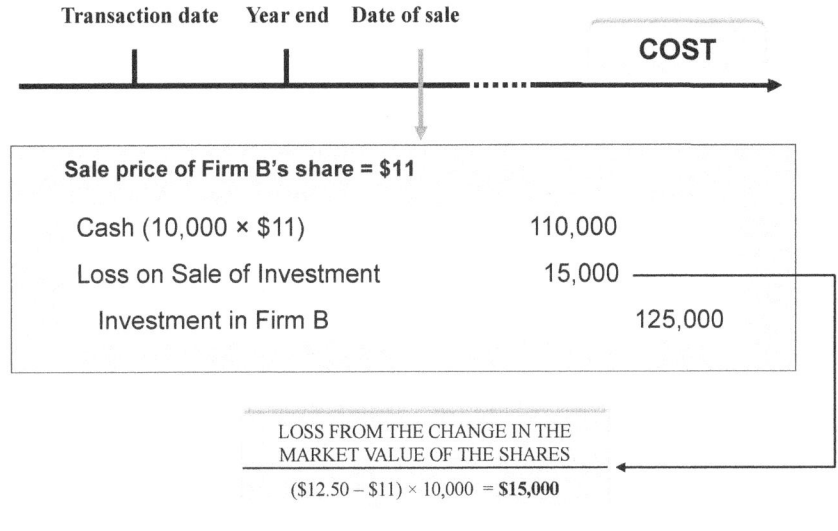

Sale price of Firm B's share = $11

Cash (10,000 × $11)	110,000	
Loss on Sale of Investment	15,000	
Investment in Firm B		125,000

LOSS FROM THE CHANGE IN THE MARKET VALUE OF THE SHARES
($12.50 − $11) × 10,000 = **$15,000**

Appendix A
ACCOUNTING FOR NON-STRATEGIC SHARE INVESTMENTS
Dividends

When Declared

Dividends Receivable	XXX	
Dividend Income		XXX

When Declared and Paid

Cash	XXX	
Dividend Income		XXX

Appendix B
Investment in Associates: Equity Methods

This publication is protected by copyright, and permission should be obtained from the publisher prior to any prohibited reproduction, storage in a retrieval system, or transmission in any form or by any means, electronic, mechanical, photocopying, recording, or otherwise.

Copyright © 2020 Parmitech

APPENDIX B
Investments in Associates: Equity Method

Objectives of this section

Review the accounting for investments in Associates.

Identify situations where a significant influence prevails.

Key concepts

- Equity method
- Significant influence
- Equity in earnings
- IAS 28

Introduction ---------- Module 1 ----------

Appendix B

INVESTMENTS IN ASSOCIATES
Context

Voting Power
A holding of 20% or more of the voting shares is taken as evidence that significant influence exists, unless evidence exists to prove otherwise.

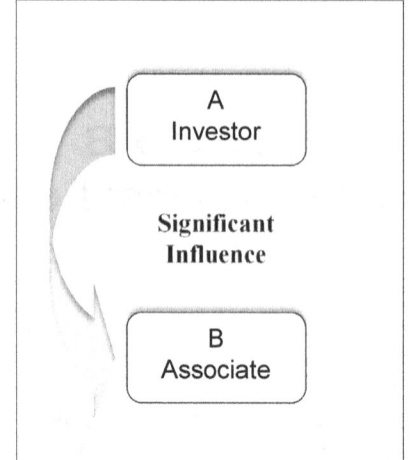

Substance over Form
A holding of less than 20% of the voting shares is indicative of lack of significant influence unless evidence exists to prove otherwise.

Firm A, the Investor, has a significant influence over Firm B, the Associate.

Appendix B

INVESTMENTS IN ASSOCIATES
Significant Influence
Operational Definition

- **LEGAL DIMENSION**

    $20\% < \text{VOTING SHARES} < 50\%$

- **SUBSTANCE OF THE RELATIONSHIP**

    ➡ COMPOSITION OF THE BOARD OF DIRECTORS

    ➡ EXTENT OF INTERCORPORATE TRANSACTIONS

    ➡ PARTICIPATION IN POLICY-MAKING PROCESSES

    ➡ INTERCHANGE OF MANAGERIAL PERSONNEL

    ➡ PROVISION OF TECHNICAL ASSISTANCE

Appendix B

INVESTMENTS IN ASSOCIATES
Significant Influence
Substance over Form

Determinant Factor

In applying professional judgment, representation on the board of directors is probably the most reliable indicator of the ability of the investor corporation to exercise significant influence.

If the investor company is able to elect one or more members to the investee's board, it would generally be clear that influence is present.

Appendix B

INVESTMENTS IN ASSOCIATES
Significant Influence
Share of Earnings

Influence

The investor plays a part in the earnings process of the investee.

Share of Earnings — Equity in Earnings

I/S

Appendix B

INVESTMENTS IN ASSOCIATES
Significant Influence
Share of Dividends

Influence

Dividends of the Investee are treated as a recovery of the equity investment.

Share of Dividends   Decrease of Equity Investment

SFP

Introduction ---------- Module 1 ---------- 7

Appendix B

INVESTMENTS IN ASSOCIATES
Equity Method
Journal Entries

PROPORTIONATE SHARE OF EARNINGS

1

Investment in B	XX	
Equity in earnings of B (I/S)		XX

PROPORTIONATE SHARE OF DIVIDENDS

2

Cash	XX	
Investment in B		XX

Proportionate share of the change of B' retained earnings

Introduction ---------- Module 1 ---------- 8

Appendix B

INVESTMENTS IN ASSOCIATES
Equity Method
Investment Account Reconciliation

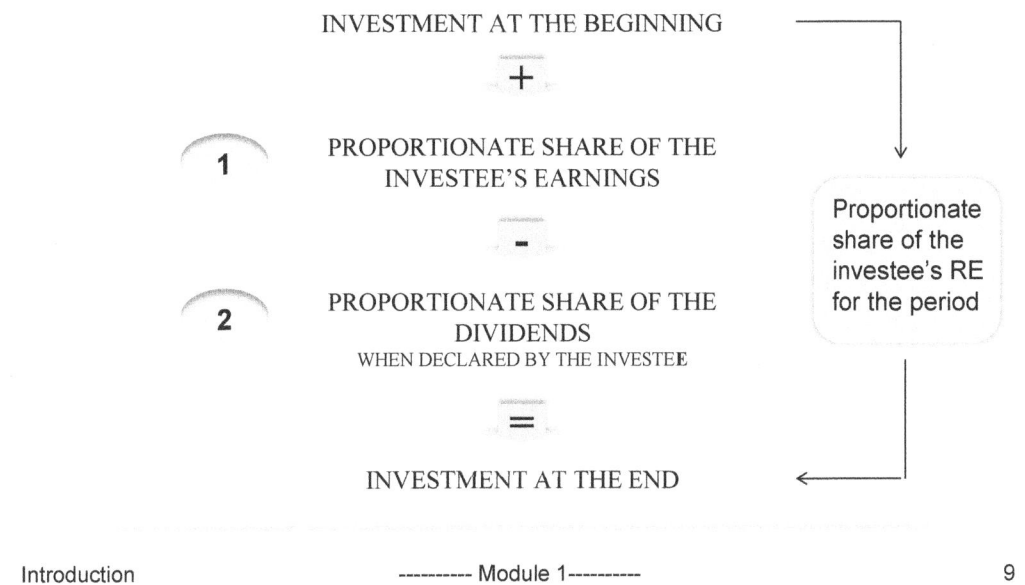

Introduction ---------- Module 1----------

Appendix B

INVESTMENTS IN ASSOCIATES
Equity Method
Illustration

Assume that on December 31 X1, Call Company purchases 30 percent of the outstanding voting shares of the Tell Company for $500,000. The investment gives Call significant influence over Tell.

Both companies have a year end on December 31. The Tell's Comprehensive Income and Dividends for each of the two years are as follows:

Year	Comprehensive Income	Dividends
X2	$ 1,200,000	$300,000
X3	800,000	100,000
Total	**$ 2,000,000**	**$ 400,000**

Introduction ---------- Module 1----------

Appendix B

INVESTMENTS IN ASSOCIATES
Equity Method
Illustration - X2

Provide the journal entries on the books of Call to account for its investment in Tell for X2 under the equity method.

PROPORTIONATE SHARE OF EARNINGS

1

Investment in Tell	360,000	
Equity in earnings of Tell		360,000

PROPORTIONATE SHARE OF DIVIDENDS

2

Cash	90,000	
Investment in Tell		90,000

Proportionate share of the change of Tell' retained earnings for X2: ($1,200,000 - $300,000) × 30% = **$270,000**

Introduction ---------- Module 1---------- 11

Appendix B

INVESTMENTS IN ASSOCIATES
Equity Method
Illustration - Balance of the Equity Investment at the End of X2

Initial investment				$500,000
◆ Share of earnings (30%)	X2	($1,200,000 × 30%)	360,000	
◆ Share of dividends (30%)	X2	(300,000 × 30%)	(90,000)	
Investment at the end of X2			**$770,000**	

30% of the change in Tell's retained earnings since acquisition

Introduction ---------- Module 1---------- 12

Appendix B

INVESTMENTS IN ASSOCIATES
Equity Method
Illustration - X3

Provide the journal entries on the books of Call to account for its investment in Tell for X3 under the equity method.

PROPORTIONATE SHARE OF EARNINGS

1
Investment in Tell	240,000	
Equity in earnings of Tell		240,000

PROPORTIONATE SHARE OF DIVIDENDS

2
Cash	30,000	
Investment in Tell		30,000

Proportionate share of the change of Tell' retained earnings for X3: ($800,000 - $100,000) × 30% = **$210,000**

Appendix B

INVESTMENTS IN ASSOCIATES
Equity Method
Illustration - Balance of the Equity Investment at the End of X3

Initial investment				$500,000
◆ Share of earnings (30%)	X2	$1,200,000		
	X3	800,000		
		2,000,000 × 30%		600,000
◆ Share of dividends (30%)	X2	300,000		
	X3	100,000		
		400,000 × 30%		(120,000)
Investment at the end of X3				**$980,000**

30% of the change in Tell's retained earnings since acquisition

Appendix B

INVESTMENTS IN ASSOCIATES
Equity Method
Summary

- The Equity Investment is initially reported at its purchase price.
- Dividends are treated as a recovery of the investment and, as a result, reduce the Equity investment account.
- The investor reports income equal to its percentage share of the investee's reported income (Equity in Earnings).
- Reporting the share of earnings as revenue makes sense since the investor plays a part in the earnings process of the investee.
- As a result, the Equity Investment account varies to reflect corresponding variations of the investee's retained earnings: share of earnings *minus* share of dividends.
- Changes in fair value of the Equity Investment are not recognized.

Introduction ---------- Module 1 ---------- 15

Appendix B

EQUITY METHOD
Closely Related to Consolidation

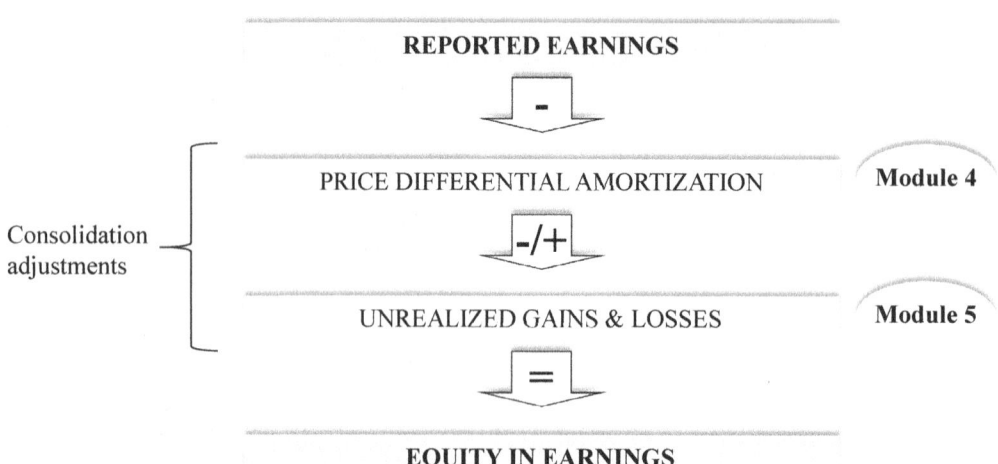

Note that the equity in earnings should be computed by the consolidation method. Since consolidation adjustments must be captured under the equity method, equity method and consolidation are closely related. This point will be illustrated in the following modules.

Introduction ---------- Module 1 ---------- 16

Appendix B

PART 2
Concept Check

> Justify the use of the equity method for investments in associates.

_____
_____
_____
_____
_____
_____
_____

Copyright © 2020, Parmitech, Ottawa. Parmitech. All rights reserved.

Exercise 1-1
Cost versus Equity Reporting

West Corporation purchased 40 percent of the stock of Full Company on January 1, X2, at underlying book value. The companies reported the following operating results and dividend payments during the first three years of intercorporate ownership:

Year	West Corporation Comp. Income	West Corporation Dividends	Full Company Comp. Income	Full Company Dividends
X2	$100,000	$40,000	$70,000	$30,000
X3	60,000	80,000	40,000	60,000
X4	250,000	120,000	25,000	50,000

Required
Compute the comprehensive income reported by West for each of the three years, assuming West accounts for its investment in full using the following methods:

a) The cost method
b) The equity method

Cost Method

$X_2 = 100,000 + (0.4 \times 30,000) = 112,000$

$X_3 = 60,000 + (60,000 \times 0.4) = 84,000$

$X_4 = 250,000 + 0.4 \times 50,000 = 270,000$

Equity Method

$X_2 = 100,000 + 0.4 \times 70,000 = 128,000$

$X_3 = 60,000 + 0.4 \times 40,000 = 76,000$

$X_4 = 250,000 + 0.4 \times 25,000 = 260,000$

Copyright © 2020, Parmitech, Ottawa. Parmitech. All rights reserved.

Exercise 1-2
Acquisition Price

Phil Company bought 40 percent ownership in Brown Company on January 1, X1, at underlying book value. In X1, X2, and X3, Brown reported comprehensive income of $8,000, $12,000, $20,000, and dividends of $15,000, $10,000, and $10,000, respectively.

The balance in Phil Company's investment account on December 31, X3, was $54,000.

Required
In each of the following independent cases, determine the amount that Phil paid for its investment in Brown stock assuming that Phil accounted for its investment in Brown using the following methods:

  a) The cost method
  b) The equity method

Cost Method

$X_1 = 8000 \quad X_2 = 12,000 \quad X_3 = 20,000$
$D_1 = 15,000 \quad D_2 = 10,000 \quad D_3 = 10,000$

purchase price: $54,000.

Equity Method

purchase price $= 54,000 - \{0.4 \times (8000 + 12,000 + 20,000) + 0.4 \times (15K + 10K + 10K)\}$

$= \$52,000.$

Exercise 1-3
Investment Income

Draft Corporation purchased 30 percent of the stock of Water Company for $90,000 on January 1, X6, when Water had capital stock of $240,000 and retained earnings of $60,000. The following data were reported by the companies for the years X6 through X9:

Year	Comprehensive Income Draft	Comprehensive Income Water	Dividends Declared Draft	Dividends Declared Water
X6	$140,000	$30,000	$70,000	$20,000
X7	80,000	50,000	70,000	40,000
X8	220,000	10,000	90,000	40,000
X9	160,000	40,000	100,000	20,000

Required
Compute the comprehensive income reported by Draft for each of the years, assuming it accounts for its investment in Water using:

a) The cost method
b) The equity method

(margin notes: stock 240,000; 30% for 90,000; earnings 60,000)

Cost Method

$X_6 = 140,000 + 0.3 \times 20,000 = 146,000$

$X_7 = 80,000 + 0.3 \times 40,000 = 92,000$

$X_8 = 220,000 + 0.3 \times 40000 = 232,000$

$X_9 = 160,000 + 0.3 \times 20,000 = 166,000$

Equity Method

$X_6 = 140,000 + 0.3 \times 30,000 = 149,000$

$X_7 = 80,000 + 0.3 \times 50,000 = 95,000$

$X_8 = 220,000 + 0.3 \times 10,000 = 223,000$

$X_9 = 160,000 + 0.3 \times 40,000 = 172,000$

Exercise 1-4
Journal Entries under the Equity Method

Investor Corporation purchased 14,400 common shares of Investee Corporation for $9 per share. The shares represent 25% ownership in Investee which gives Investor a significant influence over Investee.

- Investee reports net income of $96,000.
- Investor receives a cash dividend of $1.50 per common share from Investee.
- Investor sells all 14,400 common shares for $144,600.

Required
Present the journal entries to account for the transactions above.

14,400 at $9 per share.
25%

Initial Purchase		
Dr Investment	129,600	
Cr Cash		129,600

Share of Earnings		
Dr Investment	24,000	
Cr Equity in earnings		24,000

Share of Dividends		
Dr Cash	21,600	
Cr Investment		21,600

Sale of 14,400 Shares		
Dr Cash	144,600	
Cr Investment		132,000
Cr Gain		12,600

Copyright © 2020, Parmitech, Ottawa. Parmitech. All rights reserved.

Solutions to Exercises

1-1

a)
- X2 $100,000 + (40\% \times \$30,000) = \$112,000$
- X3 $\$60,000 + (40\% \times \$60,000) = \$84,000$
- X4 $\$250,000 + (40\% \times \$50,000) = \$270,000$

b)
- X2 $\$100,000 + (40\% \times \$70,000) = \$128,000$
- X3 $\$60,000 + (40\% \times \$40,000) = \$76,000$
- X4 $\$250,000 + (40\% \times \$25,000) = \$260,000$

1-2

a)   Purchase price = $54,000

b)   Purchase price = $54,000 − 40% ($8,000 + $12,000 + $20,000)
                       + 40% ($15,000 + $10,000 + $10,000)
Purchase price = $52,000

1-3

a)
- X6 $\$140,000 + (30\% \times \$20,000) = \$146,000$
- X7 $\$80,000 + (30\% \times \$40,000) = \$92,000$
- X8 $\$220,000 + (30\% \times \$40,000) = \$232,000$
- X9 $\$160,000 + (30\% \times \$20,000) = \$166,000$

b)
- X6 $\$140,000 + (30\% \times \$30,000) = \$149,000$
- X7 $\$80,000 + (30\% \times \$50,000) = \$95,000$
- X8 $\$220,000 + (30\% \times \$10,000) = \$223,000$
- X9 $\$160,000 + (30\% \times \$40,000) = \$172,000$

1-4

Investment in Investee	129,600	
Cash (14,400 × $9)		129,600
Investment in Investee	24,000	
Equity in Earnings		24,000
Cash (14,400 × $1.50)	21,600	
Investment in Investee		21,600
Cash	144,600	
Investment in Investee		132,000
Gain on Sale of Shares		12,600

Consolidation of Parent Founded Subsidiaries

Module 2

What you will find in this section

- How to Walk Through Module 2
- Slides
- Exercises and Solutions

Module 2
Consolidation of Parent Founded Subsidiaries

How to Walk Through Module 2

◇ Readings

1- Book "Consolidation of Financial Statements": Chapters 1 and 4
2- Student Manual "Advanced Accounting": Module 2
   PART 1: CONSOLIDATION OF PARENT FOUNDED SUBSIDIARIES AT THE DATE OF CREATION: THE DOUBLE-COUNTING ISSUE
   PART 2: INTERCOMPANY TRANSACTIONS: INTRODUCTION
   PART 3: CONSOLIDATION OF PARENT FOUNDED SUBSIDIARIES IN PERIODS SUBSEQUENT TO THE DATE OF CREATION
   PART 4: EQUITY METHOD

◇ Assignments

3- Student Manual: End-of module review and quiz questions
4- Student Manual: Exercises 1 to 6
5- Book: Cases 1 and 2

When you have completed this module successfully you will be able to do the following:

- Define a parent founded subsidiary;

- Demonstrate the mechanics of consolidating a parent founded subsidiary in periods subsequent to the date of creation;

- Account for the impact of intercompany transactions on the consolidation process. Focus on transactions that result in reciprocal balances;

- Discuss the general approach to consolidation under the worksheet approach and the direct approach;

- Discuss the financial reporting implications of using the cost method, the equity method, or full consolidation;

- Present the additional consolidation entries required to eliminate the investment account when the equity method is employed by Parent Company in non-consolidated financial statements.

CONSOLIDATION OF PARENT FOUNDED SUBSIDIARIES
Module 2

Copyright © 2020 Parmitech

Advanced Accounting: Student Manual

Copyrighted Material

Editor: Parmitech

This publication is protected by copyright, and permission should be obtained from the publisher prior to any prohibited reproduction, storage in a retrieval system, or transmission in any form or by any means, electronic, mechanical, photocopying, recording, or otherwise.

Corresponding Author

Richard Bozec Ph.D., CPA, CGA
bozec@telfer.uottawa.ca

Copyright © Parmitech

CORRESPONDING CHAPTERS in *Bozec*
"Consolidation of Financial Statements under IFRS"

Chapter 1 — Parent Founded Subsidiaries

Chapter 4 — Intercompany Dividends

Cases — 1, 2

TEACHING MATERIAL
Exercises

Module 2

2.1	Transfer of Net Assets at the Establishment of a New Subsidiary
2.2	Data from Consolidated Income Statement of Newly Established Subsidiary
2.3	Investment Account in a Newly Established Subsidiary
2.4	Accounting for a Newly Established Subsidiary
2.5	Consolidation One Year Post-Creation
2.6	Newly Established Subsidiary and Equity Method

FOCUS OF THIS MODULE: PARENT FOUNDED SUBSIDIARIES

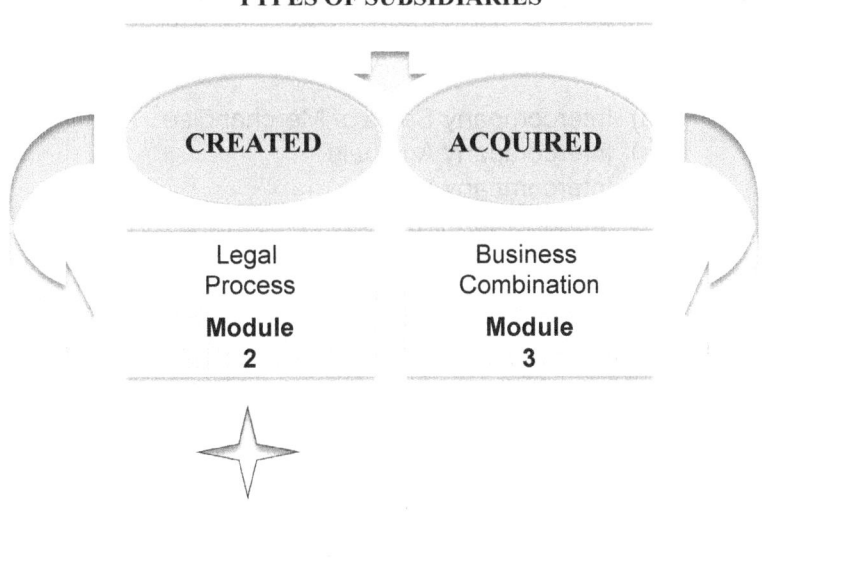

FOCUS OF THIS MODULE: DOUBLE-COUNTING

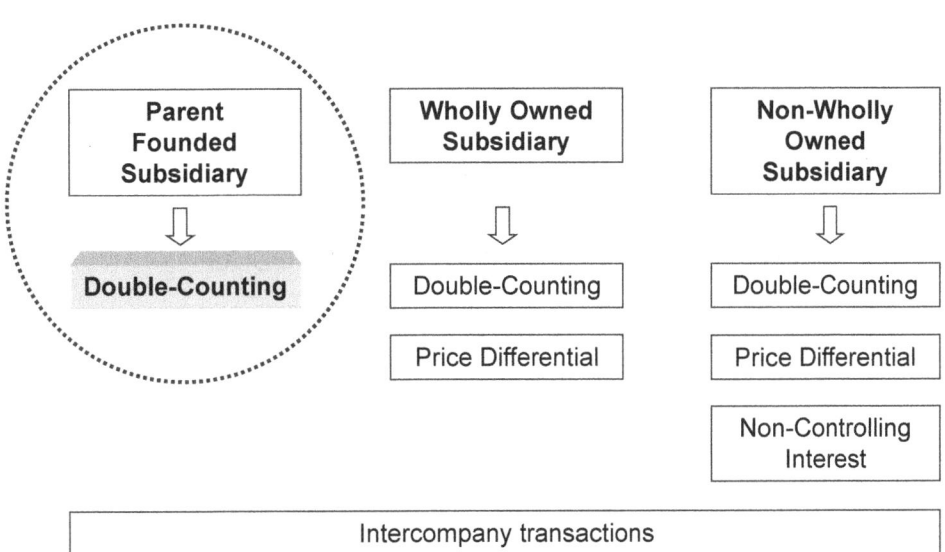

OUTLINE OF THE PRESENTATION

1 CONSOLIDATION OF PARENT FOUNDED SUBSIDIARIES AT THE DATE OF CREATION: THE DOUBLE-COUNTING ISSUE

2 INTERCOMPANY TRANSACTIONS: INTRODUCTION

    a) Intercompany Sales of Merchandise
    b) Intercompany Accruals
    c) Intercompany Loans
    d) Management Fees
    e) Intercompany Rentals
    f) Intercompany Dividends

3 CONSOLIDATION OF PARENT FOUNDED SUBSIDIARIES IN PERIODS SUBSEQUENT TO THE DATE OF CREATION

4 EQUITY METHOD

RECAP

5 REVIEW QUESTIONS

6 QUIZ QUESTIONS

7 KEY TERMS INTRODUCED IN THIS MODULE

8 RECAP ON THE OBJECTIVES OF THIS MODULE

PART 1
Consolidation of Parent Founded Subsidiaries at the Date of Creation: The Double-Counting Issue

Part 1

Objectives of this section

Introduce the basic characteristics of parent founded subsidiaries.

Illustrate the double-counting issue through consolidation at the date of creation.

Key concepts

- Parent founded subsidiary
- Double-counting in the statement of financial position
- Working paper entries

PARENT FOUNDED SUBSIDIARIES
Characteristics

Part 1

- **Legal process**
  Company founded by another company

- **Common practice**
  The vast majority of subsidiaries are founded (not acquired).

- **Created for strategic reasons**
  Risk management, branding, tax purposes, investment opportunities.

- **Controlled entities**
  Usually wholly owned (100%) by the Parent Company

To the public, subsidiaries are associated with acquired companies since business combinations get lots of attention by the media. However, the number of acquired subsidiaries is quite small compared with the number of parent founded subsidiaries.

Part 1

PARENT FOUNDED SUBSIDIARIES
Group Structure or Single Entity

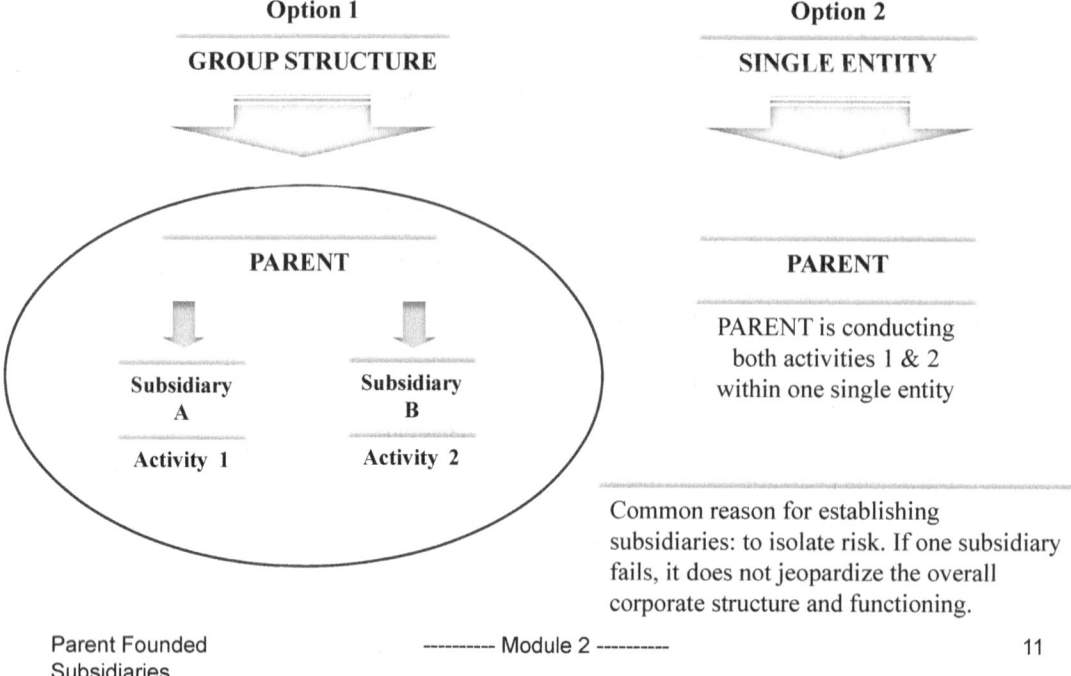

Common reason for establishing subsidiaries: to isolate risk. If one subsidiary fails, it does not jeopardize the overall corporate structure and functioning.

Part 1

MAIN ADVANTAGE TO CREATING SUBSIDIARIES
Limited Liability of the Parent

This is the most popular reason for companies to form subsidiaries. As long as corporate formalities between the parent company and the subsidiary are respected, then the potential losses of the parent company can be limited by using the subsidiary or subsidiaries as a liability shield.

This strategy is actually very common in the movie industry. Most films are independent corporate entities. The production house is the parent company. Even though the production company will benefit from the profits that the movie has made, it will also be protected from such occurrences as lawsuits from the production.

CREATING SUBSIDIARIES
Other Advantages

The Management Is Separated
Forming a subsidiary offers the advantage of having multiple entities in the same business, each with its own management structure that could adapt better to local market and culture.

Different Branding and Identities
This is quite common among clothing companies, which may want to form different clothing lines, each with its own identity that's separate from that of the parent company.

Tax Purposes
A multinational can take advantage of the lower tax rates in another company by incorporating subsidiaries in those countries.

IN THE NEWS
Washington Business Journal - June 2012

The reasoning behind Ensco Inc.'s decision to establish its avionics business as a subsidiary is simple: If an engine on an aircraft that used the company's avionics software malfunctioned, causing a crash, Ensco can't be sued for its entire $100 million in assets.

"A number of our business areas provide services that are critical to sustaining life," said CEO Greg Young. "Without some way to manage those businesses independently, we have no protection."

Limited liability is not the only reason that the Falls Church-based company initiated a corporate restructuring Jan. 4 that established Ensco Avionics Inc. and Ensco Rails Inc. as wholly owned subsidiaries. As in many companies, particularly those that serve both commercial and government markets, the legal separation of divisions provides a host of benefits, from more targeted branding opportunities to greater potential for new investors and merger activities down the road.

PARENT FOUNDED SUBSIDIARIES
Three-Step Process

Part 1

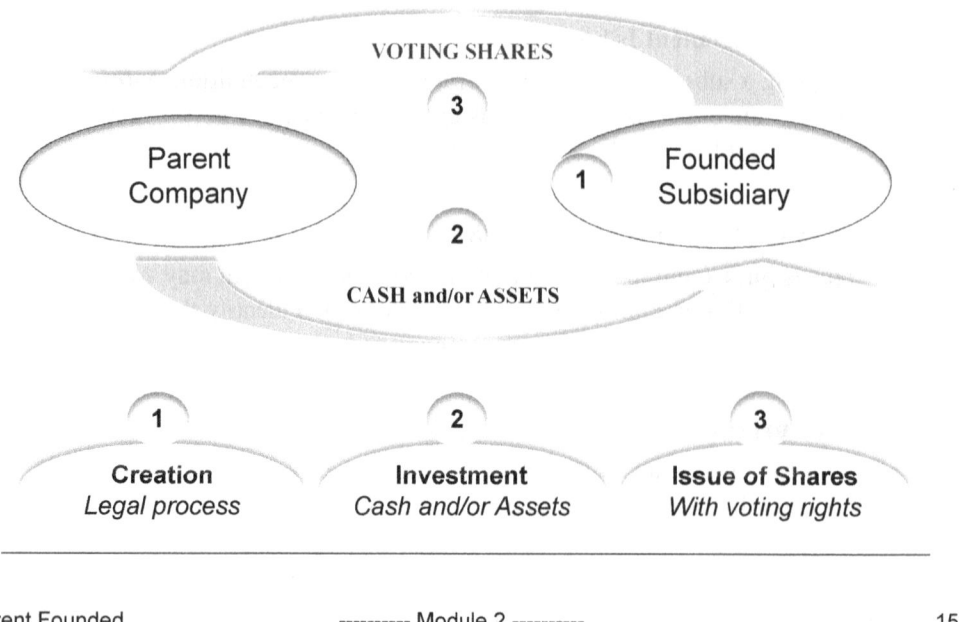

1	2	3
Creation	**Investment**	**Issue of Shares**
Legal process	*Cash and/or Assets*	*With voting rights*

CONSOLIDATION OF PARENT FOUNDED SUBSIDIARIES AT THE DATE OF CREATION
Illustration 1 - Cash Investment

Part 1

In X10, Parent Company establishes a subsidiary by creating a new corporation named Subsidiary Company. Subsidiary issues common shares to Parent in return for $80,000 cash paid by Parent.

Required
Prepare the consolidated statement of financial position of Parent Company at the date of creation.

> This illustration is oversimplified. It serves one objective: to illustrate the double-counting issue and present the core elimination entry required to remove it.

Part 1
ILLUSTRATION 1
Journal Entries at the Date of Creation

Parent

Dr Investments   80,000
  Cr Cash   80,000

Subsidiary

Dr Cash   80,000
  Cr Common Shares   80,000

Parent Founded Subsidiaries — Module 2 —

Part 1
ECONOMIC ENTITY FOLLOWING THE CREATION OF SUBSIDIARY

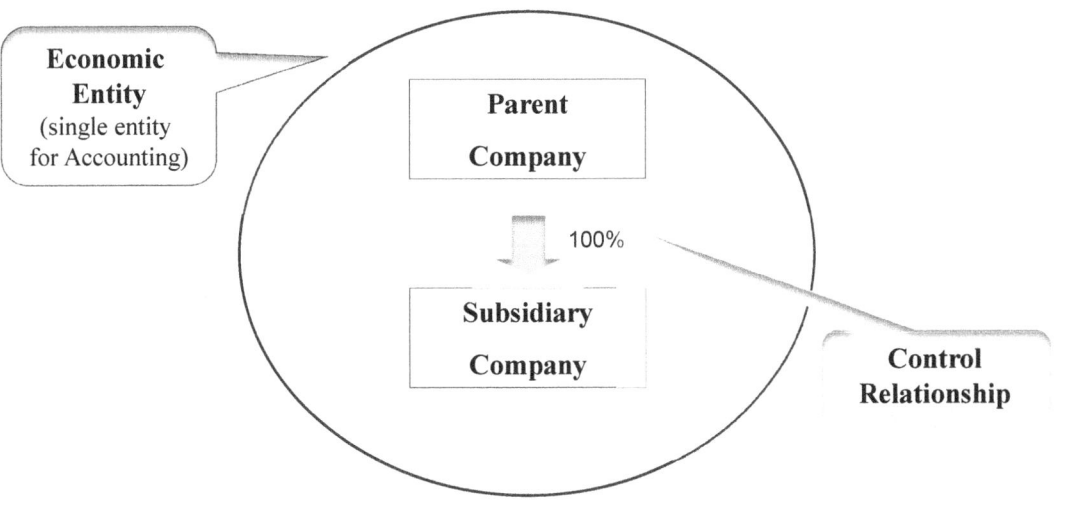

For external reporting purposes, Parent Company and Subsidiary Company are viewed as a single entity namely, the economic entity. Consolidation is then required.

Parent Founded Subsidiaries — Module 2 —

Part 1

CONSOLIDATION OF PARENT FOUNDED SUBSIDIARIES AT THE DATE OF CREATION - ILLUSTRATION 1
Double-Counting

Parent Company

ASSETS	EQUITY
INVESTMENT $80,000	
	LIABILITIES

Subsidiary Company

ASSETS	EQUITY Common Shares $80,000
Cash: $80,000	
	LIABILITIES

---------- DOUBLE-COUNTING ----------

Parent Founded Subsidiaries ---------- Module 2 ---------- 19

Part 1

CONSOLIDATION OF PARENT FOUNDED SUBSIDIARIES AT THE DATE OF CREATION
Double-Counting - Equation

Investment in Subsidiary (Parent)

=

Equity or NBV (Subsidiary)

=

Assets – Liabilities (Subsidiary)

Reciprocal investment and equity accounts at the date of creation must be eliminated to avoid double-counting.

Parent Founded Subsidiaries ---------- Module 2 ---------- 20

CONSOLIDATION OF PARENT FOUNDED SUBSIDIARIES AT THE DATE OF CREATION - ILLUSTRATION 1
Core Consolidation Entry

Complete this slide

Working Paper

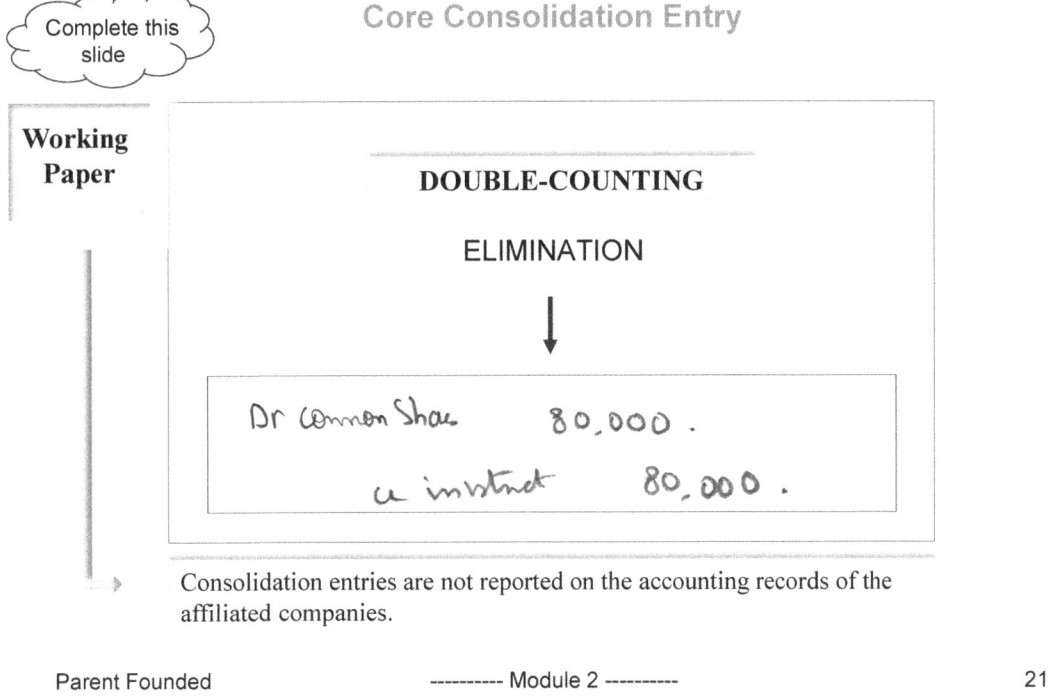

DOUBLE-COUNTING ELIMINATION

Dr Common Shares   80,000
   Cr Investment   80,000

- Consolidation entries are not reported on the accounting records of the affiliated companies.

Parent Founded Subsidiaries — Module 2 —   21

CONSOLIDATION OF PARENT FOUNDED SUBSIDIARIES AT THE DATE OF CREATION
Illustration 2 - Transfer of Assets

In X10, Parent Company establishes a subsidiary by creating a new corporation named Subsidiary Company. Subsidiary issues common shares to Parent in return for the following assets:

	BV	FV
➢ Inventory	60,000	75,000
➢ Land	50,000	90,000
➢ Buildings (net)	150,000	240,000

Required
Prepare the consolidated statement of financial position of Parent Company at the date of creation.

Parent Founded Subsidiaries — Module 2 —   22

Part 1

ILLUSTRATION 2
Journal Entries at the Date of Creation

Book value is used to transfer assets to a newly founded subsidiary in the absence of an arm's length transaction.

Parent

Investment in Subsidiary	260,000	
Inventory (BV)		60,000
Land (BV)		50,000
Buildings (BV)		150,000

Subsidiary

Inventory	60,000	
Land	50,000	
Buildings	150,000	
Common Shares		260,000

Part 1

CONSOLIDATION OF PARENT FOUNDED SUBSIDIARIES AT THE DATE OF CREATION - ILLUSTRATION 2
Double-Counting

Parent Company

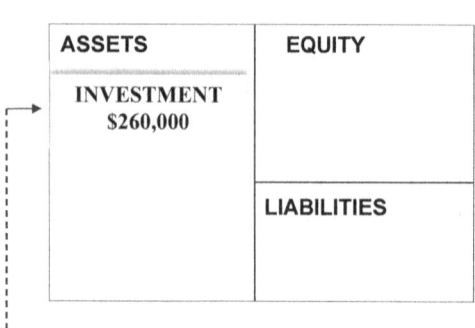

Subsidiary Company

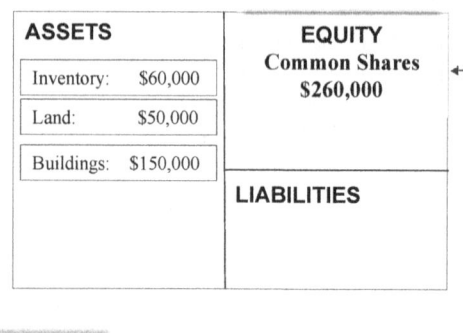

DOUBLE-COUNTING

CONSOLIDATION OF PARENT FOUNDED SUBSIDIARIES AT THE DATE OF CREATION - ILLUSTRATION 2
Core Consolidation Entry

Working Paper

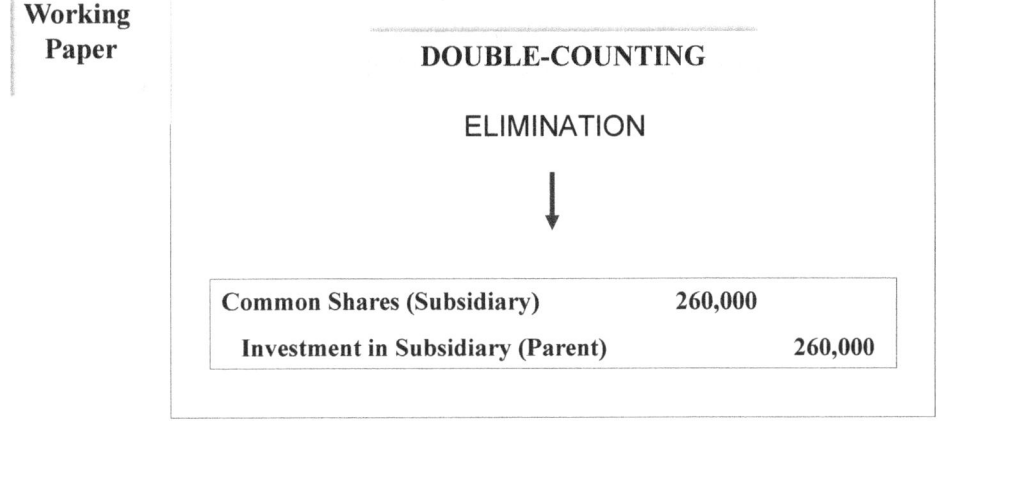

Common Shares (Subsidiary)	260,000	
Investment in Subsidiary (Parent)		260,000

Parent Founded Subsidiaries ---------- Module 2 ----------

CONSOLIDATION OF PARENT FOUNDED SUBSIDIARIES AT THE DATE OF CREATION
Double-Counting - Consolidation Process

Investment in Subsidiary (Parent)

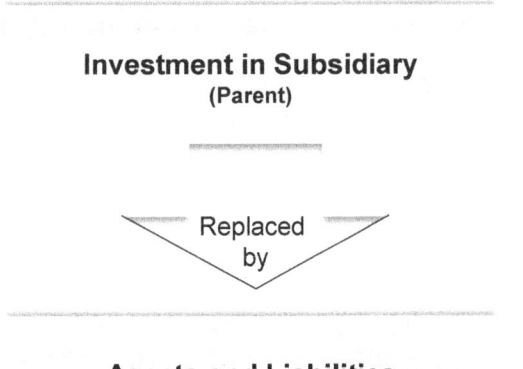

Replaced by

Assets and Liabilities (Subsidiary)

One can view the consolidation process as replacing the investment account by the Subsidiary's detailed assets and liabilities accounts.

Parent Founded Subsidiaries ---------- Module 2 ----------

PART 1
Concept Check

> What is "double-counting" in the context of consolidation?

OUTLINE OF THE PRESENTATION

1 CONSOLIDATION OF PARENT FOUNDED SUBSIDIARIES AT THE DATE OF CREATION : THE DOUBLE-COUNTING ISSUE

2 INTERCOMPANY TRANSACTIONS: INTRODUCTION

    a) Intercompany Sales of Merchandise
    b) Intercompany Accruals
    c) Intercompany Loans
    d) Management Fees
    e) Intercompany Rentals
    f) Intercompany Dividends

3 CONSOLIDATION OF PARENT FOUNDED SUBSIDIARIES IN PERIODS SUBSEQUENT TO THE DATE OF CREATION

4 EQUITY METHOD

PART 2
Intercompany Transactions: Introduction

Objective of this section

Illustrate the impact of intercompany transactions on the consolidation process. Focus on transactions that result in reciprocal balances. Intercompany transactions involving intercompany gains and losses will be introduced in Module 5.

Key concepts

- Intercompany transactions
- Intercompany dividends
- Upstream and downstream transactions
- Reciprocal balances
- Double-counting of subsidiary's earnings

INTERCOMPANY TRANSACTIONS
Basic Principles

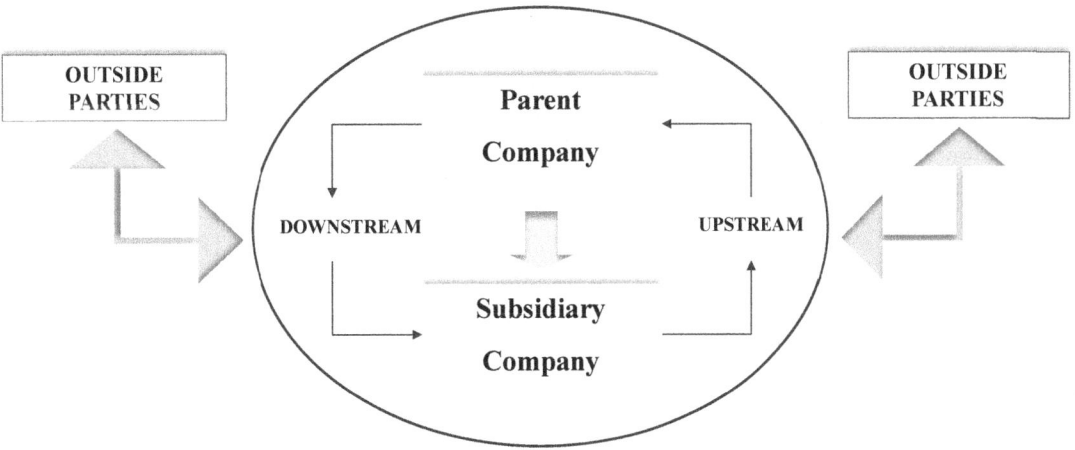

Only transactions conducted between the combined entity and outsiders must be reported in the consolidated F/S. Therefore, we need to carefully examine transfers within the group in order to remove any excess. Intercompany transactions are either **downstream** (Parent to Subsidiary) or **upstream** (Subsidiary to Parent).

Part 2

INTERCOMPANY TRANSACTIONS
Illustrations Covered Next

➡ **RECIPROCAL BALANCES**
   a) Intercompany Sales of Merchandise
   b) Intercompany Accruals (Receivables – Payables)
   c) Intercompany Loans
   d) Management Fees
   e) Intercompany Rentals

➡ **INTERCOMPANY DIVIDENDS**

Module 5 will review in more details the consolidation adjustments required in the context of intercompany gains and losses following transfers of assets (land, inventory, depreciable assets). Instead, this section focuses on intercompany transactions which result in **reciprocal balances**, that is, offsetting balances reported by both Parent and Subsidiary (Receivable-Payable). Since reciprocal balances cannot be neutralized by simply cross-adding the individual F/S of the affiliated companies through consolidation, they must be eliminated. Such eliminations are required in order to avoid overstating the consolidated balances.

Part 2

INTERCOMPANY SALES OF MERCHANDISE
Illustration 1 - Basic Information

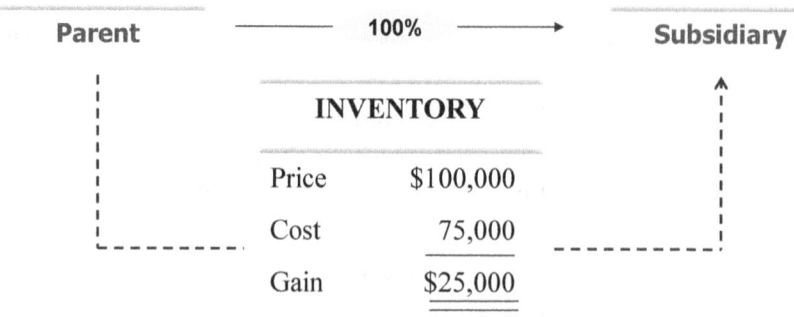

	INVENTORY	
Price	$100,000	
Cost	75,000	
Gain	$25,000	

Parent sold merchandise to Subsidiary (downstream transaction) for $100,000, all of which was sold by Subsidiary for $120,000 to external parties prior to the end of the current accounting period (X1).

Part 2

INTERCOMPANY SALES OF MERCHANDISE
Illustration 1 - Main Issue

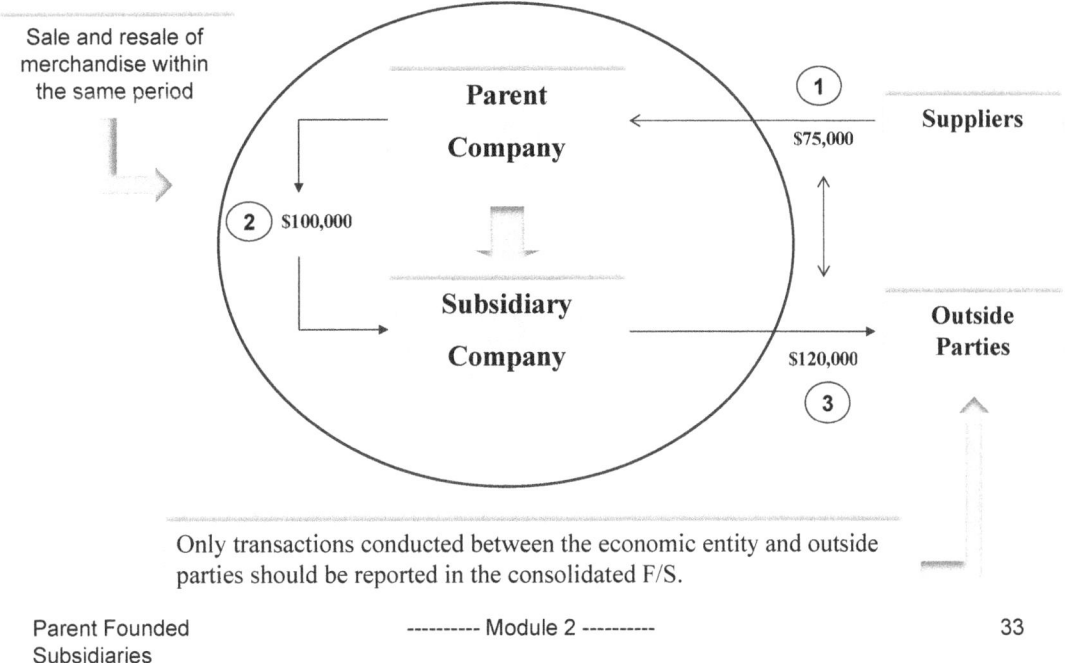

Only transactions conducted between the economic entity and outside parties should be reported in the consolidated F/S.

Part 2

INTERCOMPANY SALES OF MERCHANDISE
Illustration 1 - Journal Entries

Parent			Subsidiary		
Cash	100,000		Inventory	100,000	
Sales		100,000	Cash		100,000
Cost of Goods Sold	75,000		Cash	120,000	
Inventory		75,000	Sales		120,000
			Cost of Goods Sold	100,000	
			Inventory		100,000

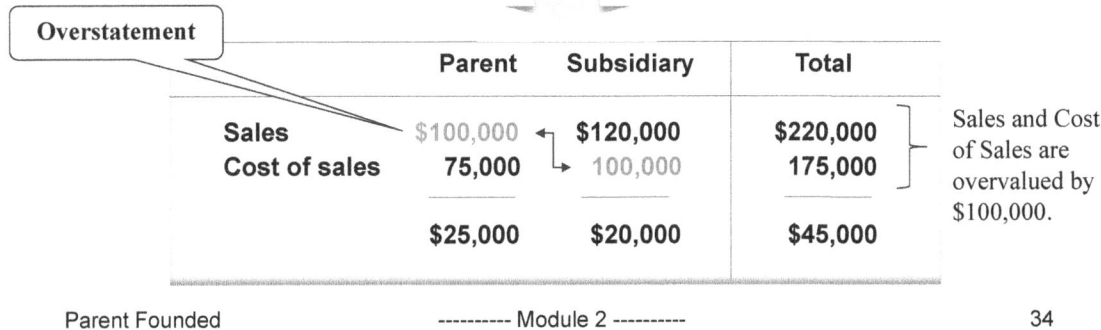

Part 2
INTERCOMPANY SALES OF MERCHANDISE
Illustration 1 - Consolidation Entry - X1

Working Paper

Dr Sales (parent) 100,000
  Cr COGS (subsidiary) 100,000

Overstatement of *Sales* and *Cost of Sales* is based on the transfer price of the units being resold by Subsidiary ($100,000). The elimination of the overstatement has no impact on the consolidated comprehensive income and, consequently, on the consolidated net value (SFP).

Part 2
INTERCOMPANY SALES OF MERCHANDISE
Illustration 1 - Impact of the Elimination on the Consolidated F/S - X1

I/S

➤ Revenues	- 100,000
➤ Expenses	- 100,000
Profit	-

Overstatement

SFP

➤ Assets	-
➤ Liabilities	-
Net value	-

Part 2

INTERCOMPANY SALES OF MERCHANDISE
Illustration 1 - Takeaways

From the standpoint of the economic entity, only transactions realized with parties outside the consolidated group are important. This illustration shows how it could be misleading to rely exclusively on the individual financial statements of the affiliated companies.

This is especially true if the parent company intentionally improves its apparent sales level by requiring (or forcing) the subsidiary to purchase unneeded quantities of goods. Parent company could also boost artificially other revenue by charging high management fees to the subsidiary. In any case, consolidated statements eliminate the potential benefit of such intragroup transactions.

Note that consolidated income is not affected when we proceed with the elimination of an equal amount of revenues and expenses (reciprocal balances).

Part 2

INTERCOMPANY SALES OF MERCHANDISE
Illustration 2 - Basic Information

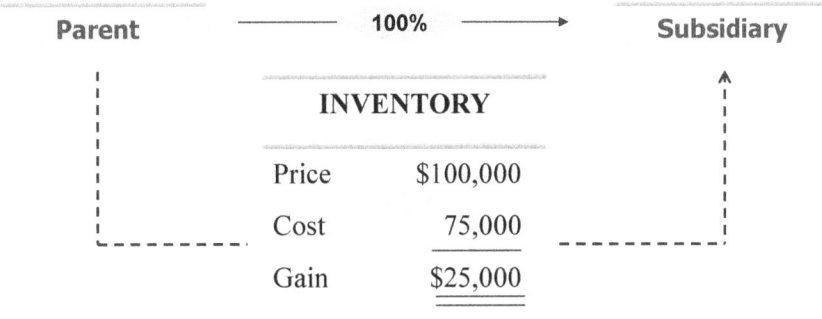

Parent sold merchandise to Subsidiary for $100,000, all of which was kept by Subsidiary at the end of the current accounting period (X1).

Part 2

INTERCOMPANY SALES OF MERCHANDISE
Illustration 2 - Main Issue

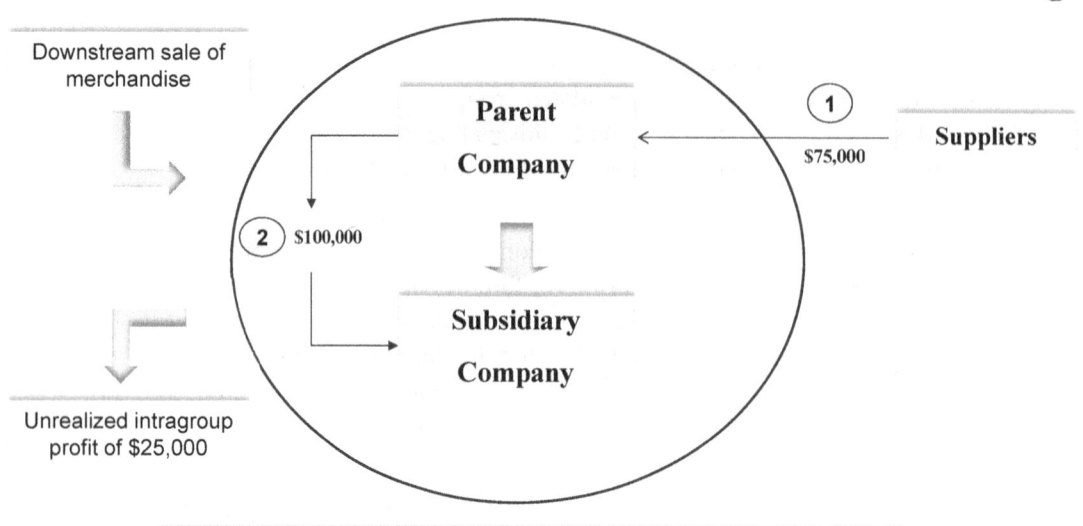

Downstream sale of merchandise

Unrealized intragroup profit of $25,000

① Suppliers $75,000

② $100,000

Parent Company

Subsidiary Company

Only transactions conducted between the economic entity and outside parties should be reported in the consolidated F/S.

Parent Founded Subsidiaries ---------- Module 2 ---------- 39

Part 2

INTERCOMPANY SALES OF MERCHANDISE
Illustration 2 - Journal Entries

Parent

Cash	100,000	
Sales		100,000
Cost of Goods Sold	75,000	
Inventory		75,000

Subsidiary

Inventory	100,000	
Cash		100,000

	Parent	Subsidiary	Total	
Sales	$100,000	-	$100,000	From the viewpoint of the group, this transaction does not exist.
Cost of sales	75,000	-	75,000	
Unrealized Profit	$25,000	-	$25,000	

Parent Founded Subsidiaries ---------- Module 2 ---------- 40

Part 2

INTERCOMPANY SALES OF MERCHANDISE
Illustration 2 - Consolidation Entry - X1

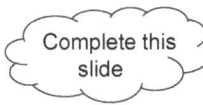

Working Paper

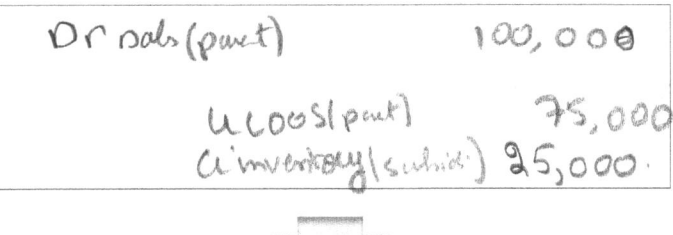

Dr Sales (parent)   100,000
  Cr COGS (parent)   75,000
  Cr inventory (subsid.)   25,000

Unrealized profit ($25,000) is eliminated and removed from the inventory as if the intercompany sales never occurred. Note that such elimination affects not only the current profit, but also the consolidated net value. We will return to this issue in Module 5.

Part 2

INTERCOMPANY SALES OF MERCHANDISE
Illustration 2 - Impact of the Elimination on the Consolidated F/S - X1

I/S

- Revenues   - 100,000
- Expenses   - 75,000

Profit   - 25,000 ← Unrealized Profit

SFP

- Assets   - 25,000
- Liabilities   -

Net value   - 25,000

INTERCOMANY ACCRUALS
Illustration

Intercompany transfers of inventory can give rise to reciprocal receivable and payable balances. Following downstream sale of inventory from Parent, assume such balances to be equal to $10,000 at the end of the accounting period X1.

	Parent	Subsidiary	Total
➢ Receivable from Subsidiary	$10,000		$10,000
➢ Due to Parent		$10,000	$10,000

Receivable and Payable are overvalued by $10,000.

Part 2 — Parent Founded Subsidiaries — Module 2 — 43

INTERCOMPANY ACCRUALS
Consolidation Entry - X1

Complete this slide

Working Paper

Dr Due To parent (subsidiary)   10,000
  Cr Receivables from subsidiary (parent)   10,000

This entry eliminates the overstatement of current assets and current liabilities. It has no impact on the consolidated net value. Intercompany accruals can often be visually identified by analyzing the individual F/S of the affiliated companies.

Part 2 — Parent Founded Subsidiaries — Module 2 — 44

INTERCOMPANY ACCRUALS
Impact of the Elimination on the Consolidated F/S - X1

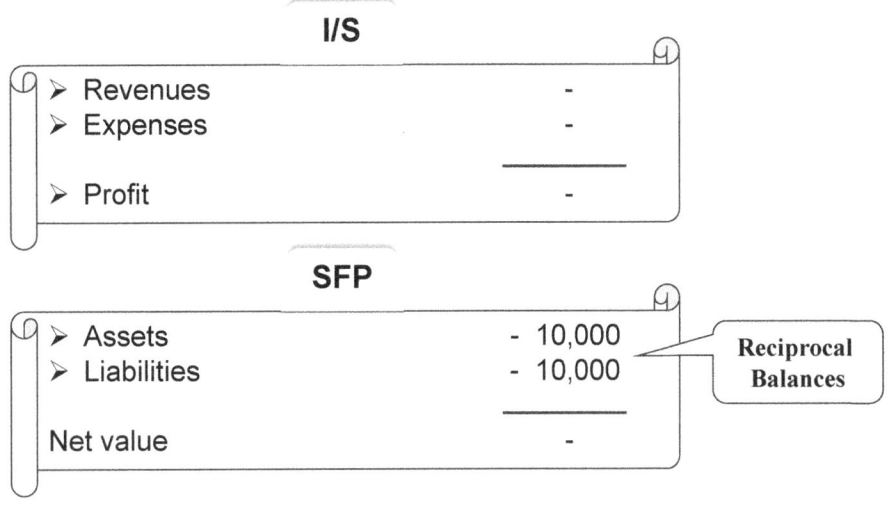

INTERCOMPANY LOANS
Illustration

Assume that Parent loans **$100,000** to Subsidiary and receives a note payable on demand with interest at **10 percent**.

- The loan is issued during the current period on June 30, X1.
- The interest is payable once a year on June 30.
- The loan is paid in full on June 30, X3.

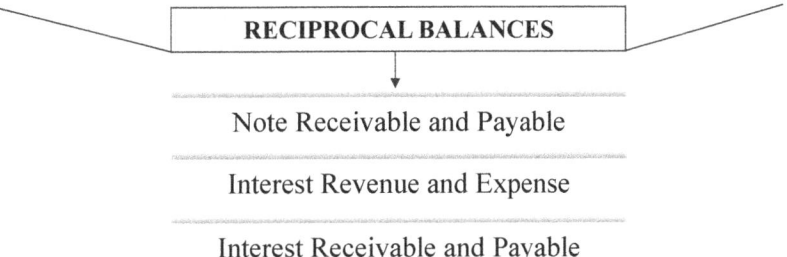

Note Receivable and Payable

Interest Revenue and Expense

Interest Receivable and Payable

INTERCOMPANY LOANS
Entries on the Books of the Affiliated Companies - X1

Part 2

PARENT

June 30

Note Receivable	100,000	
Cash		100,000

SUBSIDIARY

Cash	100,000	
Note Payable		100,000

December 31

Interest Receivable	5,000	
Interest Revenue		5,000

Interest Expense	5,000	
Interest Payable		5,000

ALL RECIPROCAL BALANCES MUST BE ELIMINATED

Parent Founded Subsidiaries — Module 2 — 47

INTERCOMPANY LOANS
Consolidation Entries

Part 2

Complete this slide

Working Paper

Note Receivable and Payable

Dr Note payable (sub)   100,000
  Cr Note receivable (parent)   100,000

Interest Revenue and Expense — 6 months

Dr Interest revenue (parent)   5,000
  Cr Interest expense   5,000

Interest Receivable and Payable — 6 months

Dr Interest payable   5,000
  Cr Interest receivable   5,000

Parent Founded Subsidiaries — Module 2 — 48

Part 2

INTERCOMPANY LOANS
Impact of the Eliminations on the Consolidated F/S - X1

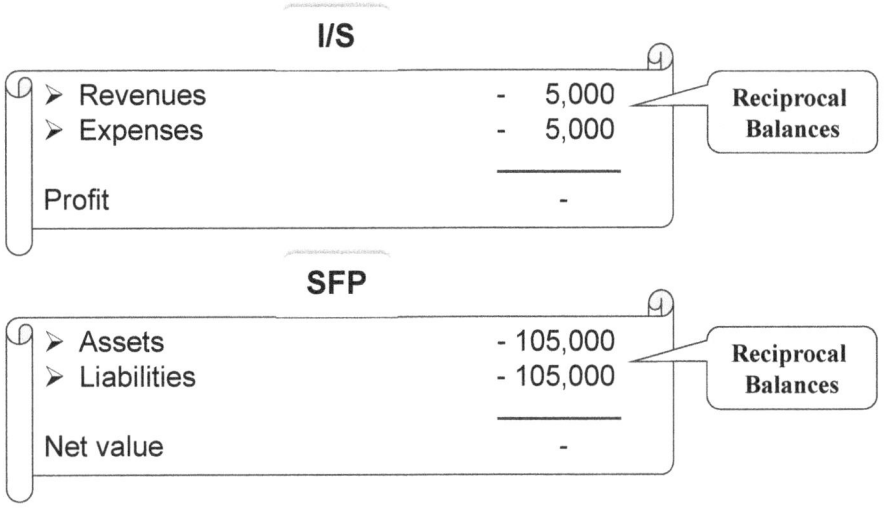

Part 2

INTERCOMPANY LOANS
Entries on the Books of the Affiliated Companies - X2

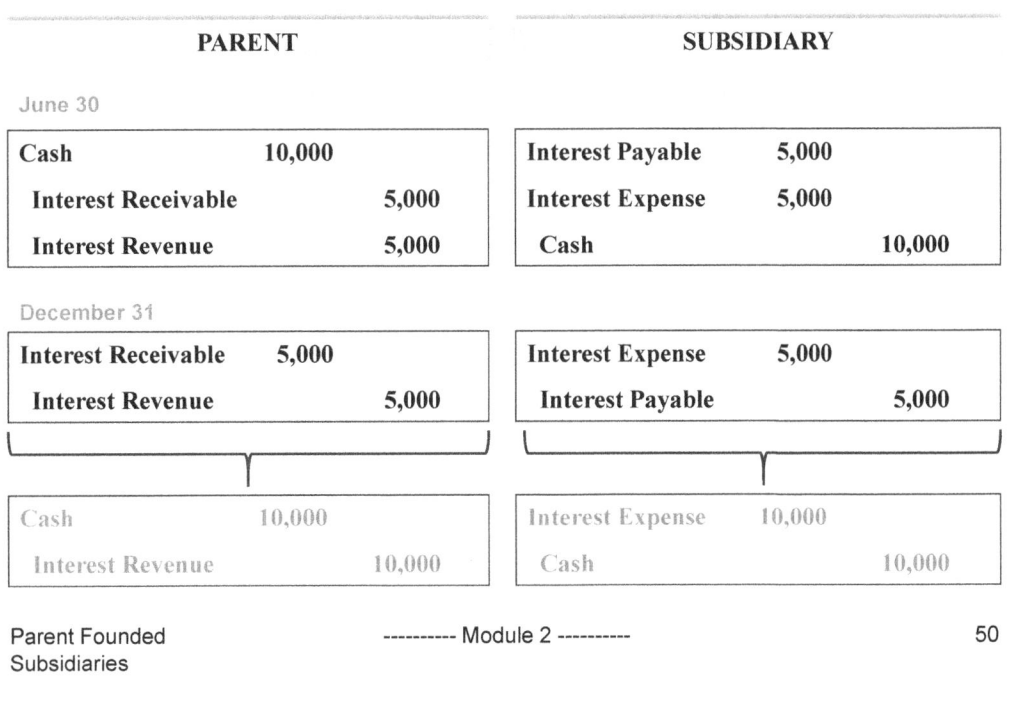

INTERCOMPANY LOANS
Consolidation Entries - X2

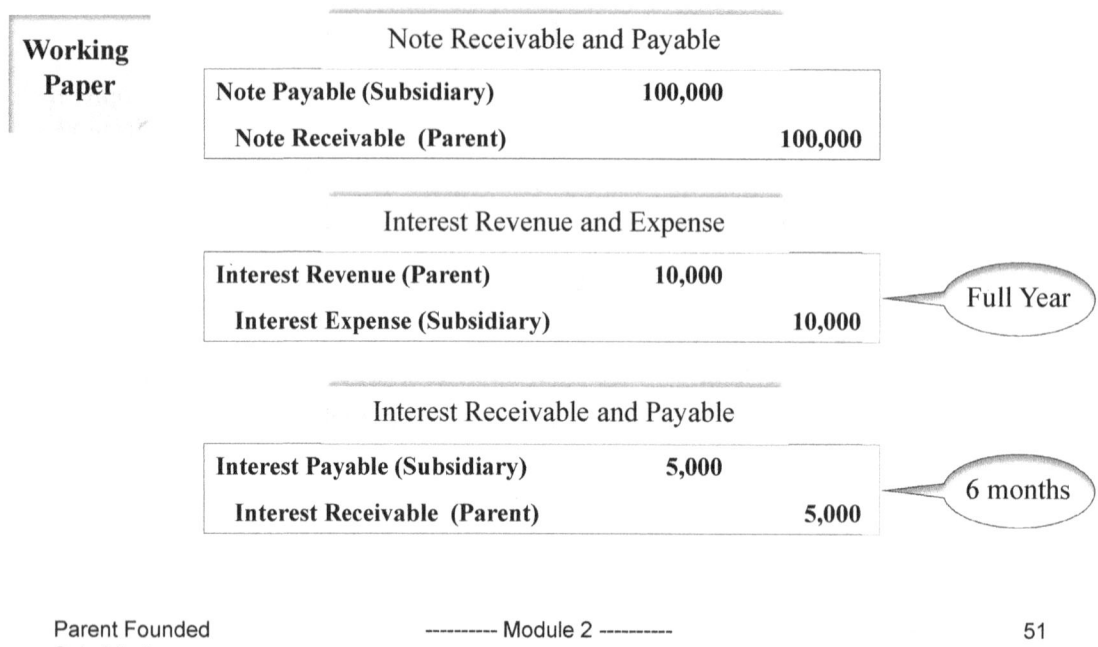

Working Paper

Note Receivable and Payable

Note Payable (Subsidiary)	100,000	
Note Receivable (Parent)		100,000

Interest Revenue and Expense

Interest Revenue (Parent)	10,000	
Interest Expense (Subsidiary)		10,000

Full Year

Interest Receivable and Payable

Interest Payable (Subsidiary)	5,000	
Interest Receivable (Parent)		5,000

6 months

INTERCOMPANY LOANS
Impact of the Eliminations on the Consolidated F/S - X2

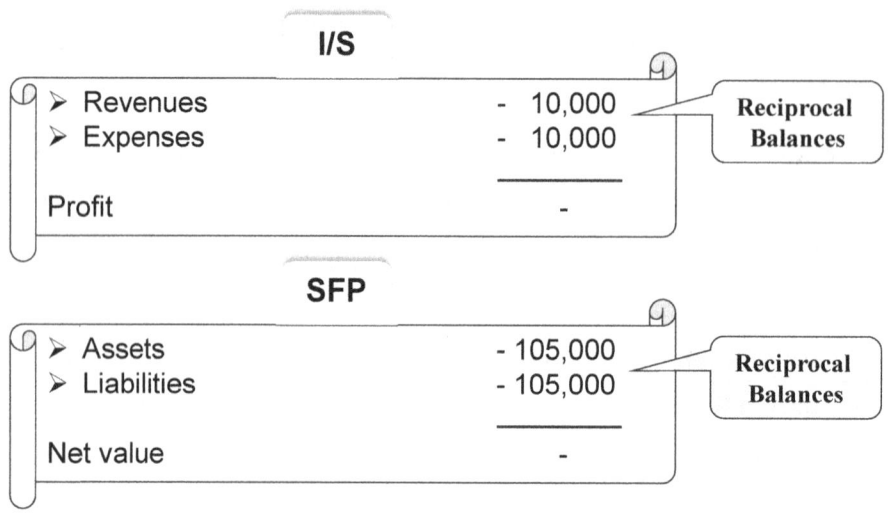

I/S
- Revenues: − 10,000
- Expenses: − 10,000
- Profit: −

Reciprocal Balances

SFP
- Assets: − 105,000
- Liabilities: − 105,000
- Net value: −

Reciprocal Balances

Part 2

INTERCOMPANY LOANS
Entries on the Books of the Affiliated Companies - X3

PARENT

June 30

Cash	110,000	
Interest Receivable		5,000
Interest Revenue		5,000
Note Receivable		100,000

SUBSIDIARY

Interest Payable	5,000	
Interest Expense	5,000	
Note Payable	100,000	
Cash		110,000

YEAR OF SETTLEMENT

Parent Founded Subsidiaries

Part 2

INTERCOMPANY LOANS
Consolidation Entry - X3

Working Paper

Interest Revenue and Expense

Interest Revenue (Parent)	5,000	
Interest Expense (Subsidiary)		5,000

(6 months)

Since the loan is paid in full, there are no reciprocal balances remaining in the SFP (Note and Accrued Interest). Only Interest Revenue and Interest Expense for the first six months of X3 ($5,000) need to be removed from the I/S of Parent and Subsidiary, respectively.

Parent Founded Subsidiaries

Part 2

INTERCOMPANY LOANS
Impact of the Elimination on the Consolidated F/S - X3

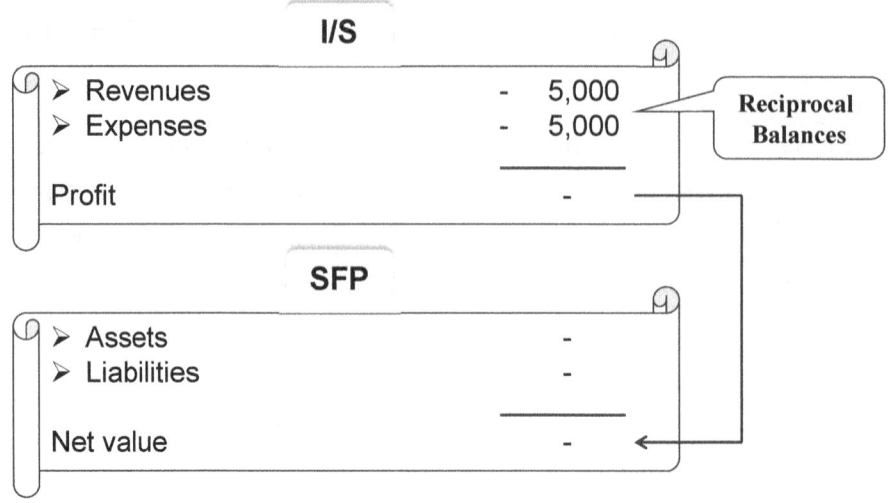

I/S
- Revenues — 5,000
- Expenses — 5,000

Profit —

Reciprocal Balances

SFP
- Assets —
- Liabilities —

Net value —

Part 2

MANAGEMENT FEES
Consolidation Entries

MANAGEMENT FEE REVENUE AND EXPENSE

Often the parent company will charge its subsidiaries a yearly management fee as a means of allocating head office costs to all the affiliated companies. This transaction results in intercompany management fee revenue (Parent) and expense (Subsidiary).

ELIMINATION

Management Fee Revenue (Parent)	XXX
Management Fee Expense (Subsidiary)	XXX

INTERCOMPANY RENTALS
Consolidation Entries

RENTAL REVENUE AND EXPENSE

Occasionally buildings or equipment owned by one company are used by another affiliated company. In such a case, the affiliated companies will agree on a yearly rental to be charged. This transaction results in intercompany rental revenue and expense.

ELIMINATION

Rental Revenue	XXX	
Rental Expense		XXX

INTERCOMPANY DIVIDENDS
Illustration - Basic Information

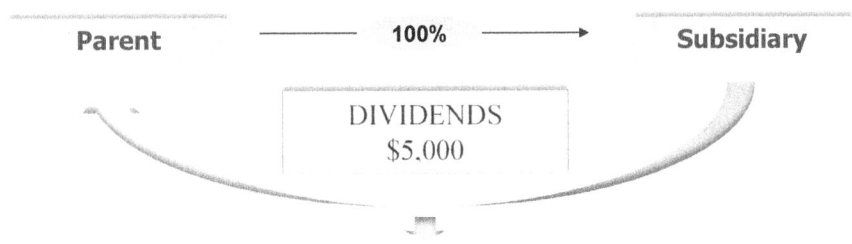

Parent — 100% → Subsidiary

DIVIDENDS $5,000

Parent is using the cost method to account for its investment in Subsidiary.

Textbook - Chapter 4
Intercompany Dividends

INTERCOMPANY DIVIDENDS
Illustration - Journal Entries

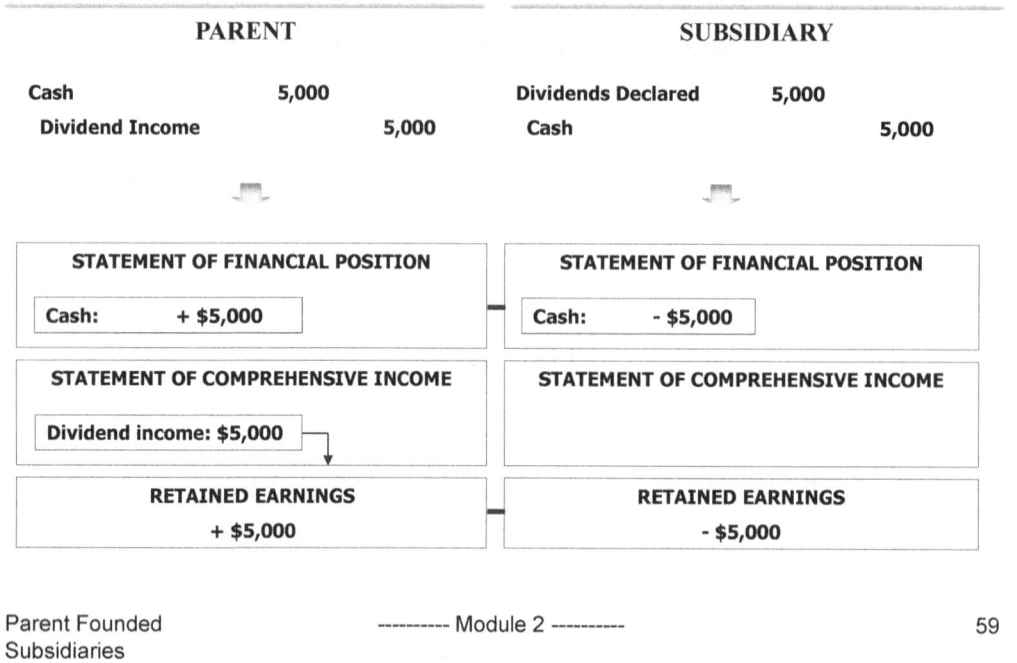

INTERCOMPANY DIVIDENDS
Illustration - Notes

As evidenced by the previous slide, when the investment in Subsidiary is reported by the cost method, dividends declared and paid by the subsidiary have no impact on the consolidated Cash account and consolidated Retained Earnings (In & Out Effect). Consequently, as a general rule, intercompany dividends do not affect the consolidated net value (SFP).

However, since dividends declared by Subsidiary are reported as revenue by Parent, double-counting is created in the consolidated statement of comprehensive income. Dividend income of $5,000 must be eliminated so as to avoid repeating Subsidiary's earnings (see entry next).

Refer to Chapter 4 from your Textbook for more details.

Part 2

INTERCOMPANY DIVIDENDS
Consolidation Entry - X1
(Under the Cost Method)

Working Paper

DOUBLE-COUNTING
↓
ELIMINATION

Dr Dividend income (profit)   5,000
 Cr Dividend declared   5,000

This elimination has no impact on the ending balance of consolidated RE and, therefore, on the consolidated net value (see next slide).

Parent Founded Subsidiaries ---------- Module 2 ---------- 61

Part 2

INTERCOMPANY DIVIDENDS
Impact of the Elimination on the Consolidated F/S - X1

I/S
- Revenues   - 5,000
- Expenses   -
                  _____
Profit   - 5,000

SFP
- Assets   -
- Liabilities   -
                  _____
Net value   -

RE + 5,000

No impact on the Net Value

Parent Founded Subsidiaries ---------- Module 2 ---------- 62

Part 2

MAIN ADVANTAGES OF CONSOLIDATED F/S
Recall from Module 1

1. Provide **Relevant** Information
2. Provide **Comparable** Information
3. Ensure **Accountability**
4. Report **Risks and Benefits**

Part 2

ADDITIONAL ADVANTAGES OF CONSOLIDATED F/S
Takeaways from the Previous Illustrations

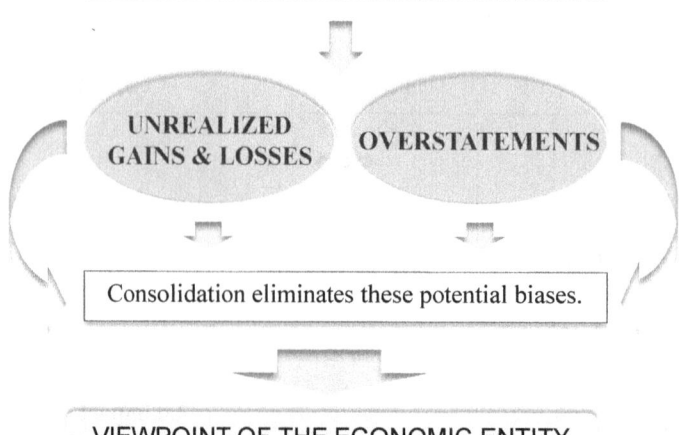

INTERCOMPANY TRANSACTIONS
Potential impact on individual records

UNREALIZED GAINS & LOSSES — OVERSTATEMENTS

Consolidation eliminates these potential biases.

VIEWPOINT OF THE ECONOMIC ENTITY

ADVANTAGES OF CONSOLIDATED FINANCIAL STATEMENTS
Additional Notes

Consolidated F/S are useful in particular when affiliated companies engage in transactions among themselves. As illustrated previously, individual records might capture benefits from intercompany transactions potentially leading to a biased view of the financial activities of the group. Consolidation eliminates most of these biases adding reliability to the F/S.

Consolidated F/S continue to grow in importance. Most publicly held companies own one or more subsidiaries. Consolidated F/S present in a single report the financial reality of the group.

However, since the information provided on a consolidated basis is aggregated, the following limitations are expected with consolidated F/S (next slide).

MAIN LIMITATIONS OF CONSOLIDATED FINANCIAL STATEMENTS
Aggregated Information

- POOR PERFORMANCE OR POSITION OF ONE OR MORE AFFIALITED COMPANIES MAY BE HIDDEN BY THE GOOD PERFORMANCE OR POSITION OF OTHERS

- WHEN HIGHLY DIVERSIFIED COMPANIES OPERATE ACROSS SEVERAL INDUSTRIES, THE COMBINATION OF DISSIMILAR DATA DECREASE THE USEFULNESS OF CONSOLIDATED F/S

- FINANCIAL RATIOS BASED ON CONSOLIDATED STATEMENTS ARE CALCULATED ON AGGREGATED INFORMATION

- NOT ALL THE CONSOLIDATED RETAINED EARNINGS BALANCE IS NECESSARILY AVAILABLE FOR DIVIDENDS OF THE PARENT

NEED FOR ADDITIONAL DISCLOSURE
(Footnotes)

PART 2
Concept Check

> Consolidated information might be biased when a parent company and its subsidiary engage in transactions among themselves. Explain.

_____
_____
_____
_____
_____
_____
_____

Parent Founded Subsidiaries ---------- Module 2---------- 67

OUTLINE OF THE PRESENTATION
Part 3

 **1** CONSOLIDATION OF PARENT FOUNDED SUBSIDIARIES AT THE DATE OF CREATION : THE DOUBLE-COUNTING ISSUE

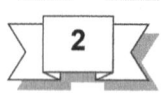 **2** INTERCOMPANY TRANSACTIONS: INTRODUCTION

      a) Intercompany Sales of Merchandise
      b) Intercompany Accruals
      c) Intercompany Loans
      d) Management Fees
      e) Intercompany Rentals
      f) Intercompany Dividends

 **3** **CONSOLIDATION OF PARENT FOUNDED SUBSIDIARIES IN PERIODS SUBSEQUENT TO THE DATE OF CREATION**

 **4** EQUITY METHOD

Parent Founded Subsidiaries ---------- Module 2 ---------- 68

PART 3
Consolidation of Parent Founded Subsidiaries in Periods Subsequent to the Date of Creation

Objectives of this section

Illustrate the consolidation process of parent founded subsidiaries in periods subsequent to the date of creation.

Discuss the general approach to consolidation under the worksheet approach and the direct approach as well.

Key concepts

- Worksheet approach
- Direct approach

CONSOLIDATION OF PARENT FOUNDED SUBSIDIARIES IN PERIODS SUBSEQUENT TO THE DATE OF CREATION
Preliminary Analysis

➢ Get the complete set of F/S of Parent and Subsidiary for the current year;

➢ From the SFP of Parent, take a look at the *Investment in Subsidiary* to determine if Parent is using either the *Cost Method* or the *Equity Method*;

➢ If the *Cost Method* is used, check the I/S of Parent for any *Dividend Income* as a result of current-year *Intercompany Dividends* (double-counting in I/S);

➢ Examine carefully the F/S of the affiliated companies to identify any additional *Reciprocal Balances* (such as Receivables/Payables; Revenues/Expenses) as a result of current and/or prior-year *Intercompany Transactions;*

➢ Enquire additional information that may be relevant for consolidation (intercompany transfers).

Part 3

CONSOLIDATION OF PARENT FOUNDED SUBSIDIARIES IN PERIODS SUBSEQUENT TO THE DATE OF CREATION
Consolidation Steps Under the Cost Method

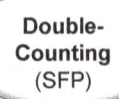
- Eliminate the double-counting in the SFP: elimination of the *Investment in Subsidiary* (Parent) and *Share Capital* or *Common Shares* (Subsidiary);

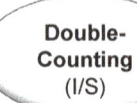
- If Intercompany Dividends, eliminate the double-counting in the I/S: elimination of *Dividend Income* (Parent) and *Dividends Declared* (Subsidiary);

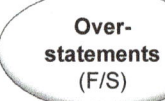
- Eliminate any additional reciprocal balances (*Overstatements*) as a result of Intercompany Transactions from current and prior years.

Part 3

CONSOLIDATION OF PARENT FOUNDED SUBSIDIARIES IN PERIODS SUBSEQUENT TO THE DATE OF CREATION
Illustration

Refer to previous illustration.

Recall that in X10, Parent Company establishes a subsidiary by creating a new corporation named Subsidiary Company. Subsidiary issues common shares to Parent in return for $80,000 cash paid by Parent.

Required
Prepare the consolidated financial statements of Parent Company for the period ending December 31, X15.

CONSOLIDATION OF PARENT FOUNDED SUBSIDIARIES IN PERIODS SUBSEQUENT TO THE DATE OF CREATION
Timeline

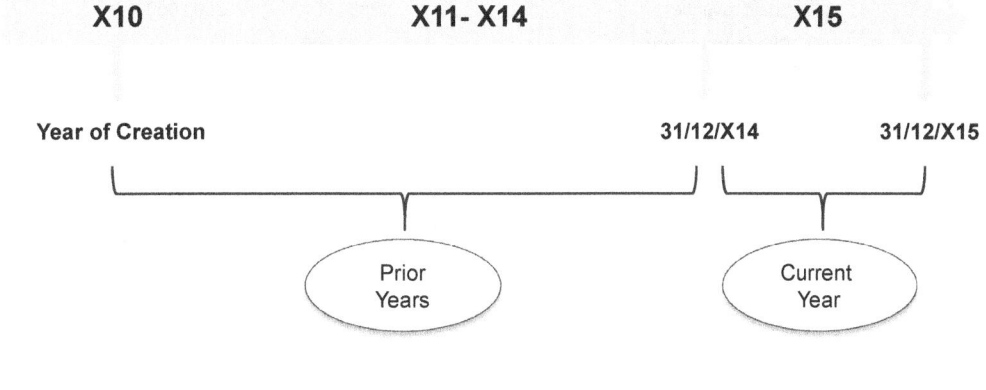

Parent Founded Subsidiaries ---------- Module 2 ----------

STATEMENT OF FINANCIAL POSITION
At December 31, X15

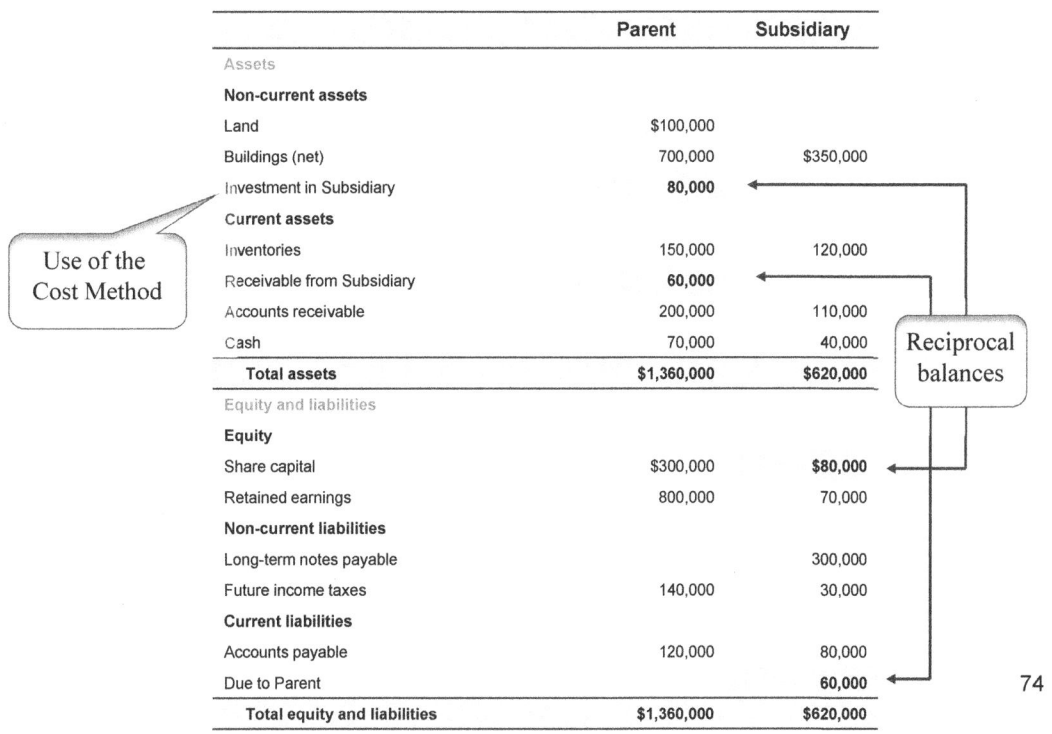

	Parent	Subsidiary
Assets		
Non-current assets		
Land	$100,000	
Buildings (net)	700,000	$350,000
Investment in Subsidiary	80,000	
Current assets		
Inventories	150,000	120,000
Receivable from Subsidiary	60,000	
Accounts receivable	200,000	110,000
Cash	70,000	40,000
Total assets	$1,360,000	$620,000
Equity and liabilities		
Equity		
Share capital	$300,000	$80,000
Retained earnings	800,000	70,000
Non-current liabilities		
Long-term notes payable		300,000
Future income taxes	140,000	30,000
Current liabilities		
Accounts payable	120,000	80,000
Due to Parent		60,000
Total equity and liabilities	$1,360,000	$620,000

Use of the Cost Method

Reciprocal balances

Part 3

INCOME STATEMENT
Year Ended December 31, X15

	Parent	Subsidiary
Sales revenue	$800,000	$400,000
Dividend income	**20,000**	
Cost of sales	480,000	280,000
Depreciation expense	130,000	30,000
Income tax expense	32,000	20,000
Other expenses	110,000	40,000
Profit for the year	**$68,000**	**$30,000**

Consistent with the use of the Cost Method

Part 3

STATEMENT OF CHANGES IN EQUITY
Year Ended December 31, X15

	Parent			Subsidiary		
	Share Capital	Retained Earnings	Total	Share Capital	Retained Earnings	Total
Balance at Dec. 31, X14	$300,000	$762,000	$1,062,000	$80,000	$60,000	$140,000
Profit for the year		68,000	68,000		30,000	30,000
Dividends		(30,000)	(30,000)		(20,000)	(20,000)
Balance at Dec. X15	**$300,000**	**$800,000**	**$1,100,000**	**$80,000**	**$70,000**	**$150,000**

Intercompany Dividends

Increase of Subsidiary's net book value (NBV) since creation

ILLUSTRATION
Additional information

Part 3

Intercompany Sales of Merchandise

The sales of Parent include $100,000 of merchandise sold to Subsidiary, all of which was resold by Subsidiary during the year to external parties.

Do we need more details regarding this downstream sale of merchandise in order to proceed with the consolidation of F/S?

_____
_____
_____
_____
_____

Parent Founded Subsidiaries ---------- Module 2 ---------- 77

ILLUSTRATION
Required Consolidation Entries: Recap

Part 3

1. **Double-Counting** — *In the Statement of Financial Position* — $80,000

2. **Double-Counting** — *of Subsidiary's earnings* — $20,000

3. **Overstatement** — *of Sales and COGS* — $100,000

4. **Reciprocal Accruals** — *Receivable and Payable* — $60,000

Parent Founded Subsidiaries ---------- Module 2 ---------- 78

Part 3

ILLUSTRATION
Core Consolidation Entry
Elimination of Reciprocal Investment and Equity Balances

Working Paper

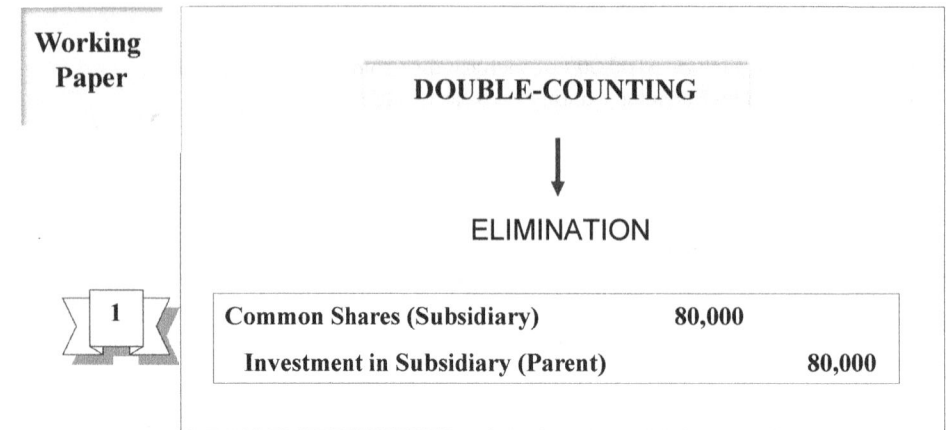

1	Common Shares (Subsidiary)	80,000
	Investment in Subsidiary (Parent)	80,000

Parent Founded Subsidiaries ---------- Module 2 ---------- 79

Part 3

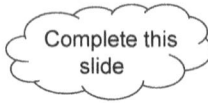
Complete this slide

ILLUSTRATION
Additional Consolidation Entries
Following Intercompany Transactions

Working Paper

2 Dr Dividend income   20,000
     Cr Dividend declared   20,000

3 Dr Sales   100,000
     Cr COGS   100,000

4 Dr Due to parents   60,000
     Cr Receivable from subsidiaries   60,000

Parent Founded Subsidiaries ---------- Module 2 ---------- 80

CONSOLIDATION PROCESS
UNDER THE WORKSHEET APPROACH

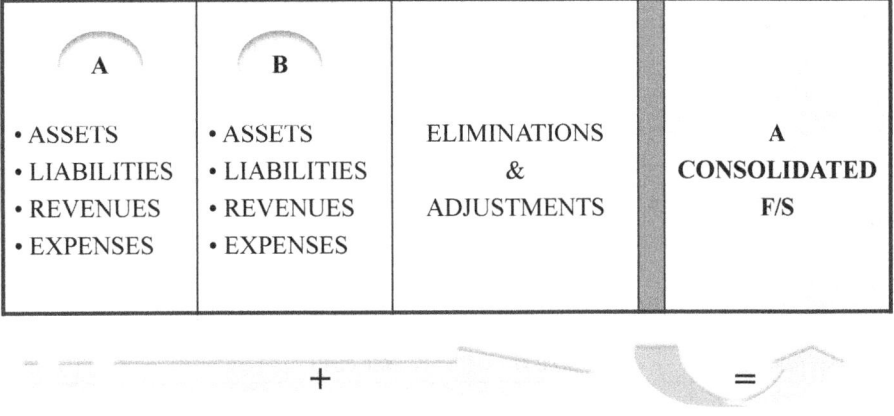

Parent Founded Subsidiaries

CONSOLIDATION WORKSHEET OF PARENT COMPANY
As of December 31, X15

	Parent	Subsidiary	Conso. Entries	Consolidated
Assets				
Land	$100,000			$100,000
Buildings (net)	700,000	$350,000		1,050,000
Investment in Subsidiary	80,000		(1) (80,000)	-
Inventories	150,000	120,000		270,000
Receivable from Subsidiary	60,000		(4) (60,000)	-
Accounts receivable	200,000	110,000		310,000
Cash	70,000	40,000		110,000
Total assets	**$1,360,000**	**$620,000**		**$1,840,000**
Equity and liabilities				
Share capital	$300,000	$80,000	(1) (80,000)	$300,000
Retained earnings	800,000	---------- 70,000	-------------------------->	870,000
Long-term notes payable		300,000		300,000
Future income taxes	140,000	30,000		170,000
Accounts payable	120,000	80,000		200,000
Due to Parent		60,000	(4) (60,000)	-
Total equity & liabilities	**$1,360,000**	**$620,000**		**$1,840,000**

Parent Founded Subsidiaries

Part 3

CONSOLIDATION WORKSHEET OF PARENT COMPANY
(continued...)
As of December 31, X15

	Parent	Subsidiary	Conso. Entries	Consolidated
Sales revenue	$800,000	$400,000	(3) (100,000)	$1,100,000
Dividend income	20,000		(2) (20,000)	-
Cost of sales	480,000	280,000	(3) (100,000)	660,000
Depreciation expense	130,000	30,000		160,000
Income tax expense	32,000	20,000		52,000
Other expenses	110,000	40,000		150,000
Profit for the year	**$68,000**	**$30,000**		**$78,000**
Retained earnings (beginning)	$762,000	$60,000		$822,000
Dividends declared	(30,000)	(20,000)	(2) (20,000)	(30,000)
Retained earnings (end)	**$800,000**	**$70,000**	-	**$870,000**

No impact of the consolidation adjustments on the ending balance of Retained Earnings.

Part 3

APPROACHES TO CONSOLIDATION

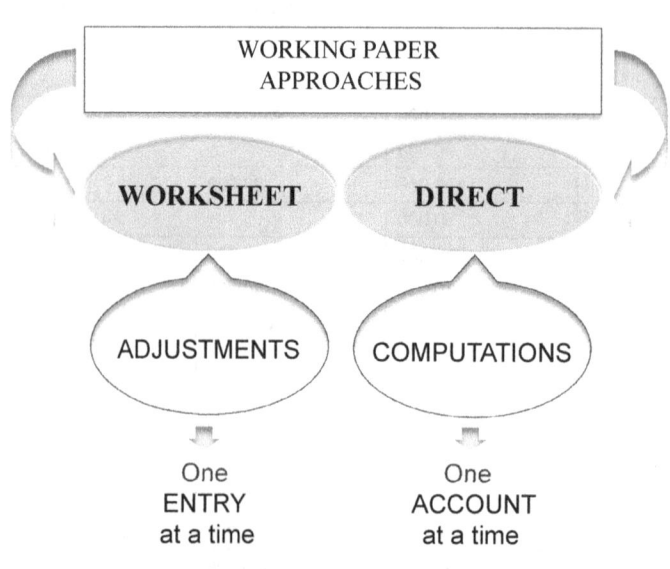

APPROACHES TO CONSOLIDATION
Recall from Module 1

Worksheet approach
The worksheet approach uses a multi-columnar worksheet to enter the trial balances of the parent and each subsidiary. Then, eliminations and adjustments are entered onto the worksheet, and the accounts are cross-added to determine the consolidated figures.

Direct approach
The direct approach prepares the consolidated statements by computing each balance directly.

RATIONALE UNDERLYING WORKSHEET APPROACH (1)

	Parent	Subsidiary
Assets		
Land	$100,000	
Buildings (net)	700,000	$350,000
Investment in Subsidiary	80,000	
Inventories	150,000	120,000
Receivable from Subsidiary	60,000	
Accounts receivable	200,000	110,000
Cash	70,000	40,000
Total assets	$1,360,000	$620,000
Equity and liabilities		
Share capital	$300,000	$80,000
Retained earnings	800,000	70,000
Long-term notes payable		300,000
Future income taxes	140,000	30,000
Accounts payable	120,000	80,000
Due to Parent		60,000
Total equity & liabilities	$1,360,000	$620,000

F/S - Parent
+
F/S - Subsidiary
−
Excess
=
Consolidaded F/S

RATIONALE UNDERLYING WORKSHEET APPROACH (2)

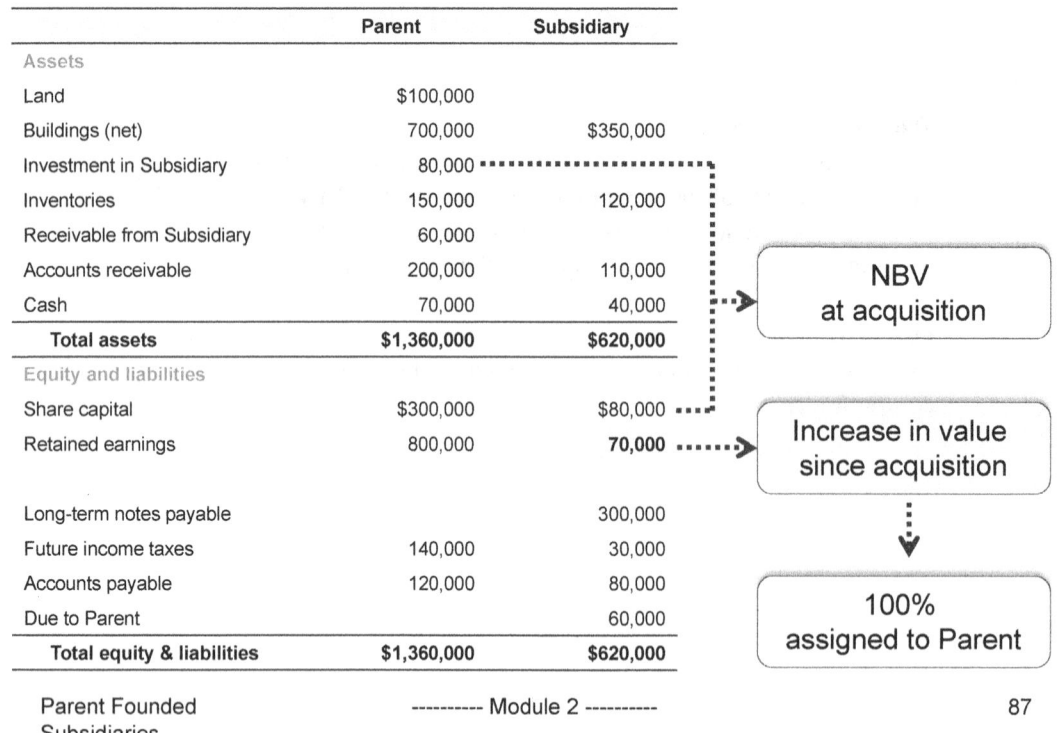

	Parent	Subsidiary
Assets		
Land	$100,000	
Buildings (net)	700,000	$350,000
Investment in Subsidiary	80,000	
Inventories	150,000	120,000
Receivable from Subsidiary	60,000	
Accounts receivable	200,000	110,000
Cash	70,000	40,000
Total assets	**$1,360,000**	**$620,000**
Equity and liabilities		
Share capital	$300,000	$80,000
Retained earnings	800,000	70,000
Long-term notes payable		300,000
Future income taxes	140,000	30,000
Accounts payable	120,000	80,000
Due to Parent		60,000
Total equity & liabilities	**$1,360,000**	**$620,000**

DIRECT APPROACH
Computation Process for Each Balance

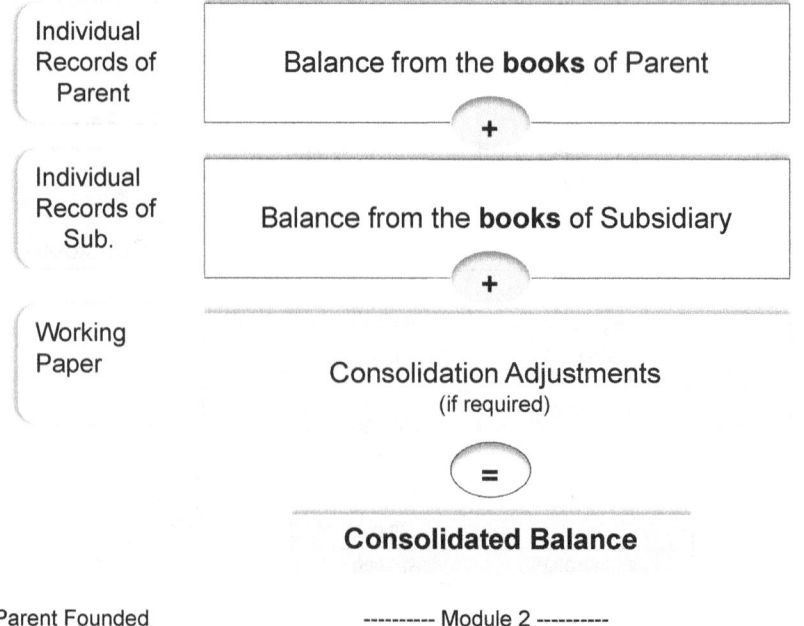

DIRECT APPROACH
Non-Current Assets

Part 3

Land
- Parent $100,000

Buildings (net)
- Parent $700,000
- Subsidiary   350,000
- Total $1,050,000

Investment in Subsidiary

✗ *Ignore what is not relevant*

For this illustration, computation of the consolidated figures is straightforward. Often calculation involves a simple addition of the balances from the affiliated companies' separate-entity accounting records.

Parent Founded Subsidiaries

DIRECT APPROACH
Current Assets

Part 3

Cash
- Parent $70,000
- Subsidiary   40,000
- Total $110,000

Accounts Receivable
- Parent $200,000
- Subsidiary   110,000
- Total $310,000

Receivable from Subsidiary

✗ *Versus Due to Parent*

Inventories
- Parent $150,000
- Subsidiary   120,000
- Total $270,000

Parent Founded Subsidiaries

Part 3

DIRECT APPROACH
Equity

Common Shares		Retained Earnings	
➢ Parent	$300,000	➢ Parent	$800,000
		➢ Subsidiary	70,000
		Total	$870,000

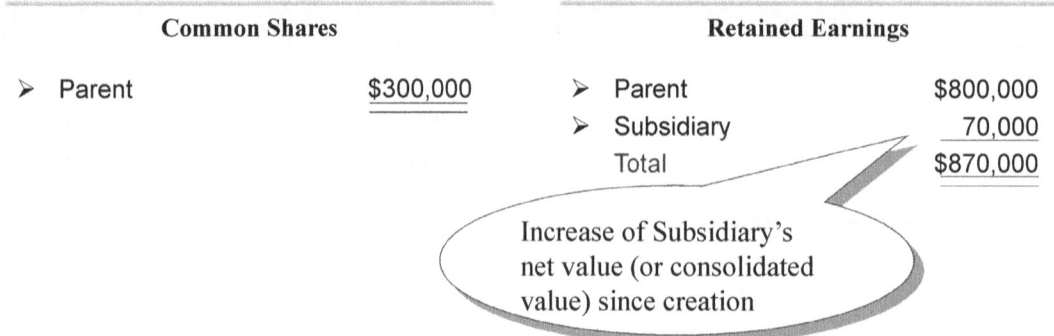

Increase of Subsidiary's net value (or consolidated value) since creation

Consolidated RE is merely an addition of the balances from the books of the affiliated companies. Recall that Subsidiary's RE reflects Subsidiary's NBV increase since creation. 100% of Subsidiary's increase in value is assigned to Parent through consolidation.

Parent Founded Subsidiaries ---------- Module 2 ---------- 91

Part 3

DIRECT APPROACH
Current and Non-Current Liabilities

Long-Term Notes Payable		Future Income Taxes	
➢ Subsidiary	$300,000	➢ Parent	$140,000
		➢ Subsidiary	30,000
		Total	$170,000

Accounts Payable		Due to Parent	
➢ Parent	$120,000		✗
➢ Subsidiary	80,000		
Total	$200,000		

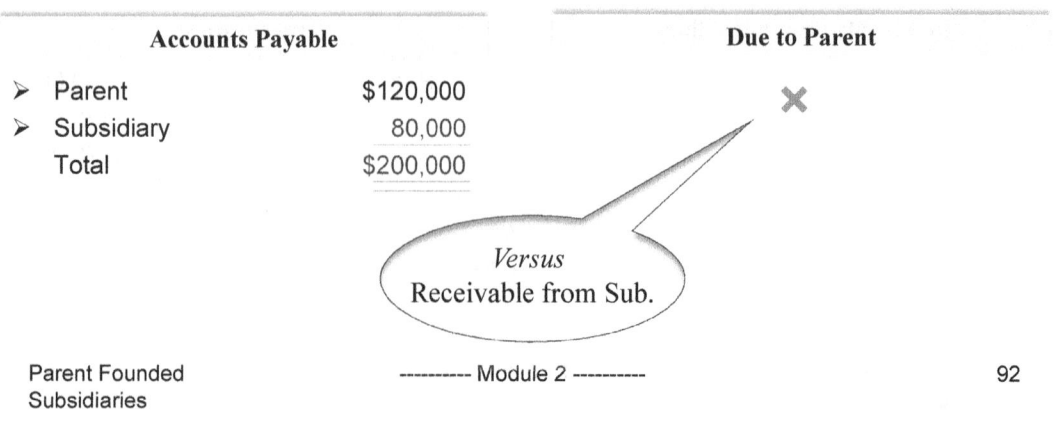

Versus Receivable from Sub.

Parent Founded Subsidiaries ---------- Module 2 ---------- 92

Part 3

DIRECT APPROACH
Income Statement

Sales Revenue

- Parent — $800,000
- Subsidiary — 400,000
- Intercompany sales — (100,000)
- Total — $1,100,000

Dividends Income

✗

Cost of Sales

- Parent — $480,000
- Subsidiary — 280,000
- Intercompany sales — (100,000)
- Total — $660,000

Depreciation Expense

- Parent — $130,000
- Subsidiary — 30,000
- Total — $160,000

Part 3

DIRECT APPROACH
Income Statement (continued...)

Income Tax Expense

- Parent — $32,000
- Subsidiary — 20,000
- Total — $52,000

Other Expenses

- Parent — $110,000
- Subsidiary — 40,000
- Total — $150,000

Part 3

DIRECT APPROACH
Consolidated Profit

1 Adjusted profit of Parent

- Profit of Parent for the period $68,000
- Intercompany dividends   (20,000) $48,000

2 Adjusted profit of Subsidiairy

- Profit of Subsidiary for the period   30,000

Consolidated profit ----------------------------> **$78,000**

Part 3

PART 3
Concept Check

> Why is double-counting in the balance sheet a recurrent issue in consolidation?

_____
_____
_____
_____
_____
_____

OUTLINE OF THE PRESENTATION

Part 4

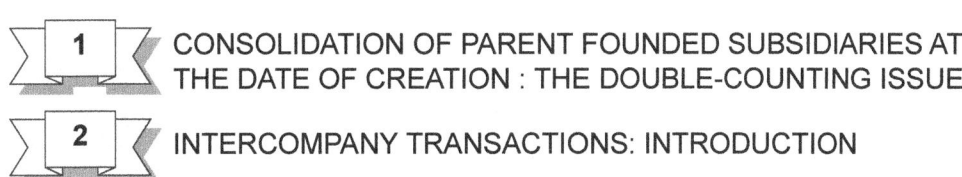 CONSOLIDATION OF PARENT FOUNDED SUBSIDIARIES AT THE DATE OF CREATION : THE DOUBLE-COUNTING ISSUE

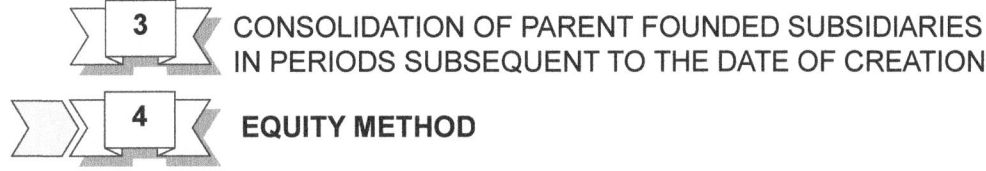 INTERCOMPANY TRANSACTIONS: INTRODUCTION

- a) Intercompany Sales of Merchandise
- b) Intercompany Accruals
- c) Intercompany Loans
- d) Management Fees
- e) Intercompany Rentals
- f) Intercompany Dividends

3 CONSOLIDATION OF PARENT FOUNDED SUBSIDIARIES IN PERIODS SUBSEQUENT TO THE DATE OF CREATION

4 EQUITY METHOD

PART 4
Equity Method

Part 4

Objectives of this section

Discuss the equity-basis reporting when Parent Company uses the equity method in its separate-entity financial statements.

Illustrate the approach to compute the investment in Subsidiary in non-consolidated financial statements under the equity method.

Present the financial reporting implications of using either the cost method, the equity method or full consolidation.

Present the additional consolidation entries required to eliminate the investment account when the equity method is employed by Parent Company in non-consolidated financial statements.

EQUITY METHOD FOR CONTROLLED ENTITIES
Internal Recording

Part 4

It is possible, but rare, for a parent company to use the equity method for internal recording purposes. In fact, a parent company is more likely to carry its subsidiaries' investment accounts on the cost basis even if the investments will be reported on the equity method for unconsolidated reporting (individual financial statements). The main reason is that the consolidation process is much easier with the cost method than with the equity method.

However, for completeness, we assume next that Parent is using the equity method for its investment in Subsidiary.

Recall that the equity method is required in the context of joint ventures (IFRS 11). We will return to this issue in Module 8.

EQUITY METHOD
What you need to know

Part 4

1. HOW TO **REPORT** THE BASIC JOURNAL ENTRIES;

2. HOW TO **COMPUTE** THE BALANCE OF THE INVESTMENT ACCOUNT AT THE END OF A PERIOD;

3. HOW TO **PRESENT** THE F/S UNDER THE EQUITY METHOD;

4. HOW TO **ELIMINATE** THE INVESTMENT ACCOUNT THROUGH CONSOLIDATION.

EQUITY METHOD
Journal Entries for X15

Part 4

PROPORTIONATE SHARE OF EARNINGS

Investment in Subsidiary	30,000	
Equity in Earnings of Subsidiary		30,000

PROPORTIONATE SHARE OF DIVIDENDS

Cash	20,000	
Investment in Subsidiary		20,000

Proportionate share of the change of Subsidiary's retained earnings during X15

Parent Founded Subsidiaries — Module 2 — 101

EQUITY METHOD
Balance of the Investment Account
As of December 31, X15

Part 4

INITIAL INVESTMENT (X10)	$80,000	Cost Method
100% OF SUBSIDIARY'S NET ADJUSTED VALUE SINCE CREATION (that is, the balance of RE at the end of the year)	70,000	↕
INVESTMENT AT THE END (X15)	$150,000	Equity Method

Net Book Value of Sub

Parent Founded Subsidiaries — Module 2 — 102

STATEMENT OF FINANCIAL POSITION - PARENT COMPANY
At December 31, X15
Under Different Reporting Practices

	Cost basis	Equity basis	Consolidated
Assets			
Non-current assets			
Land	$100,000	$100,000	$100,000
Buildings (net)	700,000	700,000	1,050,000
Investment in Subsidiary	80,000	150,000	
Current assets			
Inventories	150,000	150,000	270,000
Receivable from Subsidiary	60,000	60,000	
Accounts receivable	200,000	200,000	310,000
Cash	70,000	70,000	110,000
Total assets	$1,360,000	$1,430,000	$1,840,000
Equity and liabilities			
Equity			
Share capital	$300,000	$300,000	$300,000
Retained earnings	800,000	870,000	870,000
Non-current liabilities			
Long-term notes payable			300,000
Future income taxes	140,000	140,000	170,000
Current liabilities			
Accounts payable	120,000	120,000	200,000
Total equity and liabilities	$1,360,000	$1,430,000	$1,840,000

Net Book Value of Sub

STATEMENT OF FINANCIAL POSITION - PARENT COMPANY
At December 31, X15
Equity vs. Consolidation

- The net value is the same, whereas the assets and liabilities reported are different.

- Under the equity method, only the accounts of Parent are reported. Under full consolidation, the accounts of Parent and Subsidiary are combined.

- One can see the process of consolidation as disaggregating the Investment account into the subsidiary's detailed assets and liabilities.

Equity Method = One-line consolidation

INCOME STATEMENT - PARENT COMPANY
Year Ended December 31, X15
Under Different Reporting Practices

	Cost basis	Equity basis	Consolidated
Sales revenue	$800,000	$800,000	$1,100,000
Dividend income	20,000		
Equity in earnings		**30,000**	
Cost of sales	480,000	480,000	660,000
Depreciation expense	130,000	130,000	160,000
Income tax expense	32,000	32,000	52,000
Other expenses	110,000	110,000	150,000
Profit for the year	**$68,000**	**$78,000**	**$78,000**

Profit of Sub

Parent Founded Subsidiaries — Module 2 —

INCOME STATEMENT - PARENT COMPANY
Year Ended December 31, X15
Equity vs. Consolidation

- Profit is the same, whereas the revenues and expenses reported are different.

- Under the equity method, only the accounts of Parent are reported. Under full consolidation, the accounts of Parent and Subsidiary are combined.

- One can see the process of consolidation as disaggregating the Equity in Earnings account into the subsidiary's detailed revenues and expenses.

Equity Method = One-line consolidation

Parent Founded Subsidiaries — Module 2 —

STATEMENT OF CHANGES IN EQUITY - PARENT COMPANY
Year Ended December 31, X15
Under Different Reporting Practices

Part 4

	Cost basis			Equity basis			Consolidated		
	SC	RE	Total	SC	RE	Total	SC	RE	Total
Balance (beginning)	300,000	762,000	1,062,000	300,000	822,000	1,122,000	300,000	822,000	1,122,000
Profit for the year		68,000	68,000		78,000	78,000		78,000	78,000
Dividends declared		(30,000)	(30,000)		(30,000)	(30,000)		(30,000)	(30,000)
Balance (end)	300,000	800,000	1,100,000	300,000	870,000	1,170,000	300,000	870,000	1,170,000

Parent Founded Subsidiaries — Module 2 — 107

EQUITY METHOD
One-Line Consolidation

Part 4

Statement of Financial Position

Balance of the investment account = NBV of Subsidiary

$150,000

Income Statement

Equity in earnings of Subsidiary = Net income of Subsidiary

$30,000

In this case, note that the Net Book Value (NBV) of Subsidiary is equal to the Net Adjusted Value or consolidated value (see Module 4).

Parent Founded Subsidiaries — Module 2 — 108

EQUITY METHOD
One-Line Consolidation - Basic Journal Entries

	Equity basis	Subsidiary
Assets		
Non-current assets		
Land	$100,000	
Buildings (net)	700,000	$350,000
Investment in Subsidiary	150,000	
Current assets		
Inventories	150,000	120,000
Receivable from Subsidiary	60,000	
Accounts receivable	200,000	110,000
Cash	70,000	40,000
Total assets	$1,430,000	$620,000
Equity and liabilities		
Equity		
Share capital	$300,000	$80,000
Retained earnings	870,000	70,000
Non-current liabilities		
Long-term notes payable		300,000
Future income taxes	140,000	30,000
Current liabilities		
Accounts payable	120,000	80,000
Due to Parent		60,000
Total equity and liabilities	$1,430,000	$620,000

Creation $80,000

Since creation $70,000

(+) Share of Earnings

(−) Share of Dividends

EQUITY METHOD
One-Line Consolidation - SFP

	Equity basis	Subsidiary
Assets		
Non-current assets		
Land	$100,000	
Buildings (net)	700,000	$350,000
Investment in Subsidiary	150,000	
Current assets		
Inventories	150,000	120,000
Receivable from Subsidiary	60,000	
Accounts receivable	200,000	110,000
Cash	70,000	40,000
Total assets	$1,430,000	$620,000
Equity and liabilities		
Equity		
Share capital	$300,000	$80,000
Retained earnings	870,000	70,000
Non-current liabilities		
Long-term notes payable		300,000
Future income taxes	140,000	30,000
Current liabilities		
Accounts payable	120,000	80,000
Due to Parent		60,000
Total equity and liabilities	$1,430,000	$620,000

One can view the process of consolidation as disaggregating the Investment account into the subsidiary's detailed assets and liabilities.

EQUITY METHOD
One-Line Consolidation - I/S

	Equity basis	Subsidiary
Sales revenue	$800,000	$400,000
Dividend income		
Equity in earnings	30,000	
Cost of sales	480,000	280,000
Depreciation expense	130,000	30,000
Income tax expense	32,000	20,000
Other expenses	110,000	40,000
Profit for the year	**$78,000**	**$30,000**

One can see the process of consolidation as disaggregating the Equity in Earnings account into the subsidiary's detailed revenues and expenses.

EQUITY METHOD IN THE CONTEXT OF CONSOLIDATION
Procedure to Eliminate the Investment Account

1 BREAK DOWN THE BALANCE OF THE INVESTMENT ACCOUNT AT END OF THE PERIOD:

1. Initial Investment;
2. Increase of the Investment up to the beginning of the current period;
3. Share of Earnings – Current period;
4. Share of Dividends – Current period.

2 ELIMINATE EACH COMPONENT OF THE INVESTMENT ACCOUNT

Part 4

EQUITY METHOD
Breakdown of the Investment Account

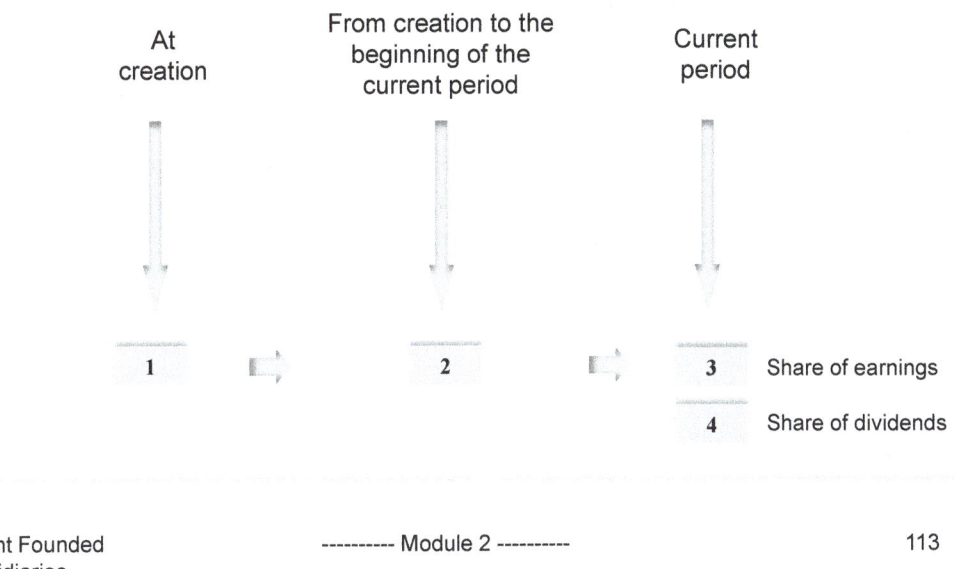

Balance of the Investment under the Equity Method

- At creation → 1
- From creation to the beginning of the current period → 2
- Current period → 3 Share of earnings
- 4 Share of dividends

Part 4

EQUITY METHOD
Breakdown of the Investment Account of $150,000

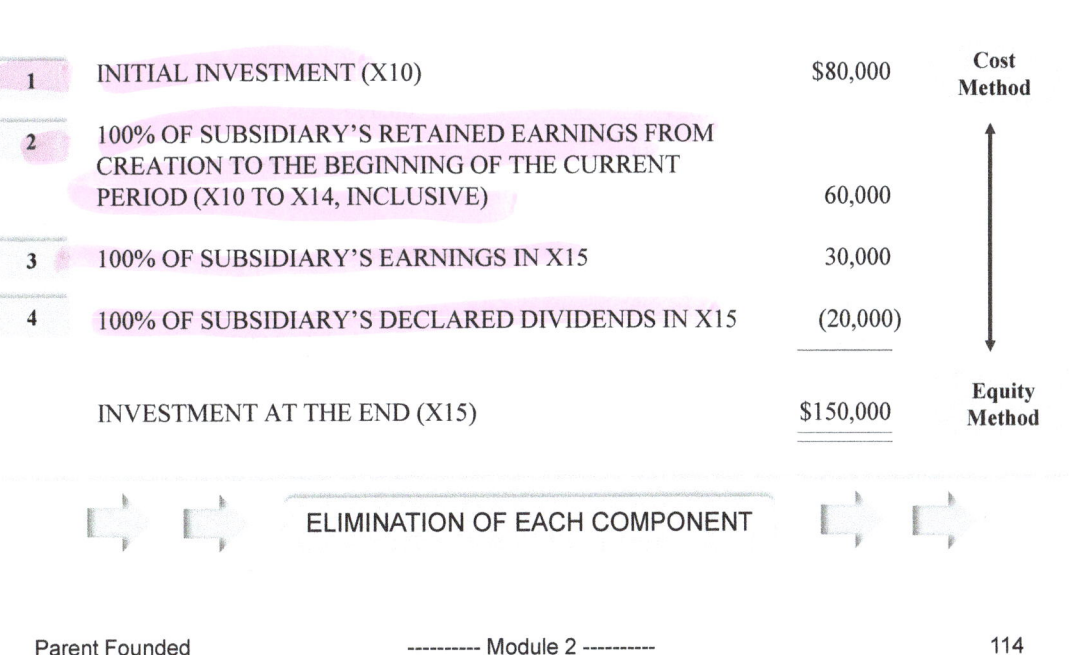

1	INITIAL INVESTMENT (X10)	$80,000	Cost Method
2	100% OF SUBSIDIARY'S RETAINED EARNINGS FROM CREATION TO THE BEGINNING OF THE CURRENT PERIOD (X10 TO X14, INCLUSIVE)	60,000	
3	100% OF SUBSIDIARY'S EARNINGS IN X15	30,000	
4	100% OF SUBSIDIARY'S DECLARED DIVIDENDS IN X15	(20,000)	
	INVESTMENT AT THE END (X15)	$150,000	Equity Method

ELIMINATION OF EACH COMPONENT

Part 4

EQUITY METHOD
Consolidation Entries Required to Eliminate the Investment Account of $150,000 (1)

Common Shares	80,000
Investment in Subsidiary	80,000

Double-counting
Same entry required under the cost method.

Part 4

EQUITY METHOD
Consolidation Entries Required to Eliminate the Investment Account of $150,000 (2)

Retained Earnings	60,000
Investment in Subsidiary	60,000

This entry eliminates the increase of the investment account from date of creation to the beginning of the current period ($60,000). This increase consists of the balance of Subsidiary's RE at the beginning of the current period.

Part 4

EQUITY METHOD
Consolidation Entries Required to Eliminate the Investment Account of $150,000 (3 & 4)

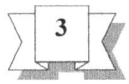

Equity in Earnings	30,000	
Investment in Subsidiary		30,000

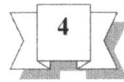

Investment in Subsidiary	20,000	
Dividends Declared		20,000

Current journal entries
These consolidation entries are cancelling out the two journal entries that were originally recorded by Parent during the year. Entry #4 replaces entry #2 previously considered under the cost method.

Part 4

PART 4
Concept Check

In the context of a parent founded subsidiary, explain how consolidation and equity method are closely related.

___
___
___
___
___
___

CONSOLIDATION OF PARENT FOUNDED SUBSIDIARIES
Module 2 - Recap

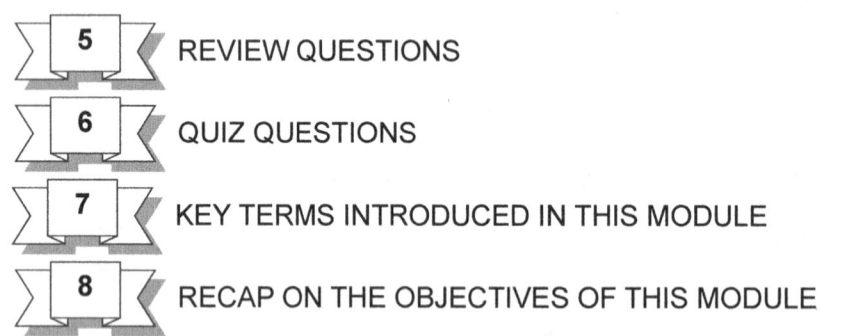

5 REVIEW QUESTIONS

6 QUIZ QUESTIONS

7 KEY TERMS INTRODUCED IN THIS MODULE

8 RECAP ON THE OBJECTIVES OF THIS MODULE

Part 5

PART 5
Review Questions

1 Define or explain the following terms:

- Intercompany transactions
- Intercompany dividends
- Upstream and downstream transactions
- Reciprocal balances
- Double-counting of subsidiary's earnings
- Parent founded subsidiary
- Double-counting in the statement of financial position
- Worksheet approach
- Direct approach

2 What are the two general approaches to preparing consolidated financial statements? Which one is the most commonly used in practice? Why?

REVIEW QUESTIONS
(continued...)

Part 5

3. What amount of capital stock is usually reported in a consolidated statement of financial position?

4. Name some reciprocal accounts that might be found in the separate records of a parent company and its subsidiaries.

5. Why reciprocal balances must be eliminated in the preparation of consolidated financial statements?

6. What effect does the elimination of reciprocal sales and cost of goods sold have on consolidated comprehensive income?

7. What effect does the elimination of reciprocal receivables and payables have on the net consolidated value?

8. What effect does the elimination of intercompany dividends have on the net consolidated value?

REVIEW QUESTIONS
(continued...)

Part 5

9. Why is the investment account on the parent's records eliminated as part of consolidation process?

10. Are working paper adjustments and eliminations entered on the affiliated companies' records? Explain.

11. The balance of retained earnings on the books of a parent company that employs the equity method is different from the balance that will be shown in the consolidated statement of financial position. Comment.

12. Why is the equity method of accounting for equity investments frequently referred to as a one-line consolidation?

13. Is there a difference between the amount of a parent company's comprehensive income under the equity method and the consolidated comprehensive income for the same parent company?

Part 5

REVIEW QUESTIONS
(continued...)

14. How are consolidated financial statements affected by the manner in which the parent company accounts for its subsidiary investment?

15. What are the differences in the eliminating entries if parent company employs the equity method instead of the cost method to account for its investment in subsidiary?

16. Why do many corporations carry out their operations through multiple subsidiaries?

17. Discuss the limitations of consolidated financial statements.

Part 6

PART 6
Quiz Questions

On December X8, Large Inc. established a subsidiary named Small Inc. The initial cash investment amounted to $250,000. Since its establishment, Small had the following earnings and paid the following dividends:

Year	Comprehensive income	Dividends
X9	$30,000	$8,000
X10	25,000	10,000
X11	50,000	20,000

Large's equity section at the end of year X11 consists of Common Shares of $800,000 and Retained Earnings of $350,000. Large's comprehensive income and dividends declared for X11 amount to $150,000 and $50,000, respectively.

With the exception of intercompany dividends, Large and Small did not engage in transactions amongst themselves.

Part 6

QUIZ QUESTIONS

1

Assume that Large is using the <u>equity method</u> to report its investment in Small. Determine the balance of the investment account on the books of Large at the end of X11.

◇

◇

◇

Parent Founded Subsidiaries — Module 2 — 125

Part 6

QUIZ QUESTIONS

2

Assume that Large is using the <u>cost method</u> to report its investment in Small. If the total comprehensive income reported by Large for X11 is $150,000, what amount would be reported had Large been using the equity method instead?

◇ Comprehensive income for X11 under the cost method $150,000

◇ *Extra dividend for X15.*   (50,000)

◇ *Comprehensive income for (X9-X10-X11)*   105,000

Comprehensive income for X11 under the equity method   205,000

Parent Founded Subsidiaries — Module 2 — 126

Part 6

QUIZ QUESTIONS
3

Assume that Large is using the <u>cost method</u> to report its investment in Small. Determine the amount that will be reported as *Retained Earnings* in Large's consolidated statement of financial position at the end of X11.

- Comprehensive income X11   150,000
- Dividend Share   20,000
                                ―――――――
                                170,000

Parent Founded Subsidiaries ---------- Module 2 ---------- 127

Part 6

QUIZ QUESTIONS
4

Assume that Large is using the <u>cost method</u> to report its investment in Small. List the consolidation entries required to consolidate the financial statements of Large for X11.

1. Dr Common Shares   250,000
     Cr Investment in Small   250,000

2. Dr Investment in subsidiary   50,000
     Cr Dividend declared   50,000

Parent Founded Subsidiaries ---------- Module 2 ---------- 128

Part 6

QUIZ QUESTIONS

5

Assume that Large is using the equity method to report its investment in Small. List the consolidation entries required to consolidate the financial statements of Large for X11.

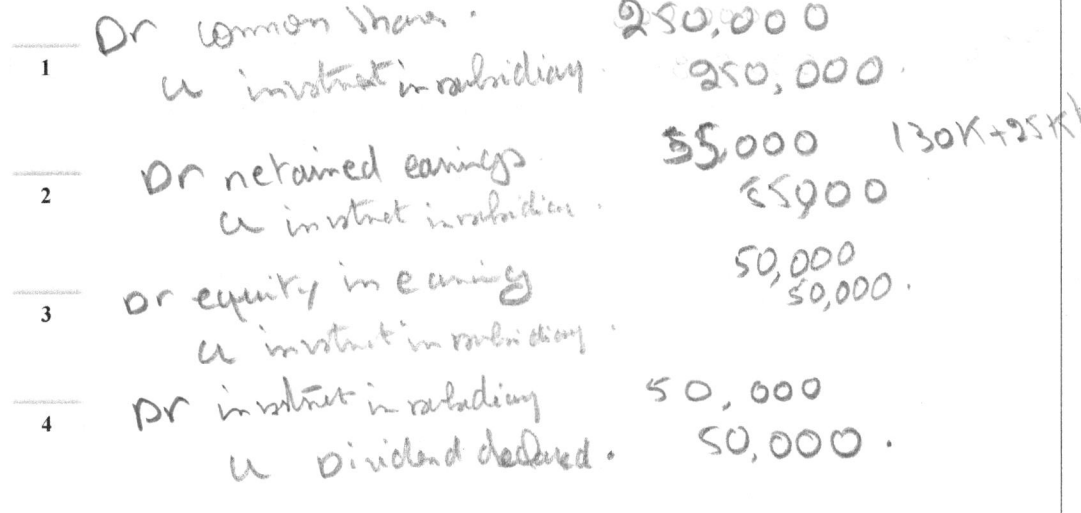

1. Dr Common shares 250,000
   Cr Investment in subsidiary 250,000

2. Dr Retained earnings 55,000 (30K + 25K)
   Cr Investment in subsidiary 55,000

3. Dr Equity in earnings 50,000
   Cr Investment in subsidiary 50,000

4. Dr Investment in subsidiary 50,000
   Cr Dividend declared 50,000

Part 7

KEY TERMS INTRODUCED IN THIS MODULE

• Parent founded subsidiary • Double-counting in the statement of financial position • Working paper entries	Part 1
• Intercompany transactions • Intercompany dividends • Upstream and downstream transactions • Reciprocal balances • Double-counting of subsidiary's earnings	Part 2
• Worksheet approach • Direct approach	Part 3

RECAP ON THE OBJECTIVES OF THIS MODULE

Part 8

Part 1 Introduce the basic characteristics of parent founded subsidiaries.

Illustrate the double-counting issue through consolidation at the date of creation.

Part 2 Illustrate the impact of intercompany transactions on the consolidation process. Focus on transactions that result in reciprocal balances. Intercompany transactions involving intercompany gains and losses will be introduced in Module 5.

Part 3 Illustrate the consolidation process of parent founded subsidiaries in periods subsequent to the date of creation.

Discuss the general approach to consolidation under the worksheet approach and the direct approach as well.

RECAP ON THE OBJECTIVES OF THIS MODULE

Part 8

Part 4 Discuss the equity-basis reporting when Parent Company uses the equity method in its separate-entity financial statements: the case of parent founded subsidiaries.

Illustrate the approach to compute the investment in Subsidiary in non-consolidated financial statements under the equity method.

Present the financial reporting implications of using either the cost method, the equity method or full consolidation.

Present the additional consolidation entries required to eliminate the investment account when the equity method is employed by Parent Company in non-consolidated financial statements.

Copyright © 2020, Parmitech, Ottawa. Parmitech. All rights reserved.

Exercise 2-1
Transfer of Net Assets at the Establishment of a New Subsidiary

Salvage Corporation decided to create a new corporation named Wild Corporation by transferring some of its existing assets and liabilities to the new entity. In exchange, Wild Corporation issued Salvage Corporation 30,000 common shares. The following information is provided on the assets and liabilities transferred (in $):

	Cost	Book Value	Fair Value
Cash	25,000	25,000	25,000
Inventory	70,000	70,000	70,000
Land	60,000	60,000	90,000
Buildings	170,000	130,000	240,000
Equipment	90,000	80,000	105,000
Acc. payable	45,000	45,000	45,000

Required

a) Give the journal entry that Salvage recorded for the transfer of net assets to Wild.
b) Give the journal entry that Wild recorded for the receipt of net assets from Salvage
c) Give the consolidation entry required to consolidate Salvage's statement of financial position at the date of creation.

Journal Entry - Salvage

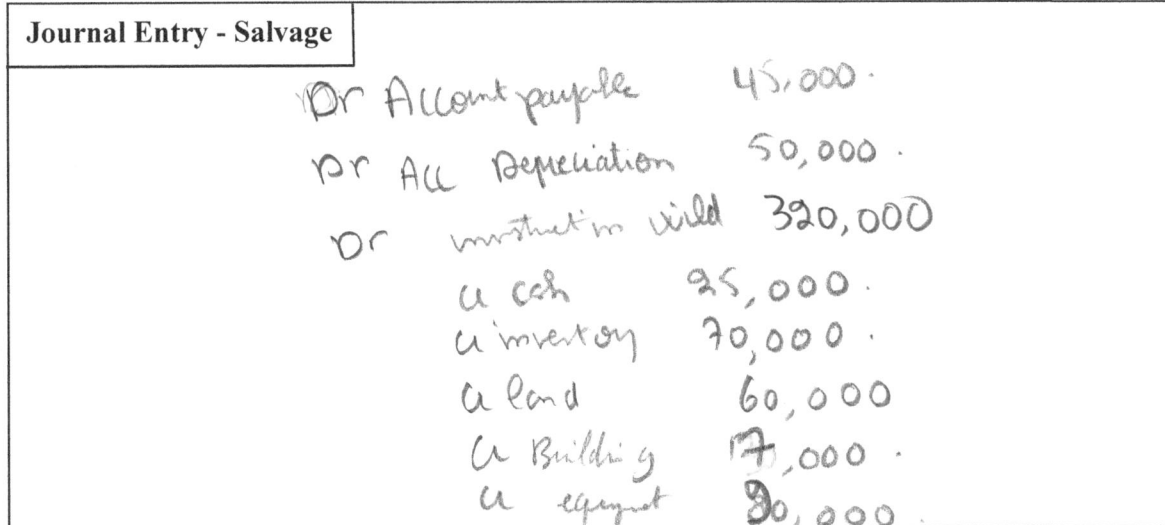

Journal Entry - Wild

Dr Cash 25,000
Dr Inv 70,000
Dr Land 60,000
Dr Building 130,000
Dr Equipment 80,000

Cr A/c payable 48,000
Cr Common Share 320,000

Consolidation Entry

Dr Common Shares 320,000
Cr Investment in subs 320,000

Copyright © 2020, Parmitech, Ottawa. Parmitech. All rights reserved.

Exercise 2-2
Data from Consolidated Income Statement of Newly Established Subsidiary

Father Corporation established a new corporation named Daughter Company during X1. During X7, Father purchased inventory for $20,000 and sold the full amount to Daughter Company for $30,000. Also, during X7, Daughter purchased inventory for $50,000 and sold all the units to Father for $80,000. Prior to the end of the year, all the transferred units have been resold to external parties. As a result of these intercompany sales, reciprocal receivables and payables amounted to $25,000 as of December 31, X7.

The following presents the summary income statement data for the affiliated companies for the year ended December 31, X7 (in $):

	Father Corporation	Daughter Company
Sales	400,000	200,000
Income from Daughter	25,000	
Cost of goods sold (COGS)	250,000	120,000
Other expenses	70,000	35,000
Profit for the year	105,000	45,000

Required

a) Compute the amount to be reported as **sales** in the X7 consolidated income statement.
b) Compute the amount to be reported as **cost of goods sold** (COGS) in the X7 consolidated income statement.
c) What amount will be reported as consolidated **profit for X7**?

[Handwritten annotations:]
20,000 → 30,000
50,000 add 80,000.

Consolidated Sales

400,000 + 200,000 − 30,000 − 80,000

sales: = 490,000

Consolidated COGS

COGS = 250,000 + 120,000 − 30,000 − 80,000 =
= 260,000.

Consolidated Profit

= 105,000 + 45,000 = 150,000

Exercise 2-3
Investment Account in a Newly Established Subsidiary

On January 1, X5, Alpha Corporation established a new corporation named Beta Corporation by transferring the following assets in exchange for 10,000 common shares (in $):

	Cost	Book Value	Fair Value
Cash	50,000	50,000	50,000
Inventory	50,000	50,000	60,000
Land	40,000	40,000	75,000
Buildings	150,000	110,000	220,000

In X5 and X6, Beta reported comprehensive income of $10,000 and $20,000, and dividends of $5,000 and $10,000, respectively.

Required
In each of the following independent cases, calculate the balance in Alpha Company's investment account on December 31, X6, assuming that Alpha accounted for its investment in Beta using:

a) The cost method
b) The equity method

Cost Method

Total BV = 250,000

Equity Method

initial investment   250,000
Share of earnings: 10,000
                     20,000
Dividend   (5,000)
                     (10,000)
                     ─────────
                     265,000

Exercise 2-4
Accounting for a Newly Established Subsidiary

Refer to Exercise 2.3.

Required

a) Give the journal entry on Alpha's records at the date of creation.
b) Give the consolidation entries required to consolidate Alpha's statement of financial position on December 31, X6, under the cost method and the equity method.

Journal Entry - Alpha

Dr Investment   250,000
Dr A/Depreciation   40,000
  Cr Cash   50,000
  Cr Inventory   50,000
  Cr Land   40,000
  Cr Building   150,000

Consolidation Entry – Cost Method

Dr Common Shares   250,000
  Cr Investment   250,000

Consolidation Entries – Equity Method

Dr Common Shares   250,000
  Cr Investment   250,000

Dr RE   20,000
  Cr Investment   20,000

Dr RE   5,000
  Cr Investment   5,000

Dr Investment   10,000
  Cr Dividend declared   10,000

Exercise 2-5
Consolidation One Year Post-Creation

On January 1, X1, Pari Corporation established a new corporation named Sol Corporation. Sol issued common shares to Pari in return for $150,000 cash paid by Pari.

The following presents the statements of financial position of the affiliated companies a year post-creation.

Separate Entity Statements of Financial Position
At December 31, X1

	Pari	Sol
Assets		
Cash	$ 18,100	$ 20,600
Accounts receivable ($10,000 from Sol)	27,700	50,000
Inventory	25,000	46,000
Investment in Sol (at cost)	150,000	
Land, building and equipment	209,500	104,000
Cumulated depreciation	(86,000)	(30,000)
Total assets	**$344,300**	**$190,600**
Liabilities		
Current liabilities ($10,000 payable to Pari)	$ 51,000	$ 38,600
Shareholder's equity		
Share capital	225,000	150,000
Retained earnings (January 01)	45,500	-
Net income	42,800	13,000
Dividends (paid cash)	(20,000)	(11,000)
Total liabilities and equity	**$344,300**	**$190,600**

Required

a) Prepare the consolidated statement of financial position of Pari Corporation on December 31, X1. Complete the following worksheet.
b) Calculate the consolidated (or adjusted) net value of Sol on December 31, X1.

Pari Corporation
Consolidated Statements of Financial Position
At December 31, X1

	Pari	Sol	Adjustments	F/S
Assets				
Cash	$ 18,100	$ 20,600		38,700
Accounts receivable	27,700	50,000	(10,000)	67,700
Inventory	25,000	46,000		71,000
Investment in Sol (at cost)	150,000		(150,000)	
Land, building and equipment	209,500	104,000		313,500
Cumulated depreciation	(86,000)	(30,000)		(116,000)
Total assets	$344,300	$190,600		374,200
Liabilities				
Current liabilities	$ 51,000	$ 38,600	(10,000)	79,600
Shareholder's equity				
Share capital	225,000	150,000	(150,000)	225,000
Retained earnings	68,300	2,000		70,300
Total liabilities and equity	$344,300	$190,600		374,900

Consolidated Net Value

initial investment + Sol RE

150,000 + 2,000 = $152,000

Exercise 2-6
Newly Established Subsidiary and Equity Method

Refer to exercise 2.5.

Required

a) Calculate the balance in Pari Corporation's investment account on December 31, X1, assuming that Pari is using the equity method for its investment in Sol.
b) Provide all the journal entries for X1 under the equity method.

Balance of Investment

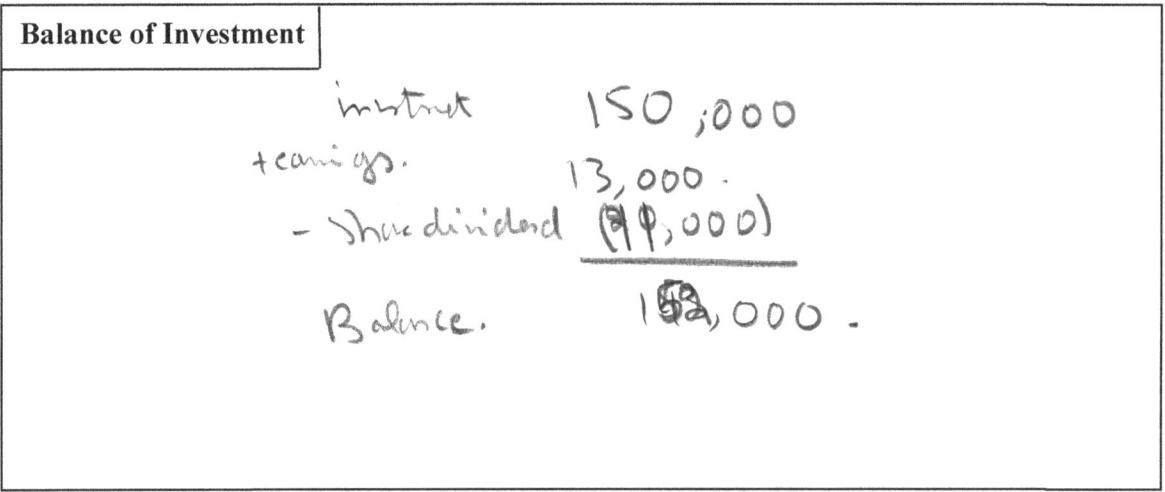

Journal Entries

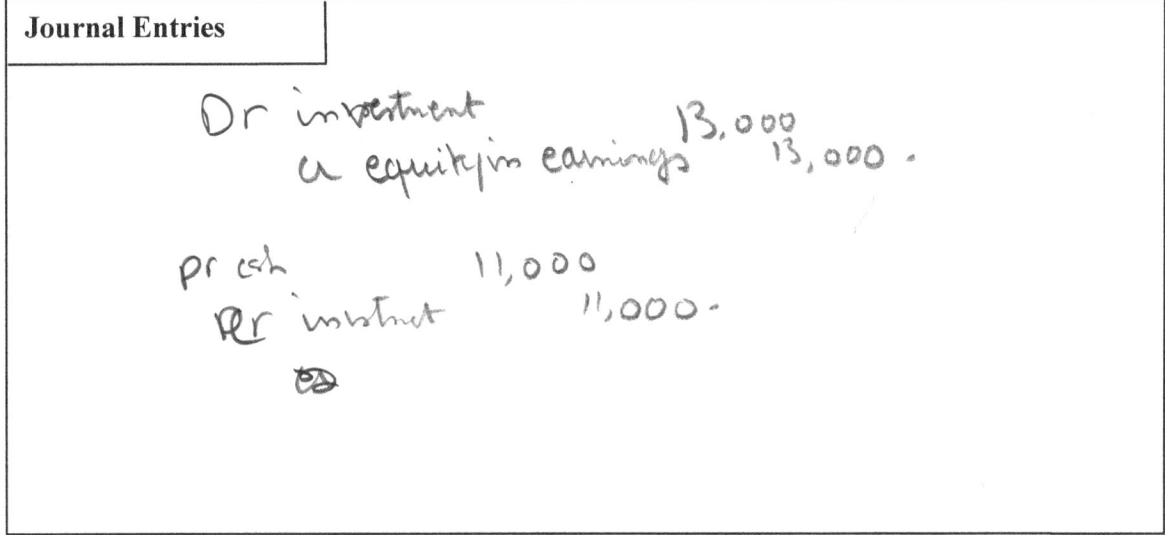

Solutions to Exercises

2-1
a) Journal entry on Salvage's records:

Investment in Wild	320,000	
Accounts Payable	45,000	
Accumulated Depreciation	50,000	
Cash		25,000
Inventory		70,000
Land		60,000
Buildings		170,000
Equipment		90,000

b) Journal entry on Wild's records:

Cash	25,000	
Inventory	70,000	
Land	60,000	
Buildings	130,000	
Equipment	80,000	
Accounts Payable		45,000
Common Shares		320,000

c) Consolidation entry:

Common Shares (Wild)	320,000	
Investment in Wild (Salvage)		320,000

2-2
a) Consolidated sales for X7:
Sales of Father ($400,000) + Sales of Daughter ($200,000) – Downstream current-year sales ($30,000) – Upstream current-year sales ($80,000) = **$490,000**

b) Consolidated cost of goods sold for X7:
Cost of goods sold of Father ($250,000) + Cost of goods sold of Daughter ($120,000) – Downstream current-year sales ($30,000) – Upstream current-year sales ($80,000) = **$260,000**

c) Consolidated profit for X7:
Profit of Father ($105,000) + Profit of Daughter ($45,000) = **$150,000** Note that Income from Daughter ($25,000) should be offset by a corresponding expense on the books of Daughter. Therefore, there is no impact on the consolidated profit.

2-3

a) Balance of the investment account under the cost method
   Initial Investment at date of creation which consists of the BV of the transferred assets:
   $250,000

b) Balance of the investment account under the equity method

Initial investment		$250,000
Share of earnings –	X5	10,000
	X6	20,000
Share of dividends –	X5	(5,000)
	X6	(10,000)
		$265,000

2-4

a) Journal entry on Alpha's records:

Investment in Beta	250,000	
Accumulated Dep. – Buildings	40,000	
Cash		50,000
Inventory		50,000
Land		40,000
Buildings		150,000

Journal entry on Beta's records (optional):

Cash	50,000	
Inventory	50,000	
Land	40,000	
Buildings	110,000	
Common Shares		250,000

b) Consolidation entry under the cost method:

Common Shares (Beta)	250,000	
Investment in Beta (Alpha)		250,000

Consolidation entries under the equity method:

Common Shares (Beta)	250,000	
Investment in Beta (Alpha)		250,000
Retained Earnings (Alpha)	5,000	
Investment in Beta (Alpha)		5,000
Equity in Earnings (Alpha)	20,000	
Investment in Beta (Alpha)		20,000
Investment in Beta (Alpha)	10,000	
Dividends Declared (Beta)		10,000

2-5
Consolidated F/S of Pari on December 31, X1.

	Pari	Sol	Adjustments	F/S
Assets				
Cash	$ 18,100	$ 20,600		38,700
Accounts receivable	27,700	50,000	(10,000)	67,700
Inventory	25,000	46,000		71,000
Investment in Sol (at cost)	150,000		(150,000)	-
Land, building and equipment	209,500	104,000		313,500
Cumulated depreciation	(86,000)	(30,000)		(116,000)
Total assets	**$344,300**	**$190,600**		**$374,900**
Liabilities				
Current liabilities	$ 51,000	$ 38,600	(10,000)	79,600
Shareholder's equity				
Share capital	225,000	150,000	(150,000)	225,000
Retained earnings	68,300	2,000		70,300
Total liabilities and equity	**$344,300**	**$190,600**		**$374,900**

Net Adjusted Value of Sol (consolidated value):
Initial Investment ($150,000) + Sol's RE ($2,000) = **$152,000**

2-6
a) Balance of the investment account under the equity method

Initial investment	$150,000
Share of earnings – X1	13,000
Share of dividends – X1	(11,000)
	$152,000

b) Journal entries under the equity method

Investment in Sol	13,000	
Equity in Earnings		13,000
Cash	11,000	
Investment in Sol		11,000

Business Combinations

Module 3

What you will find in this section

- How to Walk Through Module 3
- Slides
- Exercises and Solutions

Module 3
Business Combinations

How to Walk Through Module 3

◇ <u>Readings</u>

1- <u>Book</u> "Consolidation of Financial Statements": Chapter 2, Part 1
2- <u>Student Manual</u> "Advanced Accounting": Module 3

    PART 1: INTRODUCTION TO BUSINESS COMBINATIONS

    PART 2: ACCOUNTING FOR BUSINESS COMBINATIONS

    PART 3: PURCHASE OF NET ASSETS: ILLUSTRATION

    PART 4: PURCHASE OF SHARES: CONSOLIDATION OF WHOLLY OWNED SUBSIDIARIES AT THE DATE OF ACQUISITION

    PART 5: MERGER

◇ <u>Assignments</u>

3- <u>Student Manual</u>: End-of module review and quiz questions
4- <u>Student Manual</u>: Exercises 1 to 9
5- <u>Book</u>: Case 3

◇ <u>Additional readings</u>

6- <u>IFRS</u> 3

When you have successfully completed this module, you will be able to do the following:

- Define a business combination and its context;

- Discuss the different legal forms of business combinations;

- Explain the general accounting approach to business combinations;

- Demonstrate the mechanics of consolidating a wholly owned subsidiary at the date of acquisition.

BUSINESS COMBINATIONS
Module 3

Copyright © 2020 Parmitech

Advanced Accounting: Student Manual

Copyrighted Material

Editor: Parmitech

This publication is protected by copyright, and permission should be obtained from the publisher prior to any prohibited reproduction, storage in a retrieval system, or transmission in any form or by any means, electronic, mechanical, photocopying, recording, or otherwise.

Corresponding Author

Richard Bozec Ph.D., CPA, CGA
bozec@telfer.uottawa.ca

Copyright © Parmitech

CORRESPONDING CHAPTERS in *Bozec*
"Consolidation of Financial Statements under IFRS"

Chapter 2   Wholly Owned Subsidiaries (Part 1)

Case   3

IFRS

IFRS 3   Business Combinations

TEACHING MATERIAL
Exercises

Module 3

- 3.1   Stock Acquisition with Cash
- 3.2   Stock Acquisition with Bonds
- 3.3   Purchase of Net Assets with Cash
- 3.4   Consolidation at Date of Acquisition (no Goodwill)
- 3.5   Purchase of Net Assets: Post-Acquisition SFPs
- 3.6   Negative Goodwill
- 3.7   Stock Acquisition versus Purchase of Net Assets
- 3.8   From Case 3: Global Inc.
- 3.9   Consolidation at Date of Acquisition (with Goodwill)

FOCUS OF THIS MODULE : ACQUIRED SUBSIDIARIES

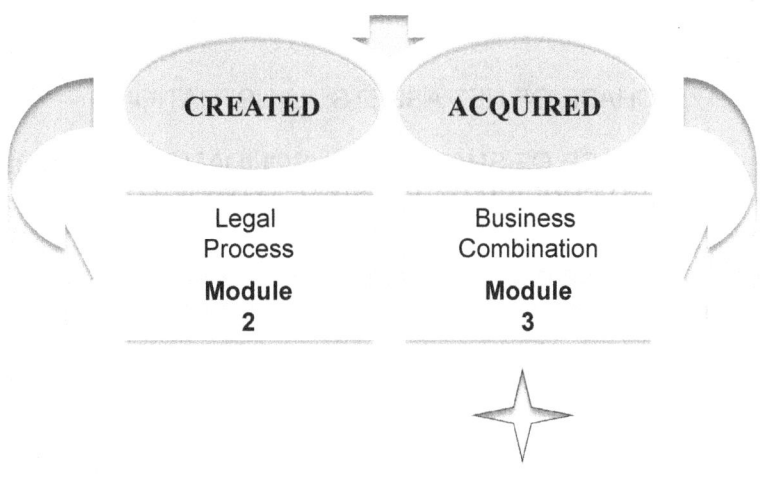

Business Combinations ---------- Module 3 ----------

FOCUS OF THIS MODULE: PRICE DIFFERENTIAL

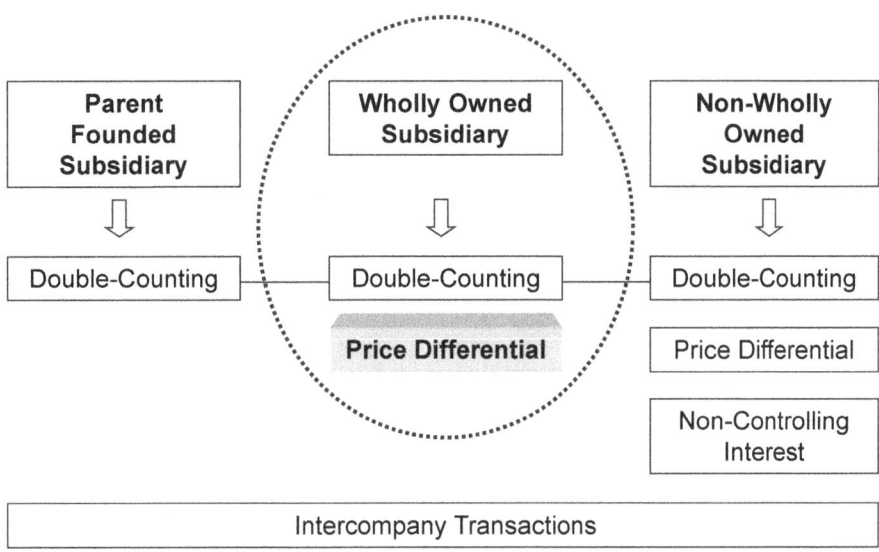

Business Combinations ---------- Module 3 ----------

OUTLINE OF THE PRESENTATION

1. INTRODUCTION TO BUSINESS COMBINATIONS
2. ACCOUNTING FOR BUSINESS COMBINATIONS
3. PURCHASE OF NET ASSETS: ILLUSTRATION
4. PURCHASE OF SHARES: CONSOLIDATION OF WHOLLY OWNED SUBSIDIARIES AT THE DATE OF ACQUISITION
5. MERGER

RECAP

6. REVIEW QUESTIONS
7. QUIZ QUESTIONS
8. KEY TERMS INTRODUCED IN THIS MODULE
9. RECAP ON THE OBJECTIVES OF THIS MODULE

PART 1
Introduction to Business Combinations

Objectives of this section

Define a business combination and its context.

Present the different legal forms of business combinations.

Key concepts

- Business; Business combination
- Purchase of net assets
- Purchase of shares
- Merger; Statutory merger; Statutory consolidation
- Reverse takeover; Hostile takeover

BUSINESS COMBINATIONS
A Multidisciplinary Topic

LEGAL — Transfer of ownership

FINANCE — Valuation

AUDITING — Audit risk and work

ACCOUNTING — Measuring and reporting

TAXATION — Impact for buyers/sellers

BUSINESS COMBINATIONS

BUSINESS COMBINATIONS
Business Expansion

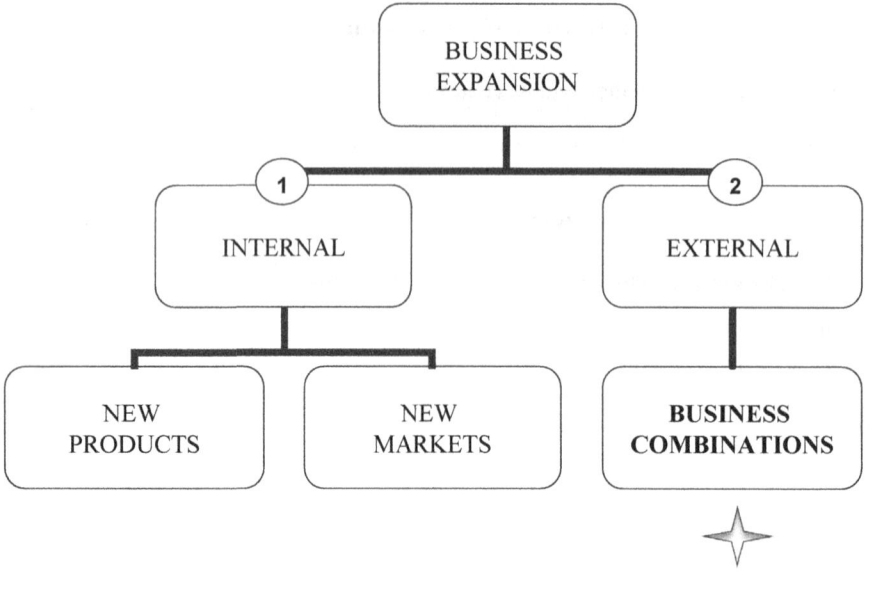

BUSINESS COMBINATIONS
Internal vs. External Expansion

Businesses can expand internally and/or externally. Internal expansion is achieved through the development and marketing of new products or by selling new or existing products in new markets. External expansion is achieved through business combinations.

Management often chooses to expand externally because it is quicker and potentially cheaper to buy a sales force, a complementary product line or a product facility than it is to build one. Internal expansion takes time since the entity may be required to develop a distribution system, generate demand for its new product. Internal expansion is also risky since the development and marketing of new products are often difficult tasks.

BUSINESS
Key Elements

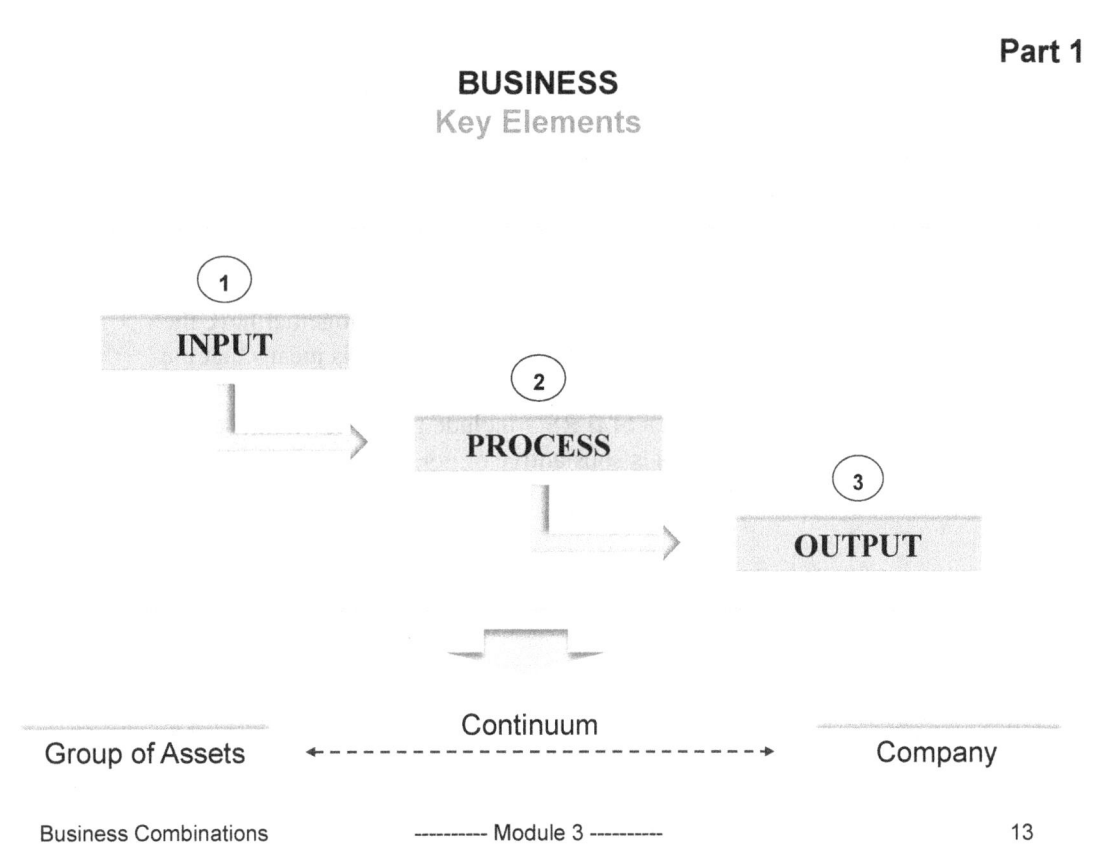

BUSINESS COMBINATIONS
Definition - Amendments to IFRS 3

Defining a business is important. This is because the financial reporting requirements for the acquisition of a business are different from the requirements for the purchase of a group of assets that does not constitute a business.

On October 22, 2018, the IASB issued *Definition of a Business (Amendments to IFRS 3)* aimed at resolving the difficulties that arise when an entity determines whether it has acquired a business or a group of assets. The amendments are effective for business combinations for which the acquisition date is on or after the beginning of the first annual reporting period beginning on or after January 1, 2020.

BUSINESS COMBINATIONS
Definition - Amendments to IFRS 3 (continued)

For the IASB, the most critical distinction between a business and a non-business is the existence of a process. Thus, a business must include, at a minimum, an input and a process that together have the "ability to contribute to the creation of outputs". This means that the transaction needs to contain inputs and at least one substantive process. The amendments of IFRS 3 include guidance on how can one assess whether a process is substantive or not.

BUSINESS COMBINATIONS
Potential Economic Advantages

- Expansion can be achieved more rapidly (compared to the development of new products and/or new markets).

- Provide an established, experienced management group immediately.

- May lead to economies of scale.

- May reduce the cost of capital because the size of the entity increases.

- Increase control over market share.

RAPID EXPANSION

Part 1

BUSINESS COMBINATIONS
Probability of Failure

- External growth is extremely competitive.

- The probability of increasing shareholders' wealth via such growth is low.

- The probability of success for the average buyer is only 50/50 at best.

- The shareholders of acquired companies are usually the big winners, receiving on average a 20 percent premium in a friendly merger and 35 percent premium in a hostile takeover.

Takeover premium
Excess of the amount offered in an acquisition over the prior stock price of the acquired firm.

Part 1

HISTORY OF BUSINESS COMBINATIONS

1880 — **HORIZONTAL COMBINATION**

- **Definition**: A combination involving two or more entities that are in competition in the same industry
- **Objective**: Dominate or monopolize particular industries

1920 — **VERTICAL COMBINATION**

- **Definition**: A combination involving two or more entities that have a potential buyer-seller relationship
- **Objective**: Improve the efficiency of operations by gaining control over the suppliers and/or distributors (or retailers)

1950 — **CONGLOMERATE COMBINATION**

- **Definition**: A combination that occurs when the acquired company is in an unrelated business
- **Objective**: Diversify the asset base so to increase income stability

NATURE OF THE BUSINESS COMBINATION

Part 1

FRIENDLY

When the boards of directors of the potential combining companies negotiate mutually agreeable terms of a proposed combination.

UNFRIENDLY

When the board of directors of a company targeted for acquisition resists the combination. Many tactics can be used in this context to curb or block a combination.

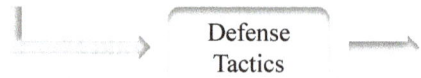
Defense Tactics

DEFENCE TACTICS

Part 1

Poison pill	Issuing stock rights to the existing shareholders so as to enable them to purchase additional shares at a price below market value, but exercisable only in the event of a potential takeover.
Greenmail	The purchase of any shares held by the would-be acquiring company at a price substantially in excess of their value.
White knight	Encouraging a third firm more acceptable to the target company management to acquire or merge with the target company.
Pac-man defense	Attempting an unfriendly takeover of the would-be acquiring company.
Selling the crown jewels	The sale of valuable assets to others to make the firm less attractive to the would-be acquirer.
Leverage buyouts	The purchase of a controlling interest in the target firm by its managers and third-party investors, who usually incur substantial debt in the process and subsequently take the firm private.

BUSINESS COMBINATIONS
Legal Forms

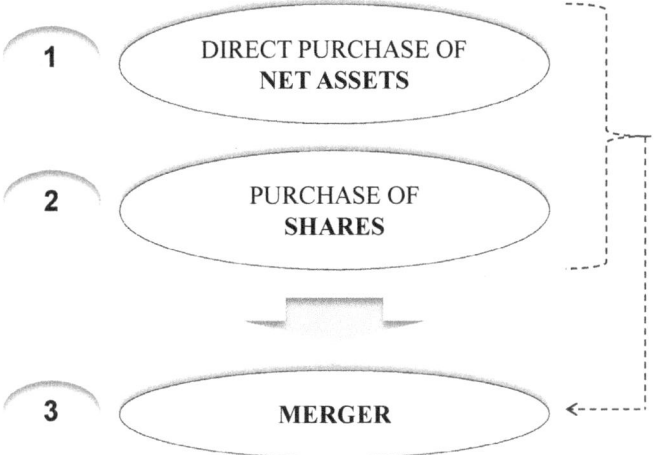

1. DIRECT PURCHASE OF **NET ASSETS**
2. PURCHASE OF **SHARES**
3. **MERGER**

LEGAL FORMS OF BUSINESS COMBINATIONS
Purchase of Net Assets

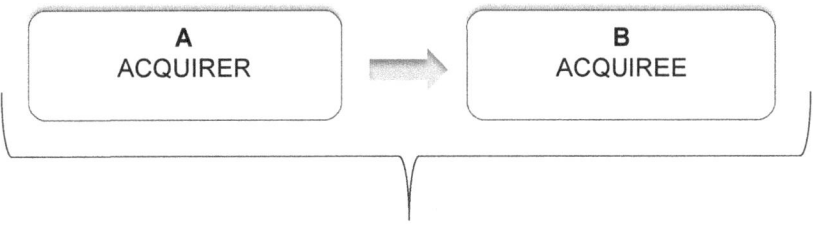

A ACQUIRER → B ACQUIREE

LEGAL TRANSFER
of all the assets and liabilities from B to A

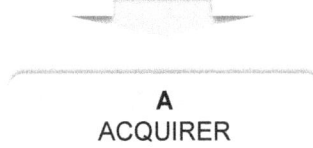

A ACQUIRER

LEGAL FORMS OF BUSINESS COMBINATIONS
Purchase of Shares

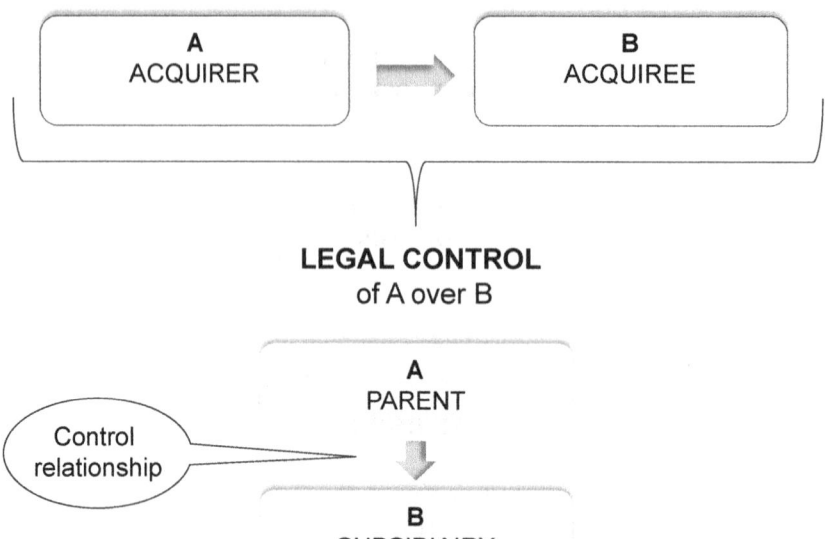

Business Combinations ---------- Module 3 ----------

LEGAL FORMS OF BUSINESS COMBINATIONS
Merger

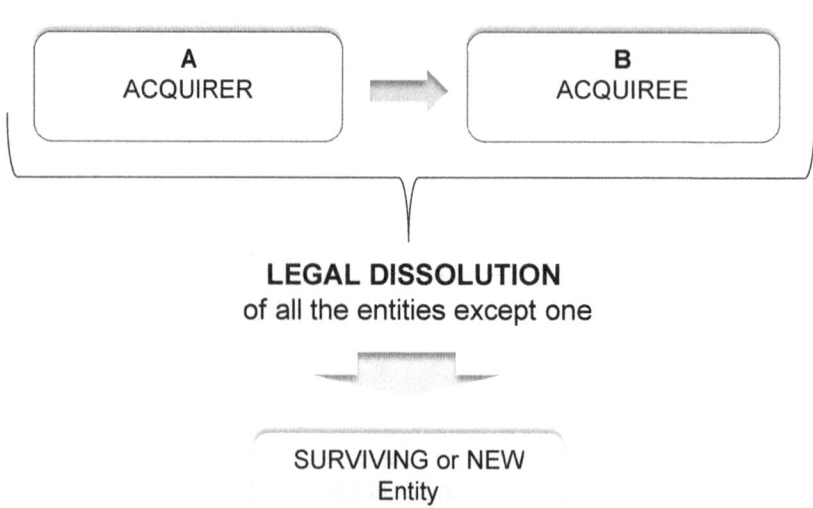

Business Combinations ---------- Module 3 ----------

BUSINESS COMBINATIONS
Consideration Given

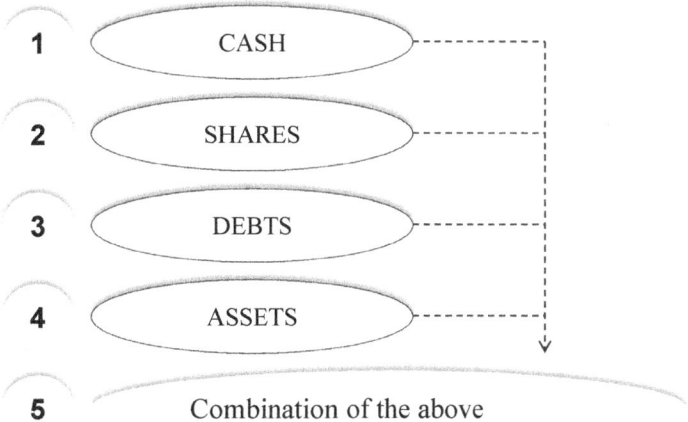

1. CASH
2. SHARES
3. DEBTS
4. ASSETS
5. Combination of the above

When the consideration given is with shares, the number of shares outstanding increases. Therefore, the existing shareholders of the acquiring company own a smaller, or diluted, percentage of their company. See next slides for illustrations.

Business Combinations ---------- Module 3 ---------- 25

BUSINESS COMBINATIONS
Scenarios Covered Next

Business Combinations	Consideration Given	
Légal process	$	Shares
➤ PURCHASE OF NET ASSETS	1	2
➤ PURCHASE OF SHARES	3	4
➤ MERGER	→ 5 ←	

Business Combinations ---------- Module 3 ---------- 26

DIRECT PURCHASE OF NET ASSETS
Affiliation Structure
Consideration Given is with Cash

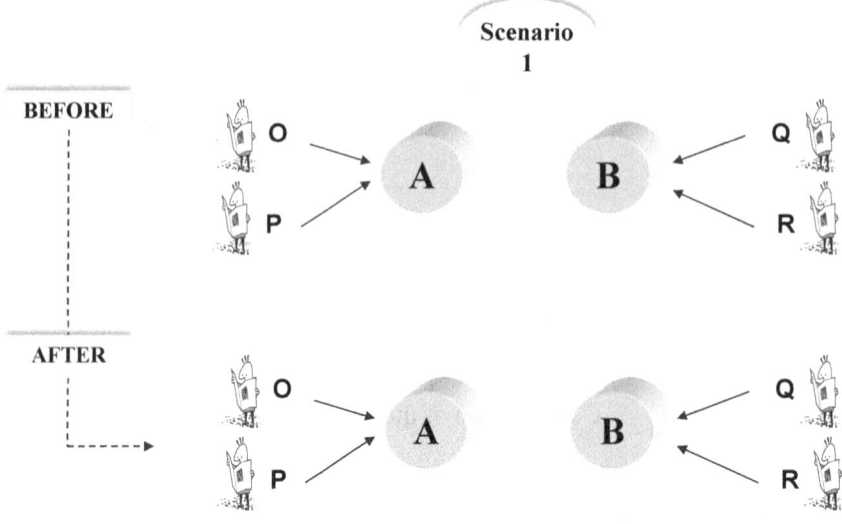

Part 1

DIRECT PURCHASE OF NET ASSETS
Affiliation Structure
Consideration Given is with Cash - Overview

Part 1

- Who is the other party to this transaction?
  - B
  - Shareholders of B
  - Outside party

- How is the combination of A and B achieved in accounting?
  - Through the books of A
  - On working paper
  - A and B are not combined

- What are the assets remaining in the post-acquisition SFP of B?
  - Only Cash
  - Only Investment in A
  - No change

- Is a reverse takeover possible?

DIRECT PURCHASE OF NET ASSETS
Affiliation Structure
Consideration Given is with Shares

Part 1

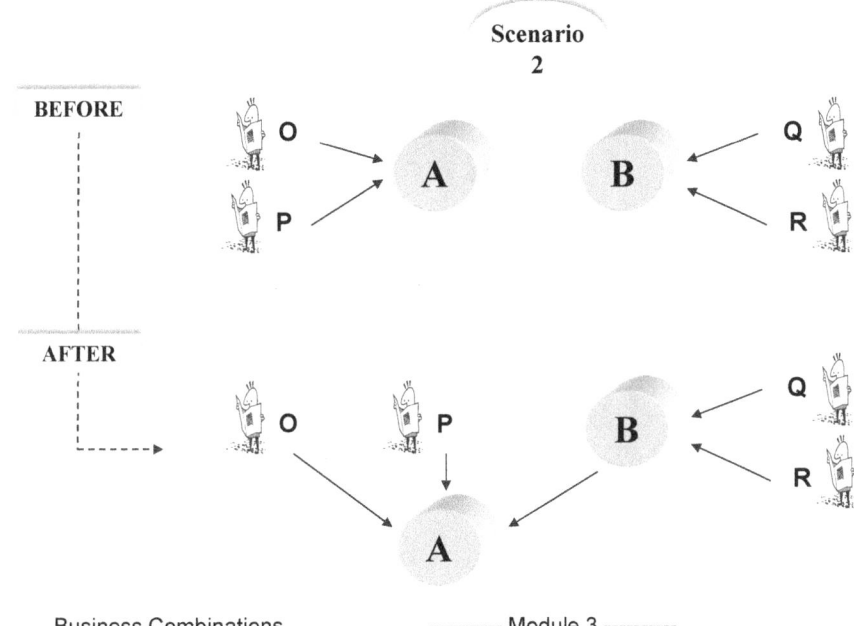

DIRECT PURCHASE OF NET ASSETS
Affiliation Structure
Consideration Given is with Shares - Overview

Part 1

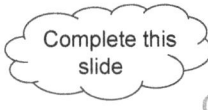

- Who is the other party to this transaction?
  - B
  - Shareholders of B
  - Outside party

- How is the combination of A and B achieved in accounting?
  - Through the books of A
  - On working paper
  - A and B are not combined

- What are the assets remaining in the post-acquisition SFP of B?
  - Only Cash
  - Only Investment in A
  - No change

- Is a reverse takeover possible?

PURCHASE OF SHARES
Affiliation Structure
Consideration Given is with Cash

Part 1

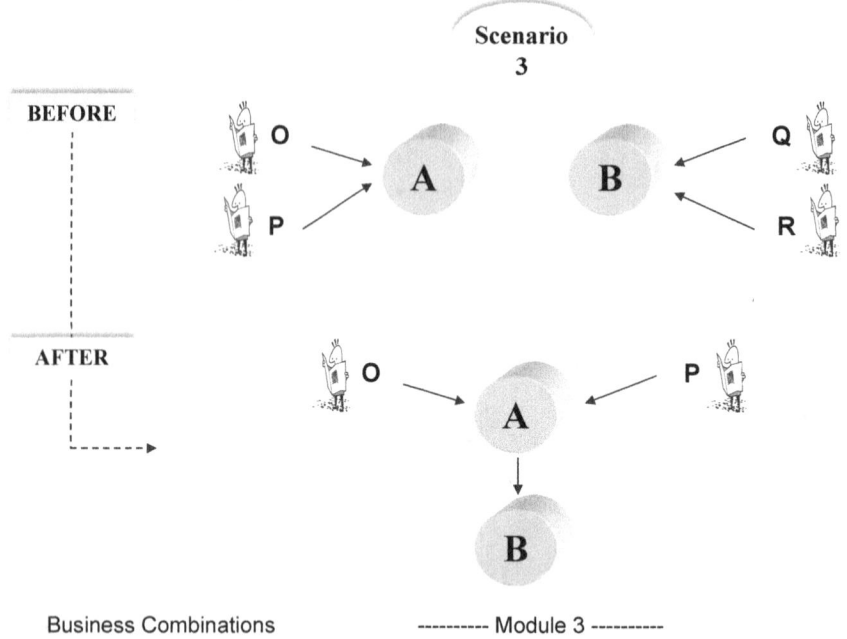

BEFORE

AFTER

PURCHASE OF SHARES
Affiliation Structure
Consideration Given is with Cash - Overview

Part 1

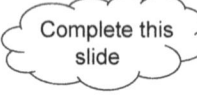
Complete this slide

- Who is the other party to this transaction?
  - B
  - Shareholders of B
  - Outside party

- How is the combination of A and B achieved in accounting?
  - Through the books of A
  - On working paper
  - A and B are not combined

- What are the assets remaining in the post-acquisition SFP of B?
  - Only Cash
  - Only Investment in A
  - No change

- Is a reverse takeover possible?

PURCHASE OF SHARES
Affiliation Structure
Consideration Given is with Shares - Exchange of Shares

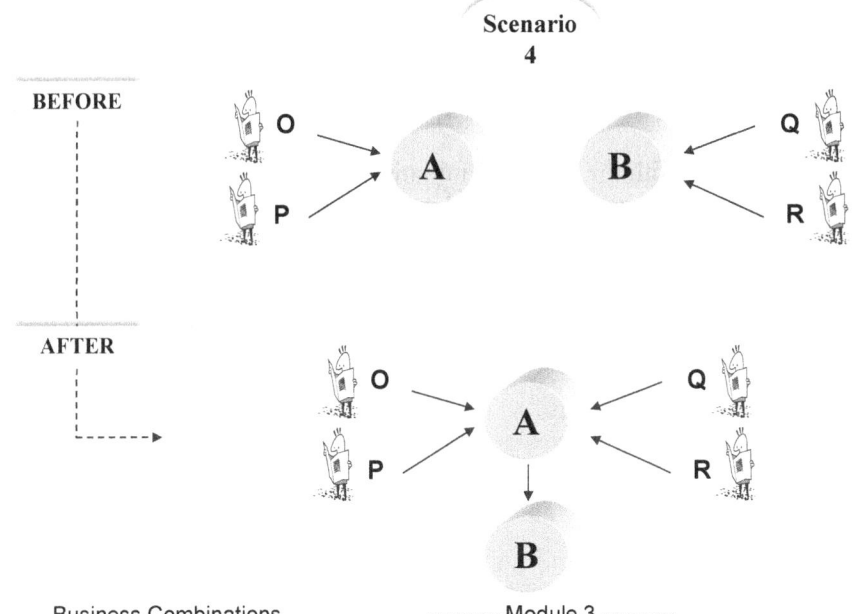

Business Combinations — Module 3 —

PURCHASE OF SHARES
Affiliation Structure
Consideration Given is with Shares - Overview

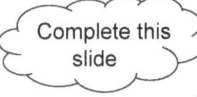 *Complete this slide*

- Who is the other party to this transaction?
  - B
  - Shareholders of B
  - Outside party

- How is the combination of A and B achieved in accounting?
  - Through the books of A
  - On working paper
  - A and B are not combined

- What are the assets remaining in the post-acquisition SFP of B?
  - Only Cash
  - Only Investment in A
  - No change

- Is a reverse takeover possible?

Business Combinations — Module 3 —

PURCHASE OF SHARES
Conditions for a Reverse Takeover

Consideration given must necessarily be with voting shares. Moreover, number of voting shares issued must be higher than number of outstanding voting shares prior to the acquisition.

Legally, control resides with the company initiating the purchase. In substance, control resides with the shareholders of the target company.

PURCHASE OF SHARES
Reverse Takeover - Illustration

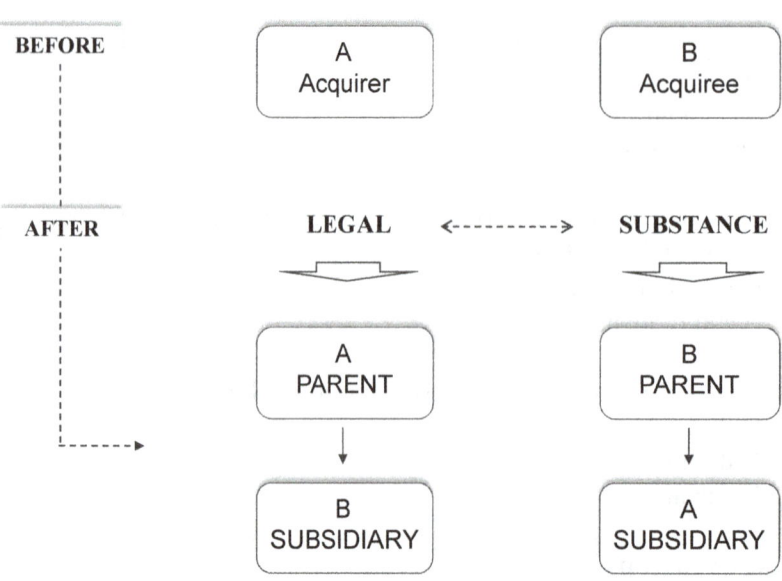

Part 1

PURCHASE OF SHARES
Main Reason for a Reverse Takeover

The main reason for a reverse takeover is to acquirer a stock exchange listing.

For instance, if Company A is a shell company (or a dormant company) and Company B wants to be listed without going through the trouble and expense of applying to security commission and stock exchange for listing, a reverse takeover could be arranged.

Company A becomes the legal acquirer or the legal parent, whereas, in substance, the acquirer is Company B. In accounting, we will report in accordance with the substance of the combination, as we always do. Therefore, we will proceed with the consolidation of Company B, the parent, and Company A, the subsidiary.

Part 1

PURCHASE OF SHARES
Advantages Over Purchase of Net Assets

Main Advantage

--- Control can be obtained at less cost --

Because less financing is needed as only a majority of shares is required for control over 100% of the net assets.

Other Advantages

- Possible to acquirer shares when the stock market is depressed, thereby, paying less than the FV of the identifiable assets of the investee.

- Publicly traded shares are more liquid than would be the individual assets of the investee.

- Easier to go around a company's management in a hostile takeover.

- The affiliated companies continue to exist as two separate legal entities which provide an element of protection of the parent's assets from attachment by creditors of the subsidiary.

MERGER
Typology

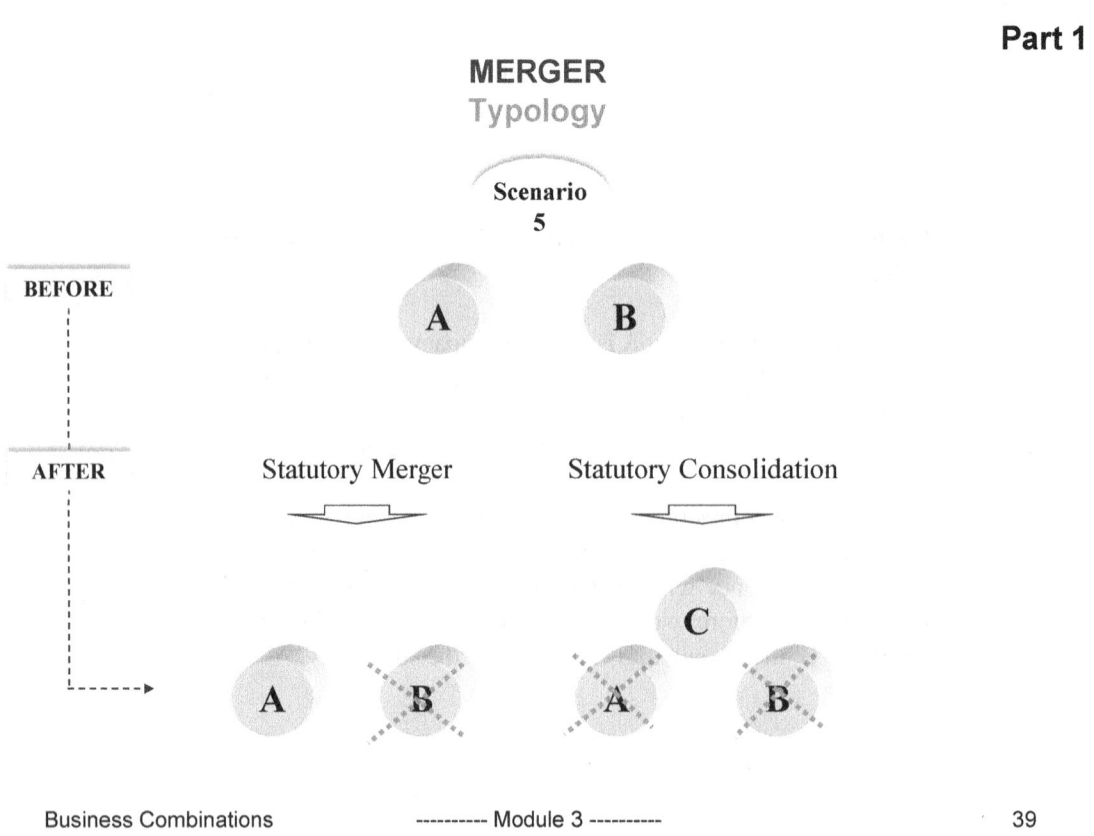

MERGER
Accounting Point of View

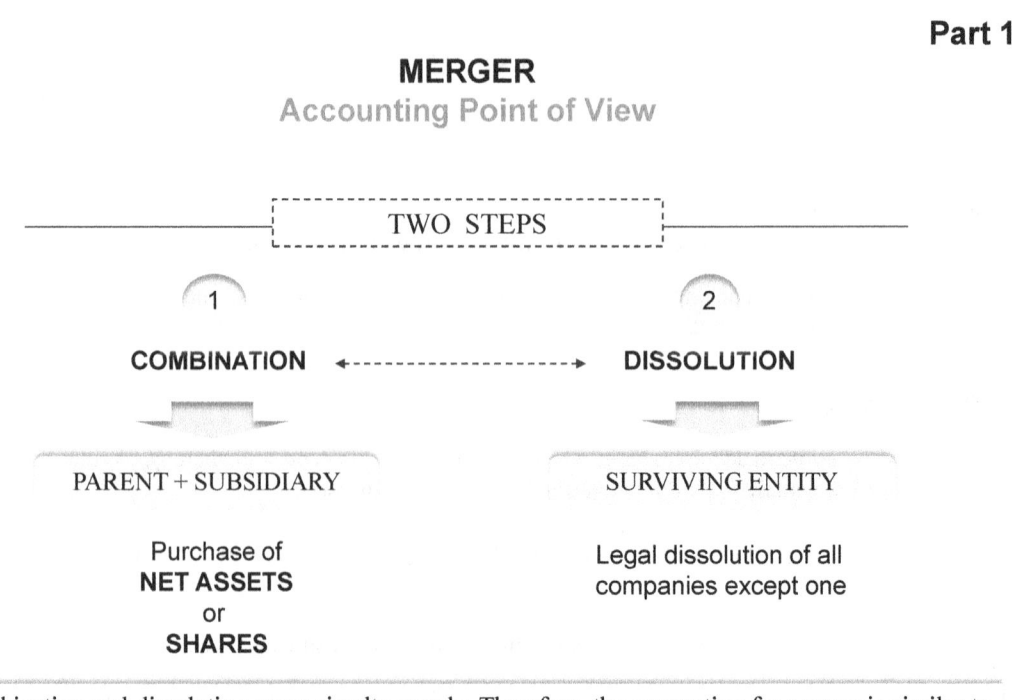

Combination and dissolution occur simultaneously. Therefore, the accounting for merger is similar to the accounting for a business combination effected through the purchase of either shares or net assets. The only difference resides in the dissolution process.

PURCHASE OF SHARES
From a Tax Viewpoint

Part 1

May benefit the **SELLER**

- Any gain to the seller on a sale of shares will be taxed as a capital gain. However, if the assets are sold, gains may be subject to tax at full rates.

- Note that the acquired company may have substantial tax loss carryforwards, the benefits of which are unlikely to be realized. The purchaser may be able to take advantage of these carryforwards.

PURCHASE OF NET ASSETS
From a Tax Viewpoint

Part 1

May benefit the **BUYER**

- When the assets are purchased directly, their cost to the acquiring company becomes the basis for their tax treatment. Since CCA is based of FV, tax deductions increase when FVs are greater than BVs.

- Similarly, goodwill purchased is treated as *Eligible Capital Property*, and 100% of the goodwill is subject to CCA (Class 14.1: 5% on a declining basis).

- However, in the context of a stock acquisition, there is no change in the tax basis for the assets of the target company, and goodwill is not tax deductible.

PART 1
Concept Check

Describe the three legal forms of business combinations.

_____
_____
_____
_____
_____
_____
_____
_____

OUTLINE OF THE PRESENTATION

1. INTRODUCTION TO BUSINESS COMBINATIONS
2. **ACCOUNTING FOR BUSINESS COMBINATIONS**
3. PURCHASE OF NET ASSETS: ILLUSTRATION
4. PURCHASE OF SHARES: CONSOLIDATION OF WHOLLY OWNED SUBSIDIARIES AT THE DATE OF ACQUISITION
5. MERGER

PART 2
Accounting for Business Combinations

Objectives of this section

Present and compare the methods of accounting for a business combination.

Outline the requirements for applying the acquisition method.

Key concepts

- Acquisition method
- Pooling of interests
- New entity
- Purchase price allocation; Price differential
- Goodwill, Negative goodwill;
- Fair value increment; Fair value decrement
- Control premium

ACCOUNTING FOR BUSINESS COMBINATIONS
Substance over Form

LEGAL FORMS	ACCOUNTING METHODS
Purchase of net assets	Pooling of interests
Purchase of shares	Acquisition
Merger	New entity

BUSINESS COMBINATIONS SHOULD BE REPORTED IN ACCORDANCE WITH THE SUBSTANCE OF THE COMBINATION, NOT WITH ITS LEGAL FORM

ACCOUNTING FOR BUSINESS COMBINATIONS
Overview

Methods	Net Assets of Parent Company		Net assets of Subsidiary
Pooling of Interests	BV	+	BV
Acquisition *(Under IFRS)*	BV	+	FV
New Entity	FV	+	FV

ACCOUNTING FOR BUSINESS COMBINATIONS
Pooling of Interests

Pooling of Interests is no longer accepted in Canada and the US for business combinations occurring after July 2001. This method was permitted only when an acquirer could not be identified, that is, when the shareholdings were evenly split between the shareholders of the two pre-acquisition companies.

Since there is no acquirer, the two companies are viewed as a single company, a combined economic entity that is merely a continuation under common ownership of two previously separated going concerns. Therefore, fair values are ignored in the consolidation process.

Current accounting standards do not recognize this specific situation. Indeed, under the acquisition method, the first step consist of identifying the acquirer (see next).

ACQUISITION METHOD
General Approach

Part 2

1. IDENTIFYING THE ACQUIRER
2. MEASURING THE COST OF THE PURCHASE
3. DETERMINING FAIR VALUES OF NET IDENTIFIABLE ASSETS
4. ALLOCATING THE COST

RECORDING THE TRANSACTION

Business Combinations ---------- Module 3 ---------- 49

ACQUISITION METHOD
Step 1
Identifying the Acquirer

Part 2

CONSIDERATION GIVEN	THE ACQUIRER WOULD BE:
Cash or assets	The company making the payment or transferring assets.
Shares	The company holding more than 50% of the voting shares of the combined entity.
	Often the company that issues shares.
	Often the larger company.
	If each group of shareholders owns the same percentage, then the makeup of the board of directors and senior management is examined.

Business Combinations ---------- Module 3 ---------- 50

ACQUISITION METHOD
Step 2
Measuring the Cost of the Purchase

CONSIDERATION GIVEN	FAIR VALUE
Cash	Cash paid
Assets	FV of assets transferred
Debts	Present value of any promises to pay cash in the future
Shares	Fair market value at the date of combination

Business Combinations — Module 3 — 51

ACQUISITION METHOD
Direct and Indirect Costs

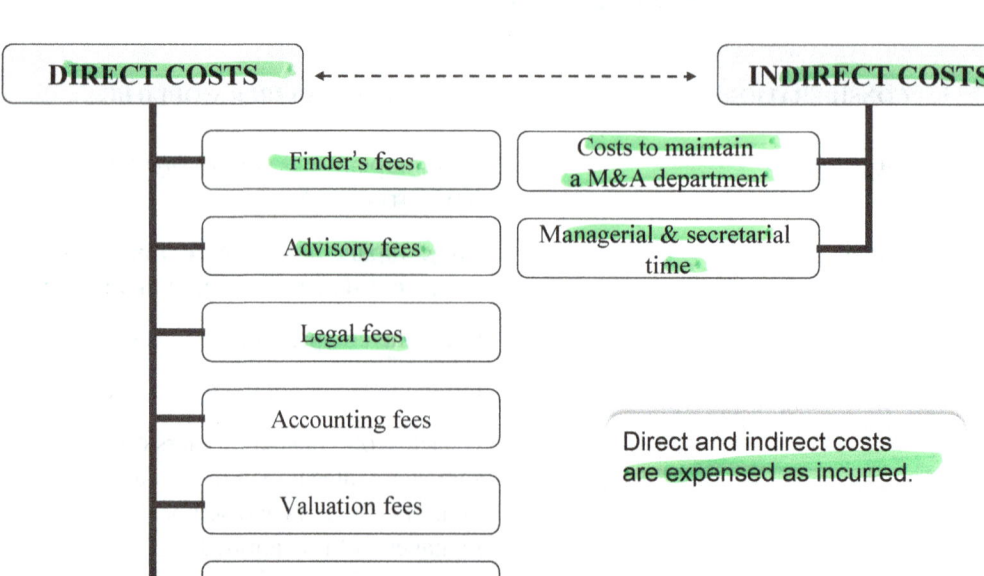

DIRECT COSTS
- Finder's fees
- Advisory fees
- Legal fees
- Accounting fees
- Valuation fees
- Professional & consulting

INDIRECT COSTS
- Costs to maintain a M&A department
- Managerial & secretarial time

Direct and indirect costs are expensed as incurred.

Business Combinations — Module 3 — 52

Part 2

ACQUISITION METHOD
Step 3
Determining Fair Values of Net Identifiable Assets: IFRS 13

- Use of exit values for non-financial assets, that is, the price that would be received to sell an asset or paid to transfer a liability.

- Determination of highest and best use (for non-financial assets).

- Incorporation of market participant assumptions about the use of non-financial assets.

- Consideration of multiple valuation techniques when measuring the fair value of assets and liabilities:

  - Market approach
  - Cost approach
  - Income approach

Part 2

ACQUISITION METHOD
Step 4
Allocating the Cost

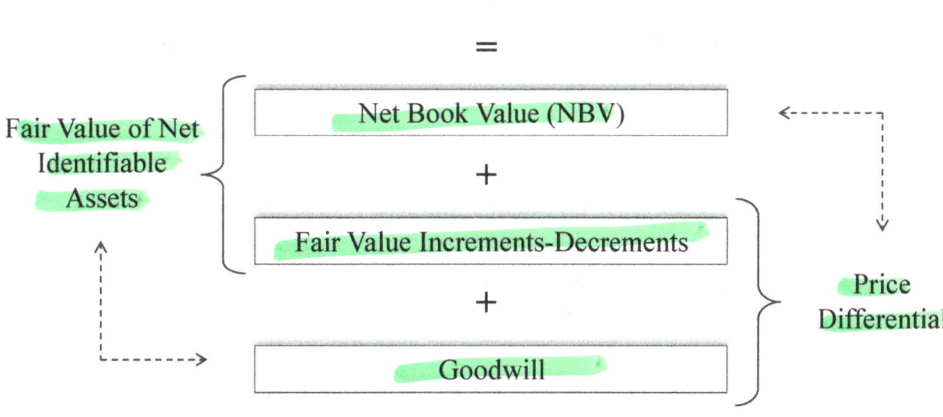

ACQUISITION METHOD
Step 4
Allocating the Cost - Key Definitions

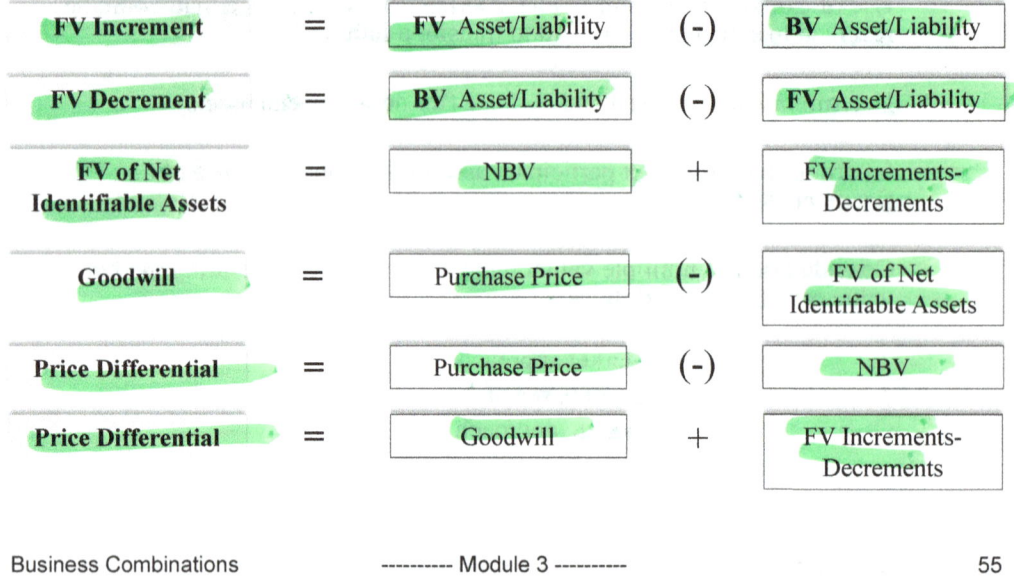

INTANGIBLES versus GOODWILL

- Intangibles should be recognized apart from goodwill when the asset:

    - Results from contractual or legal rights,
      CONTRACTUAL-LEGAL CRITERION

    - Can be sold, transferred, licensed, rented, or exchanged.
      SEPARABILITY CRITERION

- Acquired intangibles other than goodwill:
    - Limited useful life: should be amortized over its useful economic life and be reviewed for impairment.
    - Indefinite life: should not be amortized but should be tested for impairment annually.

It is very important not to use Goodwill as a catch-all item. Instead, we must carefully recognize apart from goodwill intangibles that qualify to either the contractual-legal criterion or separability criterion. Besides, the accounting for intangibles and goodwill is different.

INTANGIBLES OTHER THAN GOODWILL
Examples

Part 2

CONTRACTUAL-LEGAL CRITERION	SEPARABILITY CRITERION
• Royalties • Lease agreements • Franchise agreements • Trademarks • Tradenames • Technology patents	• Customer lists • Databases

The existence of significant unrecorded intangible assets may be both a major reason why a given acquisition may occur and a major factor in determining the purchase price. Most of these intangibles are developed during the pre-acquisition life of the investee, and few of them are recorded as assets on the investee's books. Therefore, it is critical to identify these intangibles at date of acquisition and report them apart from goodwill.

WHAT GOODWILL MIGHT INCLUDE
Examples

Part 2

Goodwill

  Skilled workforce

  Premium to achieve control

  Firm value of expected synergies

  Business network

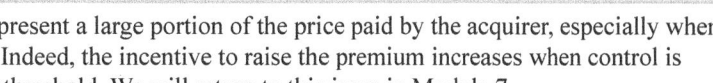

Control premium could represent a large portion of the price paid by the acquirer, especially when control is less than 100%. Indeed, the incentive to raise the premium increases when control is achieved close to the 50% threshold. We will return to this issue in Module 7.

NEGATIVE GOODWILL

- Occurs when the price paid is less than the FV of identifiable net assets acquired.

- Reported in the statement of comprehensive income of the acquirer as a **gain on purchase**.

- Considered as a **bargain purchase**.

Under the *Acquisition Method*, identifiable net assets of the acquired company are always reported at their FV at date of acquisition. Any excess of the price paid over the net FV is considered as a gain for the acquirer. Indeed, the transaction is viewed as a bargain purchase. The accounting for negative goodwill is illustrated in part 3.

PART 2
Concept Check

> Explain how the accounting principle "substance over form" applies to business combinations.

_____
_____
_____
_____
_____
_____

OUTLINE OF THE PRESENTATION

Part 3

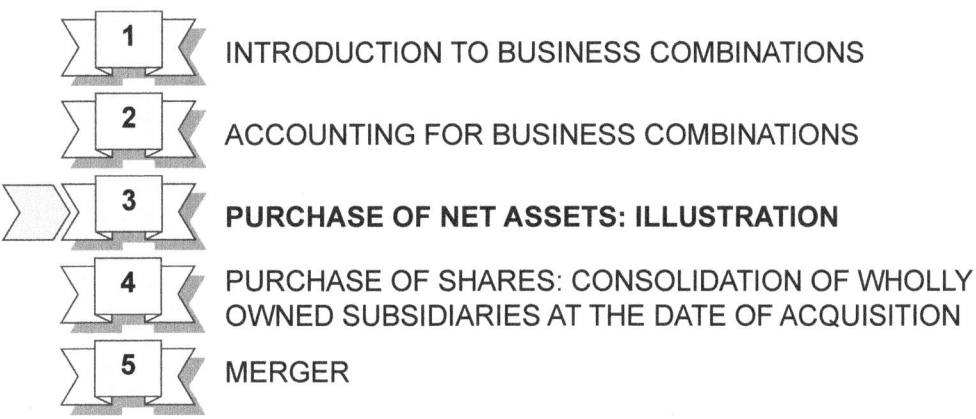

1. INTRODUCTION TO BUSINESS COMBINATIONS
2. ACCOUNTING FOR BUSINESS COMBINATIONS
3. **PURCHASE OF NET ASSETS: ILLUSTRATION**
4. PURCHASE OF SHARES: CONSOLIDATION OF WHOLLY OWNED SUBSIDIARIES AT THE DATE OF ACQUISITION
5. MERGER

Part 3

PART 3
Purchase of Net Assets: Illustration

Objective of this section

Illustrate the accounting for a purchase-of-net assets business combination.

DIRECT PURCHASE OF NET ASSETS
Illustration

On December 31, X1, Parent Company purchased all the net assets and liabilities of Subsidiary Company by issuing 40,000 voting shares. Before the transaction, Parent Company had 160,000 common shares outstanding. On December 31, X1, Parent's common shares had a closing market price of $30 on a national stock exchange.

Required

a) Report the acquisition on the books of Parent and Subsidiary, respectively.

b) Prepare post-acquisition statement of financial position of Parent and Subsidiary, respectively.

DIRECT PURCHASE OF NET ASSETS
Affiliation Structure

BEFORE

PARENT   SUBSIDIARY

AFTER

Parent's shareholders
160,000 shares
(80%)

SUBSIDIARY

40,000 shares
(20%)

PARENT

Part 3

FAIR VALUES OF SUBSIDIARY COMPANY
At December 31, X1

	Book Values	Fair Values	
Assets			
Non-current assets			
Land	$300,000	$400,00	+ 100,000
Buildings (net)	350,000	550,000	+ 200,000
Current assets			
Inventories	50,000	50,000	
Accounts receivable	150,000	150,000	
Cash	50,000	50,000	
Total assets	**$900,000**		
Equity and liabilities			
Equity			
Share capital	$200,000		
Retained earnings	600,000		
Liabilities			
Accounts payable	100,000	100,000	
Total equity and liabilities	**$900,000**		

Business Combinations ---------- Module 3 ---------- 65

Part 3

DIRECT PURCHASE OF NET ASSETS
Acquisition Method - Recap

Complete this slide

1 IDENTIFYING THE ACQUIRER:

Parent company.

2 MEASURING THE COST OF THE PURCHASE:

40,000 × 30 = 1,200,000

3 DETERMINING FAIR VALUES OF NET IDENTIFIABLE ASSETS:

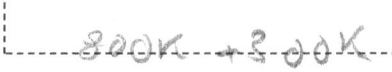
800K + 300K

4 ALLOCATING THE COST:
See next.

Business Combinations ---------- Module 3 ---------- 66

DIRECT PURCHASE OF NET ASSETS
Allocation of Purchase Price

Part 3

Purchase price $1,200 000

Net book value of Subsidiary:
- Common shares   200,000
- Retained earnings   600,000   800,000

Price differential   400,000

Fair value increments:
- Land   (100,000)
- Buildings   (200,000)   (300,000)

Goodwill   100,000

ALLOCATION OF PURCHASE PRICE
Recap

Part 3

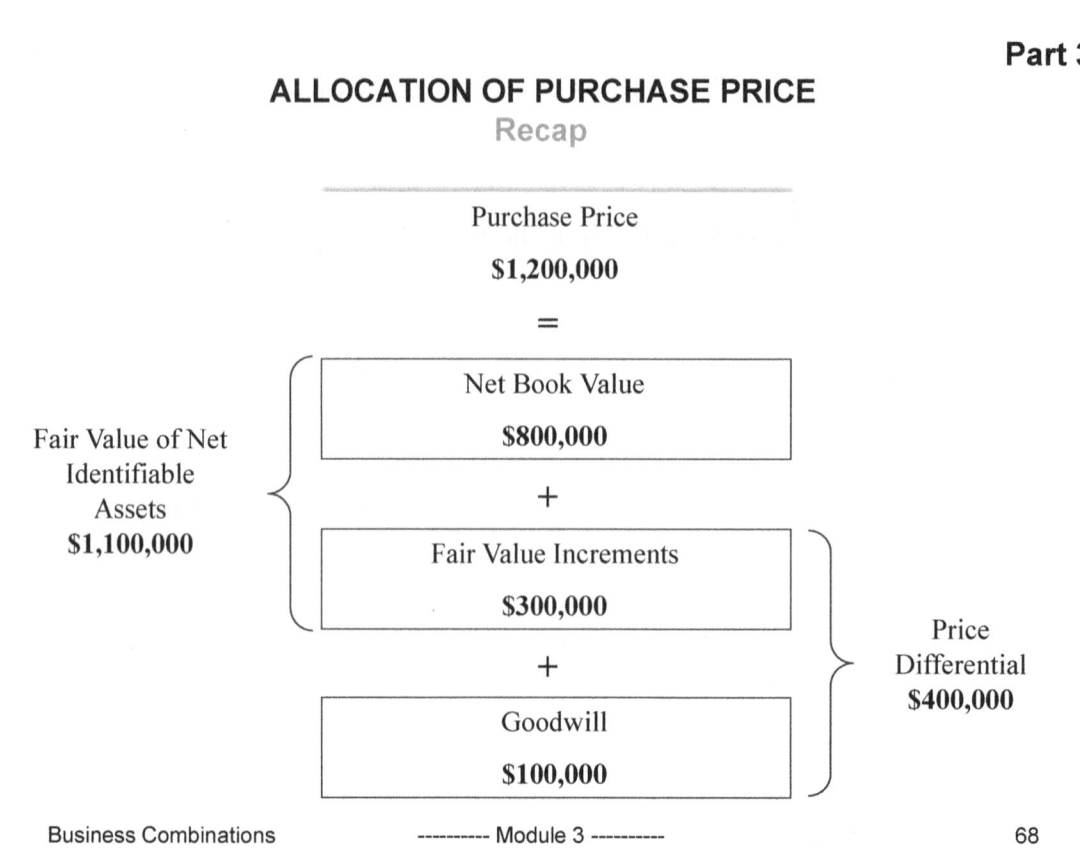

DIRECT PURCHASE OF NET ASSETS
On the Books of Parent

Complete this slide

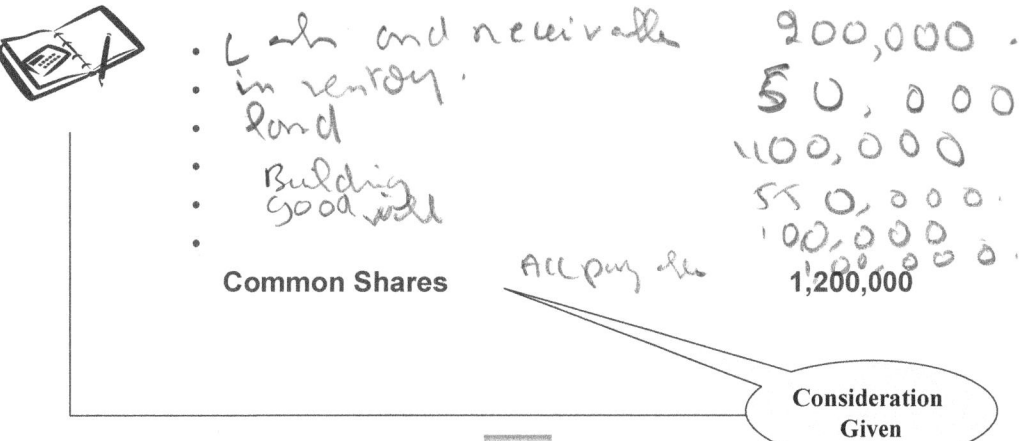

- Cash and receivable   200,000
- Inventory   50,000
- Land   400,000
- Building   550,000
- Goodwill   100,000

Acc payable

Common Shares   1,200,000

Consideration Given

Fair value of Subsidiary, including goodwill, is reported by Parent Company.
(Journal Entry)

POST-TRANSACTION STATEMENT OF FINANCIAL POSITION OF PARENT COMPANY

	Pre-acquisition	Acquisition	Post-acquisition
Assets			
Non-current assets			
Land	$1,000,000	400,000	$1,400,000
Buildings (net)	1,800,000	550,000	2,350,000
Goodwill		100,000	100,000
Current assets			
Inventories	200,000	50,000	250,000
Accounts receivable	2,000,000	150,000	2,150,000
Cash	1,000,000	50,000	1,050,000
Total assets	$6,000,000		$7,300,000
Equity and liabilities			
Equity			
Share capital	$2,600,000	1,200,000	$3,800,000
Retained earnings	2,000,000		2,000,000
Liabilities			
Long-term notes payable	400,000		400,000
Accounts payable	1,000,000	100,000	1,100,000
Total equity and liabilities	$6,000,000		$7,300,000

DIRECT PURCHASE OF NET ASSETS
On the Books of Subsidiary

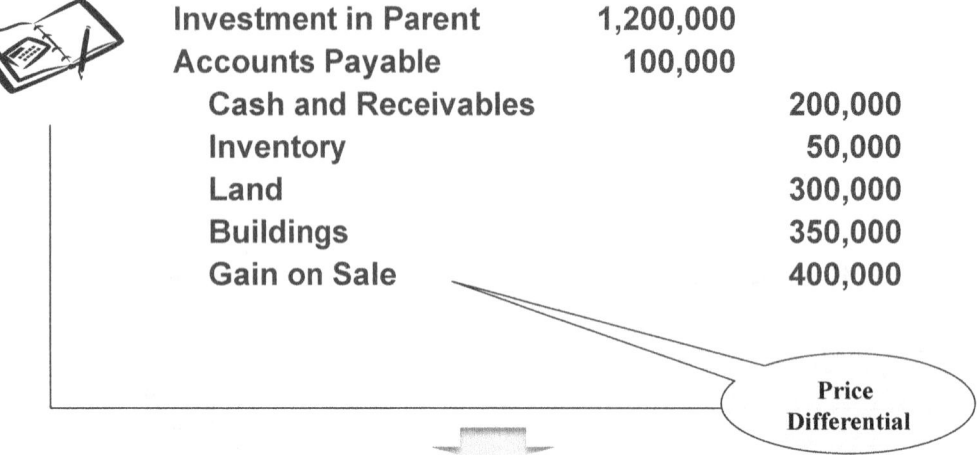

Investment in Parent	1,200,000	
Accounts Payable	100,000	
Cash and Receivables		200,000
Inventory		50,000
Land		300,000
Buildings		350,000
Gain on Sale		400,000

Price Differential

The Gain on sale ($400,000) is equivalent to the price differential, that is, the difference between the purchase price ($1,200,000) and the net book value of Subsidiary ($800,000) at date of acquisition.

POST-TRANSACTION STATEMENT OF FINANCIAL POSITION OF SUBSIDIARY COMPANY

	Pre-acquisition	Acquisition	Post-acquisition
Assets			
Non-current assets			
Land	$300,000	(300,000)	
Buildings (net)	350,000	(350,000)	
Investment in Parent		1,200,000	$1,200,000
Current assets			
Inventories	50,000	(50,000)	
Accounts receivable	150,000	(150,000)	
Cash	50,000	(50,000)	
Total assets	$900,000		$1,200,000
Equity and liabilities			
Equity			
Share capital	$200,000		$200,000
Retained earnings	600,000	(Gain) 400,000	1,000,000
Liabilities			
Accounts payable	100,000	(100,000)	
Total equity and liabilities	$900,000		$1,200,000

DIRECT PURCHASE OF NET ASSETS
Negative Goodwill

Part 3

If the purchase price was $1,000,000 instead of $1,200,000

Purchase price		$1,000,000
Net book value of Subsidiary:		
- Common shares	$200,000	
- Retained earnings	600,000	800,000
Price differential		200,000
Fair value increments:		
- Land	(100,000)	
- Buildings	(200,000)	(300,000)
Negative Goodwill		**($100,000)**

NEGATIVE GOODWILL
Under the Acquisition Method

Part 3

Fair Value of Net Assets

$1,100,000

=

Purchase Price
$1,000,000

+

Gain on Acquisition
$100,000

} Negative Goodwill

Negative goodwill ($100,000) occurs when the price paid ($1,000,000) is less than the FV of identifiable net assets acquired ($1,100,000). Under IFRS, negative goodwill is considered as a bargain purchase (see journal entry next).

Part 3

NEGATIVE GOODWILL
On the Books of Parent

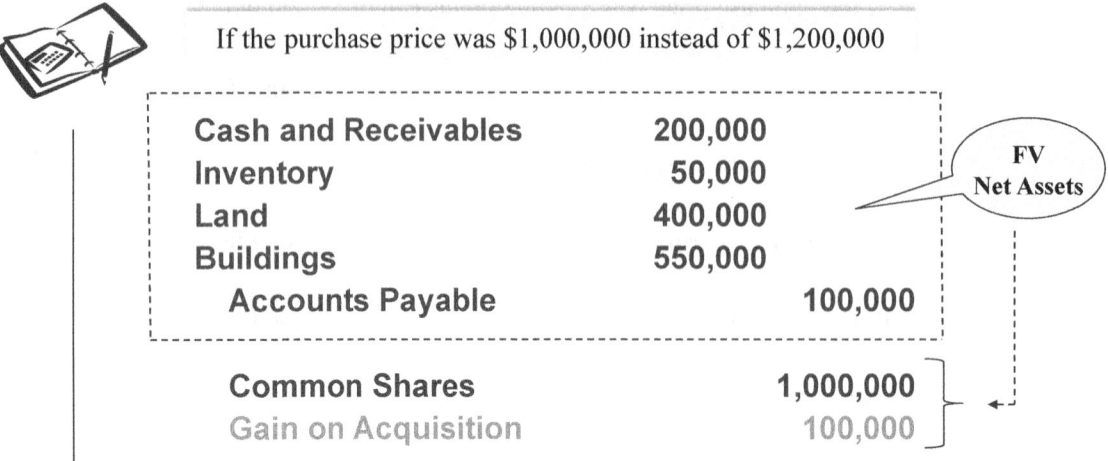

If the purchase price was $1,000,000 instead of $1,200,000

Cash and Receivables	200,000
Inventory	50,000
Land	400,000
Buildings	550,000
Accounts Payable	100,000
Common Shares	1,000,000
Gain on Acquisition	100,000

FV Net Assets

Under the acquisition method, identifiable net assets of the acquired company are always reported at their FV. Any excess over the purchase price is reported as a gain.

Business Combinations ---------- Module 3 ---------- 75

Part 3

POST-TRANSACTION STATEMENT OF FINANCIAL POSITION OF PARENT COMPANY - NEGATIVE GOODWILL

	Pre-acquisition	Acquisition	Post-acquisition
Assets			
Non-current assets			
Land	$1,000,000	400,000	$1,400,000
Buildings (net)	1,800,000	550,000	2,350,000
Current assets			
Inventories	200,000	50,000	250,000
Accounts receivable	2,000,000	150,000	2,150,000
Cash	1,000,000	50,000	1,050,000
Total assets	**$6,000,000**		**$7,200,000**
Equity and liabilities			
Equity			
Share capital	$2,600,000	1,000,000	$3,600,000
Retained earnings	2,000,000	(Gain) 100 000	2,100,000
Liabilities			
Long-term notes payable	400,000		400,000
Accounts payable	1,000,000	100,000	1,100,000
Total equity and liabilities	**$6,000,000**		**$7,200,000**

Business Combinations ---------- Module 3 ---------- 76

PART 3
Concept Check

> What is the post-acquisition affiliation structure between the acquirer and the acquiree when the combination is effected through a purchase of net assets?

OUTLINE OF THE PRESENTATION

1. INTRODUCTION TO BUSINESS COMBINATIONS
2. ACCOUNTING FOR BUSINESS COMBINATIONS
3. PURCHASE OF NET ASSETS: ILLUSTRATION
4. **PURCHASE OF SHARES: CONSOLIDATION OF WHOLLY OWNED SUBSIDIARIES AT THE DATE OF ACQUISITION**
5. MERGER

PART 4
Purchase of Shares:
Consolidation of Wholly Owned Subsidiaries at the Date of Acquisition

---

Objective of this section

Illustrate the consolidation process of wholly owned subsidiaries at the date of acquisition.

PURCHASE OF SHARES
Illustration

On December 31, X1, Parent Company purchased all the outstanding voting stock of Subsidiary Company by issuing 40,000 voting shares. Before the transaction, Parent Company had 160,000 common shares outstanding. On December 31, X1, Parent's common shares had a closing market price of $30 on a national stock exchange.

Required

Prepare the consolidated statement of financial position of Parent at the date of acquisition.

PURCHASE OF SHARES
On the Books of Parent

Dr Investment in subsidiary 1,200,000
   Cr Common Shares   1,200,000

Note that there is no entry on the books of Subsidiary since Subsidiary is not a party to the transaction. In contrast to an acquisition of net assets, a stock acquisition is a transaction involving the shareholders of the target entity, not the entity itself.

POST-TRANSACTION STATEMENT OF FINANCIAL POSITION OF PARENT COMPANY

	Pre-acquisition	Acquisition	Post-acquisition
Assets			
Non-current assets			
Land	$1,000,000		$1,000,000
Buildings (net)	1,800,000		1,800,000
Investment in Subsidiary		1,200,000	1,200,000
Current assets			
Inventories	200,000		200,000
Accounts receivable	2,000,000		2,000,000
Cash	1,000,000		1,000,000
Total assets	**$6,000,000**		**$7,200,000**
Equity and liabilities			
Equity			
Share capital	$2,600,000	1,200,000	$3,800,000
Retained earnings	2,000,000		2,000,000
Liabilities			
Long-term notes payable	400,000		400,000
Accounts payable	1,000,000		1,000,000
Total equity and liabilities	**$6,000,000**		**$7,200,000**

PURCHASE OF SHARES
Affiliation Structure

BEFORE

PARENT   SUBSIDIARY

AFTER

Parent's shareholders
160,000 shares
(80%)
→ PARENT ←
Subsidiary's shareholders
40,000 shares
(20%)

↓ 100%

SUBSIDIARY

DOUBLE-COUNTING AND PRICE DIFFERENTIAL
At the Date of Acquisition

	Parent	Subsidiary
Assets		
Land	$1,000,000	$300,000
Buildings (net)	1,800,000	350,000
Investment in Subsidiary	1,200,000	
Inventories	200,000	50,000
Accounts receivable	2,000,000	150,000
Cash	1,000,000	50,000
Total assets	**$7,200,000**	**$900,000**
Equity and liabilities		
Share capital	$3,800,000	$200,000
Retained earnings	2,000,000	600,000
Long-term notes payable	400,000	
Accounts payable	1,000,000	100,000
Total equity & liabilities	**$7,200,000**	**$900,000**

Price Differential $400,000 — 1b
Double-Counting $800,000 — 1a

Part 4

CONSOLIDATION AT THE DATE OF ACQUISITION
Consolidation Entries
Elimination of the Investment Account

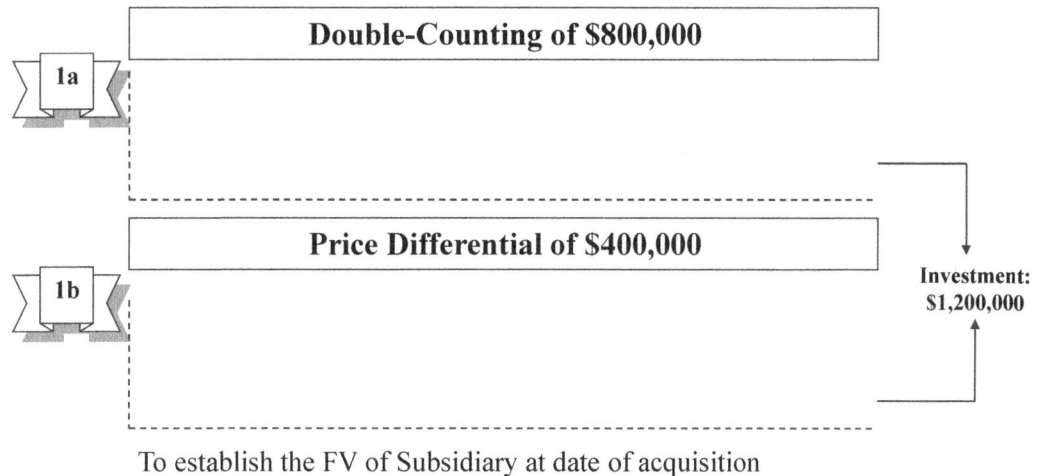

To establish the FV of Subsidiary at date of acquisition

Business Combinations ---------- Module 3 ----------

Part 4

CONSOLIDATION WORKSHEET OF PARENT COMPANY
At the Date of Acquisition

	Parent	Subsidiary	Eliminations	Consolidated
Assets				
Land	$1,000,000	$300,000	(1b) 100,000	$1,400,000
Buildings (net)	1,800,000	350,000	(1b) 200,000	2,350,000
Goodwill			(1b) 100,000	100,000
Investment in Subsidiary	1,200,000		(1a) (800,000) (1b) (400,000)	
Inventories	200,000	50,000		250,000
Accounts receivable	2,000,000	150,000		2,150,000
Cash	1,000,000	50,000		1,050,000
Total assets	**$7,200,000**	**$900,000**		**$7,300,000**
Equity and liabilities				
Share capital	$3,800,000	$200,000	(1a) (200,000)	$3,800,000
Retained earnings	2,000,000	600,000	(1a) (600,000)	2,000,000
Long-term notes payable	400,000			400,000
Accounts payable	1,000,000	100,000		1,100,000
Total equity & liabilities	**$7,200,000**	**$900,000**		**$7,300,000**

Business Combinations ---------- Module 3 ----------

Part 4
CONSOLIDATION AT THE DATE OF ACQUISITION - DIRECT APPROACH
Computation Process for Assets and Liabilities

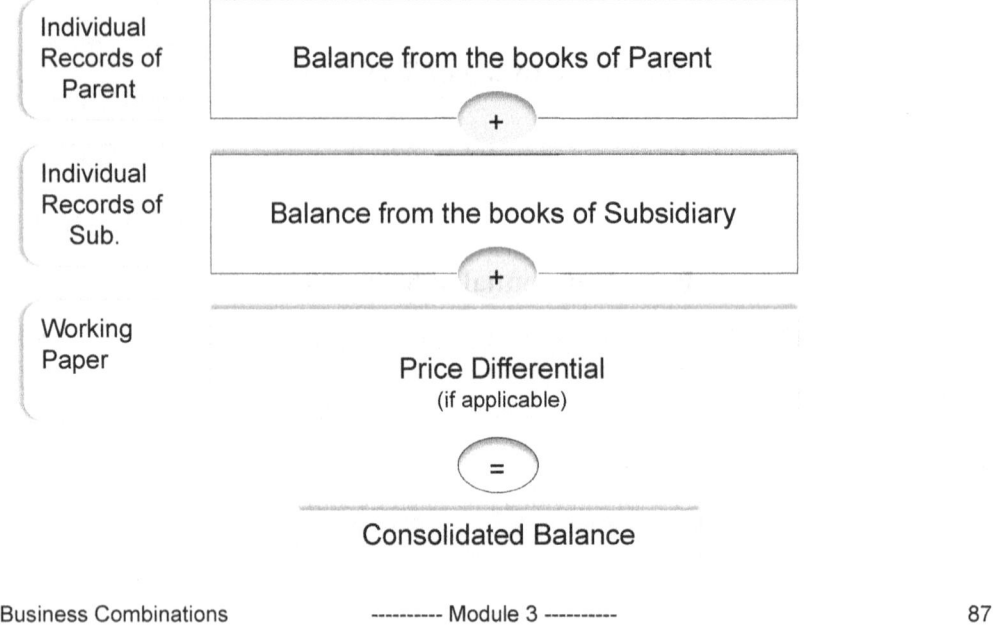

Business Combinations — Module 3 —

Part 4
CONSOLIDATION AT THE DATE OF ACQUISITION - DIRECT APPROACH
Non-current Assets

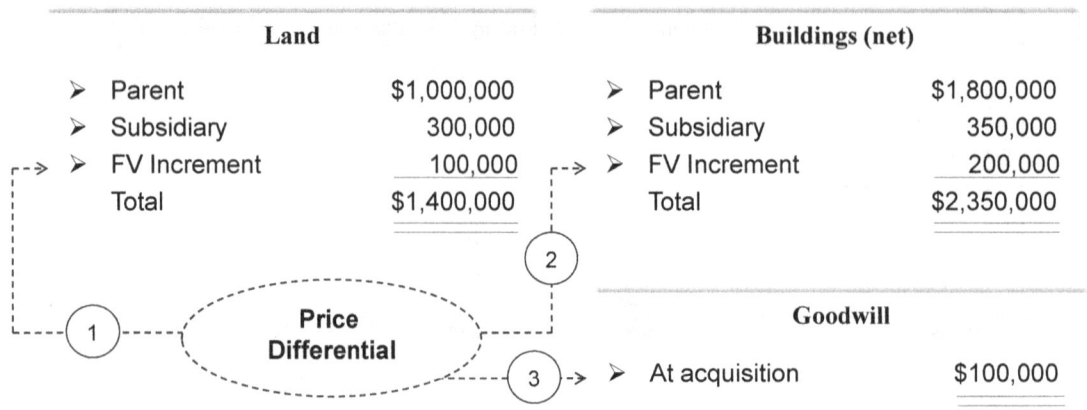

Business Combinations — Module 3 —

Part 4

CONSOLIDATION AT THE DATE OF ACQUISITION - DIRECT APPROACH
Current Assets

Cash
- Parent: $1,000,000
- Subsidiary: 50,000
- Total: $1,050,000

Accounts Receivable
- Parent: $2,000,000
- Subsidiary: 150,000
- Total: $2,150,000

Inventories
- Parent: $200,000
- Subsidiary: 50,000
- Total: $250,000

Part 4

CONSOLIDATION AT THE DATE OF ACQUISITION - DIRECT APPROACH
Equity and Liabilities

Share Capital
- Parent: $3,800,000

Retained Earnings
- Parent: $2,000,000

Accounts Payable
- Parent: $1,000,000
- Subsidiary: 10,000
- Total: $1,100,000

LT Notes Payable
- Parent: $400,000

Consolidated Share Capital and Retained Earnings only consist of Parent's balances since the equity section of Subsidiary is always eliminated through consolidation (double-counting).

Part 4

SFP OF PARENT COMPANY
At the Date of Acquisition
Stock Acquisition vs. Purchase of Net Assets

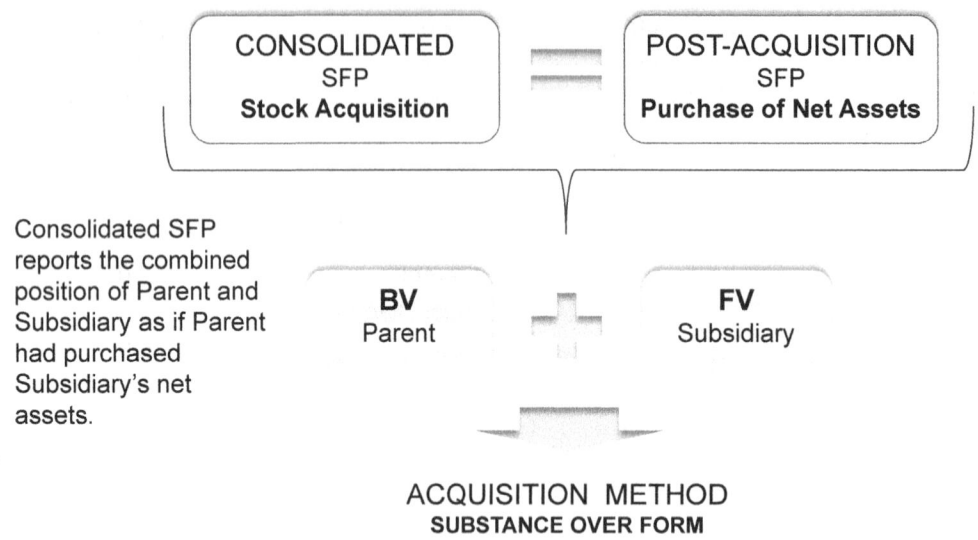

Consolidated SFP reports the combined position of Parent and Subsidiary as if Parent had purchased Subsidiary's net assets.

ACQUISITION METHOD
SUBSTANCE OVER FORM

Business Combinations ---------- Module 3 ---------- 91

Part 4

SFP OF PARENT COMPANY
At the Date of Acquisition
Purchase of Net Assets

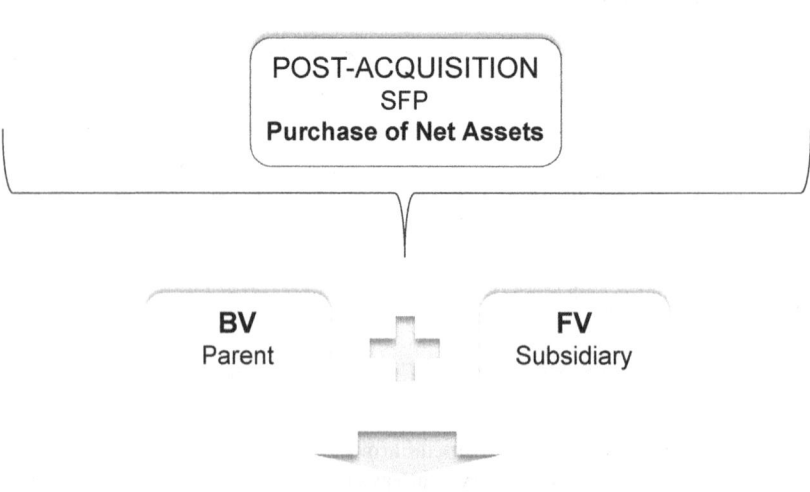

THROUGH THE BOOKS OF PARENT
WORKING PAPER ENTRY

Business Combinations ---------- Module 3 ---------- 92

Part 4

POST-TRANSACTION SFP OF PARENT COMPANY
Purchase of Net Assets - FV of Subsidiary

	Pre-acquisition	Acquisition	Post-acquisition
Assets			
Non-current assets			
Land	$1,000,000	400,000	$1,400,000
Buildings (net)	1,800,000	550,000	2,350,000
Goodwill		100,000	100,000
Current assets			
Inventories	200,000	50,000	250,000
Accounts receivable	2,000,000	150,000	2,150,000
Cash	1,000,000	50,000	1,050,000
Total assets	$6,000,000		$7,300,000
Equity and liabilities			
Equity			
Share capital	$2,600,000	1,200,000	$3,800,000
Retained earnings	2,000,000		2,000,000
Liabilities			
Long-term notes payable	400,000		400,000
Accounts payable	1,000,000	100,000	1,100,000
Total equity and liabilities	$6,000,000		$7,300,000

FV of Subsidiary At acquisition

Part 4

SFP OF PARENT COMPANY
At the Date of Acquisition
Stock Acquisition

Consolidation consists of replacing the investment account by the FV of Subsidiary at the date of acquisition.

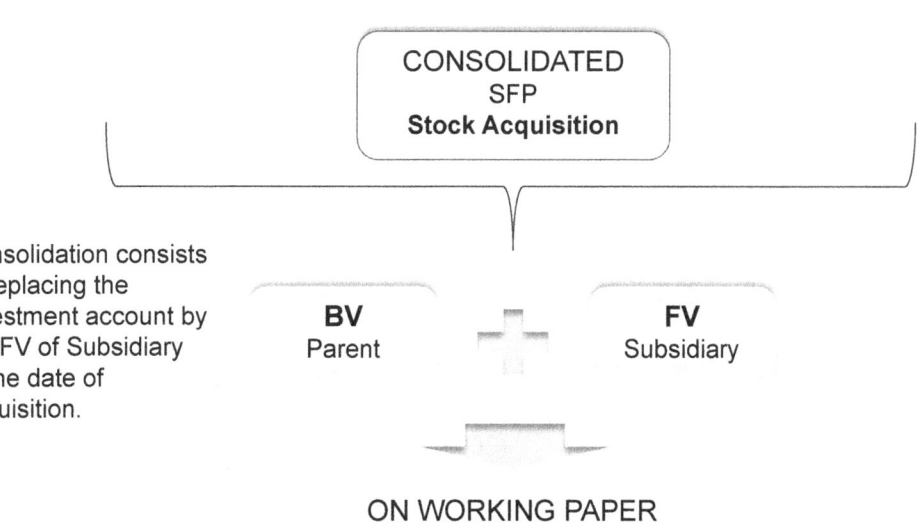

CONSOLIDATED SFP
Stock Acquisition

BV Parent + **FV** Subsidiary

ON WORKING PAPER
CONSOLIDATION OF F/S

Business Combinations ---------- Module 3 ----------

CONSOLIDATION WORKSHEET OF PARENT COMPANY
Stock Acquisition - FV of Subsidiary

Part 4

	Parent	Subsidiary	Eliminations	Consolidated
Assets				
Land	$1,000,000	$300,000	(1b) 100,000	$1,400,000
Buildings (net)	1,800,000	350,000	(1b) 200,000	2,350,000
Goodwill			(1b) 100,000	100,000
Investment in Subsidiary	1,200,000		(1a) (800,000)	
			(1b) (400,000)	
Inventories	200,000	50,000		250,000
Accounts receivable	2,000,000	150,000		2,150,000
Cash	1,000,000	50,000		1,050,000
Total assets	**$7,200,000**	**$900,000**		**$7,300,000**
Equity and liabilities				
Share capital	$3,800,000	$200,000	(1a) (200,000)	$3,800,000
Retained earnings	2,000,000	600,000	(1a) (600,000)	2,000,000
Long-term notes payable	400,000			400,000
Accounts payable	1,000,000	100,000		1,100,000
Total equity & liabilities	**$7,200,000**	**$900,000**		**$7,300,000**

FV of Subsidiary: BV + Price Differential

PURCHASE OF SHARES
Negative Goodwill

Part 4

If the purchase price was $1,000,000 instead of $1,200,000

- Purchase price $1,000 000

- Net book value of Subsidiary:
  - Common shares $200,000
  - Retained earnings 600,000   800,000

- Price differential   200,000

- Fair value increments:
  - Land   (100,000)
  - Buildings   (200,000)   (300,000)

Negative Goodwill   **($100,000)**

NEGATIVE GOODWILL
On the Books of Parent

Part 4

If the purchase price was $1,000,000 instead of $1,200,000

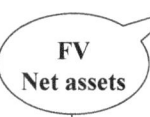
FV Net assets

Investment in Subsidiary	1,100,000	
Common Shares		1,000,000
Gain on Acquisition		100,000

Under the acquisition method, identifiable net assets of the acquired company are always reported at their FV. Therefore, the net FV of Subsidiary at date of acquisition ($1,100,000) is reported by Parent in its investment account. Any excess of the net FV of Subsidiary over the purchase price ($1,000,000) is accounted for as a gain in the income statement ($100,000).

Business Combinations ---------- Module 3 ----------

POST-TRANSACTION STATEMENT OF FINANCIAL POSITION OF PARENT COMPANY - NEGATIVE GOODWILL

Part 4

	Pre-acquisition	Acquisition	Post-acquisition
Assets			
Non-current assets			
Land	$1,000,000		$1,000,000
Buildings (net)	1,800,000		1,800,000
Investment in Subsidiary		1,100,000	1,100,000
Current assets			
Inventories	200,000		200,000
Accounts receivable	2,000,000		2,000,000
Cash	1,000,000		1,000,000
Total assets	$6,000,000		$7,100,000
Equity and liabilities			
Equity			
Share capital	$2,600,000	1,000,000	$3,600,000
Retained earnings	2,000,000	(Gain) 100 000	2,100,000
Liabilities			
Long-term notes payable	400,000		400,000
Accounts payable	1,000,000		1,000,000
Total equity and liabilities	$6,000,000		$7,100,000

NEGATIVE GOODWILL
Elimination of the Investment Account

If the purchase price was $1,000,000 instead of $1,200,000

Double-Counting of $800,000

1a
Common Shares (Subsidiary)	200,000	
Retained Earnings (Subsidiary)	600,000	
Investment in Subsidiary (Parent)		800,000

Price Differential of $300,000

1b
Land (Subsidiary)	100,000	
Buildings (Subsidiary)	200,000	
Investment in Subsidiary (Parent)		300,000

Investment: $1,100,000

CONSOLIDATION WORKSHEET OF PARENT COMPANY
At the Date of Acquisition - Negative Goodwill

	Parent	Subsidiary	Eliminations	Consolidated
Assets				
Land	$1,000,000	$300,000	(1b) 100,000	$1,400,000
Buildings (net)	1,800,000	350,000	(1b) 200,000	2,350,000
Investment in Subsidiary	1,100,000		(1a) (800,000) (1b) (300,000)	
Inventories	200,000	50,000		250,000
Accounts receivable	2,000,000	150,000		2,150,000
Cash	1,000,000	50,000		1,050,000
Total assets	**$7,100,000**	**$900,000**		**$7,200,000**
Equity and liabilities				
Share capital	$3,600,000	$200,000	(1a) (200,000)	$3,600,000
Retained earnings	2,100,000	600,000	(1a) (600,000)	2,100,000
Long-term notes payable	400,000			400,000
Accounts payable	1,000,000	100,000		1,100,000
Total equity & liabilities	**$7,100,000**	**$900,000**		**$7,200,000**

Part 4

PART 4
Concept Check

> What is the rationale underlying the elimination of the investment account through consolidation?

_____
_____
_____
_____
_____
_____
_____
_____

Business Combinations ---------- Module 3---------- 101

Part 5

OUTLINE OF THE PRESENTATION

1. INTRODUCTION TO BUSINESS COMBINATIONS
2. ACCOUNTING FOR BUSINESS COMBINATIONS
3. PURCHASE OF NET ASSETS: ILLUSTRATION
4. PURCHASE OF SHARES: CONSOLIDATION OF WHOLLY OWNED SUBSIDIARIES AT THE DATE OF ACQUISITION
5. **MERGER**

Business Combinations ---------- Module 3 ---------- 102

PART 5
Merger

Objectives of this section

Illustrate the accounting for mergers.

Show a merger as a business combination effected through either a stock acquisition or a purchase of net assets followed by a legal dissolution of all the entities except one.

MERGER
Illustration

On December 31, X1, Parent Company merged with Subsidiary Company (statutory merger). Parent issued 40,000 voting shares as consideration given. Before the transaction, Parent Company had 160,000 common shares outstanding. On December 31, X1, Parent's common shares had a closing market price of $30 on a national stock exchange.

Required

Prepare the statement of financial position of Parent at the date of merger.

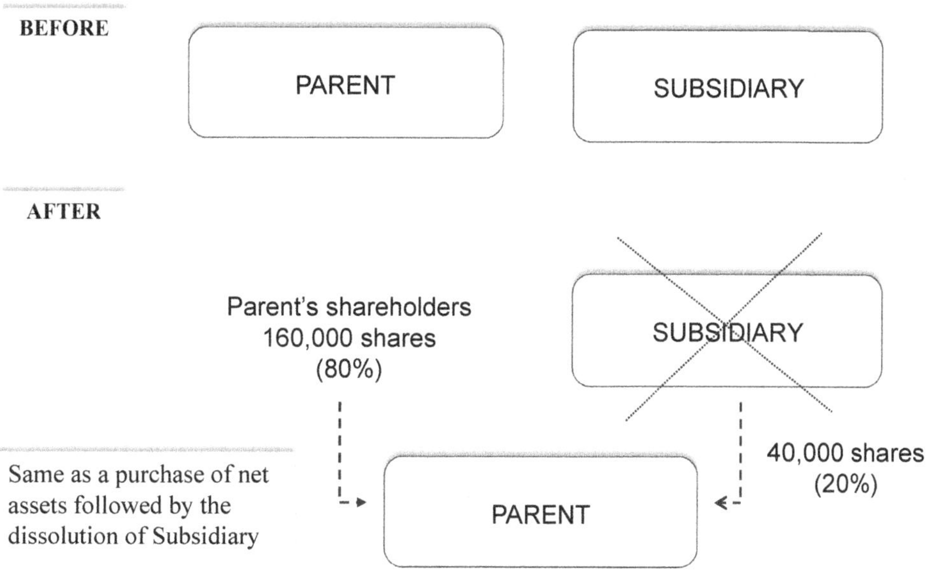

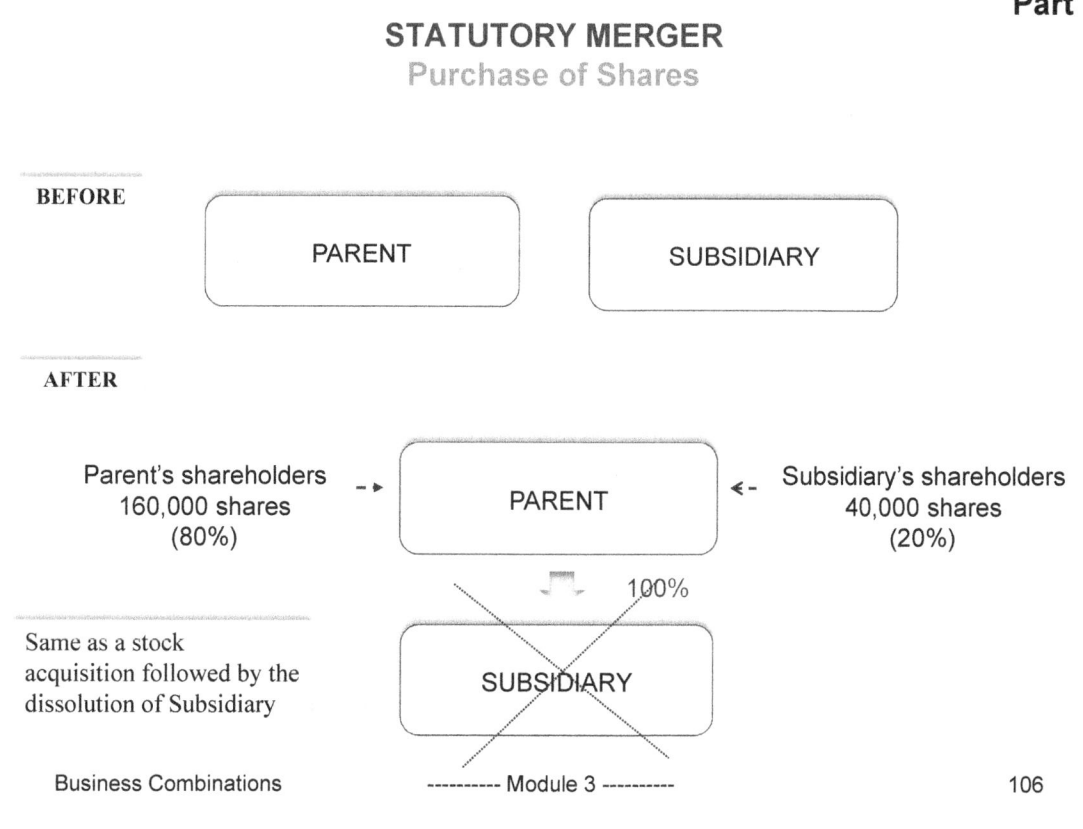

Part 5

STATUTORY MERGER
Post-Dissolution SFP

Parent's shareholders
160,000 shares
(80%)

Subsidiary's shareholders
40,000 shares
(20%)

PARENT

=

Consolidated SFP of Parent

=

SFP of Parent following the purchase of net assets

Business Combinations ---------- Module 3 ----------

Part 5

STATUTORY MERGER
Post-Dissolution SFP
If the Consideration Given Would Have Been Cash instead of Shares

Parent's shareholders
160,000 shares
(100%)

PARENT

=

Consolidated SFP of Parent

=

SFP of Parent following the purchase of net assets

Business Combinations ---------- Module 3 ----------

ACCOUNTING FOR BUSINESS COMBINATIONS
At the Date of Acquisition
Recap

Part 5

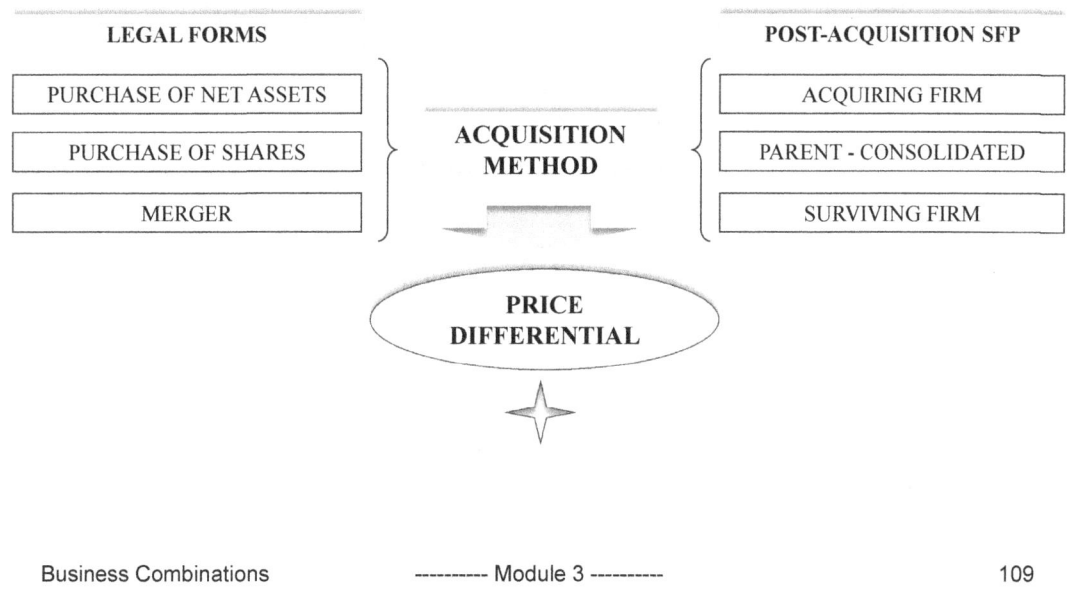

ACCOUNTING FOR BUSINESS COMBINATIONS
At the Date of Acquisition
Combination Process of Parent and Subsidiary

Part 5

LEGAL FORMS	COMBINATION PROCESS
PURCHASE OF NET ASSETS	THROUGH THE BOOKS OF PARENT - **JOURNAL ENTRY**
PURCHASE OF SHARES	ON WORKING PAPER - **CONSOLIDATION**
MERGER	BEFORE THE DISSOLUTION OF ALL THE ENTITIES EXCEPT ONE

Post-acquisition SFPs are the same

ACCOUNTING FOR BUSINESS COMBINATIONS
Disclosure Requirements

Part 5

1. THE NAME, A DESCRIPTION OF THE ACQUIREE, AND THE ACQUISITION DATE.

2. THE PERCENTAGE OF VOTING EQUITY INSTRUMENTS ACQUIRED.

3. THE PRIMARY REASONS FOR THE BUSINESS COMBINATION, INCLUDING A DESCRIPTION OF THE FACTORS THAT CONTRIBUTED TO THE RECOGNITION OF GOODWILL.

4. THE FAIR VALUE OF THE ACQUIREE AND THE BASIS FOR MEASURING THAT VALUE AT THE DATE OF ACQUISITION.

5. THE FAIR VALUE OF THE CONSIDERATION TRANSFERRED, INCLUDING THE FAIR VALUE OF EACH MAJOR CLASS OF CONSIDERATION.

6. THE AMOUNTS RECOGNIZED AT THE ACQUISITION DATE FOR EACH MAJOR CLASS OF ASSETS ACQUIRED AND LIABILITIES ASSUMED IN THE FORM OF CONDENSED BALANCE SHEET.

7. THE MAXIMUM POTENTIAL AMOUNT OF FUTURE PAYMENTS THE ACQUIRER COULD BE REQUIRED TO MAKE UNDER THE TERMS OF THE ACQUISITION AGREEMENT.

ACCOUNTING FOR BUSINESS COMBINATIONS
Additional Considerations

Part 5

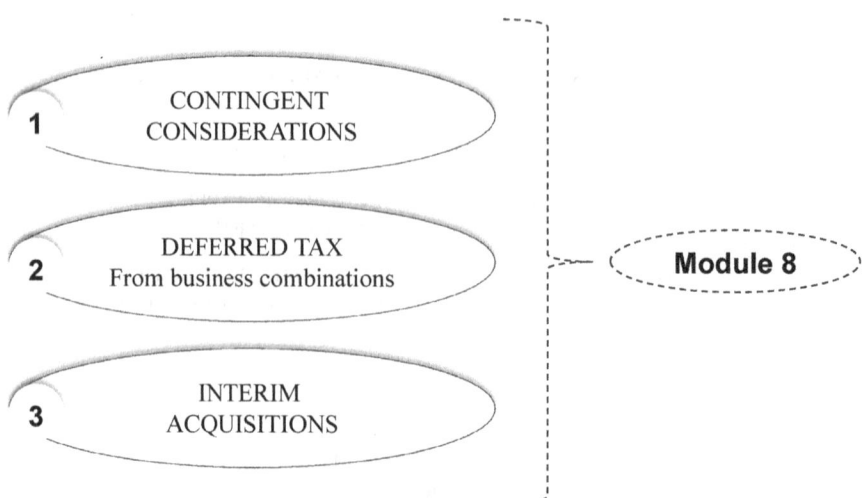

1. CONTINGENT CONSIDERATIONS
2. DEFERRED TAX — From business combinations
3. INTERIM ACQUISITIONS

Module 8

PART 5
Concept Check

> Explain why the post-acquisition statements of financial position are the same whether the combination is effected through a stock acquisition, a purchase of net assets or a merger.

Business Combinations ---------- Module 3----------

BUSINESS COMBINATIONS
Module 3 - Recap

6	REVIEW QUESTIONS
7	QUIZ QUESTIONS
8	KEY TERMS INTRODUCED IN THIS MODULE
9	RECAP ON THE OBJECTIVES OF THIS MODULE

PART 6
Review Questions

1. Define or explain the following terms:
- Acquisition method
- Pooling of interests
- New entity
- Purchase price allocation
- Price differential
- Goodwill, fair value increment, fair value decrement
- Business combination
- Purchase of net assets, purchase of shares, merger
- Reverse takeover

2. When does a corporation become a subsidiary of another?

REVIEW QUESTIONS
(continued...)

3. What are the forms of consideration that can be used in a business combination?

4. What are the three legal forms of business combinations?

5. What is the most common reason for a combination of a public company and a private company accomplished by means of a reverse takeover?

6. When an acquirer buys the net assets of another company by issuing shares, what is the relationship between the two companies once the transaction is complete?

7. What are the advantages for the acquirer of obtaining control over assets by a purchase of shares rather than by a direct purchase of assets?

8. What is the name of the accounting method for business combinations? Describe it.

Part 6

REVIEW QUESTIONS
(continued...)

9. What are the accounting implications of purchasing the net assets instead of purchasing the voting shares?

10. How should direct costs incurred in a business combination be accounted for?

11. What happens to the purchase price differential in the consolidation process as of the date of combination?

12. In what general ledger would you expect to find the account *Goodwill* from consolidation?

13. What is the appropriate accounting for negative goodwill?

14. Identify the major reasons firms combine.

15. Identify defensive tactics used to attempt to block business combinations.

Business Combinations — Module 3 — 117

Part 7

PART 7
Quiz Questions

On December 31, X8, Large Inc. acquired Small Inc. for $560,000. At the date of acquisition, Small's buildings have a market value $50,000 greater than book value and an estimated remaining economic life of 10 years (straight line). The statements of financial positions of Large and Small prior to the combination are presented below:

	Large	Small
Assets		
Land	$300,000	$100,000
Buildings (net)	950,000	400,000
Accounts receivable	50,000	30,000
Cash	650,000	10,000
Total assets	$1,950,000	$540,000
Equity and liabilities		
Equity		
Share capital	$950,000	200,000
Retained earnings	900,000	250,000
Liabilities		
Accounts payable	100,000	90,000
Total equity and liabilities	$1,950,000	$540,000

(handwritten annotations: "FV" and "+50,000" next to Buildings)

Business Combinations — Module 3 — 118

Part 7

QUIZ QUESTIONS

1

Provide the purchase price allocation. Complete the following table.

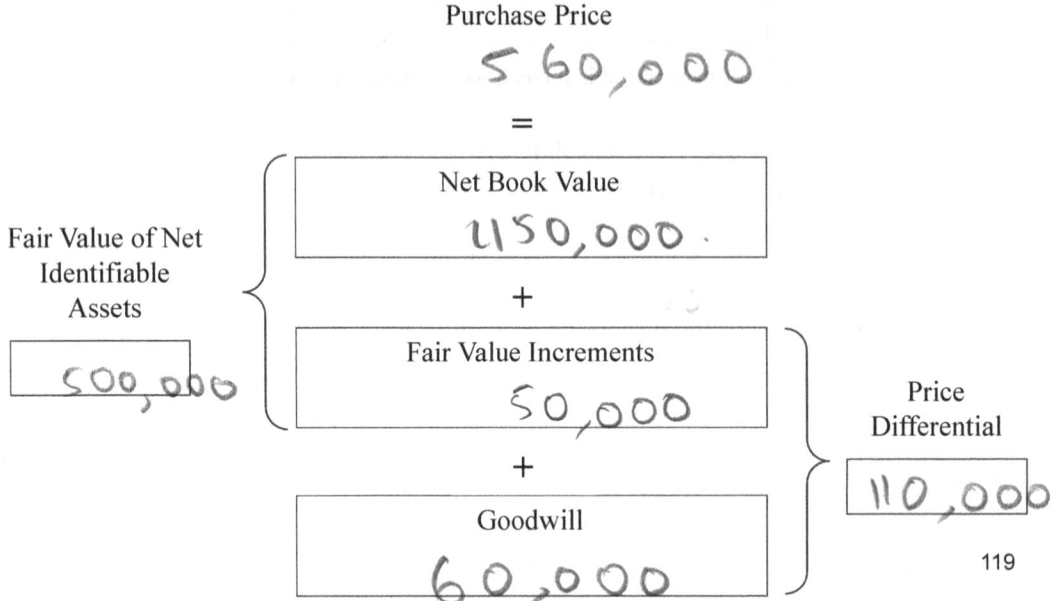

Part 7

QUIZ QUESTIONS

2

Assume that Large purchased the net assets of Small. Provide the journal entries required to account for the acquisition in the books of Large.

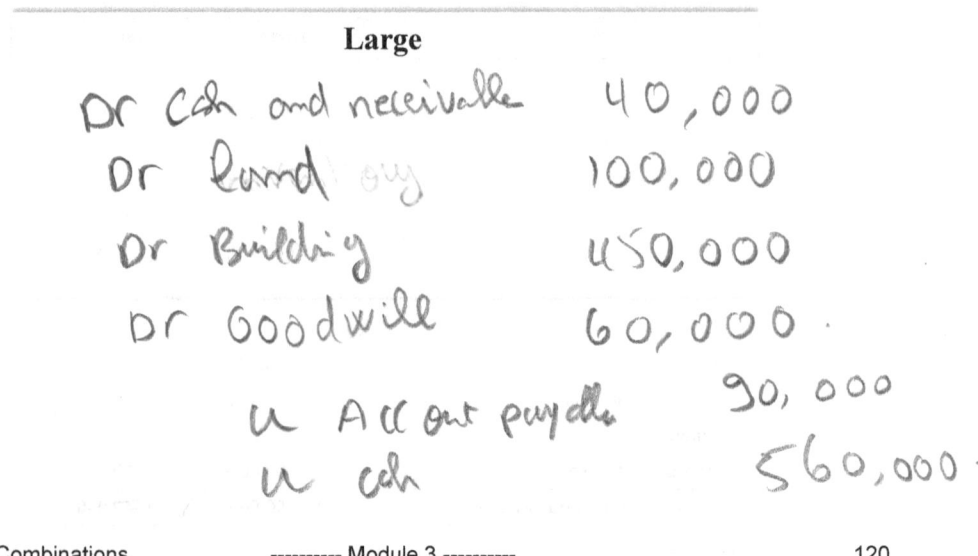

Part 7

QUIZ QUESTIONS

3

Assume that Large purchased the net assets of Small. Provide the journal entries required to account for the acquisition in the books of Small.

Small

Dr investment in parent 560,000
Dr Account payable 90,000
  Cr Cash and receivables 40,000
  Cr Land 100,000
  Cr Building 450,000
  Cr Gain on sale 60,000

Part 7

QUIZ QUESTIONS

4

Provide the consolidated statement of financial position of Large at date of combination assuming the combination is effected through a stock acquisition.

Large
Consolidated Statement of Financial Position
December 31, X8

Assets		
Land	400,000	
Buildings (net)	1,400,000	
Goodwill	60,000	
Accounts receivable	80,000	
Cash	100,000	+560,000
Total assets	2,040,000	
Equity and liabilities		
Equity		
Share capital	950,000	+560,000
Retained earnings	500,000	
Liabilities		
Accounts payable	130,000	
Total equity and liabilities	2,040,000	

224

Part 7

QUIZ QUESTIONS

5

Provide the post-acquisition statement of financial position of Large assuming the acquisition is effected through a purchase of the net assets.

Large
Post-Acquisition Statement of Financial Position
December 31, X8

Assets	
Land	400,000
Buildings (net)	1,400,000
Goodwill	60,000
Accounts receivable	80,000
Cash	660,000
Total assets	**2,600,000**
Equity and liabilities	
Equity	
Share capital	1,510,000
Retained earnings	900,000
Liabilities	
Accounts payable	190,000
Total equity and liabilities	**2,600,000**

Part 7

QUIZ QUESTIONS

6

Provide the post-acquisition statement of financial position of Large assuming the acquisition is effected through a merger.

Large
Post-Acquisition Statement of Financial Position
December 31, X8

Assets	
Land	400,000
Buildings (net)	1,400,000
Goodwill	60,000
Accounts receivable	80,000
Cash	660,000
Total assets	**2,600,000**
Equity and liabilities	
Equity	
Share capital	1,510,000
Retained earnings	900,000
Liabilities	
Accounts payable	190,000
Total equity and liabilities	**2,600,000**

Part 7

QUIZ QUESTIONS

7

Provide the post-acquisition statement of financial position of Large assuming the consideration given is with shares instead of cash.

Large
Post-Acquisition Statement of Financial Position
December 31, X8

Assets	
Land	100,000
Buildings (net)	1,400,000
Goodwill	60,000
Accounts receivable	80,000
Cash	660,000
Total assets	**2,300,000**
Equity and liabilities	
Equity	
Share capital	1,210,000
Retained earnings	900,000
Liabilities	
Accounts payable	190,000
Total equity and liabilities	**2,300,000**

Business Combinations — 125

Part 7

QUIZ QUESTIONS

8

Provide the post-acquisition statement of financial position of Large assuming the consideration given is $400,000 instead of $560,000 (the consideration given is with cash).

Large
Post-Acquisition Statement of Financial Position
December 31, X8

Assets	
Investment in subsidiary	500,000
Land	300,000
Buildings (net)	950,000
Accounts receivable	50,000
Cash	650,000
Total assets	**2,450,000**
Equity and liabilities	
Equity	
Share capital	1,350,000
Retained earnings (+ Gain of $100,000)	1,000,000
Liabilities	
Accounts payable	100,000
Total equity and liabilities	**2,450,000**

Business Combinations — 126

Part 8
KEY TERMS INTRODUCED IN THIS MODULE

Part 1
- Business; Business combination
- Purchase of net assets
- Purchase of shares
- Merger; Statutory merger; Statutory consolidation
- Reverse takeover; Hostile takeover

Part 2
- Acquisition method
- Pooling of interests
- New entity
- Purchase price allocation; Price differential
- Goodwill, Negative goodwill;
- Fair value increment; Fair value decrement
- Control premium

Part 9
RECAP ON THE OBJECTIVES OF THIS MODULE

Part 1
Define a business combination and its context.
Present the different legal forms of business combinations.

Part 2
Present and compare the methods of accounting for a business combination.
Outline the requirements for applying the acquisition method.

Part 3
Illustrate the accounting for a purchase-of-net assets business combination.

Part 4
Illustrate the consolidation process of wholly owned subsidiaries at the date of acquisition.

Part 5
Illustrate the accounting for mergers.
Show a merger as a business combination effected through either a stock acquisition or a purchase of net assets followed by a legal dissolution of all the entities except one.

Exercise 3-1
Stock Acquisition with Cash

Parent Company purchased 100 percent of Subsidiary Corporation's stock on January 2, X8, for $150,000 cash. Summarized statements of financial position of the companies on December 31, X7, are presented below.

	Parent	Subsidiary
Assets		
Cash	$200,000	$50,000
Other assets	400,000	120,000
Total assets	**$600,000**	**$170,000**
Liabilities and equity		
Current liabilities	$100,000	$80,000
Share capital	200,000	50,000
Retained earnings	300,000	40,000
Total liabilities and equity	**$600,000**	**$170,000**

Fair values of Subsidiary were equal to book values except for buildings, which had a fair value of $50,000 in excess of net book value.

Required
Prepare a consolidated statement of financial position immediately following the acquisition. Provide first the allocation of the purchase price.

Allocation of Purchase Price
Dr Investment in subsidiary 150,000
Cr Cash 150,000

Parent Company
Consolidated SFP at date of acquisition

	Parent	Subsidiary	Adjustments	F/S
Assets				
Cash				100,000
Other assets				570,000
Goodwill				10,000
Total assets				680,000
Liabilities and equity				
Current liabilities				180,000
Share capital				200,000
Retained earnings				300,000
Total liabilities and equity				680,000

Exercise 3-2
Stock Acquisition with Bonds

Refer to Exercise 3-1.

Assume instead that Parent Company purchased 100 percent of Subsidiary Corporation's voting stock on January 2, X8, by issuing bonds with par value of $140,000 and a fair value of $150,000 in exchange for the shares.

Required
Prepare a consolidated statement of financial position immediately following the acquisition.

Parent Company
Consolidated SFP at date of acquisition

Assets	
Cash	250,000
Other assets	570,000
Goodwill	10,000
Total assets	830,000
Liabilities and equity	
Current liabilities	180,000
Bonds payable	150,000
Share capital	~~140,000~~ 200,000
Retained earnings	300,000
Total liabilities and equity	

Exercise 3-3
Purchase of Net Assets with Cash

Refer to Exercise 3-1.

Assume instead that Parent Company purchased Subsidiary Corporation's net assets (instead of the stocks) on January 2, X8, for $150,000 cash.

Required
Prepare the post-acquisition statements of financial position (SFP) of Parent and Subsidiary.

Post-acquisition SFP of Parent Company

Assets	
Cash	100,000
Other assets	570,000
Goodwill	10,000
Total assets	
Liabilities and equity	
Current liabilities	180,000
Share capital	300,000
Retained earnings	300,000
Total liabilities and equity	

Post-acquisition SFP of Subsidiary Corporation

Assets	
Cash	150,000
Total assets	150,000
Liabilities and equity	
Share capital	50,000
Retained earnings	100,000
Total liabilities and equity	150,000

Exercise 3-4
Consolidation at Date of Acquisition (no Goodwill)

Tree Corporation purchased 100 percent of Plant Corporation's voting stock on December 31, X8, for $189,000 cash. At the date of combination, Plant's net assets and liabilities approximated fair value except for inventory, which had a fair value of $84,000 and buildings and equipment (net), which had a fair value of $165,000.

The following presents the statements of financial position of the two companies as of the date of acquisition.

	Tree	Plant
Assets		
Cash	$26,000	$18,000
Accounts receivable	87,000	37,000
Inventories	110,000	60,000
Buildings & equipment (net)	220,000	150,000
Investment in Plant	189,000	
Total assets	**$632,000**	**$265,000**
Liabilities and equity		
Accounts payable	$92,000	$35,000
Long-term note payable	150,000	80,000
Share capital	100,000	60,000
Retained earnings	290,000	90,000
Total liabilities and equity	**$632,000**	**$265,000**

Required
Prepare the consolidated statement of financial position of Tree Corporation at the date of acquisition.

Tree Corporation
Allocation of Purchase Price

Dr investment in subsidiary   189,000
  Cr cash   189,000

Tree Corporation
Consolidated SFP at date of acquisition

	Tree	Plant	Adjustments	F/S
Assets				
Cash				44,000
Accounts receivables				124,000
Inventories				194,000
Buildings & equipment (net)				385,000
Goodwill				7,000
Total assets				754,000
Liabilities and equity				
Current liabilities				127,000
Long-term note payable				230,000
Share capital				100,000
Retained earnings				290,000
Total liabilities and equity				754,000

Exercise 3-5
Purchase of Net Assets: Post-Acquisition SFPs

Refer to Exercise 3-4 and assume instead that Tree Corporation purchased Plant Corporation's net assets on December 31, X8, for $189,000 cash.

Handwritten journal entry:
Dr Net assets 265,000
Dr goodwill / accumulated depr. 35,000
  Cr Cash 189,000

Required
Prepare the post-acquisition statements of financial position of Tree and Plant.

Post-acquisition SFP of Tree Corporation

Assets	
Cash	44,000
Accounts receivables	124,000
Inventories	194,000
Buildings and equipment (net)	385,000
Total assets	
Liabilities and equity	
Accounts payable	127,000
Long-term note payable	230,000
Share capital	100,000
Retained earnings	290,000
Total liabilities and equity	

Post-acquisition SFP of Subsidiary Corporation

Assets	
Cash	189,000
Total assets	
Liabilities and equity	
Share capital	60,000
Retained earnings	129,000
Total liabilities and equity	189,000

Exercise 3-6
Negative Goodwill

Sun Corporation purchased all Grugger Company's voting stock on January 1, X8, for $365,000. At the date of combination, Crugger reported common stock outstanding of $80,000 and retained earnings of $130,000.

The book values of Crugger's assets and liabilities approximated their fair values, except for land, which had a book value of $80,000 and fair value of $100,000, and buildings, which had a net book value of $220,000 and a fair value of $400,000.

Required

a) Report the acquisition on the books of Sun Corporation.
b) Give the consolidation entries required to consolidate Sun's statement of financial position at the date of acquisition.

Journal Entry - Sun

Dr Investment in Crugger   410,000
  Cr Cash   365,000
  Cr Gain   45,000

Consolidation Entry

Dr CS   80,000
Dr RE   130,000
Dr Land   20,000
Dr Building   180,000
  Cr Investment in Crugger   410,000

Copyright © 2020, Parmitech, Ottawa. Parmitech. All rights reserved.

Exercise 3-7
Stock Acquisition versus Purchase of Net Assets

On January 1, X6, Green Company acquired 100% of the outstanding common shares of Blue Inc. by issuing 10,000 common shares. The book values and the fair values of both companies immediately <u>before</u> the acquisition were as follows:

	Green Company		Blue Inc.	
	Book values	Fair values	Book values	Fair values
Assets	**2,175,000**	2,400,000	**900,000**	1,042,500
Liabilities	1,155,000	1,132,000	375,000	405,000
Common shares	450,000		97,500	
Retained earnings	570,000		427,500	
	2,175,000		**900,000**	

Immediately before the acquisition transaction, Green Company had 20,000 common shares outstanding and Blue Inc. had 6,500 common shares outstanding. Green's shares were actively trading at $75.00 on the date of the acquisition.

Required
Complete the consolidated statement of financial position of Green at date of combination.

Green Company
Consolidated SFP at date of acquisition

Assets	3,330,000
Liabilities	1,560,000
Common shares	1,200,000
Retained earnings	570,000
Total liabilities and equity	3,330,000

What if
Complete the post-acquisition statement of financial position of Green assuming the combination is effected through a purchase of net assets (instead of a purchase of shares).

Post-acquisition SFP of Green Company
Purchase of Net Assets

Assets	3,330,000
Liabilities	1,560,000
Common shares	1,200,000
Retained earnings	570,000
Total liabilities and equity	3,300,000

What if
Complete the consolidated statement of financial position of Green at date of combination assuming that the consideration given is with cash (instead of shares).

Green Company
Consolidated SFP at date of acquisition

Assets	2,580,000
Liabilities	1,560,000
Common shares	450,000
Retained earnings	570,000
Total liabilities and equity	2,580,000

Copyright © 2020, Parmitech, Ottawa. Parmitech. All rights reserved.

Exercise 3-8
From Case 3: Global Inc.

Go to case 3: **Global Inc.** (Textbook, p. 278) and consider the following scenarios.

Scenario 1
Assume that Global purchased the net assets of Local (instead of the shares) for cash of $485,000. Answer the following questions.

a) Present the journal entry to account for the transaction in the books of Global.

b) Present the journal entry to account for the transaction in the books of Local.

c) Present the post-acquisition SFP of Global. Complete the following table.

Post-acquisition SFP of Global

Assets	
Liabilities	
Common shares	
Retained earnings	
Total liabilities and equity	

d) Present the post-acquisition SFP of Local. Complete the following table.

Post-acquisition SFP of Local

Assets	
Liabilities	
Common shares	
Retained earnings	
Total liabilities and equity	

Scenario 2

Assume that the consideration given by Global to purchase the shares of Local is **$360,000** instead of $485,000. Present the journal entry to account for the transaction in the books of Global.

Exercise 3-9
Consolidation at Date of Acquisition (with Goodwill)

On January 1, X3, the Most Company purchased 100% of the outstanding voting shares of the Least Company for $1.6 million in cash. On that date, Least's statement of financial position and the fair values of its identifiable assets and liabilities were as follows:

	Carrying	Fair
Cash	$ 25,000	$ 25,000
Accounts receivable	310,000	290,000
Inventories	650,000	600,000
Plant and equipment (net)	2,015,000	2,050,000
Total assets	**$3,000,000**	
Current liabilities	$ 300,000	$ 300,000
Long-term liabilities	1,200,000	1,100,000
Common stock	500,000	
Retained earnings	1,000,000	
Total liabilities and equity	**$3,000,000**	

On January 1, X3, Least's plant and equipment had a remaining useful life of eight years. Its long-term liabilities matured on January 1, X7. Goodwill, if any, is to be tested yearly for impairment.

The statement of financial position of Most prior to the date of combination is the following:

Cash	$ 2,500,000
Accounts receivable	500,000
Inventories	600,000
Plant and equipment (net)	2,400,000
Total assets	**$6,000,000**
Current liabilities	$ 500,000
Long-term liabilities	1,500,000
Common stock	1,000,000
Retained earnings	3,000,000
Total liabilities and equity	**$6,000,000**

Required
Present the consolidated statement of financial position of Most at date of combination.
Complete the following statements.

Most Company
Allocation of Purchase Price

```
purchase price = 1,600,000
                    20,000
                    50,000
                   (35,000)
                  (100,000)   (65,000)
                              _____
                              
                   goodwill 35,000
```

Most Company
Consolidated SFP at date of acquisition

	Most	Least	Adjustments	F/S
Assets				
Cash				925,000
Accounts receivables				750,000
Inventories				1,200,000
Plant and equipment (net)				4,150,000
Goodwill				35,000
Total assets				
Liabilities and equity				
Current liabilities				800,000
Long-term liabilities				2,600,000
Share capital				1,000,000
Retained earnings				3,000,000
Total liabilities and equity				7,400,000

Solutions to Exercises

3-1
Journal entry on the books of Parent to report the acquisition (not accounted for in the balance sheet provided):

Investment in Subsidiary	150,000	
Cash		150,000

Consolidated figures of Parent at the date of acquisition (in $):
- Cash　　　　　　　　100,000
- Other assets　　　　　570,000
- Goodwill　　　　　　　10,000
- Current liabilities　　　180,000
- Common shares　　　　200,000
- Retained earnings　　　300,000

3-2
Journal entry on the books of Parent to report the acquisition (not accounted for in the balance sheet provided):

Investment in Subsidiary	150,000	
Bonds Payable		150,000

Consolidated figures of Parent at the date of acquisition (in $):
- Cash　　　　　　　　250,000
- Other assets　　　　　570,000
- Goodwill　　　　　　　10,000
- Current liabilities　　　180,000
- Bonds payable　　　　150,000
- Common shares　　　　200,000
- Retained earnings　　　300,000

3-3
Journal entry on the books of Parent to report the acquisition:

Other Assets	170,000	
Goodwill	10,000	
Current Liabilities		80,000
Cash (150,000 – 50,000)		100,000

Statement of financial position figures of Parent following the acquisition of Subsidiary's net assets (in $):
- Cash　　　　　　　　100,000
- Other assets　　　　　570,000
- Goodwill　　　　　　　10,000

- Current liabilities 180,000
- Common shares 200,000
- Retained earnings 300,000

Statement of financial position figures of Subsidiary following the acquisition of net assets by Parent (in $):
- Cash 150,000
- Common shares 50,000
- Retained earnings 100,000 = ($40,000 + Gain on sale of $60,000)

3-4

Consolidated figures of Tree at the date of acquisition (in $):
- Cash 44,000
- Accounts receivable 124,000
- Inventories 194,000
- Buildings and equip. 385,000
- Accounts payable 127,000
- LT notes payable 230,000
- Common shares 100,000
- Retained earnings 290,000

3-5

Journal entry on the books of Tree to report the acquisition:

Accounts Receivable	37,000	
Inventory	84,000	
Buildings and Equip.	165,000	
Accounts Payable		35,000
Long–Term Notes Payable		80,000
Cash ($189,000 – $18,000)		171,000

Statement of financial position figures of Tree following the acquisition of Plant's net assets (in $):
- Cash 44,000
- Accounts receivable 124,000
- Inventories 194,000
- Buildings and equip. 385,000
- Accounts payable 127,000
- LT notes payable 230,000
- Common shares 100,000
- Retained earnings 290,000

Statement of financial position figures of Plant following the acquisition of net assets by Tree (in $):
- Cash　　　　　　　　189,000
- Common shares　　　60,000
- Retained earnings　　129,000 = ($90,000 + Gain on sale of $39,000)

3-6
a) Journal entry on the books of Sun to account for the acquisition of Crugger:

Investment in Crugger	410,000	
Cash		365,000
Gain on Acquisition		45,000

The gain of $45,000 reflects negative goodwill at acquisition. Under IFRS, negative goodwill represents a bargain purchase and must be reported as a gain in the income statement of the acquirer. Consequently, the value assigned to the investment of Sun in Crugger ($410,000) consists of the purchase price ($365,000) plus negative goodwill ($45,000). $410,000 reflects Crugger's net fair value at the date of acquisition which consists of Crugger's net book value ($210,000), plus FV increment on land ($20,000), plus FV increment on buildings ($180,000).

b) Combined consolidation entry at the date of acquisition:

Common Shares (Crugger)	80,000	
Retained Earnings (Crugger)	130,000	
Land (Crugger)	20,000	
Buildings (Crugger)	180,000	
Investment in Crugger (Sun)		410,000

3-7
Goodwill ($112,500) = Purchase price (10,000 shares × $75 = $750,000) – FV of nets assets acquired ($1,042,500 - $405,000 = $637,500)

Consolidated figures of Green at the date of acquisition (in $):
- Assets　　　　　　　　3,330,000　($2,175,000 + $1,042,500 + **$112,500**)
- Liabilities　　　　　　1,560,000　($1,155,000 + $405,000)
- Common shares　　　1,200,000
- Retained earnings　　　570,000
- Total liabilities & eq.　3,330,000

Post-acquisition SFP of Green (purchase of net assets):
- Assets　　　　　　　　3,330,000
- Liabilities　　　　　　1,560,000
- Common shares　　　1,200,000
- Retained earnings　　　570,000
- Total liabilities & eq.　3,330,000

Consolidated figures of Green at the date of acquisition when consideration is with Cash:
- Assets 2,580,000
- Liabilities 1,560,000
- Common shares 450,000
- Retained earnings 570,000
- Total liabilities & eq. 2,580,000

3-8

a) Journal entry on Global's records:

Cash	70,000	
Accounts Receivables	21,000	
Inventory	5,600	
Land	40,000	
Buildings and Equip.	550,000	
Goodwill	118,400	
Current Liabilities		20,000
Long-Term Liabilities		300,000
Cash		485,000

b) Journal entry on Local's records:

Current Liabilities	20,000	
Long-Term Liabilities	250,000	
Cash	485,000	
Cash		70,000
Accounts Receivables		21,000
Inventory		5,600
Land		25,000
Buildings and Equip.		500,000
Gain on Sale		133,400

c) Post-acquisition SFP of Global (in $):
- Assets 2,015,000
- Liabilities 1,510,000
- Common shares 200,000
- Retained earnings 305,000
- Total liabilities & eq. 2,015,000

d) Post-acquisition SFP of Local (in $):
- Assets 485,000
- Liabilities -
- Common shares 100,000
- Retained earnings 385,000
- Total liabilities & eq. 485,000

Journal entry on Global's records if consideration given is $360,000 (stock acquisition):

Investment in Local	366,600	
Gain on Acquisition		6,600
Cash		360,000

3-9
Allocation of purchase price

Cost of 100% of Least		$1,600,000
Book value of Least:		
Common shares	$500,000	
Retained earnings	1,000,000	
	1,500,000	
Most's ownership	100%	1,500,000
Price differential		100,000
Allocated:		
◆ Accounts rec.	20,000	
◆ Inventory	50,000	
◆ Plant & Equip.	(35,000)	
◆ LT Liabilities	(100,000)	(65,000)
Balance – goodwill		**$35,000**

Consolidated figures of Most at the date of acquisition (in $):
- Cash   925,000
- Accounts receivables   790,000
- Inventory   1,200,000
- Buildings and equip.   4,450,000
- Goodwill   **35,000**
- Current liabilities   800,000
- Long-term liabilities   2,600,000
- Common shares   1,000,000
- Retained earnings   3,000,000

Wholly-Owned Subsidiaries: Reporting Subsequent to Acquisition

Module 4

What you will find in this section

- How to Walk Through Module 4
- Slides
- Exercises and Solutions

Module 4
Wholly-Owned Subsidiaries: Reporting Subsequent to Acquisition

---
How to Walk Through Module 4

◇ Readings

    1- Book "Consolidation of Financial Statements": Chapter 2, Part 2
    2- Student Manual "Advanced Accounting": Module 4
        PART 1: CONSOLIDATION OF WHOLLY OWNED SUBSIDIARIES IN PERIODS
            SUBSEQUENT TO THE DATE OF ACQUISITION: ILLUSTRATION
        PART 2: EQUITY METHOD
        PART 3: PRICE DIFFERENTIAL: ADDITIONNAL CONSIDERATIONS

◇ Assignments

    3- Student Manual: End-of module review and quiz questions
    4- Student Manual: Exercises 1 to 4
    5- Book: Case 4

◇ Additional readings

6- IAS 36, 38

When you have successfully completed this module, you will be able to do the following:

- Demonstrate the mechanics of consolidating a wholly owned subsidiary in periods subsequent to the date of acquisition (when there are no intercompany transactions);

- Present the additional consolidation entries required to eliminate the investment account when the equity method is employed by Parent Company in non-consolidated financial statements: the case of wholly owned subsidiaries.

WHOLLY OWNED SUBSIDIARIES: REPORTING SUBSEQUENT TO ACQUISITION
Module 4

Copyright © 2020 Parmitech

Advanced Accounting: Student Manual

Copyrighted Material

Editor: Parmitech

This publication is protected by copyright, and permission should be obtained from the publisher prior to any prohibited reproduction, storage in a retrieval system, or transmission in any form or by any means, electronic, mechanical, photocopying, recording, or otherwise.

Corresponding Author

Richard Bozec Ph.D., CPA, CGA
bozec@telfer.uottawa.ca

Copyright © Parmitech

TEACHING MATERIAL
Exercises

Module 4

4.1	Consolidated versus Separate-Entity Statements
4.2	Equity Method Subsequent to Acquisition (with no intercompany transactions)
4.3	Equity Method and Net Adjusted Value Subsequent to Acquisition (with no intercompany transactions)
4.4	Worksheet Approach and Equity Method Subsequent to Acquisition (with no intercompany transactions)

CORRESPONDING CHAPTERS in *Bozec*
"Consolidation of Financial Statements under IFRS"

Chapter 2 — Wholly Owned Subsidiaries (Part 2)

Case — 4

IFRS

IAS 36 — Impairment Assets

IAS 38 — Intangible Assets

FOCUS OF THIS MODULE: PRICE DIFFERENTIAL

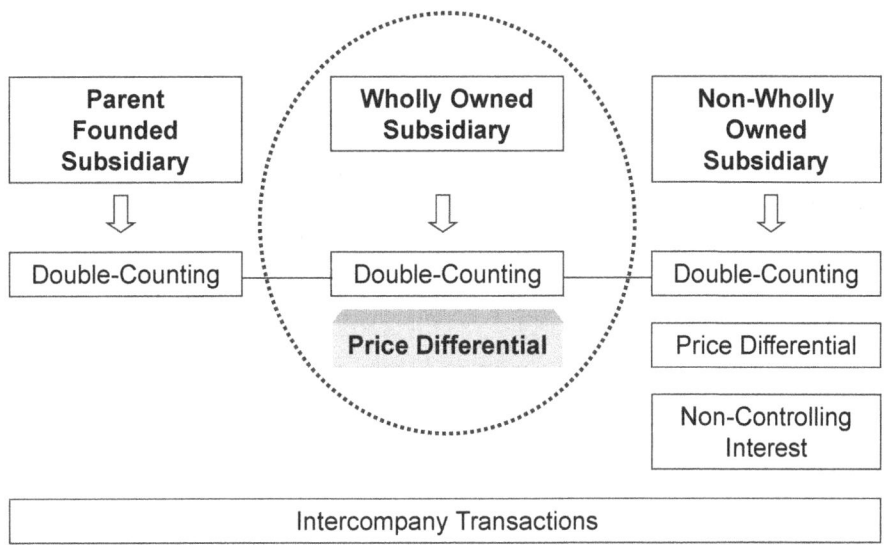

OUTLINE OF THE PRESENTATION

1. CONSOLIDATION OF WHOLLY OWNED SUBSIDIARIES IN PERIODS SUBSEQUENT TO THE DATE OF ACQUISITION: ILLUSTRATION
2. EQUITY METHOD
3. PRICE DIFFERENTIAL: ADDITIONAL CONSIDERATIONS

RECAP

4. REVIEW QUESTIONS
5. QUIZ QUESTIONS
6. KEY TERMS INTRODUCED IN THIS MODULE
7. RECAP ON THE OBJECTIVES OF THIS MODULE

Part 1

PART 1
Consolidation of Wholly Owned Subsidiaries in Periods Subsequent to the Date of Acquisition

Objectives of this section

Illustrate the consolidation process of wholly owned subsidiaries in periods subsequent to the date of acquisition. <u>Note</u>: the investment in Subsidiary is accounted for on a cost basis and there are no intercompany transactions.

Illustrate the consolidation process under the worksheet approach and the direct approach as well.

Key concepts

- Price differential amortization
- Goodwill impairment
- Net adjusted value of Subsidiary

Part 1

ACCOUNTING FOR BUSINESS COMBINATIONS
In periods Subsequent to Acquisition

LEGAL FORMS OF ACQUISITION	ACCOUNTING SUBSEQUENT TO ACQUISITION
PURCHASE OF NET ASSETS	X
PURCHASE OF SHARES	CONSOLIDATION
MERGER	X

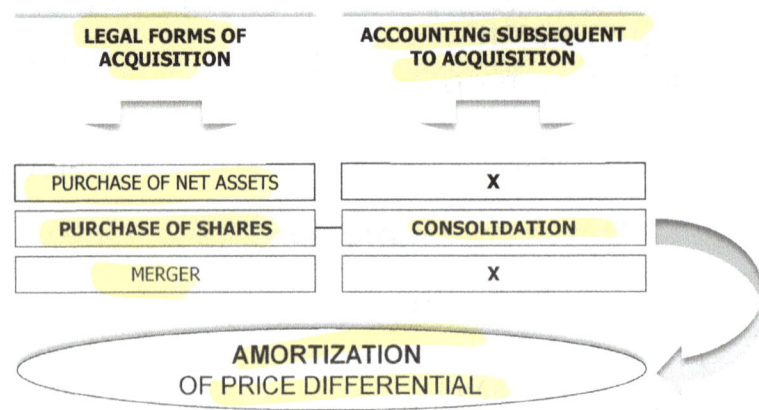

AMORTIZATION OF PRICE DIFFERENTIAL

Module 4 continues the development of Parent and Subsidiary (from Module 3). Accountants must follow up on business combinations in post-acquisition periods when combinations are initially structured as a purchase of shares. Indeed, for as long as a control relationship is sustained between the parent and its subsidiaries, consolidation is required. In this case, price differential amortization will add a new complexity to the consolidation process.

Part 1

CONSOLIDATION OF ACQUIRED SUBSIDIARIES IN PERIODS SUBSEQUENT TO ACQUISITION
Preliminary Analysis (1/2)

- Check if control of Parent over Subsidiary is maintained;

- If control is sustained, consolidation of F/S is still required. Then, return to the date of acquisition to prepare or retrieve the allocation of the purchase price;

    → **ALLOCATION OF THE PURCHASE PRICE**

- Follow up on the price differential from date of acquisition to the current year (amortization and/or realization of the FV increments/decrements and goodwill impairment);

    → **PRICE DIFFERENTIAL AMORTIZATION SCHEDULE**

- Get the complete set of F/S of Parent and Subsidiary for the current year;

- From the SFP of Parent, take a look at the *Investment in Subsidiary* to determine if Parent is using either the *Cost Method* or the *Equity Method*;

Wholly Owned Subsidiaries — Module 4 —

Part 1

CONSOLIDATION OF ACQUIRED SUBSIDIARIES IN PERIODS SUBSEQUENT TO ACQUISITION
Preliminary Analysis (2/2)

- If the *Cost Method* is used, check the I/S of Parent for any *Dividend Income* as a result of current-year *Intercompany Dividends* (double-counting in I/S);

- Examine carefully the F/S of the affiliated companies to identify any additional *Reciprocal Balances* (such as Receivables/Payables; Revenues/Expenses) as a result of current and/or prior-year *Intercompany Transactions*;

- Enquire additional information that may be relevant for consolidation (intercompany transfers).

Wholly Owned Subsidiaries — Module 4 —

CONSOLIDATION OF ACQUIRED SUBSIDIARIES IN PERIODS SUBSEQUENT TO ACQUISITION
Consolidation Steps Under the Cost Method

- Eliminate the double-counting in the SFP: elimination of the *Investment in Subsidiary* (Parent) and the *Equity* section (Subsidiary);

- Establish the FV of Subsidiary at date of acquisition (price differential);

- Take into account the portion of the price differential that has been amortized and/or realized since acquisition;

- If Intercompany Dividends, eliminate the double-counting in the I/S: elimination of *Dividend Income* (Parent) and *Dividends Declared* (Subsidiary);

- Eliminate any additional reciprocal balances (*Overstatements*) as a result of Intercompany Transactions from current and prior years.

PURCHASE OF SHARES
Illustration - Parent & Subsidiary: Two Years Post-Acquisition

Refer to previous illustration (Module 3).

Recall that on December 31, X1, Parent Company purchased all the outstanding voting stock of Subsidiary Company by issuing 40,000 voting shares worth $1,200,000.

Assume that the affiliated companies never engaged in transactions between themselves.

Parent still controls 100% of Subsidiary.

Required
Prepare the consolidated financial statements of Parent at December 31, X3.

CONSOLIDATION OF PARENT COMPANY IN YEAR SUBSEQUENT TO ACQUISITION
Affiliation Structure at December 31, X3

Part 1

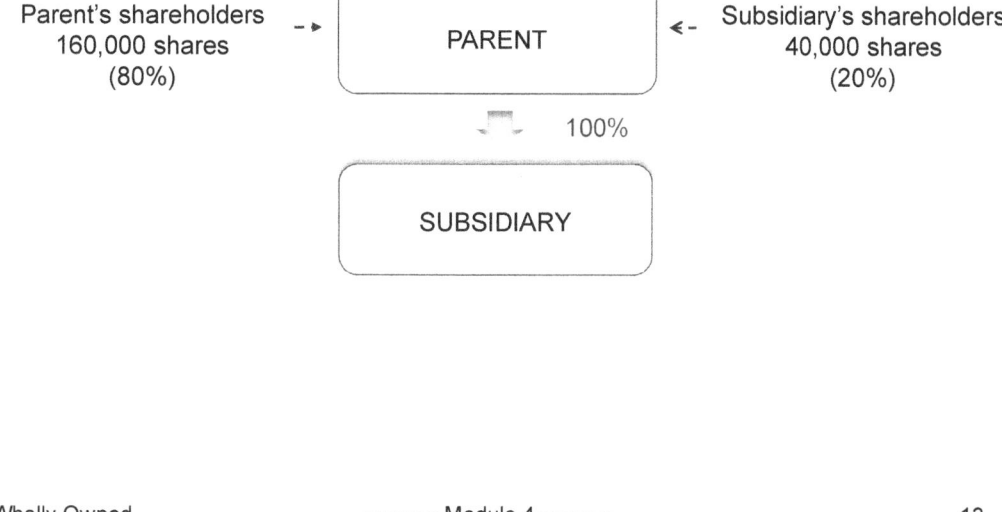

Wholly Owned Subsidiaries

---------- Module 4 ----------

CONSOLIDATION OF PARENT COMPANY IN YEAR SUBSEQUENT TO ACQUISITION
Timeline

Part 1

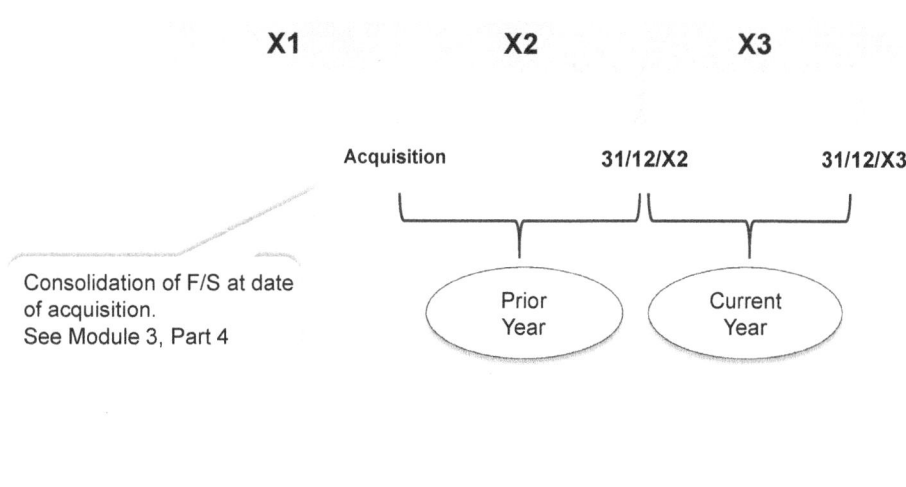

Wholly Owned Subsidiaries

---------- Module 4 ----------

Part 1

CONSOLIDATION OF PARENT COMPANY
IN YEAR SUBSEQUENT TO ACQUISITION
Basic Information at Acquisition - From Module 3

	Book Values	Fair Values	
Assets			
Non-current assets			
Land	$300,000	$400,00	+ 100,000
Buildings (net)	350,000	550,000	+ 200,000
Current assets			
Inventories	50,000	50,000	
Accounts receivable	150,000	150,000	
Cash	50,000	50,000	
Total assets	**$900,000**		
Equitiy and liabilities			
Equity			
Share capital	$200,000		
Retained earnings	600,000		
Liabilities			
Accounts payable	100,000	100,000	
Total equity and liabilities	**$900,000**		

Wholly Owned Subsidiaries

15

Part 1

CONSOLIDATION OF PARENT COMPANY
IN YEAR SUBSEQUENT TO ACQUISITION
Allocation of Purchase Price - From Module 3

Purchase price $1,200 000

Net book value of Subsidiary:
- Common shares $200,000
- Retained earnings 600,000   800,000

Price differential 400,000

Fair value increments:
- Land (100,000)
- Buildings (200,000) (300,000)

Goodwill $100,000

Wholly Owned Subsidiaries

---------- Module 4 ----------

16

CONSOLIDATION OF PARENT COMPANY IN YEAR SUBSEQUENT TO ACQUISITION

Separate-Entity Statements of Financial Position
At December 31, X3

	Parent	Subsidiary
Assets		
Non-current assets		
Land	$1,450,000	$300,000
Buildings (net)	2,400,000	280,000
Investment in Subsidiary	1,200,000	
Current assets		
Inventories	300,000	60,000
Accounts receivable	1,900,000	475,000
Cash	490,000	70,000
Total assets	$7,740,000	$1,185,000
Equity and liabilities		
Equity		
Share capital	$3,800,000	$200,000
Retained earnings	2,575,000	835,000
Liabilities		
Long-term notes payable	500,000	-
Accounts payable	865,000	150,000
Total equity and liabilities	$7,740,000	$1,185,000

CONSOLIDATION OF PARENT COMPANY IN YEAR SUBSEQUENT TO ACQUISITION

Separate-Entity Income Statements
For the Period Ended December 31, X3

	Parent	Subsidiary
Sales revenue	$3,020,000	$550,000
Cost of sales	2,100,000	220,000
Depreciation expense	100,000	35,000
Other expenses	440,000	75,000
Profit for the year	**$380,000**	**$220,000**

CONSOLIDATION OF PARENT COMPANY
IN YEAR SUBSEQUENT TO ACQUISITION

Separate-Entity Statements of Changes in Equity
For the Period Ended December 31, X3

	Parent			Subsidiary		
	Share Capital	Retained Earnings	Total	Share Capital	Retained Earnings	Total
Balance at Dec. 31, X2	$3,800,000	$2,330,000	$6,130,000	$200,000	$615,000	$815,000
Profit for the year		380,000	380,000		220,000	220,000
Dividends		(135,000)	(135,000)			
Balance at Dec. X3	$3,800,000	$2,575,000	$6,375,000	$200,000	$835,000	$1,035,000

Wholly Owned Subsidiaries ---------- Module 4 ---------- 19

CONSOLIDATION OF PARENT COMPANY
IN YEAR SUBSEQUENT TO ACQUISITION

Consolidation Entries - Elimination of the Investment Account

Double-Counting of $800,000

1a
```
Common Shares (Subsidiary)          200,000
Retained Earnings (Subsidiary)      600,000
   Investment in Subsidiary (Parent)           800,000
```

Price Differential of $400,000

1b
```
Land (Subsidiary)                   100,000
Buildings (Subsidiary)              200,000
Goodwill (Subsidiary)               100,000
   Investment in Subsidiary (Parent)           400,000
```

Investment: $1,200,000

To establish the FV of Subsidiary at date of acquisition

Wholly Owned Subsidiaries ---------- Module 4 ---------- 20

CONSOLIDATION OF PARENT COMPANY
IN YEAR SUBSEQUENT TO ACQUISITION
Follow-Up on Price Differential

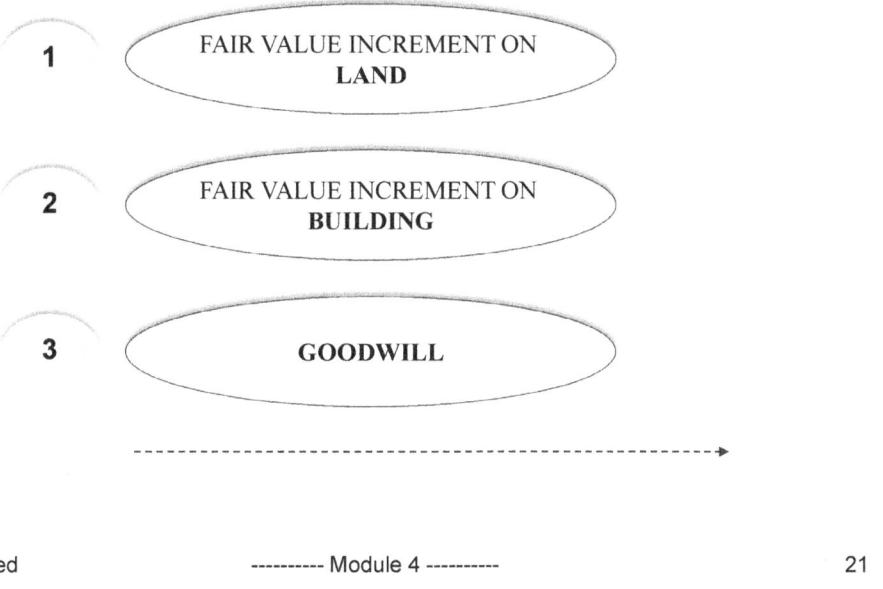

1. FAIR VALUE INCREMENT ON **LAND**
2. FAIR VALUE INCREMENT ON **BUILDING**
3. **GOODWILL**

CONSOLIDATION OF PARENT COMPANY
IN YEAR SUBSEQUENT TO ACQUISITION
Fair Value Increment on Land

- Land is reported by Subsidiary at BV.

- FV of Land is considered on working paper via adjustment 1b.

- No consideration need be given the land in post-acquisition periods for as long as the land is not sold to an unrelated party (this scenario is explored in Module 6).

- Since land is a non-depreciable asset, the FV increment assigned to land at date of acquisition remains unchanged.

THE FV INCREMENT WILL BE REALIZED WHENEVER LAND IS SOLD

Part 1

 Complete this slide

CONSOLIDATION OF PARENT COMPANY IN YEAR SUBSEQUENT TO ACQUISITION
Fair Value Increment on Buildings

AMORTIZATION ON THE BOOKS OF 'SUBSIDIARY'
Net Book Value

350,000/10 = 35,000

AMORTIZATION ON CONSOLIDATED F/S
Fair Value

550,000/10 = 55,000

ADJUSTMENT REQUIRED

55,000 − 35,000 = 20,000

Amortization of buildings
10 years on a straight-line basis.

Wholly Owned Subsidiaries ---------- Module 4 ---------- 23

Part 1

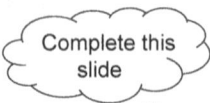 Complete this slide

CONSOLIDATION OF PARENT COMPANY IN YEAR SUBSEQUENT TO ACQUISITION
Consolidation Entry - Amortization of FVI on Buildings

Amortization of the Fair Value Increment on Buildings since Acquisition

② Dr Depreciation Expense 20,000
   Dr RE 20,000
      Cr Building 40,000

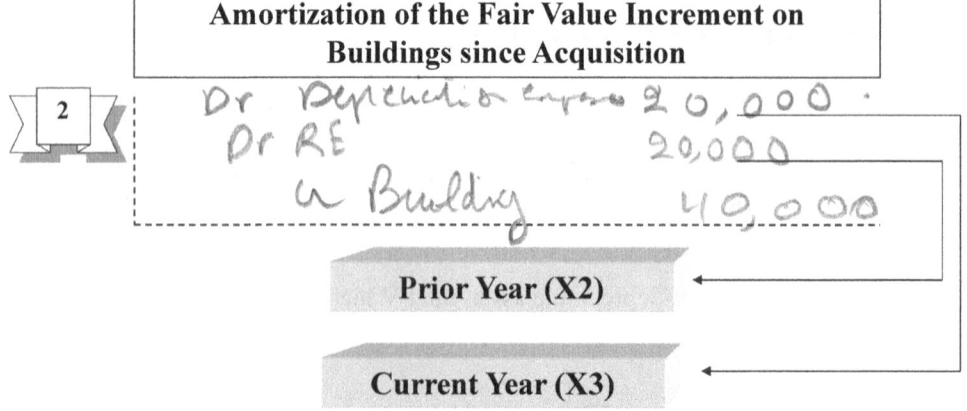

Prior Year (X2)
Current Year (X3)

This entry is required to account for the cumulative amortization of the FVI on Buildings ($40,000). Since consolidation is made on working paper, beginning consolidated RE is adjusted for the amount of the FVI amortized in prior consolidation period ($20,000).

Wholly Owned Subsidiaries ---------- Module 4 ---------- 24

CONSOLIDATION OF PARENT COMPANY
IN YEAR SUBSEQUENT TO ACQUISITION
Goodwill

Part 1

GOODWILL

Goodwill established at date of acquisition will be carried forward unless it is impaired.

IMPAIRMENT TEST

GOODWILL IMPAIRMENT TEST
Goodwill must be allocated to the acquirer's Cash-Generating Units (CGU)

Part 1

RECOVERABLE AMOUNT
OF THE CGU

CARRYING AMOUNT
OF THE CGU

GOODWILL IMPAIRMENT TEST
Recoverable Amount

The higher of:

1 FAIR VALUE LESS COSTS
Amount obtainable from the sale of the CGU in an arm's length transaction between knowledgeable, willing parties, less the costs of disposal.

2 VALUE IN USE
Present value of the future cash flows expected to be derived from the CGU.

GOODWILL IMPAIRMENT TEST
If Goodwill is Impaired

RECOVERABLE AMOUNT
OF THE CGU

<

CARRYING AMOUNT
OF THE CGU

The excess amount (Impairment Loss) must be allocated as follows:

1 GOODWILL

2 OTHER ASSETS OF THE CGU
(on a pro-rata based on the carrying amount of each asset)

Part 1

GOODWILL IMPAIRMENT
From Bombardier - 2016 Annual Report, page 121

Goodwill is related to the DaimlerChrysler Rail Systems GmbH (Adtranz) acquisition in May 2001. This goodwill is monitored by management at the Transportation operating segment level. An impairment assessment is performed at least annually, and whenever circumstances such as significant declines in expected sales, earnings or cash flows indicate that it is more likely than not that goodwill might be impaired. We selected the fourth quarter to perform an annual impairment assessment of goodwill.

During the fourth quarter of 2016, an impairment test was completed. The recoverable amount of the Transportation operating segment was calculated based on fair value less cost to sell using a discounted cash flow model. We did not identify any impairment.

Part 1

PRICE DIFFERENTIAL AMORTIZATION SCHEDULE

Price Differential Items	Balance at Acquisition	Amortization Prior Year (X2)	Amortization Current Year (X3)	Unamortized Excess at December 31, X3
Land	100,000			100,000
Buildings	200,000	(20,000)	(20,000)	160,000
Goodwill	100,000			100,000
Total	400,000	(20,000)	(20,000)	360,000

Complete this slide

PORTION BEING CONSUMED SINCE ACQUISITION
$40,000

CONSOLIDATION OF PARENT COMPANY
Price Differential - Collapsing Entries

Items	Price Differential Balance at Acquisition	Amortization Prior Year (X2)	Amortization Current Year (X3)	Unamortized Excess at December 31, X3
Land	$100,000			$100,000
Buildings	200,000	($20,000)	($20,000)	160,000
Goodwill	100,000			100,000
Total	$400,000	($20,000)	($20,000)	$360,000

1b

Retained Earnings	20,000	
Depreciation Expense	20,000	
Land	100,000	
Buildings	160,000	
Goodwill	100,000	
Investment in Subsidiary		400,000

CONSOLIDATION WORKSHEET OF PARENT COMPANY
For the Year Ended December 31, X3

	Parent	Subsidiary	Conso. Entries	Consolidated
Assets				
Land	$1,450,000	$300,000	(1b) 100,000	$1,850,000
Buildings (net)	2,400,000	280,000	(1b) 200,000 (2) (40,000)	2,840,000
Goodwill			(1b) 100,000	100,000
Investment in Subsidiary	1,200,000		(1a) (800,000) (1b) (400,000)	
Inventories	300,000	60,000		360,000
Accounts receivable	1,900,000	475,000		2,375,000
Cash	490,000	70,000		560,000
Total assets	$7,740,000	$1,185,000		$8,085,000
Equity and liabilities				
Share capital	$3,800,000	$200,000	(1a) (200,000)	$3,800,000
Retained earnings	2,575,000	835,000	(640,000)	2,770,000
Long-term notes payable	500,000	-		500,000
Accounts payable	865,000	150,000		1,015,000
Total equity and liabilities	$7,740,000	$1,185,000		$8,085,,000

Part 1
CONSOLIDATION WORKSHEET OF PARENT COMPANY (continued…)
For the Year Ended December 31, X3

	Parent	Subsidiary	Conso. Entries	Consolidated
Sales revenue	$3,020,000	$550,000		$3,570,000
Cost of sales	2,100,000	220,000		2,320,000
Depreciation expense	100,000	35,000	(2) 20,000	155,000
Other expenses	440,000	75,000		515,000
Profit for the year	**$380,000**	**$220,000**	**(20,000)**	**$580,000**
Retained earnings (beginning)	$2,330,000	$615,000	(1a) (600,000) (2) (20,000)	$2,325,000
Dividends declared	(135,000)			(135,000)
Retained earnings (end)	**$2,575,000**	**$835,000**	**(640,000)**	**$2,770,000**

Net impact of the consolidation adjustments on the ending balance of Retained Earnings. To be transferred in the statement of financial position

---

Part 1
DIRECT APPROACH
Non-Current Assets

Buildings

Parent	$2,400,000
Subsidiary	280,000
Unamortized portion of the fair value increment (200,000 * 8/10)	**160,000**
Total	$2,840,000

Goodwill

At acquisition	$100,000

Land

Parent	$1,450,000
Subsidiary	300,000
Fair value increment at acquisition	**100,000**
Total	$1,850,000

DIRECT APPROACH
Current Assets

Cash

Parent	$490,000
Subsidiary	70,000
Total	$560,000

Accounts Receivable

Parent	$1,900,000
Subsidiary	475,000
Total	$2,375,000

Inventories

Parent	$300,000
Subsidiary	60,000
Total	$360,000

DIRECT APPROACH
Equity

Common Shares

Parent	$3,800,000

Retained Earnings

Parent		$2,575,000
Subsidiary's net adjusted value since acquisition:		
• Retained earnings increase since acquisition ($835,000 - $600,000)	$235,000	
• Price differential amortization since acquisition	(40,000)	195,000
Total		$2,770,000

Net Adjusted Value or Consolidated Value of Subsidiary since acquisition

DIRECT APPROACH
Liabilities

Accounts Payable

Parent	$865,000
Subsidiary	150,000
Total	$1,015,000

Long-Term Notes Payable

Parent	$500,000

DIRECT APPROACH
Consolidated Profit

- Profit of Parent — $380,000

- Adjusted profit of Subsidiary:
  - Profit of Subsidiary for the period — $220,000
  - **Current-year price differential amortization** — (20,000)   200,000

   Total — $580,000

CONSOLIDATION OF PARENT COMPANY IN YEAR SUBSEQUENT TO ACQUISITION
Recap

PARENT
BV at year-end

+

SUBSIDIARY
NET ADJUSTED VALUE or CONSOLIDATED VALUE at year-end

=

PARENT
Consolidated F/S

Wholly Owned Subsidiaries — Module 4 — 39

NET ADJUSTED VALUE OF SUBSIDIARY
In Post-Acquisition Periods

Individual Records of Subsidiary

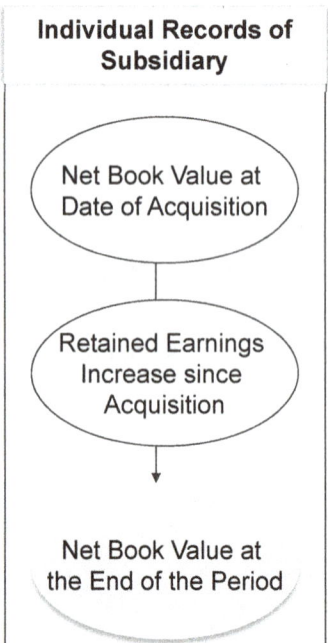

Consolidation Adjustments

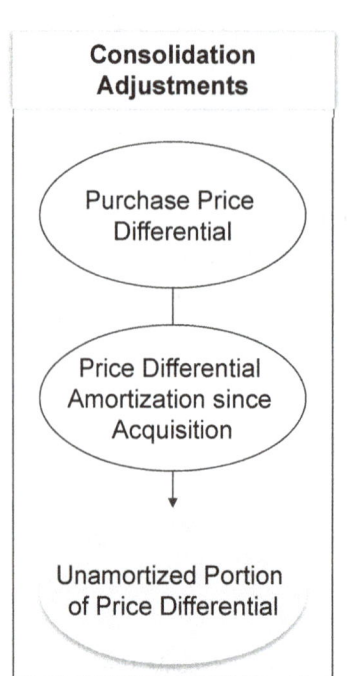

Consolidated Value of Subsidiary

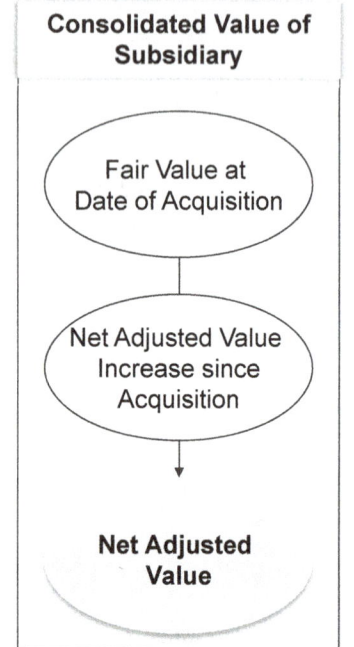

Part 1

NET ADJUSTED VALUE OF SUBSIDIARY
At December 31, X3

	Individual Records of Subsidiary	Consolidation Adjustments	Consolidated Value of Subsidiary
At Date of Acquisition December 31, X1	Net Book Value 800,000	Purchase Price Differential 400,000	Purchase Price 1,200,000
Since Acquisition	Retained Earnings Increase 235K	Price Differential Amortization (40,000)	Net Adjusted Value Increase 195,000
At December 31, X3	Net Book Value 1,035,000	Unamortized Portion of Price Differential 360,000	Net Adjusted Value 1,395,000

Wholly Owned Subsidiaries ---------- Module 4 ---------- 41

Part 1

CONSOLIDATION IN YEAR SUBSEQUENT TO ACQUISITION
Accounting Methods and Fiscal Periods

- A difference in accounting methods between a parent and its subsidiary generally should have no effect on the decision to consolidate that subsidiary.

- In any event, adequate disclosure of the various accounting methods used must be given in the notes to the financial statements.

- A difference in the fiscal periods of a parent and subsidiary should not preclude consolidation of that subsidiary.

- Often the fiscal period of the subsidiary, if different from the parent's, is changed to coincide with that of the parent.

- Another alternative is to adjust the financial statement data of the subsidiary each period to place the data on a basis consistent with the fiscal period of the parent.

Wholly Owned Subsidiaries ---------- Module 4 ---------- 42

PART 1
Concept Check

> What is the "net adjusted value" or "consolidated value" of Subsidiary in the consolidation process?

OUTLINE OF THE PRESENTATION

1 — CONSOLIDATION OF WHOLLY OWNED SUBSIDIARIES IN PERIODS SUBSEQUENT TO THE DATE OF ACQUISITION: ILLUSTRATION

2 — **EQUITY METHOD**

3 — PRICE DIFFERENTIAL: ADDITIONAL CONSIDERATIONS

RECAP

4 — REVIEW QUESTIONS

5 — QUIZ QUESTIONS

6 — KEY TERMS INTRODUCED IN THIS MODULE

7 — RECAP ON THE OBJECTIVES OF THIS MODULE

PART 2
Equity Method

Objectives of this section

Discuss the equity-basis reporting when Parent Company uses the equity method in its separate-entity financial statements.

Illustrate the approach to compute the investment in Subsidiary in non-consolidated financial statements under the equity method.

Present the financial reporting implications of using either the cost method, the equity method or full consolidation.

Present the additional consolidation entries required to eliminate the investment account when the equity method is employed by Parent Company in non-consolidated financial statements.

EQUITY METHOD
What you need to know - Recall

1. HOW TO **REPORT** THE BASIC JOURNAL ENTRIES;

2. HOW TO **COMPUTE** THE BALANCE OF THE INVESTMENT ACCOUNT AT THE END OF A PERIOD;

3. HOW TO **PRESENT** THE F/S UNDER THE EQUITY METHOD;

4. HOW TO **ELIMINATE** THE INVESTMENT ACCOUNT THROUGH CONSOLIDATION.

Part 2

EQUITY METHOD
Closely Related to Consolidation - Recall

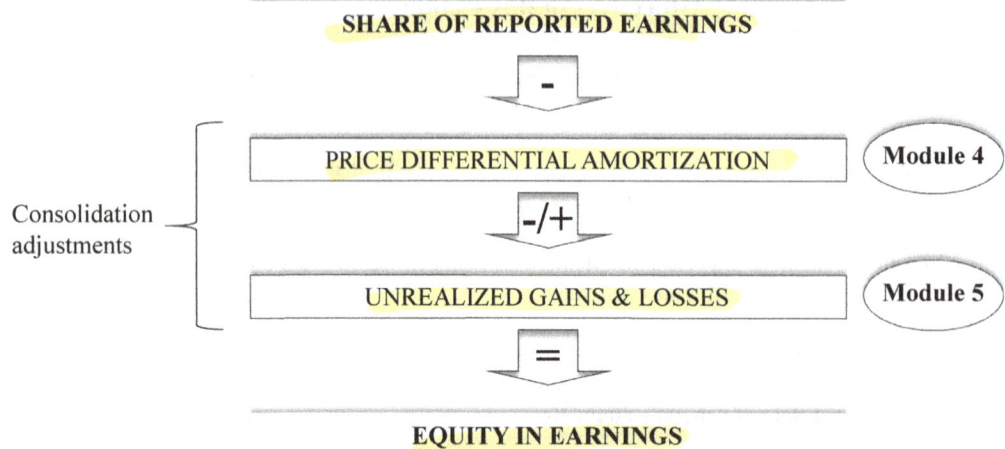

Wholly Owned Subsidiaries ---------- Module 4 ---------- 47

Part 2

EQUITY METHOD
Journal Entries for X3

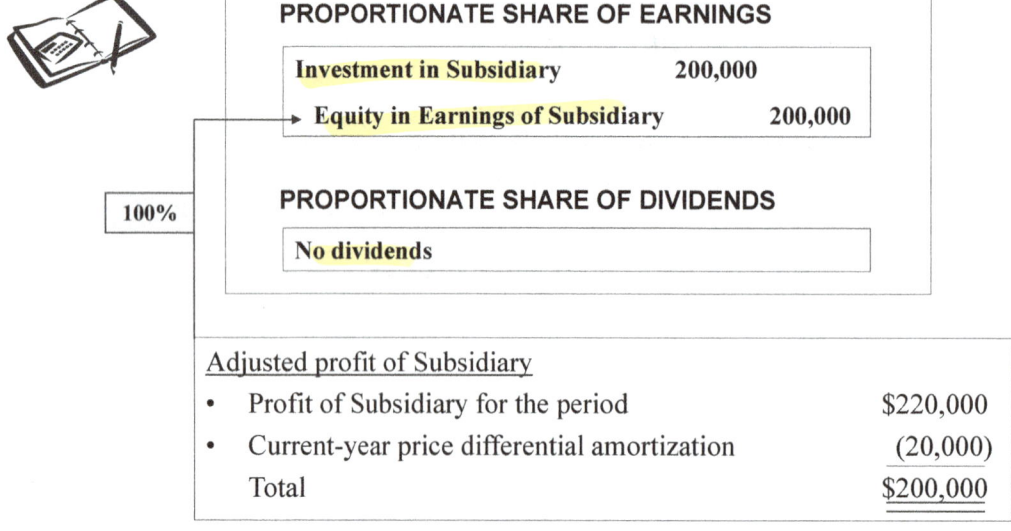

Wholly Owned Subsidiaries ---------- Module 4 ---------- 48

Part 2

EQUITY METHOD
Balance of the Investment Account
As of December 31, X3

INITIAL INVESTMENT (X1)		$1,200,000	Cost Method
SUBSIDIARY'S NET ADJUSTED VALUE SINCE ACQUISITION		195,000	↕
INVESTMENT AT THE END (X3)		$1,395,000	Equity Method

100% Subsidiary's net adjusted value since acquisition
- Retained earnings increase since acquisition ($835,000 - $600,000) $235,000
- Price differential amortization since acquisition .... (40,000)
- Total $195,000

Net Adjusted Value of Sub

Wholly Owned Subsidiaries ---------- Module 4 ---------- 49

Part 2

STATEMENT OF FINANCIAL POSITION - PARENT COMPANY
At December 31, X3
Under Different Reporting Practices

	Cost basis	Equity basis	Consolidated
Assets			
Non-current assets			
Land	$1,450,000	$1,450,000	$1,850,000
Buildings (net)	2,400,000	2,400,000	2,840,000
Goodwill			100,000
Investment in Subsidiary	1,200,000	1,395,000	
Current assets			
Inventories	300,000	300,000	360,000
Accounts receivable	1,900,000	1,900,000	2,375,000
Cash	490,000	490,000	560,000
Total assets	$7,740,000	$7,935,000	$8,085,000
Equity and liabilities			
Equity			
Share capital	$3,800,000	**$3,800,000**	$3,800,000
Retained earnings	2,575,000	**2,770,000**	2,770,000
Liabilities			
Long-term notes payable	500,000	500,000	500,000
Accounts payable	865,000	865,000	1,015,000
Total equity and liabilities	$7,740,000	$7,935,000	$8,085,,000

Net Adjusted Value of Sub

50

STATEMENT OF FINANCIAL POSITION - PARENT COMPANY
At December 31, X3
Equity vs. Consolidation

- The net value is the same, whereas the assets and liabilities reported are different.

- Under the equity method, only the accounts of Parent are reported. Under full consolidation, the accounts of Parent and Subsidiary are combined.

- One can see the process of consolidation as disaggregating the Investment account into the subsidiary's detailed assets and liabilities, **including the unamortized portion of price differential**.

Equity Method = One-line consolidation

INCOME STATEMENT - PARENT COMPANY
Year Ended December 31, X3
Under Different Reporting Practices

	Cost basis	Equity basis	Consolidated	
Sales revenue	$3,020,000	$3,020,000	$3,570,000	
Equity in earnings		200,000		Adjusted Profit of Sub
Cost of sales	2,100,000	2,100,000	2,320,000	
Depreciation expense	100,000	100,000	155,000	
Other expenses	440,000	440,000	515,000	
Profit for the year	**$380,000**	**$580,000**	**$580,000**	

Part 2

INCOME STATEMENT - PARENT COMPANY
Year Ended December 31, X3
Equity vs. Consolidation

- Profit is the same, whereas the revenues and expenses reported are different.

- Under the equity method, only the accounts of Parent are reported. Under full consolidation, the accounts of Parent and Subsidiary are combined.

- One can see the process of consolidation as disaggregating the Equity in Earnings account into the subsidiary's detailed revenues and expenses, **including the amortized portion of price differential for the current period**.

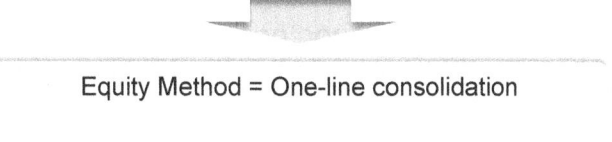

Equity Method = One-line consolidation

Wholly Owned Subsidiaries ---------- Module 4 ---------- 53

Part 2

STATEMENT OF CHANGES IN EQUITY - PARENT COMPANY
Year Ended December 31, X3
Under Different Reporting Practices

	Cost basis			Equity basis			Consolidated		
	SC	RE	Total	SC	RE	Total	SC	RE	Total
Balance (beginning)	3,800,000	2,330,000	6,130,000	3,800,000	2,325,000	6,125,000	3,800,000	2,325,000	6,125,000
Profit for the year		380,000	380,000		580,000	580,000		580,000	580,000
Dividends declared		(135,000)	(135,000)		(135,000)	(135,000)		(135,000)	(135,000)
Balance (end)	**3,800,000**	**2,575,000**	**6,375,000**	**3,800,000**	**2,770,000**	**6,570,000**	**3,800,000**	**2,770,000**	**6,570,000**

Wholly Owned Subsidiaries ---------- Module 4 ---------- 54

EQUITY METHOD
One-Line Consolidation

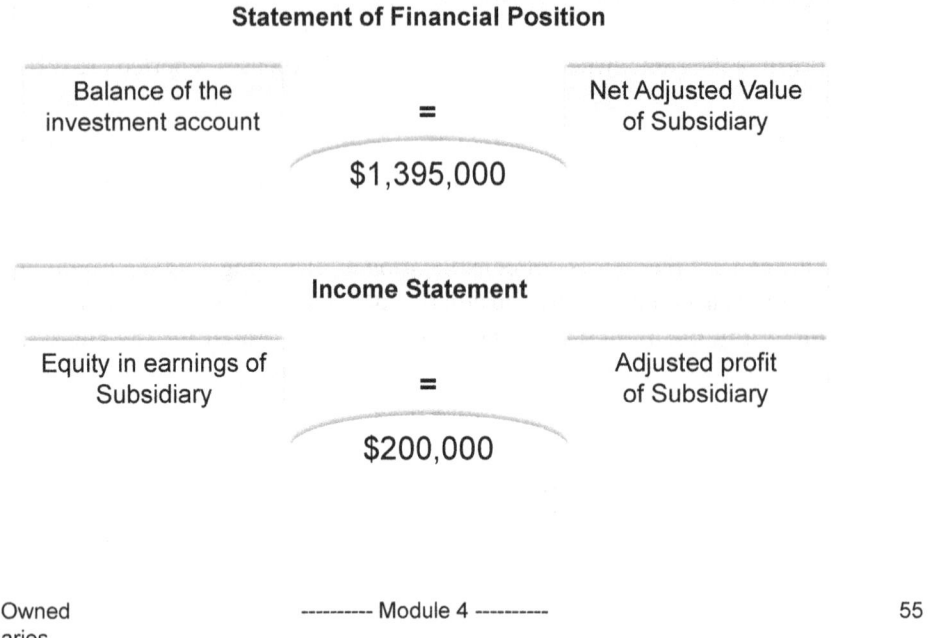

Statement of Financial Position

Balance of the investment account = Net Adjusted Value of Subsidiary

$1,395,000

Income Statement

Equity in earnings of Subsidiary = Adjusted profit of Subsidiary

$200,000

EQUITY METHOD IN THE CONTEXT OF CONSOLIDATION
Procedure to Eliminate the Investment Account - Recall

1 BREAK DOWN THE BALANCE OF THE INVESTMENT ACCOUNT AT END OF THE PERIOD:

1. Initial Investment;
2. Increase of the Investment up to the beginning of the current period;
3. Share of Earnings – Current period;
4. Share of Dividends – Current period.

2 ELIMINATE EACH COMPONENT OF THE INVESTMENT ACCOUNT

Part 2

EQUITY METHOD
Breakdown of the Investment Account

Balance of the Investment under the Equity Method

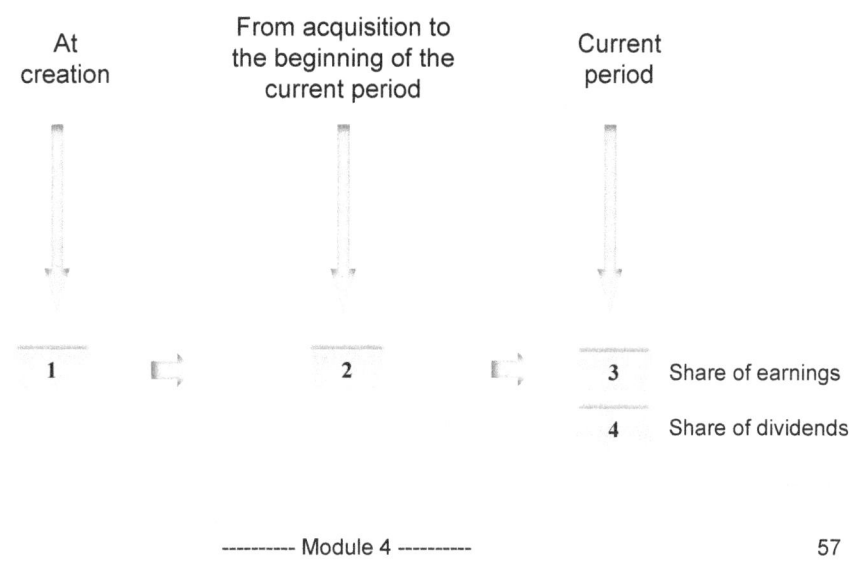

At creation	From acquisition to the beginning of the current period	Current period
1	2	3 Share of earnings
		4 Share of dividends

Wholly Owned Subsidiaries

Part 2

EQUITY METHOD
Breakdown of the Investment Account of $1,395,000

1	INITIAL INVESTMENT (X1)	$1,200,000	Cost Method
2	SUBSIDIARY'S NET ADJUSTED VALUE FROM ACQUISITION TO THE BEGINNING OF X3 (see next slide)	(5,000)	↕
3	SUBSIDIARY'S ADJUSTED EARNINGS IN X3	200,000	
	INVESTMENT AT THE END (X3)	$1,395,000	Equity Method

Wholly Owned Subsidiaries

Part 2
EQUITY METHOD
Subsidiary's Net Adjusted Value from Acquisition to the Beginning of X3

- Retained earnings increase from 31-12-X1 to 31-12-X2 $15,000
  ($615,000 - $600,000)

- Price differential amortization (X2)   (20,000)

    Net adjusted value decrease $(5000)

OPTIONAL

Wholly Owned Subsidiaries ---------- Module 4 ---------- 59

Part 2
EQUITY METHOD
Consolidation Entries Required to Eliminate the Investment Account of $1,395,000

		Debit	Credit
1	Common Shares	200,000	
	Retained Earnings	600,000	
	Land	100,000	
	Buildings	200,000	
	Goodwill	100,000	
	Investment in Subsidiary		1,200,000
2	Investment in Subsidiary	5,000	
	Retained earnings		5,000
3	Equity in Earnings	200,000	
	Investment in Subsidiary		200,000

Entries 2 and 3: Additional Consolidation Entries

Wholly Owned Subsidiaries ---------- Module 4 ---------- 60

PART 2
Concept Check

> In the context of wholly owned subsidiaries, explain how consolidation and equity method are closely related.

_____
_____
_____
_____
_____
_____
_____

OUTLINE OF THE PRESENTATION

1 CONSOLIDATION OF WHOLLY OWNED SUBSIDIARIES IN PERIODS SUBSEQUENT TO THE DATE OF ACQUISITION: ILLUSTRATION

2 EQUITY METHOD

3 **PRICE DIFFERENTIAL: ADDITIONAL CONSIDERATIONS**

RECAP

4 REVIEW QUESTIONS

5 QUIZ QUESTIONS

6 KEY TERMS INTRODUCED IN THIS MODULE

7 RECAP ON THE OBJECTIVES OF THIS MODULE

Part 3

PART 3
Price Differential: Additional Considerations

Objective of this section

Illustrate the impact on consolidation when Fair Value Increments (FVI) and Fair Value Decrements (FVD) affect simultaneously Subsidiary's assets and liabilities at date of combination.

Part 3

PRICE DIFFERENTIAL
Impact of FVI/FVD (Assets-Liabilities) on the Net Fair Value and Goodwill

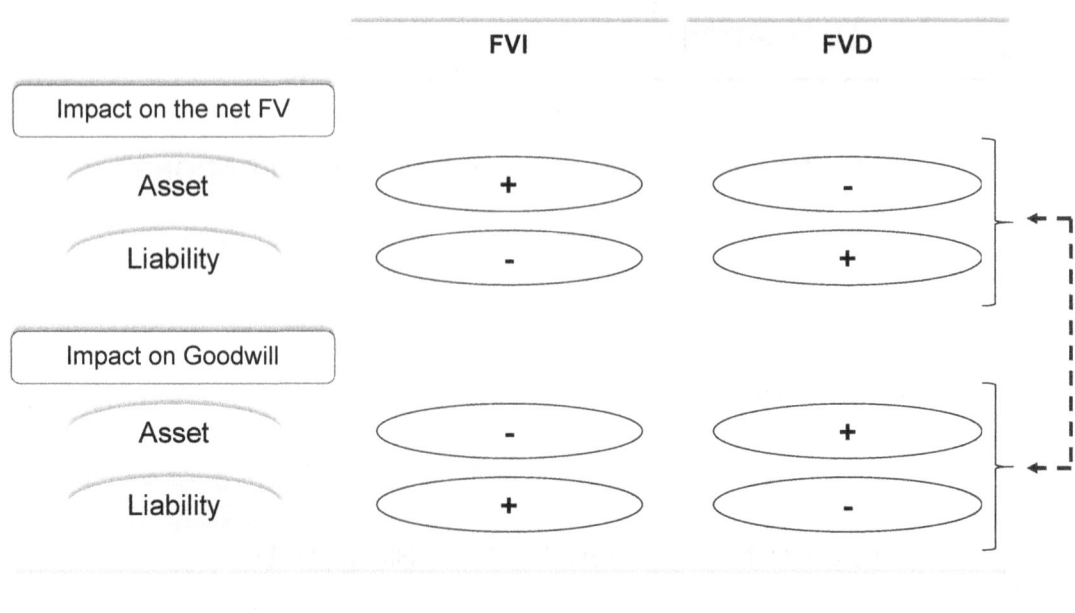

PRICE DIFFERENTIAL
Impact of FVI and FVD on Goodwill - Illustration

December 31, X1	Book Values	Fair Values	
Assets			
Non-current assets			
Land	$300,000	$300,00	
Buildings (net) (remaining useful life: 10 years)	**350,000**	**250,000**	- 100,000
Current assets			
Inventories	**50,000**	**60,000**	+ 10,000
Accounts receivable	150,000	150,000	
Cash	50,000	50,000	
Total assets	**$900,000**		
Equity and liabilities			
Equity			
Share capital	$200,000		
Retained earnings	600,000		
Liabilities			
LT payable (maturity: 10 years)	100,000	50,000	- 50,000
Total equity and liabilities	**$900,000**		

PRICE DIFFERENTIAL
Illustration - Allocation of Purchase Price of $1,200,000

Purchase price		$1,200 000
Net book value of Subsidiary:		
- Common shares	$200,000	
- Retained earnings	600,000	800,000
Price differential		400,000
Fair value increments:		
- Inventory	(10,000)	
Fair value decrements:		
- Buildings	100,000	
- LT liabilities	(50,000)	40,000
Goodwill		$440,000

PRICE DIFFERENTIAL
Illustration - Price Differential Amortization - X2 and X3

Price Differential Items	Balance at Acquisition	Amortization Prior Year (X2)	Amortization Current Year (X3)	Unamortized Excess at December 31, X3
Inventory (FVI)	$10,000	($10,000)	-	-
Buildings (FVD)	(100,000)	10,000	$10,000	(80,000)
LT liabilities (FVD)	50,000	(5,000)	(5,000)	40,000
Goodwill	440,000	-	-	440,000
Total	$400,000	($5,000)	$5,000	$400,000

CONSOLIDATION ENTRIES
Price Differential - Collapsing Entries

Retained Earnings	5,000	
Interest Expense	5,000	
LT Liabilities	40,000	
Goodwill	440,000	
Buildings		80,000
Depreciation Expense		10,000
Investment in Subsidiary		400,000

WHOLLY OWNED SUBSIDIARIES: REPORTING SUBSEQUENT TO ACQUISITION
Module 4 - Recap

- **4** REVIEW QUESTIONS
- **5** QUIZ QUESTIONS
- **6** KEY TERMS INTRODUCED IN THIS MODULE
- **7** RECAP ON THE OBJECTIVES OF THIS MODULE

PART 4
Review Questions

Part 4

1. Define or explain the following terms:
   - Price differential amortization
   - Goodwill impairment
   - Net adjusted value of Subsidiary since acquisition

2. How is goodwill arising from a business combination accounted for in time periods subsequent to acquisition?

3. Describe the steps that may be required to determine if goodwill has been impaired?

4. In what general ways will consolidation of a wholly owned subsidiary differ from consolidation of a parent founded subsidiary?

5. Why are purchase price differentials amortized in consolidation periods subsequent to the date of acquisition?

REVIEW QUESTIONS
(continued...)

6. What type of adjustment must be made in preparing the consolidation workpaper if a differential is assigned to land and the subsidiary disposes of the land in the current period?

7. What type of adjustment must be made in preparing the consolidation workpaper if a differential is assigned to inventory and the subsidiary disposes of the inventory in the current period?

8. What type of adjustment must be made in preparing the consolidation workpaper if a differential is assigned to land and the subsidiary disposed of the land in a prior period?

9. What type of adjustment must be made in preparing the consolidation workpaper if a differential is assigned to inventory and the subsidiary disposed of the inventory in a prior period?

PART 5
Quiz Questions

On December 31, X8, Large Inc. acquired all the outstanding voting shares of Small Inc. for $250,000. At the date of acquisition, Small had Common Shares and Retained Earnings of $100,000 and $50,000, respectively. Small's plant assets have a market value $60,000 greater than book value and an estimated remaining economic life of six years (straight line).

In post-acquisition periods, Small had the following earnings and paid the following dividends:

Year	Comprehensive income	Dividends
X9	$30,000	$8,000
X10	25,000	10,000
X11	50,000	20,000

Large's equity section at the end of year X11 consists of Common Shares of $800,000 and Retained Earnings of $350,000. Large's comprehensive income and dividends declared for X11 amount to $150,000 and $50,000, respectively.

With the exception of intercompany dividends, Large and Small did not engage in transactions amongst themselves. In addition, Goodwill has not been impaired.

Part 5

QUIZ QUESTIONS

1

Provide the purchase price allocation. Complete the following table.

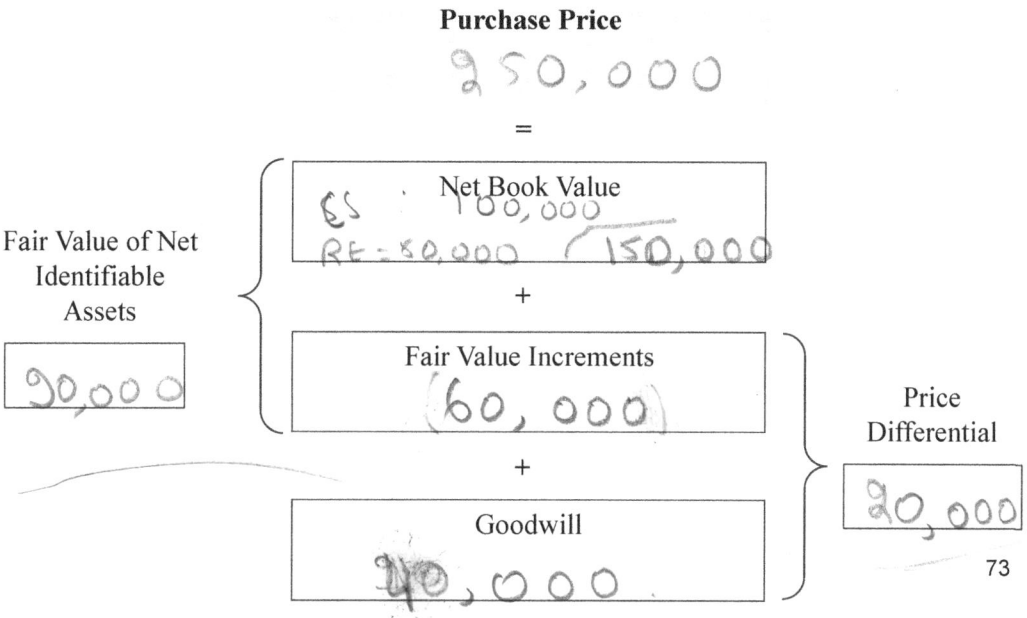

Purchase Price 250,000

Fair Value of Net Identifiable Assets: 90,000

Net Book Value: CS 100,000 / RE = 50,000 → 150,000

Fair Value Increments: 60,000

Goodwill: 40,000

Price Differential: 20,000

Part 5

QUIZ QUESTIONS

2

Provide the price differential amortization schedule. Complete the following table.

Price Differential Items	Balance at Acquisition	Amortization Prior Years (X9-X10)	Amortization Current Year (X11)	Unamortized Excess at December 31, X11
Plant	60,000	(10,000)	(10,000)	40,000
Goodwill	40,000			40,000
Total	100,000	(10,000)	(10,000)	80,000

60,000 ÷ 6 years = 10,000

Wholly Owned Subsidiaries ---------- Module 4 ----------

Part 5

QUIZ QUESTIONS

3

Compute the net adjusted value of Small at December 31, X11. Complete the following table.

	Individual Records of Subsidiary	Consolidation Adjustments	
At Date of Acquisition December 31, X8	Net Book Value 150,000	Purchase Price Differential 100,000	Purchase Price 250,000
Since Acquisition	Retained Earnings Increase 67,000	Price Differential Amortization (20,000)	Net Adjusted Value Increase 47,000
At December 31, X11	Net Book Value 217,000	Unamortized Portion of Price Differential 80,000	Net Adjusted Value 297,000

67,000   297,000

= Comprehensive income − Dividend

Part 5

QUIZ QUESTIONS

4

Assume that Large is using the **equity method** to report its investment in Small. Determine the balance of the investment account on the books of Large at the end of X11.

INITIAL INVESTMENT (X8)	$250,000
SUBSIDIARY'S NET ADJUSTED VALUE SINCE ACQUISITION	47,000
INVESTMENT AT THE END (X11)	297,000

100% Subsidiary net value since Acquisition
       RE increase since Acquisition   67,000
       price differential Amortization   (20,000)
              Total   47,000

QUIZ QUESTIONS

Part 5

5

Assume that Large is using the <u>cost method</u> to report its investment in Small. If the total comprehensive income reported by Large for X11 is $150,000, what amount would be reported had Large been using the equity method instead?

- Comprehensive income for X11 under the cost method $150,000
- *comprehensive for Small*   50,000   *(slide 8)*
- *less dividend X11*   (20,000)
- Comprehensive income for X11 under the equity method   180,000

QUIZ QUESTIONS

Part 5

6

slide 19

Assume that Large is using the <u>cost method</u> to report its investment in Small. Determine the amount that will be reported as *Retained Earnings* in Large's consolidated statement of financial position at the end of X11.

- RE at Dec 31 X0   250,000
- profit for the year
- RE at the end of X11   67,000

RE at Dec X11   317,000

Share of earnings   67,000

Part 5

QUIZ QUESTIONS
7

Assume that Large is using the cost method to report its investment in Small. List the consolidation entries required to eliminate this account for the consolidation of X11.

1a — Double-Counting of $150,000

Dr Common Shares (sub) 100,000
Dr Retained earnings (sub) 50,000
  Cr Investment in subsidiary (parent) 150,000

1b — Price Differential of $100,000

Dr Plant (sub) 60,000
Dr Goodwill (sub) 40,000
  Cr Investment in subsidiary (parent) 100,000

Investment: $250,000

Wholly Owned Subsidiaries — Module 4 — 79

Part 5

QUIZ QUESTIONS
8

List the consolidation entries required to account for price differential amortization since acquisition.

slide 24

Amortization of the Fair Value Increment on Plant Assets since Acquisition

Dr Depreciation expense 10,000
Dr Retained earnings 10,000
  Cr Plant 20,000

Prior Years (X9-X10)

Current Year (X11)

Wholly Owned Subsidiaries — Module 4 — 80

Part 5

QUIZ QUESTIONS
9

Assume that Large is using the equity method to report its investment in Small. Provide the journal entries to account for the investment for X11.

PROPORTIONATE SHARE OF EARNINGS

Dr investment in subsidiary   40,000
  Cr equity in earnings of subsidiary 40,000

100%

PROPORTIONATE SHARE OF DIVIDENDS

Dr investment in subsidiary   20,000
  Cr Dividend declared   20,000

Adjusted profit of subsidiary:
  Profit for sub   50,000
  Amortization   (10,000)
  Total   40,000

297,000
311,000

Part 5

QUIZ QUESTIONS
10

Assume that Large is using the equity method to report its investment in Small. List the consolidation entries required to eliminate this account for the consolidation of X11.

slide 60

1. Dr Common Shares   100,000
   Dr RE   50,000
   Dr plant   60,000
   Dr goodwill   40,000
     Cr investment in subsidiary 250,000

2. Dr RE   27,000   (30,000 - 8000)
     Cr investment in sub. 27,000 + (25K - 10k)
                                   = 31,000
                                   - 10,000
                                   - 17,000

3. Dr equity in earnings 40,000
     Cr investment in subsidiary 40,000

4. Dr equity in earnings 20,000
     Cr investment in sub 20,000

KEY TERMS INTRODUCED IN THIS MODULE

Part 6

> - Price differential amortization
> - Goodwill impairment
> - Net adjusted value of Subsidiary

Part 1

RECAP ON THE OBJECTIVES OF THIS MODULE

Part 7

Part 1 Illustrate the consolidation process of wholly owned subsidiaries in periods subsequent to the date of acquisition. <u>Note</u>: the investment in Subsidiary is accounted for on a cost basis and there are no intercompany transactions.

Illustrate the consolidation process under the worksheet approach and the direct approach as well.

Part 2 Discuss the equity-basis reporting when Parent Company uses the equity method in its separate-entity financial statements: <u>the case of subsidiaries being acquired</u>.

Illustrate the approach to compute the investment in Subsidiary in non-consolidated financial statements under the equity method.

Present the financial reporting implications of using either the cost method, the equity method or full consolidation.

Present the additional consolidation entries required to eliminate the investment account when the equity method is employed by Parent Company in non-consolidated financial statements.

Part 3 Illustrate the impact on consolidation when Fair Value Increments (FVI) and Fair Value Decrements (FVD) affect simultaneously Subsidiary's assets and liabilities at date of combination.

Copyright © 2020, Parmitech, Ottawa. Parmitech. All rights reserved.

Exercise 4-1
Consolidated versus Separate-Entity Statements

Consider the following transactions:

- January 1, X1
  Small Ltd. purchased a truck for $100,000. The useful life of the truck is 10 years.

- December 31, X1
  Total Inc. acquired all the outstanding common shares of Small. The fair value of Small's truck on this date was estimated at $108,000.

Required

Determine the account balances for *Truck* (net value) and *Amortization Expense - Truck* for years X1 and X2 for three sets of financial statements, that is, separate-entity statements for Total and Small and consolidated statements.

Complete the following table.

	Truck (net value)	Amortization expense
December 31, 20X1		
➢ Total	0	0
➢ Small	90,000	10,000
➢ Consolidated	108,000	0
December 31, 20X2		
➢ Total	0	0
➢ Small	80,000	10,000
➢ Consolidated	96,000	12,000

Exercise 4-2
Equity Method Subsequent to Acquisition
(with no intercompany transactions)

On January 01, X3, Supra Ltd acquired 100% of the outstanding common shares of Pen Ltd. On that date, Pen had $12,000 in retained earnings and no subsequent transaction has been reported in its common shares' account.

At the date of acquisition, the book value of each of Pen's assets was equal to its fair market value except for the following:

	Book Value	Fair Value
➢ Inventory	$50,000	$32,000
➢ Patent	- 0 -	14,000

- ➢ The patent had a remaining legal life of 8 years at January 01, X3.
- ➢ The value of goodwill has not been impaired since acquisition.

Required
If Supra Ltd were using the equity method instead of the cost method to report its investment in Pen Ltd:

a) Calculate the amount of Supra's *Investment in Pen* at the end of X7.
b) Calculate Supra's *Equity in Earnings of Pen* for the year ended December 31, X7.
c) Present the journal entries for X7 on the books of Supra under the equity method.

The following presents the financial statements of Supra Ltd and its subsidiary, Pen Ltd as of December 31, X7:

Separate Entity Statements of Financial Position
At December 31, X7

	Supra	Pen
Assets		
Cash	$ 18,100	$ 20,600
Accounts receivable	27,700	55,000
Inventory	35,000	46,000
Investment in Pen (at cost)	161,500	
Land, building and equipment	198,000	104,000
Cumulated depreciation	(86,000)	(30,000)
Total assets	**$354,300**	**$195,600**
Liabilities		
Current liabilities	$ 56,000	$ 70,100
Dividends payable	5,000	5,500
Shareholder's equity		
Share capital	225,000	50,000
Retained earnings (January 01)	45,500	68,000
Net income	42,800	13,000
Dividends	(20,000)	(11,000)
Total liabilities and equity	**$354,300**	**$195,600**

Separate Entity Income Statements
Year Ended December 31, X7

	Supra	Pen
Sales	$534,300	$270,000
Dividend income	11,000	-
	$545,300	$270,000
Cost of goods sold	364,000	206,000
Selling expenses	78,400	24,100
Administrative expenses	60,100	26,900
(including depreciation)	$502,500	$257,000
Profit for the year	**$ 42,800**	**$ 13,000**

Allocation of Purchase Price

Cost of 100% of Pen: 161,500

Book value of Pen:
  Common shares 50,000
  Retained earnings 12,000

Supra's ownership: 62,000

Price differential: 99,500

Allocated:
- inventory 18,000
- patent 14,000   4,000

Balance – goodwill: 103,500

Follow-up on Price Differential

	Balance at acquisition Jan. 1/X3	Amortization X3-X6	Amortization X7	Remaining at Dec. 31/X7
➢ Patent	14,000	(7,000)	(1,750)	5,250
➢ Inventory	(18,000)	18,000	0	0
➢ Goodwill	103,500	—	—	103,500
Total	99,500	11,000	(1,750)	108,750

Investment in Pen

purchase price 161,500

RE increase

Equity in Earnings

net income for sub   13,000
Amortization   1,750
                     _____
                     11,250

Journal Entries

Dr investment in pen   11,250
   Cr equity in earnings   11,250

Dr cash   5,500
Dr AR   5,500
   Cr investment in pen   11,000

Exercise 4-3
Equity Method and Net Adjusted Value Subsequent to Acquisition
(with no intercompany transactions)

On January 1, X3, Grant Corporation bought 100 percent of the outstanding common shares of Lee Company for $100,000 cash. On that date, Lee had $25,000 of common shares outstanding and $30,000 retained earnings. Also on that date, the book value of each of Lee's identifiable assets and liabilities was equal to its fair value except for the following:

	Book Value	Fair Value
➢ Inventory	$50,000	$55,000
➢ Patent	10,000	20,000

The patent had an estimated useful life of 5 years at January 1, X3, and the entire inventory was sold during X3. Grant uses the cost method to account for its investment.

Additional information

1. The fair value of goodwill was determined to be $10,000 on December 31, X6. The impairment occurred in the current period.

2. Grant's accounts receivable contain $30,000 owing from Lee.

3. The affiliated companies did not engage in transactions amongst themselves since acquisition.

4. The balance of Lee's retained earnings at the end of X6 is $75,000. Lee's profit for the year X6 amounts to $30,000.

Required

a) Present the **purchase price allocation** for the above business combination.
b) Provide the **price differential amortization schedule** for the consolidation of Grant as of December 31, X6.
c) Compute the **net adjusted value** of Lee as of December 31, X6.
d) Calculate the balance of Grant's **Investment in Lee** on December 31, X6, under the equity method.
e) Calculate Grant's **Equity in Earnings of Lee** for the year ended December 31, X6.
f) Present the **journal entries** on the books of Grant under the equity method for the year ended December 31, X6.

Price Allocation

purchase price = net Book value + NV in assets + goodwill
100,000 = 55,000 + 15,000 + 30,000

FV identifiable cont. = 40,000
price diff = (15,000)

Schedule - Price Diff.

	Balance at acquisition Jan 1, x3	Amort x3-x5	Am x6	Balance at Dec 31
patent	10,000	(6,000)	(2,000)	2,000
inventory	5,000	5,000	—	—
goodwill	30,000	—	(20,000)	10,000
Total	45,000	(11,000)	(22,000)	12,000

Net Adjusted Value

purchase price   100,000
RE increase   45,000
price diff net of amortization (33,000)
                         _____
                          12,000
NAV   112,000

Investment in Lee under the Equity Method

Same as Before.
112,000.

Equity in Earnings

Dr investment in subsidiary 8,000
   Cr equity in earning   8,000

Journal Entries under the Equity Method

profit 30,000
less amortization for 6 22,000
                      ─────────
                       8,000

Exercise 4-4
Worksheet Approach and Equity Method Subsequent to Acquisition
(with no intercompany transactions)

On June 30, X1, Parent Corporation acquired 100% of the outstanding common shares of Sub Ltd. for $3,350,000 in cash. On the date of acquisition, the fair values and book values of each of Sub's assets were equal, except for inventory that was undervalued by $225,000, and capital assets (net) that were overvalued by $1,000,000. The shareholder's equity of Sub at that time was $3,440,000, consisting of Common Shares of $2,900,000 and Retained Earnings of $540,000.

Statements of financial position at June 30, X5, are as follows:

	Parent Corp.	Sub Ltd.
Assets		
Cash and marketable securities	$4,432,000	$321,000
Accounts and other receivables	2,153,000	950,000
Inventory	1,764,000	1,206,000
Capital assets (net)	17,064,000	7,161,000
Other long-term investments	3,038,000	2,240,000
Investment in Sub Ltd.	3,350,000	-
Total assets	**$34,153,000**	**$11,878,000**
Liabilities		
Current liabilities	$3,025,000	$2,090,000
Mortgage note payable	12,135,000	4,000,000
Total liabilities	15,160,000	6,090,000
Shareholders' equity		
Share capital	10,000,000	2,900,000
Retained earnings	8,993,000	2,888,000
Total shareholders' equity	18,993,000	5,788,000
Total liabilities and shareholders' equity	**$34,153,000**	**$11,878,000**

Additional information

The capital assets that were overvalued on the date of acquisition had a remaining useful life of 20 years. Both companies follow the straight-line method for depreciating capital assets. The controller of Parent has informed that to date, there has been no impairment in goodwill and no intercompany transactions.

Required:

a) Present the consolidation entries required to consolidate the financial statements of Parent Corporation and its subsidiary, Sub Ltd., as of June 30, X5.

b) Had Parent Corporation been using the equity method instead of the cost method to account for its investment in Sub, what would have been the balance of the investment account as of June 30, X5?

Allocation of Purchase Price

Cost of 100% of Sub: **3,350,000**
Book value of Sub:
  Common shares: 2,900,000
  Retained earnings: 510,000

Parent's ownership: 3,440,000
Price differential: 90,000

Allocated:
- (225,000)
- 1,000,000 → 775,000

Balance – goodwill: **685,000**

Follow-up on Price Differential

	Balance at acquisition June 30/X1	Amortization Prior	Amortization Current	Remaining at June 30/X5
➢ Capital assets	(1,000,000)	150,000	50,000	(800,000)
➢ Inventory	225,000	(225,000)	—	—
➢ Goodwill	685,000	—	—	—
Total	(90,000)	(75,000)	50,000	(115,000)

Investment Account

Dr Common Shares 2,900,000
Dr RE 560,000
  Cr investment in parent 3,440,000

Dr inv 225,000
Dr goodwill 685,000
Dr institutional 90,000
  Cr capital asset 1,000,000

Price Differential

Dr RE 225,000
  Cr inventory 225,000

Dr capital assets (sub) 200,000
  Cr RE 150,000
  Cr other expense 50,000

Investment in Sub under the Equity Method

purchase price   3,350,000
increase in RE   2,340,000
price differential amortization (25,000)
                        —————————
                        5,673,000

Solutions to Exercises

4-1

	Truck (net value)	Amortization expense
December 31, X1		
• Total	0	0
• Small	$90,000	$10,000
• Consolidated	$108,000	0
December 31, X2		
• Total	0	0
• Small	$80,000	$10,000
• Consolidated	$96,000	$12,000

4-2

Note 1: Allocation of purchase price

Cost of 100% of Pen		$161,500
Book value of Pen:		
Common shares	$50,000	
Retained earnings	12,000	62,000
Price differential		99,500
Allocated:		
♦ Patent	(14,000)	
♦ Inventory	18,000	4,000
Balance – goodwill		$103,500

Note 2: Purchase discrepancy amortization schedule

	Balance at acquisition Jan. 1/X3	Amortization X3-X6	Amortization X7	Remaining at Dec. 31/X7
Patent (Note 1)	$14,000	$(7,000)	$(1,750)	$5,250
Inventory (Note 1)	(18,000)	18,000	-	-
Goodwill (Note 1)	103,500	-	-	103,500
Total	$99,500	$11,000	$(1,750)	$108,750

a) Balance of the investment account on equity basis as of December 31, X7

Purchase price		$161,500
Net adjusted value of Pen since acquisition:		
• RE increase since acquisition ($70,000 - $12,000)	$58,000	
• Price differential amortization since acquisition	9,250	67,250
Total		**$228,750**

b) Equity in Earnings of Pen for X7

Supra's share (100%) of Pen adjusted profit:		
• Pen's profit for the year	$13,000	
• Current-year price differential amortization (Note 2)	(1,750)	**$11,250**

c) Journal entries for X7

Investment in Pen	11,250	
Equity in Earnings of Pen		11,250
Cash	5,500	
Acc. Receivable	5,500	
Investment in Pen		11,000

4-3

a) Allocation of purchase price

Cost of 100% of Lee		$100,000
Book value of Lee:		
Common shares	$25,000	
Retained earnings	30,000	
	55,000	
Grant's ownership	100%	55,000
Price differential		45,000
Allocated:		
• Patent	(5,000)	
• Inventory	(10,000)	(15,000)
Balance – goodwill		$30,000

b) Purchase discrepancy amortization schedule

	Balance at acquisition Jan. 1/X3	Amortization X3-X5	Amortization X6	Remaining at Dec.31/X6
Patent	$10,000	$(6,000)	$(2,000)	$2,000
Inventory	5,000	(5,000)	-	-
Goodwill	30,000	-	(20,000)	10,000
Total	**$45,000**	**$(11,000)**	**$(22,000)**	**$12,000**

c) Net adjusted value of Lee

Purchase price		$100,000
Net adjusted value of Lee since acquisition:		
• RE increase since acquisition ($75,000 - $30,000)	45,000	
• Price differential amortization since acquisition	(33,000)	12,000
Total		**$112,000**

d) Balance of the investment account on equity basis as of December 31, X6

Initial investment		$100,000
Net adjusted value of Lee since acquisition:		
• RE increase since acquisition ($75,000 - $30,000)	45,000	
• Price differential amortization since acquisition	(33,000)	12,000
Total		**$112,000**

e) Equity in Earnings of Lee for X6

Grant's share (100%) of Lee adjusted profit:
• Lee's profit for the year	$30,000	
• Current-year price differential amortization	(22,000)	**$8,000**

f) Journal entry for X6

Investment in Lee	8,000	
Equity in Earnings of Lee		8,000

4-4

Note 1: Allocation of purchase price

Cost of 100% of Sub		$3,350,000
Book value of Sub:		
Common shares	$2,900,000	
Retained earnings	540,000	
	3,440,000	
Parent's ownership	100%	3,440,000
Price differential		(90,000)
Allocated:		
◆ Inventory.	(225,000)	
◆ Capital assets	1,000,000	775,000
Balance – goodwill		**$685,000**

Note 2: Purchase discrepancy amortization schedule

	Balance at acquisition June 30, X1	Amortization Prior	Amortization Current	Remaining at June 30, X5
Capital assets (Note 1)	$(1,000,000)	$150,000	$50,000	$(800,000)
Inventory (Note 1)	225,000	(225,000)	-	-
Goodwill (Note 1)	685,000	-	-	685,000
Total	**$(90,000)**	**$(75,000)**	**$50,000**	**$(115,000)**

a) Consolidation entries

Investment account

To eliminate reciprocal investment and equity accounts at the date of acquisition.
Common Shares (Sub)	2,900,000	
Retained Earnings (Sub)	540,000	
Investment in Sub (Parent)		3,440,000

To allocate the price differential.
Inventory (Sub)	225,000	
Goodwill	685,000	
Investment in Sub (Parent)	90,000	
Capital Assets (Sub)		1,000,000

Price differential amortization		
To recognize prior-year realization of the fair value increment on inventory.		
Retained Earnings (Sub)	225,000	
Inventory (Sub)		225,000
To amortize the fair value decrement on Capital Assets.		
Capital Assets (Sub)	200,000	
Retained Earnings (Sub)		150,000
Other Expenses (Sub)		50,000

b) Balance of the investment account under the equity method.

Purchase price		$3,350,000
Net adjusted value of Sub since acquisition:		
• RE increase since acquisition ($2,888,000 - $540,000)	2,348,000	
• Price differential amortization since acquisition	(25,000)	2,323,000
Total		**$5,673,000**

Intercompany Transactions

Module 5

What you will find in this section

- How to Walk Through Module 5
- Slides
- Exercises and Solutions

Module 5
Intercompany Transactions

How to Walk Through Module 5

◇ Readings

1- Book "Consolidation of Financial Statements": Chapters 5, 6 and 7
2- Student Manual "Advanced Accounting": Module 5
   PART 1: INTERCOMPANY TRANSACTIONS: BASIC PRINCIPLES
   PART 2: INTERCOMPANY SALES OF NON-DEPRECIABLE ASSETS
   PART 3: INTERCOMPANY SALES OF INVENTORY
   PART 4: INTERCOMPANY SALES OF DEPRECIABLE ASSETS
   PART 5: INTERCOMPANY LOSSES

◇ Assignments

3- Student Manual: End-of module review and quiz questions
4- Student Manual: Exercises 1 to 12

When you have successfully completed this module, you will be able to do the following:

- Discuss the basic principles supporting adjustments for intercompany transactions when preparing consolidated financial statements;

- Illustrate and account for the effect of intercompany transactions on the consolidation process for transfers involving non-depreciable assets, inventory and depreciable assets.

INTERCOMPANY TRANSACTIONS
Module 5

Copyright © 2020 Parmitech

Advanced Accounting: Student Manual

Copyrighted Material

Editor: Parmitech

This publication is protected by copyright, and permission should be obtained from the publisher prior to any prohibited reproduction, storage in a retrieval system, or transmission in any form or by any means, electronic, mechanical, photocopying, recording, or otherwise.

Corresponding Author

Richard Bozec Ph.D., CPA, CGA
bozec@telfer.uottawa.ca

Copyright © Parmitech

CORRESPONDING CHAPTERS in *Bozec*
"Consolidation of Financial Statements under IFRS"

Chapter 5	Intercompany Sales of Land
Chapter 6	Intercompany Sales of Inventory
Chapter 7	Intercompany Sales of Depreciable Assets

TEACHING MATERIAL
Exercises

Module 5

5.1	Downstream Sale of Truck
5.2	Upstream Sale of Land
5.3	Downstream Sale of Equipment (1)
5.4	Downstream Sale of Equipment (2)
5.5	Upstream Sale of Equipment & Consolidated Comprehensive Income
5.6	Downstream Sale of Land & Consolidated Comprehensive Income
5.7	Downstream Sale of Inventory
5.8	Upstream Sale of Inventory
5.9	Consolidated versus Separate-Entity Statements
5.10	Intercompany Transactions and Worksheet Adjustments (1)
5.11	Intercompany Transactions and Worksheet Adjustments (2)

FOCUS OF THIS MODULE:
INTERCOMPANY TRANSACTIONS

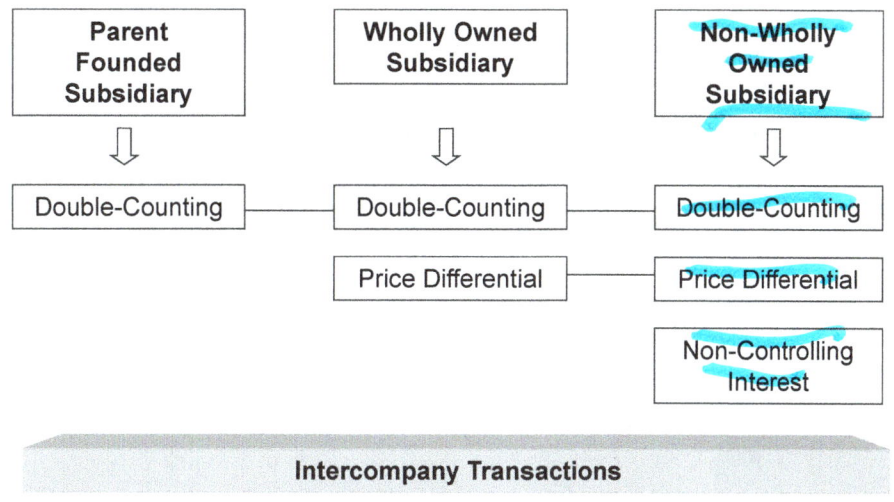

OUTLINE OF THE PRESENTATION

1. INTERCOMPANY TRANSACTIONS: BASIC PRINCIPLES
2. INTERCOMPANY SALES OF NON-DEPRECIABLE ASSETS
3. INTERCOMPANY SALES OF INVENTORY
4. INTERCOMPANY SALES OF DEPRECIABLE ASSETS
5. INTERCOMPANY LOSSES

RECAP

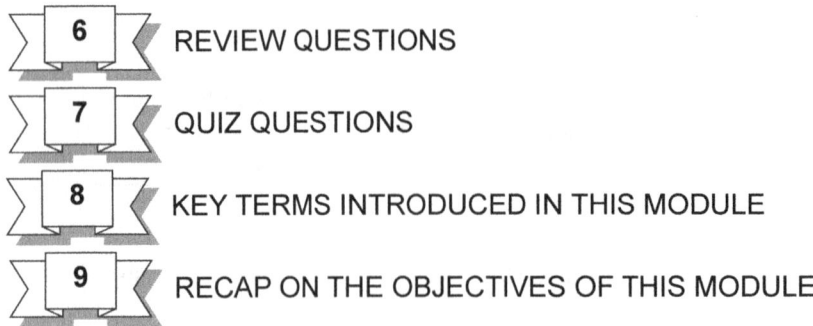

- **6** REVIEW QUESTIONS
- **7** QUIZ QUESTIONS
- **8** KEY TERMS INTRODUCED IN THIS MODULE
- **9** RECAP ON THE OBJECTIVES OF THIS MODULE

Intercompany Transactions ---------- Module 5 ---------- 7

PART 1

Intercompany Transactions: Basic Principles

Objective of this section

Introduce the basic principles supporting adjustments for intercompany transactions when preparing consolidated financial statements.

Key concepts

- Unrealized gain
- Unrealized loss
- Realization of intercompany gains and losses

Intercompany Transactions ---------- Module 5 ---------- 8

INTERCOMPANY SALES
Viewpoint of the Economic Entity

Part 1

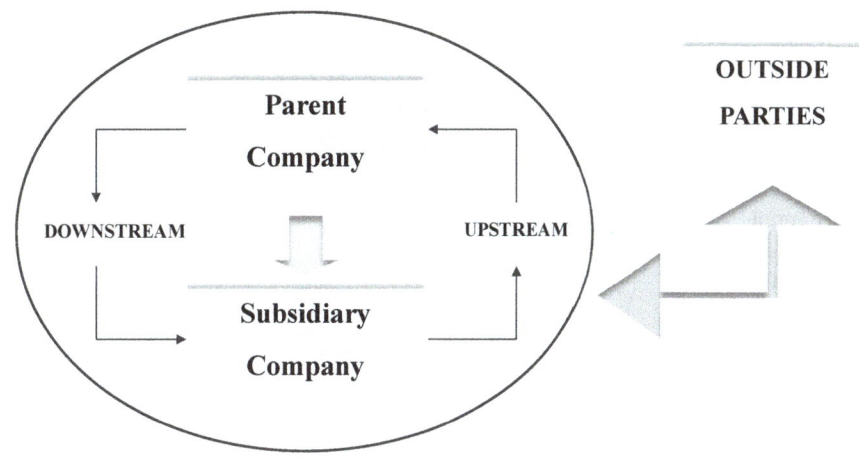

Recall that consolidated F/S must reflect only the results of transactions with outside parties.

INTERCOMPANY SALES
General Rule for Gains

Part 1

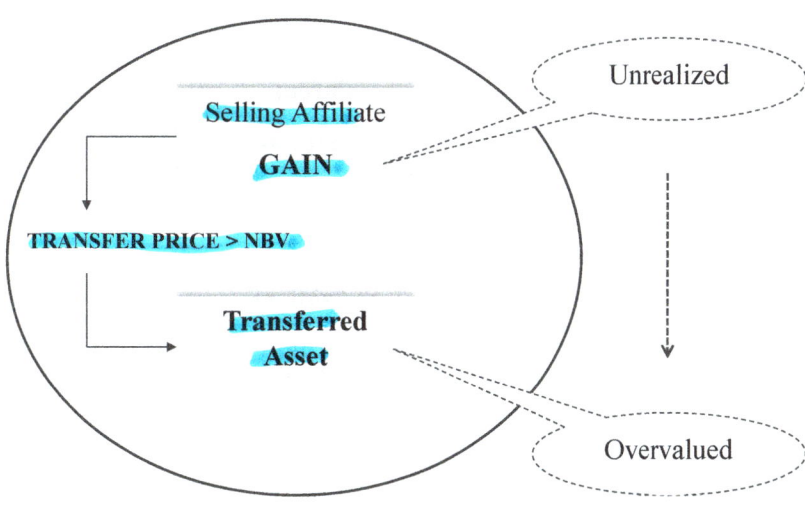

In this case, the **intercompany gain** must be removed, and the value of the transferred asset returned to its original cost (**downward** adjustment).

INTERCOMPANY SALES
General Rule for Losses

Part 1

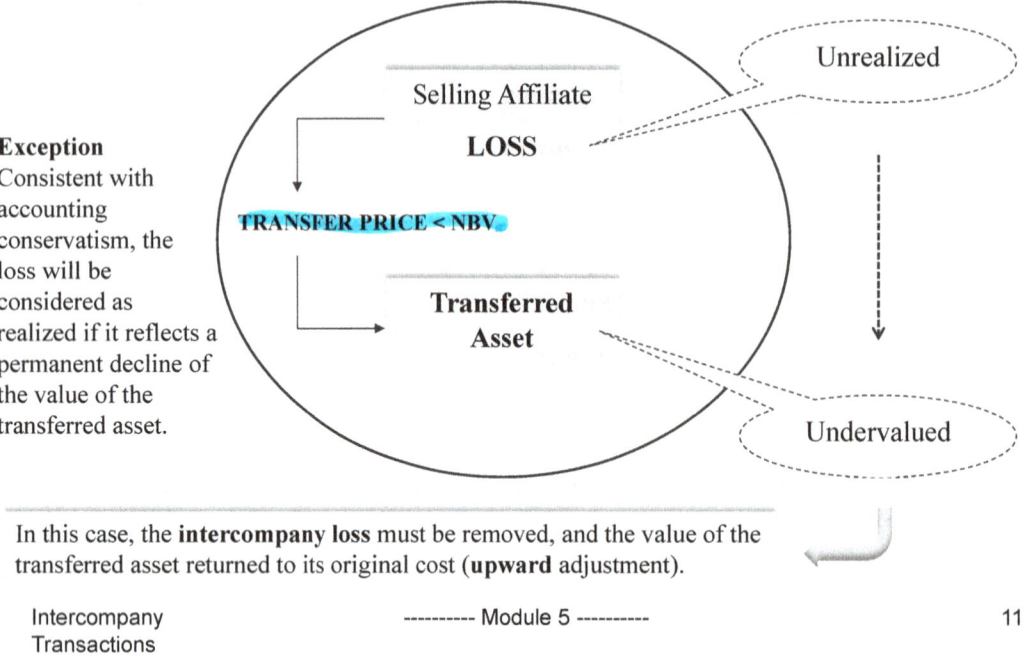

Exception
Consistent with accounting conservatism, the loss will be considered as realized if it reflects a permanent decline of the value of the transferred asset.

In this case, the **intercompany loss** must be removed, and the value of the transferred asset returned to its original cost (**upward** adjustment).

Intercompany Transactions — Module 5 — 11

INTERCOMPANY SALES
Unrealized Gains and Losses: What to Do Next?

Part 1

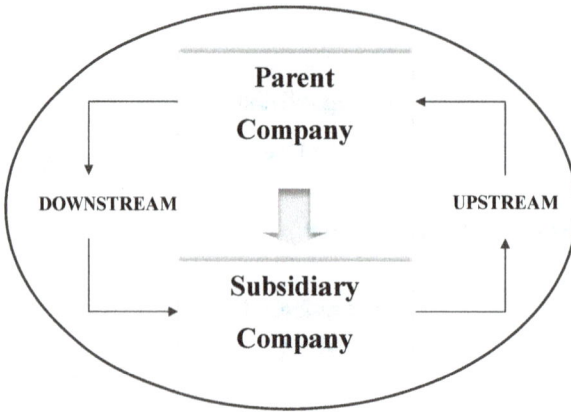

Having recognized a gain or a loss as being unrealized for consolidation purposes prompts the question of when and how will the intercompany gain or loss be realized. Realization depends ultimately on the type of assets being transferred.

Intercompany Transactions — Module 5 — 12

INTERCOMPANY SALES
Type of Assets

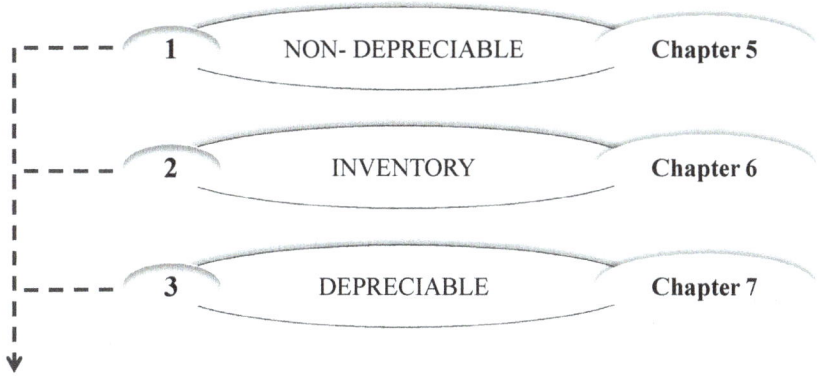

As a general rule, intercompany gains and losses will be realized through consolidation whenever the asset being transferred is resold to an outside party (most likely scenario for merchandise) or used by the purchasing affiliate to generate revenue (most likely scenario for depreciable assets).

INTERCORPORATE SALES OF ASSETS
Impact on the Consolidation Process

Type of Assets	Characteristics	Intercorporate Gain or Loss
Non-Depreciable Assets (Land)	Use to generate revenue or as an investment	Unrealized until the asset is sold to an outsider (could take many years)
Inventory	Use within company's operations or resold to external parties	Unrealized until the asset is sold to an outsider (usually within one year)
Depreciable Assets	Use to generate revenue	Is being realized over the remaining useful life of the asset

PART 1
Concept Check

> Describe how intercompany gains and losses are being realized for consolidation purposes.

_____
_____
_____
_____
_____
_____
_____

Intercompany Transactions ---------- Module 5 ---------- 15

OUTLINE OF THE PRESENTATION

1. INTERCOMPANY TRANSACTIONS: BASIC PRINCIPLES
2. **INTERCOMPANY SALES OF NON-DEPRECIABLE ASSETS**
3. INTERCOMPANY SALES OF INVENTORY
4. INTERCOMPANY SALES OF DEPRECIABLE ASSETS
5. INTERCOMPANY LOSSES

Intercompany Transactions ---------- Module 5 ---------- 16

PART 2

Intercompany Sales of Non-Depreciable Assets

Objectives of this section

Illustrate the effect of intercompany sales of **non-depreciable assets** on the affiliated companies' financial statements.

Illustrate the adjustments required in the consolidation of financial statements when the affiliated companies engaged in intercompany sales of non-depreciable assets.

INTERCOMPANY SALE OF LAND
Illustration

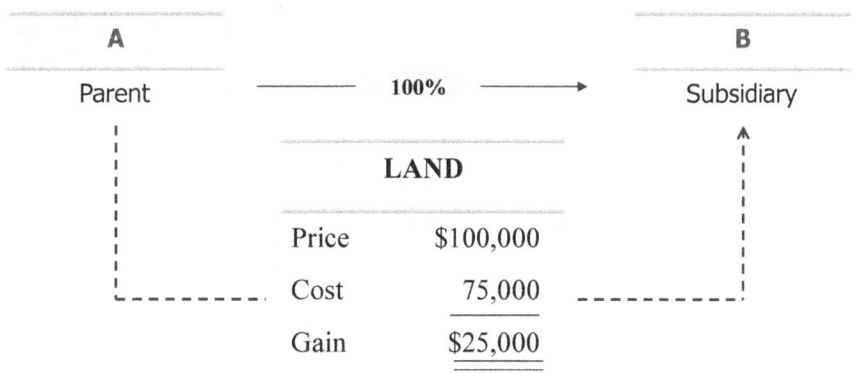

During X1, Parent sold land to Subsidiary for $100,000. The initial cost of the land for Parent is $75,000.

INTERCOMPANY SALE OF LAND
Potential Scenarios

Part 2

	Year of Transfer	Year Subsequent to Year of Transfer
The Land is Held Within the Consolidated Group at the End of the Accounting Period	1	3
The land is Resold by the Purchasing Affiliate to an External Party	2	4

Consolidation adjustments regarding the sale of land will depend on whether the consolidation is conducted for the year of transfer or for a period subsequent to year of transfer, and whether or not the asset has been resold by the purchasing affiliate to an outside party. This leaves us with four potential scenarios. However, scenarios 3 and 4 may only be possible following scenario 1.

INTERCOMPANY SALE OF LAND
Scenario 1

Part 2

	Year of Transfer	Year Subsequent to Year of Transfer
The Land is Held Within the Consolidated Group at the End of the Accounting Period	1	3
The land is Resold by the Purchasing Affiliate to an External Party	2	4

INTERCOMPANY SALES OF LAND
Year of Transfer - No Resale (Scenario 1)

A			B		
Cash	100,000		Land	100,000	
Land		75,000	Cash		100,000
Gain on Sale of Land		25,000			

STATEMENT OF FINANCIAL POSITION
Land: $75,000 → Land: $100,000

STATEMENT OF COMPREHENSIVE INCOME
Gain on sale: $25,000

RETAINED EARNINGS
+ $25,000

STATEMENT OF FINANCIAL POSITION

STATEMENT OF COMPREHENSIVE INCOME

RETAINED EARNINGS

INTERCOMPANY SALE OF LAND
Scenario 1 - Consolidation Entry

Complete this slide

Dr gain   25,000
   u land   25,000

This working paper entry returns the value of the land to its original cost ($75,000) and eliminates the gain on sale ($25,000) recognized by Parent following the downstream transfer. From the viewpoint of the economic entity, this transaction never occurred.

Part 2

INTERCOMPANY SALE OF LAND
Scenario 1 - Impact of the Elimination on the Consolidated F/S

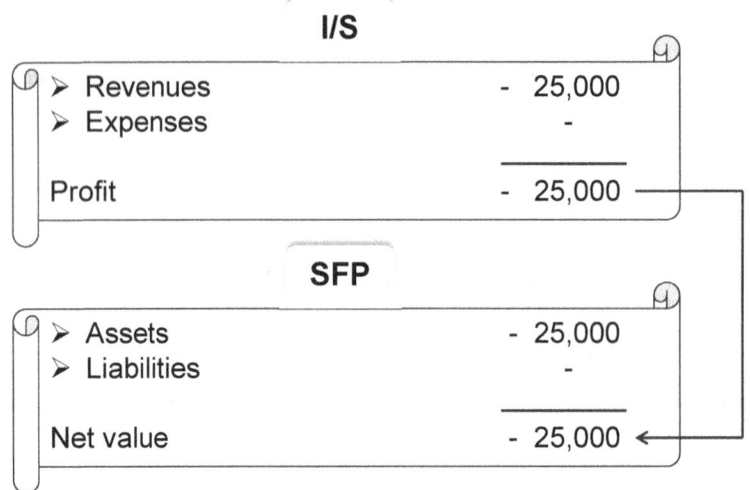

I/S
- Revenues   - 25,000
- Expenses   -
- Profit   - 25,000

SFP
- Assets   - 25,000
- Liabilities   -
- Net value   - 25,000

Part 2

INTERCOMPANY SALE OF LAND
Scenario 2

	Year of Transfer	Year Subsequent to Year of Transfer
The Land is Held Within the Consolidated Group at the End of the Accounting Period	1	3
The land is Resold by the Purchasing Affiliate to an External Party	2	4

INTERCOMPANY SALE OF LAND
Year of Transfer - Resale for $150,000 (Scenario 2)

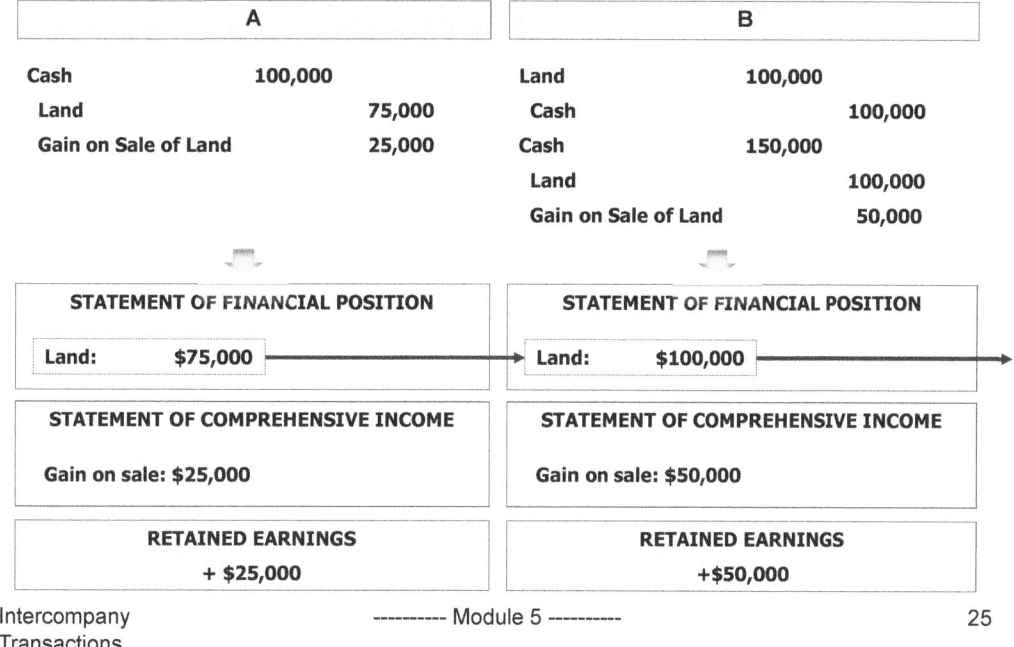

INTERCOMPANY SALE OF LAND
Scenario 2 - Consolidation Entry

NO ENTRY REQUIRED

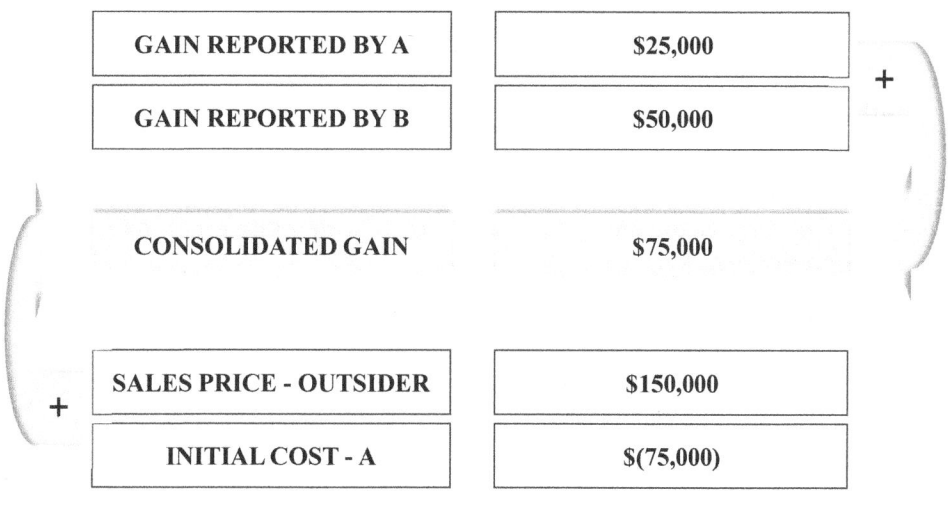

INTERCOMPANY SALE OF LAND
Scenario 3

	Year of Transfer	Year Subsequent to Year of Transfer
The Land is Held Within the Consolidated Group at the End of the Accounting Period	1 ----→	3
The land is Resold by the Purchasing Affiliate to an External Party	2	4

INTERCOMPANY SALE OF LAND
Subsequent Year - No Resale (Scenario 3)

A	B
STATEMENT OF FINANCIAL POSITION	**STATEMENT OF FINANCIAL POSITION** Land: $100,000
STATEMENT OF COMPREHENSIVE INCOME	**STATEMENT OF COMPREHENSIVE INCOME**
RETAINED EARNINGS $25,000 gain from prior year	**RETAINED EARNINGS**

→ The gain recognized by Parent in prior year (X1) is now included in the opening balance of Parent's RE.

INTERCOMPANY SALE OF LAND
Scenario 3 - Consolidation Entry

Part 2

Dr Retained earnings 25,000
   Cr Land   25,000

This consolidation entry removes the unrealized prior-year gain ($25,000) from Parent's opening RE and restates the value of the land to its initial cost for the combined entity ($75,000). We will need to repeat such adjustment in future consolidation exercises for as long as the land is not resold by Subsidiary to an external party.

INTERCOMPANY SALE OF LAND
Scenario 3 - Impact of the Elimination on the Consolidated F/S

Part 2

I/S
- Revenues — -
- Expenses — -
- Profit — -

SFP
- Assets — - 25,000
- Liabilities — -
- Net value — - 25,000

Part 2

INTERCOMPANY SALE OF LAND
Scenario 4

	Year of Transfer	Year Subsequent to Year of Transfer
The Land is Held Within the Consolidated Group at the End of the Accounting Period	1	3
The land is Resold by the Purchasing Affiliate to an External Party	2	4

Intercompany Transactions ---------- Module 5 ---------- 31

Part 2

INTERCOMPANY SALE OF LAND
Subsequent Year - Resale for $150,000 (Scenario 4)

A	B
	Cash 150,000
	Land 100,000
	Gain on Sale of Land 50,000

A:
- STATEMENT OF FINANCIAL POSITION
- STATEMENT OF COMPREHENSIVE INCOME
  - Gain on sale: $25,000
- RETAINED EARNINGS
  - $25,000 gain from prior year

B:
- STATEMENT OF FINANCIAL POSITION
  - Land: $100,000
- STATEMENT OF COMPREHENSIVE INCOME
  - Gain on sale: $50,000
- RETAINED EARNINGS
  - +$50,000

Intercompany Transactions ---------- Module 5 ---------- 32

INTERCOMPANY SALE OF LAND
Scenario 4 - Consolidation Entry

Dr RE   25,000
   Cr gain on sale of land 25,000.

This consolidation entry accounts for the realization of the prior-year gain on intercompany sale of land ($25,000). Note that the adjustment does not affect the consolidated net value (*in and out effect*). Indeed, the gain has only been transferred from the opening balance of RE to the I/S. This way, we synchronize the reporting of the two gains within the same accounting period ($75,000), that is, Parent's gain ($25,000) from year of transfer and Subsidiary's gain ($50,000) from the current period (as if land would have been sold by Parent to an outside party for $150,000 in the current period). Now that the gain is realized, the intercompany sale of land has no impact in future consolidation periods.

INTERCOMPANY SALE OF LAND
Scenario 4 - Impact of the Elimination on the Consolidated F/S

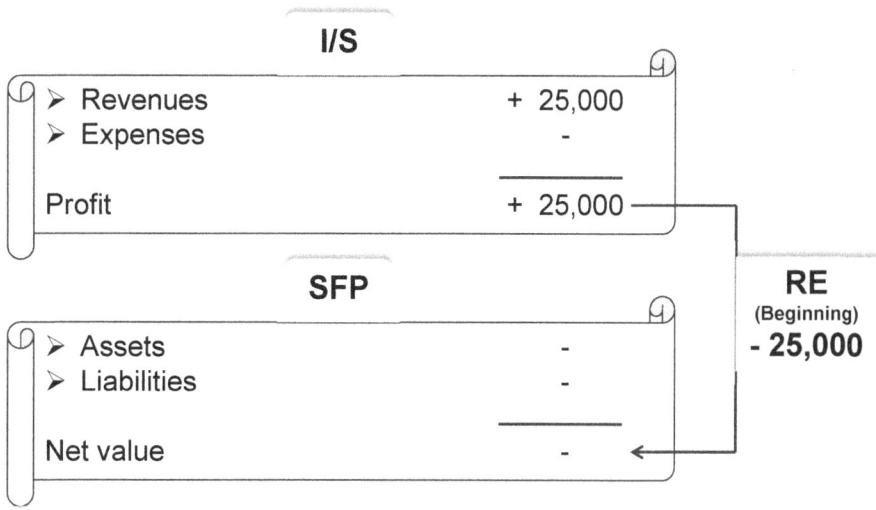

INTERCOMPANY SALE OF LAND
Impact of the Eliminations on the Consolidated F/S - Recap

Part 2

Scenario	RE Beginning	Profit	RE End
Year of transfer			
➢ Scenario 1	-	($25,000)	($25,000)
➢ Scenario 2	-	-	-
Post year of transfer			
➢ Scenario 3	($25,000)	-	(25,000)
➢ Scenario 4	(25,000)	25,000	-

PART 2
Concept Check

Part 2

> What, in general, is the current-year adjustment for consolidation-related adjustments and eliminations made in previous year(s)?

Part 3

OUTLINE OF THE PRESENTATION

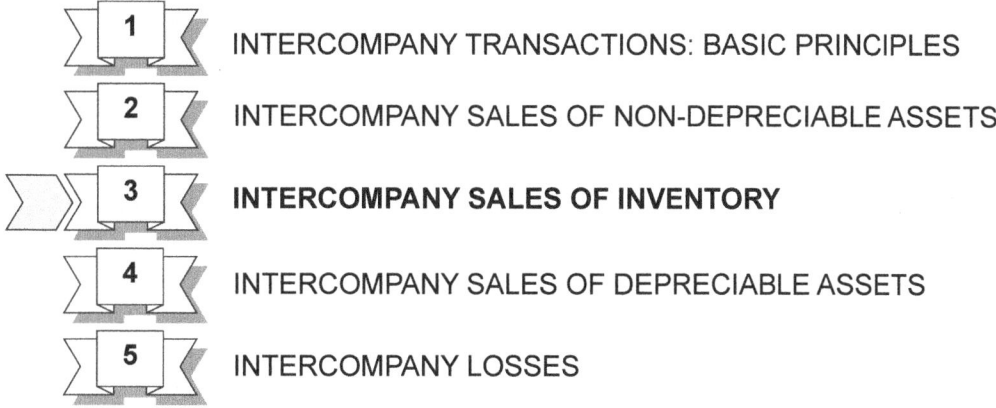

1. INTERCOMPANY TRANSACTIONS: BASIC PRINCIPLES
2. INTERCOMPANY SALES OF NON-DEPRECIABLE ASSETS
3. **INTERCOMPANY SALES OF INVENTORY**
4. INTERCOMPANY SALES OF DEPRECIABLE ASSETS
5. INTERCOMPANY LOSSES

PART 3
Intercompany Sales of Inventory

Objectives of this section

Illustrate the effect of intercompany sales of **inventory** on the affiliated companies' financial statements.

Illustrate the adjustments required in the consolidation of financial statements when the affiliated companies engaged in intercompany sales of inventory.

INTERCOMPANY SALE OF INVENTORY
Illustration

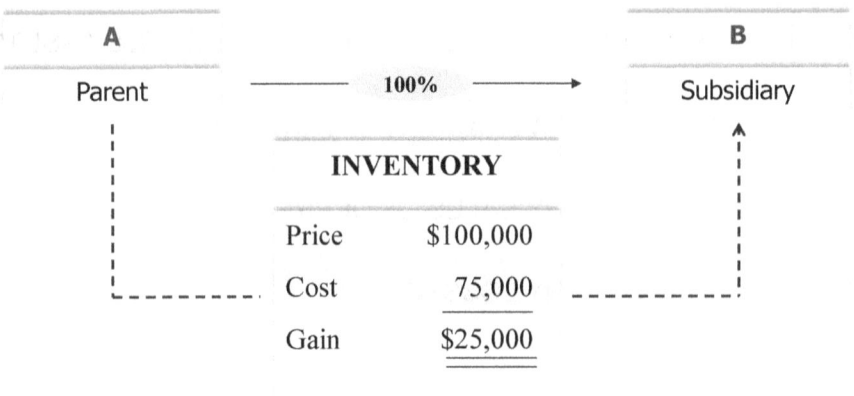

During X1, Parent sold merchandise to Subsidiary for $100,000. The initial cost of the inventory for Parent is $75,000.

INTERCOMPANY SALE OF INVENTORY
Potential Scenarios

	Year of Transfer	Year Subsequent to Year of Transfer
All the Inventory is Held Within the Consolidated Group at the End of the Accounting Period	1	
All the Inventory is Resold by the Purchasing Affiliate to External Parties	2	4
A Portion Only of the Inventory is Resold by the Purchasing Affiliate to External Parties	3	

Assume that any remaining inventory from year of transfer is resold the next year.

INTERCOMPANY SALE OF INVENTORY
Scenario 1

Part 3

	Year of Transfer	Year Subsequent to Year of Transfer
All the Inventory is Held Within the Consolidated Group at the End of the Accounting Period	1	
All the Inventory is Resold by the Purchasing Affiliate to External Parties	2	4
A Portion Only of the Inventory is Resold by the Purchasing Affiliate to External Parties	3	

INTERCOMPANY SALE OF INVENTORY
Year of Transfer - No Resale (Scenario 1)

Part 3

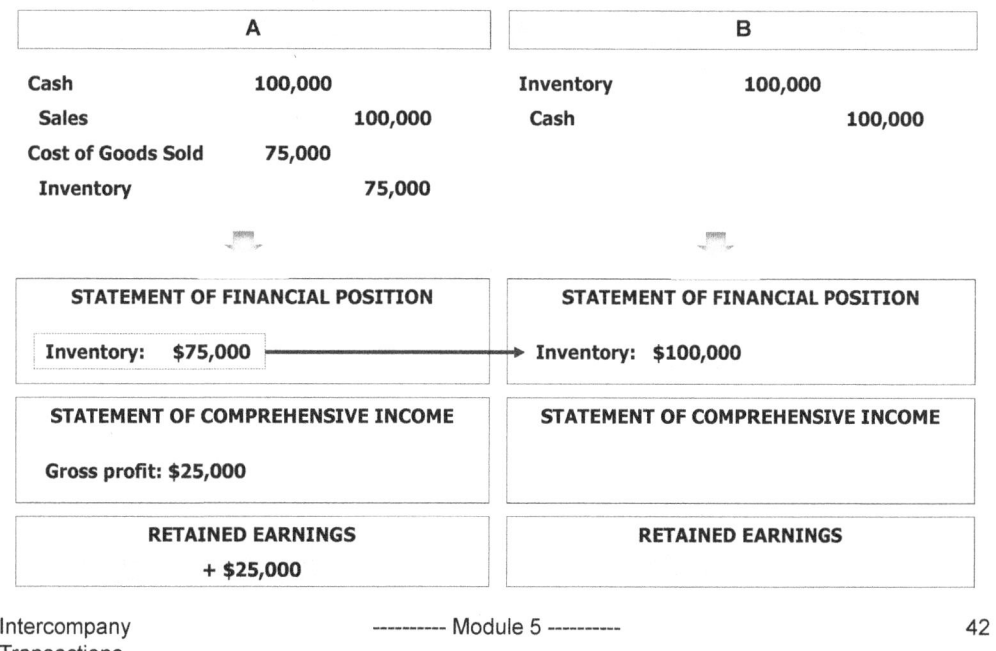

Part 3

INTERCOMPANY SALE OF INVENTORY
Scenario 1 - Consolidation Entry

Sales (A)	100,000	
Cost of Goods Sold (A)		75,000
Inventory (B)		25,000

Same as in Module 2
We must return the value of the transferred inventory to its original cost for Parent ($75,000) and eliminate the profit ($25,000) recognized by Parent following the transfer. The unrealized profit is eliminated while decreasing Sales by $100,000 and COGS by $75,000.

Intercompany Transactions — Module 5 —

Part 3

INTERCOMPANY SALE OF INVENTORY
Scenario 1 - Impact of the Elimination on the Consolidated F/S

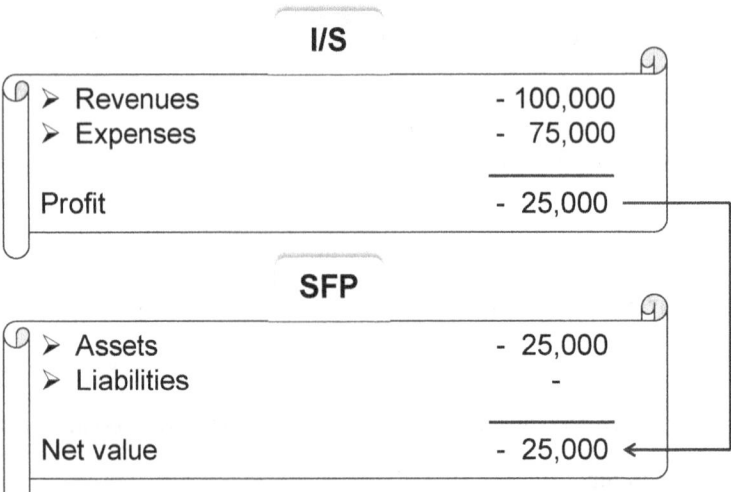

I/S
- Revenues   - 100,000
- Expenses   - 75,000

Profit   - 25,000

SFP
- Assets   - 25,000
- Liabilities   -

Net value   - 25,000

Intercompany Transactions — Module 5 —

INTERCOMPANY SALE OF INVENTORY
Scenario 2

Part 3

	Year of Transfer	Year Subsequent to Year of Transfer
All the Inventory is Held Within the Consolidated Group at the End of the Accounting Period	1	
All the Inventory is Resold by the Purchasing Affiliate to External Parties	2	4
A Portion Only of the Inventory is Resold by the Purchasing Affiliate to External Parties	3	

Intercompany Transactions — Module 5 — 45

INTERCOMPANY SALE OF INVENTORY
Year of Transfer - Resale for $150,000 (Scenario 2)

Part 3

A
Cash	100,000
Sales	100,000
Cost of Goods Sold	75,000
Inventory	75,000

B
Inventory	100,000
Cash	100,000
Cash	150,000
Sales	150,000
Cost of Goods Sold	100,000
Inventory	100,000

STATEMENT OF FINANCIAL POSITION
Inventory: $75,000

STATEMENT OF FINANCIAL POSITION
Inventory: $100,000

STATEMENT OF COMPREHENSIVE INCOME
Gross profit: $25,000

STATEMENT OF COMPREHENSIVE INCOME
Gross profit: $50,000

RETAINED EARNINGS
+ $25,000

RETAINED EARNINGS
+ $50,000

Intercompany Transactions — Module 5 — 46

Part 3

INTERCOMPANY SALE OF INVENTORY
Scenario 2 - Reciprocal Balances

Parent sold merchandise to Subsidiary for $100,000, all of which was sold by Subsidiary for $150,000 to external parties prior to the end of the current accounting period. The cost of sales for Parent amounts to $75,000.

	A	B	Total
Sales	$100,000	$150,000	$250,000
Cost of sales	75,000	100,000	175,000
	$25,000	$50,000	$75,000

Intercompany Transactions — Module 5 — 47

Part 3

INTERCOMPANY SALE OF INVENTORY
Scenario 2 - Consolidation Entry

Sales (A)	100,000	
Cost of Goods Sold (B)		100,000

Same as in Module 2

Recall that the sale and resale of merchandise within the same accounting period create an overstatement of *Sales* and *Cost of Goods Sold*. Such excess is equal to the transfer price of the units being resold ($100,000). However, no adjustment is required in the consolidated SFP.

Intercompany Transactions — Module 5 — 48

Part 3

INTERCOMPANY SALE OF INVENTORY
Scenario 2 - Impact of the Elimination on the Consolidated F/S

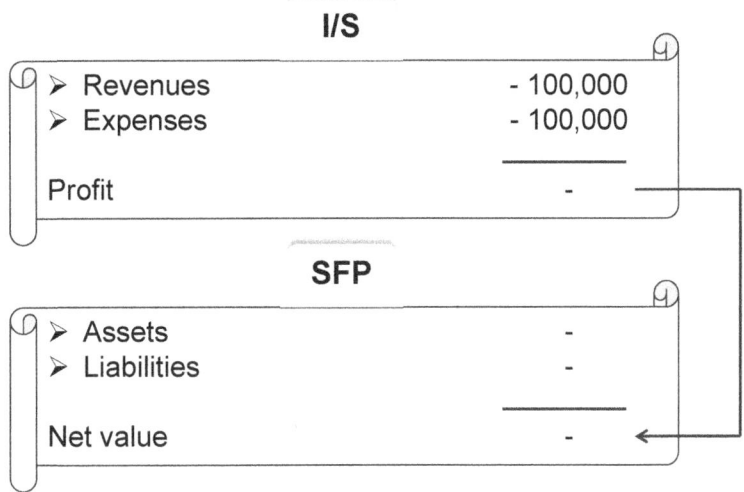

I/S
- Revenues   - 100,000
- Expenses   - 100,000

Profit   —

SFP
- Assets   —
- Liabilities   —

Net value   —

Intercompany Transactions — Module 5 — 49

Part 3

INTERCOMPANY SALE OF INVENTORY
Scenario 3

	Year of Transfer	Year Subsequent to Year of Transfer
All the Inventory is Held Within the Consolidated Group at the End of the Accounting Period	1	
All the Inventory is Resold by the Purchasing Affiliate to External Parties	2	4
A Portion Only of the Inventory is Resold by the Purchasing Affiliate to External Parties	3	

Intercompany Transactions — Module 5 — 50

INTERCOMPANY SALE OF INVENTORY
Year of Transfer - Resale of 75% for $110,000 (Scenario 3)

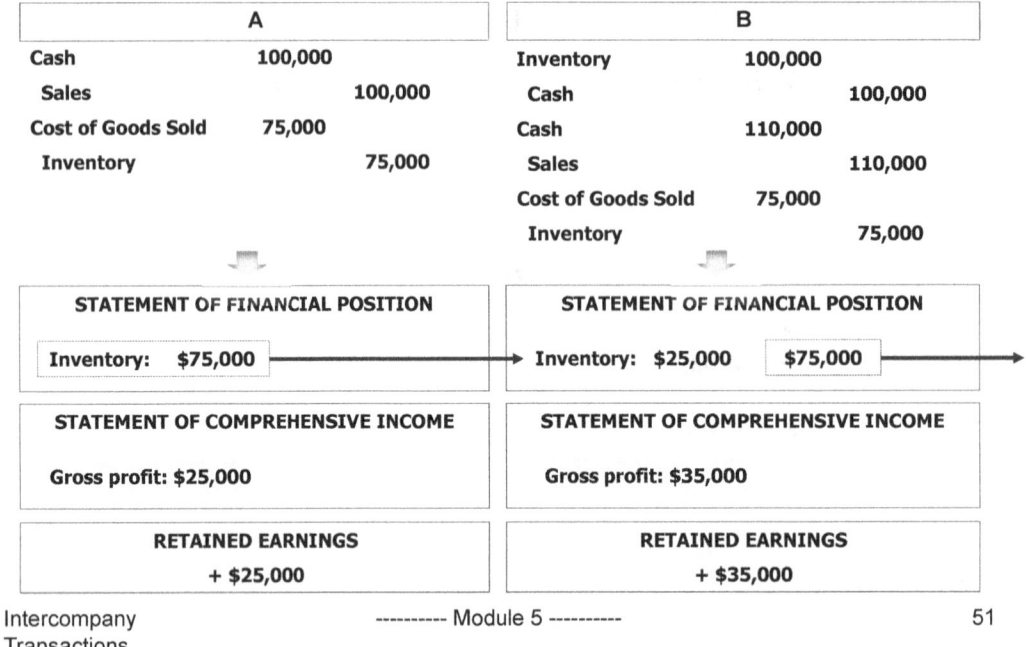

INTERCOMPANY SALE OF INVENTORY
Scenario 3 - Consolidation Issues

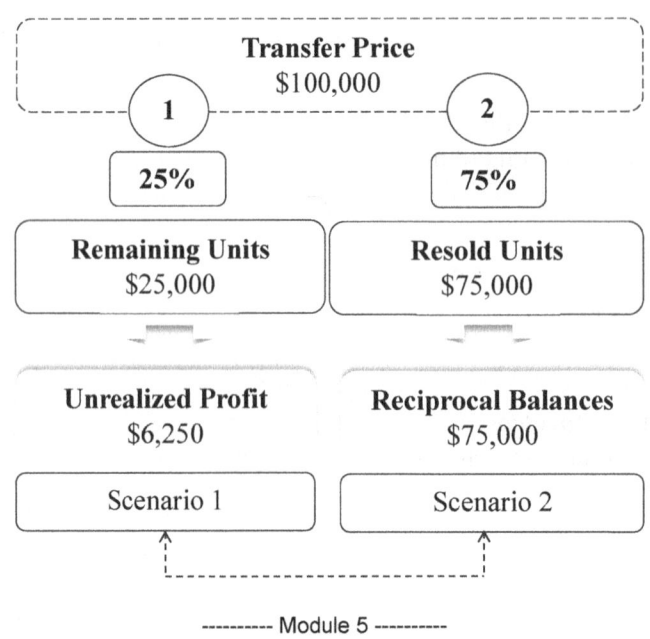

INTERCOMPANY SALE OF INVENTORY
Scenario 3 - Unrealized Profit and Reciprocal Balances

Parent sold merchandise to Subsidiary for $100,000. 75% of the transferred units is resold by Subsidiary for $110,000 prior to the end of the current accounting period. The cost of sales for Parent amounts to $75,000.

	A Units sold to B and Held by B (25%)	A Resold by B (75%)	B
Sales	$25,000	$75,000	$110,000
Cost of sales	18,750	56,250	75,000
Profit (25%)	$6,250	$18,750	$35,000

↑ Unrealized Profit   ↑ Realized Profits

INTERCOMPANY SALE OF INVENTORY
Scenario 3 - Consolidation Entries

Complete this slide

Unrealized Profit (1) — Scenario 1

Sales (A)	25,000	
Cost of Goods Sold (A)		18,750
Inventory (B)		6,250

Reciprocal Balances (2) — Scenario 2

Sales (A)	75,000	
Cost of Goods Sold (B)		75,000

Combined Entry (1+ 2) — Scenario 3

Dr Sales 100,000
   Cr COGS   93,750
   Cr Inventory 6,250

Part 3

INTERCOMPANY SALE OF INVENTORY
Scenario 3 - Impact of the Elimination on the Consolidated F/S

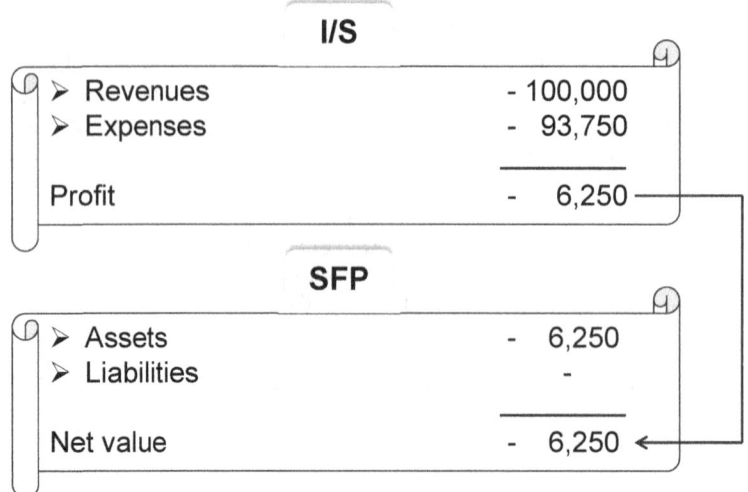

I/S
- Revenues   - 100,000
- Expenses   - 93,750

Profit   - 6,250

SFP
- Assets   - 6,250
- Liabilities   -

Net value   - 6,250

Intercompany Transactions — Module 5 — 55

Part 3

INTERCOMPANY SALE OF INVENTORY
Scenario 4 (from scenario 1)

	Year of Transfer	Year Subsequent to Year of Transfer
All the Inventory is Held Within the Consolidated Group at the End of the Accounting Period	1	
All the Inventory is Resold by the Purchasing Affiliate to External Parties	2	4
A Portion Only of the Inventory is Resold by the Purchasing Affiliate to External Parties	3	

Intercompany Transactions — Module 5 — 56

Part 3

INTERCOMPANY SALE OF INVENTORY
Subsequent Year - Resale for $150,000

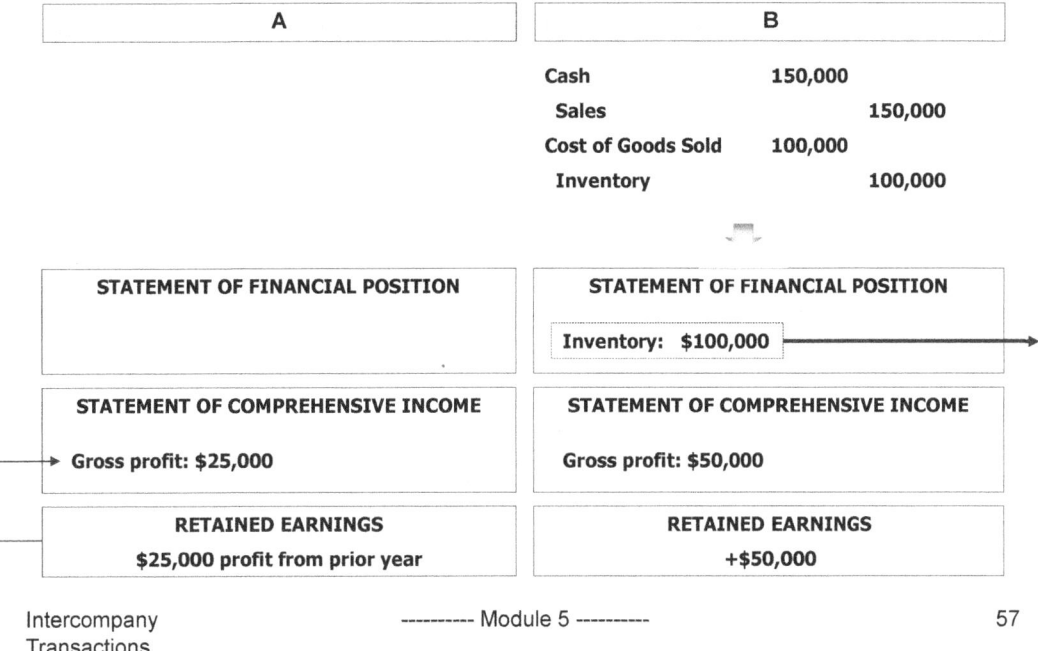

A	B
	Cash 150,000
	Sales 150,000
	Cost of Goods Sold 100,000
	Inventory 100,000

STATEMENT OF FINANCIAL POSITION | **STATEMENT OF FINANCIAL POSITION**
Inventory: $100,000

STATEMENT OF COMPREHENSIVE INCOME | **STATEMENT OF COMPREHENSIVE INCOME**
Gross profit: $25,000 | Gross profit: $50,000

RETAINED EARNINGS | **RETAINED EARNINGS**
$25,000 profit from prior year | +$50,000

Intercompany Transactions — Module 5 — 57

Part 3

Complete this slide

INTERCOMPANY SALE OF INVENTORY
Scenario 4 - Consolidation Entry

Dr RE   25,000
    Cr COGS   25,000

Since the beginning inventory ($100,000) contains the prior-year unrealized profit ($25,000), the cost of sales of the current period is inflated following the resale by Subsidiary. Therefore, we recognize prior-year profit by decreasing current-year COGS.

Intercompany Transactions — Module 5 — 58

INTERCOMPANY SALE OF INVENTORY
Scenario 4 - Impact of the Elimination on the Consolidated F/S

Part 3

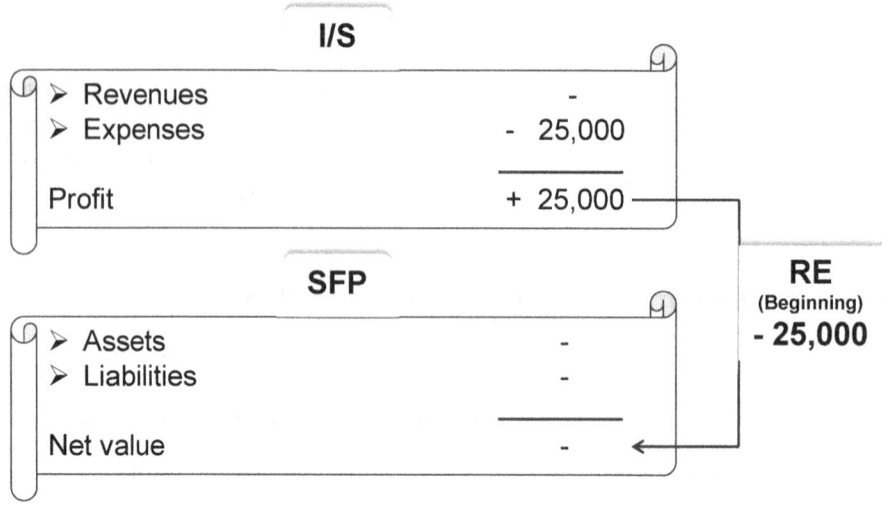

I/S
- Revenues — -
- Expenses — - 25,000

Profit — + 25,000

SFP
- Assets — -
- Liabilities — -

Net value — -

RE (Beginning) - 25,000

INTERCOMPANY SALE OF INVENTORY
Scenario 4 (from scenario 3)

Part 3

	Year of Transfer	Year Subsequent to Year of Transfer
All the Inventory is Held Within the Consolidated Group at the End of the Accounting Period	1	
All the Inventory is Resold by the Purchasing Affiliate to External Parties	2	4
A Portion Only of the Inventory is Resold by the Purchasing Affiliate to External Parties	3	

INTERCOMPANY SALE OF INVENTORY
Subsequent Year - Resale of Remaining Units for $35,000

A	B

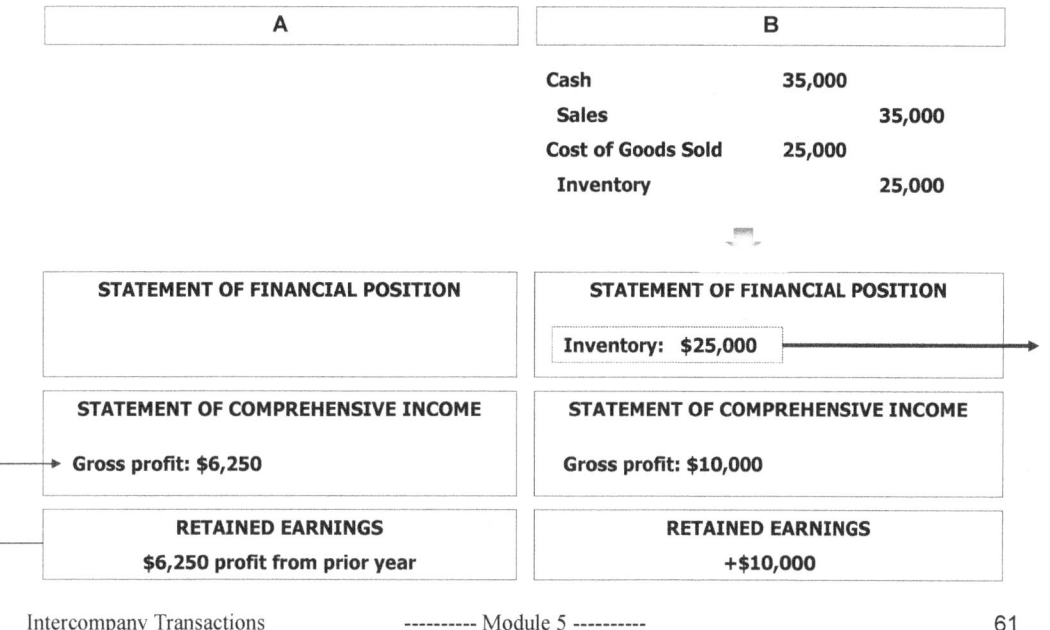

STATEMENT OF FINANCIAL POSITION	STATEMENT OF FINANCIAL POSITION
	Inventory: $25,000
STATEMENT OF COMPREHENSIVE INCOME	**STATEMENT OF COMPREHENSIVE INCOME**
Gross profit: $6,250	Gross profit: $10,000
RETAINED EARNINGS	**RETAINED EARNINGS**
$6,250 profit from prior year	+$10,000

INTERCOMPANY SALE OF INVENTORY
Scenario 4 - Consolidation Entry

Retained Earnings (A)	6,250	
Cost of Goods Sold		6,250

Since the beginning inventory ($25,000) contains the prior-year unrealized profit ($6,250), the cost of sales of the current period is inflated following the resale by Subsidiary. Therefore, we recognize prior-year profit by decreasing current-year COGS.

Part 3

INTERCOMPANY SALE OF INVENTORY
Scenario 4 - Impact of the Elimination on the Consolidated F/S

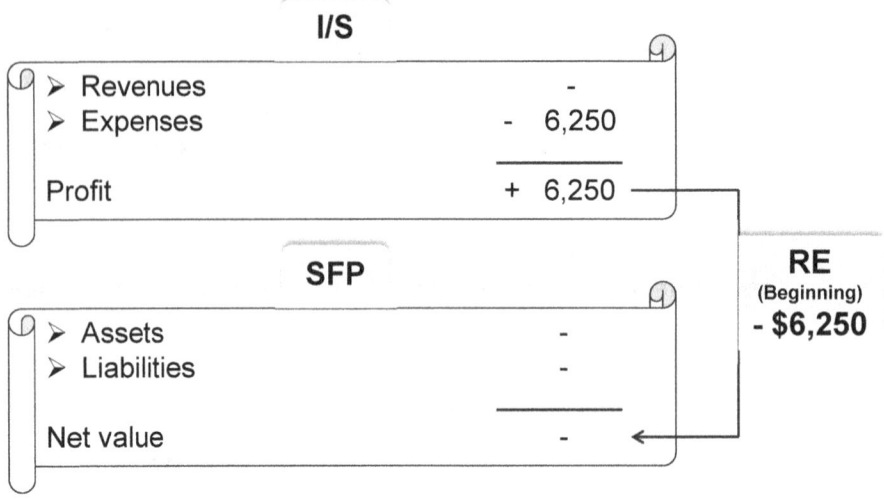

I/S
- Revenues — -
- Expenses — - 6,250
- Profit — + 6,250

SFP
- Assets — -
- Liabilities — -
- Net value — -

RE (Beginning) - $6,250

Part 3

INTERCOMPANY SALE OF INVENTORY
Impact of the Eliminations on the Consolidated F/S - Recap

Scenario	RE Beginning	Profit	RE End
Year of transfer			
Scenario 1	-	($25,000)	($25,000)
Scenario 2	-	-	-
Scenario 3		(6,250)	(6,250)
Post year of transfer			
Scenario 4	($25,000)	25,000	-
	(6,250)	6,250	-

PART 3
Concept Check

> What is the current-year adjustment for the unrealized profit on the intercompany sale of inventory in the previous year?

Part 4

OUTLINE OF THE PRESENTATION

1. INTERCOMPANY TRANSACTIONS: BASIC PRINCIPLES
2. INTERCOMPANY SALES OF NON-DEPRECIABLE ASSETS
3. INTERCOMPANY SALES OF INVENTORY
4. **INTERCOMPANY SALES OF DEPRECIABLE ASSETS**
5. INTERCOMPANY LOSSES

PART 4
Intercompany Sales of Depreciable Assets

Part 4

Objectives of this section

Illustrate the effect of intercompany sales of **depreciable assets** on the affiliated companies' financial statements.

Illustrate the adjustments required in the consolidation of financial statements when the affiliated companies engaged in intercompany sales of depreciable assets.

Intercompany Transactions ---------- Module 5 ---------- 67

INTERCOMPANY SALES OF DEPRECIABLE ASSETS
Offsetting Effect - Intercompany Gains

Part 4

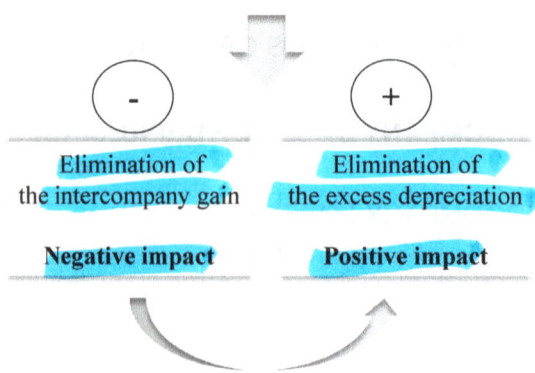

Offsetting effect taking place over the remaining useful life of the asset from the date of transfer.

Intercompany Transactions ---------- Module 5 ---------- 68

Part 4

INTERCOMPANY SALES OF DEPRECIABLE ASSETS
Offsetting Effect - Intercompany Losses

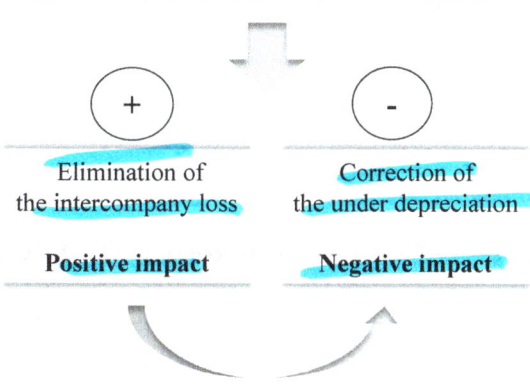

Offsetting effect taking place over the remaining useful life of the asset from the date of transfer.

Part 4

INTERCOMPANY SALE OF EQUIPEMENT
Illustration

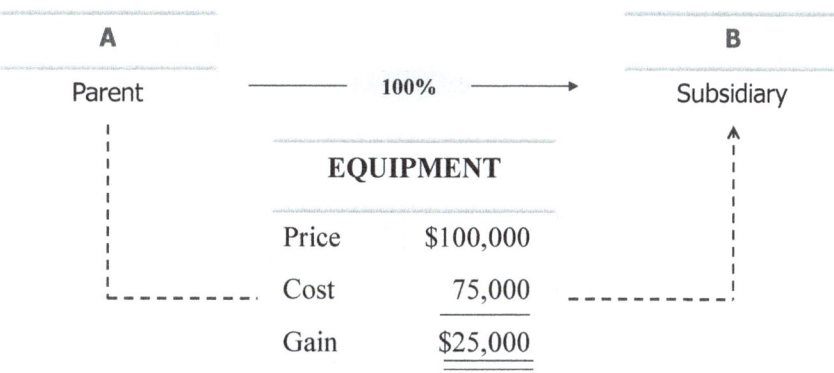

At the begiginning of X1, Parent sold equipment to Subsidiary for $100,000. The initial cost of the equipment for Parent is $75,000. Subsidiary is using the equipment to generate revenue.
Amortization of equipment: 10 years on a straight-line basis.

INTERCOMPANY SALE OF EQUIPEMENT
Year of Transfer

Part 4

A

Cash	100,000
Equipment	75,000
Gain on Sale	25,000

B

Equipment	100,000
Cash	100,000

STATEMENT OF FINANCIAL POSITION
Equipment: $75,000 → Equipment: $100,000

STATEMENT OF COMPREHENSIVE INCOME
Gain on sale: $25,000

STATEMENT OF COMPREHENSIVE INCOME

RETAINED EARNINGS
+ $25,000

RETAINED EARNINGS

INTERCOMPANY SALE OF EQUIPMENT
Year of Transfer - Consolidation Entry

Part 4

Gain on Sale of Equipment (A) 25,000
    Equipment (B)   25,000

We must return the value of the equipment to its original cost ($75,000) and eliminate the gain on sale recognized by Parent ($25,000) following the transfer. Next, as a result of this downward adjustment, the excess depreciation expense on the equipment must be removed. Indeed, the expense should be based on the original cost of the equipment ($75,000) instead of the transfer price ($100,000). A similar adjustment would apply if we were dealing with a FV decrement on a depreciable asset. See details next.

INTERCOMPANY SALE OF EQUIPMENT
Year of Transfer - Excess Depreciation

AMORTIZATION ON THE BOOKS OF 'B'
(Acquisition cost for B)
($100,000/10 years) = $10,000

AMORTIZATION ON CONSOLIDATED F/S
(Acquisition cost for A)
($75,000/10 years) = $7,500

ADJUSTMENT REQUIRED

($10,000 − $7,500) = $2,500
or
(Intercompany gain of $25,000/10 years) = $2,500

INTERCOMPANY SALE OF EQUIPMENT
Year of Transfer - Consolidation Entry

Equipment (net) (B)	2,500	
Depreciation Expense (B)		2,500

Or Accumulated Depreciation – Equipment

Removing the excess depreciation has a positive impact on the consolidated profit. Because of this reversal effect taking place on working paper, one can view the initial unrealized intercompany gain ($25,000) as being realized (or consumed) over the remaining useful life of the transferred asset (realization over 10 years, at a rate of $2,500 a year).

Part 4

INTERCOMPANY SALE OF EQUIPMENT
Impact of the Eliminations on the Consolidated F/S

I/S
- Revenues   - 25,000
- Expenses   - 2,500

Profit   - 22,500

SFP
- Assets   - 22,500
- Liabilities   -

Net value   - 22,500

Intercompany Transactions — Module 5 — 75

Part 4

INTERCOMPANY SALE OF EQUIPMENT
Realization of the Intercorporate Gain

| Gain on Sale Following Transfer |
| $25,000 |

| Unrealized Portion of the Gain at the End of Year of Transfer (Year 1) | $2,500 |
| $22,500 | |

| Unrealized Portion of the Gain at the End of Year 2 | $5,000 |
| $20,000 | |

| Unrealized Portion of the Gain at the End of Year 3 | $7,500 |
| $17,500 | |

Realized Portion of the Gain at the End of Year 10
$25,000

Intercompany Transactions — Module 5 — 76

INTERCOMPANY SALE OF EQUIPMENT
Year 2 - Consolidation Entries

Part 4

Unrealized Portion of the Gain at the Beginning

Years 2 to 10
($2,500 × 9)
=
$22,500

Retained Earnings (A-B)	22,500	
Equipment (net) (B)		22,500

Excess Depreciation of the Current Period

Equipment (net) (B)	2,500	
Depreciation Expense (B)		2,500

Intercompany Transactions ---------- Module 5 ---------- 77

INTERCOMPANY SALE OF EQUIPMENT
Year 2 - Alternative Consolidation Entries

Part 4

Unrealized Portion of the Gain at the Beginning

Retained Earnings (A-B)	22,500	
Accumulated Dep. Equip. (B)	2,500	
Equipment (B)		25,000

Excess Depreciation of the Current Period

Accumulated Dep. Equip. (B)	2,500	
Depreciation Expense (B)		2,500

Intercompany Transactions ---------- Module 5 ---------- 78

INTERCOMPANY SALE OF EQUIPMENT
Impact of the Eliminations on the Consolidated F/S - Year 2

Part 4

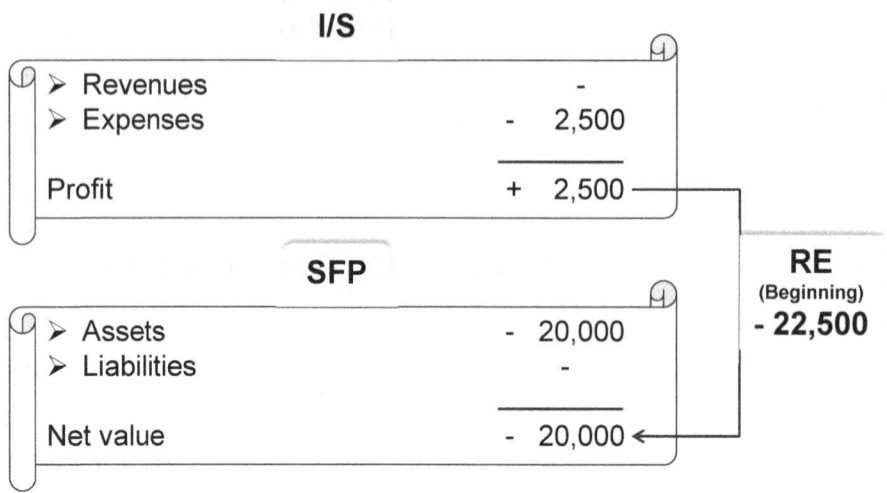

I/S
- Revenues — -
- Expenses — - 2,500
- Profit — + 2,500

SFP
- Assets — - 20,000
- Liabilities — -
- Net value — - 20,000

RE (Beginning) — - 22,500

Intercompany Transactions — Module 5

INTERCOMPANY SALE OF EQUIPMENT
Year 5 - Consolidation Entries

Part 4

Unrealized Portion of the Gain at the Beginning

Years 5 to 10
($2,500 × 6)
=
$15,000

Retained Earnings (A-B)	15,000	
Equipment (net) (B)		15,000

Excess Depreciation of the Current Period

Equipment (net) (B)	2,500	
Depreciation Expense (B)		2,500

Intercompany Transactions — Module 5

INTERCOMPANY SALE OF EQUIPMENT
Year 5 - Alternative Consolidation Entries

Unrealized Portion of the Gain at the Beginning

Retained Earnings (A-B)	15,000	
Accumulated Dep. Equip. (B)	10,000	
Equipment (B)		25,000

Excess Depreciation of the Current Period

Accumulated Dep. Equip. (B)	2,500	
Depreciation Expense (B)		2,500

INTERCOMPANY SALE OF EQUIPMENT
Impact of the Eliminations on the Consolidated F/S - Year 5

INTERCOMPANY SALE OF EQUIPMENT
If the Equipment is Resold by Subsidiary at the Beginning of Year 5

Part 4

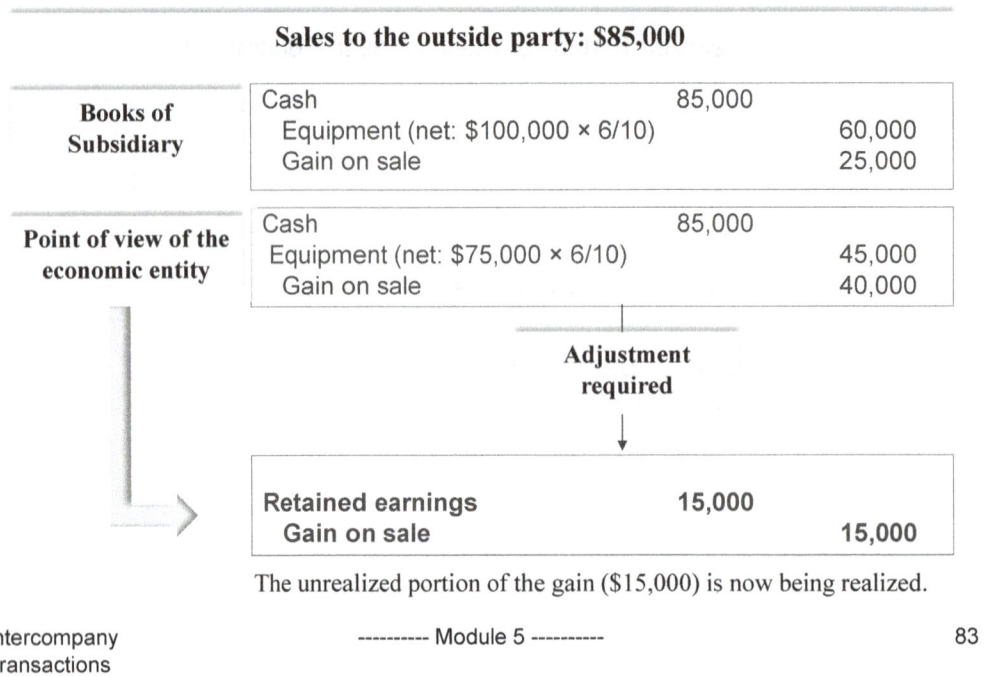

RESALE OF EQUIPMENT
Impact of the Eliminations on the Consolidated F/S - Year 5

Part 4

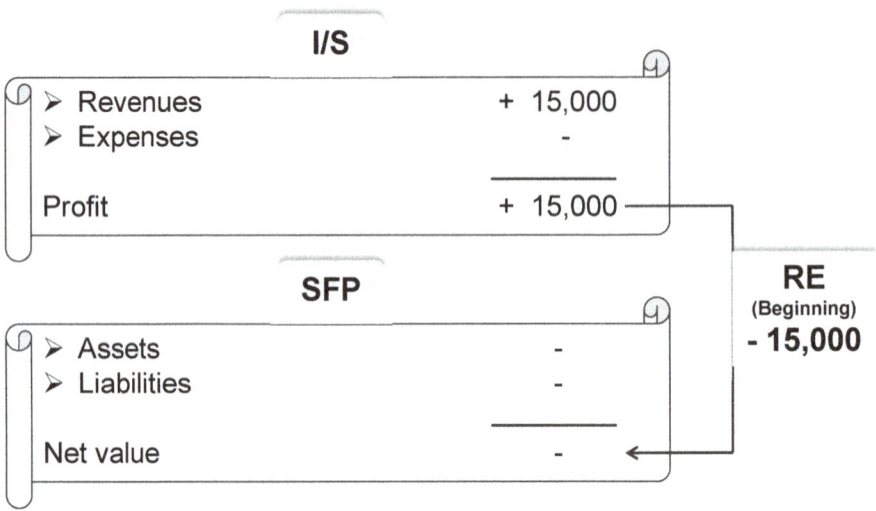

PART 4
Concept Check

> Explain how unrealized gains on intercompany sales of depreciable assets are being realized for consolidation purposes.

_____
_____
_____
_____
_____
_____
_____

Part 5

OUTLINE OF THE PRESENTATION

1. INTERCOMPANY TRANSACTIONS: BASIC PRINCIPLES
2. INTERCOMPANY SALES OF NON-DEPRECIABLE ASSETS
3. INTERCOMPANY SALES OF INVENTORY
4. INTERCOMPANY SALES OF DEPRECIABLE ASSETS
5. **INTERCOMPANY LOSSES**

PART 5
Intercompany Losses

Objectives of this section

Illustrate the effect of intercompany losses on the affiliated companies' financial statements.

Illustrate the adjustments required in the consolidation of financial statements when intercompany transactions result in losses.

INTERCOMPANY SALES OF NON-DEPRECIABLE ASSETS
Illustration

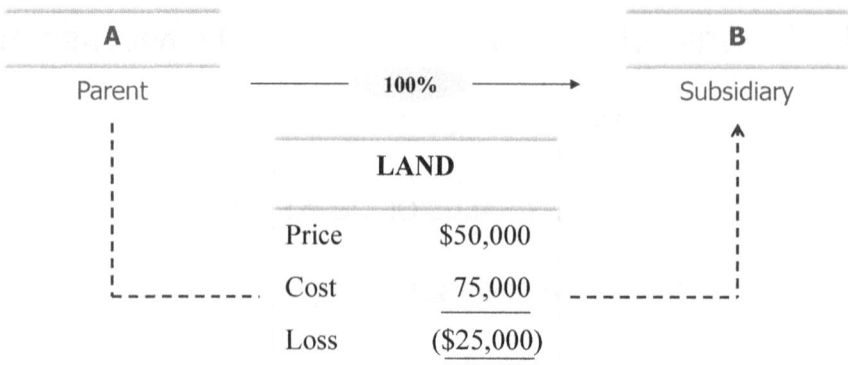

During X1, Parent sold land to Subsidiary for $50,000. The initial cost of the land for Parent is $75,000.

INTERCOMPANY SALE OF LAND
Scenario 1 - Consolidation Entry

Part 5

Land (B)	**25,000**	
Loss on Sale of Land (A)		**25,000**

INTERCOMPANY SALE OF LAND
Scenario 1 - Impact of the Elimination on the Consolidated F/S

Part 2

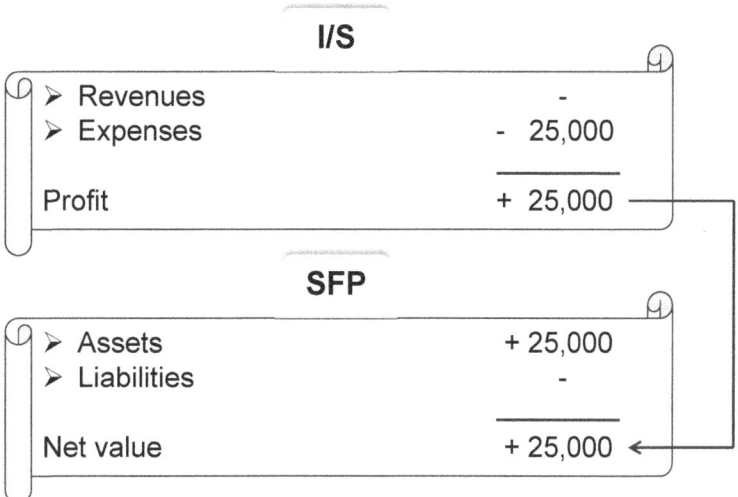

Part 5

INTERCOMPANY SALE OF LAND
Scenario 2 - Consolidation Entry

NO ENTRY REQUIRED

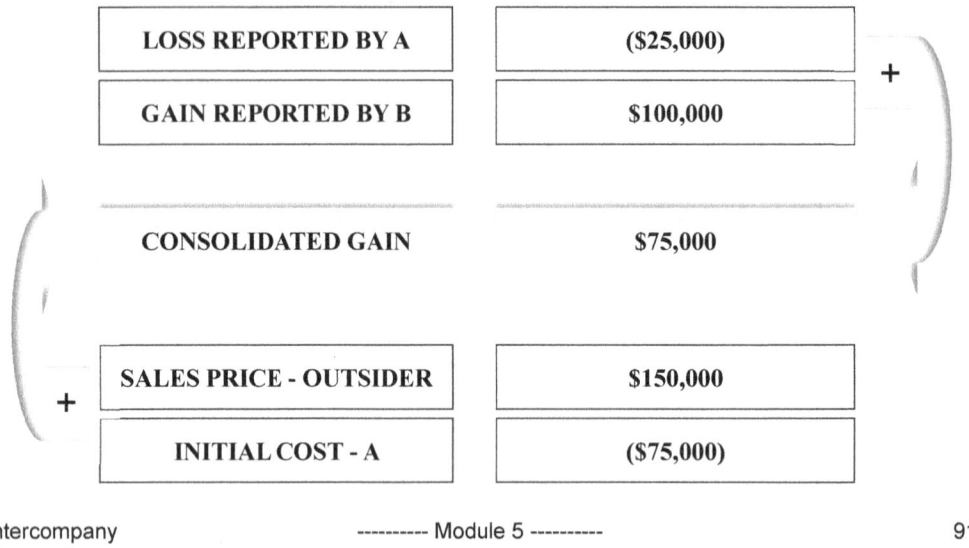

LOSS REPORTED BY A	($25,000)
GAIN REPORTED BY B	$100,000
CONSOLIDATED GAIN	$75,000
SALES PRICE - OUTSIDER	$150,000
INITIAL COST - A	($75,000)

Part 5

INTERCOMPANY SALE OF LAND
Scenario 3 - Consolidation Entry

Land (B)	25,000	
Retained Earnings (A)		25,000

Part 2

INTERCOMPANY SALE OF LAND
Scenario 3 - Impact of the Elimination on the Consolidated F/S

I/S
- Revenues —
- Expenses —

Profit —

SFP
- Assets + 25,000
- Liabilities —

Net value + 25,000

Part 5

INTERCOMPANY SALE OF LAND
Scenario 4 - Consolidation Entry

Loss on Sale of Land (A)	25,000	
Retained earnings (A)		25,000

Part 5
INTERCOMPANY SALE OF LAND
Scenario 4 - Impact of the Elimination on the Consolidated F/S

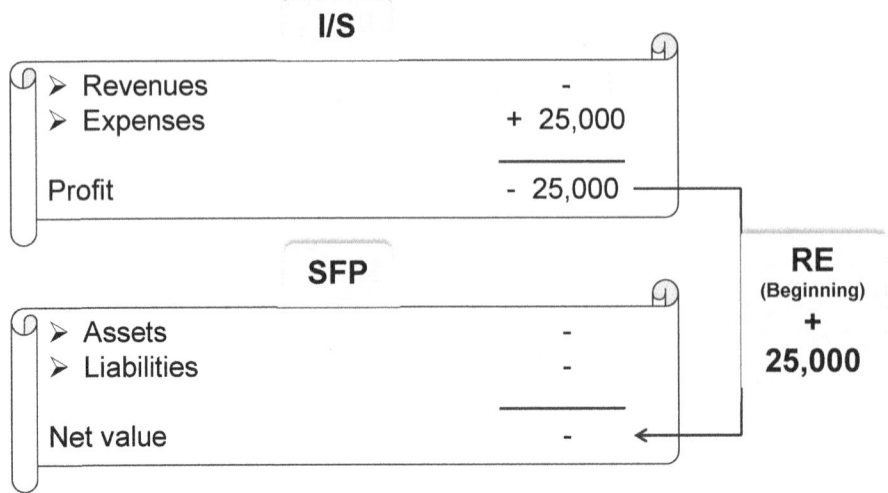

Part 5
INTERCOMPANY SALES OF INVENTORY
Illustration

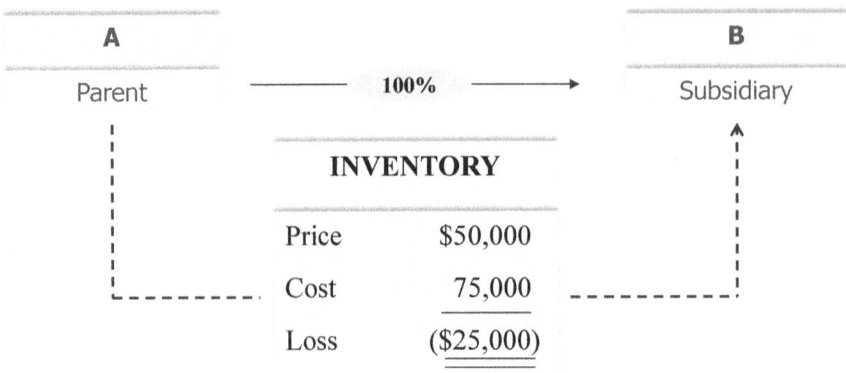

During X1, Parent sold merchandise to Subsidiary for $50,000. The initial cost of the inventory for Parent is $75,000.

Part 5

INTERCOMPANY SALE OF INVENTORY
Scenario 1 - Consolidation Entry

Sales (A)	50,000	
Inventory (B)	25,000	
Cost of Goods Sold (A)		75,000

Part 5

INTERCOMPANY SALE OF INVENTORY
Scenario 1 - Impact of the Elimination on the Consolidated F/S

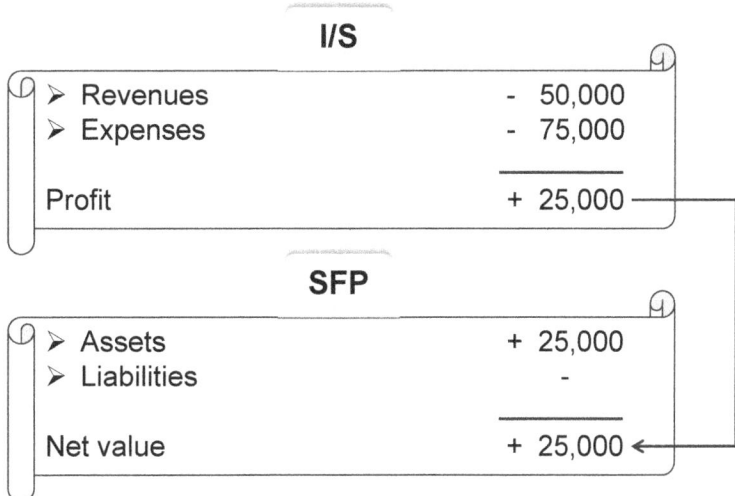

I/S
- Revenues — 50,000
- Expenses — 75,000

Profit + 25,000

SFP
- Assets + 25,000
- Liabilities -

Net value + 25,000

Part 5

INTERCOMPANY SALE OF INVENTORY
Scenario 2 - Reciprocal Balances

Parent sold merchandise to Subsidiary for **$50,000**, all of which was sold by Subsidiary for $150,000 to external parties prior to the end of the current accounting period. The cost of sales for Parent amounts to $75,000.

	A	B	Total
Sales	$50,000	$150,000	$200,000
Cost of sales	75,000	50,000	125,000
	($25,000)	$100,000	$75,000

Part 5

INTERCOMPANY SALE OF INVENTORY
Scenario 2 - Consolidation Entry

Sales (A)	50,000	
Cost of Goods Sold (B)		50,000

Part 5

INTERCOMPANY SALE OF INVENTORY
Scenario 2 - Impact of the Elimination on the Consolidated F/S

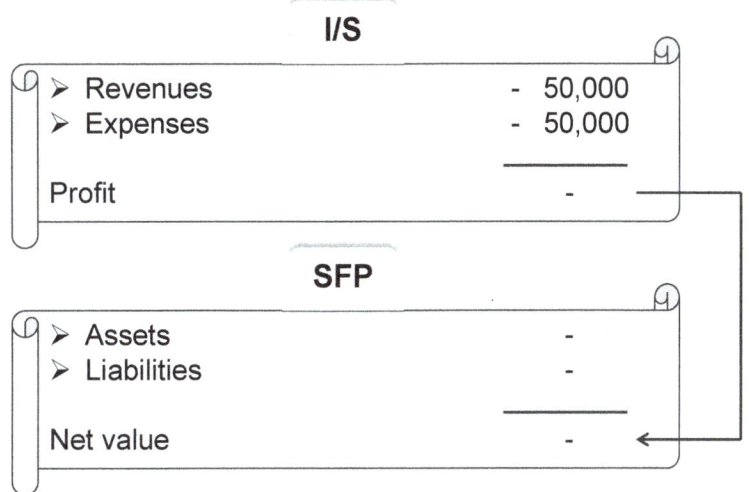

Intercompany Transactions ---------- Module 5 ---------- 101

Part 5

INTERCOMPANY SALE OF INVENTORY
Scenario 3 - Unrealized Loss and Reciprocal Balances

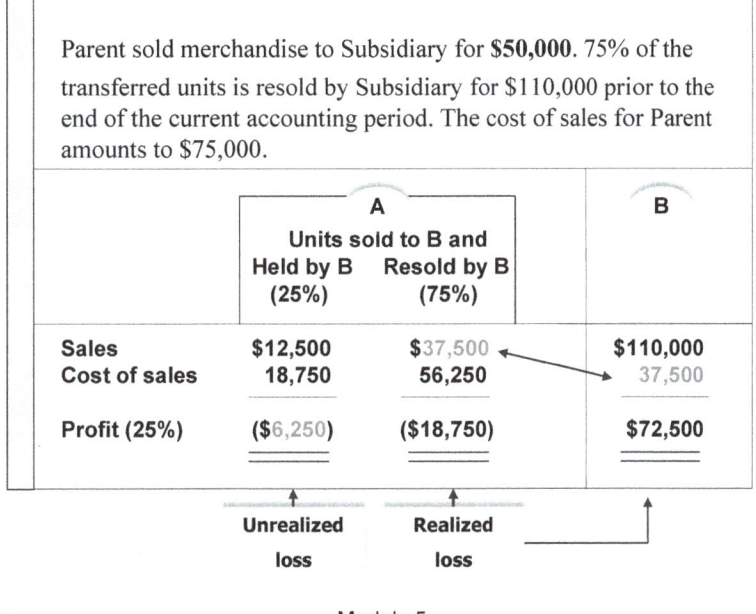

Intercompany Transactions ---------- Module 5 ---------- 102

INTERCOMPANY SALE OF INVENTORY
Scenario 3 - Consolidation Entries

Part 5

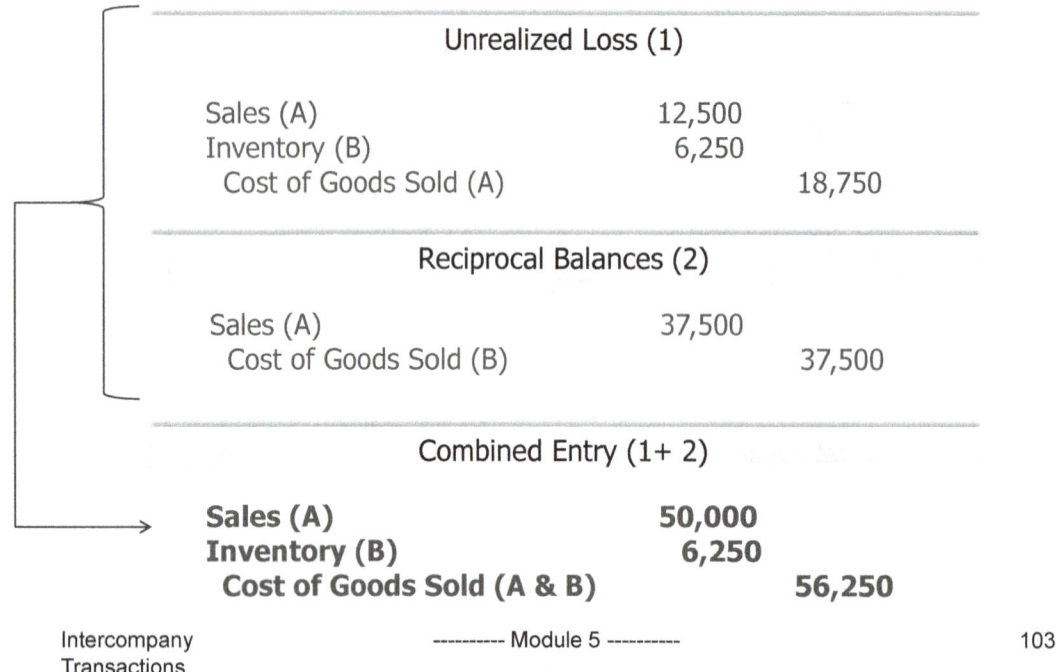

Unrealized Loss (1)

Sales (A)	12,500	
Inventory (B)	6,250	
Cost of Goods Sold (A)		18,750

Reciprocal Balances (2)

Sales (A)	37,500	
Cost of Goods Sold (B)		37,500

Combined Entry (1+ 2)

Sales (A)	**50,000**	
Inventory (B)	**6,250**	
Cost of Goods Sold (A & B)		**56,250**

INTERCOMPANY SALE OF INVENTORY
Scenario 3 - Impact of the Elimination on the Consolidated F/S

Part 5

I/S

- Revenues   - 50,000
- Expenses   - 56,250

Profit   + 6,250

SFP

- Assets   + 6,250
- Liabilities   -

Net value   + 6,250

Part 5

INTERCOMPANY SALE OF INVENTORY
Scenario 4 - Consolidation Entry

Cost of Goods Sold	25,000	
Retained Earnings (A)		25,000

Part 5

INTERCOMPANY SALE OF INVENTORY
Scenario 4 - Impact of the Elimination on the Consolidated F/S

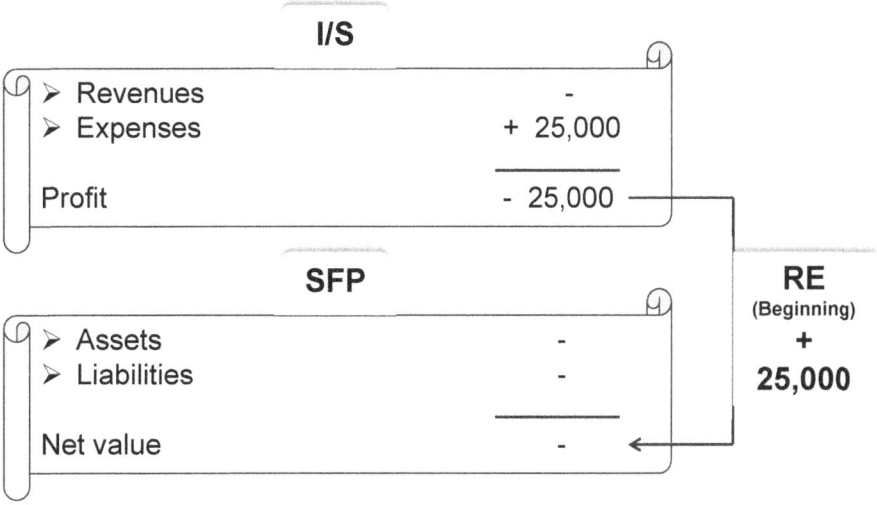

I/S
- Revenues — -
- Expenses — + 25,000
- Profit — - 25,000

SFP
- Assets — -
- Liabilities — -
- Net value — -

RE (Beginning) + 25,000

INTERCOMPANY SALES OF DEPRECIABLE ASSETS
Illustration

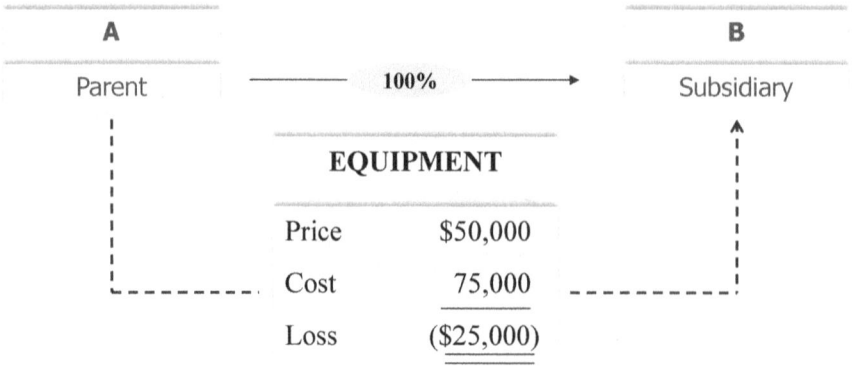

At the begiginning of X1, Parent sold equipment to Subsidiary for $50,000. The initial cost of the equipment for Parent is $75,000. Subsidiary is using the equipment to generate revenue.

Amortization of equipment: 10 years on a straight-line basis.

INTERCOMPANY SALE OF EQUIPMENT
Year of Transfer - Consolidation Entry

Equipment (B)   25,000
    Loss on Sale of Equipment (A)   25,000

INTERCOMPANY SALE OF EQUIPMENT
Year of Transfer - Under Depreciation

AMORTIZATION ON THE BOOKS OF 'B'
(Acquisition cost for B)
($50,000/10 years) = $5,000

AMORTIZATION ON CONSOLIDATED F/S
(Acquisition cost for A)
($75,000/10 years) = $7,500

ADJUSTMENT REQUIRED

($5,000 − $7,500) = ($2,500)
or
(Intercompany loss of $25,000/10 years) = ($2,500)

INTERCOMPANY SALE OF EQUIPMENT
Year of Transfer - Consolidation Entry

Depreciation Expense (B)	2,500	
Equipment (net) (B)		2,500

Part 5

INTERCOMPANY SALE OF EQUIPMENT
Impact of the Eliminations on the Consolidated F/S

I/S
- Revenues — -
- Expenses — - 22,500

Profit — + 22,500

SFP
- Assets — + 22,500
- Liabilities — -

Net value — + 22,500

Intercompany Transactions ---------- Module 5 ---------- 111

INTERCOMPANY TRANSACTIONS
Module 5 - Recap

6	REVIEW QUESTIONS
7	QUIZ QUESTIONS
8	KEY TERMS INTRODUCED IN THIS MODULE
9	RECAP ON THE OBJECTIVES OF THIS MODULE

PART 6
Review Questions

1. Define or explain the following terms:
   - Unrealized gain
   - Unrealized loss
   - Realization of intercompany gains and losses

2. When are unrealized intercompany gains or losses on sales of non-depreciable assets realized from the viewpoint of the consolidated entity?

3. When are unrealized intercompany gains or losses on sales of depreciable assets realized from the viewpoint of the consolidated entity?

4. When is it necessary to eliminate intercompany profits for consolidation purposes?

REVIEW QUESTIONS
(continued...)

5. Which company may have unrealized profits on its books in an upstream sale?

6. Which company may have unrealized profits on its books in a downstream sale?

7. How are unrealized gains on sale of land treated in the consolidated financial statements if the intercorporate sale occurred in a prior period and the transferred land is sold to an external party in the current period?

8. How are unrealized gains on sale of land treated in the consolidated financial statements if the intercorporate sale occurred in a prior period and the transferred land remains in the consolidated group at the end of the current period?

9. Is the effect of unrealized intercorporate profits on consolidated comprehensive income different between an upstream and a downstream sale?

REVIEW QUESTIONS
(continued...)

10. Why is there need for an eliminating entry when an intercompany inventory transfer is made at cost?

11. What is the basic consolidation entry needed when inventory is sold to an affiliate and resold the same year to outsiders?

12. How does unrealized profit in the beginning inventory affect the consolidated comprehensive income, if the inventory has been sold during the year?

13. What is the basic consolidation entry needed when land is sold to an affiliate and resold the same year to an outsider?

14. 'Intercompany losses recorded on the sale of assets to an affiliate within the consolidated entity should always be eliminated when consolidated financial statements are prepared.' Do you agree with this statement? Explain.

PART 7
Quiz Questions

On January 1, X1, Total Company acquired 100% of the outstanding voting shares of Partial Company. Ten years later, that is, on December 31, X10, Total still controls 100% of Partial. The following transactions occurred between the two companies:

- Total sold a **land** to Partial in X3 for $75,000. The original cost of the land to Total is $70,000. Partial keeps the land for its own use.

- Partial Company sells **merchandise** to Total Company at a price that provides Partial with a gross margin of 50% of the sales price. During X10, these sales amounted to $1,000,000. The December 31, X10, inventories of Total contain $200,000 of these purchases while the December 31, X9, inventories of Total contained $100,000 in merchandise purchased from Partial.

- During X7, the Total Company sold **equipment** to the Partial Company for $550,000. At the time of the sale, the equipment had a net book value in Total's records of $450,000. The remaining useful life of the asset on this date was 10 years.

Required
Present the consolidation adjustments for X10 related to the intercompany transactions.

Part 7

QUIZ QUESTIONS
INTERCOMPANY SALE OF LAND FROM X3
Consolidation Entry - Unrealized Prior-Year Intercompany Gain

Dr gain   5,000
  cr land.   5,000

Part 7

QUIZ QUESTIONS
INTERCOMPANY SALES OF INVENTORY FROM X9
Consolidation Entry - Recognition of Prior-Year Intercompany Profit

Dr sales   1,400,000
  cr cost of goods sold   50,000
  cr inventory   50,000

slide 43

Part 7

QUIZ QUESTIONS
INTERCOMPANY SALES OF INVENTORY FROM X10
Unrealized Profit and Reciprocal Balances

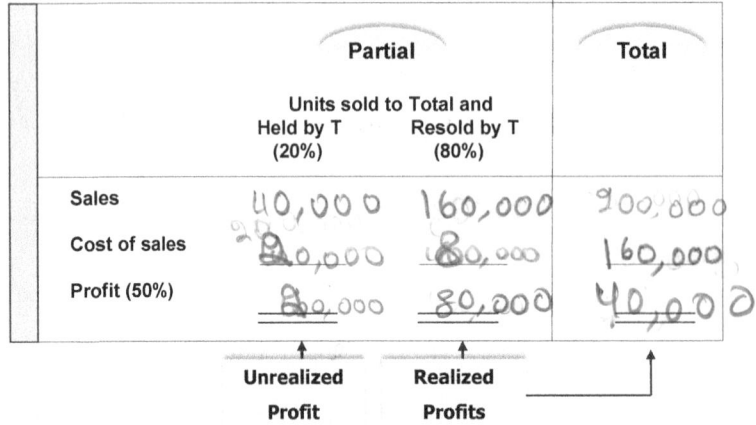

Part 7

QUIZ QUESTIONS
INTERCOMPANY SALES OF INVENTORY FROM X10
Consolidation entries

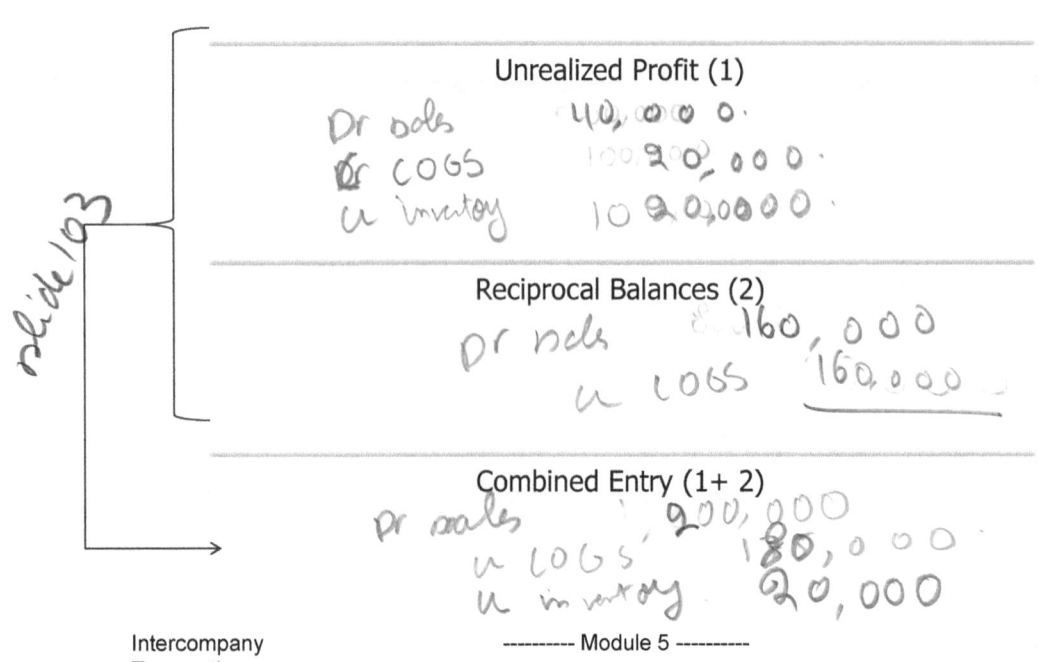

QUIZ QUESTIONS
INTERCOMPANY SALE OF EQUIPMENT
Consolidation Entries

Part 7

Handwritten annotations:
- X7
- sch 550,000
- NBV 450,000
- UL: 10 years

$X_7 \rightarrow X_{10}$

Unrealized Portion of the Gain at the Beginning

4 × 10K = 40,000

Dr Retained earnings   40,000
   Cr equipment   40,000

Excess Depreciation of the Current Period

Dr equipment   10,000
   Cr depreciation expense   10,000

$\frac{550,000}{10} = 55,000$

$\frac{450,000}{10} = 45,000$

$55,000 - 45,000 = 10,000$

Intercompany Transactions — Module 5 — 121

Part 8

KEY TERMS INTRODUCED IN THIS MODULE

• Unrealized gain • Unrealized loss • Realization of intercompany gains and losses	Part 1

RECAP ON THE OBJECTIVES OF THIS MODULE

Part 9

Part 1 — Introduce the basic principles supporting adjustments for intercompany transactions when preparing consolidated financial statements.

Part 2 — Illustrate the effect of intercompany sales of **non-depreciable assets** on the affiliated companies' financial statements.

Illustrate the adjustments required in the consolidation of financial statements when the affiliated companies engaged in intercompany sales of non-depreciable assets.

Part 3 — Illustrate the effect of intercompany sales of **inventory** on the affiliated companies' financial statements.

Illustrate the adjustments required in the consolidation of financial statements when the affiliated companies engaged in intercompany sales of inventory.

RECAP ON THE OBJECTIVES OF THIS MODULE

Part 9

Part 4 — Illustrate the effect of intercompany sales of **depreciable assets** on the affiliated companies' financial statements.

Illustrate the adjustments required in the consolidation of financial statements when the affiliated companies engaged in intercompany sales of depreciable assets.

Part 5 — Illustrate the effect of intercompany losses on the affiliated companies' financial statements.

Illustrate the adjustments required in the consolidation of financial statements when intercompany transactions result in losses.

Copyright © 2020, Parmitech, Ottawa. Parmitech. All rights reserved.

Exercise 5-1
Downstream Sale of Truck

Parent Corporation holds 100 percent ownership of Subsidiary Corporation. On December 31, X6, Subsidiary paid Parent $40,000 for a truck that Parent had purchased for $45,000 on January 1, X2. The truck was considered to have a 15-year life from January 1, X2, and no residual value. Both companies depreciate trucks using the straight-line method.

40,000 truck. p=45,000. 15/year.

Required

a) Give the workpaper eliminating entries needed on December 31, X6, to remove the effects of the intercompany sale of truck.
b) Give the workpaper eliminating entries needed on December 31, X7, to remove the effects of the intercompany sale of truck.

Elimination for X6

Transfer price 40,000
Cost   30,000
gain   10,000

Dr gain on sale   10,000
  Cr truck   10,000

Elimination for X7

Realized gain X6   10,000
              X7   0
                    10,000

Dr Retained earnings 10,000
  Cr Truck   10,000

10,000/10 years = 1,000

Dr Acc Depreciation   1,000
  Cr Depreciation exp.   1,000

1

Exercise 5-2
Upstream Sale of Land

Para Corporation holds 100 percent ownership of Sub Corporation. On March 15, X2, Sub sold land it had purchased for $140,000 to Para for $185,000. Para plans to build a new warehouse on the property in X3.

Cost 140,000 for 185,000.

Required

a) Give the workpaper eliminating entries needed on December 31, X2, to remove the effects of the intercompany sale of land.
b) Give the workpaper eliminating entries needed on December 31, X3, to remove the effects of the intercompany sale of land.

Elimination for X2

transfer price 185,000
cost   140,000
gain   45,000

Dr gain 45,000
   cr land 45,000

Elimination for X3

unrealized gain for X2   45,000
            X3   0
                          45,000

Dr RE   45,000
   cr land 45,000

Exercise 5-3
Downstream Sale of Equipment (1)

Allan Corporation holds 100 percent ownership of Min Corporation. On January 1, X5, Allan received $245,000 from Min for an equipment Allan had purchased on January 1, X2 for $300,000. The equipment was considered to have a 10-year life from January 1, X2, and no residual value. Both companies depreciate equipment using the straight-line method.

Required

a) Give the workpaper eliminating entries needed on December 31, X5, to remove the effects of the intercompany sale of equipment.
b) Give the workpaper eliminating entries needed on December 31, X6, to remove the effects of the intercompany sale of equipment.

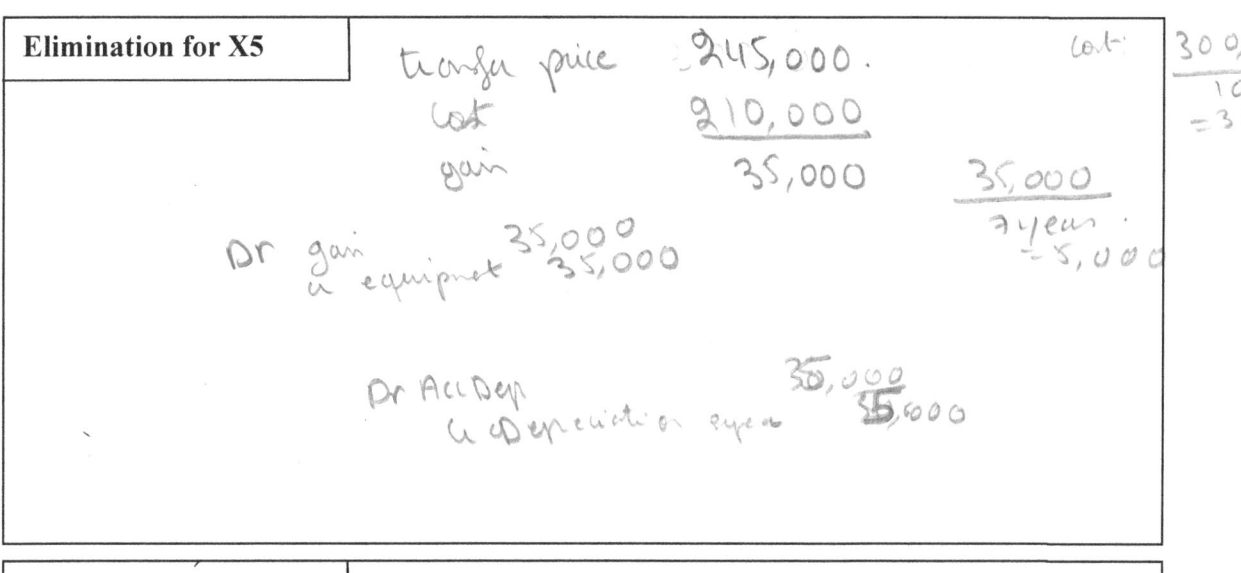

Exercise 5-4
Downstream Sale of Equipment (2)

Ralf Corporation holds 100 percent ownership of Local Corporation. On January 1, X7, Ralf sold to Local equipment it had purchased for $150,000 and used for eight years. Ralf recorded a gain of $14,000 on the sale. The equipment has a total useful life of 15 years and is depreciated on a straight-line basis.

Required

a) Give the journal entries made by Ralf on January 1, X7, to record the sale of equipment.
b) Give the journal entries recorded by Local during X7 to account for the purchase of equipment and year-end depreciation expense.
c) Give the workpaper eliminating entries needed on December 31, X7, to remove the effects of the intercompany sale of equipment.
d) Give the workpaper eliminating entries needed on December 31, X8, to remove the effects of the intercompany sale of equipment.

Journal Entry - Ralf

Dr Cash   84,000
Dr Acc Depreciation   80,000
    Cr Equipment   150,000
    Cr Gain on sale   14,000

Journal Entry - Local

Dr Equipment   84,000
    Cr Cash   84,000

Dr Depreciation expense 12,000
    Cr Acc Depreciation   12,000

Elimination for X7

$\dfrac{14,000}{7} = 2,000$

Dr gain 14,000
 Cr equipment 14,000

Dr Acc Dep 2,000
 Cr Depreciation exp 2,000

Elimination for X8

Dr RE 12,000
 Cr equipment 12,000

Dr Acc Dep 2,000
 Cr Depreciation exp 2,000

Exercise 5-5
Upstream Sale of Equipment & Consolidated Comprehensive Income

Barn Corporation purchased 100 percent ownership of Tool Corporation on January X0, at underlying book value. On January 1, X6, Barn paid Tool $270,000 to acquire equipment that Tool had purchased on January 1, X3, for $300,000. The equipment was considered to have a 15-year life from January 1, X3, and no residual value. Both companies depreciate equipment using the straight-line method.

Barn reported comprehensive income of $100,000 for X8 and paid dividends of $40,000. Tool reported comprehensive income of $40,000 in X8.

Required

a) Compute the amount reported as consolidated comprehensive income for X8.
b) Give the workpaper eliminating entries needed on December 31, X8, to remove the effects of the intercompany sale of equipment.

Profit for X8

transfer price 270,000   2,500
               240,000   = 30,000
       gain   30,000   ─────
                                     12

comprehensive income = 100,000 + 40,000 + 2,500
                     = 142,500

Elimination for X8

Dr RE   25,000
   cr equipment   25,000

Dr A/D Depc   2,500
   cr Depreciation expense   2,500

Exercise 5-6
Downstream Sale of Land & Consolidated Comprehensive Income

Bulk Corporation purchased 100 percent ownership of Task Corporation on January X0, at underlying book value. On June 1, X4, Bulk sold land to Task for $120,000. The land had a book value of $95,000 at the time of sale.

Bulk reported comprehensive income from its separate operations of $90,000 and $110,000 for X4 and X5, respectively. Task reported comprehensive income of $60,000 and $40,000 in X4 and X5, respectively.

Required
Compute the amount reported as consolidated comprehensive income for X4 and X5.

Profit for X4

120,000
95,000
gain 25,000

CI = 90,000 + 60,000 − 25,000 = 125,000

Profit for X5

CI = 110,000 + 40,000 = 150,000

Exercise 5-7
Downstream Sale of Inventory

Loft Corporation holds 100 percent ownership of Built Corporation. During X4, Loft purchased 40,000 chairs for $24 each and sold 25,000 of the chairs to Built for $30 each. Built sold 18,000 of the transferred chairs to retail establishments prior to December 31, X4, for $45 each. Both companies use perpetual inventory systems.

40,000 × 24
25,000 × 30

Required

a) Give all journal entries made by Loft in X4 for the purchase of inventory and resale to Built.
b) Give the journal entries recorded by Built in X4 for the purchase of inventory and resale to retail establishments.
c) Give the workpaper eliminating entries needed on December 31, X4, to remove the effects of the intercompany sale of inventory.

Journal Entry - Loft

Dr inventory 960,000
  Cr AP 960,000

Dr AR 750K
  Cr Sales 750K

Dr COGS 600K
  Cr inventory 600K

Journal Entry - Built

Dr inventory 750K
  Cr AP 750K

Dr AR 810K
  Cr Sales 810K

Dr COGS 540,000
  Cr inventory 540,000

Elimination for X4

Dr Sales 750,000
  Cr COGS 708,000
  Cr inventory 42,000

Exercise 5-8
Upstream Sale of Inventory

Pratt Corporation holds 100 percent ownership of Bear Corporation. During X7, Bear produced 25,000 computer desks at a cost of $82 each and sold 10,000 desks to Pratt for $94 each. Pratt sold 7,000 of the desks to unrelated parties for $130 each prior to December 31, X7, and sold the remainder in early X8 for $140 each. Both companies use perpetual inventory systems.

Required

a) Give the amounts of cost of goods sold (COGS) recorded by Pratt and Bear in X7.
b) Give the amount of consolidated cost of goods (COGS) sold for X7.
c) Give the workpaper eliminating entries needed on December 31, X7, to remove the effects of the intercompany sale of inventory.
d) Give the workpaper eliminating entries needed on December 31, X8, to remove the effects of the intercompany sale of inventory.

COGS - Pratt

Dr COGS 658,000
 Cr inventory 658,000

COGS - Bear

Dr COGS 820,000
 Cr inventory 820,000

Consolidated COGS

574,000.

Elimination for X7

Dr Sales 940,000
  Cr COGS   904,000
  Cr Inventory 36,000

Elimination for X8

Dr RE 36,000
  Cr COGS 36,000

Exercise 5-9
Consolidated versus Separate-Entity Statements

Consider the following transactions:

1. <u>January 1, X1</u>: Small Ltd. purchased land for $100,000.
2. <u>December 31, X1</u>: Total Inc. acquired all the outstanding common shares of Small. The fair value of Small's land on this date was $115,000.
3. <u>December 31, X2</u>: Small sold its land to Total for $125,000.
4. <u>December 31, X3</u>: Total sold the land to an arm's-length party for $130,000.

Required
Determine the account balances for *Land* and *Gain on Sale of Land* for years X1, X2, and X3 for three sets of financial statements, that is, separate-entity statements for Total and Small and consolidated statements. Complete the following table.

	Land	Gain on sale
December 31, X1		
➤ Total	0	0
➤ Small	100,000	0
➤ Consolidated	115,000	0
December 31, X2		
➤ Total	125,000	0
➤ Small		25,000
➤ Consolidated	115,000	0
December 31, X3		
➤ Total	0	5,000
➤ Small	0	
➤ Consolidated	0	15,000

Exercise 5-10
Intercompany Transactions and Worksheet Adjustments (1)

On June 30, X1, Parent Corporation acquired 100% of the outstanding common shares of Sub Ltd. for $3,350,000 in cash.

On the date of acquisition, the fair values and book values of each of Sub's assets were equal, except for inventory that was undervalued by $225,000, and capital assets (net) that were overvalued by $1,000,000.

The shareholder's equity of Sub at that time was $3,440,000, consisting of Common Shares of $2,900,000 and Retained Earnings of $540,000.

For each of the following intercompany transaction, provide the consolidation entries required to consolidate the financial statements of Parent Corporation and its subsidiary, Sub Ltd., as of June 30, X5.

a) Dividends of $480,000 were declared by Sub during the fiscal year but were not paid until August 12, X5.

> Dr Dividend income   480,000
>   Cr Dividend declared   480,000
>
> a) Dr A/C payable   480,000
>   Cr A/R   480,000

b) Sub sold goods to Parent during the year ended June 30, X4, at a gross profit margin of 25%. The opening inventory of Parent at July 1, X4, included items purchased from Sub in the amount of $160,000. There were no sales from Sub to Parent during the year ended June 30, X5.

> Dr RE   40,000
>   Cr COGS   40,000

c) Parent sold goods to Sub during the current fiscal year at a gross profit margin of 30%. Of the $750,000 of sales, goods worth $200,000 were in Sub's closing inventory at June 30, X5. None of these intercompany sales still in inventory had been paid for at the fiscal year-end.

```
Dr Sales          750,000
   cr COGS              690,000
   cr Inventory           60,000

Dr AP             200,000
   cr AR                 200,000
```

d) On July 1, X1, Sub acquired equipment at a cost of $120,000. At this time the equipment was expected to have a useful life of five years with no anticipated net salvage value. On June 30, X3, the equipment is sold to Parent for $90,000. At the time of this sale, the remaining useful life of the equipment is estimated to be three years.

```
Dr RE             12,000
   cr equipment         12,000

Dr Accum Dep       6,000
   cr Depr expense       6,000
```

e) During the year ended June 30, X2, Parent sold land to Sub for $600,000. The land originally cost Parent $500,000. During the year ended June 30, X4, Sub sold the land to an outsider for $300,000.

```
NA
```

Exercise 5-11
Intercompany Transactions and Worksheet Adjustments (2)

On January 1, X3, Grant Corporation bought 100 percent of the outstanding common shares of Lee Company for $100,000 cash. On that date, Lee had $25,000 of common shares outstanding and $30,000 retained earnings.

The following presents the intercompany transactions that took place during X7.

a) Lee made a payment of $25,000 to Grant for management fees for the year X7.
b) Lee made sales of $100,000 to Grant. The December 31, X7 inventory of Grant contained merchandise purchased from Lee amounting to $30,000. Lee's sales to Grant are priced to provide it with a gross profit of 20% (gross profit on sales).
c) On July 1, X7, Lee borrowed $55,000 from Grant and signed a note bearing interest at 12% per annum. The interest on this note was paid on December 31, X7.
d) During X7, Lee sold a land to Grant and recorded a gain of $25,000 on the transaction. This land is being held by Grant on December 31, X7.
e) During X7, Grant sold equipment to Lee and recorded a loss of $10,000. The equipment was resold by Lee the same year to an outside party. Lee recorded a gain on sale of equipment of $30,000. The remaining useful life of the equipment at date of intercompany sale is 5 years.
f) Dividends declared by Lee during X7 amount to $20,000. These dividends are still unpaid at the end of X7.

Required

For each of the above intercompany transactions, provide the consolidation entries required to consolidate the financial statements of Grant and its subsidiary, Lee, as of December 31, X7.

a) Management fees

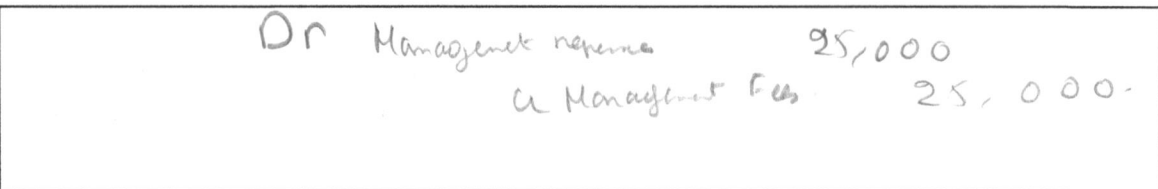

b) Sales of merchandise to Grant

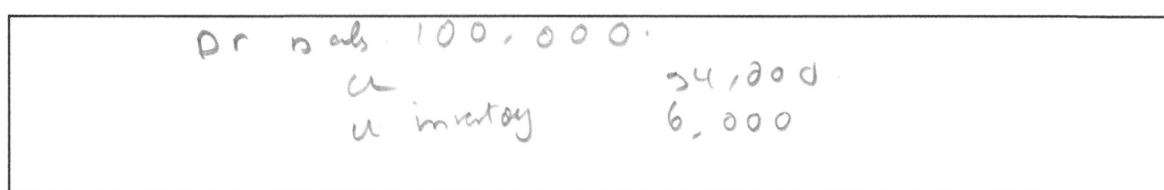

c) Intercompany loan

```
Dr interest revenue      3,300
   Cr interest expense       3,300
Dr NP                   55,000
   Cr NR                    55,000
```

d) Sale of land to Grant

```
Dr gain    25,000
   Cr land    25,000
```

e) Sale of equipment to Lee

no required entry.

f) Intercompany dividends

```
Dr Dividend income        20,000
   Cr Dividend declared      20,000
Dr Dividend payable       20,000
   Cr Dividend receivable    20,000
```

15

Exercise 5-12
Intragroup Transactions & Consolidated Comprehensive Income

Kim Corporation purchased 100 percent ownership of Slim Corporation on July 30, X1, at underlying book value. The companies reported the following data with respect to intercompany sales of inventory in X4 and X5. Unsold units at the end of the year are usually sold at the beginning of the subsequent year. Figures are reported in $.

Year	Purchased by	Price	Sold to	Sale Price	Unsold at the end
X4	Slim	120,000	Kim	180,000	45,000
X5	Slim	90,000	Kim	135,000	30,000
X5	Kim	140,000	Slim	280,000	110,000

Kim reported comprehensive income (excluding income from its investment in Slim) of $160,000 and $220,000 in X4 and X5, respectively. Slim reported comprehensive income of $90,000 and $85,000 in X4 and X5, respectively.

Required

a) Compute consolidated comprehensive income in X4.
b) Compute consolidated comprehensive income in X5.

Profit for X4

Profit for X5

Solutions to Exercises

5-1

a) Unrealized gain on sale of truck on December 31, X6:

- Transfer price $40,000
- Net Book Value at the time of sale
 ($45,000 × 10/15) (30,000)
 Gain on sale **$10,000**

Consolidation entry:
Gain on sale 10,000
 Truck (net) 10,000

Alternative
Gain on sale 10,000
Truck 5,000
 Accumulated Dep. Truck 15,000

b) Unrealized portion of the gain at the beginning of X7:

- Initial gain (X6) $10,000
- Portion realized in X6 -
 Unrealized gain **$10,000**

Consolidation entry:
Retained earnings 10,000
 Truck (net) 10,000

Alternative
Retained Earnings 10,000
Truck 5,000
 Accumulated Dep. Truck 15,000

Portion of the gain being realized in X7:
($10,000 /10) = **$1,000**

Consolidation entry:
Truck (net) 1,000
 Depreciation Expense 1,000

Alternative
Accumulated Dep. Truck 1,000
 Depreciation Expense 1,000

5-2

a) Unrealized gain on sale of land on March 15, X2:

- Transfer price $185,000
- Net Book Value at the time of sale (140,000)
  Gain on sale $45,000

Consolidation entry:
Gain on Sale	45,000	
Land		45,000

b) Consolidation entry:
Retained Earnings	45,000	
Land		45,000

5-3

a) Unrealized gain on sale of equipment on January 1, X5:

- Transfer price $245,000
- Net Book Value at the time of sale
  ($300,000 × 7/10) (210,000)
  Gain on sale $35,000

Consolidation entry:
Gain on Sale	35,000	
Equipment (net)		35,000

Alternative
Gain on Sale	35,000	
Equipment	55,000	
Accumulated Dep. Equipment		90,000

Portion of the gain being realized in X5:
($35,000 / 7) = **$5,000**

Consolidation entry:
Equipment (net)	5,000	
Depreciation Expense		5,000

Alternative
Accumulated Dep. Equip.	5,000	
Depreciation Expense		5,000

b) Unrealized portion of the gain at the beginning of X6:

- Initial gain (X5) $35,000
- Portion realized in X5   5,000
- Unrealized gain   **$30,000**

Consolidation entry:
Retained Earnings   30,000
    Equipment (net)   30,000

Alternative
Retained Earnings   30,000
Equipment   55,000
    Accumulated Dep. Equipment   85,000

Consolidation entry to account for the portion of the gain being realized in X6:
Equipment (net)   5,000
    Depreciation Expense   5,000
($35,000 /7) = **$5,000**

Alternative
Accumulated Dep. Equip.   5,000
    Depreciation Expense   5,000

5-4

a) Unrealized gain on sale of equipment on January 1, X7:

- Transfer price   **$84,000**
- Net Book Value at the time of sale
  ($150,000 × 7/15)   (70,000)
  Gain on sale $14,000

Journal entry made by Ralf:
Cash   84,000
Accumulated Depreciation   80,000
    Equipment   150,000
    Gain on Sale   14,000

b) Journal entries made by Local in X7:
Equipment   84,000
    Cash   84,000

Depreciation Expense   12,000
    Equipment (net)   12,000

c) Consolidation entry to remove the intercompany gain on sale of equipment in X7:

Gain on Sale	14,000	
Equipment (net)		14,000

Alternative

Gain on Sale	14,000	
Equipment	66,000	
Accumulated Dep. Equipment		80,000

Consolidation entry to account for the portion of the gain being realized in X7:

Equipment (net)	2,000	
Depreciation Expense		2,000
($14,000 /7) = **$2,000**		

Alternative

Accumulated Dep. Equip.	2,000	
Depreciation Expense		2,000

d) Unrealized portion of the gain at the beginning of X8:

- Initial gain (X7) $14,000
- Portion realized in X7   2,000
- Unrealized gain   **$12,000**

Consolidation entry:

Retained Earnings	12,000	
Equipment (net)		12,000

Alternative

Retained Earnings	12,000	
Equipment	66,000	
Accumulated Dep. Equipment		78,000

Consolidation entry to account for the portion of the gain being realized in X8:

Equipment (net)	2,000	
Depreciation Expense		2,000
($14,000 /7) = **$2,000**		

Alternative

Accumulated Dep. Equip.	2,000	
Depreciation Expense		2,000

5-5

a) Unrealized gain on sale of equipment on January 1, X6:

- Transfer price $270,000
- Net Book Value at the time of sale
  ($300,000 × 12/15) (240,000)
  Gain on sale **$30,000**

Consolidated comprehensive income for X8:
Comprehensive income of Barn ($100,000) + Comprehensive income of Tool ($40,000) + Portion of the intercompany gain on sale of equipment being realized in X8 ($2,500) = **$142,500**

b) Unrealized portion of the gain at the beginning of X8:

- Initial gain (X6) $30,000
- Portion realized in X6 and X7
  ($30,000/12 × 2 years) 5,000
  Unrealized gain **$25,000**

Consolidation entry:
Retained Earnings 25,000
  Equipment (net) 25,000

Consolidation entry to account for the portion of the gain being realized in X8:
Equipment (net) 2,500
  Depreciation Expense 2,500
($30,000 /12) = **$2,500**

5-6

Unrealized gain on sale of land on June 1, X4:

- Transfer price $120,000
- Net Book Value at the time of sale (95,000)
  Gain on sale **$25,000**

Consolidated comprehensive income for X4:
Comprehensive income of Bulk ($90,000) + Comprehensive income of Task ($60,000) – Unrealized intercompany gain on sale of land ($25,000) = **$125,000**

Consolidated comprehensive income for X5:
Comprehensive income of Bulk ($110,000) + Comprehensive income of Task ($40,000) = **$150,000**

5-7

a) Journal entries made by Loft in X4:

Inventory	960,000	
Accounts Payable		960,000

(40,000 × $24) = $960,000

Accounts Receivable	750,000	
Sales		750,000

(25,000 × $30) = $750,000

Cost of Goods Sold	600,000	
Inventory		600,000

(25,000 × $24) = $600,000

b) Journal entries made by Built in X4:

Inventory	750,000	
Accounts Payable		750,000

(25,000 × $30) = $750,000

Accounts Receivable	810,000	
Sales		810,000

(18,000 × $45) = $810,000

Cost of Goods Sold	540,000	
Inventory		540,000

(18,000 × $30) = $540,000

c) Consolidation entry for X4:

Sales	**750,000**	
Cost of Goods Sold		**708,000**
Inventory		**42,000**

Unrealized profit:
- Profit per unit realized by Loft: ($30 − $24) = $6
- Units remaining in the consolidated group at the end of X4: (25,000 − 18,000) = 7,000
- Unrealized profit: (7,000 × $6) = **$42,000**

5-8

a) Cost of goods sold reported by Bear in X7:

Cost of Goods Sold	820,000	
Inventory		820,000

(10,000 × $82) = $820,000

Cost of goods sold reported by Pratt in X7:
Cost of Goods Sold   658,000
  Inventory   658,000
(7,000 × $94) = $658,000

b) Consolidated cost of goods sold for X7:
COGS of Pratt ($658,000) + COGS of Bear ($820,000) − Intercompany sales ($940,000) + Unrealized intercompany profit ($36,000) = **$574,000**

c) Consolidation entry for X7:
Sales   940,000
  Cost of Goods Sold   904,000
  Inventory   36,000

Unrealized profit:
- Profit per unit realized by Bear: ($94 − $82) = $12
- Units remaining in the consolidated group at the end of X7: (10,000 − 7,000) = 3,000
- Unrealized profit: (3,000 × $12) = **$36,000**

d) Consolidation entry for X8:
Retained Earnings   36,000
  Cost of Goods Sold   36,000

5-9

	Land	Gain on sale
December 31, X1		
• Total	0	0
• Small	$100,000	0
• Consolidated	$115,000	0
December 31, X2		
• Total	$125,000	0
• Small	0	$25,000
• Consolidated	$115,000	0
December 31, X3		
• Total	0	$5,000
• Small	0	0
• Consolidated	0	$15,000

5-10

a)

Dividends Income (Parent)	480,000	
Dividends Declared (Sub)		480,000
Accounts Payable (Sub)	480,000	
Accounts Receivable (Parent)		480,000

b)

Retained Earnings (Sub)	40,000	
Cost of Goods Sold (Sub)		40,000

($160,000 × 25%) = $40,000

c)

Sales (Parent)	750,000	
Cost of Goods Sold (Parent-Sub))		690,000
Inventory (Sub)		60,000
Accounts Payable (Sub)	200,000	
Accounts Receivable (Parent)		200,000

d)

Retained Earnings (Parent-Sub)	12,000	
Equipment (Sub)		12,000
Equipment (Sub)	6,000	
Other Expenses (Sub)		6,000

<u>Initial gain</u>: $90,000 – ($120,000 × 3/5) = $18,000
<u>Amortization</u>: $18,000 / 3 years = $6,000

e)   No adjustments required

5-11

a)

Management Revenue (Grant)	25,000	
Management Fees (Lee)		25,000

b)

Sales (Lee)	100,000	
COGS (Grant & Lee)		94,000
Inventory (Grant)		6,000

c)	*Interest - Revenue (Grant)*	3,300	
	Interest - Expensses (Lee)		3,300
	Note Payable (Lee)	55,000	
	Note Receivable (grant)		55,000
d)	*Gain on Sale of Land (Lee)*	25,000	
	Land(Grant)		25,000
e)	No adjustments required		
f)	*Dividends Revenue (Grant)*	20,000	
	Dividends Declared (Lee)		20,000
	Dividends Payable (Lee)	20,000	
	Dividends Receivable (Grant)		20,000

5-12

a) Consolidated net income in X4:
Comprehensive income of Kim ($160,000) + Comprehensive income of Slim ($90,000) – Current-year upstream intercompany profit ($15,000) = **$235,000**

Deferred upstream profit:
- Profit margin over sales: (180,000 -120,000)/180,000 = 33,3%
- Unrealized profit: ($45,000 × 33,3%) = $15,000

b) Consolidated net income in X5:
Comprehensive income of Kim ($220,000) + Comprehensive income of Slim ($85,000) – Current-year upstream intercompany profit ($10,000) – Current-year downstream intercompany profit ($55,000) + Prior-year upstream intercompany profit ($15,000) = **$255,000**

Deferred upstream profit:
- Profit margin over sales: ($135,000 - $90,000)/$135,000 = 33,3%
- Unrealized profit: ($30,000 × 33,3%) = $10,000

Deferred downstream profit:
- Profit margin over sales: ($280,000 - $140,000)/$280,000 = 50%
- Unrealized profit: ($110,000 × 50%) = $55,000

Consolidation of Wholly Owned Subsidiaries Subsequent to Acquisition: Comprehensive Illustration

Module 6

What you will find in this section

- How to Walk Through Module 6
- Slides
- Exercises and Solutions

Module 6
Consolidation of Wholly Owned Subsidiaries Subsequent to Acquisition: Comprehensive Illustration

---

How to Walk Through Module 6

◇ <u>Readings</u>

1- <u>Book</u> "Consolidation of Financial Statements": Chapter 8
2- <u>Student Manual</u> "Advanced Accounting": Module 6
   PART 1: COMPREHENSIVE ILLUSTRATION: BASIC INFORMATION
   PART 2: ADJUSTMENTS RELATED TO CONTROLLING OWNERSHIP
   PART 3: ADJUSTMENTS RELATED TO INTERCOMPANY TRANSACTIONS
   PART 4: EQUITY METHOD

◇ <u>Assignments</u>

3- <u>Student Manual</u>: End-of module quiz questions
4- <u>Student Manual</u>: Exercises 1 to 8
5- <u>Book</u>: Cases 5, 6 and 7

When you have successfully completed this module, you will be able to do the following:

- Demonstrate the mechanics of consolidating wholly owned subsidiaries in periods subsequent to acquisition (case involving intercompany transactions)

- Consolidate financial statements in post-acquisition periods using the worksheet approach and the direct approach

- Consolidate financial statements under the cost and the equity method

CONSOLIDATION OF WHOLLY OWNED SUBSIDIARIES SUBSEQUENT TO ACQUISITION: COMPREHENSIVE ILLUSTRATION
Module 6

Copyright © 2020 Parmitech

Advanced Accounting: Student Manual

Copyrighted Material

Editor: Parmitech

This publication is protected by copyright, and permission should be obtained from the publisher prior to any prohibited reproduction, storage in a retrieval system, or transmission in any form or by any means, electronic, mechanical, photocopying, recording, or otherwise.

Corresponding Author

Richard Bozec Ph.D., CPA, CGA
bozec@telfer.uottawa.ca

Copyright © Parmitech

CORRESPONDING CHAPTERS in *Bozec*
"Consolidation of Financial Statements under IFRS"

Chapter 8   **Practical Guide**

Cases   (5) (6) (7)

TEACHING MATERIAL
Exercises

Module 6

6.1	Multiple-Choice Questions
6.2	Consolidation Subsequent to Acquisition: Direct Approach and Equity Method
6.3	Consolidation Subsequent to Acquisition: Direct Approach
6.4	Consolidation Subsequent to Acquisition: Worksheet Approach
6.5	Continuation of Plus Inc. (Case 7) in Year X8
6.6	Continuation of Plus Inc. (Case 7) in Year X9
6.7	Consolidated Retained Earnings
6.8	Consolidation Subsequent to Acquisition and Negative Goodwill

FOCUS OF THIS MODULE: INTEGRATION OF PRIOR MODULES

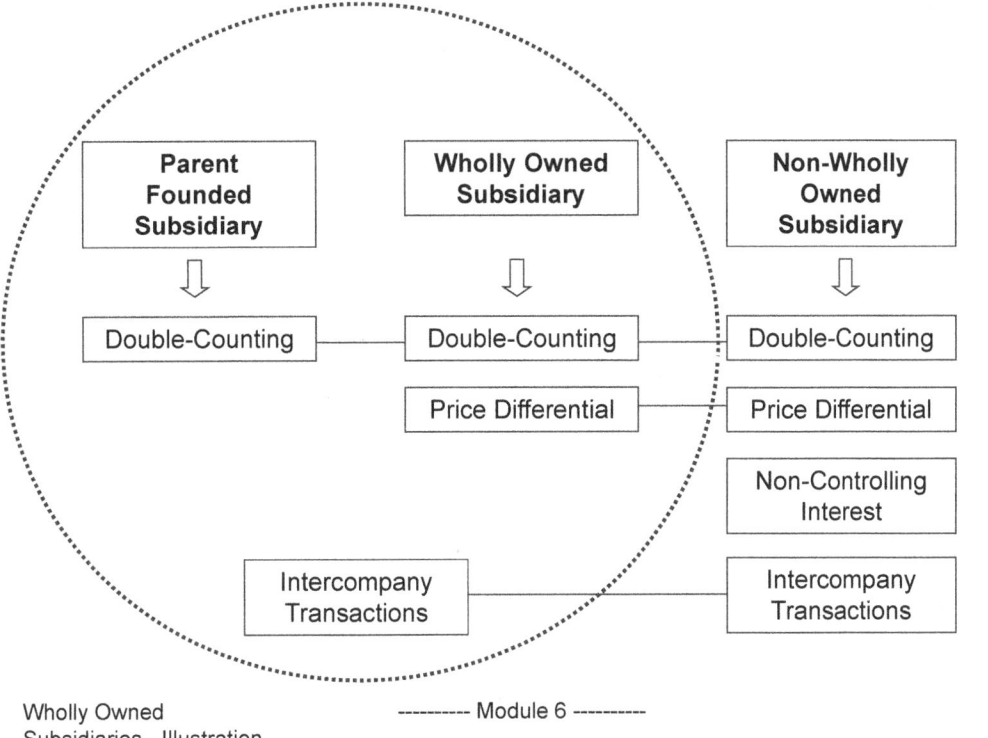

Wholly Owned Subsidiaries - Illustration

OBJECTIVES OF THIS MODULE

- Illustrate the consolidation process of wholly owned subsidiaries in periods subsequent to acquisition using the worksheet approach and the direct approach. Discuss the general approach to consolidation when the parent has used either the cost method or the equity method to account for its investment.

- Discuss a comprehensive case that integrates all the basic consolidation techniques and procedures introduced thus far. The case includes price differential and intercompany transactions.

- Prepare for the midterm exam.

INTEGRATION OF PRIOR MODULES

Wholly Owned Subsidiaries - Illustration

OUTLINE OF THE PRESENTATION

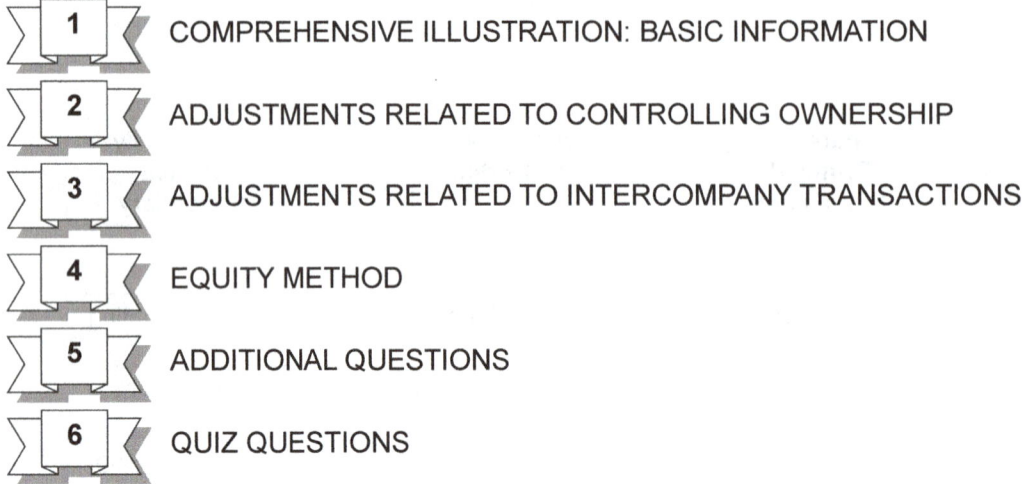

1. COMPREHENSIVE ILLUSTRATION: BASIC INFORMATION
2. ADJUSTMENTS RELATED TO CONTROLLING OWNERSHIP
3. ADJUSTMENTS RELATED TO INTERCOMPANY TRANSACTIONS
4. EQUITY METHOD
5. ADDITIONAL QUESTIONS
6. QUIZ QUESTIONS

Part 1

CONSOLIDATION OF ACQUIRED SUBSIDIARIES IN PERIODS SUBSEQUENT TO ACQUISITION
Preliminary Analysis (1/2)

- Check if control of Parent over Subsidiary is maintained;

- If control is sustained, consolidation of F/S is still required. Then, return to the date of acquisition to prepare or retrieve the allocation of the purchase price;

    → **ALLOCATION OF THE PURCHASE PRICE**

- Follow up on the price differential from date of acquisition to the current year (amortization and/or realization of the FV increments/decrements and goodwill impairment);

    → **PRICE DIFFERENTIAL AMORTIZATION SCHEDULE**

- Get the complete set of F/S of Parent and Subsidiary for the current year;

- From the SFP of Parent, take a look at the *Investment in Subsidiary* to determine if Parent is using either the *Cost Method* or the *Equity Method*;

Part 1

CONSOLIDATION OF ACQUIRED SUBSIDIARIES
IN PERIODS SUBSEQUENT TO ACQUISITION
Preliminary Analysis (2/2)

- If the *Cost Method* is used, check the I/S of Parent for any *Dividend Income* as a result of current-year *Intercompany Dividends* (double-counting in I/S);

- Examine carefully the F/S of the affiliated companies to identify any additional *Reciprocal Balances* (such as Receivables/Payables; Revenues/Expenses) as a result of current and/or prior-year *Intercompany Transactions;*

- Enquire additional information regarding *Intercompany Transactions*. Assess the impact of each transaction (upstream and downstream) on the current profit and RE.

    ➥ RECAP ON INTERCOMPANY TRANSACTIONS

Wholly Owned Subsidiaries - Illustration

Part 1

CONSOLIDATION OF ACQUIRED SUBSIDIARIES
IN PERIODS SUBSEQUENT TO ACQUISITION
Consolidation Steps Under the Cost Method (1/2)

- Eliminate the double-counting in the SFP: elimination of the *Investment in Subsidiary* (Parent) and the *Equity* section (Subsidiary);

- Establish the FV of Subsidiary at date of acquisition (price differential);

- Take into account the portion of the price differential that has been amortized and/or realized since acquisition;

- If Intercompany Dividends, eliminate the double-counting in the I/S: elimination of *Dividend Income* (Parent) and *Dividends Declared* (Subsidiary);

- Eliminate any additional reciprocal balances (*Overstatements*) as a result of Intercompany Transactions from current and prior years.

Wholly Owned Subsidiaries - Illustration

CONSOLIDATION OF ACQUIRED SUBSIDIARIES IN PERIODS SUBSEQUENT TO ACQUISITION
Consolidation Steps Under the Cost Method (2/2)

- Eliminate any unrealized gains and losses from upstream and downstream transactions.

- Account for any unrealized gains and losses from prior-year transactions that are now being realized.

PART 1
Comprehensive Illustration: Basic Information

1. INITIAL ACQUISITION
2. FINANCIAL STATEMENTS OF THE AFFILIATED COMPANIES
3. ADDITIONAL INFORMATION
4. PURCHASE PRICE ALLOCATION
5. PRICE DIFFERENTIAL AMORTIZATION SCHEDULE

Part 1

BASIC INFORMATION
Initial Acquisition

On December 31, X1, Parent Company acquires all the outstanding voting shares of Subsidiary by issuing 40,000 shares with a market value of $30, or $1,200,000 total, in exchange.

At the date of combination, the fair values of Subsidiary's land and buildings exceeded their book values by $100,000 and $200,000, respectively. The fair values of all of Subsidiary's other assets and liabilities were equal to their book values.

Subsidiary had common shares of $200,000 and retained earnings of $600,000 at the date of acquisition.

The remaining useful life of the buildings from the date of acquisition is ten years. Subsidiary uses the straight-line method to calculate amortizations.

Required

Prepare the consolidated financial statements of Parent Company for the year ended December 31, X5.

Part 1

BASIC INFORMATION
Affiliation Structure

BEFORE

[PARENT]   [SUBSIDIARY]

AFTER

Parent's shareholders   Subsidiary's shareholders
160,000 shares → [PARENT] ← 40,000 shares
(80%)   (20%)

↓ 100%

[SUBSIDIARY]

Part 1

CONSOLIDATION OF PARENT COMPANY IN YEAR SUBSEQUENT TO ACQUISITION
Timeline

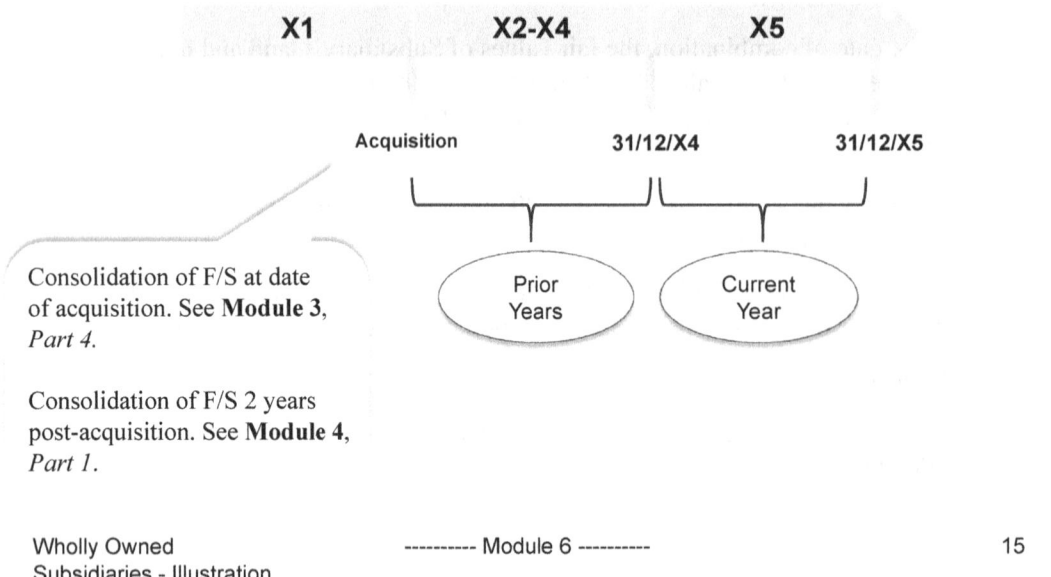

Consolidation of F/S at date of acquisition. See **Module 3**, *Part 4*.

Consolidation of F/S 2 years post-acquisition. See **Module 4**, *Part 1*.

Wholly Owned Subsidiaries - Illustration

---------- Module 6 ----------

Part 1

CONSOLIDATION OF PARENT COMPANY IN YEAR SUBSEQUENT TO ACQUISITION
Basic Information at Acquisition - From Module 3

	Book Values	Fair Values	
Assets			
Non-current assets			
Land	$300,000	$400,00	+ 100,000
Buildings (net)	350,000	550,000	+ 200,000
Current assets			
Inventories	50,000	50,000	
Accounts receivable	150,000	150,000	
Cash	50,000	50,000	
Total assets	**$900,000**		
Equity and liabilities			
Equity			
Share capital	$200,000		
Retained earnings	600,000		
Liabilities			
Accounts payable	100,000	100,000	
Total equity and liabilities	**$900,000**		

Wholly Owned Subsidiaries - Illustration

Part 1

CONSOLIDATION OF PARENT COMPANY IN YEAR SUBSEQUENT TO ACQUISITION
Allocation of Purchase Price - From Module 3

Purchase price		$1,200 000
Net book value of Subsidiary:		
- Common shares	$200,000	
- Retained earnings	600,000	800,000
Price differential		400,000
Fair value increments:		
- Land	(100,000)	
- Buildings	(200,000)	(300,000)
Goodwill		$100,000

Part 1

BASIC INFORMATION
Separate-Entity Statements of Financial Position
At December 31, X5

	Parent	Subsidiary
Assets		
Non-current assets		
Land	$1,250,000	-
Buildings & equipment (net)	3,400,000	$210,000
Investment in Subsidiary	1,200,000	
Current assets		
Inventories	500,000	230,000
Accounts receivable	1,800,000	780,000
Cash	590,000	170,000
Total assets	**$8,740,000**	**$1,390,000**
Equity and liabilities		
Equity		
Share capital	$3,800,000	$200,000
Retained earnings	3,600,000	1,100,000
Liabilities		
Long-term notes payable	1,000,000	-
Accounts payable	340,000	90,000
Total equity and liabilities	**$8,740,000**	**$1,390,000**

BASIC INFORMATION
Separate-Entity Income Statements
For the Period Ended December 31, X5

	Parent	Subsidiary
Sales revenue	$3,100,000	$570,000
Dividend income	20,000	
Cost of sales	2,300,000	420,000
Depreciation expense	200,000	35,000
Other expenses	440,000	85,000
Profit for the year	**$180,000**	**$30,000**

Wholly Owned Subsidiaries - Illustration

BASIC INFORMATION
Separate-Entity Statements of Changes in Equity
For the Period Ended December 31, X5

	Parent			Subsidiary		
	Share Capital	Retained Earnings	Total	Share Capital	Retained Earnings	Total
Balance at Dec. 31, X4	$3,800,000	$3,520,000	$7,320,000	$200,000	$1,090,000	$1,290,000
Profit for the year		180,000	180,000		30,000	30,000
Dividends		(100,000)	(100,000)		(20,000)	(20,000)
Balance at Dec. X5	$3,800,000	$3,600,000	$7,400,000	$200,000	$1,100,000	$1,300,000

Wholly Owned Subsidiaries - Illustration

CONSOLIDATION OF PARENT COMPANY
Additional Information

Intercompany Transactions

1. In X5, Parent had sales of $60,000 to Subsidiary. Parent's X5 gross margin was 45%; $10,000 (sales price) of the transferred units are in Subsidiary's inventory on December 31, X5.

2. In X4, Parent had sales of $20,000 to Subsidiary. Parent's X4 gross margin was 30%; $6,000 (sales price) of the transferred units was in Subsidiary's inventory on December 31, X4.

3. In X4, Subsidiary had sales of $50,000 to Parent. Subsidiary's X4 gross margin was 35%; all the transferred units were resold to external parties by the end of X4.

4. Subsidiary sold an equipment to Parent on January 1, X4, for $30,000. The net book value of the equipment at the time of transfer was equal to $20,000, that is, the original cost for Subsidiary. The estimated useful life of the equipment is 10 years.

CONSOLIDATION OF PARENT COMPANY
Additional Information (continued...)

Price Differential

5. Subsidiary sold its land to an outside party in X4 for $450,000. The land originally cost Subsidiary $300,000, and its fair value at the date of Parent's acquisition was $400,000.

6. Impairment test for X5 revealed that Goodwill should be $80,000.

Part 1

BASIC INFORMATION
Price Differential Amortization Schedule

Items	Price Differential — Balance at Acquisition	Amortization — Prior Years (X2-X4)	Amortization — Current Year (X5)	Unamortized Excess at December 31, X5
Land	$100,000	($100,000)	-	-
Buildings	200,000	(60,000)	(20,000)	$120,000
Goodwill	100,000	-	(20,000)	80,000
Total	$400,000	($160,000)	($40,000)	$200,000

PORTION BEING CONSUMED SINCE ACQUISITION
$200,000

Wholly Owned Subsidiaries - Illustration ---------- Module 6 ----------

---

Part 1

BASIC INFORMATION
Price Differential Amortization Schedule - Notes

The price differential amortization schedule summarizes the information regarding the price differential amortization-realization since acquisition, that is, from X2 to X5 inclusive.

- The land has been sold in X4 (Additional Information 5). Therefore, the asset-related fair value increment at acquisition ($100,000) is fully realized.
- Buildings-related fair value increment ($200,000) must be amortized over 10 years in order to adjust for the annual underdepreciation expense ($20,000).
  Prior years: (3 × $20,000) = $60,000.
- Goodwill has been impaired in X5. Therefore, $20,000 must be expensed (Additional Information 6).

Wholly Owned Subsidiaries - Illustration ---------- Module 6 ----------

BASIC INFORMATION
Recap on Intercompany Gains - Impact for X5

Part 1

Transaction	RE Beginning	Profit	RE End
Downstream			
➢ Unrealized profit from sale of merchandise in X5	-	($4,500)	($4,500)
➢ Unrealized profit from sale of merchandise in X4	($1,800)	1,800	-
Upstream			
➢ Sale and resale of merchandise in X4	-	-	-
➢ Sale of equipment in X4	(9,000)	1,000	(8,000)

CONSOLIDATION OF PARENT COMPANY
Practical Guide
Bozec, Chapter 8

Part 1

Scenarios	Description
2.2	Consolidation of a wholly owned subsidiary subsequent to acquisition
4.1	Intercompany dividends (X5)
6.1	Intercompany sale of inventory in current year (X5)
6.2	Intercompany sale of inventory in prior year (X4)
7.2	Intercompany sale of equipment in prior year (X4)

Part 2

OUTLINE OF THE PRESENTATION

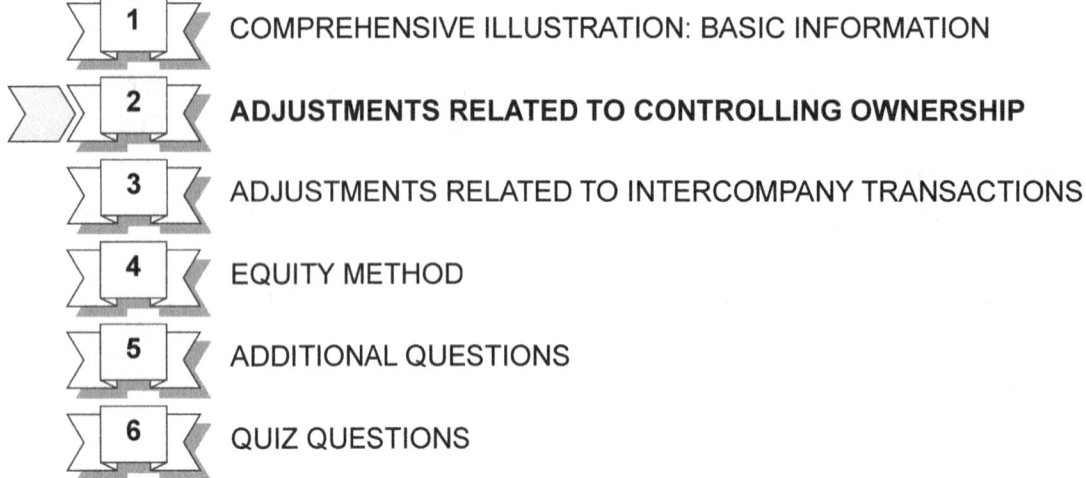

1. COMPREHENSIVE ILLUSTRATION: BASIC INFORMATION
2. **ADJUSTMENTS RELATED TO CONTROLLING OWNERSHIP**
3. ADJUSTMENTS RELATED TO INTERCOMPANY TRANSACTIONS
4. EQUITY METHOD
5. ADDITIONAL QUESTIONS
6. QUIZ QUESTIONS

Part 2

PART 2
Adjustments Related to Controlling Ownership

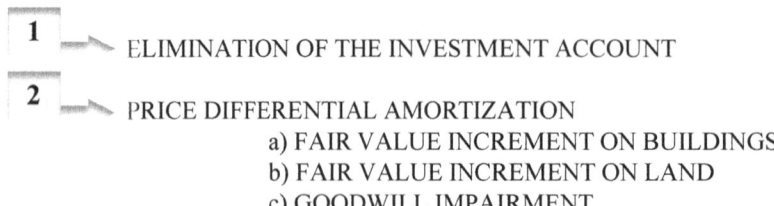

1. ELIMINATION OF THE INVESTMENT ACCOUNT
2. PRICE DIFFERENTIAL AMORTIZATION
   a) FAIR VALUE INCREMENT ON BUILDINGS
   b) FAIR VALUE INCREMENT ON LAND
   c) GOODWILL IMPAIRMENT

Part 2

ADJUSTMENTS RELATED TO CONTROLLING OWNERSHIP
Elimination of the Investment Account

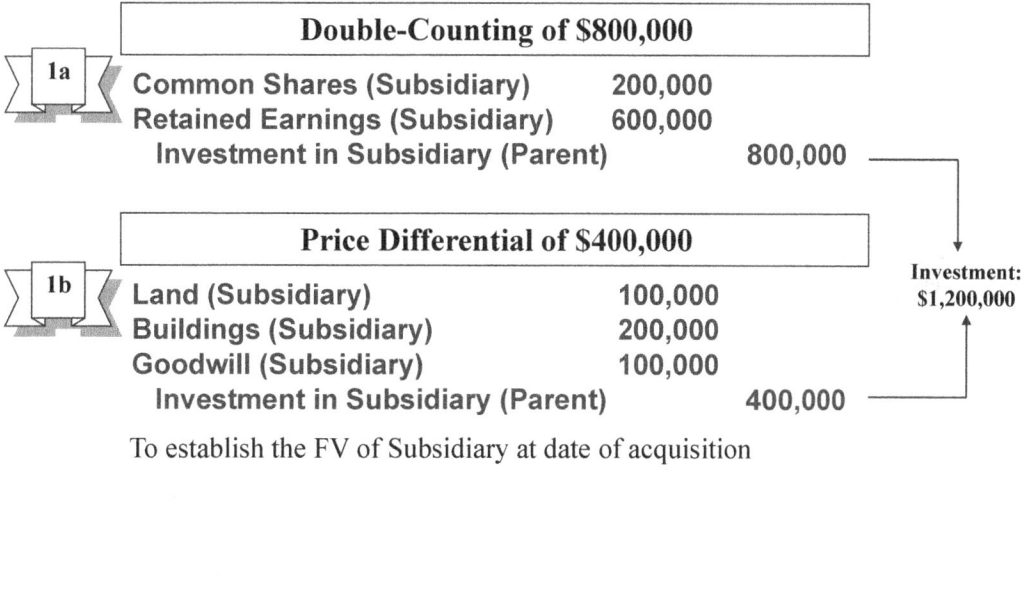

Double-Counting of $800,000

1a Common Shares (Subsidiary)   200,000
    Retained Earnings (Subsidiary)   600,000
        Investment in Subsidiary (Parent)   800,000

Price Differential of $400,000

1b Land (Subsidiary)   100,000
    Buildings (Subsidiary)   200,000
    Goodwill (Subsidiary)   100,000
        Investment in Subsidiary (Parent)   400,000

Investment: $1,200,000

To establish the FV of Subsidiary at date of acquisition

Wholly Owned Subsidiaries - Illustration ———— Module 6 ————

Part 2

ADJUSTMENTS RELATED TO CONTROLLING OWNERSHIP
Price Differential - Fair Value Increment on Buildings

Amortization of the Fair Value Increment on Buildings since Acquisition

2a Depreciation Expense (Subsidiary)   20,000
    Retained Earnings (Subsidiary)   60,000
        Buildings (Subsidiary)   80,000

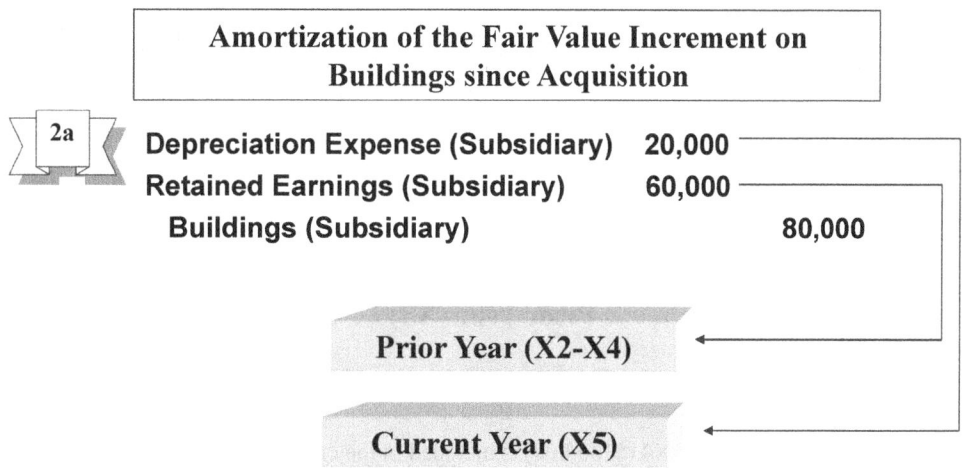

Prior Year (X2-X4)

Current Year (X5)

Wholly Owned Subsidiaries - Illustration ———— Module 6 ————

Part 2

ADJUSTMENTS RELATED TO CONTROLLING OWNERSHIP
Price Differential - Fair Value Increment on Land
Impact on X4

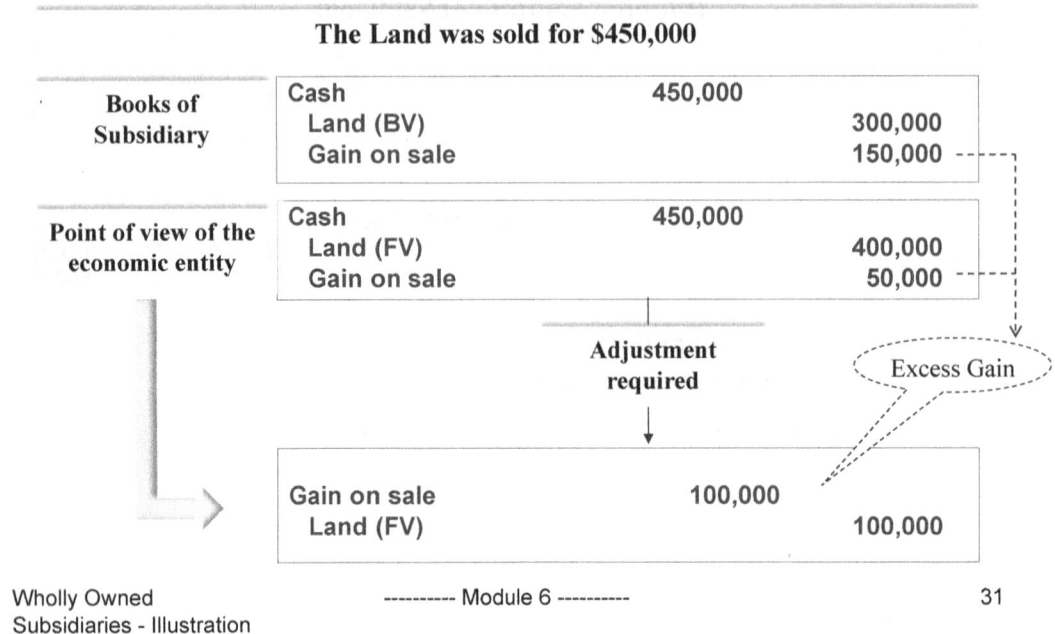

Part 2

ADJUSTMENTS RELATED TO CONTROLLING OWNERSHIP
Price Differential - Fair Value Increment on Land

Realization of the Fair Value Increment on Land

2b

	Debit	Credit
Retained Earnings (Subsidiary)	100,000	
Land (Subsidiary)		100,000

Prior Year (X4)

In X5, the excess gain on sale of X4 ($100,000) is included in the opening balance of Subsidiary's RE. Therefore, we must decrease Subsidiary's RE by $100,000 in the current period so as to correct for the overstatement. Next, consistent with entry 1b, which accounts for price differential, we must decrease Land by $100,000 (FVI at the date of acquisition). This consolidation entry must be repeated in the future.

Part 2

ADJUSTMENTS RELATED TO CONTROLLING OWNERSHIP
Price Differential - Goodwill

Goodwill Impairment

2c Other Expenses (Subsidiary)   20,000
      Goodwill (Subsidiary)   20,000

Current Year (X5)

Wholly Owned Subsidiaries - Illustration ---------- Module 6 ----------

---

Part 2

ADJUSTMENTS RELATED TO CONTROLLING OWNERSHIP
Price Differential - Collapsing Entries

Price Differential		Amortization		Unamortized Excess at December 31, X5
Items	Balance at Acquisition	Prior Years (X2-X4)	Current Year (X5)	
Land	$100,000	($100,000)	-	-
Buildings	200,000	(60,000)	(20,000)	$120,000
Goodwill	100,000	=	(20,000)	80,000
Total	$400,000	($160,000)	($40,000)	$200,000

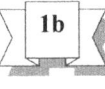

Retained Earnings   160,000
Depreciation Expense   20,000
Other Expenses   20,000
Buildings   120,000
Goodwill   80,000
    Investment in Subsidiary   400,000

Wholly Owned Subsidiaries - Illustration ---------- Module 6 ----------

Part 3

OUTLINE OF THE PRESENTATION

1. COMPREHENSIVE ILLUSTRATION: BASIC INFORMATION
2. ADJUSTMENTS RELATED TO CONTROLLING OWNERSHIP
3. **ADJUSTMENTS RELATED TO INTERCOMPANY TRANSACTIONS**
4. EQUITY METHOD
5. ADDITIONAL QUESTIONS
6. QUIZ QUESTIONS

Part 3

PART 3
Adjustments Related to Intercompany Transactions

1. DOWNSTREAM SALE OF INVENTORY IN THE CURRENT PERIOD
2. DOWNSTREAM SALE OF INVENTORY IN A PRIOR PERIOD
3. UPSTREAM SALE OF INVENTORY IN A PRIOR PERIOD
4. UPSTREAM SALE OF EQUIPMENT IN A PRIOR PERIOD
5. INTERCOMPANY DIVIDENDS

Part 3
ADJUSTMENTS RELATED TO INTERCOMPANY TRANSACTIONS
Downstream Sale of Inventory in X5 – Impact on the Affiliates' Income Statements

In X5, Parent had sales of $60,000 to Subsidiary. Parent's X5 gross margin was 45%; $10,000 (sales price) of the transferred units are in Subsidiary's inventory on December 31, X5 (Additional Information #1).

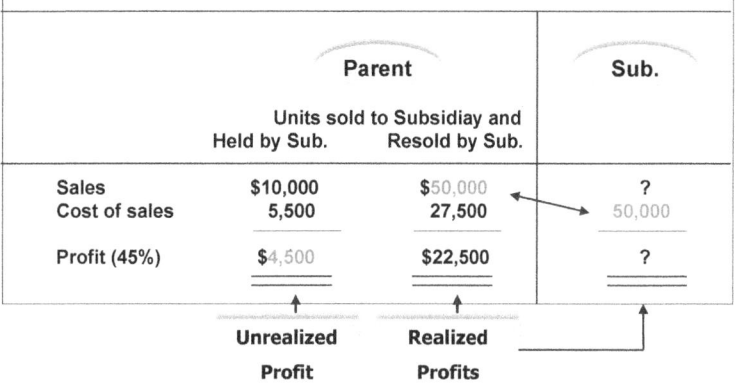

Wholly Owned Subsidiaries - Illustration

Part 3
ADJUSTMENTS RELATED TO INTERCOMPANY TRANSACTIONS
Downstream Sale of Inventory in X5 - Consolidation Entries

(1) Unrealized Profit

Sales (Parent)	10,000	
Cost of Goods Sold (Parent)		5,500
Inventory (Subsidiary)		4,500

(2) Reciprocal Balances

Sales (Parent)	50,000	
Cost of Goods Sold (Subsidiary)		50,000

Combined Entry (1 + 2)

Sales (Parent)	60,000	
Cost of Goods Sold (Parent & Sub.)		55,500
Inventory (Subsidiary)		4,500

Wholly Owned Subsidiaries - Illustration

Part 3
ADJUSTMENTS RELATED TO INTERCOMPANY TRANSACTIONS
Downstream Sale of Inventory in X4 - Consolidation Entry

In X4, Parent had sales of $20,000 to Subsidiary. Parent's X4 gross margin was 30%; $6,000 (sales price) of the transferred units was in Subsidiary's inventory on December 31, X4 (Additional Information #2).

Realization of Prior-Year Profit on Sale of Inventory		

Retained Earnings (Parent)	1,800	
Cost of Goods Sold		1,800

Wholly Owned Subsidiaries - Illustration ---------- Module 6 ---------- 39

Part 3
ADJUSTMENTS RELATED TO INTERCOMPANY TRANSACTIONS
Upstream Sale of Inventory in X4

In X4, Subsidiary had sales of $50,000 to Parent. Subsidiary's X4 gross margin was 35%; all the transferred units were resold to external parties by the end of X4 (Additional Information #3).

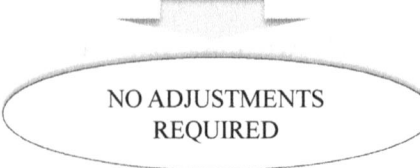

NO ADJUSTMENTS REQUIRED

Wholly Owned Subsidiaries - Illustration ---------- Module 6 ---------- 40

Part 3
ADJUSTMENTS RELATED TO INTERCOMPANY TRANSACTIONS
Upstream Sale of Equipment in X4

Subsidiary sold an equipment to Parent on January 1, X4, for $30,000. The net book value of the equipment at the time of transfer was equal to $20,000, that is, the original cost for Subsidiary. The estimated useful life of the equipment is 10 years (Additional Information #4).

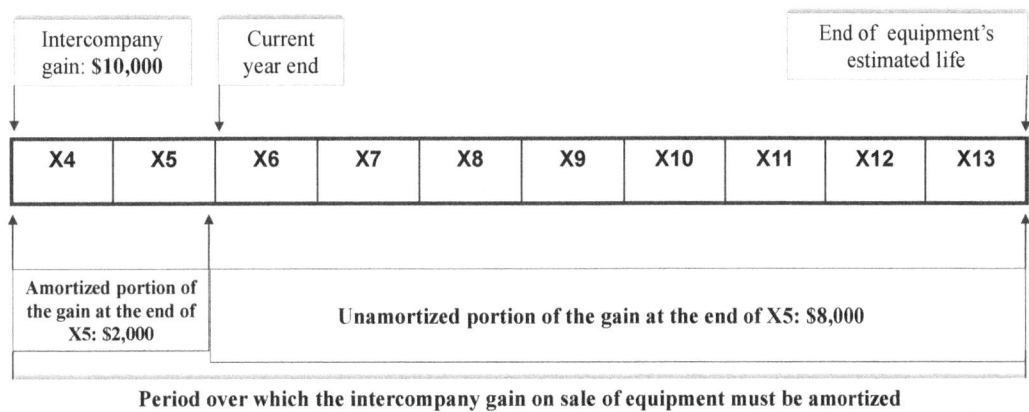

Period over which the intercompany gain on sale of equipment must be amortized

---

Part 3
ADJUSTMENTS RELATED TO INTERCOMPANY TRANSACTIONS
Upstream Sale of Equipment in X4 - Consolidation Entries

Unrealized Portion of the Gain at the Beginning of X5

5a) Retained Earnings (Parent & Sub.)   9,000
        Buildings & Equip. (net) (Parent)   9,000

Excess Depreciation of the Current Period

5b) Buildings & Equip. (net) (Parent)   1,000
        Depreciation Expenses (Parent)   1,000

Part 3

ADJUSTMENTS RELATED TO INTERCOMPANY TRANSACTIONS
Equipment - Alternative Consolidation Entries

Unrealized Portion of the Gain at the Beginning of X5

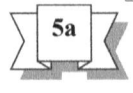

Retained Earnings (Parent & Sub.)	9,000	
Accumulated D. B & Equip. (Parent)	1,000	
Buildings & Equip. (Parent)		10,000

Excess Depreciation of the Current Period

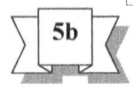

Accumulated D. B & Equip. (Parent)	1,000	
Depreciation Expenses (Parent)		1,000

Part 3

ADJUSTMENTS RELATED TO INTERCOMPANY TRANSACTIONS
What if the Equipment was Resold by Parent at the Beginning of X5

Sales to the outside party: $50,000

Books of Parent

Cash	50,000	
Equipment (net: $30,000 × 9/10)		27,000
Gain on sale		23,000

Point of view of the economic entity

Cash	50,000	
Equipment (net: $20,000 × 9/10)		18,000
Gain on sale		32,000

Adjustment required ↓

Retained earnings	9,000	
Gain on sale		9,000

Part 3

ADJUSTMENTS RELATED TO INTERCOMPANY TRANSACTIONS
Intercompany Dividends

Double-Counting of Subsidiary's Earnings

6 Dividend Income (Parent)   20,000
       Dividends Declared (Subsidiary)   20,000

Wholly Owned Subsidiaries - Illustration ---------- Module 6 ----------

---

Part 3

CONSOLIDATION WORKSHEET OF PARENT COMPANY
For the Year Ended December 31, X5

	Parent	Subsidiary	Conso. Entries	Consolidated
Assets				
Land	$1,250,000	-	(1b) 100,000 (2b) (100,000)	$1,250,000
Buildings & equipment (net)	3,400,000	$210,000	(1b) 200,000 (2a) (80,000) (5a) (9,000) (5b) 1,000	3,722,000
Goodwill			(1b) 100,000 (2c) (20,000)	80,000
Investment in Subsidiary	1,200,000		(1a) (800,000) (1b) (400,000)	-
Inventories	500,000	230,000	(3) (4,500)	725,500
Accounts receivable	1,800,000	780,000		2,580,000
Cash	590,000	170,000		760,000
Total assets	**$8,740,000**	**$1,390,000**		**$9,117,500**
Equity and liabilities				
Share capital	$3,800,000	$200,000	(1a) (200,000)	$3,800,000
Retained earnings	3,600,000	1,100,000	(812,500)	3,887,500
Long-term notes payable	1,000,000	-		1,000,000
Accounts payable	340,000	90,000		430,000
Total equity and liabilities	**$8,740,000**	**$1,390,000**		**$9,117,500**

CONSOLIDATION WORKSHEET OF PARENT COMPANY (continued…)
For the Year Ended December 31, X5

Part 3

	Parent	Subsidiary	Conso. Entries	Consolidated
Sales revenue	$3,100,000	$570,000	(3) (60,000)	$3,610,000
Dividend income	20,000		(6) (20,000)	-
Cost of sales	2,300,000	420,000	(3) (55,500) (4) (1,800)	2,662,700
Depreciation expense	200,000	35,000	(2a) 20,000 (5b) (1,000)	254,000
Other expenses	440,000	85,000	(2c) 20,000	545,000
Profit for the year	**$180,000**	**$30,000**	**(61,700)**	**$148,300**
Retained earnings (beginning)	$3,520,000	$1,090,000	(1a) (600,000) (2a) (60,000) (2b) (100,000) (4) (1,800) (5a) (9,000)	$3,839,200
Dividends declared	(100,000)	(20,000)	(6) 20,000	(100,000)
Retained earnings (end)	**$3,600,000**	**$1,100,000**	**(812,500)**	**$3,887,500**

Net impact of the consolidation adjustments on the ending balance of Retained Earnings. To be transferred in the statement of financial position

---

DIRECT APPROACH
Non-Current Assets

Part 3

Buildings & Equipment (net)

Parent	$3,400,000
Subsidiary	210,000
Unamortized portion of the:	
• Fair value increment on Buildings ($200,000 × 6/10)	**120,000**
• Upstream gain on sale of Equip. ($10,000 × 8/10)	**(8,000)**
Total	$3,722,000

Goodwill

At acquisition	$100,000
Portion impaired	**(20,000)**
Total	$80,000

Land

Parent	$1,250,000

DIRECT APPROACH
Current Assets

Cash

Parent	$590,000
Subsidiary	170,000
Total	$760,000

Accounts Receivable

Parent	$1,800,000
Subsidiary	780,000
Total	$2,580,000

Inventories

Parent	$500,000
Subsidiary	230,000
Unrealized profit on downstream sale	**(4,500)**
Total	$725,500

DIRECT APPROACH
Equities

Common Shares

Parent	$3,800,000

PRICE DIFFERENTIAL AMORTIZATION SCHEDULE

RECAP ON INTERCOMPANY TRANSACTIONS

Retained Earnings

Parent		$3,600,000
Unrealized profit on **downstream** sale of inventory		(4,500)
Subsidiary's net adjusted value since acquisition		
• Retained earnings increase since acquisition ($1,100,000 - $600,000)	$500,000	
• Price differential amortization since acquisition	(200,000)	
• Unrealized portion of the gain on **upstream** sale of equipment ($10,000 × 8/10)	(8,000)	292,000
Total		$3,887,500

DIRECT APPROACH - CONSOLIDATED BALANCE OF RE
Classification of Upstream vs. Downstream Adjustments

Part 3

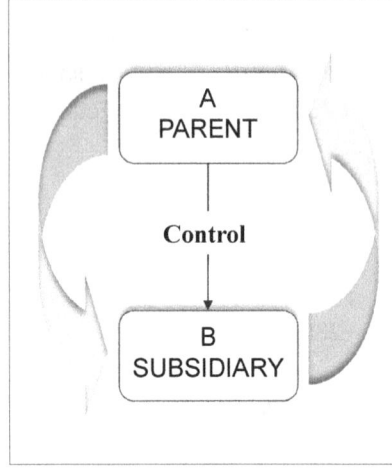

Consolidation adjustments from **downstream** transactions affect **Parent**.

Consolidation adjustments from **upstream** transactions affect the net adjusted value (or consolidated value) of **Subsidiary**.

The distinction between upstream and downstream transactions is critical in control relationships of less than 100% ownership. We will return to this issue in Module 7.

DIRECT APPROACH
Liabilities

Part 3

Accounts Payable	
Parent	$340,000
Subsidiary	90,000
Total	$430,000

Long-Term Notes Payable	
Parent	$1,000,000

Part 3

DIRECT APPROACH
Consolidated Profit

- Adjusted profit of Parent:
  - Profit of Parent for the period $180,000
  - Unrealized current-year profit on **downstream** sale of inventory (4,500)
  - Realized profit from prior-year **downstream** sale of inventory 1,800
  - Intercompany dividends (20,000) $157,300

- Adjusted profit of Subsidiary:
  - Profit of Subsidiary for the period $30,000
  - Current-year price differential amortization (40,000)
  - Realized portion of prior-year **upstream** sale of equipment ($10,000/10) 1,000   (9,000)
  - Total $148,300

Wholly Owned Subsidiaries - Illustration

Part 3

DIRECT APPROACH - CONSOLIDATED PROFIT
Classification of Upstream vs. Downstream Adjustments

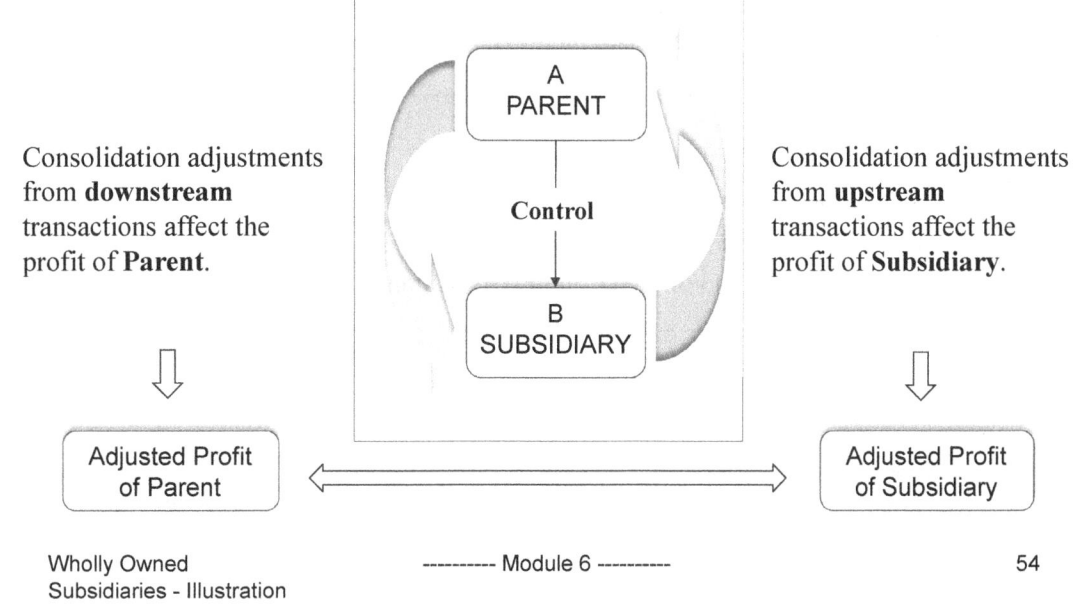

Consolidation adjustments from **downstream** transactions affect the profit of **Parent**.

Consolidation adjustments from **upstream** transactions affect the profit of **Subsidiary**.

Wholly Owned Subsidiaries - Illustration

NET ADJUSTED VALUE OF SUBSIDIARY
At December 31, X5

	Individual Records of Subsidiary	Consolidation Adjustments		Purchase Price
At Date of Acquisition December 31, X1	Net Book Value $800,000	Purchase Price Differential $400,000		$1,200,000
Since Acquisition	Retained Earnings Increase $500,000	Price Differential Amortization ($200,000)	Unrealized Gain- Sale of Equipment ($8,000)	Net Adjusted Value Increase $292,000
At December 31, X5	Net Book Value $1,300,000	Unamortized Portion of Price Differential $200,000	Unrealized Gains on Upstream Transactions ($8,000)	Net Adjusted Value $1,492,000

Wholly Owned Subsidiaries - Illustration

DIRECT APPROACH - RECAP
How to Compute Retained Earnings

1
- Retained earnings of Parent
- Unrealized profits and/or losses on **downstream** transactions

2
- Net Adjusted Value of Subsidiary since Acquisition:
  - Retained earnings increase of Subsidiary since acquisition
  - Price differential amortization since acquisition
  - Unrealized profits and/or losses on **upstream** transactions

Wholly Owned Subsidiaries - Illustration

Part 3

DIRECT APPROACH - RECAP
How to Compute the Consolidated Profit

1

- Adjusted profit of Parent:
    - Profit of Parent for the period
    - Unrealized current-year profits and/or losses on **downstream** transactions
    - Realized profits and/or losses from prior-year **downstream** transactions
    - Intercompany dividends

2

- Adjusted profit of Subsidiary:
    - Profit of Subsidiary for the period
    - Current-year price differential amortization (see amortization schedule)
    - Unrealized current-year profits and/or losses on **upstream** transactions
    - Realized profits and/or losses from prior-year **upstream** transactions

---

Part 4

OUTLINE OF THE PRESENTATION

1. COMPREHENSIVE ILLUSTRATION: BASIC INFORMATION
2. ADJUSTMENTS RELATED TO CONTROLLING OWNERSHIP
3. ADJUSTMENTS RELATED TO INTERCOMPANY TRANSACTIONS
4. **EQUITY METHOD**
5. ADDITIONAL QUESTIONS
6. QUIZ QUESTIONS

PART 4
Equity Method

Part 4

1 → JOURNAL ENTRIES
2 → COMPUTATION OF THE INVESTMENT BALANCE ACCOUNT
3 → FINANCIAL STATEMENTS PRESENTATION
4 → CONSOLIDATION ENTRIES

Wholly Owned Subsidiaries - Illustration ---------- Module 6 ---------- 59

EQUITY METHOD
Basic Journal Entries - Review

Part 4

PROPORTIONATE SHARE OF EARNINGS

1

Investment in B	XX	
Equity in earnings of B (I/S)		XX

PROPORTIONATE SHARE OF DIVIDENDS

2

Cash	XX	
Investment in B		XX

Proportionate share of the change of B'retained earnings

Wholly Owned Subsidiaries - Illustration ---------- Module 6 ---------- 60

EQUITY METHOD
Closely Related to Consolidation - Recall

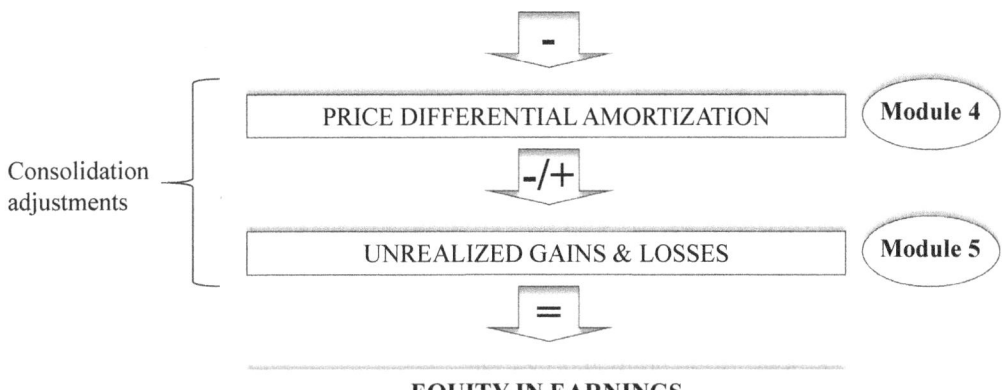

Consolidation adjustments:
- PRICE DIFFERENTIAL AMORTIZATION — Module 4
- UNREALIZED GAINS & LOSSES — Module 5

SHARE OF REPORTED EARNINGS − PRICE DIFFERENTIAL AMORTIZATION −/+ UNREALIZED GAINS & LOSSES = EQUITY IN EARNINGS

- Wholly Owned Subsidiaries - Illustration

EQUITY METHOD
Equity in Earnings for X5

- Adjusted profit of Subsidiary:
  - Profit of Subsidiary for the period $30,000
  - Current-year price differential amortization   (40,000)
  - Realized portion of prior-year **upstream** sale of equipment ($10,000/10)   1,000   (9,000)

- Unrealized current-year profit on **downstream** sale of inventory   (4,500)
- Realized profit from prior-year **downstream** sale of inventory   1,800

  Total   **(11 700)**

EQUITY METHOD
Equity in Earnings vs. Consolidated Profit

- Adjusted profit of Parent:
  - Profit of Parent for the period $180,000
  - Unrealized current-year profit on downstream sale of inventory .... (4,500)
  - Realized profit from prior-year downstream sale of inventory 1,800
  - Intercompany dividends .... (20,000) $157,300

- Adjusted profit of Subsidiary:
  - Profit of Subsidiary for the period $30,000
  - Current-year price differential amortization .... (40,000)
  - Realized portion of prior-year upstream sale of equipment ($10,000/10) 1,000   (9,000)
  - Total $148,300

(11,700)

EQUITY METHOD
Journal Entries on the Books of Parent for X5

PROPORTIONATE SHARE OF LOSSES

1

Equity in Earnings of Subsidiary	11,700	
Investment in Subsidiary		11,700

PROPORTIONATE SHARE OF DIVIDENDS

2

Cash	20,000	
Investment in Subsidiary		20,000

EQUITY METHOD
Balance of the Investment Account
As of December 31, X5

INITIAL INVESTMENT (X1)	$1,200,000	Cost Method
SUBSIDIARY'S NET ADJUSTED VALUE SINCE ACQUISITION	292,000	
UNREALIZED PROFIT FROM DOWNSTREAM SALE OF INVENTORY	(4,500)	
INVESTMENT AT THE END (X5)	$1,487,500	Equity Method

100% — **Subsidiary's net adjusted value since acquisition**
- Retained earnings increase since acquisition ($1,100,000 - $600,000) $500,000
- Price differential amortization since acquisition .... (200,000)
- Unrealized portion of the gain on <u>upstream</u> sale of equipment ($10,000 × 8/10) .... (8,000)
- Total **$292,000**

Net Adjusted Value of Sub (+) Downstream adjustments

Wholly Owned Subsidiaries - Illustration ---------- Module 6 ---------- 65

EQUITY METHOD
Investment Account vs. Consolidated Retained Earnings

Retained Earnings

Parent		$3,600,000
Unrealized profit on <u>downstream</u> sale of inventory		**(4,500)**
Subsidiary's net adjusted value since acquisition:		
• Retained earnings increase since acquisition ($1,100,000 - $600,000)	$500,000	
• Price differential amortization since acquisition	(200,000)	
• Unrealized portion of the gain on <u>upstream</u> sale of equipment ($10,000 × 8/10)	(8,000)	**292,000**
Total		$3,887,500

Balance of the investment account under Equity vs. Cost Method
Difference of $287,500: ($292,000 - $4,500)

Wholly Owned Subsidiaries - Illustration ---------- Module 6 ---------- 66

Part 4

STATEMENT OF FINANCIAL POSITION - PARENT COMPANY
At December 31, X5
Equity Basis vs. Consolidation

	Equity Basis	Consolidated
Assets		
Non-current assets		
Land	$1,250,000	$1,250,000
Buildings & equipment (net)	3,400,000	3,722,000
Goodwill		80,000
Investment in Subsidiary	1,487,500	
Current assets		
Inventories	500,000	725,500
Accounts receivable	1,800,000	2,580,000
Cash	590,000	760,000
Total assets	**$9,027,500**	**$9,117,500**
Equity and liabilities		
Equity		
Share capital	$3,800,000	$3,800,000
Retained earnings	3,887,500	3,887,500
Liabilities		
Long-term notes payable	1,000,000	1,000,000
Accounts payable	340,000	430,000
Total equity and liabilities	**$9,027,500**	**$9,117,500**

Net Adjusted Value of Sub
(+)
Downstream adjustments

Part 4

STATEMENT OF FINANCIAL POSITION - PARENT COMPANY
At December 31, X5
Equity vs. Consolidation

- The net value is the same, whereas the assets and liabilities reported are different.

- Under the equity method, only the accounts of Parent are reported. Under full consolidation, the accounts of Parent and Subsidiary are combined.

- One can see the process of consolidation as disaggregating the Investment account into the subsidiary's detailed assets and liabilities, **including the unamortized portion of price differential and any unrealized intercompany gains and losses at the end of the period.**

Equity Method = One-line consolidation

Wholly Owned Subsidiaries - Illustration   ---------- Module 6 ----------

Part 4

INCOME STATEMENT - PARENT COMPANY
Year Ended December 31, X5
Equity Basis vs. Consolidation

	Equity Basis	Consolidated	
Sales revenue	$3,100,000	$3,610,000	**Adjusted Profit** of Sub
Equity in earnings	(11,700)		
Cost of sales	2,300,000	2,662,700	
Depreciation expense	200,000	254,000	
Other expenses	440,000	545,000	(+) Downstream adjustments
Profit for the year	**$148,300**	**$148,300**	

Wholly Owned Subsidiaries - Illustration — Module 6 — 69

Part 4

INCOME STATEMENT - PARENT COMPANY
Year Ended December 31, X5
Equity vs. Consolidation

- Profit is the same, whereas the revenues and expenses reported are different. Under the equity method, only the accounts of Parent are reported. Under full consolidation, the accounts of Parent and Subsidiary are combined.

- One can see the process of consolidation as disaggregating the Equity in Earnings account into the subsidiary's detailed revenues and expenses, **including the current-year amortized portion of price differential, any unrealized intercompany gains and losses from the current period, and any realized gains and losses from prior-year transactions.**

Equity Method = One-line consolidation

Wholly Owned Subsidiaries - Illustration — Module 6 — 70

STATEMENT OF CHANGES IN EQUITY - PARENT COMPANY
Year Ended December 31, X5
Equity Basis vs. Consolidation

	Equity Basis			Consolidated		
	Share Capital	Retained Earnings	Total	Share Capital	Retained Earnings	Total
Balance at Dec. 31, X4	$3,800,000	$3,839,200	$7,639,200	$3,800,000	$3,839,200	$7,639,200
Profit for the year		$148,300	$148,300		$148,300	$148,300
Dividends		(100,000)	(100,000)		(100,000)	(100,000)
Balance at Dec. X5	$3,800,000	$3,887,500	$7,687,500	$3,800,000	$3,887,500	$7,687,500

Wholly Owned Subsidiaries - Illustration ---------- Module 6 ---------- 71

Part 4

EQUITY METHOD
One-Line Consolidation

Statement of Financial Position

Balance of the investment account = Net Adjusted Value of Subsidiary

$1,487,500

(+) Downstream adjustments

Income Statement

Equity in earnings of Subsidiary = Adjusted profit of Subsidiary

($11,700)

(+) Downstream adjustments

Wholly Owned Subsidiaries - Illustration ---------- Module 6 ---------- 72

EQUITY METHOD IN THE CONTEXT OF CONSOLIDATION
Procedure to Eliminate the Investment Account - Recall

Part 4

1 — BREAK DOWN THE BALANCE OF THE INVESTMENT ACCOUNT AT END OF THE PERIOD:

1. Initial Investment;
2. Increase of the Investment up to the beginning of the current period;
3. Share of Earnings – Current period;
4. Share of Dividends – Current period.

2 — ELIMINATE EACH COMPONENT OF THE INVESTMENT ACCOUNT

Wholly Owned Subsidiaries - Illustration ---------- Module 6 ---------- 73

EQUITY METHOD
Breakdown of the Investment Account

Part 4

1	INITIAL INVESTMENT (X1)	$1,200,000	Cost Method
2	100% OF SUBSIDIARY'S NET ADJUSTED VALUE FROM ACQUISITION TO THE BEGINNING OF THE CURRENT PERIOD (X2 TO X4, INCLUSIVE) (see next slide)	319,200	
3	100% OF SUBSIDIARY'S ADJUSTED EARNINGS IN X5	(11,700)	
4	100% OF SUBSIDIARY'S DECLARED DIVIDENDS IN X5	(20,000)	
	INVESTMENT AT THE END (X5)	$1,487,500	Equity Method

Wholly Owned Subsidiaries - Illustration ---------- Module 6 ---------- 74

Part 4

EQUITY METHOD
Subsidiary's Net Adjusted Value from Acquisition to the Beginning of X5
(Optional)

◆	Retained earnings increase from 31-12-X1 to 31-12-X4 ($1,090,000 - $600,000)	$490,000
◆	Price differential amortization (X2-X3-X4)	(160,000)
◆	Unrealized gain on sale of equipment	(9,000)
◆	Unrealized profit on downstream sale of inventory (X4)	(1,800)
	Net adjusted value increase	**$319,200**

Wholly Owned Subsidiaries - Illustration ---------- Module 6 ---------- 75

Part 4

EQUITY METHOD
Consolidation Entries Required to Eliminate the Investment Account

1 See consolidation adjustments 1a and 1b under cost basis.

2
Retained Earnings	319,200	
Investment in Subsidiary		319,200

3
Investment in Subsidiary	11,700	
Equity in Earnings		11,700

4
Investment in Subsidiary	20,000	
Dividends Declared		20,000

} Additional Consolidation Entries

Wholly Owned Subsidiaries - Illustration ---------- Module 6 ---------- 76

OUTLINE OF THE PRESENTATION

Part 5

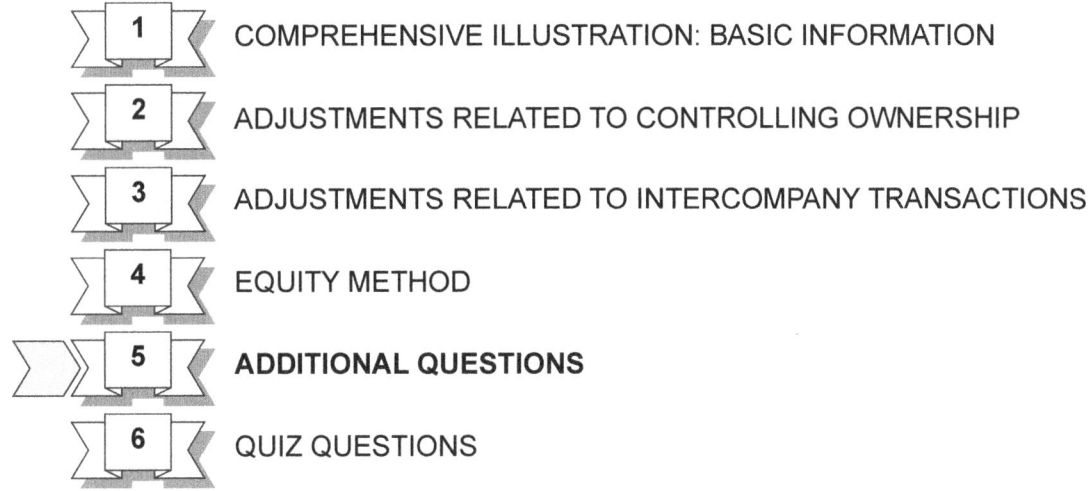

1. COMPREHENSIVE ILLUSTRATION: BASIC INFORMATION
2. ADJUSTMENTS RELATED TO CONTROLLING OWNERSHIP
3. ADJUSTMENTS RELATED TO INTERCOMPANY TRANSACTIONS
4. EQUITY METHOD
5. **ADDITIONAL QUESTIONS**
6. QUIZ QUESTIONS

Part 5

ADDITIONAL QUESTIONS
Continuation of Parent and Subsidiary in X6

Refer to the basic information from X5. We are now preparing the consolidated financial statements of Parent Company for the year ended December 31, X6. Assume that there are no intercompany transactions and no goodwill impairment in X6.

Required

1- Using the direct approach, compute the following balances:

- Retained Earnings (ending balance for Parent: $3,800,000; Subsidiary: $1,150,000)
- Profit for X6 (Parent: $200,000; Subsidiary: $50,000)
- Buildings and Equipment (ending balance for Parent: $4,000,000; Subsidiary: $300,000)

2- Provide the list of all the consolidation adjustments for X6.

Part 5

ADDITIONAL QUESTIONS
Price Differential Amortization Schedule - X6

Price Differential		Amortization		Unamortized Excess at December 31, X6
Items	Balance at Acquisition	Prior Years (X2-X5)	Current Year (X6)	
Land	$100,000	($100,000)	-	-
Buildings	200,000	(80,000)	(20,000)	$100,000
Goodwill	100,000	(20,000)	-	80,000
Total	$400,000	($200,000)	($20,000)	$180,000

Wholly Owned Subsidiaries - Illustration

Part 5

ADDITIONAL QUESTIONS
Recap on Intercompany Gains: Impact for X6

Transaction	RE Beginning	Profit	RE End
Downstream			
➤ Unrealized profit from sale of merchandise in X5	($4,500)	$4,500	-
Upstream			
➤ Sale of equipment in X4	(8,000)	1,000	(7,000)

Wholly Owned Subsidiaries - Illustration

ADDITIONAL QUESTIONS
Retained Earnings - X6

Parent $3,800,000

Subsidiary's net adjusted value since acquisition:
- Retained earnings increase since acquisition
  ($1,150,000 - $600,000) $550,000
- Price differential amortization since acquisition (220,000)
- Unrealized portion of the gain on <u>upstream</u> sale
  of equipment ($10,000 × 7/10)   (7,000)   223,000
Total $4,023,000

ADDITIONAL QUESTIONS
Consolidated Profit for X6

Adjusted profit of Parent:
- Profit of Parent for the period $200,000
- Realized profit from prior-year **downstream**
  sale of inventory   4,500 $204,500

Adjusted profit of Subsidiary:
- Profit of Subsidiary for the period $50,000
- Current-year price differential amortization (20,000)
- Realized portion of prior-year **upstream** sale
  of equipment ($10,000/10)   1,000   31,000
  Total $235,500

ADDITIONAL QUESTIONS
Buildings and Equipment - X6

Parent	$4,000,000
Subsidiary	300,000
Unamortized portion of the:	
• Fair value increment on Buildings ($200,000 × 5/10)	100,000
• Upstream gain on sale of Equipment ($10,000 × 7/10)	(7,000)
Total	$4,393,000

ADDITIONAL QUESTIONS
Consolidation Entries for X6

1a
Common Shares (Subsidiary)	200,000	
Retained Earnings (Subsidiary)	600,000	
Investment in Subsidiary (Parent)		800,000

1b
Land (Subsidiary)	100,000	
Buildings (Subsidiary)	200,000	
Goodwill (Subsidiary)	100,000	
Investment in Subsidiary (Parent)		400,000

2a
Depreciation Expense (Subsidiary)	20,000	
Retained Earnings (Subsidiary)	80,000	
Buildings (Subsidiary)		100,000

2b
Retained Earnings (Subsidiary)	100,000	
Land (Subsidiary)		100,000

Part 5

ADDITIONAL QUESTIONS
Consolidation Entries for X6 (continued...)

2c	Retained Earnings (Subsidiary)	20,000	
	Goodwill (Subsidiary)		20,000
3	Retained Earnings (Parent)	4,500	
	Cost of Goods Sold		4,500
4a	Retained Earnings (Parent & Sub.)	8,000	
	Buildings & Equip. (net) (Parent)		8,000
4b	Buildings & Equip. (net) (Parent)	1,000	
	Depreciation Expenses (Parent)		1,000

Part 6

OUTLINE OF THE PRESENTATION

1. COMPREHENSIVE ILLUSTRATION: BASIC INFORMATION
2. ADJUSTMENTS RELATED TO CONTROLLING OWNERSHIP
3. ADJUSTMENTS RELATED TO INTERCOMPANY TRANSACTIONS
4. EQUITY METHOD
5. ADDITIONAL QUESTIONS
6. **QUIZ QUESTIONS**

PART 6
Quiz Questions

On December X8, Large Inc. acquired all the outstanding voting shares of Small Inc. for $250,000. At the date of acquisition, Small had Common Shares and Retained Earnings of $100,000 and $50,000, respectively. Small's plant assets have a market value $60,000 greater than book value and an estimated remaining economic life of six years (straight line).

In post-acquisition periods, Small had the following earnings and paid the following dividends:

Year	Comprehensive income	Dividends
X9	$30,000	$8,000
X10	25,000	10,000
X11	50,000	20,000

Large's equity section at the end of year X11 consists of Common Shares of $800,000 and Retained Earnings of $350,000. Large's comprehensive income and dividends declared for X11 amount to $150,000 and $50,000, respectively.

PART 6
Quiz Questions (continued...)

Goodwill has not been impaired since acquisition.

Small sold land to Large in X10 for $100,000. The land originally cost Small $90,000. The land is kept by Large since then.

In X11, Large had sales of $40,000 to Small. Large's X11 gross margin was 50%; $10,000 (sales price) of the transferred units are in Small's inventory on December 31, X11.

250,000 = 150,000 + 60,000 + 40,000
                    ⎧‾‾‾‾‾210,000‾‾‾‾‾⎫
                                                    100,000

Part 6

QUIZ QUESTIONS

1

Compute the net adjusted value of Small at December 31, X11. Complete the following table.

	Individual Records of Subsidiary	Consolidation Adjustments		
At Date of Acquisition December 31, X8	Net Book Value 150,000	Purchase Price Differential 100,000	✗	Purchase Price 250,000
Since Acquisition	Retained Earnings Increase 67,000	Price Differential Amortization (30,000)	Unrealized Gain- Sale of Land 37,000	Net Adjusted Value Increase 37,000
At December 31, X11	Net Book Value 217,000	Unamortized Portion of Price Differential 70,000	Unrealized Gains on Upstream Transactions 287,000	Net Adjusted Value 287,000

Wholly Owned Subsidiaries - Illustration ---------- Module 6 ----------

slide 55.

Part 6

QUIZ QUESTIONS

2

Assume that Large is using the equity method to report its investment in Small. Determine the balance of the investment account on the books of Large at the end of X11.

INITIAL INVESTMENT (X8)	$250,000
SUBSIDIARY'S NET ADJUSTED VALUE SINCE ACQUISITION	37,000
UNREALIZED PROFIT ON SALE OF INVENTORY	(5,000)
INVESTMENT AT THE END (X11)	

100%

Retained earnings increase   67,000
less price differential Amort (30,000)
Total   37,000

slide 65

Part 6

QUIZ QUESTIONS

3

Assume that Large is using the <u>cost method</u> to report its investment in Small. If the total comprehensive income reported by Large for X11 is $150,000, what amount would be reported had Large been using the equity method instead?

- Comprehensive income for X11 under the cost method $150,000

- ADD share of Small Retained earnings
  Small comprehensive income 50,000
  less current year price differential amort (10,000)   40,000
- Share of dividend   (20,000)
- profit   5,000

Comprehensive income for X11 under the equity method

Wholly Owned Subsidiaries - Illustration ---------- Module 6 ---------- 91

Part 6

QUIZ QUESTIONS

4

Assume that Large is using the <u>cost method</u> to report its investment in Small. Determine the amount that will be reported as *Retained Earnings* in Large's consolidated statement of financial position at the end of X11.

- Balance of retained earnings at end of X11   350,000
- Share of small net adjusted value   37,000
- unrealised profit on sale of inventory   (15,000)

  consolidation RE at the end of X11

RE since acquisition   67,000
less price differential amortization   (30,000)
Total   37,000

92

QUIZ QUESTIONS

5

Assume that Large is using the <u>equity method</u> to report its investment in Small. List the consolidation entries required to eliminate this account for the consolidation of Large for X11.

1. Dr CS   100,000
    Dr RE   50,000
    Dr plant   60,000
    Dr goodwill   40,000
        Cr investment   250,000

2. Dr RE   12,000
        Cr investment in small   12,000

3. Dr equity in earnings of small   40,000
        Cr investment in small   40,000

4. Dr investment in small   20,000
        Cr Dividend declared   20,000

QUIZ QUESTIONS

6

List the consolidation entries required to account for intercompany transactions.

Intercompany Sale of Inventory

Dr sale   40,000
    Cr inventory   5,000
    Cr COGS   35,000

Prior-Year Gain on Sale of Land

Dr gain on sale of land   10,000
    Cr land   10,000

Intercompany Dividends

Dr investment in small   20,000
    Cr Dividend declared   20,000

Exercise 6-1
Multiple-Choice Questions

1. When a parent uses the acquisition method to consolidate a wholly owned subsidiary, what amount will appear as "common shares" in the equity section of the consolidated balance sheet?

   a) The book value of the parent's common shares plus the book value of the subsidiary's common shares.
   b) The book value of the parent's common shares plus the fair value of the subsidiary's common shares.
   c) The fair value of the parent's common shares on the date of the purchase of the subsidiary.
   d) The book value of the parent's common shares at the date of consolidation. ✓

2. P Company acquires 100% of the common shares of S Company by issuing non-voting preferred shares. For both P Company and S Company, the FV of all assets is greater than recorded book values. Which of the following approaches to consolidation will show the highest total asset value on the consolidated balance sheet on the date of acquisition?

   a) Pooling of interest.
   b) Acquisition method.
   c) New entity. ✓
   d) Cannot be determined based on the information provided.

The following data should be used for Questions 3 and 4.

Harper Corp. has only three assets:

	Book value	Fair value
➤ Inventory	$ 165,000	$ 225,000
➤ Land	1,050,000	900,000
➤ Buildings	1,050,000	1,350,000

Kandon Inc. purchases Harper's assets by issuing 100,000 common shares with a market value of $30 per share.

3. At what amount will the inventory, land, and buildings respectively appear on Kandon's balance sheet?

   a) $165,000, $900,000, $1,350,000
   b) $165,000, $1,050,000, $1,050,000
   c) $225,000, $900,000, $1,350,000 ✓
   d) $225,000, $1,050,000, $1,350,000

4. What is the amount of goodwill from this business combination?

   a) $525,000
   b) Negative $525,000
   c) $735,000
   d) Nil

The following data should be used for Questions 5 and 6.

On January 1, X6, Green Company acquired 100% of the outstanding common shares of Blue Inc. by issuing 10,000 common shares. The book values and the fair values of both companies immediately <u>before</u> the acquisition were as follows:

	Green Company Book values	Fair values	Blue Inc. Book values	Fair values
Assets	**$2,175,000**	$2,400,000	**$900,000**	$1,042,500
Liabilities	1,155,000	$1,132,000	375,000	$405,000
Common shares	450,000		97,500	
Retained earnings	570,000		427,500	
	$2,175,000		**$900,000**	

Immediately before the acquisition transaction, Green Company had 20,000 common shares outstanding and Blue Inc. had 6,500 common shares outstanding. Green's shares were actively trading at $75.00 on the date of the acquisition.

5. What amount would Green Company report on its consolidated financial statements immediately after the acquisition transaction for "assets"?

   a) $3,075,000
   b) $3,217,500
   c) $3,330,000
   d) $3,442,500

6. What amount would Green Company report on its consolidated financial statements immediately after the acquisition transaction for "common shares"?

   a) $450,000
   b) $547,500
   c) $1,200,000
   d) $1,297,500

7. When one company controls another company, the *CICA Handbook* recommends that the parent reports the subsidiary on a consolidated basis. Which of the following best describes the primary reason for this recommendation?

    a) To report the combined retained earnings of the two companies, allowing shareholders to better predict dividend payments.
    b) To allow for taxation of the combined entity.
    c) To report the total resources of the economic entity under the control of the parent's shareholders.
    d) To meet the requirements of federal and provincial securities commissions.

8. Which of the following best describes the accounting treatment acceptable under IFRS for negative goodwill?

    a) It should be disclosed as a long-term credit on the consolidated financial statements.
    b) It should be reported as a gain in the income statement the year of acquisition.
    c) It should be disclosed as a separate line item in consolidated shareholders' equity.
    d) It should reduce the values assigned in the purchase transaction to noncurrent assets.

9. At December 31, X5, Alpha Company has 20,000 common shares outstanding while Beta Inc. has 10,000 common shares outstanding. Alpha wishes to enter into a reverse takeover of Beta to gain its listing on the stock exchange. Which one of the following describes how many shares would have to be issued, and by which company, for this to occur? Assume that the transaction involves a purchase of shares.

    a) Alpha would have to issue more than 10,000 shares.
    b) Alpha would have to issue more than 20,000 shares.
    c) Beta would have to issue more than 10,000 shares.
    d) Beta would have to issue more than 20,000 shares.

10. Parent Inc. purchased all of the outstanding shares of Sub Ltd on January 1, Year 1, for $214,000. Annual amortization of the purchase price differential amounted to $16,000. Parent Inc. reported net income of $100,000 in Year 1 and $110,000 in Year 2, and paid $40,000 in dividends each year. Sub Ltd reported net income of $33,000 in Year 1 and $39,000 in Year 2, and paid $8,000 in dividends each year.

    What is the Investment in Sub Ltd. balance on Parent's books as at December 31, Year 2, if the equity method has been used?

    a) $238,000
    b) $246,000
    c) $278,000
    d) $286,000

11. Burns Ltd. purchased 100% of the outstanding shares of Simon Inc. on January 1, Year 1, at a price that was in excess of the subsidiary's fair market value. On that date, Burn's equipment had a book value of $300,000 and a fair market value of $400,000. Simon had equipment with a book value of $200,000 and a fair value of $300,000 (10-year life). Burns uses the equity method to record its investment. On December 31, Year 3, Burns has equipment with a book value of $210,000 and a fair value of $333,000. Simon has equipment with a book value of $140,000 and a fair value of $270,000.

    What is the balance of equipment on the consolidated balance sheet on December 31, Year 3?

    a) $600,000
    b) $490,000
    c) $480,000
    d) $420,000

12. Albany Ltd. negotiated the purchase of all of the outstanding shares of Gerrard Inc. on January 1, X4, for $1,200,000. The price resulted in a $90,000 allocation to equipment and goodwill of $75,000. Because the subsidiary earned especially high profits, Albany was required to pay an additional $200,000 at the date of acquisition. How should this extra amount be reported?

    a) The $200,000 additional payment is reflected as a reduction in consolidated retained earnings.
    b) The amount of $200,000 must be expensed in X4.
    c) Consolidated goodwill at date of acquisition must be increased by $200,000.
    d) None of the above.

13. When a company uses the Equity Method to record its investment in a subsidiary during the year, which of the following will be included in the journal entry to record the parent's share of the subsidiary's dividends when they are declared?

    a) Debit dividend income.
    b) Credit dividend income.
    c) Debit investment in subsidiary.
    d) Credit investment in subsidiary.

14. Which of the following best describes why a company would use the cost method to record its investment in a subsidiary rather than the equity method?

    a) It results in the same net income and retained earnings as consolidation.
    b) It is easy and inexpensive to use.
    c) It is required by the *CICA Handbook*.
    d) It is required by the Canada Revenue Agency (CRA) for tax purposes.

Exercise 6-2
Consolidation Subsequent to Acquisition:
Direct Approach and Equity Method

On December 31, X1, the Big Ltd. purchased 100% of the outstanding common shares of the Small Ltd. for $9.5 million in cash. On that date, the shareholders' equity of Small totalled $8 million and consisted of $1 million in Common Stock and $7 million in retained earnings. Both companies use the straight-line method to calculate amortization.

For the year ending December 31, X6, the income statements for Big and Small were as follows:

	Big	Small
Sales	$21,000,000	$9,100,000
Other revenue	1,500,000	700,000
Total sales and other revenue	22,500,000	9,800,000
Expenses		
Cost of goods sold	16,000,000	5,000,000
Amortization expense	2,500,000	2,000,000
Other expenses	1,800,000	1,200,000
Profit for the year	**$2,200,000**	**$1,600,000**

As at December 31, X6, the condensed statements of financial position for the two companies were as follows:

	Big	Small
Building	$17,000,000	$1,500,000
Accumulated depreciation	(9,500,000)	(825,000)
Investment in Small	9,500,000	- 0 -
Other Assets	12,500,000	12,825,000
Total assets	**$31,000,000**	**$13,500,000**
Liabilities	$5,000,000	$1,200,000
Share capital	12,100,000	1,000,000
Retained earnings	13,900,000	11,300,000
Total liabilities and equities	**$31,000,000**	**$13,500,000**

Additional information

1. Fair market values of Small were equal to their book values at the date of acquisition.

2. During X5, Small sold merchandise to Big for $200,000, a price that includes a gross profit of 30% based on sales price. During X5, 60% of this merchandise was resold by Big and the other 40% remains in its December 31, X5 inventories. On December 31, X5, the inventories of Small contained merchandise purchased from Big on which Big had recognized a gross profit in the amount of $20,000.

3. During X6, Big sold merchandise to Small for $100,000, a price that includes a gross profit of 40% based on sales price. During X6, 30% of this merchandise was resold by Small and the other 70% remains in its December 31, X6 inventories. On December 31, X6, the inventories of Big contained merchandise purchased from Small on which Small had recognized a gross profit in the amount of $30,000. Total sales to Big from Small were $50,000 for the year.

4. During X6, Big declared and paid dividends of $300,000 while Small declared and paid dividends of $100,000.

5. In each of the years since Big acquired control over Small, the goodwill arising on this business combination transaction has been tested for impairment. After completing the annual impairment tests, it was determined that the goodwill impairment loss for X4 was $60,000 and for X6 it was $80,000. No impairment was found in any of the other years since acquisition.

6. The retained earnings of Big as at December 31, X5, were $12,000,000. On that date, Small had retained earnings of $9,800,000. Small has not issued any common stock since its acquisition by Big.

Required

a) Using the direct approach, compute the consolidated balance of Retained Earnings as of December 31, X6.
b) Using the direct approach, compute the consolidated profit for the year ended December 31, X6.
c) Had Big Ltd. been using the equity method instead of the cost method to account for its investment in Sub, what would have been the *journal entries* on the books of Big for the current year (report the journal entries, not the consolidation entries)?

Copyright © 2020, Parmitech, Ottawa. Parmitech. All rights reserved.

Exercise 6-3
Consolidation Subsequent to Acquisition: Direct Approach

On January 1, X6, the Parent Ltd. purchased 100% of the outstanding common shares of the Sub Ltd. for $1.5 million in cash. On that date, the shareholders' equity of Sub totaled $725,000 and consisted of $350,000 in Common Stock and $375,000 in Retained Earnings. Both companies use the straight-line method to calculate amortization.

For the year ending December 31, X7, the income statements for Parent and Sub were as follows:

	Parent	Sub
Sales and other revenue	$1,420,000	$800,000
Cost of goods sold	680,000	325,000
Other expenses	250,000	195,000
Profit for the year	**$490,000**	**$280,000**

As at December 31, X7, the condensed statements of financial position for the two companies were as follows:

	Parent	Sub
Total assets	**$3,077,000**	**$1,175,000**
Liabilities	$177,000	$90,000
Share capital	960,000	350,000
Retained earnings	1,940,000	735,000
Total liabilities and equity	**$3,077,000**	**$1,175,000**

Additional Information

1. On January 1, X6, Sub had Plant and Equipment with a fair value that was $150,000 greater than its carrying value. The plant and equipment had an estimated remaining useful life of 10 years.

2. On January 1, X6, Sub had inventory with a fair value that was $50,000 greater than its carrying value. One-half of the inventory was sold in X6, the remainder was sold in X7.

3. At the end of X6, Parent had in its ending inventory $60,000 of merchandise it had purchased from Sub during the year. Sub sold the merchandise at a markup of 25% over sales.

4. During X7, Parent sold merchandise to Sub for $310,000 at a markup of 20% of the selling price. At December 31, X7, Sub still had merchandise that it purchased from Parent for $82,000 in its inventory.

5. During X7, Parent declared and paid dividends of $50,000 while Sub declared and paid dividends of $25,000.

6. Parent accounts for its investment in Sub using the cost method.

7. The balance of retained earnings of Parent as at December 31, X6, was equal to $1,500,000. On that date, Sub had retained earnings of $480,000. Sub has not issued any common stock since its acquisition by Parent.

8. Goodwill has not been impaired since acquisition.

Required

Using the direct approach, provide the computation for the following consolidated balances for the period ended December 31, X7:

a) Total Assets
b) Liabilities
c) Profit for the year
d) Share capital
e) Retained Earnings

Exercise 6-4
Consolidation Subsequent to Acquisition: Worksheet Approach

Refer to Exercise 6.3.

Required
Present all the consolidation entries required for the consolidation of X7.

Exercise 6-5
Continuation of Plus Inc. (Case 7) in Year X8

Continue the case of Plus Inc. (see Textbook, p. 344) in the subsequent year (X8).

Additional Information

1. There are no intercompany transactions during X8.
2. Plus did not declare dividends in X8.
3. Land sold to Lortis in X7 remains within the group at the end of X8.
4. Goodwill impairment tests resulted in no losses since acquisition.
5. Profits for X8 were $3,000,000 (Plus) and $1,500,000 (Lortis).

Required
Calculate the Profit for X8, the consolidated balance of Retained Earnings at the end of the year, and the Investment in Lortis under the equity method.

Exercise 6-6
Continuation of Plus Inc. (Case 7) in Year X9

Continuation of Exercise 6.5 in year X9.

Additional Information

1. On July 1, X9, Plus sold a parcel of land to Lortis for $100,000. Plus had purchased this land in X4 for $150,000. On September 30, X9, Lortis sold the property to another company for $190,000. In addition, Land sold to Lortis in X7 has been sold by Lortis in X9 to an outside party.

2. During X9, $1 million of Plus's sales were to Lortis. Of these sales, $200,000 remains in the December 31, X9, inventories of Lortis. Plus' sales to Lortis are priced to provide it with a gross profit of 20% (gross profit on sales).

3. During X9, $2.5 million of Lortis' sales were to Plus. Of these sales, $500,000 remains in the December 31, X9, inventories of Plus. Lortis' sales are priced to provide it with a gross profit of 30% (gross profit on sales).

4. Dividends declared on December 31, X9, were $350,000 (Plus) and $100,000 (Lortis).

5. Goodwill impairment tests resulted in no losses since acquisition.

Required
Present all the consolidation entries required for the consolidation of X9.

Exercise 6-7
Consolidated Retained Earnings

On January 1, X3, the Most Company purchased 100% of the outstanding voting shares of the Least Company for $1.6 million in cash. On that date, Least's statement of financial position and the fair values of its identifiable assets and liabilities were as follows:

	Carrying	Fair
Cash	$ 25,000	$ 25,000
Accounts receivable	310,000	290,000
Inventories	650,000	600,000
Plant and equipment (net)	2,015,000	2,050,000
Total assets	**$3,000,000**	2,965,000
Current liabilities	$ 300,000	$ 300,000
Long-term liabilities	1,200,000	1,100,000
Common stock	500,000	
Retained earnings	1,000,000	
Total liabilities and equity	**$3,000,000**	

On January 1, X3, Least's plant and equipment had a remaining useful life of eight years. Its long-term liabilities matured on January 1, X7. Goodwill, if any, is to be tested yearly for impairment.

The statements of financial position as at December 31, X9, for the two companies are as follows:

Statements of Financial Position
At December 31, X9

	Most	Least
Cash	$ 500,000	$ 40,000
Accounts receivables	1,700,000	500,000
Inventories	2,300,000	1,200,000
Plant and equipment (net)	8,200,000	4,000,000
Investment in Least (at cost)	1,600,000	-
Land	700,000	260,000
Total assets	**$15,000,000**	**$6,000,000**
Current liabilities	$ 600,000	$ 200,000
Long-term liabilities	3,000,000	3,000,000
Common stock	1,000,000	500,000
Retained earnings	10,400,000	2,300,000
Total liabilities and equity	**$15,000,000**	**$6,000,000**

Change in RE for X9

Balance, January 1, X9	$ 9,750,000	$2,000,000
Net income, X9	1,000,000	400,000
	10,750,000	2,400,000
Dividends, X9	350,000	100,000
Balance, December 31, X9	$10,400,000	$2,300,000

Additional Information

1. The inventories of both companies have a maximum turnover period of one year. Receivables have a maximum turnover period of 62 days.

2. During X9, $2 million of Most's sales were to Least. Of these sales, $500,000 remains in the December 31, X9, inventories of Least. The December 31, X8, inventories of Least contained $312,500 of merchandise purchased from Most. Most's sales to Least are priced to provide it with a gross profit of 20% (gross profit on sales).

3. During X9, $1.5 million of Least's sales were to Most. Of these sales, $714,280 remains in the December 31, X9, inventories of Most. The December 31, X8, inventories of Most contained $857,140 of merchandise purchased from Least. Least's sales are priced to provide it with a gross profit of 30% (gross profit on sales).

4. Dividends declared on December 31, X9, were #350,000 (Most) and $100,000 (Least)

5. Goodwill has not been impaired since acquisition.

Required

Under the direct approach, compute the consolidated Retained Earnings of Most as of December 31, X9.

Exercise 6-8
Consolidation Subsequent to Acquisition and Negative Goodwill

Paper Corp. purchased 100% of the outstanding shares of Sand Ltd. on January 01, X2, at a cost of $84,000. Paper has always used the cost method to account for its strategic investments.

On January 01, Year 2, Sand had common shares of $50,000 and retained earnings of $30,000, and fair values were equal to carrying values for all its net assets except inventory (fair value was $9,000 less than book value) and equipment (fair value was $24,000 greater than book value). The equipment had an estimated remaining life of 6 years on January 01, X2.

The following are the financial statements of Paper Corp. and its subsidiary Sand Ltd. as at December 31, X5:

Statements of Financial Position
At December 31, X5

	Paper	Sand
Cash	$ -	$10,000
Accounts receivable	25,000	30,000
Note receivable	-	40,000
Inventory	66,000	44,000
Equipment (net)	220,000	76,000
Investment in Sand	95,000	--
Land	150,000	30,000
Total assets	**$556,000**	**$230,000**
Bank indebtedness	90,000	-
Accounts payable	50,000	60,000
Notes payable	40,000	-
Share capital	150,000	50,000
Retained Earnings	226,000	120,000
Total liabilities and equity	**$556,000**	**$230,000**

Change in RE for X5

Retained earnings, January 01, Year 5	$106,000	$ 86,000
Net income	120,000	48,000
	226,000	134,000
Dividends	-	14,000
Retained earnings, December 31, Year 5	**$226,000**	**$120,000**

Income Statements
For the Year Ended December 31, X5

	Paper	Sand
Sales	$798,000	$300,000
Management fee revenue	24,000	-
Other income	14,000	3,600
Gain on sale of land	-	20,000
	836,000	323,600
Cost of sales	480,000	200,000
Amortization	40,000	12,000
Interest expense	10,000	-
Miscellaneous expenses	186,000	63,600
	716,000	275,600
Profit for the year	**$120,000**	**$48,000**

Additional information

1. During X5, Sand made a cash payment of $2,000 per month to Paper for management fees, which is included in Sand's "Miscellaneous expenses".

2. During X5, Paper made intra-group sales of $100,000 to Sand. The December 31, X5, inventory of Sand contained goods purchased from Paper amounting to $30,000. These sales had a gross profit of 35%.

3. On April 01, X5, Paper acquired land from Sand for $40,000. This land has been recorded on Sand's books at a net book value of $20,000. Paper paid for the land by signing a $40,000 notes payable to Sand, bearing yearly interest at 8%. Interest for X5 was paid by Paper in cash on December 31, X5. This land was still being held by Paper on December 31, X5.

Required

a) Present the journal entry to account for the acquisition in the books of Paper.
b) Present the journal entry to account for the acquisition in the books of Sand.
c) Using a direct approach, compute the consolidated RE at the end of Year 5.
d) Using a direct approach, compute the consolidated profit for Year 5.
e) Using a direct approach, compute the following consolidated balances at the end of Year 5: (1) Accounts Receivables, (2) Inventory, (3) Equipment.
f) Present all the consolidation entries to account for intercompany transactions for Year 5.

Solutions to Exercises

6-1
Multiple-choice questions

1	D	6	C	11	D
2	C	7	C	12	C
3	C	8	B	13	D
4	A	9	C	14	B
5	C (see 3.7)	10	A		

6-2

a) Retained Earnings

Big		$13,900,000
Unrealized profit on <u>downstream</u> sale of inventory		(28,000)
Small's net adjusted value since acquisition:		
• Retained earnings increase since acquisition ($11,300,000 - $7,000,000)	$4,300,000	
• Price differential amortization since acquisition	(140,000)	
• Unrealized portion of the gain on <u>upstream</u> sale of inventory	(30,000)	4,130,000
Total		**$18,002,000**

b) Profit for the year

Adjusted profit of Big:		
• Profit of Big for the period	$2,200,000	
• Unrealized current-year profit on <u>downstream</u> sale of inventory	(28,000)	
• Realized profit from prior-year <u>downstream</u> sale of inventory	20,000	
• Intercompany dividends	(100,000)	$2,092,000
Adjusted profit of Small:		
• Profit of Small for the period	$1,600,000	
• Current-year price differential amortization	(80,000)	
• Unrealized current-year profit on <u>upstream</u> sale of inventory	(30,000)	
• Realized portion of prior-year <u>upstream</u> sale of inventory	24,000	1,514,000
Total		**$3,606,000**

c) Journal entries under the equity method.

Investment in Small	1,506,000	
Equity in Earnings		1,506,000
Cash	100,000	
Investment in Small		100,000

- Adjusted Profit of Small $1,514,000
- Unrealized current-year profit on downstream sale of inventory   (28,000)
- Realized profit from prior-year downstream sale of inventory   20,000

Equity in Earnings   **$1,506,000**

6-3

Note 1: Allocation of purchase price

Cost of 100% of Sub			$1,500,000
Book value of Sub:			
Common shares		$350,000	
Retained earnings		375,000	
		725,000	
Parent's ownership		100%	725,000
Price differential			775,000
Allocated:			
• Plant & Equip.		(150,000)	
• Inventory		(50,000)	(200,000)
Balance – goodwill			**$575,000**

Note 2: Purchase discrepancy amortization schedule

	Balance at acquisition Jan. 1, X6	Amortization X6	Amortization X7	Remaining at Dec. 31, X7
Plant & Equip. (Note 1)	$150,000	$(15,000)	$(15,000)	$120,000
Inventory (Note 1)	50,000	(25,000)	(25,000)	-
Goodwill (Note 1)	575,000	-	-	575,000
Total	**$775,000**	**$(40,000)**	**$(40,000)**	**$695,000**

Note 3: Intercompany profits

- *Beginning inventory*
  Sub selling ($60,000 x 25%) $15,000

- *Ending inventory*
  Parent selling ($82,000 x 20%) $16,400

a) Total Assets

• Parent	$3,077,000
• Investment in Sub	(1,500,000)
• Sub	1,175,000
• Unamortized portion of FVI on P&E (15,000 × 8/10)	120,000
• Goodwill	575,000
• Unrealized profit on downstream sale of inventory	(16,400)
	$3,430,600

b) Liabilities

• Parent	$177,000
• Sub	90,000
	$267,000

c) Profit for the year

Adjusted profit of Parent:
- Profit – Parent $490,000
- Dividends from Sub   (25,000)
- Unrealized profit from downstream sale of inventory (16,400) $448,600

Adjusted profit of Sub:
- Profit – Sub   280,000
- Current-year price differential amortization (Note 2)   (40,000)
- Realized profit on prior-year upstream sale of inv.   15,000   255,000

Consolidated profit   **$703,600**

d) Common Shares

Parent	**$960,000**

e) Retained Earnings

Parent's retained earnings, Dec. 31/X7		$1,940,000
Unrealized profit on downstream sale of inventory		(16,400)

Net adjusted value of Sub since acquisition:
- Sub's retained earnings, Dec. 31/X7 $735,000
- Sub's retained earnings, Jan. 1/X6   375,000
  Change in retained earnings since acquisition   360,000
- Cumulative amortization of price differential (Note 2)(80,000)   280,000

Consolidated retained earnings, Dec. 31/X7   **$2,203,600**

6-4

1. Investment account

    To eliminate reciprocal investment and equity accounts at the date of acquisition.
Common Shares (Sub)	*350,000*	
Retained Earnings (Sub)	*375,000*	
Investment in Sub (Parent)		*725,000*

    To allocate the price differential.
Plant & Equip. (Sub)	*150,000*	
Inventory (Sub)	*50,000*	
Goodwill	*575,000*	
Investment in Sub (Parent)		*775,000*

2. Price differential amortization

    To recognize the prior-year realization of the fair value increment on inventory.
Retained Earnings (Sub)	*25,000*	
COGS (Sub)	*25,000*	
Inventory (Sub)		*50,000*

    To amortize the fair value increment on P & E.
Retained Earnings (Sub)	*15,000*	
Other Expenses (Sub)	*15,000*	
Plant & Equip. (Sub)		*30,000*

3. Downstream sale of merchandise

Sales (Parent)	*310,000*	
Cost of Goods Sold (Parent-Sub)		*293,600*
Inventory (Sub)		*16,400*

4. Upstream sale of merchandise

   Retained Earnings (Sub)   15,000
    Cost of Goods Sold (Sub)   15,000

5. Intercompany dividends

   Sales & Other Revenue (Parent) 25,000
    Dividends Declared (Sub)   25,000

6-5

a) Profit for X8

Profit – Plus		$3,000,000
Adjusted profit of Lortis:		
• Profit – Lortis	$1,500,000	
• Current-year price differential amortization	50,000	
• Realized profit on prior-year upstream sale of inv.	150,000	1,700,000
Consolidated profit		**$4,700,000**

b) Retained Earnings

Plus's retained earnings, Dec. 31/X8		$18,300,000
Unrealized profit on downstream sale of land		(500,000)
Net adjusted value of Lortis since acquisition:		
• Lortis' retained earnings, Dec. 31/X8	$9,200,000	
• Lortis' retained earnings, at acquisition	4,000,000	
Change in retained earnings since acquisition	5,200,000	
• Cumulative amortization of price differential	(1,200,000)	4,000,000
Consolidated retained earnings, Dec. 31/X8		**$21,800,000**

c) Balance of the investment account under the equity method.

Purchase price		$9,750,000
Net adjusted value of Lortis since acquisition (see b)	$4,000,000	
Unrealized profit on downstream sale of land	(500,000)	3,500,000
Total		**$13,250,000**

6-6

1. Investment account

    <u>To eliminate reciprocal investment and equity accounts at the date of acquisition.</u>
Common Shares (Lortis)	3,000,000	
Retained Earnings (Lortis)	4,000,000	
Investment in Sub (Plus)		7,000,000

    <u>To allocate the price differential.</u>
Inventory (Lortis)	1,000,000	
Buildings (Lortis)	2,000,000	
Patents (Lortis)	500,000	
Goodwill	1,250,000	
Land (Lortis)		500,000
Long-Term Liabilities (Lortis)		1,500,000
Investment in Lortis (Plus)		2,750,000

2. Price differential amortization

    <u>To recognize the prior-year realization of the fair value increment on inventory.</u>
Retained Earnings (Lortis)	1,000,000	
Inventory (Lortis)		1,000,000

    <u>To amortize the fair value increment on buildings.</u>
Retained Earnings (Lortis)	600,000	
Other Expenses (Lortis)	100,000	
Buildings (Lortis)		700,000

    <u>To recognize the prior-year realization of the fair value increment on software.</u>
Retained Earnings (Lortis)	500,000	
Patents (Lortis)		500,000

    <u>To amortize the fair value increment on liabilities.</u>
Long-Term Liabilities (Lortis)	1,050,000	
Retained Earnings (Lortis)		900,000
Other Expenses (Lortis)		150,000

3. Downstream sale of land – X9

> *No entry required since Land has been resold the same year to an outside party*

4. Sale of land – X7

Retained Earnings (Lortis)	500,000	
Gain on Sale (Lortis)		500,000

5. Downstream sale of merchandise – X9

Sales (Plus)	1,000,000	
Cost of Goods Sold		960,000
Inventory (Lortis)		40,000

6. Upstream sale of merchandise – X9

Sales (Lortis)	2,500,000	
Cost of Goods Sold		2,350,000
Inventory (Plus)		150,000

7. Intercompany dividends

Revenue (Plus))	100,000	
Dividends Declared (Plus)		100,000

6-7

Note 1: Allocation of purchase price

Cost of 100% of Least			$1,600,000
Book value of Least:			
Common shares		$500,000	
Retained earnings		1,000,000	
		1,500,000	
Most's ownership		100%	1,500,000
Price differential			100,000
Allocated:			
♦ Accounts rec.		20,000	
♦ Inventory		50,000	
♦ Plant & Equip.		(35,000)	
♦ LT Liabilities		(100,000)	(65,000)
Balance – goodwill			**$35,000**

Note 2: Purchase discrepancy amortization schedule

	Balance at acquisition Jan. 1, X3	Amortization X3-X8	Amortization X9	Remaining at Dec. 31, X9
Accounts Rec.	$(20,000)	$20,000	$ -	$ -
Inventory	(50,000)	50,000	-	-
Plant & Equip.	35,000	(26,250)	(4,375)	4,375
LT Liabilities	100,000	(100,000)	-	-
Goodwill	35,000	-	-	35,000
Total	**$100,000**	**$(56,250)**	**$(4,375)**	**$39,375**

Consolidated Retained Earnings – X9

Most's retained earnings, Dec. 31/X9		$10,400,000
Unrealized profit on downstream sale of merchandise		(100,000)
Net adjusted value of Least since acquisition:		
♦ Least's retained earnings, Dec. 31/X9	$2,300,000	
♦ Least's retained earnings, at acquisition	1,000,000	
Change in retained earnings since acquisition	1,300,000	
♦ Cumulative amortization of price differential	(60,625)	
♦ Unrealized profit on upstream sale of merchandise	(214,284)	1,025,091
Consolidated retained earnings, Dec. 31/X8		**$11,325,091**

6-8

Note 1: Allocation of purchase price

Cost of 100% of Sand			$84,000
Book value of Sand:			
Common shares		$50,000	
Retained earnings		30,000	
		80,000	
Parent's ownership		100%	80,000
Price differential			4,000
Allocated:			
♦ Equipment		(24,000)	
♦ Inventory		9,000	(15,000)
Balance – goodwill			**$(11,000)**

Note 2: Purchase discrepancy amortization schedule

	Balance at acquisition Jan. 1, X2	Amortization X2-X4	Amortization X5	Remaining at Dec. 31, X5
Equipment (Note 1)	$24,000	$(12,000)	$(4,000)	$8,000
Inventory (Note 1)	(9,000)	9,000	-	-
Total	**$15,000**	**$(3,000)**	**$(4,000)**	**$8,000**

a) Journal entry to account for the acquisition in the books of Paper

Investment in Sand	95,000	
Cash		84,000
Gain on acquisition		11,000

b) Journal entry to account for the acquisition in the books of Sand

> *No entry since Sand is not a party to the transaction.*

c) Consolidated RE at the end of Year 5

Parent (Paper)			$226,000
100% of Sand's net adjusted value since acquisition:			
• Retained earnings increase since acquisition: ($120,000 - $30,000)	$90,000		
• Total price differential amortization	(7,000)		
• Upstream unrealized gain on sale of land	(20,000)		
	$63,000		
		100%	63,000
Unrealized portion of gain on downstream sale of inventory			(10,500)
Total			**$278,500**

d) Consolidated Profit for Year 5

Paper's net adjusted profit:		
• Paper's profit	$120,000	
• Current-year unrealized downstream profit	(10,500)	
• Intercompany dividends	(14,000)	$95,500
Sand's net adjusted profit:		
• Sand's profit	$48,000	
• Current-year unrealized gain on upstream sale of land	(20,000)	
• Current-year price differential amortization	(4,000)	24,000
Total profit		**$119,500**

e) Consolidated balances

1. Accounts receivable	($25,000 + $30,000)		$55,000
2. Inventory	($66,000 + $44,000 - $10,500)		$99,500
3. Equipment	($220,000 + $76,000 + $8,000)		$304,000

f) Consolidation entries – intercompany transactions

<u>Intercompany dividends</u>

Other Income	14,000	
Dividends Declared		14,000

<u>Management fees</u>

Management Fee Revenue	24,000	
Miscellaneous Expenses		24,000

<u>Current-year unrealized profit on downstream sale of inventory</u>

Revenues	100,000	
COGS		89,500
Inventory		10,500

<u>Current-year unrealized gain on upstream sale of Land</u>

Gain on Sale of Land	20,000	
Land		20,000
Note Payable	40,000	
Note Receivable		40,000
Other Income	2,400	
Interest Expense		2,400

Consolidation of Non-Wholly Owned Subsidiaries

Module 7

What you will find in this section

- How to Walk Through Module 7
- Slides
- Exercises and Solutions

Module 7
Consolidation of Non-Wholly Owned Subsidiaries

How to Walk Through Module 7

◇ <u>Readings</u>

1- <u>Book</u> "Consolidation of Financial Statements": Chapters 3, 8 and 9
2- <u>Student Manual</u> "Advanced Accounting": Module 7

    PART 1: CONSOLIDATION THEORIES

    PART 2: CONSOLIDATION OF NON-WHOLLY OWNED SUBSIDIARIES AT THE DATE OF ACQUISITION

    PART 3: CONSOLIDATION OF NON-WHOLLY OWNED SUBSIDIARIES SUBSEQUENT TO THE DATE OF ACQUISITION

    PART 4: EQUITY METHOD

APPENDIX: CONSOLIDATION OF NON-WHOLLY OWNED SUBSIDIARIES UNDER THE BV APPROACH

◇ <u>Assignments</u>

3- <u>Student Manual</u>: End-of module review and quiz questions
4- <u>Student Manual</u>: Exercises 1 to 10
5- <u>Book</u>: Cases 8, 9 and 10

When you have successfully completed this module, you will be able to do the following:

- Explain why some subsidiaries are non-wholly owned;

- Discuss the conceptual alternatives for consolidating non-wholly owned subsidiaries and explain their differences;

- Illustrate the techniques and procedures involved in establishing non-controlling interest in consolidated financial statements at the date of acquisition and in periods subsequent to acquisition under the full and partial goodwill alternatives;

- Present the additional consolidation entries required to eliminate the investment account when the equity method is employed by Parent Company in non-consolidated financial statements: the case of non-wholly owned subsidiaries.

CONSOLIDATION OF NON-WHOLLY OWNED SUBSIDIARIES
Module 7

Copyright © 2020 Parmitech

Advanced Accounting: Student Manual

Copyrighted Material

Editor: Parmitech

This publication is protected by copyright, and permission should be obtained from the publisher prior to any prohibited reproduction, storage in a retrieval system, or transmission in any form or by any means, electronic, mechanical, photocopying, recording, or otherwise.

Corresponding Author

Richard Bozec Ph.D., CPA, CGA
bozec@telfer.uottawa.ca

Copyright © Parmitech

CORRESPONDING CHAPTERS in *Bozec*
"Consolidation of Financial Statements under IFRS"

Chapter 3 — Non-Wholly Owned Subsidiaries

Chapter 8 — Practical Guide

Chapter 9 — Comprehensive Illustration

Cases — 8, 9, 10

TEACHING MATERIAL
Exercises

Module 7

7.1	Partial Control: Direct Approach and Worksheet Approach
7.2	Valuation of NCI at Date of Acquisition
7.3	Consolidation Subsequent to Acquisition: NCI, Profit, and Retained Earnings
7.4	Consolidation Subsequent to Acquisition with NCI: Worksheet Approach
7.5	Consolidated F/S, NCI, Profit, and Retained Earnings
7.6	Partial Control: Consolidation and Equity Method
7.7	Partial Control: Worksheet/Direct Approach - Equity Method (Year 5)
7.8	Partial Control: Worksheet/Direct Approach - Equity Method (Year 6)
7.9	Partial Control: Worksheet/Direct Approach - Equity Method (Year 7)
7.10	Partial Control: Direct Approach - Equity Method

FOCUS OF THIS MODULE: NON-CONTROLLING INTEREST

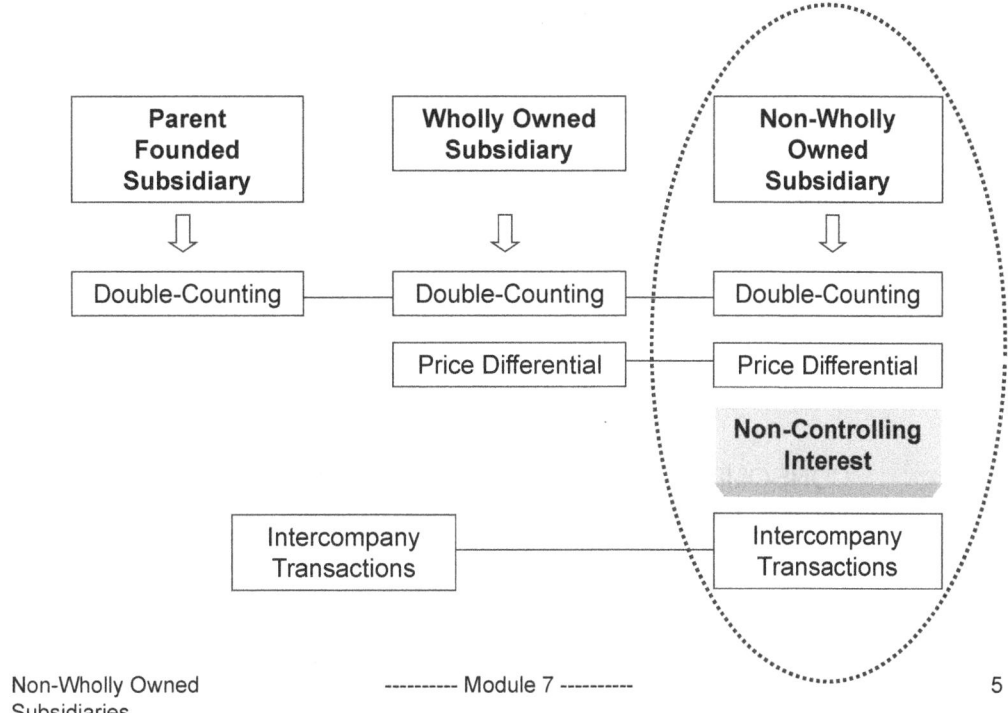

OUTLINE OF THE PRESENTATION

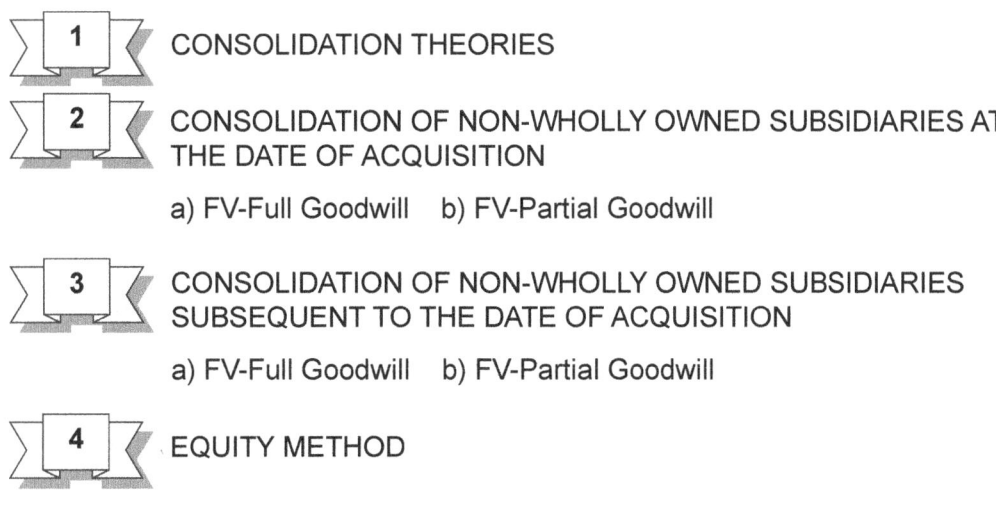

1 CONSOLIDATION THEORIES

2 CONSOLIDATION OF NON-WHOLLY OWNED SUBSIDIARIES AT THE DATE OF ACQUISITION

    a) FV-Full Goodwill   b) FV-Partial Goodwill

3 CONSOLIDATION OF NON-WHOLLY OWNED SUBSIDIARIES SUBSEQUENT TO THE DATE OF ACQUISITION

    a) FV-Full Goodwill   b) FV-Partial Goodwill

4 EQUITY METHOD

RECAP

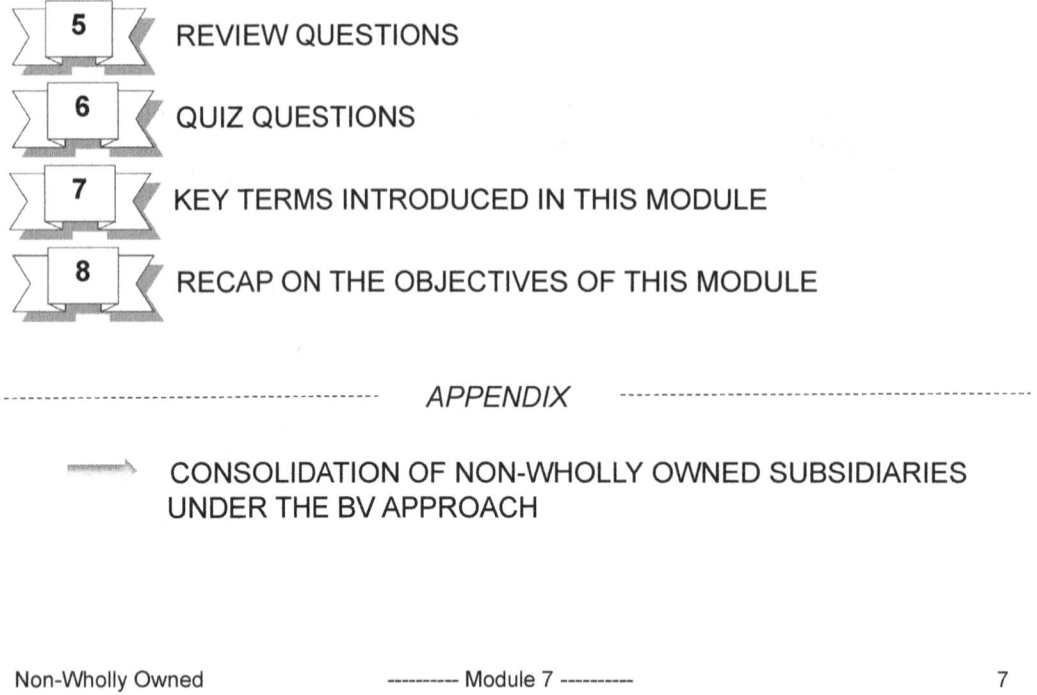

- **5** REVIEW QUESTIONS
- **6** QUIZ QUESTIONS
- **7** KEY TERMS INTRODUCED IN THIS MODULE
- **8** RECAP ON THE OBJECTIVES OF THIS MODULE

--------------- *APPENDIX* ---------------

→ CONSOLIDATION OF NON-WHOLLY OWNED SUBSIDIARIES UNDER THE BV APPROACH

PART 1
Consolidation Theories

Part 1

Objective of this section

Introduce the conceptual alternatives for consolidating non-wholly owned subsidiaries and explain their differences.

Key concepts

- Non-wholly owned subsidiary
- Non-controlling interest
- Entity theory; Full / Partial goodwill approach
- Parent company approach
- Proportionate consolidation

WHY OWN LESS THAN 100%?

- IF SUBSIDIARY IS IN A FOREIGN COUNTRY WHICH PROHIBITS OUTSIDERS FROM GAINING FULL CONTROL OF DOMESTIC BUSINESSES

- IF FEW SHAREHOLDERS OF THE SUBSIDIARY HAVE ELECTED NOT TO SELL THEIR SHARES

- IF THE PARENT FORMS A SUBSIDIARY WITH THE INVOLVEMENT OF A NON-CONTROLLING PARTNER WHO IS PROVIDING SPECIALIZED EXPERTISE, MANAGEMENT ABILITY, MARKET ACCESS, ...

- IF THE PARENT WANTS TO EITHER CONSERVE ITS LIQUID RESSOURCES (IF THE PURCHASE IS FOR CASH) OR REDUCE ITS SHARE DILUTION (IF THE PURCHASE WAS FOR AN EXCHANGE OF SHARES)

Control of 100% of subsidiary's resources with less than 100% ownership

---

CONSOLIDATION THEORIES
Approaches to Reporting Non-Controlling Interest (NCI)

SHOULD WE CONSIDER NCI?	VALUE ASSIGNED TO NCI	NAME OF THE APPROACH
NO	-	PROPORTIONATE CONSOLIDATION
YES	BOOK VALUE	PARENT COMPANY
YES	FAIR VALUE (Partial Goodwill Approach)	ENTITY (modified)
YES	FAIR VALUE (Full Goodwill Approach)	ENTITY

CONSOLIDATION THEORIES
Breakdown of the FV of Subsidiary at Date of Acquisition

Components	FV of Subsidiary — At date of acquisition	
	Portion assigned to:	
	Parent	**NCI**
BV — Book value of Subsidiary's net assets	◯	◯
FVI - FVD — Fair value increments & decrements	◯	◯
GOODWILL	◯	◯

Non-Wholly Owned Subsidiaries

Part 1

CONSOLIDATION THEORIES
Valuation of NCI through Consolidation

	Nil		Book Value		FV Partial Goodwill Approach		FV Full Goodwill Approach	
	Parent	NCI	Parent	NCI	Parent	NCI	Parent	NCI
BV	◯		◯	X	◯	X	◯	X
FVI - FVD	↑		↑		↑	X	↑	X
GOODWILL								X

Parent's portion of subsidiary's value is fully represented under all approaches.
Only the value assigned to NCI varies.

Non-Wholly Owned Subsidiaries

Part 1

Part 1

CONSOLIDATION THEORIES
Impact on the Consolidation Process

- The chart illustrates the Parent and NCI's portions of Subsidiary's full fair value under each consolidation approach.

- The full fair value of Subsidiary is broken down into the following 3 core components: 1) BV; 2) FVI/D; 3) Goodwill.

- Under the *Proportionate Consolidation*, no value is assigned to NCI.

- Under the *BV Approach*, NCI is measured at BV.

- Under the *Partial Goodwill Approach*, no goodwill is assigned to NCI (this represents one option under IFRS).

- Under the *Full Goodwill Approach*, the full FV of subsidiary (including full goodwill) is assigned proportionally to Parent and NCI.

Non-Wholly Owned Subsidiaries ---------- Module 7 ---------- 13

Part 1

CONSOLIDATION THEORIES
Valuation of Subsidiary through Consolidation

	Nil		Book Value		FV Partial Goodwill Approach		FV Full Goodwill Approach	
	Parent	NCI	Parent	NCI	Parent	NCI	Parent	NCI
BV	+		100% - BV		100% FV Net Assets		100% Full FV	
FVI - FVD	+		+					
GOODWILL	+		+		+			

Non-Wholly Owned Subsidiaries ---------- Module 7 ---------- 14

Part 1

CURRENT PRACTICE
Value Assigned to NCI at the Date of Acquisition

UNDER	VALUE ASSIGNED TO NCI CONSISTS OF NCI'S SHARE OF SUBSIDIARY'S	NAME OF THE APPROACH
CANADIAN STANDARDS (prior to 2011)	NET BOOK VALUE	PARENT COMPANY
2005 EXPOSURE DRAFT Joint Project IASB, AcSB & FASB	FULL FAIR VALUE **Full Goodwill Approach**	ENTITY
IFRS (since 2011)	FAIR VALUE OF IDENTIFIABLE NET ASSETS or FV of NCI **Partial Goodwill Approach**	ENTITY (Modified)

Part 1

CONSOLIDATION THEORIES
Parent vs. Entity

	PARENT COMPANY	ENTITY
➢ Viewpoint	Controlling shareholder	Consolidated entity
➢ Non-controlling interest	Liability	Part of the equity
➢ Value assigned to the net assets of subsidiary in the consolidation process	Limited to the cost to the parent company	Full fair market value at the date of acquisition
➢ Consolidated net income	Combined profit after deducting non-controlling interest in profit	Combined profit and allocation to controlling and non-controlling interest

CONSOLIDATION THEORIES - CONCEPTUAL VIEWPOINT
Parent Company

Part 1

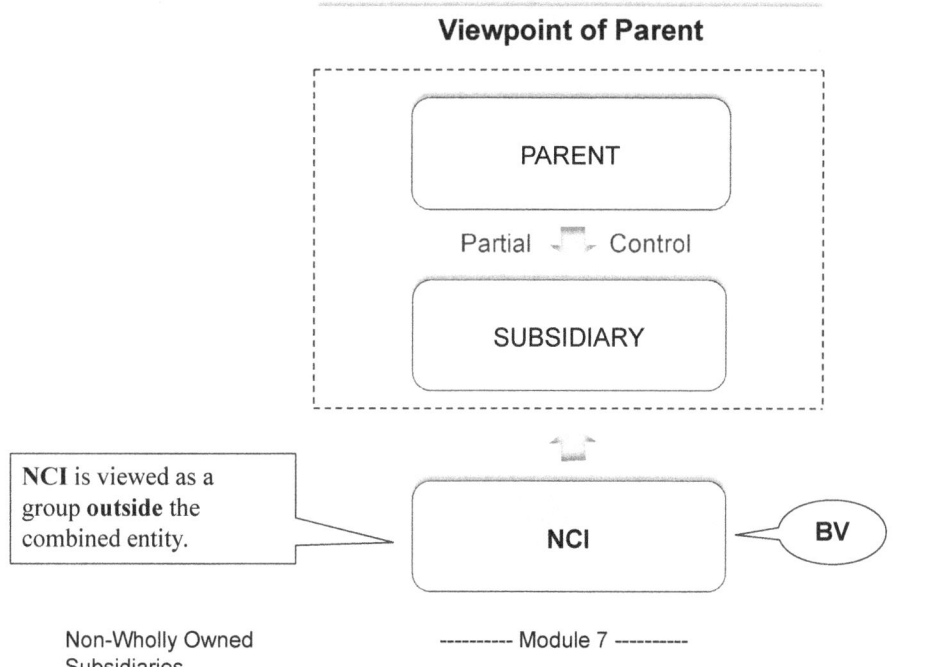

Part 1

CONSOLIDATION THEORIES - CONCEPTUAL VIEWPOINT
Entity

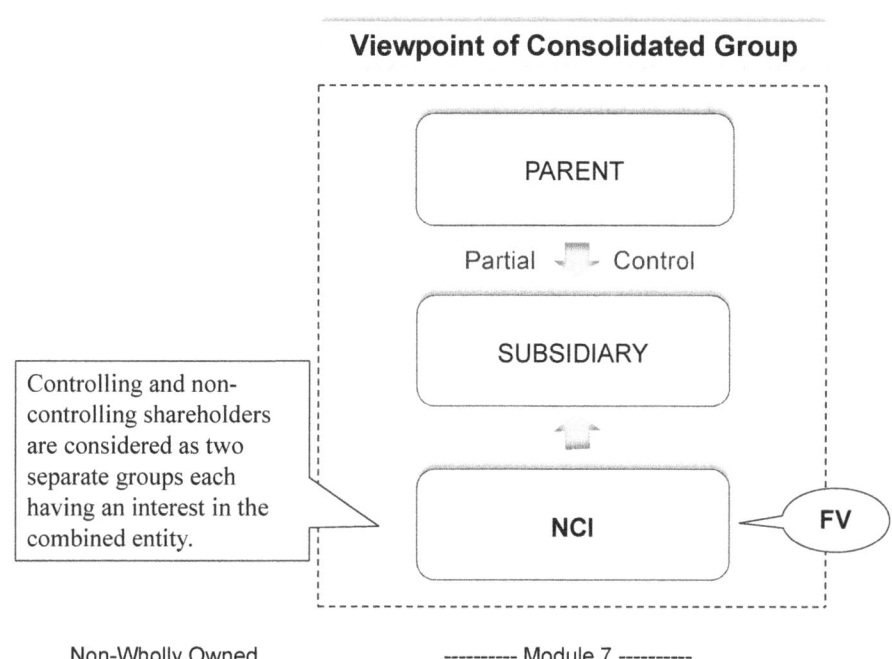

PART 1
Concept Check

> Compare the Parent Company approach with the Entity approach.

_____
_____
_____
_____
_____
_____
_____

OUTLINE OF THE PRESENTATION

1 CONSOLIDATION THEORIES

2 CONSOLIDATION OF NON-WHOLLY OWNED SUBSIDIARIES AT THE DATE OF ACQUISITION

  a) FV-Full Goodwill   b) FV-Partial Goodwill

3 CONSOLIDATION OF NON-WHOLLY OWNED SUBSIDIARIES SUBSEQUENT TO THE DATE OF ACQUISITION

  a) FV-Full Goodwill   b) FV-Partial Goodwill

4 EQUITY METHOD

PART 2 a
Consolidation of Non-Wholly Owned Subsidiaries at the Date of Acquisition
Fair Value - Full Goodwill Approach

Objective of this section

Illustrate techniques and procedures involved in establishing non-controlling interest (NCI) in consolidated financial statements at the date of acquisition when NCI is measured at fair value under the **Full Goodwill Approach**.

Key concepts

- Implied purchase price
- Implied price differential
- Full goodwill
- Full fair value increment and decrement

BASIC INFORMATION
Initial Acquisition

On December 31, X1, Parent Company acquires **90%** of the outstanding voting shares of Subsidiary by issuing 36,000 shares with a market value of $30, or **$1,080,000** total, in exchange.

At the date of combination, the fair values of Subsidiary's land and buildings exceeded their book values by $100,000 and $200,000, respectively. The fair values of all of Subsidiary's other assets and liabilities were equal to their book values.

Subsidiary had common shares of $200,000 and retained earnings of $600,000 at the date of acquisition.

The remaining useful life of the buildings from the date of acquisition is ten years. Subsidiary uses the straight-line method to calculate amortizations.

Required

Prepare the consolidated statement of financial position of Parent Company at the date of acquisition.

Part 2a

BASIC INFORMATION
Affiliation Structure

BEFORE

PARENT   SUBSIDIARY

AFTER

Parent's shareholders
160,000 shares
(82%) → PARENT ← Subsidiary's shareholders
36,000 shares
(18%)

↓ 90%

SUBSIDIARY ← Minority Shareholders (10%)

Non-Wholly Owned Subsidiaries ---------- Module 7 ---------- 23

Part 2a

FAIR VALUE - FULL GOODWILL
Process

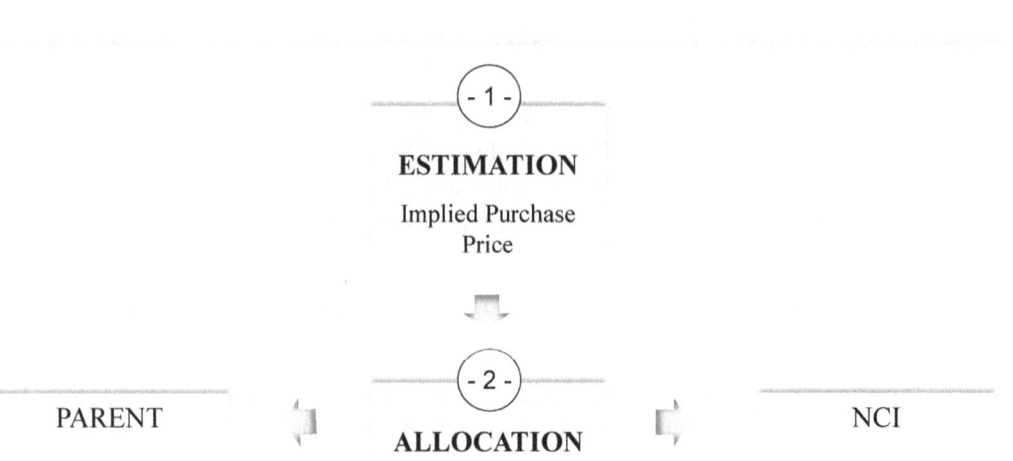

- 1 -
ESTIMATION
Implied Purchase Price

- 2 -
PARENT ⇨ **ALLOCATION** ⇨ NCI

Non-Wholly Owned Subsidiaries ---------- Module 7 ---------- 24

ESTIMATION OF IMPLIED PURCHASE PRICE
Definition and Formula

Part 2a

Definition

PURCHASE PRICE THAT PARENT COMPANY WOULD HAVE PAID HAD PARENT PURCHASED 100% OF THE VOTING STOCK OF SUBSIDIARY INSTEAD OF 90%

Formula

$$\frac{\text{PRICE PAID } \$1,080,000}{\text{PERCENTAGE ACQUIRED } 0.90} = \text{IMPLIED VALUE } \$1,200,000 \quad (100\%)$$

IMPLIED PURCHASE PRICE
Assumption

Part 2a

Assumption made

Goodwill for the subsidiary as a whole is a linear extrapolation of what the parent paid for its share of goodwill.

This assumption is not valid when the purchase price includes a control premium, which is usually the case when control is achieved close to 50%. Recall that control premium is the bonus an acquiring company is willing to pay in order to gain control. That is when tender offers or takeover bids propose a high price, but offer to buy only enough of the outstanding shares to gain control. When the buyer pays a premium, the uncomplicated and apriori simplistic method of calculating the implied value under the Full Goodwill alternative could lead to an overstatement of the overall FV of the target entity. This first critical step could therefore compromise the consolidation process that follows. Besides, this is one of the main reasons why the Entity Theory is currently not in use, at least in its pure form.

ALLOCATION OF IMPLIED PURCHASE PRICE
Full Goodwill Approach

Part 2a

	Implied (100%)	Parent (90%)	NCI (10%)
Purchase price	$1,200,000	$1,080,000	$120,000
Net book value of Subsidiary:			
- Common shares $200,000			
- Retained earnings 600,000	800,000	720,000	80,000
Price differential	400,000	360,000	40,000
Fair value increments:			
- Land (100,000)			
- Buildings (200,000)	(300,000)	(270,000)	(30,000)
Goodwill	$100,000	$90,000	$10,000

Non-Wholly Owned Subsidiaries — Module 7 — 27

GOODWILL ASSIGNED TO NCI
Residual of Residual

Part 2a

	Implied (100%)	Parent (90%)	NCI (10%)
Goodwill →	$100,000	$90,000	$10,000
	(1) ---→	(2) ---→	(1 – 2)
	From the Implied Value	From the Puchase Price	
	$1,200,000	$1,080,000	

Goodwill is by definition a residual. Therefore, goodwill assigned to the NCI under the Full Goodwill Approach ($ 10,000) becomes a residual of a residual ($100,000$ - $90,000)

Non-Wholly Owned Subsidiaries — Module 7 — 28

Part 2a

CONSOLIDATION ENTRIES
Elimination of the Investment Account

Double-Counting of $720,000

1a
Common Shares (Subsidiary)	180,000	
Retained Earnings (Subsidiary)	540,000	
Investment in Subsidiary (Parent)		720,000

Implied Price Differential Allocated to Parent (90%)

1b
Land (Subsidiary)	90,000	
Buildings (Subsidiary)	180,000	
Goodwill (Subsidiary)	90,000	
Investment in Subsidiary (Parent)		360,000

Investment: $1,080,000

Part 2a

CONSOLIDATION ENTRIES
Non-Controlling Interest

Complete this slide

Implied Purchase Price Allocated to NCI (10%)

2
- Common Shares — 20,000
- RE — 60,000
- Land — 10,000
- Building — 20,000
- Goodwill — 10,000

Non-Controlling Interest   120,000

The full FV of Subsidiary at date of acquisition ($1,200,000), including full goodwill ($100,000), is assigned proportionally to Parent (90%) and NCI (10%).

CONSOLIDATION WORKSHEET OF PARENT COMPANY
At the Date of Acquisition

Part 2a

	Parent	Subsidiary	Eliminations	Consolidated
Assets				
Land	$1,000,000	$300,000	(1b) 90,000 (2) 10,000	$1,400,000
Buildings (net)	1,800,000	350,000	(1b) 180,000 (2) 20,000	2,350,000
Goodwill			(1b) 90,000 (2) 10,000	100,000
Investment in Subsidiary	1,080,000		(1a) (720,000) (1b) (360,000)	
Inventories	200,000	50,000		250,000
Accounts receivable	2,000,000	150,000		2,150,000
Cash	1,000,000	50,000		1,050,000
Total assets	**$7,080,000**	**$900,000**		**$7,300,000**
Equity and liabilities				
Share capital	$3,680,000	$200,000	(1a) (180,000) (2) (20,000)	$3,680,000
Retained earnings	2,000,000	600,000	(1a) (540,000) (2) (60,000)	2,000,000
Non-controlling Interest			(2) 120,000	120,000
Long-term notes payable	400,000			400,000
Accounts payable	1,000,000	100,000		1,100,000
Total equity and liabilities	**$7,080,000**	**$900,000**		**$7,300,000**

CONSOLIDATION WORKSHEET OF PARENT COMPANY
FV of Subsidiary at Date of Acquisition

Part 2a

	Parent	Subsidiary	Eliminations	Consolidated
Assets				
Land	$1,000,000	$300,000	(1b) 90,000 (2) 10,000	$1,400,000
Buildings (net)	1,800,000	350,000	(1b) 180,000 (2) 20,000	2,350,000
Goodwill			(1b) 90,000 (2) 10,000	100,000
Investment in Subsidiary	1,080,000		(1a) (720,000) (1b) (360,000)	
Inventories	200,000	50,000		250,000
Accounts receivable	2,000,000	150,000	FV of Sub. (100%)	2,150,000
Cash	1,000,000	50,000		1,050,000
Total assets	**$7,080,000**	**$900,000**		**$7,300,000**
Equity and liabilities				
Share capital	$3,680,000	$200,000	(1a) (180,000) (2) (20,000)	$3,680,000
Retained earnings	2,000,000	600,000	(1a) (540,000) (2) (60,000)	2,000,000
Non-controlling Interest			(2) **120,000**	120,000
Long-term notes payable	400,000		NCI (10%)	400,000
Accounts payable	1,000,000	100,000		1,100,000
Total equity and liabilities	**$7,080,000**	**$900,000**		**$7,300,000**

Part 2a
CONSOLIDATED STATEMENT OF FINANCIAL POSITION - PARENT
AT THE DATE OF ACQUISITION
Wholly Owned vs. Non-Wholly Owned Subsidiary

	Wholly-Owned Subsidiary	Non-Wholly Owned Subsidiary (Full Goodwill)
Assets		
Non-current assets		
Land	$1,400,000	$1,400,000
Buildings (net)	2,350,000	2,350,000
Goodwill	100,000	100,000
Current assets		
Inventories	250,000	250,000
Accounts receivable	2,150,000	2,150,000
Cash	1,050,000	1,050,000
Total assets	**$7,300,000**	**$7,300,000**
Equity and liabilities		
Equity		
Share capital	$3,800,000	$3,680,000
Retained earnings	2,000,000	2,000,000
Non-controlling Interest		120,000
Liabilities		
Long-term notes payable	400,000	400,000
Accounts payable	1,100,000	1,100,000
Total equity and liabilities	**$7,300,000**	**$7,300,000**

Part 2b
OUTLINE OF THE PRESENTATION

1 CONSOLIDATION THEORIES

2 CONSOLIDATION OF NON-WHOLLY OWNED SUBSIDIARIES AT THE DATE OF ACQUISITION

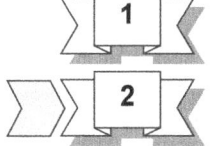

a) FV-Full Goodwill   **b) FV-Partial Goodwill**

3 CONSOLIDATION OF NON-WHOLLY OWNED SUBSIDIARIES SUBSEQUENT TO THE DATE OF ACQUISITION

a) FV-Full Goodwill   b) FV-Partial Goodwill

4 EQUITY METHOD

Non-Wholly Owned Subsidiaries ---------- Module 7 ----------

PART 2 b
Consolidation of Non-Wholly Owned Subsidiaries at the Date of Acquisition
Fair Value - Partial Goodwill Approach

Objective of this section

Illustrate techniques and procedures involved in establishing non-controlling interest (NCI) in consolidated financial statements at the date of acquisition when NCI is measured at fair value under the **Partial Goodwill Approach** (IFRS).

CURRENT STANDARDS
Partial Goodwill Approach

The NCI in a subsidiary is measured as either:

1. The fair value of the NCI as a whole

or

2. The proportionate interest in the fair value of the identifiable net assets

FV of NCI can be measured on two different ways. Sometimes, an acquirer will be able to measure the acquisition-date fair value of NCI on the basis of active market prices for the equity shares not held by the acquirer. However, in other situations, an active market price for the equity shares will not be available. In those situations, the acquirer would measure the fair value of NCI based on the FV of the identifiable net assets at the date of acquisition. In either case, there is no risk of overstating the implied value of Subsidiary nor to compute goodwill as a residual of a residual.

PURCHASE PRICE ALLOCATION
Partial Goodwill Approach - NCI at FV of Net Assets

		Parent (90%)	NCI (10%)
Purchase price		$1,080,000	
Net book value of Subsidiary:			
- Common shares $200,000			
- Retained earnings 600,000	800,000	720,000	80,000
Price differential		360,000	
Fair value increments:			
- Land (100,000)			
- Buildings (200,000)	(300,000)	(270,000)	30,000
Goodwill		$90,000	
			$110,000

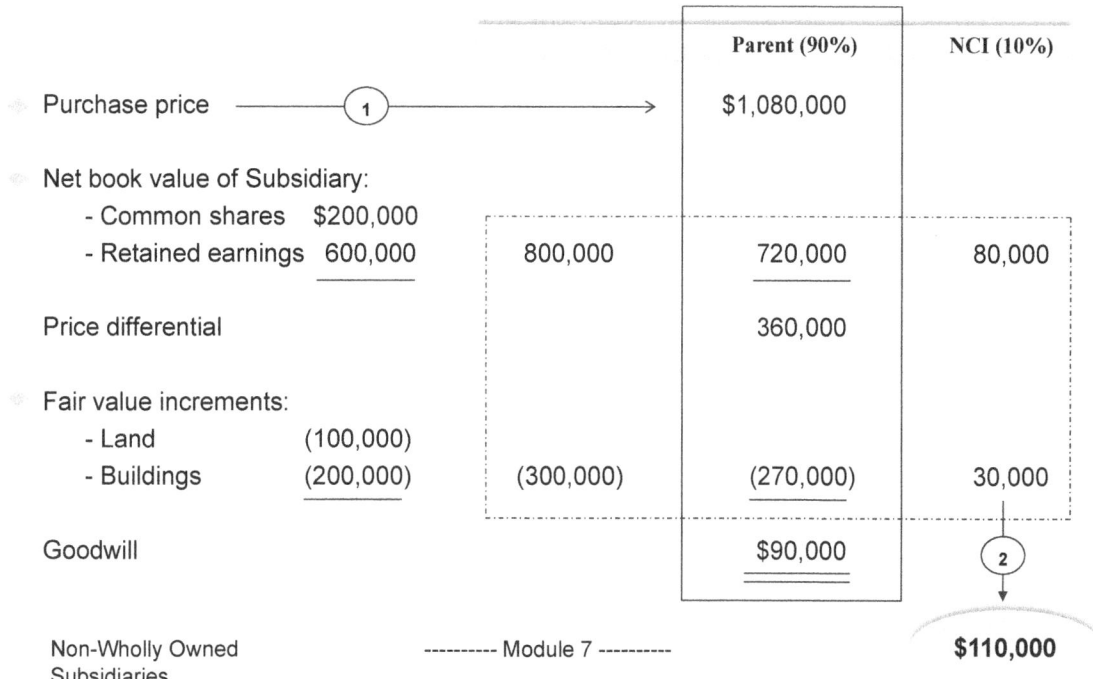

Non-Wholly Owned Subsidiaries — Module 7 —

CONSOLIDATION ENTRIES
Elimination of the Investment Account

Double-Counting of $720,000

1a
Common Shares (Subsidiary)   180,000
Retained Earnings (Subsidiary)   540,000
  Investment in Subsidiary (Parent)   720,000

Price Differential

1b
Land (Subsidiary)   90,000
Buildings (Subsidiary)   180,000
Goodwill (Subsidiary)   90,000
  Investment in Subsidiary (Parent)   360,000

Investment: $1,080,000

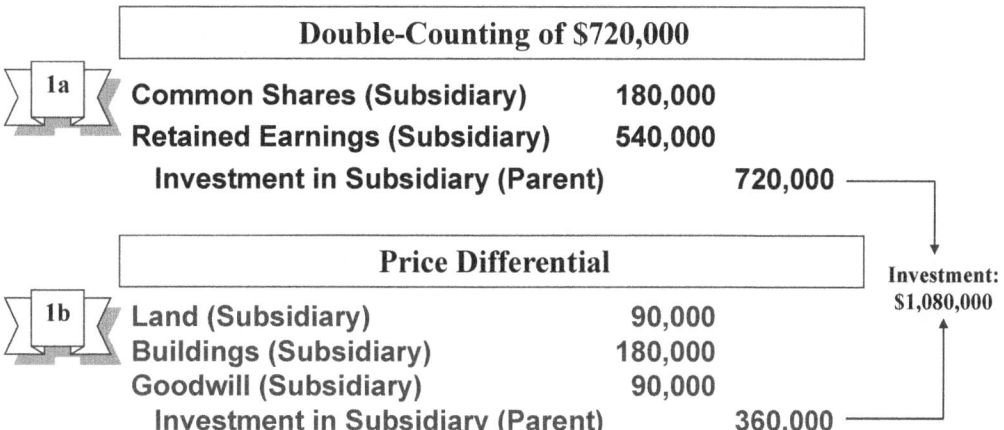

Non-Wholly Owned Subsidiaries — Module 7 — 38

Part 2b

CONSOLIDATION ENTRIES
Non-Controlling Interest at FV of Net Assets

FV of Identifiable Net Assets Allocated to NCI (10%)

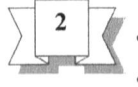

- RE   20,000
- Common Shares 60,000
- Land   10,000
- Building   20,000

Non-Controlling Interest   110,000

NCI amounts to $110,000 at date of acquisition, that is:
- $80,000 (10% of the NBV of Subsidiary: $10\% \times \$800,000$) + $30,000 (10% of FVIs: $10\% \times \$300,000$) or,
- 10% of the FV of Subsidiary's identifiable net assets: ($10\% \times \$1,100,000$).

No goodwill is assigned to NCI.

Non-Wholly Owned Subsidiaries ---------- Module 7 ----------

Part 2b

CONSOLIDATION WORKSHEET OF PARENT COMPANY
At the Date of Acquisition

	Parent	Subsidiary	Eliminations	Consolidated
Assets				
Land	$1,000,000	$300,000	(1b) 90,000 (2) 10,000	$1,400,000
Buildings (net)	1,800,000	350,000	(1b) 180,000 (2) 20,000	2,350,000
Goodwill			(1b) 90,000	90,000
Investment in Subsidiary	1,080,000		(1a) (720,000) (1b) (360,000)	
Inventories	200,000	50,000		250,000
Accounts receivable	2,000,000	150,000		2,150,000
Cash	1,000,000	50,000		1,050,000
Total assets	**$7,080,000**	**$900,000**		**$7,290,000**
Equity and liabilities				
Share capital	$3,680,000	$200,000	(1a) (180,000) (2) (20,000)	$3,680,000
Retained earnings	2,000,000	600,000	(1a) (540,000) (2) (60,000)	2,000,000
Non-controlling Interest			(2) 110,000	110,000
Liabilities				
Long-term notes payable	400,000			400,000
Accounts payable	1,000,000	100,000		1,100,000
Total equity and liabilities	**$7,080,000**	**$900,000**		**$7,290,000**

Part 2b

CONSOLIDATED STATEMENT OF FINANCIAL POSITION - PARENT
AT THE DATE OF ACQUISITION
Full Goodwill vs. Partial Goodwill (NCI at FV of Net Assets)

	Full Goodwill	Partial Goodwill
Assets		
Non-current assets		
Land	$1,400,000	$1,400,000
Buildings (net)	2,350,000	2,350,000
Goodwill	100,000	90,000
Current assets		
Inventories	250,000	250,000
Accounts receivable	2,150,000	2,150,000
Cash	1,050,000	1,050,000
Total assets	**$7,300,000**	**$7,290,000**
Equity and liabilities		
Equity		
Share capital	$3,680,000	$3,680,000
Retained earnings	2,000,000	2,000,000
Non-controlling Interest	120,000	110,000
Liabilities		
Long-term notes payable	400,000	400,000
Accounts payable	1,100,000	1,100,000
Total equity and liabilities	**$7,300,000**	**$7,290,000**

Consolidated figures are the same under both approaches except for Goodwill and NCI.

Part 2b

PURCHASE PRICE ALLOCATION
Partial Goodwill Approach - Assume FV of NCI = $115,000

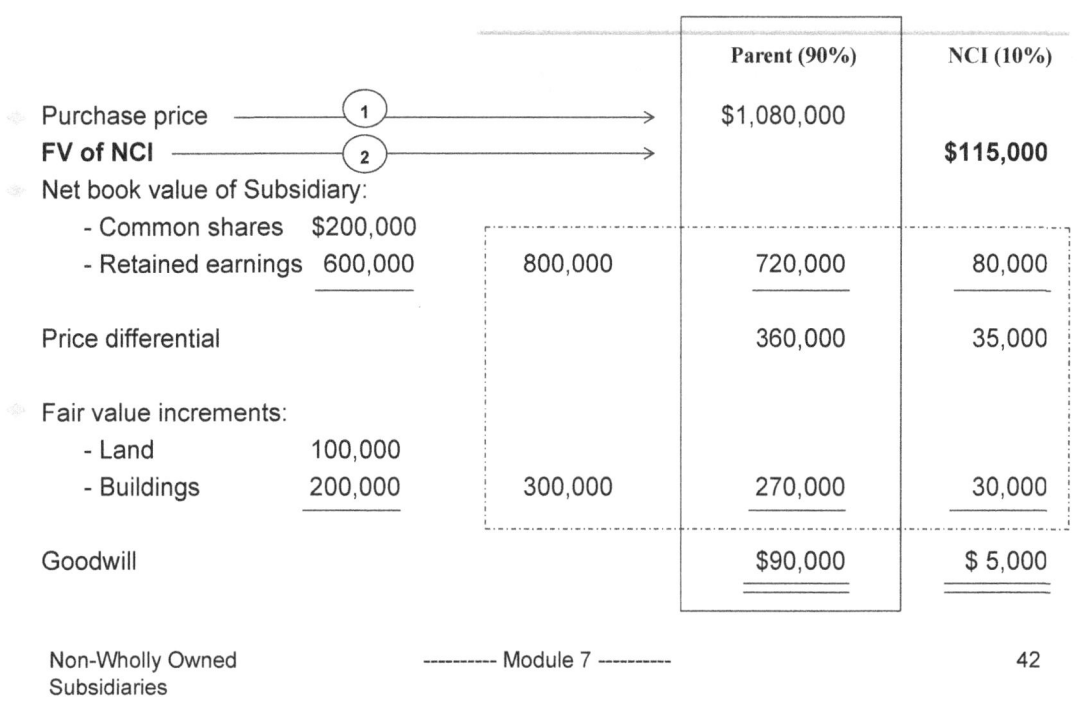

Non-Wholly Owned Subsidiaries ---------- Module 7 ----------

Part 2b

CONSOLIDATION ENTRIES
Non-Controlling Interest at FV

	FV of NCI = $115,000	
2	Common Shares (Subsidiary)	20,000
	Retained Earnings (Subsidiary)	60,000
	Land (Subsidiary)	10,000
	Buildings (Subsidiary)	20,000
	Goodwill	5,000
	Non-Controlling Interest	115,000

Here, Goodwill ($5,000) is the excess of the acquisition-date FV of NCI ($115,000) over NCI's share of Subsidiary's identifiable net assets ($110,000).

Part 2b

CONSOLIDATION PROCESS AT THE DATE OF ACQUISITION
Recap

Fair Value - Full Goodwill Approach

PARENT		SUBSIDIARY		NCI
BV	+	FULL FV (100%)	↔ ↔	FULL FV (10%)

Fair Value - Partial Goodwill Approach (NCI at FV of Net Assets)

PARENT		SUBSIDIARY		NCI
BV	+	FV of net assets (100%)	↔ ↔	FV of net assets (10%)
		Partial Goodwill (90%)		

Under the Full Goodwill approach, consolidation process is straightforward. The estimated full market value of Subsidiary at acquisition is added to the BV of Parent. Then, 10% of the implied FV is assigned to NCI. Under the Partial Goodwill approach, if NCI is valued at 10% of Subsidiary's net fair value, only Goodwill from the purchase price is entered.

PART 2
Concept Check

> How is the value of the NCI different under the full goodwill alternative and the partial goodwill alternative?

OUTLINE OF THE PRESENTATION

1 CONSOLIDATION THEORIES

2 CONSOLIDATION OF NON-WHOLLY OWNED SUBSIDIARIES AT THE DATE OF ACQUISITION

    a) FV-Full Goodwill   b) FV-Partial Goodwill

3 **CONSOLIDATION OF NON-WHOLLY OWNED SUBSIDIARIES SUBSEQUENT TO THE DATE OF ACQUISITION**

    a) FV-Full Goodwill   b) FV-Partial Goodwill

4 EQUITY METHOD

PART 3 a
Consolidation of Non-Wholly Owned Subsidiaries Subsequent to the Date of Acquisition
Fair Value - Full Goodwill Approach

Objectives of this section

Illustrate techniques and procedures involved in establishing non-controlling interest (NCI) in consolidated financial statements in periods subsequent to acquisition when NCI is measured at fair value under the **Full Goodwill Approach**.

Discuss the general approach to consolidation involving non-wholly owned subsidiaries using both the worksheet approach and the direct approach. Illustrate the process when the parent has used the cost method to account for its investment.

Key concept

Allocation of consolidated profit to majority and minority interests

---

BASIC INFORMATION
Consolidation of Parent and Subsidiary Four Years Post-Acquisition

Refer to the previous illustration.

Recall that on December 31, X1, Parent Company acquired 90% of the outstanding voting shares of Subsidiary by issuing 36,000 shares with a market value of $30, or $1,080,000 total, in exchange.

At the date of combination, the fair values of Subsidiary's land and buildings exceeded their book values by $100,000 and $200,000, respectively. Subsidiary had common shares of $200,000 and retained earnings of $600,000 at the date of acquisition.

Required

Prepare the consolidated financial statements of Parent Company for the year ended December 31, X5.

BASIC INFORMATION
Separate-Entity Statements of Financial Position
At December 31, X5

	Parent	Subsidiary
Assets		
Non-current assets		
Land	$1,250,000	-
Buildings & equipment (net)	3,400,000	$210,000
Investment in Subsidiary	**1,080,000**	
Current assets		
Inventories	500,000	230,000
Accounts receivable	1,800,000	780,000
Cash	590,000	170,000
Total assets	**$8,620,000**	**$1,390,000**
Equity and liabilities		
Equity		
Share capital	$3,680,000	$200,000
Retained earnings	3,600,000	1,100,000
Liabilities		
Long-term notes payable	1,000,000	-
Accounts payable	340,000	90,000
Total equity and liabilities	**$8,620,000**	**$1,390,000**

BASIC INFORMATION
Separate-Entity Income Statements
For the Period Ended December 31, X5

	Parent	Subsidiary
Sales revenue	$3,100,000	$570,000
Dividend income	**18,000**	
Cost of sales	2,300,000	420,000
Depreciation expense	200,000	35,000
Other expenses	440,000	85,000
Profit for the year	**$178,000**	**$30,000**

BASIC INFORMATION
Separate-Entity Statements of Changes in Equity
For the Period Ended December 31, X5

	Parent			Subsidiary		
	Share Capital	Retained Earnings	Total	Share Capital	Retained Earnings	Total
Balance at Dec. 31, X4	$3,680,000	$3,522,000	$7,202,000	$200,000	$1,090,000	$1,290,000
Profit for the year		178,000	178,000		30,000	30,000
Dividends		(100,000)	(100,000)		(20,000)	(20,000)
Balance at Dec. X5	**$3,680,000**	**$3,600,000**	**$7,280,000**	**$200,000**	**$1,100,000**	**$1,300,000**

CONSOLIDATION WITH NCI
Upstream Transactions and NCI

Only consolidation adjustments from upstream transactions affect Subsidiary's consolidated (or adjusted) value, which in turn affect the valuation of NCI.

PARENT — Partial Control — UPSTREAM — SUBSIDIARY

PARENT — NCI

Part 3a

CONSOLIDATION WITH NCI
Upstream vs. Downstream Transactions

When dealing with non-wholly owned subsidiaries, it becomes critical to distinguish clearly between upstream and downstream transactions. Indeed, only consolidation adjustments from upstream transactions affect Subsidiary's value through consolidation. Therefore, since the adjusted value of Subsidiary must be assigned proportionally to Parent and NCI, consolidation adjustments from upstream transactions will indirectly impact the valuation of NCI.

In our illustration, we need to pay close attention to the upstream transfer of the equipment in X4 for which a portion of the gain is still unrealized in the current period (X5).

See additional information next.

Part 3a

CONSOLIDATION OF PARENT COMPANY
Additional Information

1. In X5, Parent had sales of $60,000 to Subsidiary. Parent's X5 gross margin was 45%; $10,000 (sales price) of the transferred units are in Subsidiary's inventory on December 31, X5.

2. In X4, Parent had sales of $20,000 to Subsidiary. Parent's X4 gross margin was 30%; $6,000 (sales price) of the transferred units was in Subsidiary's inventory on December 31, X4.

3. In X4, Subsidiary had sales of $50,000 to Parent. Subsidiary's X4 gross margin was 35%; all the transferred units were resold to external parties by the end of X4.

4. Subsidiary sold an equipment to Parent on January 1, X4, for $30,000. The net book value of the equipment at the time of transfer was equal to $20,000, that is, the original cost for Subsidiary. The estimated useful life of the equipment is 10 years.

(Items 3 and 4: **Upstream Transactions**)

CONSOLIDATION OF PARENT COMPANY
Additional Information (continued…)

5. Subsidiary sold its land to an outside party in X4 for $450,000. The land originally cost Subsidiary $300,000, and its fair value at the date of Parent's acquisition was $400,000.

6. Impairment test for X5 revealed that Goodwill should be $80,000.

BASIC INFORMATION
Implied Price Differential Amortization Schedule

Items	Implied Price Differential Balance at Acquisition	Amortization Prior Years (X2-X4)	Amortization Current Year (X5)	Unamortized Excess at December 31, X5
Land	$100,000	($100,000)	-	-
Buildings	200,000	(60,000)	($20,000)	$120,000
Goodwill	100,000	-	(20,000)	80,000
Total	$400,000	($160,000)	($40,000)	$200,000

BASIC INFORMATION
Recap on Intercompany Gains - Impact for X5

Transaction	RE Beginning	Profit	RE End
Downstream			
➤ Unrealized profit from sale of merchandise in X5	-	$(4,500)	$(4,500)
➤ Unrealized profit from sale of merchandise in X4	$(1,800)	1,800	-
Upstream			
➤ Sale and resale of merchandise in X4	-	-	-
➤ Sale of equipment in X4	(9,000)	1,000	(8,000)

CONSOLIDATION OF PARENT COMPANY
Practical Guide
Bozec, Chapter 8

Scenarios	Description
3.2	Consolidation of a non-wholly owned subsidiary subsequent to acquisition
4.1	Intercompany dividends (X5)
6.1	Intercompany sale of inventory in current year (X5)
6.2	Intercompany sale of inventory in prior year (X4)
7.2	Intercompany sale of equipment in prior year (X4)

Part 3a

CONSOLIDATION ENTRIES
Elimination of the Investment Account

Double-Counting of $720,000

1a) Common Shares (Subsidiary)   180,000
     Retained Earnings (Subsidiary)   540,000
       Investment in Subsidiary (Parent)   720,000

Implied Price Differential Allocated to Parent (90%)

1b) Land (Subsidiary)   90,000
     Buildings (Subsidiary)   180,000
     Goodwill (Subsidiary)   90,000
       Investment in Subsidiary (Parent)   360,000

Investment: $1,080,000

Non-Wholly Owned Subsidiaries   ---------- Module 7 ----------   59

Part 3a

WORKSHEET APPROACH
Implied Price Differential
Full Fair Value Increment on Buildings

Amortization of the Full Fair Value Increment on Buildings since Acquisition

2a) Depreciation Expense (Subsidiary)   20,000
     Retained Earnings (Subsidiary)   60,000
       Buildings & Equip. (Subsidiary)   80,000

Prior Years (X2-X4)

Current Year (X5)

Non-Wholly Owned Subsidiaries   ---------- Module 7 ----------   60

Part 3a

WORKSHEET APPROACH
Implied Price Differential
Full Fair Value Increment on Land

Realization of the Full Fair Value Increment on Land

2b Retained Earnings (Subsidiary)   100,000
        Land (Subsidiary)   100,000

Prior Year (X4)

Part 3a

WORKSHEET APPROACH
Implied Price Differential
Full Goodwill

Goodwill Impairment

2c Other Expenses (Subsidiary)   20,000
        Goodwill (Subsidiary)   20,000

Current Year (X5)

Part 3a

WORKSHEET APPROACH
Non-Controlling Interest at Acquisition

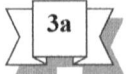

Implied Purchase Price Allocated to NCI (10%)	
Common Shares (Subsidiary)	20,000
Retained Earnings (Subsidiary)	60,000
Land (Subsidiary)	10,000
Buildings (Subsidiary)	20,000
Goodwill (Subsidiary)	10,000
Non-Controlling Interest	120,000

Non-Wholly Owned Subsidiaries ---------- Module 7 ---------- 63

Part 3a

WORKSHEET APPROACH
Allocation of Net Adjusted Value of Subsidiary since Acquisition to Non-Controlling Interest

Complete this slide

Net Adjusted Value of Subsidiary Since Acquisition

- Retained earnings increase since acquisition
  ($1,100,000 - $600,000) $500,000
- Implied price differential amortization
  since acquisition   (200,000)
- Unrealized portion of the gain on <u>upstream</u> sale
  of equipment ($10,000 × 8/10)   (8,000)
  Total $292,000

Adjustment of NCI   10%

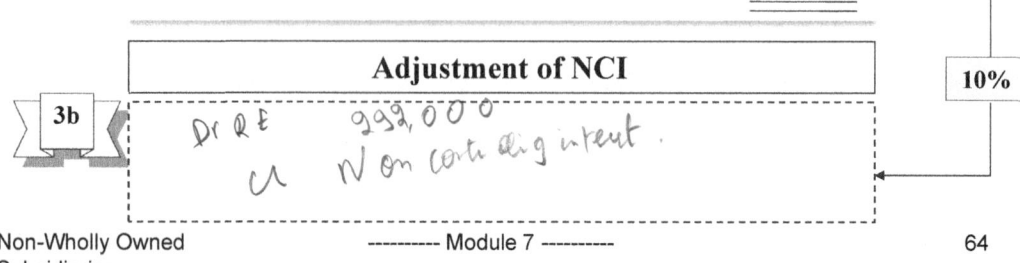

Dr RE 292,000
 Cr Non controlling interest

Non-Wholly Owned Subsidiaries ---------- Module 7 ---------- 64

Part 3a

WORKSHEET APPROACH
Adjustments Related to Intercompany Transactions
Sales of Inventory

Current-Year Downstream Sale of Inventory

4 Sales (Parent)   60,000
    Cost of Goods Sold (Parent)   55,500
    Inventory (Subsidiary)   4,500

Realization of Prior-Year Profit on Downstream Sale of Inventory

5 Retained Earnings (Parent)   1,800
    Cost of Goods Sold   1,800

Part 3a

WORKSHEET APPROACH
Adjustments Related to Intercompany Transactions
Upstream Sale of Equipment in X4

Unrealized Portion of the Gain at the Beginning of X5

6a Retained Earnings (Parent & Sub.)   9,000
    Buildings & Equip. (net) (Parent)   9,000

Excess Depreciation of the Current Period

6b Buildings & Equip. (net) (Parent)   1,000
    Depreciation Expenses (Parent)   1,000

WORKSHEET APPROACH
Adjustments Related to Intercompany Transactions
Intercompany Dividends

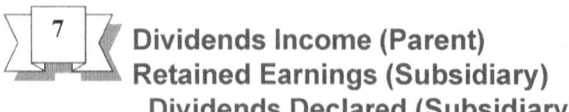

Dividends Income (Parent)	18,000	
Retained Earnings (Subsidiary)	2,000	
Dividends Declared (Subsidiary)		20,000

The adjustment to RE ($2,000) is consistent with entry 3b, which captures the NCI's share of current intercompany dividends. Moreover, the adjustment to RE is required in order to remove 100% of the dividends declared by Subsidiary ($20,000).

CONSOLIDATION WORKSHEET OF PARENT COMPANY
For the Year Ended December 31, X5

	Parent	Subsidiary	Conso. Entries	Consolidated
Assets				
Land	$1,250,000	-	(1b) 90,000 (2b) (100,000); (3a) 10,000	$1,250,000
Buildings & equipment (net)	3,400,000	$210,000	(1b) 180,000 (2a) (80,000); (3a) 20,000 (6a) (9,000); (6b) 1,000	3,722,000
Goodwill			(1b) 90,000 (2c) (20,000); (3a) 10,000	80,000
Investment in Subsidiary	1,080,000		(1a) (720,000); (1b) (360,000)	-
Inventories	500,000	230,000	(4) (4,500)	725,500
Accounts receivable	1,800,000	780,000		2,580,000
Cash	590,000	170,000		760,000
Total assets	**$8,620,000**	**$1,390,000**		**$9,117,500**
Equity and liabilities				
Share capital	$3,680,000	$200,000	(1a) (180,000); (3a) (20,000)	$3,680,000
Retained earnings	3,600,000	1,100,000	(841,700)	3,858,300
Non-controlling interest			(3a) 120,000; (3b) 29,200	149,200
Long-term notes payable	1,000,000	-		1,000,000
Accounts payable	340,000	90,000		430,000
Total equity and liabilities	**$8,620,000**	**$1,390,000**		**$9,117,500**

CONSOLIDATION WORKSHEET OF PARENT COMPANY (continued...)
For the Year Ended December 31, X5

Part 3a

	Parent	Subsidiary	Conso. Entries	Consolidated
Sales revenue	$3,100,000	$570,000	(4) (60,000)	$3,610,000
Dividend income	18,000		(7) (18,000)	-
Cost of sales	2,300,000	420,000	(4) (55,500); (5) (1,800)	2,662,700
Depreciation expense	200,000	35,000	(2a) 20,000; (6b)(1,000)	254,000
Other expenses	440,000	85,000	(2c) 20,000	545,000
Profit for the year	**$178,000**	**$30,000**	**(59,700)**	**$148,300**
Retained earnings (beginning)	$3,522,000	$1,090,000	(1a) (540,000) (2a) (60,000) (2b) (100,000) (3a) (60,000) (3b) (29,200) (5) (1,800) (6a) (9,000); (7) (2,000)	$3,810,000
Dividends declared	(100,000)	(20,000)	(7) 20,000	(100,000)
Retained earnings (end)	**$3,600,000**	**$1,100,000**	**(841,700)**	**$3,858,300**

Net impact of the consolidation adjustments on the ending balance of Retained Earnings. To be transferred into the statement of financial position.

DIRECT APPROACH
Non-Current Assets

Part 3a

Buildings & Equipment (net)

Parent	$3,400,000
Subsidiary	210,000
Unamortized portion of the:	
• Fair value increment on Buildings ($200,000 × 6/10)	**120,000**
• Upstream gain on sale of Equip. ($10,000 × 8/10)	**(8,000)**
Total	$3,722,000

Goodwill

At acquisition	$100,000
Portion impaired	**(20,000)**
Total	$80,000

Land

Parent	$1,250,000

DIRECT APPROACH
Current Assets

Cash
Parent	$590,000
Subsidiary	170,000
Total	$760,000

Accounts Receivable
Parent	$1,800,000
Subsidiary	780,000
Total	$2,580,000

Inventories
Parent	$500,000
Subsidiary	230,000
Unrealized profit on downstream sale	(4,500)
Total	$725,500

DIRECT APPROACH
Retained Earnings

- Parent — $3,600,000
- Unrealized profit on <u>downstream</u> sale of inventory — (4,500)
- Parent's share of Subsidiary's net adjusted value since acquisition: ($292,000 × 90%) — 262,800
- Total — $3,858,300

90%

Net Adjusted Value of Subsidiary Since Acquisition

- Retained earnings increase since acquisition ($1,100,000 - $600,000) — $500,000
- Implied price differential amortization since acquisition — (200,000)
- Unrealized portion of the gain on <u>upstream</u> sale of equipment ($10,000 × 8/10) — (8,000)
- Total — $292,000

DIRECT APPROACH
Non-Controlling Interest

- Minority's share of implied purchase price:
  ($1,200,000 × 10%) $120,000
- Minority's share of Subsidiary's net adjusted value since acquisition: ($292,000 × 10%) 29,200
- Total $149,200

10%

Net Adjusted Value of Subsidiary Since Acquisition

- Retained earnings increase since acquisition
  ($1,100,000 - $600,000) $500,000
- Implied price differential amortization since acquisition (200,000)
- Unrealized portion of the gain on <u>upstream</u> sale of equipment
  ($10,000 × 8/10) (8,000)
  Total $292,000

DIRECT APPROACH
Liabilities

Accounts Payable	
Parent	$340,000
Subsidiary	90,000
Total	$430,000

Long-Term Notes Payable	
Parent	$1,000,000

NET ADJUSTED VALUE OF SUBSIDIARY
At December 31, X5

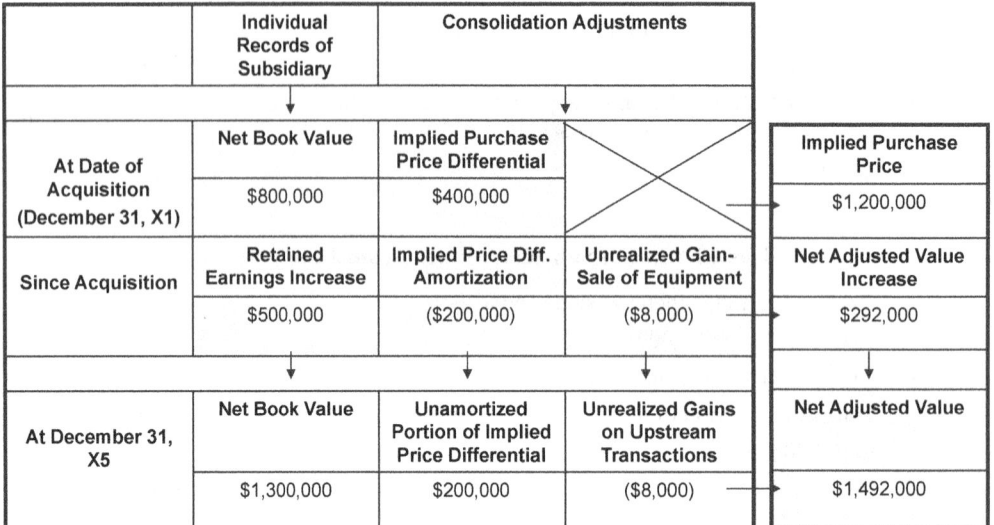

	Individual Records of Subsidiary	Consolidation Adjustments		
At Date of Acquisition (December 31, X1)	Net Book Value $800,000	Implied Purchase Price Differential $400,000		Implied Purchase Price $1,200,000
Since Acquisition	Retained Earnings Increase $500,000	Implied Price Diff. Amortization ($200,000)	Unrealized Gain- Sale of Equipment ($8,000)	Net Adjusted Value Increase $292,000
At December 31, X5	Net Book Value $1,300,000	Unamortized Portion of Implied Price Differential $200,000	Unrealized Gains on Upstream Transactions ($8,000)	Net Adjusted Value $1,492,000

NET ADJUSTED VALUE OF SUBSIDIARY
Valuation of the NCI at December 31, X5

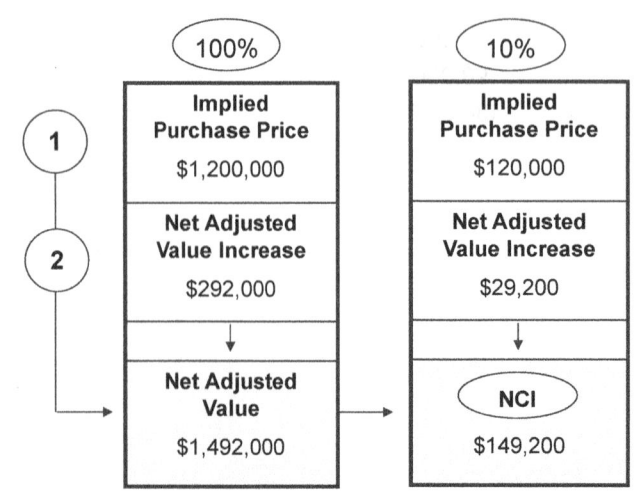

DIRECT APPROACH
Consolidated Profit

Part 3a

- Adjusted profit of Parent:
  - Profit of Parent for the period $178,000
  - Unrealized current-year profit on **downstream**
    sale of inventory   (4,500)
  - Realized profit from prior-year **downstream**
    sale of inventory   1,800
  - Intercompany dividends   (18,000) $157,300

- Adjusted profit of Subsidiary:
  - Profit of Subsidiary for the period $30,000
  - Current-year implied price differential amortization   (40,000)
  - Realized portion of prior-year **upstream** sale
    of equipment ($10,000/10)   1,000   (9,000)
  - Total $148,300

DIRECT APPROACH
Consolidated Profit Allocated to Parent and NCI

Part 3a

Complete this slide

Allocation to Parent

Adjusted profit of parent   157,300
Parent share of adjusted net loss   (8,100)   ← (9000) × 0.9
                                             149,200

Allocation to Non-Controlling Shareholders

Minority share of adjusted net loss   900   ← (9000 × 0.1)

Part 3a
CONSOLIDATED STATEMENT OF FINANCIAL POSITION - PARENT
At December 31, X5
Wholly Owned vs. Non-Wholly Owned Subsidiary

	Wholly-Owned Subsidiary	Non-Wholly Owned Subsidiary
Assets		
Non-current assets		
Land	$1,250,000	$1,250,000
Buildings (net)	3,722,000	3,722,000
Goodwill	80,000	80,000
Current assets		
Inventories	725,500	725,500
Accounts receivable	2,580,000	2,580,000
Cash	760,000	760,000
Total assets	**$9,117,500**	**$9,117,500**
Equity and liabilities		
Equity		
Share capital	$3,800,000	$3,680,000
Retained earnings	3,887,500	3,858,300
Non-controlling Interest		149,200
Liabilities		
Long-term notes payable	1,000,000	1,000,000
Accounts payable	430,000	430,000
Total equity and liabilities	**$9,117,500**	**$9,117,500**

Part 3a
CONSOLIDATED INCOME STATEMENT OF PARENT
For the Year Ended December 31, X5
Wholly Owned vs. Non-Wholly Owned Subsidiary

	Wholly-Owned Subsidiary	Non-Wholly Owned Subsidiary
Sales revenue	$3,610,000	$3,610,000
Cost of sales	2,662,700	2,662,700
Depreciation expense	254,000	254,000
Other expenses	545,000	545,000
Profit for the year	**$148,300**	**$148,300**
Allocation to:		
• Parent		149,200
• NCI		(900)

OUTLINE OF THE PRESENTATION

Part 3b

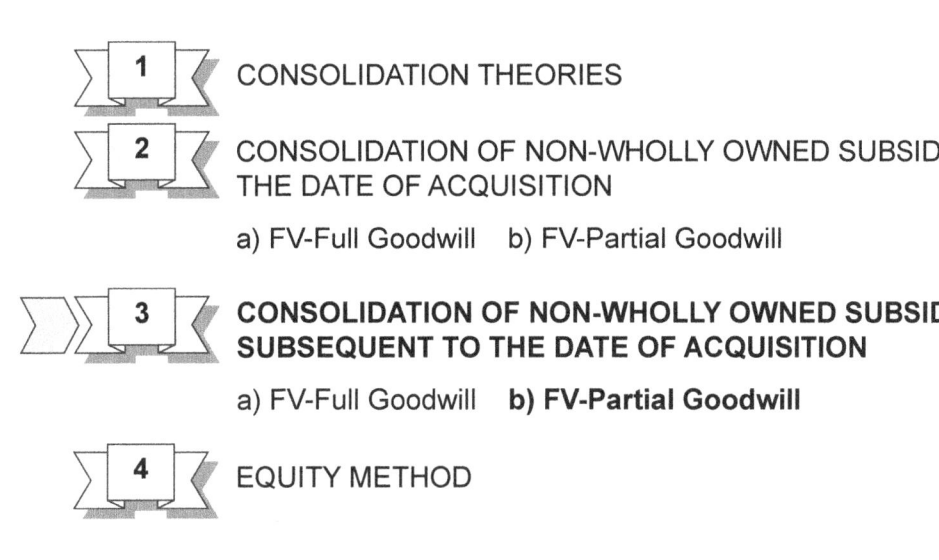

1. CONSOLIDATION THEORIES
2. CONSOLIDATION OF NON-WHOLLY OWNED SUBSIDIARIES AT THE DATE OF ACQUISITION
   a) FV-Full Goodwill   b) FV-Partial Goodwill
3. **CONSOLIDATION OF NON-WHOLLY OWNED SUBSIDIARIES SUBSEQUENT TO THE DATE OF ACQUISITION**
   a) FV-Full Goodwill   **b) FV-Partial Goodwill**
4. EQUITY METHOD

Part 3b

PART 3 b
Consolidation of Non-Wholly Owned Subsidiaries Subsequent to the Date of Acquisition
Fair Value - Partial Goodwill Approach

Objectives of this section

Illustrate techniques and procedures involved in establishing non-controlling interest (NCI) in consolidated financial statements in periods subsequent to acquisition when NCI is measured at fair value under the **Partial Goodwill Approach** (IFRS).

Discuss the general approach to consolidation involving non-wholly owned subsidiaries using both the worksheet approach and the direct approach. Illustrate the process when the parent has used the cost method to account for its investment.

BASIC INFORMATION
Price Differential - Partial Goodwill

Part 3b

Goodwill Impairment

Impairment test for X5 revealed that Goodwill should be $72,000.

**Goodwill Impairment
X5**
($90,000 - $72,000)
=
$18,000

BASIC INFORMATION
Price Differential Amortization Schedule

Part 3b

Items	Price Differential Balance at Acquisition	Amortization Prior Years (X2-X4)	Amortization Current Year (X5)	Unamortized Excess at Dec. 31, X5
Land *(Full FVI)*	$100,000	($100,000)	-	-
Buildings *(Full FVI)*	200,000	(60,000)	($20,000)	$120,000
Partial Goodwill	$90,000	-	($18,000)	$72,000
Total	**$390,000**	**($160,000)**	**($38,000)**	**$192,000**

Assigned to Parent only

Part 3b

CONSOLIDATION ENTRIES
Elimination of the Investment Account

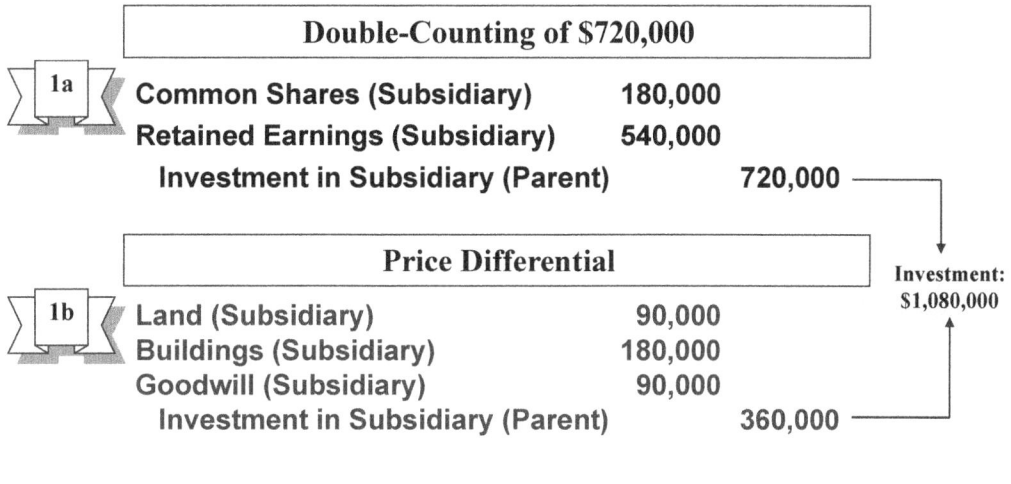

Double-Counting of $720,000

1a) Common Shares (Subsidiary)   180,000
    Retained Earnings (Subsidiary) 540,000
        Investment in Subsidiary (Parent)   720,000

Price Differential

1b) Land (Subsidiary)   90,000
    Buildings (Subsidiary) 180,000
    Goodwill (Subsidiary)   90,000
        Investment in Subsidiary (Parent)   360,000

Investment: $1,080,000

Non-Wholly Owned Subsidiaries ---------- Module 7 ---------- 85

Part 3b

WORKSHEET APPROACH
Price Differential
Full Fair Value Increment on Buildings

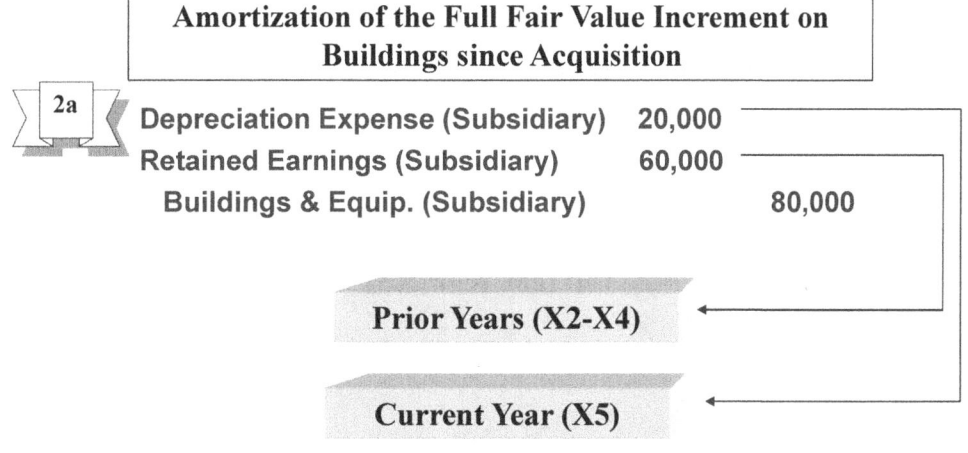

Amortization of the Full Fair Value Increment on Buildings since Acquisition

2a) Depreciation Expense (Subsidiary)   20,000
    Retained Earnings (Subsidiary)   60,000
        Buildings & Equip. (Subsidiary)   80,000

Prior Years (X2-X4)

Current Year (X5)

Non-Wholly Owned Subsidiaries ---------- Module 7 ---------- 86

Part 3b

WORKSHEET APPROACH
Price Differential
Full Fair Value Increment on Land

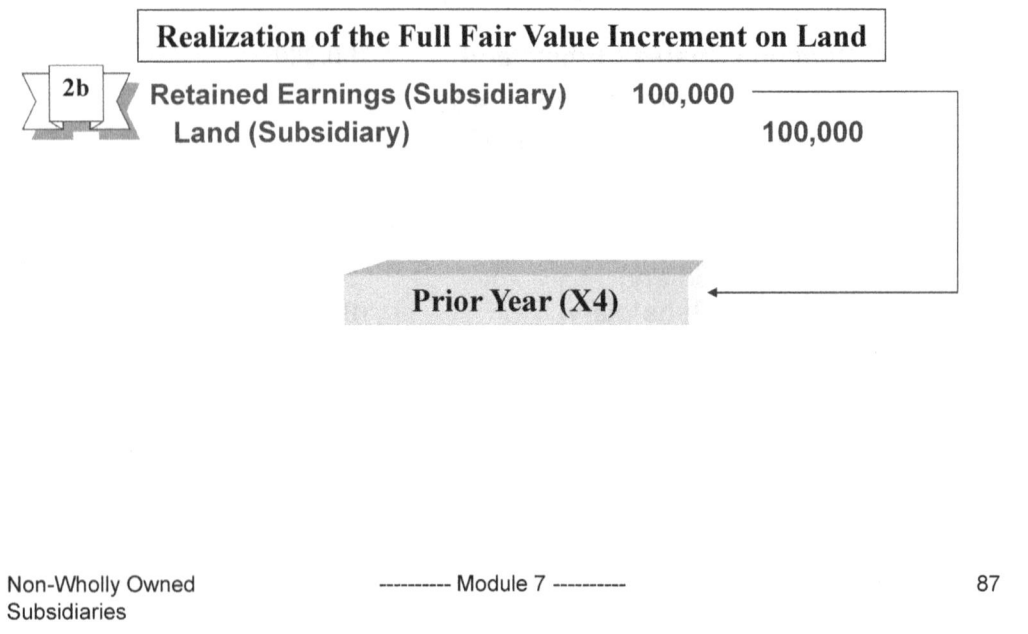

Realization of the Full Fair Value Increment on Land

| 2b | Retained Earnings (Subsidiary) | 100,000 | |
| | Land (Subsidiary) | | 100,000 |

Prior Year (X4)

Part 3b

WORKSHEET APPROACH
Price Differential
Partial Goodwill

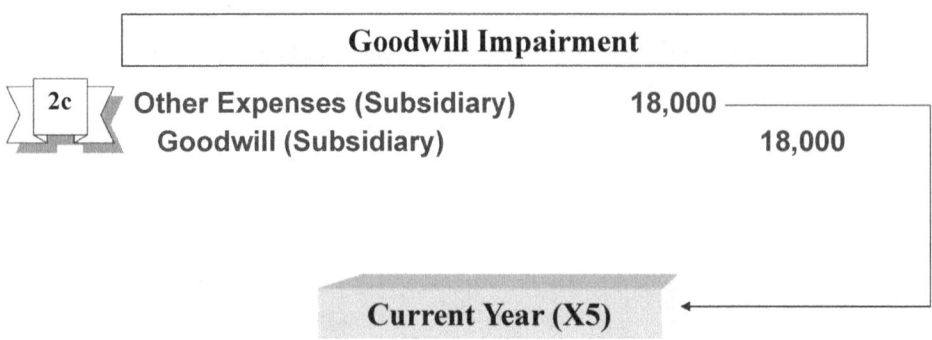

Goodwill Impairment

| 2c | Other Expenses (Subsidiary) | 18,000 | |
| | Goodwill (Subsidiary) | | 18,000 |

Current Year (X5)

Part 3b

WORKSHEET APPROACH
Non-Controlling Interest at Acquisition

FV of identifiable net assets Allocated to NCI (10%)		

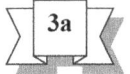

Common Shares (Subsidiary)	20,000	
Retained Earnings (Subsidiary)	60,000	
Land (Subsidiary)	10,000	
Buildings (Subsidiary)	20,000	
Non-Controlling Interest		110,000

Part 3b

WORKSHEET APPROACH
Allocation of Net Adjusted Value of Subsidiary since Acquisition to Non-Controlling Interest

Complete this slide

Net Adjusted Value of Subsidiary Since Acquisition

- Retained earnings increase since acquisition
  ($1,100,000 − $600,000) $500,000
- **FV increments amortized since acquisition**   (180,000)
  (Goodwill impairment not included)
- Unrealized portion of the gain on upstream sale
  of equipment ($10,000 × 8/10)   (8,000)
  Total   **$312,000**

Adjustment of NCI

10%

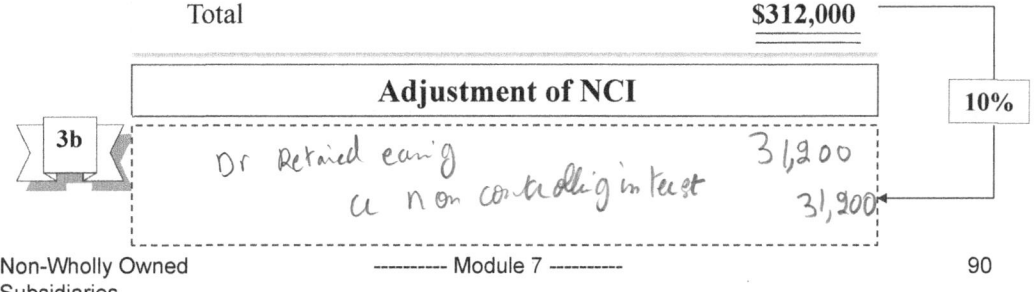

Dr Retained earning 31,200
   Cr Non controlling interest 31,200

Part 3b
WORKSHEET APPROACH
Adjustments Related to Intercompany Transactions

Consolidation Entries Relating to Intercompany Transactions
(same as under the Full Goodwill Approach).

4 Current-Year Downstream Sale of Inventory

5 Realization of Prior-Year Profit on Downstream Sale of Inventory

6a Upstream Sale of Equipment in X4:
Unrealized Portion of the Gain at the Beginning of X5

6b Upstream Sale of Equipment in X4:
Excess Depreciation of the Current Period

7 Intercompany Dividends

Part 3b
CONSOLIDATION WORKSHEET OF PARENT COMPANY
For the Year Ended December 31, X5

	Parent	Subsidiary	Conso. Entries	Consolidated
Assets				
Land	$1,250,000	-	(1b) 90,000 (2b) (100,000); (3a) 10,000	$1,250,000
Buildings & equipment (net)	3,400,000	$210,000	(1b) 180,000 (2a) (80,000); (3a) 20,000 (6a) (9,000); (6b) 1,000	3,722,000
Goodwill			(1b) 90,000 (2c) (18,000)	72,000
Investment in Subsidiary	1,080,000		(1a) (720,000); (1b) (360,000)	-
Inventories	500,000	230,000	(4) (4,500)	725,500
Accounts receivable	1,800,000	780,000		2,580,000
Cash	590,000	170,000		760,000
Total assets	**$8,620,000**	**$1,390,000**		**$9,109,500**
Equity and liabilities				
Share capital	$3,680,000	$200,000	(1a) (180,000); (3a) (20,000)	$3,680,000
Retained earnings	3,600,000	1,100,000	(841,700)	3,858,300
Non-controlling interest			(3a) 110,000; (3b) 31,200	141,200
Long-term notes payable	1,000,000	-		1,000,000
Accounts payable	340,000	90,000		430,000
Total equity and liabilities	**$8,620,000**	**$1,390,000**		**$9,109,500**

Part 3b
CONSOLIDATION WORKSHEET OF PARENT COMPANY (continued…)
For the Year Ended December 31, X5

	Parent	Subsidiary	Conso. Entries	Consolidated
Sales revenue	$3,100,000	$570,000	(4) (60,000)	$3,610,000
Dividend income	18,000		(7) (18,000)	-
Cost of sales	2,300,000	420,000	(4) (55,500); (5) (1,800)	2,662,700
Depreciation expense	200,000	35,000	(2a) 20,000; (6b)(1,000)	254,000
Other expenses	440,000	85,000	(2c) 18,000	543,000
Profit for the year	**$178,000**	**$30,000**	**(57,700)**	**$150,300**
Retained earnings (beginning)	$3,522,000	$1,090,000	(1a) (540,000) (2a) (60,000) (2b) (100,000) (3a) (60,000) (3b) (31,200) (5) (1,800) (6a) (9,000); (7) (2,000)	$3,808,000
Dividends declared	(100,000)	(20,000)	(7) 20,000	(100,000)
Retained earnings (end)	**$3,600,000**	**$1,100,000**	**(841,700)**	**$3,858,300**

Net impact of the consolidation adjustments on the ending balance of Retained Earnings. To be transferred into the statement of financial position.

Part 3b
DIRECT APPROACH
Non-Current Assets

Buildings & Equipment (net)

Parent	$3,400,000
Subsidiary	210,000
Unamortized portion of the:	
• Fair value increment on Buildings ($200,000 × 6/10)	120,000
• Upstream gain on sale of Equip. ($10,000 × 8/10)	(8,000)
Total	$3,722,000

Goodwill

At acquisition	$90,000
Portion impaired	(18,000)
Total	$72,000

Land

Parent	$1,250,000

Part 3b

DIRECT APPROACH
Current Assets

Cash

Parent	$590,000
Subsidiary	170,000
Total	$760,000

Accounts Receivable

Parent	$1,800,000
Subsidiary	780,000
Total	$2,580,000

Inventories

Parent	$500,000
Subsidiary	230,000
Unrealized profit on downstream sale	(4,500)
Total	$725,500

Part 3b

DIRECT APPROACH
Retained Earnings

- Parent — $3,600,000
- Unrealized profit on <u>downstream</u> sale of inventory — (4,500)
- Parent's share of Subsidiary's net adjusted value since
- acquisition ($312,000 × 90%) — 280,800   ← 90%
- **Goodwill impairment since acquisition** — **(18,000)**
- Total — $3,858,300

Net Adjusted Value of Subsidiary Since Acquisition

- Retained earnings increase since acquisition:
  ($1,100,000 - $600,000) — $500,000
- **FV increments amortized since acquisition** — **(180,000)**
  (Goodwill impairment not included)
- Unrealized portion of the gain on <u>upstream</u> sale of equipment
  ($10,000 × 8/10) — (8,000)
- Total — $312,000

Part 3b

DIRECT APPROACH
Non-Controlling Interest

- Minority's share of FV of Subsidiary's identifiable net assets at acquisition ($1,100,000 × 10%)   **$110,000**
- Minority's share of Subsidiary's net adjusted value since acquisition ($312,000 × 10%)   31,200
- Total   **$141,200**

10%

Net Adjusted Value of Subsidiary Since Acquisition

- Retained earnings increase since acquisition ($1,100,000 - $600,000) $500,000
- **FV increments amortized since acquisition (Goodwill impairment not included)**   (180,000)
- Unrealized portion of the gain on <u>upstream</u> sale of equipment ($10,000 × 8/10)   (8,000)
- Total $312,000

Part 3b

DIRECT APPROACH
Liabilities

Accounts Payable	
Parent	$340,000
Subsidiary	90,000
Total	$430,000

Long-Term Notes Payable	
Parent	$1,000,000

Part 3b

DIRECT APPROACH
Consolidated Profit

- Adjusted profit of Parent:
  - Profit of Parent for the period $178,000
  - Unrealized current-year profit on **downstream** sale of inventory   (4,500)
  - Realized profit from prior-year **downstream** sale of inventory   1,800
  - Intercompany dividends   (18,000) $157,300
- Adjusted profit of Subsidiary:
  - Profit of Subsidiary for the period $30,000
  - Current-year FV increment amortization   (20,000)
  - Realized portion of prior-year **upstream** sale of equipment ($10,000/10)   1,000
  - Total before Goodwill impairment   11,000
  - **Current-year Goodwill impairment**   **(18,000)**   (7,000)
- Total $150,300

Part 3b

DIRECT APPROACH
Consolidated Profit
Allocated to Parent and NCI

Allocation to Parent

- Adjusted profit of Parent $157,300
- Parent's share of adjusted profit of Subsidiary before Goodwill impairment ($11,000 × 90%)   9,900
- **Current-year goodwill impairment**   (18,000)

Total $149,200

Allocation to Non-Controlling Shareholders

Minority's share of adjusted profit of Subsidiary before Goodwill impairment ($11,000 × 10%)   **$1,100**

Non-Wholly Owned Subsidiaries

Part 3b

CONSOLIDATED STATEMENT OF FINANCIAL POSITION - PARENT
At December 31, X5
Full Goodwill vs. Partial Goodwill (NCI at FV of Net Assets)

	Full Goodwill	Partial Goodwill
Assets		
Non-current assets		
Land	$1,250,000	$1,250,000
Buildings (net)	3,722,000	3,722,000
Goodwill	**80,000**	**72,000**
Current assets		
Inventories	725,500	725,500
Accounts receivable	2,580,000	2,580,000
Cash	760,000	760,000
Total assets	**$9,117,500**	**$9,109,500**
Equity and liabilities		
Equity		
Share capital	$3,680,000	$3,680,000
Retained earnings	3,858,300	3,858,300
Non-controlling Interest	**149,200**	**141,200**
Liabilities		
Long-term notes payable	1,000,000	1,000,000
Accounts payable	430,000	430,000
Total equity and liabilities	**$9,117,500**	**$9,109,500**

Part 3b

CONSOLIDATED INCOME STATEMENT OF PARENT
For the Year Ended December 31, X5
Full Goodwill vs. Partial Goodwill (NCI at FV of Net Assets)

	Full Goodwill	Partial Goodwill
Sales revenue	$3,610,000	$3,610,000
Cost of sales	2,662,700	2,662,700
Depreciation expense	254,000	254,000
Other expenses	545,000	543,000
Profit for the year	**$148,300**	**$150,300**
Allocation to:		
• Parent	149,200	149,200
• NCI	(900)	1,100

PART 3
Concept Check

> In the case of partial control, why is it important to distinguish downstream transactions from upstream transactions?

_____
_____
_____
_____
_____
_____
_____

Part 4

OUTLINE OF THE PRESENTATION

1 CONSOLIDATION THEORIES

2 CONSOLIDATION OF NON-WHOLLY OWNED SUBSIDIARIES AT THE DATE OF ACQUISITION

   a) FV-Full Goodwill   b) FV-Partial Goodwill   c) BV

3 CONSOLIDATION OF NON-WHOLLY OWNED SUBSIDIARIES SUBSEQUENT TO THE DATE OF ACQUISITION

   a) FV-Full Goodwill   b) FV-Partial Goodwill   c) BV

4 EQUITY METHOD

PART 4
Equity Method

Objectives of this section

Discuss the equity-basis reporting when Parent Company uses the equity method in its separate-entity financial statements.

Illustrate the approach to compute the investment in Subsidiary in non-consolidated financial statements under the equity method.

Present the financial reporting implications of using either the cost method, the equity method or full consolidation.

Present the additional consolidation entries required to eliminate the investment account when the equity method is employed by Parent Company in non-consolidated financial statements.

EQUITY METHOD
Equity in Earnings for X5 Based on the Full Goodwill Alternative

- Parent's share of Subsidiary's adjusted net loss
  - Profit for the period $30,000
  - Current-year price differential amortization   (40,000)
  - Realized portion of prior-year <u>upstream</u> sale of equipment ($10,000/10)   1,000

  (9,000) × 90%   (8,100)

- Unrealized current-year profit on <u>downstream</u> sale of inventory (**100%**)   (4,500)
- Realized profit from prior-year <u>downstream</u> sale of inventory (**100%**)   1,800

  Total $(10,800)

Part 4

EQUITY METHOD
Equity in Earnings for X5 Based on the Partial Goodwill Alternative

- Parent's share of Subsidiary's adjusted net loss
  - Profit for the period $30,000
  - Current-year FVI amortization (20,000)
  - Realized portion of prior-year upstream sale of equipment ($10,000/10)   1,000
                                   11,000 × **90%** $9,900
- Current-year goodwill impairment   (18,000)
- Unrealized current-year profit on downstream sale of inventory (**100%**)   (4,500)
- Realized profit from prior-year downstream sale of inventory (**100%**)   1,800

  Total $(10,800)

Part 4

EQUITY METHOD
Journal Entries on the Books of Parent for X5

1 PROPORTIONATE SHARE OF LOSSES

Equity in Earnings of Subsidiary	10,800	
Investment in Subsidiary		10,800

2 PROPORTIONATE SHARE OF DIVIDENDS

Cash	18,000	
Investment in Subsidiary		18,000

EQUITY METHOD
Balance of the Investment Account
As of December 31, X5

INITIAL INVESTMENT (X1)	$1,080,000	Cost Method
90% OF SUBSIDIARY'S NET ADJUSTED VALUE SINCE ACQUISITION ($292,000 × 90%)	262,800	↕
UNREALIZED PROFIT FROM DOWNSTREAM SALE OF INVENTORY	(4,500)	
INVESTMENT AT THE END (X5)	$1,338,300	Equity Method

90% — **Subsidiary's net adjusted value since acquisition**
- Retained earnings increase since acquisition ($1,100,000 - $600,000) — $500,000
- Price differential amortization since acquisition — (200,000)
- Unrealized portion of the gain on <u>upstream</u> sale of equipment ($10,000 × 8/10) — (8,000)
- Total — **$292,000**

Non-Wholly Owned Subsidiaries

STATEMENT OF FINANCIAL POSITION - PARENT COMPANY
At December 31, X5
Equity Basis vs. Consolidation (Entity)

	Equity Basis	Consolidated FV – Full goodwill
Assets		
Non-current assets		
Land	$1,250,000	$1,250,000
Buildings & equipment (net)	3,400,000	3,722,000
Goodwill		80,000
Investment in Subsidiary	1,338,300	-
Current assets		
Inventories	500,000	725,500
Accounts receivable	1,800,000	2,580,000
Cash	590,000	760,000
Total assets	**$8,878,300**	**$9,117,500**
Equity and liabilities		
Equity		
Share capital	$3,680,000	$3,680,000
Retained earnings	3,858,300	3,858,300
Non-controlling interest		149,200
Liabilities		
Long-term notes payable	1,000,000	1,000,000
Accounts payable	340,000	430,000
Total equity and liabilities	**$8,878,300**	**$9,117,500**

INCOME STATEMENT OF PARENT COMPANY
Year Ended December 31, X5
Equity Basis vs. Consolidation (Entity)

	Equity Basis	Consolidated FV – Full goodwill
Sales revenue	$3,100,000	$3,610,000
Equity in earnings	(10,800)	
Cost of sales	2,300,000	2,662,700
Depreciation expense	200,000	254,000
Other expenses	440,000	545,000
Profit for the year	**$149,200**	**$148,300**
• Allocated to Parent	149,200	149,200
• Allocated to minority shareholders	-	(900)

STATEMENT OF CHANGES IN EQUITY - PARENT COMPANY
Year Ended December 31, X5
Equity Basis vs. Consolidation (Entity)

	Equity Basis			Consolidated FV – Full goodwill			
	Share Capital	Retained Earnings	Total	Share Capital	Retained Earnings	NCI	Total
Balance at Dec. 31, X4	$3,680,000	$3,809,100	$7,489,100	$3,680,000	$3,809,100	$150,100	$7,639,200
Profit for the year		$149,200	$149,200		$149,200	(900)	$148,300
Dividends		(100,000)	(100,000)		(100,000)		(100,000)
Balance at Dec. X5	$3,680,000	$3,858,300	$7,538,300	$3,680,000	$3,858,300	$149,200	$7,687,500

EQUITY METHOD
Breakdown of the Investment Account

Part 4

1	INITIAL INVESTMENT (X1)	$1,080,000	Cost Method
2	90% OF SUBSIDIARY'S NET ADJUSTED VALUE FROM ACQUISITION TO THE BEGINNING OF THE CURRENT PERIOD (X2 TO X4, INCLUSIVE)	287,100	
3	90% OF SUBSIDIARY'S ADJUSTED EARNINGS IN X5	(10,800)	
4	90% OF SUBSIDIARY'S DECLARED DIVIDENDS IN X5	(18,000)	
	INVESTMENT AT THE END (X5)	$1,338,300	Equity Method

Non-Wholly Owned Subsidiaries ---------- Module 7 ---------- 113

EQUITY METHOD
Consolidation Entries Required to Eliminate the Investment Account

Part 4

1 See consolidation adjustments 1a and 1b under cost basis.

2
Retained Earnings   287,100
    Investment in Subsidiary   287,100

3
Investment in Subsidiary   10,800
    Equity in Earnings   10,800

4
Investment in Subsidiary   18,000
Retained Earnings   2,000
    Dividends Declared   20,000

Additional Consolidation Entries

Non-Wholly Owned Subsidiaries ---------- Module 7 ---------- 114

PARTIAL CONTROL
Additional Considerations

Part 4

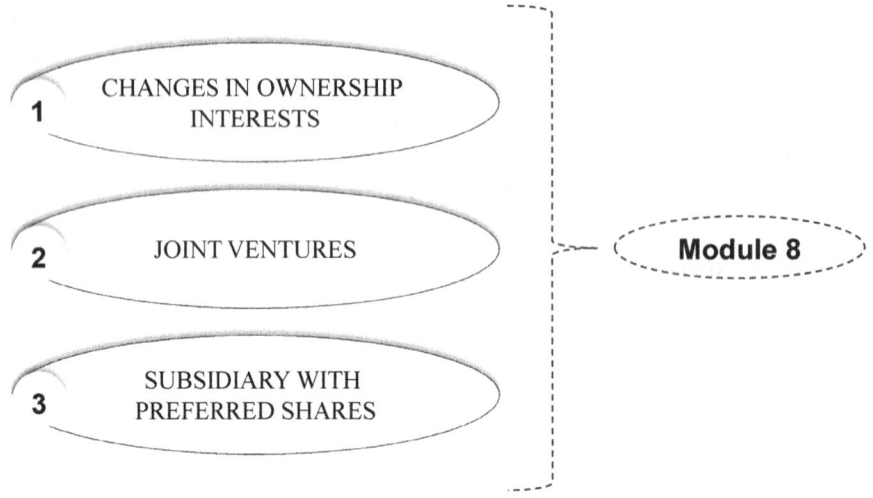

PART 4
Concept Check

Part 4

> In the context of partial control, explain how consolidation and equity method are closely related.

CONSOLIDATION OF NON-WHOLLY OWNED SUBSIDIARIES
Module 7 - Recap

5 REVIEW QUESTIONS

6 QUIZ QUESTIONS

7 KEY TERMS INTRODUCED IN THIS MODULE

8 RECAP ON THE OBJECTIVES OF THIS MODULE

Part 5

PART 5
Review Questions

1 Define or explain the following terms:

- Non-wholly owned subsidiary
- Non-controlling interest
- Entity theory
- Parent company approach
- Proportionate consolidation
- Implied purchase price
- Implied price differential
- Full goodwill,
- Full fair value increment and decrement
- Allocation of consolidated net income to majority and minority interests

2 In what general ways will consolidation of a non-wholly owned subsidiary differ from consolidation of a wholly owned subsidiary?

3 How can the inclusion of the full market value of the subsidiary on the consolidated statement of financial position be justified when the parent company owns less than 100% of the subsidiary's voting shares?

Non-Wholly Owned Subsidiaries ---------- Module 7 ---------- 118

Part 5

REVIEW QUESTIONS
(continued...)

4. What advantages are there to a parent company in owning less than 100% of the shares of their subsidiaries?

5. Describe how the total non-controlling interest at the end of an accounting period is determined.

6. How is the amount of net income assigned to non-controlling interest determined?

7. Is the amount of intercompany profit to be eliminated from consolidated financial statements affected by the existence of a minority interest? Explain.

8. Under what circumstances is non-controlling interest affected by intercompany transactions?

9. What is the view of the economic unit consolidation concept with regard to recognition of the non-controlling interest?

Non-Wholly Owned Subsidiaries ---------- Module 7 ---------- 119

Part 6

PART 6
Quiz Questions

On December X8, Large Inc. acquired **80%** of the outstanding voting shares of Small Inc. for **$200,000**. At the date of acquisition, Small had Common Shares and Retained Earnings of $100,000 and $50,000, respectively. Small's plant assets have a market value $60,000 greater than book value and an estimated remaining economic life of six years (straight line).

In post-acquisition periods, Small had the following earnings and paid the following dividends:

Year	Comprehensive income	Dividends
X9	$30,000	$8,000
X10	25,000	10,000
X11	50,000	20,000

Large's equity section at the end of year X11 consists of Common Shares of $800,000 and Retained Earnings of $350,000. Large's comprehensive income and dividends declared for X11 amount to $150,000 and $50,000, respectively.

Non-Wholly Owned Subsidiaries ---------- Module 7 ---------- 120

PART 6
Quiz Questions (continued...)

Goodwill has not been impaired since acquisition.

Small sold land to Large in X10 for $100,000. The land originally cost Small $90,000. The land is kept by Large since then.

In X11, Large had sales of $40,000 to Small. Large's X11 gross margin was 50%; $10,000 (sales price) of the transferred units are in Small's inventory on December 31, X11.

Handwritten notes:
$10,000 \times 0.5 = 5,000$

Downstream unrealized gain (5,000)

$100,000 - 90,000 =$ unrealized gain on upstream sale $10,000$

QUIZ QUESTIONS
1

Present the allocation of price differential under the Full Goodwill Approach.

	Implied (100%)	Large (80%)	NCI (20%)
Purchase price	$\frac{200,000}{0.8} = 250,000$	200,000	50,000
Net book value of Subsidiary:			
- Common shares $100,000		(150K × 0.8)	
- Retained earnings 50,000	150,000	120,000	30,000
Price differential	100,000	80,000	20,000
Fair value increment:			
- Buildings (60,000)	(60,000)	(48,000)	(12,000)
Goodwill	40,000	32,000	8,000

Part 6

QUIZ QUESTIONS

2

Assume that Large is using the <u>equity method</u> to report its investment in Small. Determine the balance of the investment account on the books of Large at the end of X11.

INITIAL INVESTMENT (X8)	$200,000
SUBSIDIARY'S NET ADJUSTED VALUE SINCE ACQUISITION 80% × 27,000	21,600
UNREALIZED PROFIT ON SALE OF INVENTORY (100%)	(5,000)
INVESTMENT AT THE END (X11)	216,600

80%

subsidiary net adjusted value since acquisition:
RE increase: 67,000
price differential Amortization: (30,000)
unrealized portion of the gain on upstream sale of ppe (10,000)
Total   27,000

60,000 ÷ 6 = 10,000

PPE 60,000   X9-X10   X11
      (20,000) (10,000) 30,000
      Total (30,000)

Part 6

QUIZ QUESTIONS

3

Assume that Large is using the <u>cost method</u> to report its investment in Small. If the total comprehensive income reported by Large for X11 is $150,000, what amount would be reported had Large been using the equity method instead?

◇ Comprehensive income for X11 under the cost method $150,000

◇ Share of small dividend for X11
   Share earnings   50,000
   current year price differential (10,000) × 0.8 =   32,000

◇ unrealized profit on downstream sale of inventory   (5,000)

◇ Share of small dividend for X11   (16,000)

Comprehensive income for X11 under the equity method   153,000

Non-Wholly Owned Subsidiaries ---------- Module 7 ----------

Part 6

QUIZ QUESTIONS

4

Assume that Large is using the cost method to report its investment in Small. Determine the amount that will be reported as *Retained Earnings* in Large's consolidated statement of financial position at the end of X11 under the Full Goodwill Approach.

◊ Balance of Large RE at end of X11   350,000
◊ unrealized profit on downstream sale of inv toy   (5,000)
◊ Share of small net adjusted value   21,600 ←

consolidated RE of large at the end of X11   366,600

Small NAV since acquisition:
RE increase   67,000
price differential amortization   (30,000)
prior year unrealized gain on sale ppd   (10,000)
                                    27,000 × 0.8

Part 6

QUIZ QUESTIONS

5

Determine the amount that will be reported as *Non-Controlling Interest* in Large's consolidated statement of financial position at the end of X11 under the Full Goodwill Approach.

Minority Shares implied purchase price   50,000
minority share of subsidiary NAV   5,400
Total   14/554,400

subsidiary net adjusted value since acq'n
Same as Q-B

Part 6

QUIZ QUESTIONS
6

Determine the amount that will be reported as *Non-Controlling Interest* in Large's consolidated statement of financial position at the end of X11 under the Partial Goodwill Approach (NCI at FV of Net Assets).

Minority Share of FV of subsidiary identifiable Net Assets: 210,000
Minority Share of subsidiary net adjusted value: 5,400
Total: 215,400

Net adjusted value since acquisition: 67,000
FV increments amortized since acquisition: (30,000)
unrealized portion of gain on upstream sale of land: (10,000)
27,000
× 0.2 = 5,400

Part 6

QUIZ QUESTIONS
7

Assume that Large is using the <u>equity method</u> to report its investment in Small. List the consolidation entries required to eliminate this account for the consolidation of Large for X11.

1

2 Dr RE   20,800
   Cr Investment in Small   20,800

3

4 Dr Dividend income   16,000
   Dr RE dividend declared   4,000
      Cr   20,000

Part 6

QUIZ QUESTIONS

8

List the consolidation entries required for X11 to account for non-controlling interest under the Full Goodwill Approach

---

Implied Purchase Price Allocated to NCI (20%)

Dr Common Share   20,000
Dr RE   10,000
Dr PPE   12,000
Dr goodwill   8,000
   Cr Non controlling interest   50,000

Share of Small's Net Adjusted Value

Dr RE   21,600
   Cr non controlling interest   21,60

Part 7

KEY TERMS INTRODUCED IN THIS MODULE

• Non-wholly owned subsidiary • Non-controlling interest • Entity theory; Full / Partial goodwill approach • Parent company approach • Proportionate consolidation	**Part 1**

• Implied purchase price • Implied price differential • Full goodwill • Full fair value increment and decrement	**Part 2a**

Allocation of consolidated profit to majority and minority interests	**Part 3a**

Part 8

RECAP ON THE OBJECTIVES OF THIS MODULE

Part 1 Introduce the conceptual alternatives for consolidating non-wholly owned subsidiaries and explain their differences.

Part 2 Illustrate techniques and procedures involved in establishing non-controlling interest in consolidated financial statements at the date of acquisition

- **2a** • when NCI is measured at fair value under the Full Goodwill Approach.

- **2b** • when NCI is measured at fair value under the Partial Goodwill Approach (IFRS).

Part 8

RECAP ON THE OBJECTIVES OF THIS MODULE

Part 3 Illustrate techniques and procedures involved in establishing non-controlling interest in consolidated financial statements in periods subsequent to acquisition

- **3a** • when NCI is measured at fair value under the Full Goodwill Approach.

- **3b** • when NCI is measured at fair value under the Partial Goodwill Approach (IFRS).

Discuss the general approach to consolidation involving non-wholly owned subsidiaries using both the worksheet approach and the direct approach. Illustrate the process when the parent has used the cost method to account for its investment.

Part 8

RECAP ON THE OBJECTIVES OF THIS MODULE

Part 4 Discuss the equity-basis reporting when Parent Company uses the equity method in its separate-entity financial statements: the case of non-wholly owned subsidiaries.

Illustrate the approach to compute the investment in Subsidiary in non-consolidated financial statements under the equity method.

Present the financial reporting implications of using either the cost method, the equity method or full consolidation.

Present the additional consolidation entries required to eliminate the investment account when the equity method is employed by Parent Company in non-consolidated financial statements.

Appendix
Consolidation of Non-Wholly Owned Subsidiaries under the BV Approach

This publication is protected by copyright, and permission should be obtained from the publisher prior to any prohibited reproduction, storage in a retrieval system, or transmission in any form or by any means, electronic, mechanical, photocopying, recording, or otherwise.

Copyright © 2020 Parmitech

Appendix

Appendix
Consolidation of Non-Wholly Owned Subsidiaries at the Date of Acquisition
NCI at Book Value

Objective of this section

Illustrate techniques and procedures involved in establishing non-controlling interest in consolidated financial statements at the date of acquisition when NCI is measured at book value, that is, as the NCI's proportionate share of the **carrying value of the acquiree's identifiable assets.**

Appendix

PURCHASE PRICE ALLOCATION
NCI at BV

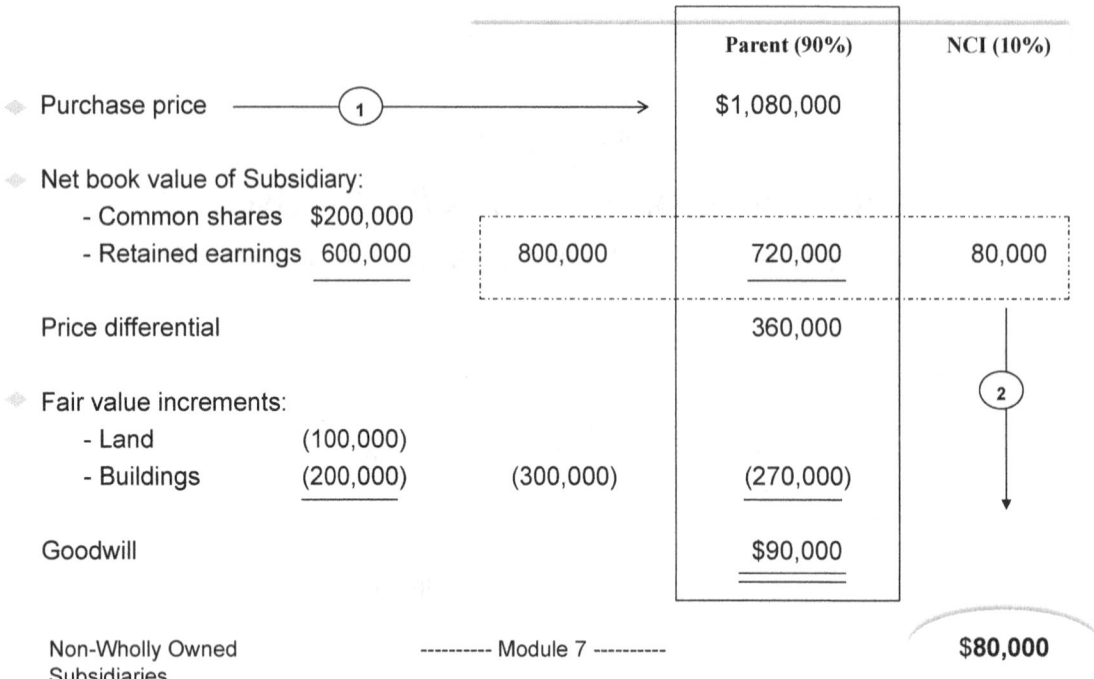

			Parent (90%)	NCI (10%)
Purchase price	①		$1,080,000	
Net book value of Subsidiary:				
- Common shares	$200,000			
- Retained earnings	600,000	800,000	720,000	80,000
Price differential			360,000	
Fair value increments:				
- Land	(100,000)			
- Buildings	(200,000)	(300,000)	(270,000)	
Goodwill			$90,000	

NCI: $80,000

Non-Wholly Owned Subsidiaries — Module 7 —

Appendix

CONSOLIDATION ENTRIES
Elimination of the Investment Account

Double-Counting of $720,000

1a
Common Shares (Subsidiary)	180,000	
Retained Earnings (Subsidiary)	540,000	
Investment in Subsidiary (Parent)		720,000

Price Differential

1b
Land (Subsidiary)	90,000	
Buildings (Subsidiary)	180,000	
Goodwill (Subsidiary)	90,000	
Investment in Subsidiary (Parent)		360,000

Investment: $1,080,000

Non-Wholly Owned Subsidiaries — Module 7 —

CONSOLIDATION ENTRIES
Non-Controlling Interest

Net Book Value Allocated to NCI (10%)

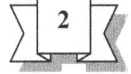

Common Shares (Subsidiary)	20,000	
Retained Earnings (Subsidiary)	60,000	
Non-Controlling Interest		80,000

Non-Wholly Owned Subsidiaries

CONSOLIDATION WORKSHEET OF PARENT COMPANY
At the Date of Acquisition

	Parent	Subsidiary	Eliminations	Consolidated
Assets				
Land	$1,000,000	$300,000	(1b) 90,000	$1,390,000
Buildings (net)	1,800,000	350,000	(1b) 180,000	2,330,000
Goodwill			(1b) 90,000	90,000
Investment in Subsidiary	1,080,000		(1a) (720,000) (1b) (360,000)	
Inventories	200,000	50,000		250,000
Accounts receivable	2,000,000	150,000		2,150,000
Cash	1,000,000	50,000		1,050,000
Total assets	**$7,080,000**	**$900,000**		**$7,260,000**
Equity and liabilities				
Share capital	$3,680,000	$200,000	(1a) (180,000) (2) (20,000)	$3,680,000
Retained earnings	2,000,000	600,000	(1a) (540,000) (2) (60,000)	2,000,000
Non-Controlling Interest			(2) 80,000	80,000
Liabilities				
Long-term notes payable	400,000			400,000
Accounts payable	1,000,000	100,000		1,100,000
Total equity and liabilities	**$7,080,000**	**$900,000**		**$7,260,000**

Non-Wholly Owned Subsidiaries

Appendix

CONSOLIDATED STATEMENT OF FINANCIAL POSITION - PARENT
AT THE DATE OF ACQUISITION
FV - Full Goodwill vs. Book Value

	Fair value (Full Goodwill)	Book Value
Assets		
Non-current assets		
Land	$1,400,000	$1,390,000
Buildings (net)	2,350,000	2,330,000
Goodwill	100,000	90,000
Current assets		
Inventories	250,000	250,000
Accounts receivable	2,150,000	2,150,000
Cash	1,050,000	1,050,000
Total assets	$7,300,000	$7,260,000
Equity and liabilities		
Equity		
Share capital	$3,680,000	$3,680,000
Retained earnings	2,000,000	2,000,000
Non-controlling interest	120,000	80,000
Liabilities		
Long-term notes payable	400,000	400,000
Accounts payable	1,100,000	1,100,000
Total equity and liabilities	$7,300,000	$7,260,000

$40,000

Appendix

Consolidation of Non-Wholly Owned Subsidiaries
Subsequent to the Date of Acquisition
NCI at Book Value

Objectives of this section

Illustrate techniques and procedures involved in establishing non-controlling interest in consolidated financial statements in periods subsequent to acquisition when NCI is measured as the NCI's proportionate share of the **carrying value of the acquiree's identifiable assets**.

Discuss the general approach to consolidation involving non-wholly owned subsidiaries using both the worksheet approach and the direct approach. Illustrate the process when the parent has used the cost method to account for its investment.

Appendix

BASIC INFORMATION
Price Differential Amortization Schedule

Items	Price Differential Balance at Acquisition	Amortization Prior Years (X2-X4)	Amortization Current Year (X5)	Unamortized Excess at December 31, X5
Land (90% of full FVI)	$90,000	($90,000)	-	-
Buildings (90% of full FVI)	180,000	(54,000)	($18,000)	$108,000
Partial Goodwill	90,000	-	(18,000)	72,000
Total	**$360,000**	**($144,000)**	**($36,000)**	**$180,000**

Assigned to Parent only

Appendix

WORKSHEET APPROACH
Elimination of the Investment Account

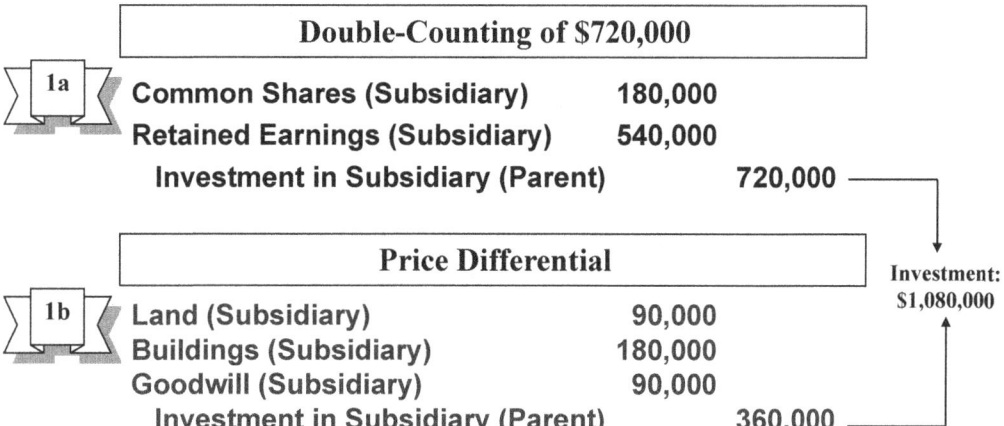

Double-Counting of $720,000

1a
- Common Shares (Subsidiary)   180,000
- Retained Earnings (Subsidiary)   540,000
-   Investment in Subsidiary (Parent)   720,000

Price Differential

1b
- Land (Subsidiary)   90,000
- Buildings (Subsidiary)   180,000
- Goodwill (Subsidiary)   90,000
-   Investment in Subsidiary (Parent)   360,000

Investment: $1,080,000

WORKSHEET APPROACH
Price Differential
Fair Value Increment on Buildings

Amortization of the Fair Value Increment on Buildings since Acquisition

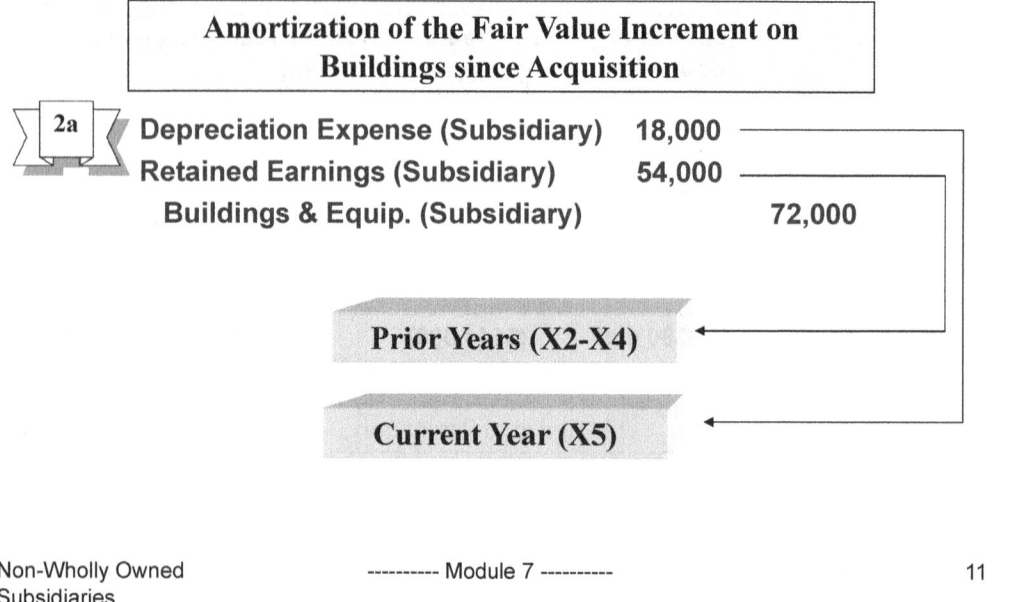

2a	Depreciation Expense (Subsidiary)	18,000	
	Retained Earnings (Subsidiary)	54,000	
	Buildings & Equip. (Subsidiary)		72,000

Prior Years (X2-X4)

Current Year (X5)

WORKSHEET APPROACH
Price Differential
Fair Value Increment on Land

Realization of the Fair Value Increment on Land

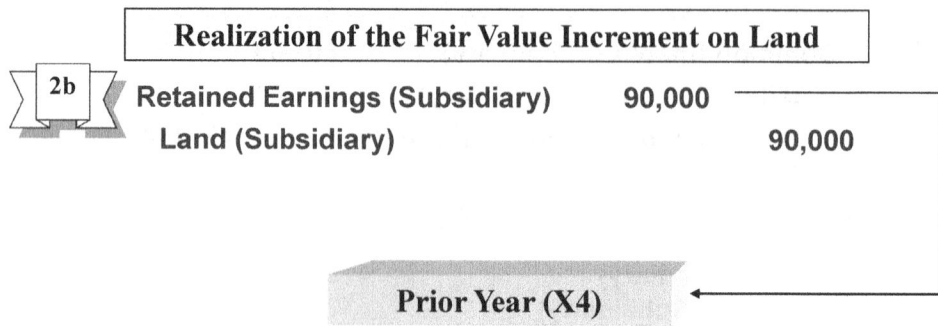

| 2b | Retained Earnings (Subsidiary) | 90,000 | |
| | Land (Subsidiary) | | 90,000 |

Prior Year (X4)

Appendix

WORKSHEET APPROACH
Price Differential
Partial Goodwill

Goodwill Impairment		
2c Other Expenses (Subsidiary)	18,000	
Goodwill (Subsidiary)		18,000

Current Year (X5)

Non-Wholly Owned Subsidiaries ---------- Module 7 ---------- 13

Appendix

WORKSHEET APPROACH
Non-Controlling Interest at Acquisition

Net Book Value Allocated to NCI (10%)		
3a Common Shares (Subsidiary)	20,000	
Retained Earnings (Subsidiary)	60,000	
Non-Controlling Interest		80,000

Non-Wholly Owned Subsidiaries ---------- Module 7 ---------- 14

Appendix

WORKSHEET APPROACH
Allocation of Net Adjusted Value of Subsidiary since Acquisition to Non-Controlling Interest

Net Adjusted Value of Subsidiary Since Acquisition

> Price differential amortization NOT included

- Retained earnings increase since acquisition
  ($1,100,000 - $600,000) $500,000
- Unrealized portion of the gain on <u>upstream</u> sale
  of equipment ($10,000 × 8/10)   (8,000)
  Total $492,000

Adjustment of NCI   10%

3b Retained Earnings (Subsidiary)   49,200
     Non-Controlling Interest   49,200

Non-Wholly Owned Subsidiaries ---------- Module 7 ---------- 15

Appendix

WORKSHEET APPROACH
Adjustments Related to Intercompany Transactions

Consolidation Entries Relating to Intercompany Transactions
(same as under the Full Goodwill Approach)

4 Current-Year Downstream Sale of Inventory

5 Realization of Prior-Year Profit on Downstream Sale of Inventory

6a Upstream Sale of Equipment in X4:
Unrealized Portion of the Gain at the Beginning of X5

6b Upstream Sale of Equipment in X4:
Excess Depreciation of the Current Period

7 Intercompany Dividends

Non-Wholly Owned Subsidiaries ---------- Module 7 ---------- 16

Appendix

CONSOLIDATION WORKSHEET OF PARENT COMPANY
For the Year Ended December 31, X5

	Parent	Subsidiary	Conso. Entries	Consolidated
Assets				
Land	$1,250,000	-	(1b) 90,000 (2b) (90,000)	$1,250,000
Buildings & equipment (net)	3,400,000	$210,000	(1b) 180,000 (2a) (72,000) (6a) (9,000); (6b) 1,000	3,710,000
Goodwill			(1b) 90,000 (2c) (18,000)	72,000
Investment in Subsidiary	1,080,000		(1a) (720,000); (1b) (360,000)	-
Inventories	500,000	230,000	(4) (4,500)	725,500
Accounts receivable	1,800,000	780,000		2,580,000
Cash	590,000	170,000		760,000
Total assets	**$8,620,000**	**$1,390,000**		**$9,097,500**
Equity and liabilities				
Share capital	$3,680,000	$200,000	(1a) (180,000); (3a) (20,000)	$3,680,000
Retained earnings	3,600,000	1,100,000	(841,700)	3,858,300
Non-controlling interest			(3a) 80,000; (3b) 49,200	129,200
Long-term notes payable	1,000,000	-		1,000,000
Accounts payable	340,000	90,000		430,000
Total equity and liabilities	**$8,620,000**	**$1,390,000**		**$9,097,500**

Appendix

CONSOLIDATION WORKSHEET OF PARENT COMPANY (continued…)
For the Year Ended December 31, X5

	Parent	Subsidiary	Conso. Entries	Consolidated
Sales revenue	$3,100,000	$570,000	(4) (60,000)	$3,610,000
Dividend income	18,000		(7) (18,000)	-
Cost of sales	2,300,000	420,000	(4) (55,500); (5) (1,800)	2,662,700
Depreciation expense	200,000	35,000	(2a) 18,000; (6b)(1,000)	252,000
Other expenses	440,000	85,000	(2c) 18,000	543,000
Profit for the year	**$178,000**	**$30,000**	**(55,700)**	**$152,300**
Retained earnings (beginning)	$3,522,000	$1,090,000	(1a) (540,000) (2a) (54,000) (2b) (90,000) (3a) (60,000) (3b) (49,200) (5) (1,800) (6a) (9,000); (7) (2,000)	$3,806,000
Dividends declared	(100,000)	(20,000)	(7) 20,000	(100,000)
Retained earnings (end)	**$3,600,000**	**$1,100,000**	**(841,700)**	**$3,858,300**

Appendix

DIRECT APPROACH
Non-Current Assets

Buildings & Equipment (net)

Parent	$3,400,000
Subsidiary	210,000
Unamortized portion of the:	
• **Fair value increment on Buildings ($180,000 × 6/10)**	108,000
• Upstream gain on sale of Equip. ($10,000 × 8/10)	(8,000)
Total	$3,710,000

Goodwill

At acquisition	**$90,000**
Portion impaired	**(18,000)**
Total	**$72,000**

Land

Parent	$1,250,000

Appendix

DIRECT APPROACH
Current Assets

Cash

Parent	$590,000
Subsidiary	170,000
Total	$760,000

Accounts Receivable

Parent	$1,800,000
Subsidiary	780,000
Total	$2,580,000

Inventories

Parent	$500,000
Subsidiary	230,000
Unrealized profit on downstream sale	(4,500)
Total	$725,500

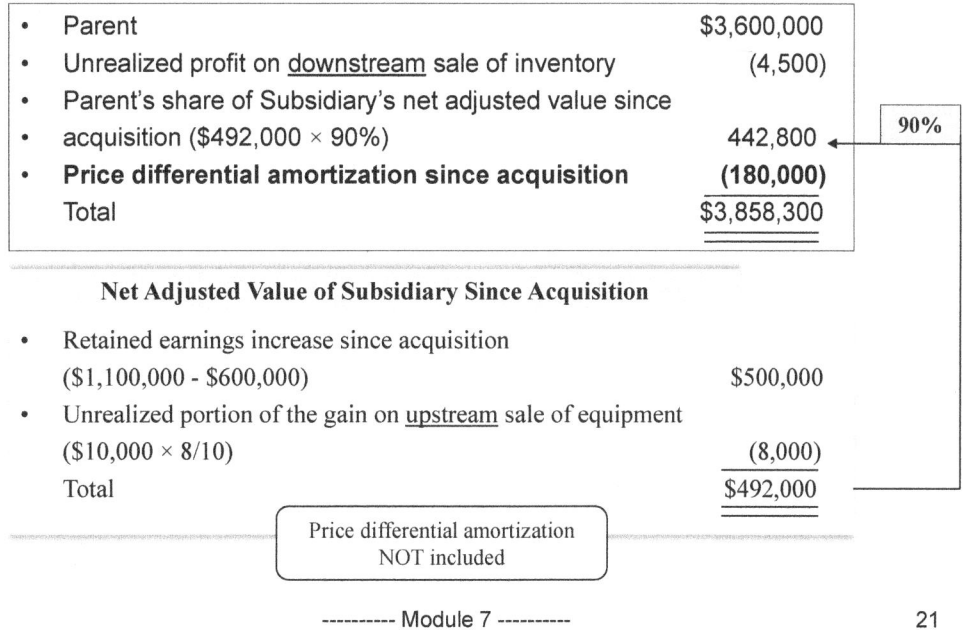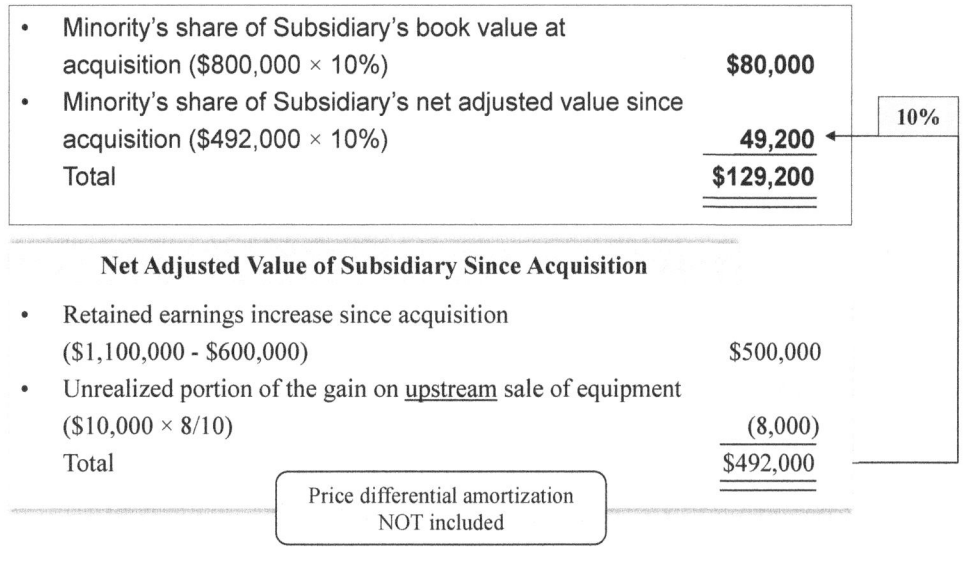

DIRECT APPROACH
Liabilities

Accounts Payable

Parent	$340,000
Subsidiary	90,000
Total	$430,000

Long-Term Notes Payable

Parent	$1,000,000

DIRECT APPROACH
Consolidated Profit

- Adjusted profit of Parent:
  - Profit of Parent for the period — $178,000
  - Unrealized current-year profit on **downstream** sale of inventory — (4,500)
  - Realized profit from prior-year **downstream** sale of inventory — 1,800
  - Intercompany dividends — (18,000) — $157,300
- Adjusted profit of Subsidiary:
  - Profit of Subsidiary for the period — $30,000
  - Realized portion of prior-year **upstream** sale of equipment ($10,000/10) — 1,000
  - Total before price differential amortization — 31,000
  - **Current-year price differential amortization** — **(36,000)** — (5,000)
  - Total — $152,300

Appendix

DIRECT APPROACH
Consolidated Profit
Allocated to Parent and NCI

Allocation to Parent

- Adjusted profit of Parent $157,300
- Parent's share of adjusted profit of Subsidiary <u>before price differential amortization</u>
  ($31,000 × 90%) 27,900
- **Current-year price differential amortization** (36,000)

  Total $149,200

Allocation to Non-Controlling Shareholders

Minority's share of adjusted profit of Subsidiary <u>before price differential amortization</u>
($31,000 × 10%) **$3,100**

Appendix

CONSOLIDATED STATEMENT OF FINANCIAL POSITION - PARENT
At December 31, X5
FV - Full Goodwill vs. Book Value

	Fair Value Full Goodwill	Book Value
Assets		
Non-current assets		
Land	$1,250,000	$1,250,000
Buildings & equipment (net)	3,722,000	3,710,000
Goodwill	80,000	72,000
Current assets		
Inventories	725,500	725,500
Accounts receivable	2,580,000	2,580,000
Cash	760,000	760,000
Total assets	**$9,117,500**	**$9,097,500**
Equity and liabilities		
Equity		
Share capital	$3,680,000	$3,680,000
Retained earnings	3,858,300	3,858,300
Non-controlling interest	149,200	129,200
Liabilities		
Long-term notes payable	1,000,000	1,000,000
Accounts payable	430,000	430,000
Total equity and liabilities	**$9,117,500**	**$9,097,500**

CONSOLIDATED INCOME STATEMENT OF PARENT
For the Year Ended December 31, X5
FV - Full Goodwill vs. Book Value

	Fair Value Full Goodwill	Book Value
Sales revenue	$3,610,000	$3,610,000
Cost of sales	2,662,700	2,662,700
Depreciation expense	254,000	252,000
Other expenses	545,000	543,000
Profit for the year	**$148,300**	**$152,300**
Allocation to:		
• Parent	149,200	149,200
• NCI	(900)	3,100

Non-Wholly Owned Subsidiaries

Copyright © 2020, Parmitech, Ottawa. Parmitech. All rights reserved.

Exercise 7-1
Partial Control: Direct Approach and Worksheet Approach

On January 1, X2, the Prime Company acquired 60 percent of the outstanding voting shares of the Sublime Company for $3 million in cash. On this date, the Sublime Company had Common Stock of $3 million and Retained Earnings of $2 million. All of Sublime's identifiable assets and liabilities had fair values that were equal to their carrying values except for the Accounts Receivable which had a total net realizable value that was $100,000 less than its stated value and a piece of equipment with a fair value that was $400,000 less than its carrying value and had a remaining useful life of 3 years.

Both Companies use the straight line method to calculate all depreciation and amortization expenses. Prime carries its investment in Sublime by the cost method.

On December 31, X3, the statements of financial position of the Prime Company and its subsidiary, the Sublime Company, are as follows:

Statements of Financial Position
At December 31, X3

	Prime	Sublime
Cash and current receivables	$ 1,600,000	$ 1,000,000
Inventories	2,400,000	1,500,000
Investment in Sublime (at Cost)	3,000,000	-
Long-term receivables	1,500,000	-
Plant and equipment (net)	14,000,000	8,500,000
Land	5,000,000	2,000,000
Total assets	**$27,500,000**	**$13,000,000**
Current liabilities	$ 4,500,000	$ 2,000,000
Long-term liabilities	5,000,000	3,000,000
Share capital	6,000,000	3,000,000
Retained earnings	12,000,000	5,000,000
Total equities	**$27,500,000**	**$13,000,000**

Additional Information

1. The Prime Company sold merchandise to the Sublime Company in X2 of which $300,000 remained in the December 31, X2 Inventories of Sublime. This merchandise was sold in X3 and Prime made no further sales of inventories to Sublime in X3. Prime's sales are priced to provide it with a 40 percent gross margin on sales price.

2. Sublime's Sales in X3 included $500,000 in sales to Prime. Of these sales, $200,000 remains in the December 31, X3 Inventories of Prime. Prime's January 1, X3 inventories contained $400,000 of merchandise purchased from Sublime. Sublime's sales are priced to provide it with a 25 percent gross margin on sales price.

3. On January 1, X3, the Prime Company sold a machine it had built for a cost of $200,000 to the Sublime Company for $150,000. The machine had an estimated useful life on January 1, X3, of 5 years.

4. The Sublime Company purchased Land for $2 million from Prime on November 1, X2. The land was originally purchased by Prime for $1 million. The purchase price is to be paid in 5 equal instalments of $400,000 on January 1 of each year subsequent to the sale.

5. During X3, Prime earned net income of $2,000,000 and paid dividends of $400,000 and Sublime earned net income of $500,000 and paid dividends of $100,000.

6. In each of the years since Prime acquired control over Sublime, the goodwill arising on this business combination transaction has been tested for impairment. No impairment was found in any of the years since acquisition.

Required

a) Provide the consolidation entries required to account for the intercompany transactions.
b) Using the direct approach, provide the calculation of the following balances as of December 31, X3, assuming that the *full goodwill approach* is used:

- Plant and Equipment (net)
- Retained Earnings
- Non-Controlling Interest (NCI)

Exercise 7-2
Valuation of NCI at Date of Acquisition

Assume that on January 1, X5, S Company has capital stock and retained earnings of $1,500,000 and $500,000, respectively, and identifiable assets and liabilities as presented below.

Identifiable Assets and Liabilities of S Company
January 1, X5

	Fair Value	Book Value
➤ Inventory	$350,000	$300,000
➤ Other current assets	450,000	450,000
➤ Equipment (net); remaining life of 10 yrs.	600,000	300,000
➤ Land	400,000	250,000
➤ Other noncurrent assets	1,000,000	1,000,000
➤ Liabilities	(300,000)	(300,000)
Identifiable net assets	**$2,500,000**	**$2,000,000**

Assume further that P Company acquires a 75% interest in S Company on January 1, X5, for $2,100,000. There is no Land on the books of P Company on January 1, X5.

Required
Complete the following table.

Consolidated value at acquisition	Proportionate Consolidation	Full Goodwill Approach	Partial Goodwill Approach	Book Value
NCI	0	700,000	625,000	500,000 (using BV)
Goodwill	225,000	300,000	225,000	225,000
Land	300,000	400,000	400,000	363,?

Note: "300,000 – goodwill" annotation near Partial Goodwill NCI.

Exercise 7-3
Consolidation Subsequent to Acquisition: NCI, Profit and Retained Earnings

Refer to Exercise 7.2.

Assume further the following:

- On December 31, X8, S Company has capital stock and retained earnings of $1,500,000 and $2,000,000, respectively.
- There were no intragroup transactions since acquisition.
- Land has been sold to an outside party by S Company prior to X8.
- Goodwill has not been impaired.
- The balance of P Company's Retained Earnings on Dec. 31, X8 amounts to $5,000,000.
- Profit for the X8 is $900,000 for P Company and $600,000 for S Company.
- P Company is using the cost method for its investments.

Required
Complete the following table.

Consolidated Value on Dec. 31, X8	Full Goodwill Approach	Partial Goodwill Approach
NCI	995,000	920,000
RE	5,885,000	5,885,000
Profit for X8	1,470,000 →	1,470,000
Allocation of profit to NCI	1,327,500 →	same
Allocation of profit to P	142,500 →	same

Exercise 7-4
Consolidation Subsequent to Acquisition with NCI: Worksheet Approach

Refer to Exercise 7.3.

The following presents all the relevant additional information regarding intragroup transactions between P Company and S Company since acquisition:

- S Company's Sales during X9 include sales of $500,000 to P Company. The December 31, X9 Inventories of the P Company contain $150,000 of this merchandise purchased from S Company during X9.
- The January 1, X9 Inventories of the P Company contained $150,000 in merchandise purchased from S Company during X8.
- All intercompany sales are priced to provide the selling company a gross margin on sales price of 25 percent.

Assume that there is no intragroup transaction in X10.

On December 31, X10, S Company has capital stock and retained earnings of $1,500,000 and $3,000,000, respectively. Goodwill has not been impaired.

Required

Provide all the consolidation entries required for the consolidation of X10.

Exercise 7-5
Consolidated F/S, NCI, Profit and Retained Earnings

On January 1, X5, the Pert Company purchases 80 percent of the outstanding shares of the Sloan Company for $3,200,000 in cash. On that date, the Sloan Company had No Par Common Stock of $2,000,000 and Retained Earnings of $1,500,000. On December 31, X9, the adjusted trial balances of the Pert Company and its subsidiary, the Sloan Company are as follows (in $000):

	Pert	Sloan
Cash	$ 500	$ 300
Current receivables	800	400
Inventories	2,500	1,700
Long-term note receivable	200	-
Investment in Sloan - At Cost	3,200	-
Land	1,500	1,000
Plant and equipment (Net)	4,500	1,900
Cost of goods sold	2,800	1,500
Amortization expense	200	100
Other expenses	364	616
Interest expense	240	84
Dividends declared	350	100
Total debits	**$17,154**	**$7,700**
Current liabilities	$ 500	$ 200
Long-term liabilities	2,000	700
No par common stock	8,000	2,000
Retained earnings (January 1)	2,550	2,300
Sales	4,000	2,500
Interest revenue	24	-
Dividend revenue	80	-
Total credits	**$17,154**	**$7,700**
January 1, X9 Retained earnings	$2,550	$2,300
X9 Net income	500	200
Dividends declared	(350)	(100)
December 31, X9 Retained earnings	**$2,700**	**$2,400**

Additional Information

1. At the date of Pert Company's acquisition of the Sloan Company's shares, all of the identifiable assets and liabilities of the Sloan Company had fair values that were equal to their carrying values except:

> Inventories which had fair values that were $100,000 more than their carrying values,
> Land with a fair value that was $150,000 less than its carrying value, and
> Plant & Equipment which had a fair value that was $250,000 greater than its carrying value.

2. The Plant and Equipment had a remaining useful life on the acquisition date of 20 years while the Inventories that were present on the acquisition date were sold during the year ending December 31, X5. The Land is still on the books of the Sloan Company on December 31, X9. Both companies use the straight line method to calculate amortization.

3. In each of the years since Pert acquired control over Sloan, the goodwill arising on this business combination transaction has been tested for impairment. No impairment was found in any of the years since acquisition.

4. Sloan Company's Sales during X9 include sales of $300,000 to Pert Company. The December 31, X9 Inventories of the Pert Company contain $100,000 of this merchandise purchased from Sloan Company during X9. In addition, the January 1, X9 Inventories of the Pert Company contained $70,000 in merchandise purchased from Sloan Company during X8. All intercompany sales are priced to provide the selling company a gross margin on sales price of 40 percent.

5. On December 31, X9, the Pert Company is holding Sloan Company's long-term note payable in the amount of $200,000. Interest at 12 percent is payable on July 1 of each year. Pert Company has been holding this note since July 1, X7.

6. During X7, the Pert Company sold Land to the Sloan Company for $100,000 in cash. The Land had a carrying value on the books of the Pert Company of $75,000.

7. During X8, the Sloan Company sold Land to the Pert Company for $150,000. This Land had a carrying value on the books of the Sloan Company of $110,000.

8. On December 31, X7, the Sloan Company sold Equipment to the Pert Company for $600,000. The Equipment had originally cost the Sloan Company $800,000 and, at the time of the intercompany sale, had accumulated amortization of $350,000. On this date, it was estimated that the remaining useful life of the Equipment was three years with no net salvage value.

Required

a) Prepare the *consolidated financial statements* of Pert Company as at December 31, X9, under the Entity approach (Full Goodwill).
b) Present the consolidated financial statements along with the direct computation of Retained Earnings, NCI and Profit for the year.

Exercise 7-6
Partial Control: Consolidation and Equity Method

On December 31, X1, the Big Ltd. purchased 80% of the outstanding common shares of the Small Ltd. for $7.6 million in cash. On that date, the shareholders' equity of Small totalled $8 million and consisted of $1 million in Common Stock and $7 million in retained earnings. Both companies use the straight-line method to calculate amortization.

For the year ending December 31, X6, the income statements for Big and Small were as follows:

	Big	Small
Sales	$21,000,000	$9,100,000
Other revenue	1,500,000	700,000
Total sales and other revenue	22,500,000	9,800,000
Cost of goods sold	16,000,000	5,000,000
Amortization expense	2,500,000	2,000,000
Other expenses	1,800,000	1,200,000
Profit for the year	**$2,200,000**	**$1,600,000**

As at December 31, X6, the condensed balance sheets for the two companies were as follows:

	Big	Small
Building	$17,000,000	$1,500,000
Accumulated depreciation	(9,500,000)	(825,000)
Investment in Small	7,600,000	- 0 -
Other assets	15,900,000	12,825,000
Total assets	$31,000,000	$13,500,000
Liabilities	$5,000,000	$1,200,000
Common stock	12,100,000	1,000,000
Retained earnings	13,900,000	11,300,000
Total liabilities and equity	**$31,000,000**	**$13,500,000**

Additional information

1. Fair market values of Small were equal to their book values at the date of acquisition.

2. During X5, Small sold merchandise to Big for $200,000, a price that includes a gross profit of 30% based on sales price. During X5, 60% of this merchandise was resold by Big and the other 40% remains in its December 31, 05 inventories.

3. On December 31, X5, the inventories of Small contained merchandise purchased from Big on which Big had recognized a gross profit in the amount of $20,000.

4. During X6, Big sold merchandise to Small for $100,000, a price that includes a gross profit of 40% based on sales price. During X6, 30% of this merchandise was resold by Small and the other 70% remains in its December 31, X6 inventories.

5. On December 31, X6, the inventories of Big contained merchandise purchased from Small on which Small had recognized a gross profit in the amount of $30,000. Total sales to Big from Small were $50,000 for the year.

6. During X6, Big declared and paid dividends of $300,000 while Small declared and paid dividends of $100,000.

7. In each of the years since Big acquired control over Small, the goodwill arising on this business combination transaction has been tested for impairment. After completing the annual impairment tests, it was determined that the goodwill impairment loss for X4 was $60,000 and for X6 it was $80,000. No impairment was found in any of the other years since acquisition.

8. The retained earnings of Big as at December 31, X5, were $12,000,000. On that date, Small had retained earnings of $9,800,000. Small has not issued any common stock since its acquisition by Big.

Required:

a) Present the consolidated financial statements of Big Ltd. as at December 31, X6, under the full goodwill alternative.
b) On a comparative basis, present the financial statements of Big Ltd. with the *Investment in Small* accounted for under the *equity method*.

Exercise 7-7
Partial Control: Worksheet/Direct Approach and Equity Method (Year 5)

Paper Corp. purchased 70% of the outstanding shares of Sand Ltd. on January 01, X2, at a cost of $84,000. Paper has always used the cost method to account for its strategic investments.

On January 01, Year 2, Sand had common shares of $50,000 and retained earnings of $30,000, and fair values were equal to carrying values for all its net assets except inventory (fair value was $9,000 less than book value) and equipment (fair value was $24,000 greater than book value). The equipment had an estimated remaining life of 6 years on January 01, X2.

The following are the financial statements of Paper Corp. and its subsidiary Sand Ltd. as at December 31, X5:

Statements of Financial Position
At December 31, X5

	Paper	Sand
Cash	$ -	$10,000
Accounts receivable	36,000	30,000
Note receivable	-	40,000
Inventory	66,000	44,000
Equipment (net)	220,000	76,000
Investment in Sand	84,000	--
Land	150,000	30,000
Total assets	**$556,000**	**$230,000**
Bank indebtedness	90,000	-
Accounts payable	50,000	60,000
Notes payable	40,000	-
Share capital	150,000	50,000
Retained Earnings	226,000	120,000
Total liabilities and equity	**$556,000**	**$230,000**

Change in RE for X5

	Paper	Sand
Retained earnings, January 01, Year 5	$106,000	$ 92,000
Net income	120,000	48,000
	226,000	140,000
Dividends	-	20,000
Retained earnings, December 31, Year 5	**$226,000**	**$120,000**

Income Statements
For the Year Ended December 31, X5

	Paper	Sand
Sales	$798,000	$300,000
Management fee revenue	24,000	-
Other income	14,000	3,600
Gain on sale of land	-	20,000
	836,000	323,600
Cost of sales	480,000	200,000
Amortization	40,000	12,000
Interest expense	10,000	-
Miscellaneous expenses	186,000	63,600
	716,000	275,600
Profit for the year	**$120,000**	**$48,000**

Additional information

1. During X5, Sand made a cash payment of $2,000 per month to Paper for management fees, which is included in Sand's "Miscellaneous expenses".

2. During X5, Paper made intra-group sales of $100,000 to Sand. The December 31, X5 inventory of Sand contained goods purchased from Paper amounting to $30,000. These sales had a gross profit of 35%.

3. On April 01, X5, Paper acquired land from Sand for $40,000. This land has been recorded on Sand's books at a net book value of $20,000. Paper paid for the land by signing a $40,000 notes payable to Sand, bearing yearly interest at 8%. Interest for X5 was paid by Paper in cash on December 31, X5. This land was still being held by Paper on December 31, X5.

4. The fair value of goodwill remained unchanged from January 01, X2, to July, X5. On July 01, X5, a valuation was performed, indicating that the FV of goodwill was $3,500. Non-controlling interest (30%) is valued based on the fair value of Sand's net assets at acquisition (Partial Goodwill).

Required:

a) Present all the consolidation entries required for X5.
b) Present the consolidated F/S of Paper as at December 31, X5.
c) On a comparative basis, present the individual F/S of Paper with the *Investment in Sand* accounted for under the *equity method*.
d) Using a direct approach, compute the consolidated RE and the profit for X5.

Exercise 7-8
Partial Control: Worksheet/Direct Approach and Equity Method (Year 6)

Continuation of Exercise 7.7 in Year 6.

The following presents the change in RE of Paper and Sand for the year ended December 31, X6.

Change in RE for X6

	Paper	Sand
Retained earnings, January 01, X6	$226,000	$120,000
Net income	250,000	75,000
	476,000	195,000
Dividends (paid cash)	50,000	10,000
Retained earnings, December 31, X6	$426,000	$185,000

Additional information

1. During X6, Sand made a cash payment of $2,000 per month to Paper for management fees, which is included in Sand's "Miscellaneous expenses".

2. During X6, Paper made intra-group sales of $200,000 to Sand. The December 31, X6 inventory of Sand contained goods purchased from Paper amounting to $50,000. These sales had a gross profit of 35%.

3. Land acquired by Paper from Sand on April 01, X5, has been sold to an outside party on March 31, X6. On the same date, the notes payable to Sand, including interest, has been paid in cash.

4. Goodwill has not been impaired in X6.

Required:

a) Present all the consolidation entries required for X6.
b) Compute the balance of the *Investment in Sand* under the *equity method.*
c) Using a direct approach, compute the consolidated RE, the profit for X6 and the NCI

Exercise 7-9
Partial Control: Worksheet/Direct Approach and Equity Method (Year 7)

Continuation of Exercise 7.8 in Year 7.

The following presents the change in RE of Paper and Sand for the year ended December 31, X7.

Change in RE for X7

	Paper	Sand
Retained earnings, January 01, X7	$426,000	$185,000
Net income	175,000	115,000
	601,000	300,000
Dividends (paid cash)	25,000	8,000
Retained earnings, December 31, X7	$576,000	$292,000

Additional information

1. During X7, Sand made a cash payment of $1,500 per month to Paper for management fees, which is included in Sand's "Miscellaneous expenses".

2. During X7, Paper made intra-group sales of $100,000 to Sand. The December 31, X7 inventory of Sand contained goods purchased from Paper amounting to $10,000. These sales had a gross profit of 35%.

3. During X7, Sand made intra-group sales of $80,000 to Paper. The December 31, X7 inventory of Paper contained goods purchased from Sand amounting to $1,000. These sales had a gross profit of 25%.

4. During X7, Sand purchased land from an outside party for $50,000 for its own use.

5. On January 01, X7, Sand sold equipment that on that date had an original cost of $200,000 and carrying value of $100,000 to Paper for $200,000. The equipment also had a future useful life of 10 years on January 01, X7.

6. Goodwill has not been impaired in X7.

Required:

a) Present all the consolidation entries for X7.
b) Compute the balance of the *Investment in Sand* under the *equity method*.
c) Using a direct approach, compute the consolidated RE, the profit for X7 and the NCI

Exercise 7-10
Partial Control: Direct Approach and Equity Method

Continuation of Exercise 7.1 in Year 4.

The following presents the change in retained earnings (RE) of Prime and Sublime for the year ended December 31, X4.

Change in RE for X4

	Prime	Sublime
Retained earnings, January 01, X4	$12,000,000	$ 5,000,000
Net income	3,225,000	975,000
	15,225,000	5,975,000
Dividends	50,000	-
Retained earnings, December 31, X4	$15,175,000	$5,975,000

Assume that there are no intercompany transactions and no goodwill impairment in X4.

Required:

a) Compute the balance of the *Investment in Sublime* under the *equity method*.
b) Using a direct approach, compute the following:

- Consolidated Retained Earnings of Prime at the end of X4,
- Consolidated Profit for X4 with the allocation to Prime and NCI,
- NCI at the end of X4.

Solutions to Exercises

7-1

a) Consolidation entries

1. Downstream sale of land (including liability outstanding)

Retained Earnings (RE)	1,000,000	
Land		1,000,000
Accounts Payable	1,600,000	
Accounts Receivable		1,600,000

2. Downstream sale of equipment

Machine	50,000	
Loss on Sale		50,000
Depreciation Expense	10,000	
Machine		10,000

3. Upstream sales of merchandise

RE	100,000	
Cost of Goods Sold (COGS)		100,000
Sales	500,000	
COGS		450,000
Inventory		50,000

4. Downstream sales of merchandise

RE	120,000	
COGS		120,000

5. Intercompany dividends

Dividend Income	60,000	
RE	40,000	
Dividends Declared		100,000

b) Direct approach

1. Plant and Equipment

• Prime	$14,000,000
• Sublime	8,500,000
• Unamortized portion of FVD	(133,333)
• Unamortized portion of downstream loss on sale of machine	40,000
Total	**$22,406,667**

2. Retained Earnings

◆ Prime		$12,000,000
◆ Unrealized gain – downstream sale of land		(1,000,000)
◆ Unrealized loss – downstream sale of machine		40,000
◆ 60% of Sublime's net adjusted value:		
- Increase of RE	3,000,000	
- Price differential amortization	366,666	
- Unrealized gain – upstream sale	(50,000)	
	3,316,666 × 60%	1,990,000
Total		**$13,030,000**

3. Non-Controlling Interest

◆ Implied purchase price		$2,000,000
◆ 40% of Sublime's net adjusted value:		
- Increase of RE	3,000,000	
- Price differential amortization	366,666	
- Unrealized gain – upstream sale	(50,000)	
	3,316,666 × 40%	1,326,666
Total		**$3,326,666**

3,000,000 ÷ 0.6 = 3,000,000 –

7-2

Allocation of the implied value

	100%	P 75%	S 25%
Implied purchase price	$2,800,000	$2,100,000	$700,000
Net book value of S			
◆ Common shares	1,500,000	1,125,000	375,000
◆ RE	500,000	375,000	125,000
Total	2,000,000	1,500,000	500,000
Price differential	800,000	600,000	200,000
FVIs			
◆ Inventory	(50,000)	(37,500)	(12,500)
◆ Equipment (net)	(300,000)	(225,000)	(75,000)
◆ Land	(150,000)	(112,500)	(37,500)
Total	(500,000)	(375,000)	(125,000)
Goodwill	**$300,000**	**$225,000**	**$75,000**

	Consolidation Approaches			
Consolidated value at date of acquisition	Proportionate Consolidation	Full Goodwill Approach	Partial Goodwill Approach	Book Value
NCI	nil	$700,000	$625,000	$500,000
Goodwill	$225,000	$300,000	$225,000	$225,000
Land	$300,000	$400,000	$400,000	$362,500

7-3

Purchase discrepancy amortization schedule – Partial goodwill

Items	Balance acquisition	Amortization X5 – X7	Amortization X8	Remaining at Dec. 31/ X8
Inventory	$50,000	$(50,000)	-	-
Equipment	300,000	(90,000)	$(30,000)	$180,000
Land	150,000	(150,000)	-	-
Goodwill	225,000	-	-	225,000
Total	**$725,000**	**$(290,000)**	**$(30,000)**	**$405,000**

Consolidated Values on Dec. 31, X8	Full Goodwill Approach (or Entity Theory)	Partial Goodwill Approach
NCI	$995,000	$920,000
RE	$5,885,000	$5,885,000
Profit for X8	$1,470,000	$1,470,000
Allocation of profit to NCI	$142,500	$142,500
Allocation of profit to P	$1,327,500	$1,327,500

Net Adjusted Value (NAV) of S:
- Increase of RE ($2,000,000 – $500,000) $1,500,000
- Price differential amortization – X5-X8   (320,000)
  Total   **$1,180,000**

NCI – Full Goodwill:
- At acquisition $700,000
- Share of NAV of S (25%)   295,000
  Total   **$995,000**

NCI – Partial Goodwill:
- At acquisition $625,000
- Share of NAV of S (25%)   295,000
  Total   **$920,000**

Consolidated RE:
- RE of S $5,000,000
- NAV of S ($1,180,000 x 75%)   885,000
  Total   **$5,885,000**

Consolidated Profit for X8:

Profit of P $900,000
Adjusted profit of S:
- Current profit $600,000
- Price differential - X8   (30,000)   570,000
  Total   **$1,470,000**

➢ **Allocation to P :**
   - Profit of P $900,000
   - Adjusted profit of S ($570,000 x 75%)   427,500
     Total   **$1,327,500**

➢ **Allocation to NCI :**
   Adjusted profit of S ($570,000 x 25%)   **$142,500**

7-4

a) Elimination of the investment and price differential amortization/realization

Investment

1a)	Common Shares	1,125,000	
	RE	375,000	
	Investment in S		1,500,000
1b)	Inventory	37,500	
	Equipment	225,000	
	Land	112,500	
	Goodwill	225,000	
	Investment in S		600,000

Price differential

	RE	50,000	
	Inventory		50,000
	RE	150,000	
	Depreciation – Equipment	30,000	
	Equipment		80,000
	RE	150,000	
	Land		150,000

b) NCI (Partial Goodwill Approach)

Common Shares	375,000	
RE	125,000	
Inventory	12,500	
Equipment	75,000	
Land	37,500	
NCI		625,000
RE	530,000	
NCI		530,000

- Share of net fair value of subsidiary at date of acquisition
  ($1,500,000 + $500,000 + $500,000) x 25% $625,000
- Share of net adjusted value of subsidiary since acquisition
  ($2,120,000 x 25%)   530,000
  Total   **$1,155,000**

Net adjusted value of subsidiary since acquisition:
- RE since acquisition ($3,000,000 – $500,000) $2,500,000
- Cumulative amortization of price differential   (380 000)
  Total   **$2,120,000**

c) Intragroup Transactions

    RE   37,500

        COGS   37,500

7-5

a) Consolidated F/S

Pert Company
Consolidated Statement of Financial Position
At December 31, X9
Full Goodwill

Cash	$ 800,000
Accounts receivables	1,188,000
Inventories	4,160,000
Plant and equipment (net)	6,537,500
Land	2,285,000
Goodwill	300,000
Total assets	**$ 15,270,500**
Current liabilities	688,000
Long-term liabilities	2,500,000
Non-controlling interest	921,500
Common stock	8,000,000
Retained earnings	3,161,000
Total liabilities and equity	**$ 15,270,500**

Pert Company
Consolidated Income Statement
For the Year Ended December 31, X9
Full Goodwill

Sales	$ 6,200,000
Cost of sales	4,012,000
	2,188,000
Interest expense	300,000
Amortization expense	262,500
Expenses (misc.)	980,000
Net income	**$ 645,500**
Allocation to:	
➤ Pert	600,400
➤ Non-controlling interest	45,100
	$ 645,500

b) Direct approach

Retained Earnings

Pert Company		$2,700,000
Unrealized gain from downstream sale of Land		(25,000)
80% of Sloan's net adjusted value since acquisition:		
◆ Retained earnings increase	$900,000	
◆ Implied cumulative PD amortization	(162,500)	
◆ Unrealized profit on upstream sale of Land	(40,000)	
◆ Unrealized profit on upstream sale of inventory	(40,000) (40,000)	
◆ Unrealized gain on upstream sale of Equip.	(50,000)	
	$607,500	
	×80%	486,000
Total		**$3,161,000**

Non-controlling Interest

◆ 20% of implied purchase price	$800,000	
◆ 20% of Sloan's net adjusted value since acquisition	121,500	
Total	**$921,500**	

Consolidated Net Income

Pert's adjusted net income:

◆ Pert net income	$500,000	
◆ Intercompany dividends	(80,000)	$420,000

Sloan's adjusted net income:

◆ Net income of subsidiary for the period	200,000	
◆ Current-year implied PD amortization	(12,500)	← where is it coming from
◆ Unrealized profit on current-year upstream sale of Inventory	(40,000)	
◆ Realized portion of prior-year upstream sales: - Equipment	50,000	?
- Inventory	28,000	225,500
Total		**$645,500**

> **Allocation to Most**

Pert's adjusted net income	420,000
80% of Sloan's adjusted net income	180,400
Total	**$600,400**

> **Allocation to Sloan**

20% of Sloan's adjusted net income	**$45,100**

7-6
Consolidated F/S - X6

Big Ldt
Consolidated Statement of Financial Position
At December 31, X6

	Full Goodwill	*Equity method*
Assets		
Buildings (net)	$8,175,000	$7,500,000
Investment in Small		10,876,000
Other assets	28,667,000	15,900,000
Goodwill	1,360,000	-
Total assets	**$38,202,000**	**$34,276,000**
Liabilities and equity		
Liabilities	$6,200,000	$5,000,000
Common stock	12,100,000	12,100,000
Retained earnings	17,176,000	17,176,000
NCI	2,726,000	-
Total liabilities and equiy	**$38,202,000**	**$34,276,000**

Big Ltd
Consolidated Income Statement
For the year ending December 31, X6

Sales	$29,950,000	$21,000,000
Equity in earnings		1,203,200
Other revenue	2,120,000	1,420,000
	32,070,000	23,623,200
Cost of goods sold	20,864,000	16,000,000
Amortization expense	4,500,000	2,500,000
Other expenses	**3,080,000**	1,800,000
	28,444,000	20,300,000
Net income	**$3,626,000**	**$3,323,200**

Allocation to:
- Parent — $3,323,200
- Minority shareholders — 302,800
- **$3,626,000**

Consolidation entries
(Optional)

ADJUSTMENTS RELATED TO CONTROLLING OWNERSHIP

1. Elimination of the Investment Account in the Subsidiary
1a To eliminate reciprocal investment and equity accounts at date of acquisition

Common Shares	800,000	
Retained Earnings	5,600,000	
Investment in Small		6,400,000

1b To allocate the implied price differential (Big's proportionate share)

Goodwill	1,200,000	
Investment in Small		1,200,000

2. Implied Price Differential Amortization Since Acquisition

Retained Earnings	60,000	
Other Expenses	80,000	
Goodwill		140,000

3. Non-Controlling Interest
3a To allocate the implied purchase price to non-controlling interest

Common Shares	200,000	
Retained Earnings	1,400,000	
Goodwill	300,000	
Non-Controlling Interest		1,900,000

3b To allocate the subsidiary's net adjusted value since acquisition to non-controlling interest

Retained Earnings	826,000	
Non-Controlling Interest		826,000

ADJUSTMENTS RELATED TO INTERCOMPANY TRANSACTIONS

4. Intercompany Dividends

Other Income	80,000	
Retained Earnings	20,000	
Dividends Declared		100,000

5. Downstream Transactions
5a Current-Year Downstream Sale of Inventory

Sales	100,000	
Cost of Goods Sold		72,000
Inventory		28,000

5b Realization of Prior-Year Profit on Downstream Sale of Inventory

Retained Earnings	20,000	
Cost of Goods Sold		20,000

6. Upstream Transactions

6a Current-Year Upstream Transaction

Sales	50,000	
Cost of Goods Sold		20,000
Inventory		30,000

6b Realization of Prior-Year Profit on Upstream Sale of Inventory

Retained Earnings	24,000	
Cost of Goods Sold		24,000

Equity in Earnings for X6

Net income of Small	$1,600,000
Current-period price differential amortization: Goodwill impairment	(80,000)
Realized portion of prior-year upstream sale of inventory	24,000
Unrealized current-year gain from upstream sale of inventory	(30,000)
Adjusted net income of Small	$1,514,000
	80%
	1,211,200
Unrealized current-year gain (loss) from **downstream** transactions	(28,000)
Prior-year deferred gain (loss) from **downstream** transactions being realized in the current period	20,000
	$1,203,200

Balance of the investment account at Dec. 31 X6

Initial Investment (X3)	$7,600,000
80% of Small's net adjusted value since acquisition	3,304,000
Unrealized profit from downstream sale of inventory (100%)	(28,000)
Investment at the end (X6)	**$10,876,000**

Note: To report the F/S of Big under the equity method, the catch is to remove from *Other revenue* the dividends income of X6, that is, $80,000. Therefore, *Other revenue* should be shown at $1,420,000.

7-7

Allocation of the purchase price

			Paper	NCI
		100%	70%	30%
Cost of investment in Sand Ltd.		$120,000	$84,000	
NBV of Sand Ltd.				
Share capital	$50,000			
Retained earnings	30,000	80,000	56,000	$24,000
Price differential			28,000	
FV Increments and decrements				
Inventory	9,000		6,300	(2,700)
Equipment	(24,000)	(15,000)	(16,800)	7,200
Goodwill			**$17,500**	

Follow-up - Price differential

Items	Balance at Acquisition	Current Year X5	Years X2-X4	Balance at 31-12-X5
Inventory	$(9,000)	$-	$9,000	$-
Equipment	24,000	(4,000)	(12,000)	8,000
Goodwill	17,500	(14,000)	-	3,500
Total	**$32,500**	**$(18,000)**	**$(3,000)**	**$11,500**

Consolidation Entries for X5

<u>Elimination of the investment</u>

Common Shares	35,000	
Retained Earnings	21,000	
Investment in Sand		56,000
Equipment	16,800	
Goodwill	17,500	
Inventory		6,300
Investment in Sand		28,000

Price differential amortization since acquisition

Inventory	9,000	
Retained Earnings		9,000
Retained Earnings	12,000	
Amortization	4,000	
Equipment		16,000
Goodwill Impairment	14,000	
Goodwill		14,000

Non-controlling interest

Common Shares	15,000	
Retained Earnings	9,000	
Equipment	7,200	
Inventory		2,700
Non-Controlling Interest		28,500
Retained Earnings	18,900	
Non-Controlling Interest		18,900

Sand's net adjusted value since acquisition

Sand's RE since acquisition ($120,000-$30,000)	$90,000
Total price differential amortization excluding Goodwill	(7,000)
Upstream unrealized gain on sale of land	(20,000)
Total	**$63,000**

NCI: ($63,000 × 30%) = **$18,900** ⬅────────────┘

Intercompany dividends

Other Income	14,000	
Retained Earnings	6,000	
Dividends Declared		20,000

Management fees

Management Fee Revenue	24,000	
Miscellaneous Expenses		24,000

Current-year unrealized profit on downstream sale of inventory

Revenues	100,000	
COGS		89,500
Inventory		10,500

Current-year unrealized gain on upstream sale of Land

Gain on Sale of Land	20,000	
Land		20,000
Note Payable	40,000	
Note Receivable		40,000
Other Income	2,400	
Interest Expense		2,400

Consolidated F/S - X5

Paper Corp.
Statement of Financial Position
At December 31, X5

Assets

Cash		$10,000
Accounts receivable	($36,000 + $30,000)	66,000
Inventory	($66,000 + $44,000 - $10,500)	99,500
Equipment	($220,000 + $76,000 + $8,000)	304,000
Land	($150,000 + $30,000 - $20,000)	160,000
Goodwill	($17,500 - $14,000)	3,500
Total Assets		**$643,000**

Liabilities and equity

Bank indebtedness		$90,000
Accounts payable	($50,000 + $60,000)	110,000
Share capital		150,000
Retained earnings	($226,000 + $120,000 - $100,400)	245,600
Non-controlling interest	($28,500 + $18,900)	47,400
Total liabilities and equity		**$643,000**

Paper Corp.
Consolidated Income Statement
For the Year Ended December 31, X5

Sales	$998,000
Other income ($3,600 - $2,400)	1,200
	$999,200
Cost of sales	$590,500
Amortization	56,000
Interest expense	7,600
Miscellaneous expense	225,600
Goodwill impairment	14,000
	$893,700
Profit for the year	**$105,500**
Allocation to	
➢ Paper	$98,300
➢ Minority shareholders	7,200
	$105,500

Equity method vs. consolidated F/S

Paper Corp.
Statement of Financial Position
For the Year Ended December 31, X5

	Equity method	Consolidated
Assets		
Cash	$ -	$10,000
Accounts receivable	36,000	66,000
Note receivable	-	-
Inventory	66,000	99,500
Equipment	220,000	304,000
Land	150,000	160,000
Goodwill	-	3,500
Investment in Sand	103,600	-
Total Assets	**$575,600**	**$643,000**

Liabilities and equity

Bank indebtedness	$90,000	$90,000
Accounts payable	50,000	110,000
Note payable	40,000	-
Share capital	150,000	150,000
Retained earnings	**245,600**	**245,600**
Non-controlling interest	-	47,400
Total liabilities and equity	**$575,600**	**$643,000**

Balance of the Investment in Sand at Dec. 31 X5

Purchase Price	$84,000
Paper's share of Sand's net adjusted value since acquisition ($63,000 × 70%)	44,100
Unrealized portion of gain from downstream sale of inventory	(10,500)
Goodwill Impairment	(14,000)
Investment at Dec. 31,X5	**$103,600**

Paper Corp.
Income Statement
For the Year Ended December 31, X5

	Equity method	*Consolidated*
Sales	$798,000	$998,000
Management fee revenue	24,000	-
Other income	-	1,200
Equity in earnings	(7,700)	-
	$814,300	$999,200
Cost of sales	$(480,000)	$(590,500)
Amortization	(40,000)	(56,000)
Interest expense	(10,000)	(7,600)
Miscellaneous expenses	(186,000)	(225,600)
Goodwill impairment	-	(14,000)
	$(716,000)	$(893,700)
Profit for the year	**$98,300**	**$105,500**
Allocation to:		
➢ Paper		$98,300
➢ Non-controlling interest		7,200
		$105,500

Equity in earnings of Paper for X5

Paper's share of Sand's net adjusted profit ($24000 × 70%)	$16,800
Unrealized portion of gain from downstream sale of inventory	(10,500)
Goodwill Impairment	(14,000)
	$(7,700)

Retained earnings at Dec. 31 X5

Parent (Paper)		$226,000
70% of Sand's net adjusted value since acquisition:		
Retained earnings increase since acquisition ($120,000 - $30,000)	$90,000	
Total price differential amortization (excluding Goodwill)	(7,000)	
Upstream unrealized gain on sale of land	(20,000)	
	$63,000	
	70%	44,100
Goodwill impairment		(14,000)
Unrealized portion of gain on downstream sale of inventory		(10,500)
Total		**$245,600**

Consolidated profit for the year X5

Paper's net adjusted profit:		
Paper's profit	$120,000	
Current-year unrealized downstream profit	(10,500)	
Intercompany dividends	(14,000)	$95,500
Sand's net adjusted profit:		
Sand's profit	$48,000	
Current-year unrealized gain on upstream sale of land	(20,000)	
Current-year price differential amortization	(4,000)	24,000
Goodwill impairment		(14,000)
Total profit		**$105,500**

Allocation to:

Paper
- Paper's net adjusted profit — $95,500
- 70% of Sand's net adjusted profit ($24,000 × 70%) — 16,800
- Goodwill impairment — (14,000)

$98,300

NCI: 30% of Sand's net adjusted profit ($24,000 × 30%) — **$7,200**

7-8

Allocation of the purchase price

		100%	Paper 70%	NCI 30%
Cost of investment in Sand Ltd.		$120,000	$84,000	
NBV of Sand Ltd.				
Share capital	$50,000			
Retained earnings	30,000	80,000	56,000	$24,000
Price differential			28,000	
FV Increments and decrements				
Inventory	9,000		6,300	(2,700)
Equipment	(24,000)	(15,000)	(16,800)	7,200
Goodwill			**$17,500**	

Follow-up - Price differential

Items	Balance at Acquisition	Current Year X6	Years X2-X5	Balance at 31-12-X6
Inventory	$(9,000)	$-	$9,000	$-
Equipment	24,000	(4,000)	(16,000)	4,000
Goodwill	17,500	-	(14,000)	3,500
Total	**$32,500**	**$(4,000)**	**$(21,000)**	**$7,500**

Consolidation Entries for X6

Elimination of the investment

Common Shares	35,000	
Retained Earnings	21,000	
Investment in Sand		56,000
Equipment	16,800	
Goodwill	17,500	
Inventory		6,300
Investment in Sand		28,000

Price differential amortization since acquisition

Inventory	9,000	
Retained Earnings		9,000
Retained Earnings	16,000	
Amortization	4,000	
Equipment		20,000
Retained Earnings	14,000	
Goodwill		14,000

Non-controlling interest

Common Shares	15,000	
Retained Earnings	9,000	
Equipment	7,200	
Inventory		2,700
Non-Controlling Interest		28,500
Retained Earnings	43,200	
Non-Controlling Interest		43,200

Sand's net adjusted value since acquisition

Sand's RE since acquisition ($185,000-$30,000)	$155,000
Total price differential amortization excluding Goodwill	(11,000)
Total	**$144,000**

NCI: ($144,000 × 30%) = **$43,200**

Intercompany dividends

Other Income	7,000	
Retained Earnings	3,000	
Dividends Declared		10,000

Management fees

Management Fee Revenue	24,000	
Miscellaneous Expenses		24,000

Current-year unrealized profit on downstream sale of inventory

Revenues	200,000	
COGS		182,500
Inventory		17,500

Prior-year gain on upstream sale of Land
Retained Earnings	20,000	
Gain on Sale of Land		20,000

Prior-year profit on downstream sale of inventory
Retained Earnings	10,500	
COGS		10,500

Intercompany interests
Other Income	800	
Interest Expense		800

Balance of the Investment in Sand at Dec. 31 X6

Purchase Price	$84,000
Paper's share of Sand's net adjusted value since acquisition ($144,000 × 70%)	100,800
Unrealized portion of gain from downstream sale of inventory	(17,500)
Goodwill Impairment	(14,000)
Investment at Dec. 31, X6	**$153,300**

Retained earnings at Dec. 31 X6

Parent (Paper)		$426,000
70% of Sand's net adjusted value since acquisition:		
Retained earnings increase since acquisition ($185,000 - $30,000)	$155,000	
Total price differential amortization (excluding Goodwill)	(11,000)	
	$144,000	
	70%	100,800
Goodwill impairment		(14,000)
Unrealized portion of gain on downstream sale of inventory		(17,500)
Total		**$495,300**

Consolidated profit for the year X6

Paper's net adjusted profit:		
Paper's profit	$250,000	
Prior-year profit on downstream sale of merchandise	10,500	
Current-year unrealized downstream profit	(17,500)	
Intercompany dividends	(7,000)	$236,000

Sand's net adjusted profit:
Sand's profit	$75,000	
Prior-year gain on upstream sale of land	20,000	
Current-year price differential amortization	(4,000)	91,000
Total profit		$327,000

Allocation to:
Paper
- Paper's net adjusted profit — $236,000
- 70% of Sand's net adjusted profit ($91,000 × 70%) — 3,700

$299,700

NCI: 30% of Sand's net adjusted profit ($91,000 × 30%) — $27,300

Non-controlling Interest
- 30% of NFV of Sand at acquisition — $28,500
- 30% of Sand's net adjusted value since acquisition — 43,200

Total — **$71,700**

7-9

Allocation of the purchase price

			Paper	NCI
		100%	70%	30%
Cost of investment in Sand Ltd.		$120,000	$84,000	
NBV of Sand Ltd.				
Share capital	$50,000			
Retained earnings	30,000	80,000	56,000	$24,000
Price differential			28,000	
FV Increments and decrements				
Inventory	9,000		6,300	(2,700)
Equipment	(24,000)	(15,000)	(16,800)	7,200
Goodwill			**$17,500**	

Follow-up - Price differential

Items	Balance at Acquisition	Current Year X7	Years X2-X6	Balance at 31-12-X7
Inventory	$(9,000)	$-	$9,000	$-
Equipment	24,000	(4,000)	(20,000)	-
Goodwill	17,500	-	(14,000)	3,500
Total	**$32,500**	**$(4,000)**	**$(25,000)**	**$3,500**

Consolidation Entries for X7

Elimination of the investment

Common Shares	35,000	
Retained Earnings	21,000	
Investment in Sand		56,000
Equipment	16,800	
Goodwill	17,500	
Inventory		6,300
Investment in Sand		28,000

Price differential amortization since acquisition

Inventory	9,000	
Retained Earnings		9,000
Retained Earnings	20,000	
Amortization	4,000	
Equipment		24,000
Retained Earnings	14,000	
Goodwill		14,000

Non-controlling interest

Common Shares	15,000	
Retained Earnings	9,000	
Equipment	7,200	
Inventory		2,700
Non-Controlling Interest		28,500

Retained Earnings	47,025	
Non-Controlling Interest		47,025

Sand's net adjusted value since acquisition

Sand's RE since acquisition ($292,000-$30,000)	$262,000
Unrealized upstream gains:	
➢ Inventory	(250)
➢ Equipment	(90,000)
Total price differential amortization excluding Goodwill	(15,000)
Total	**$156,750**

NCI: ($156,750 × 30%) = **$47,025**

<u>Intercompany dividends</u>

Other Income	5,600	
Retained Earnings	2,400	
Dividends Declared		8,000

<u>Management fees</u>

Management Fee Revenue	18,000	
Miscellaneous Expenses		18,000

<u>Current-year unrealized profit on downstream sale of inventory</u>

Revenues	100,000	
COGS		96,500
Inventory		3,500

<u>Current-year unrealized profit on upstream sale of inventory</u>

Revenues	80,000	
COGS		79,750
Inventory		250

<u>Prior-year profit on downstream sale of inventory</u>

Retained Earnings	17,500	
COGS		17,500

<u>Current-year unrealized Gain on upstream sale of equipment</u>

Gain on Sale of Equipment	100,000	
Equipment		100,000

Current-year realized gain
   Equipment   10,000
      Depreciation Expense   10,000

Balance of the Investment in Sand at Dec. 31 X7

Purchase Price	$84,000
Paper's share of Sand's net adjusted value since acquisition ($156,750 × 70%)	109,725
Unrealized portion of gain from downstream sale of inventory	(3,500)
Goodwill Impairment	(14,000)
Investment at Dec. 31, X6	**$176,225**

Retained earnings at Dec. 31 X7

Parent (Paper)	$576,000
70% of Sand's net adjusted value since acquisition: ($156,750 × 70%)	109,725
Goodwill impairment	(14,000)
Unrealized portion of gain on downstream sale of inventory	(3,500)
Total	**$668,225**

Consolidated profit for the year X7

Paper's net adjusted profit:		
Paper's profit	$576,000	
Prior-year profit on downstream sale of merchandise	17,500	
Current-year unrealized downstream profit	(3,500)	
Intercompany dividends	(5,600)	$183,400
Sand's net adjusted profit:		
Sand's profit	$115,000	
Current-year unrealized profit on upstream sale of inventory	(250)	
Current-year unrealized profit on upstream sale of equipment	(90,000)	
Current-year price differential amortization	(4,000)	20,750
Total profit		**$204,150**

Allocation to:
Paper
- Paper's net adjusted profit $183,400
- 70% of Sand's net adjusted profit ($20,750 × 70%)   14,525
                                                                                       $197,925

NCI: 30% of Sand's net adjusted profit ($20,750 × 30%)				<u>$6,225</u>

Non-controlling Interest
- 30% of NFV of Sand at acquisition $28,500
- 30% of Sand's net adjusted value since acquisition   <u>47,025</u>

Total   **$75,525**

7-10

Allocation of the purchase price

			Prime	NCI
		100%	60%	40%
Cost of investment in Sublime.			$3,000,000	
NBV of Sublime				
Share capital	$3,000,000			
Retained earnings	<u>2,000,000</u>	$5,000,000	<u>3,000,000</u>	$2,000,000
Price differential			-	
FV decrements				
A/R	100,000			
Equipment	<u>400,000</u>	500,000	<u>300,000</u>	(200 000)
Goodwill			**$300,000**	

Follow-up - Price differential

Items	Balance at Acquisition	Current Year X4	Years X2-X3	Balance at 31-12-X4
A/R	$(100,000)	$-	100,000	$-
Equipment	(400,000)	133,333	266,667	-
Goodwill	300,000	-	-	300,000
Total	$(200,000)	$133,333	$366,667	$300,000

Net Adjusted Value of Sublime since Acquisition
Retained earnings increase since acquisition ($5,975,000 - $2,000,000)	$3,975,000
FV decrements amortized since acquisition	<u>500,000</u>
Total	**$4,475,000**

Balance of the Investment in Sublime at Dec. 31 X4

Purchase Price	$3,000,000
Prime's share of Sublime's net adjusted value since acquisition ($4,475,000 × 60%)	2,685,000
Unrealized portion of loss from downstream sale of equipment	30,000
Unrealized downstream gain on sale of Land	(1,000,000)
Investment at Dec. 31,X4	**$4,715,000**

Retained earnings at Dec. 31 X4

Parent (Prime)	$15,175,000
60% of Sublime's net adjusted value since acquisition: ($4,475,000 × 60%)	2,685,000
Unrealized portion of loss from downstream sale of equipment	30,000
Unrealized downstream gain on sale of Land	(1,000,000)
Total	**$16,890,000**

Consolidated profit for the year X4

Prime's net adjusted profit:

Prime's profit	$3,225,000	
Current-year portion of loss on downstream sale of equipment	(10,000)	$3,215,000

Sublime's net adjusted profit:

Sublime's profit	$975,000	
Realized profit on prior-year upstream sale of inventory	50,000	
Current-year price differential amortization	133,333	1,158,333
Total profit		**$4,373,333**

Allocation to:
Prime

- Prime's net adjusted profit — $3,215,000
- 60% of Sublime's net adjusted profit ($1,158,333 × 60%) — 695,000

$3,910,000

NCI: 40% of Sublime's net adjusted profit ($1,158,333 × 30%) — **$463,333**

Non-controlling Interest
- 40% of NFV of Sublime at acquisition $1,800,000
- 40% of Sublime's net adjusted value since acquisition
  ($4,475,000 × 40%) 1,790,000

Total **$3,790,000**

Other Consolidation Issues

Module 8

What you will find in this section

- How to Walk Through Module 8
- Slides

Module 8
Other Consolidation Issues

How to Walk Through Module 8

◇ <u>Readings</u>

1- <u>Student Manual</u> "Advanced Accounting": Module 8
   - **PART 1**: JOINT VENTURES
   - **PART 2**: CHANGES IN OWNERSHIP INTERESTS
   - **PART 3**: MULTIPLE INVESTMENTS SITUATIONS
   - **PART 4**: INCOME TAX ALLOCATION
   - **PART 5**: PUSH-DOWN ACCOUNTING
   - **PART 6**: CONTINGENT CONSIDERATION
   - **PART 7**: INTERIM ACQUISITIONS
   - **PART 8**: SUBSIDIARY WITH PREFERRED SHARES

◇ <u>Additional readings</u>

2- <u>IFRS</u> 11

When you have successfully completed this module, you will be able to do the following:

Discuss the impact on the consolidation when:

- The company being controlled is a joint-venture;
- The ownership interest changes overtime;
- Parent controls more than one subsidiary;
- There are contingencies;
- The combination occurs during the year;
- Subsidiary holds preferred shares.

OTHER CONSOLIDATION ISSUES
Module 8

Copyright © 2020 Parmitech

Advanced Accounting: Student Manual

Copyrighted Material

Editor: Parmitech

This publication is protected by copyright, and permission should be obtained from the publisher prior to any prohibited reproduction, storage in a retrieval system, or transmission in any form or by any means, electronic, mechanical, photocopying, recording, or otherwise.

Corresponding Author

Richard Bozec Ph.D., CPA, CGA
bozec@telfer.uottawa.ca

Copyright © Parmitech

OUTLINE

1. JOINT VENTURES
2. CHANGES IN OWNERSHIP INTERESTS
3. MULTIPLE INVESTMENTS SITUATIONS
4. INCOME TAX ALLOCATION
5. PUSH-DOWN ACCOUNTING
6. CONTINGENT CONSIDERATION
7. INTERIM ACQUISITIONS
8. SUBSIDIARY WITH PREFERRED SHARES

Other Consolidation Issues ---------- Module 8 ---------- 3

Part 1

PART 1
JOINT VENTURES

PROPORTIONATE CONSOLIDATION AND EQUITY METHOD

This publication is protected by copyright, and permission should be obtained from the publisher prior to any prohibited reproduction, storage in a retrieval system, or transmission in any form or by any means, electronic, mechanical, photocopying, recording, or otherwise.

Copyright © 2020 Parmitech

TEACHING MATERIAL
Electronic Sources

IFRS

IFRS 11   Joint Arrangements

Other Consolidation Issues — Module 8 — 5

JOINT VENTURES
Definition

A **joint venture** is a contractual arrangement whereby two or more parties undertake an economic activity that is subject to **joint control**.

Joint ventures are common in certain industries, such as resource exploration and in global competition.

Potential **benefits**:

- Shared Resources and Responsibilities
- Flexibility for Participating Companies
- Shared Business Risk

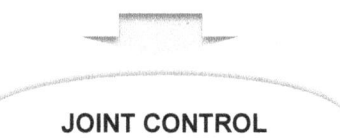

JOINT CONTROL

Other Consolidation Issues — Module 8 — 6

JOINT VENTURES
Benefits

Shared Resources and Responsibilities
More often than not, a company enters into a joint venture because it lacks the required knowledge, human capital, technology or access to a specific market that is necessary to be successful in pursuing the project on its own. Coming together with another business affords each party access to the resources of the other participating company without having to spend excessive amounts of capital to obtain it.

Flexibility for Participating Companies
Unlike a merger or acquisition, a joint venture is a temporary contract between participating companies that dissolves at a specific future date or when the project is completed. The companies entering into a joint venture are not required to create a new business entity under which the project is then completed, providing a degree of flexibility not found in more permanent business strategies.

JOINT VENTURES
Benefits (continued)

Shared Business Risk
The creation of a new product or delivery of a new service carries a great deal of risk for a business, and many companies are not able to manage that risk alone. Under a joint venture, each company contributes a portion of the resources needed to bring the product or service to market, making the heavy financial burden of research and development less of a challenge.

Part 1

JOINT ARRANGEMENTS
Forms of Organization

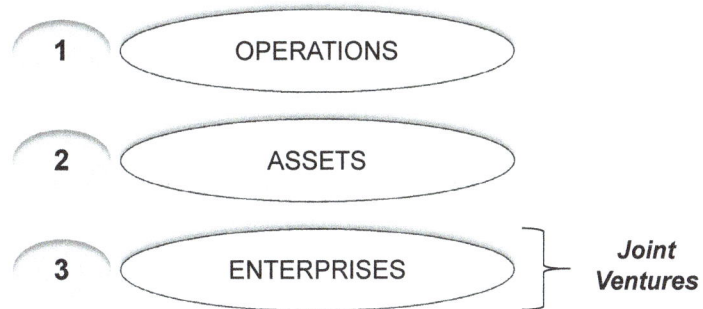

A joint venture is a type of joint arrangement. A jointly controlled entity operates in the same way as other entities, except that a contractual arrangement between the venturers establishes joint control over the economic activity of the entity.

Part 1

JOINT ARRANGEMENTS
Forms of Organization - Description

1   JOINTLY CONTROLLED OPERATIONS

Each venturer uses its own property, plant, and equipment.
Assets remain under the individual ownership and control of each venturer. The arrangement will provide for the sharing of revenues and of common expenses.

2   JOINTLY CONTROLLED ASSETS

Assets are jointly controlled by the venturers.
The arrangement will provide for the sharing of the output from the assets and of common expenses.

3   JOINTLY CONTROLLED ENTERPRISE

Establishment of a separate corporation or partnership in which each venturer has an investment interest.

JOINT ARRANGEMENTS
Accounting Methods - IFRS 11

1

JOINTLY CONTROLLED **OPERATIONS** & **ASSETS**

Proportionate Consolidation

2

JOINTLY CONTROLLED **ENTERPRISES**
(Joint Ventures)

Equity Method

Other Consolidation Issues ---------- Module 8 ---------- Part 1 11

JOINT ARRANGEMENTS
Accounting Methods - ASPE

1

JOINTLY CONTROLLED **OPERATIONS** & **ASSETS**

Proportionate Consolidation

2

JOINTLY CONTROLLED **ENTERPRISES**
(Joint Ventures)

Choice between:
Proportionate Consolidation and Equity Method

Other Consolidation Issues ---------- Module 8 ---------- Part 1 12

REPORTING JOINT VENTURES
Illustration - Proportionate Consolidation

Part 1

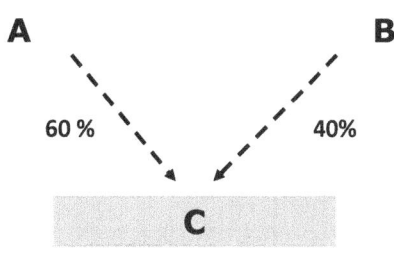

Resources invested by A and B could be financial, technical and/or administrative. For Company C to qualify as a Joint Venture, the agreement should clearly stipulate that in all areas essential to the operation of Company C, decisions must be made by, and require the consent of, both Company A and Company B.

PROPORTIONATE CONSOLIDATION
Overview of the Consolidation Process for Company A

Part 1

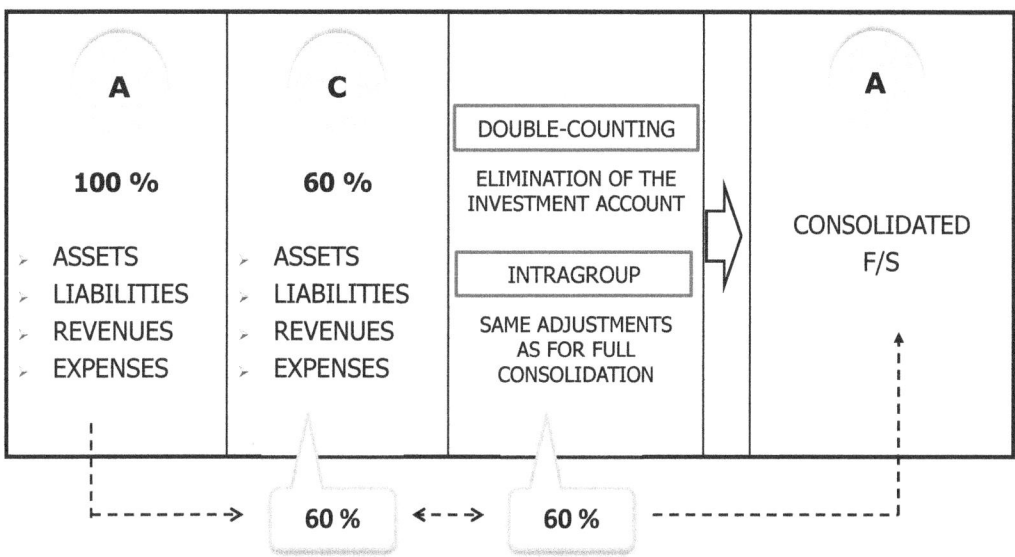

PROPORTIONATE CONSOLIDATION
Overview of the Consolidation Process for Company B

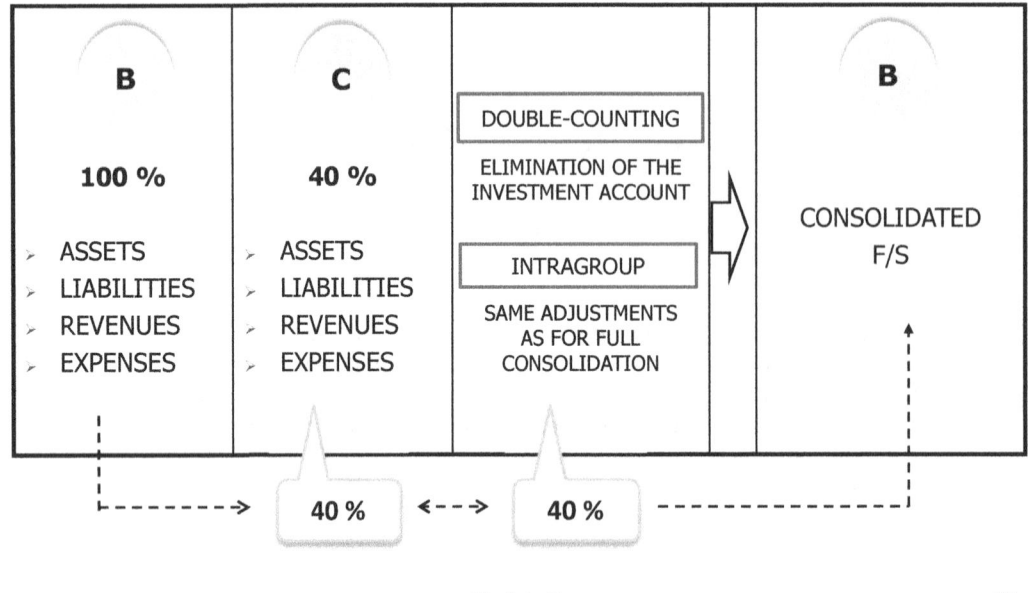

PROPORTIONATE CONSOLIDATION
vs. FULL CONSOLIDATION
Main Differences

1

NON-CONTROLLING INTEREST

Under proportionate consolidation, only the co-venturer's proportionate share in the joint venture is taken into consideration. Therefore, there is no value assigned to non-controlling interest in the consolidated financial statements.

2

GAINS (LOSSES) ON DOWNSTREAM SALES

Gains (losses) from downstream sales are recognized in the consolidation process to the extent of the interests of the other non-related venturers.

Part 1

IN THE CONTEXT OF A SUBSIDIARY
Downstream Gains & Losses - Recall

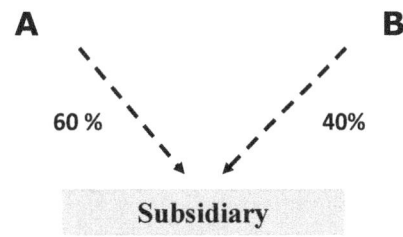

A can't sell to itself

Unilateral control of A over Subsidiary.
Downstream gains/losses will be eliminated at **100%**.

Part 1

IN THE CONTEXT OF A JOINT VENTURE
Downstream Gains & Losses

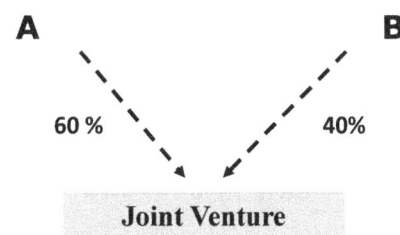

When A sells to Joint Venture, A indirectly sells to B

Joint control of A and B over Joint Venture.
Downstream gains/losses will be eliminated to the extent of A's share: **60%**. In other words, downstream gains/losses will be recognized to the extent of the other co-venture's share: **40%**.

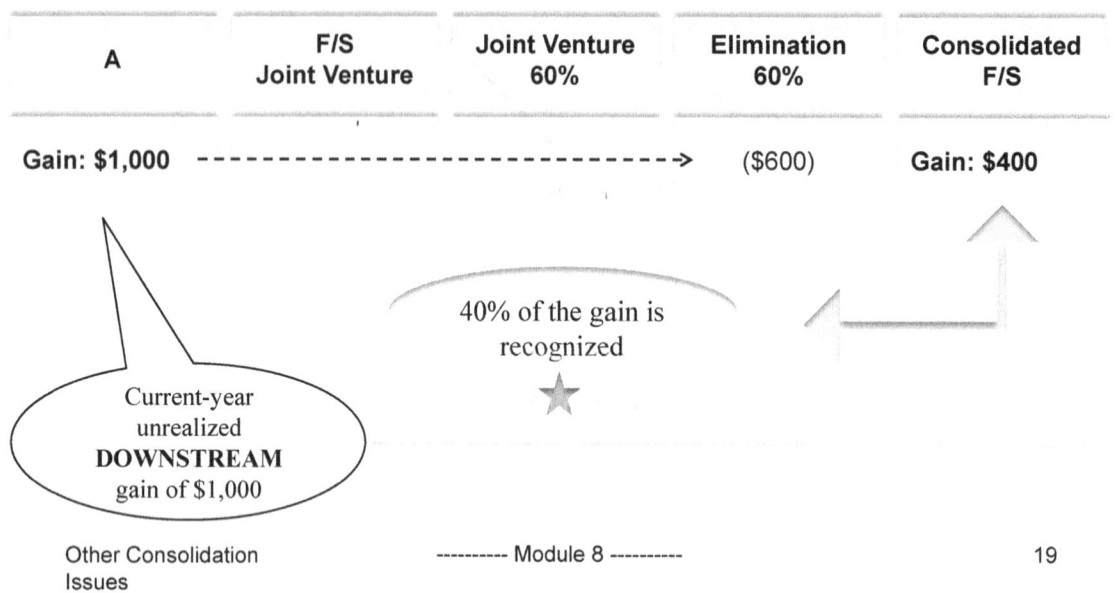

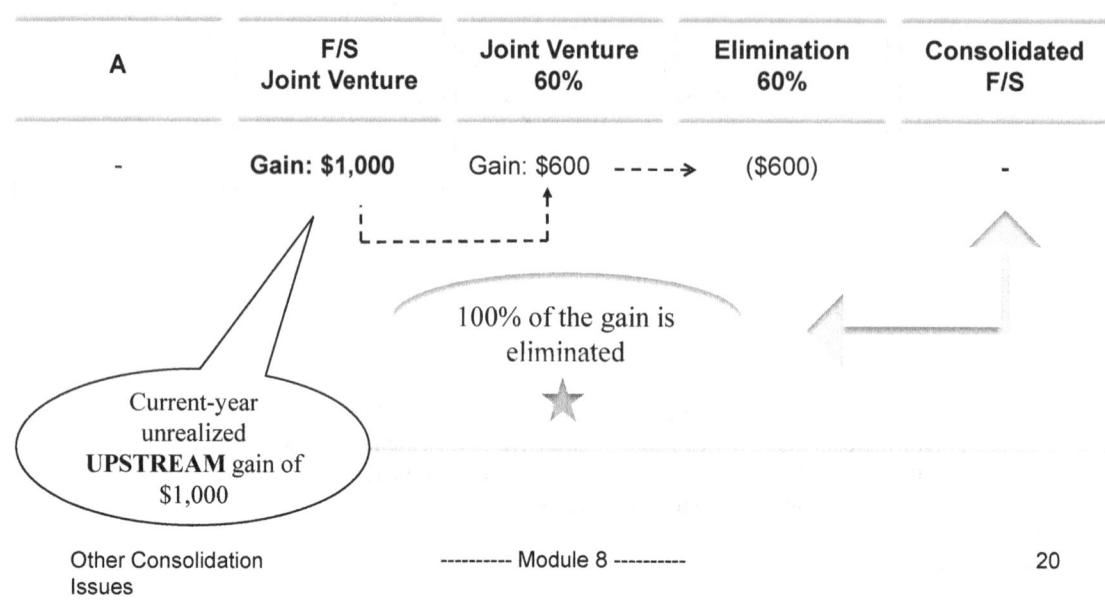

PROPORTIONATE CONSOLIDATION
Illustration

Part 1

Assume that on January 1, X5, Company A and Company B, two private enterprises, established a new company, Company C. The co-venturers signed an agreement, which specifies that *in all areas essential to the operation of Company C, decisions must be made by, and require the consent of, each of the two investor Companies*. The new company is organized to develop oil fields in northern Canada.

Company A contributed $60,000 in cash for 60% of Company C while Company B contributed $40,000 in cash for the remaining ownership (40%).

Assume that the affiliated companies did not engaged in transactions among themselves since the creation of the joint venture. Both companies are using proportionate consolidation to account for their investment in Company C.

Required

Prepare the consolidated statement of financial position of Company A and Company B at December, 31, X9.

CONSOLIDATION OF JOINT VENTURES
IN PERIODS SUBSEQUENT TO THE DATE OF CREATION
Timeline

Part 1

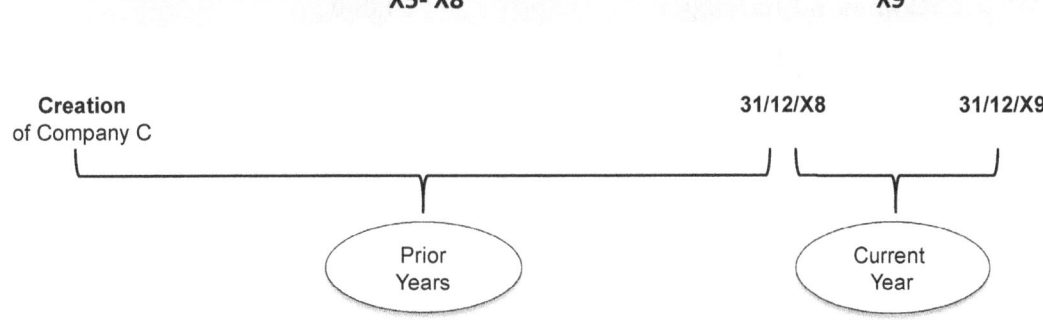

Part 1

STATEMENTS OF FINANCIAL POSITION
OF THE AFFILIATED COMPANIES
At December 31, X9

	Company A	Company B	Company C
Assets			
Cash	$100,000	$50,000	$5,000
Accounts receivable	200,000	50,000	30,000
Land	26,000	100,000	55,000
Buildings (net)	449,000	150,000	140,000
Investment in Company C	60,000	+ 40,000	
Total assets	**$835,000**	**$390,000**	**$230,000**
Liabilities and equities			
Accounts payable	$85,000	$20,000	$10,000
Share capital	500,000	200,000	100,000
Retained earnings	250,000	170,000	120,000
Total liabilities & equ.	**$835,000**	**$390,000**	**$230,000**

Cost Method → Investment in Company C

Double-Counting → Share capital

Part 1

CONSOLIDATION ENTRIES
At December 31, X9

FOR COMPANY A

Common Shares (C)	60,000	
Investment in C (A)		60,000

FOR COMPANY B

Common Shares (C)	40,000	
Investment in C (B)		40,000

Part 1

CONSOLIDATION WORKSHEET OF COMPANY A
For the Year Ended December 31, X9

	Company A	Company C	60% of C	Elimination	Consolidated
Assets					
Cash	$100,000	$5,000	$3,000		$103,000
Accounts receivable	200,000	30,000	18,000		218,000
Land	26,000	55,000	33,000		59,000
Buildings (net)	449,000	140,000	84,000		533,000
Investment in C	60,000			(60,000)	
Total assets	**$835,000**	**$230,000**	**$138,000**		**$913,000**
Liabilities and equity					
Accounts payable	$85,000	$10,000	$6,000		$91,000
Share capital	500,000	100,000	60,000	(60,000)	500,000
Retained earnings	250,000	120,000	72,000		322,000
Total L & Equity	**$835,000**	**$230,000**	**$138,000**		**$913,000**

Through the process, 60% of Company C's increase in value since creation is assigned to Company A: ending balance of RE ($120,000) × 60% = **$72,000**

Other Consolidation Issues ---------- Module 8 ---------- 25

Part 1

CONSOLIDATION WORKSHEET OF COMPANY B
For the Year Ended December 31, X9

	Company B	Company C	40% of C	Elimination	Consolidated
Assets					
Cash	$50,000	$5,000	$2,000		$52,000
Accounts receivable	50,000	30,000	12,000		62,000
Land	100,000	55,000	22,000		122,000
Buildings (net)	150,000	140,000	56,000		206,000
Investment in C	40,000			(40,000)	
Total assets	**$390,000**	**$230,000**	**$92,000**		**$442,000**
Liabilities and equity					
Accounts payable	$20,000	$10,000	$4,000		$24,000
Share capital	200,000	100,000	40,000	(40,000)	200,000
Retained earnings	170,000	120,000	48,000		218,000
Total L & Equity	**$390,000**	**$230,000**	**$92,000**		**$442,000**

Through the process, 40% of Company C's increase in value since creation is assigned to Company B: ending balance of RE ($120,000) × 40% = **$48,000**

Other Consolidation Issues ---------- Module 8 ---------- 26

REPORTING JOINT VENTURES
Equity Method

SPECIAL FEATURE

The approach is similar to the one illustrated so far in the case of subsidiaries (see prior modules) except for the treatment accorded to gains/losses arising from **downstream** transactions. These gains/losses must be eliminated only to the extent of the co-venturer's proportionate share in the joint venture.

CONSEQUENCE

Gains/losses from downstream sales are recognized in the financial statements of the co-venturer to the extent of the interests of the other non-related venturers.

JUSTIFICATION

In the context of joint control, we assume that the investors are less able to manipulate their earnings by suitably arranging intercompany transactions.

ILLUSTRATION OF THE EQUITY METHOD
Taken from Module 7 - Case Involving a Subsidiary - Recall

- Parent's share of Subsidiary's adjusted net loss
  - Profit for the period $30,000
  - Current-year price differential amortization .... (40,000)
  - Realized portion of prior-year **upstream** sale of equipment ($10,000/10) 1,000

  (9,000) × **90%** .... (8,100)

  - Unrealized current-year profit on **downstream** sale of inventory (**100%** × $4,500) .... (4,500)
  - Realized profit from prior-year **downstream** sale of inventory (**100%** × $1,800) 1,800

  Total .... $(10,800)

Downstream profits are eliminated at **100%**.

Part 1

ILLUSTRATION OF THE EQUITY METHOD
If Subsidiary is a Joint Venture Instead of a Subsidiary

<u>Parent's share of Subsidiary's adjusted net loss</u>
- Profit for the period $30,000
- Current-year price differential amortization (40,000)
- Realized portion of prior-year **upstream** sale of equipment ($10,000/10) $\underline{1,000}$

  (9,000) × **90%**   (8,100)

- Unrealized current-year profit on **downstream** sale of inventory (**90%** × $4,500)   (4,050)
- Realized profit from prior-year **downstream** sale of inventory (**90%** × $1,800) $\underline{1,620}$

Total $(10,530)

Downstream profits are recognized to the extent of the other co-ventures' share: **10%**.

Other Consolidation Issues ———— Module 8 ————   29

Part 2

Parmitech

PART 2
CHANGES IN OWNERSHIP INTERESTS

STEP ACQUISITIONS

This publication is protected by copyright, and permission should be obtained from the publisher prior to any prohibited reproduction, storage in a retrieval system, or transmission in any form or by any means, electronic, mechanical, photocopying, recording, or otherwise.

Copyright © 2020 Parmitech

CHANGES IN OWNERSHIP INTERESTS
Different Scenarios

Part 2

INCREASES
- WHEN PARENT PURCHASES ADDITIONAL SUBSIDIARY SHARES DIRECTLY FROM THIRD PARTIES: **STEP ACQUISITION**.
- WHEN THE SUBSIDIARY PURCHASES ITS SHARES FROM THIRD PARTIES.

DECREASES
- WHEN PARENT SELLS SOME SUBSIDIARY SHARES DIRECTLY TO THIRD PARTIES.
- WHEN THE SUBSIDIARY SELLS ADDITIONAL SHARES TO THIRD PARTIES.

Other Consolidation Issues ---------- Module 8 ---------- 31

STEP ACQUISITIONS
Two Cases

Part 2

Measure and recognize acquiree's identifiable assets and liabilities at 100% of their fair values on date the acquirer obtains control.

CONTROL NOT ACCHIEVED UPON THE FIRST PURCHASE

Revaluation of the initial investment to FV when control is achieved. Adjustment to income statement.

CONTROL ACCHIEVED IN THE FIRST PURCHASE

Adjustment to contributed capital of controlling interest.

Other Consolidation Issues ---------- Module 8 ---------- 32

STEP ACQUISITION
Illustration 1 - Taken from Module 7
From no control to full control

Part 2

(1) On June 30, X1, Parent Company acquires **10%** (10 000 shares) of the outstanding voting shares of Subsidiary for **$100,000** cash.

(2) On December 31, X1, Parent Company acquires **90%** (90 000 shares) of the outstanding voting shares of Subsidiary by issuing 36,000 shares with a market value of $30, or **$1,080,000** total, in exchange.

At the date of combination, the fair values of Subsidiary's land and buildings exceeded their book values by $100,000 and $200,000, respectively. The fair values of all of Subsidiary's other assets and liabilities were equal to their book values.

Subsidiary had common shares of $200,000 and retained earnings of $600,000 at the date of acquisition.

The remaining useful life of the buildings from the date of acquisition is ten years. Subsidiary uses the straight-line method to calculate amortizations.

STEP ACQUISITION
Illustration 1
From no control to full control

Part 2

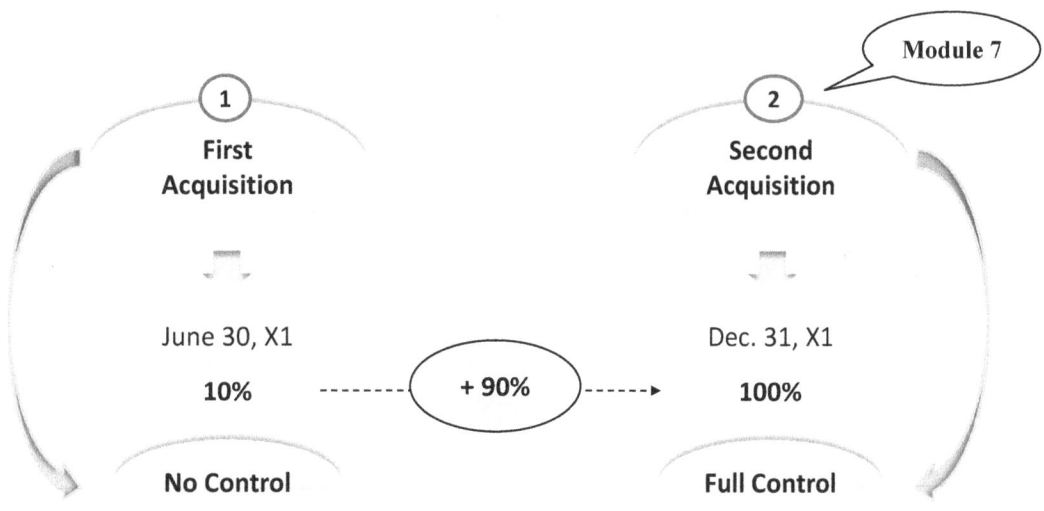

STEP ACQUISITION
Illustration 1
Overview

	First Acquisition	Second Acquisition
% acquired	10%	90%
Ownership	10%	100%
Type	Non-strategic	Full control
Method	FV	Consolidation
Particularities	Revaluation at the date of the second purchase	Consolidation from the date of the second purchase

---

STEP ACQUISITION
Illustration 1
On the books of Parent - June 30, X1

FIRST ACQUISITION (10%)

Investment in Subsidiary	100,000	
Common Shares		100,000

⬇

(Non-Strategic Investment)

STEP ACQUISITION
Illustration 1
On the books of Parent - December 31, X1

REVALUATION OF THE PREVIOUSLY HELD INVESTMENT (10%)

Investment in Subsidiary	20,000	
Income - Gain		20,000

FV of the first investment at December 31, X1:

($1,080,000/90,000 shares) = $12/share
(10,000 shares × $12) = $120,000

Gain: ($120,000 - $100,000) = $20,000

SECOND ACQUISITION (90%)

Investment in Subsidiary	1,080,000	
Common Shares		1,080,000

STEP ACQUISITION
Illustration 1
Impact on the consolidation

- Purchase price:
  - ① - FV – first acquisition (10%) $ 120,000
  - ② - Purchase price – second acquisition (90%)   1,080,000
  -                                       1,200,000   Acquisitions 1 & 2 combined

- Net book value of Subsidiary:
  - Common shares $200,000
  - Retained earnings   600,000   800,000

- Price differential   400,000

- Fair value increments:
  - Land   100,000
  - Buildings   200,000   300,000

- Goodwill $100,000

STEP ACQUISITION
Illustration 1
Consolidation at the date of the second acquisition

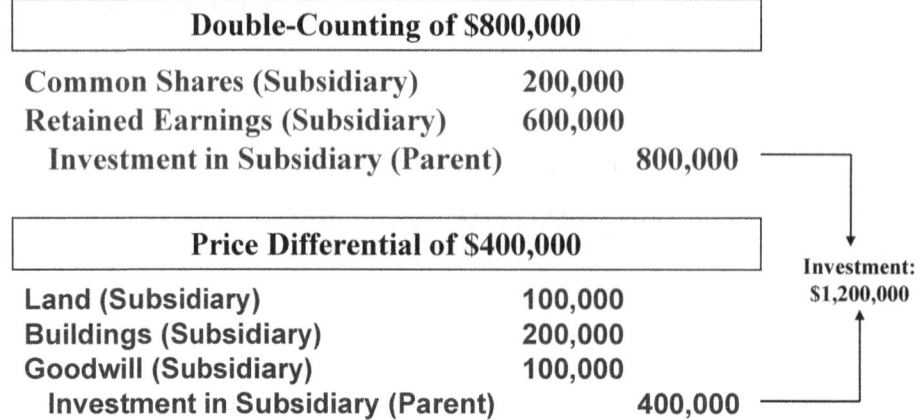

Double-Counting of $800,000		
Common Shares (Subsidiary)	200,000	
Retained Earnings (Subsidiary)	600,000	
Investment in Subsidiary (Parent)		800,000

Price Differential of $400,000		
Land (Subsidiary)	100,000	
Buildings (Subsidiary)	200,000	
Goodwill (Subsidiary)	100,000	
Investment in Subsidiary (Parent)		400,000

Investment: $1,200,000

STEP ACQUISITION
Illustration 2 - Taken from Module 7
From partial control to full control

(1)
On December 31, X1, Parent Company acquires **90%** (90 000 shares) of the outstanding voting shares of Subsidiary by issuing 36,000 shares with a market value of $30, or **$1,080,000** total, in exchange.

At the date of combination, the fair values of Subsidiary's land and buildings exceeded their book values by $100,000 and $200,000, respectively. The fair values of all of Subsidiary's other assets and liabilities were equal to their book values.

Subsidiary had common shares of $200,000 and retained earnings of $600,000 at the date of acquisition.

The remaining useful life of the buildings from the date of acquisition is ten years. Subsidiary uses the straight-line method to calculate amortizations.

(2)
On December 31, X5, Parent Company acquires **10%** (10 000 shares) of the outstanding voting shares of Subsidiary for **$100,000** cash.

STEP ACQUISITION
Illustration 2
From partial control to full control

Part 2

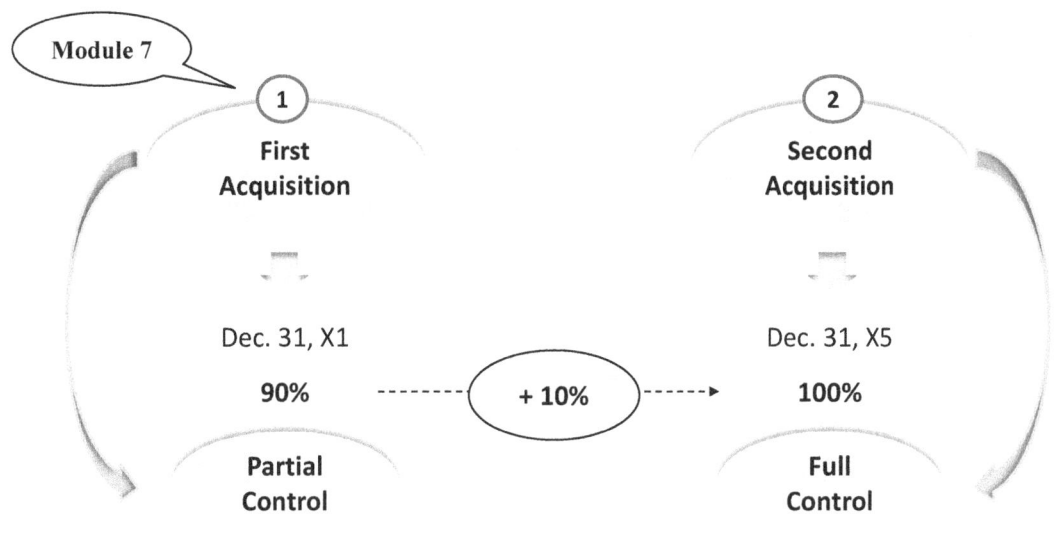

STEP ACQUISITION
Illustration 2
Overview

Part 2

	First Acquisition	Second Acquisition
% acquired	90%	10%
Ownership	90%	100%
Type	Partial control	Full control
Method	Consolidation	Consolidation
Particularities	NCI = 10%	Transfer of NCI to Parent

Module 7 illustrates the consolidation of Parent and Subsidiary at December 31, X5, which coincides with the date of the second acquisition (10%). Therefore, we return to Module 7 for the valuation of NCI in order to proceed with the transfer of NCI to Parent (see next slide).

STEP ACQUISITION
Illustration 2
Impact on the consolidation: transfer of the NCI to Parent

NCI at the date of the second acquisition (taken from Module 7)

- Minority's share of implied purchase price:
  ($1,200,000 × 10%) $120,000
- Minority's share of Subsidiary's net adjusted value since
  acquisition: ($292,000 × 10%)   29,200
  Total $149,200

Gain to Parent

- Amount transferred from NCI $149,200
- Purchase price – second acquisition   100,000
  Gain to Parent $ 49,200

STEP ACQUISITION
Illustration 2
Consolidation at the date of the second acquisition

Effect on the NCI		
Non-Controlling Interest	149,200	
Retained Earnings (Subsidiary)		49,200
Investment in Subsidiary (Parent)		100,000

This consolidation entry transfers the NCI to Parent following the second acquisition (10%). It is in continuity with the consolidation of Parent illustrated in Module 7.

Part 3

PART 3
MULTIPLE INVESTMENT SITUATIONS

MULTI-COMPANY AFFILIATION
MULTI-LEVEL AFFILIATION
RECIPROCAL HOLDINGS

This publication is protected by copyright, and permission should be obtained from the publisher prior to any prohibited reproduction, storage in a retrieval system, or transmission in any form or by any means, electronic, mechanical, photocopying, recording, or otherwise.

Copyright © 2020 Parmitech

Part 3

MULTI-COMPANY AFFILIATION

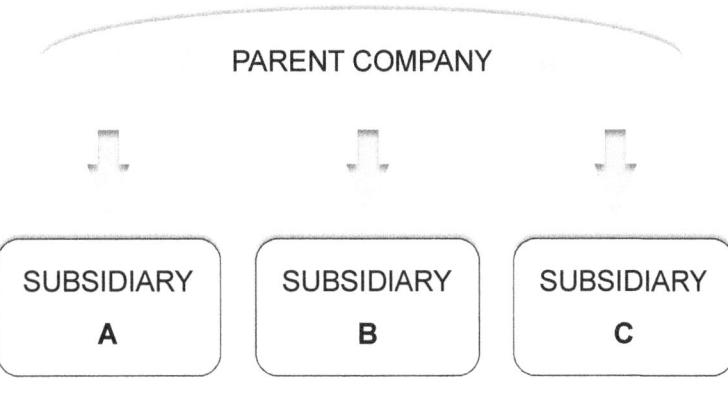

The term **multi-company affiliation** is used to describe situations in which a single company has acquired, by direct investment in each investee, two or more subsidiaries. There are no particular complications in this situation. It is simply a matter of dealing with each subsidiary and then summing the financial data. In this setting, note that intercompany transactions also encompass transactions among subsidiaries.

Other Consolidation Issues ---------- Module 8 ---------- 46

Part 3

MULTI-LEVEL AFFILIATION

Step-by-Step Consolidation

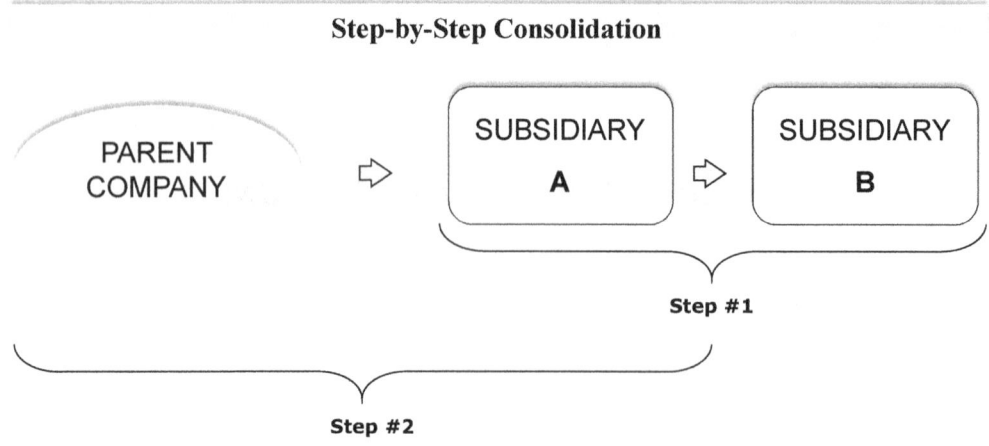

The term **multi-level affiliation** is used to describe situations in which a single company has acquired, by indirect investment, two or more subsidiaries. In this setting, one must follow a step-by-step consolidation accounting process (one level of control at a time).

Part 3

RECIPROCAL HOLDINGS

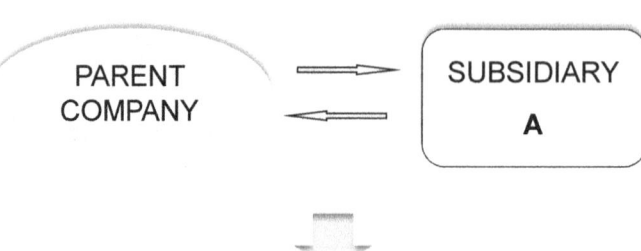

Reciprocal holdings refer to situations in which a parent has invested in a subsidiary and the subsidiary, in turn, has acquired shares of the parent. Reciprocal holdings add considerable complexity since, in order to determine the parent's share of subsidiary's net value increase since acquisition, one must determine the subsidiary's share of the parent's net value increase since the investment was made. Since the latter figure involves the former, simultaneous equations (financial econometrics) are necessary to arrive at a solution to this problem (circular causation).

HYBRID STRUCTURE
Vertical and Horizontal

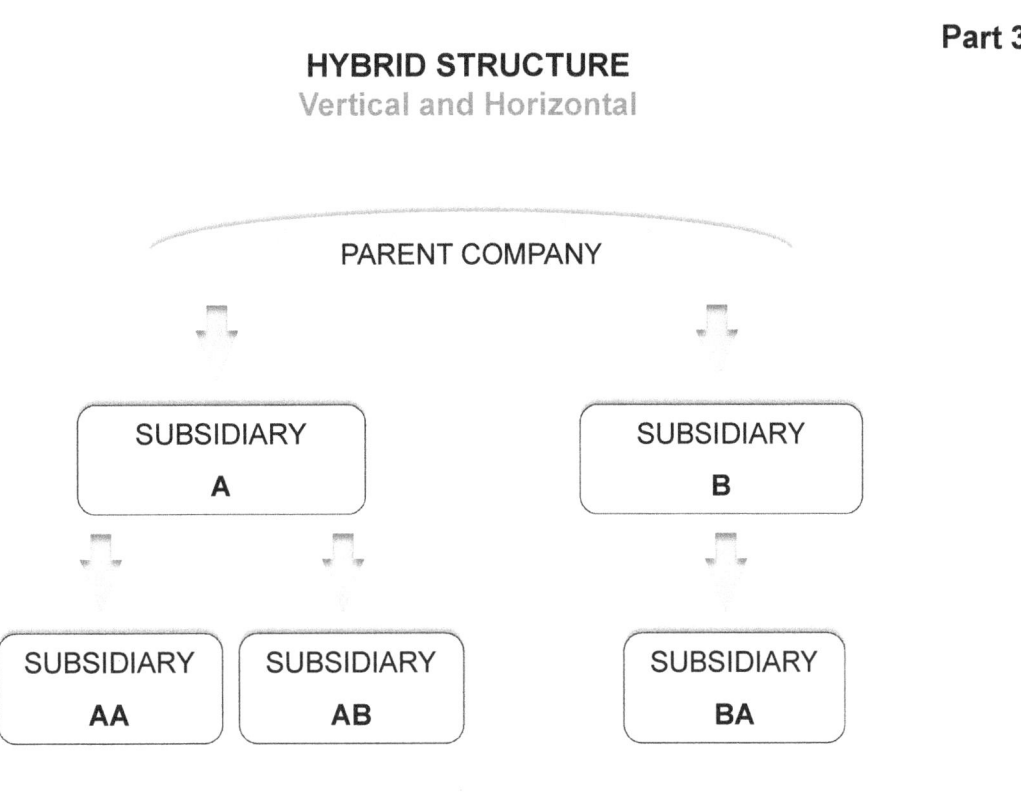

MULTI-COMPANY AFFILIATION
Illustration

Assume that on January 1, X5, Parent Company acquired **90%** of the outstanding shares of Subsidiary A for **$250,200**. Subsidiary's Common Stock and Retained Earnings at the date of acquisition amount to $200,000 and $70,000, respectively.

Parent also acquired **80%** of the outstanding common stock of Subsidiary B on January 1, X7, for **$115,000**. The net book value of Subsidiary B at the date of acquisition consists of Common Shares of $100,000 and Retained Earnings of $40,000.

Any difference between implied and the book values relates to goodwill. Goodwill has not been impaired since acquisition. Assume that the affiliated companies did not engaged in transactions among themselves.

Required

Prepare the consolidated statement of financial position of Parent Company at December 31, X9, under the *full goodwill approach*.

MULTI-COMPANY AFFILIATION
Illustration - Timeline

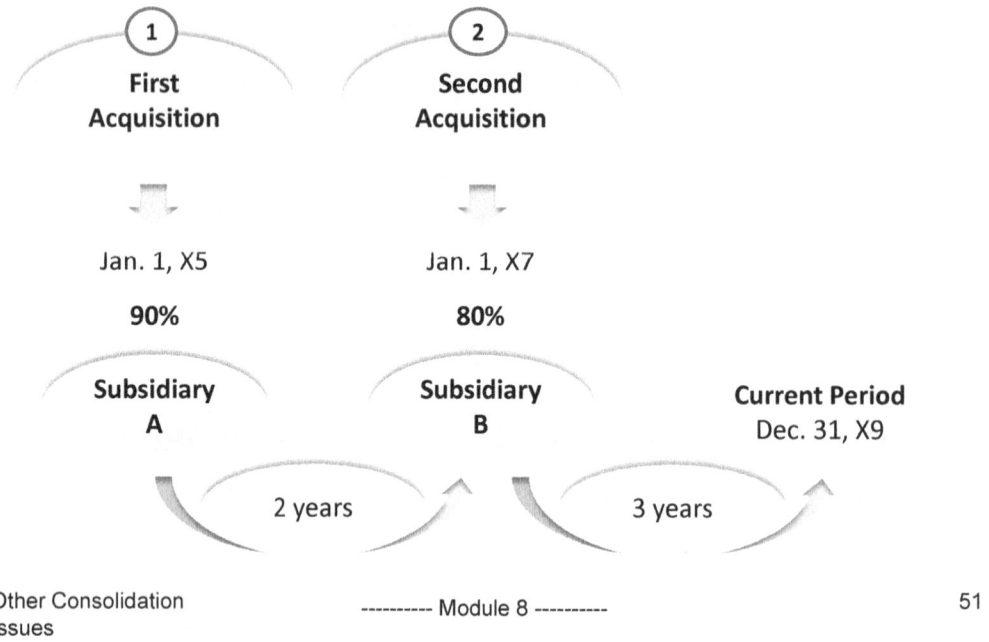

STATEMENTS OF FINANCIAL POSITION
OF THE AFFILIATED COMPANIES
At December 31, X9

	Parent	Subsidiary A	Subsidiary B
Assets			
Cash	$100,000	$50,000	$5,000
Accounts receivable	200,000	50,000	30,000
Land	26,000	100,000	55,000
Buildings (net)	143,800	190,000	140,000
Investment in Subsidiary A	250,200		
Investment in Subsidiary B	115,000		
Total assets	**$835,000**	**$390,000**	**$230,000**
Liabilities and equities			
Accounts payable	$85,000	$20,000	$10,000
Share capital	500,000	200,000	100,000
Retained earnings	250,000	170,000	120,000
Total liabilities and equ.	**$835,000**	**$390,000**	**$230,000**

(Cost Method)

ALLOCATION OF PURCHASE PRICE
FULL GOODWILL APPROACH
Subsidiary A
January 1, X5

	Implied (100%)	Parent (90%)	NCI (10%)
Purchase price	$278,000	$250,200	$27,800
Net book value of Subsidiary:			
- Common shares $200,000			
- Retained earnings 70,000	270,000	243,000	27,000
Price differential	8,000	7,200	800
Goodwill	**$ 8,000**	**$ 7,200**	**$ 800**

Implied purchase price: ($250,200/90%) = **$278,000**

ALLOCATION OF PURCHASE PRICE
FULL GOODWILL APPROACH
Subsidiary B
January 1, X7

	Implied (100%)	Parent (80%)	NCI (20%)
Purchase price	$143,750	$115,000	$28,750
Net book value of Subsidiary:			
- Common shares $100,000			
- Retained earnings 40,000	140,000	112,000	28,000
Price differential	3,750	3,000	750
Goodwill	**$ 3,750**	**$ 3,000**	**$ 750**

Implied purchase price: ($115,000/80%) = **$143,750**

Part 3

CONSOLIDATION ENTRIES
December 31, X9

SUBSIDIARY A

Common Shares (Subsidiary)	200,000	
Retained Earnings (Subsidiary)	70,000	
Goodwill (Subsidiary)	8,000	
Investment in Subsidiary (cost)		250,200
Non-Controlling Interest		27,800

10% Implied Value

SUBSIDIARY B

Common Shares (Subsidiary)	100,000	
Retained Earnings (Subsidiary)	40,000	
Goodwill (Subsidiary)	3,750	
Investment in Subsidiary (cost)		115,000
Non-Controlling Interest		28,750

20% Implied Value

Part 3

CONSOLIDATION ENTRIES
Adjustment to NCI

Net Adjusted Value of Subsidiary A Since Acquisition

Retained earnings increase since acquisition
($170,000 - $70,000) $100,000 — 10%

Net Adjusted Value of Subsidiary B Since Acquisition

Retained earnings increase since acquisition
($120,000 - $40,000) $80,000 — 20%

Adjustment to NCI

Retained Earnings	26,000	
Non-Controlling Interest		26,000

Part 3

CONSOLIDATION WORKSHEET OF PARENT COMPANY
For the Year Ended December 31, X9

	Parent	Sub. A	Sub. B	Eliminations	Consolidated
Assets					
Cash	$100,000	$50,000	$5,000		$155,000
Accounts receivable	200,000	50,000	30,000		280,000
Land	26,000	100,000	55,000		181,000
Buildings (net)	143,800	190,000	140,000		473,800
Investment in A	250,200			(250,200)	-
Investment in B	115,000			(115,000)	-
Goodwill				8,000/3,750	11,750
Total assets	**$835,000**	**$390,000**	**$230,000**	**($353,450)**	**$1,101,550**
Liabilities and equity					
Accounts payable	$85,000	$20,000	$10,000		$115,000
Share capital	500,000	200,000	100,000	(200,000) (100,000)	500,000
Retained earnings	250,000	170,000	120,000	(70,000)/(40,000) (26,000)	404,000
NCI				27,800/28,750 26,000	82,550
Total L & Equity	**$835,000**	**$390,000**	**$230,000**	**($353,450)**	**$1,101,550**

Other Consolidation Issues ---------- Module 8 ---------- 57

Part 4

PART 4
INCOME TAX ALLOCATION

BUSINESS COMBINATIONS
INTERCOMPANY TRANSFERS

This publication is protected by copyright, and permission should be obtained from the publisher prior to any prohibited reproduction, storage in a retrieval system, or transmission in any form or by any means, electronic, mechanical, photocopying, recording, or otherwise.

Copyright © 2020 Parmitech

DEFERRED TAX
In your Textbook - Bozec (2016)

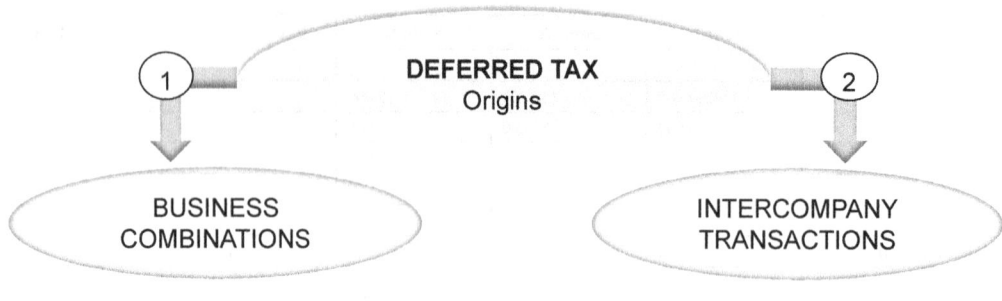

COMPUTATION OF INCOME TAX PAYABLE
General Approach - Review

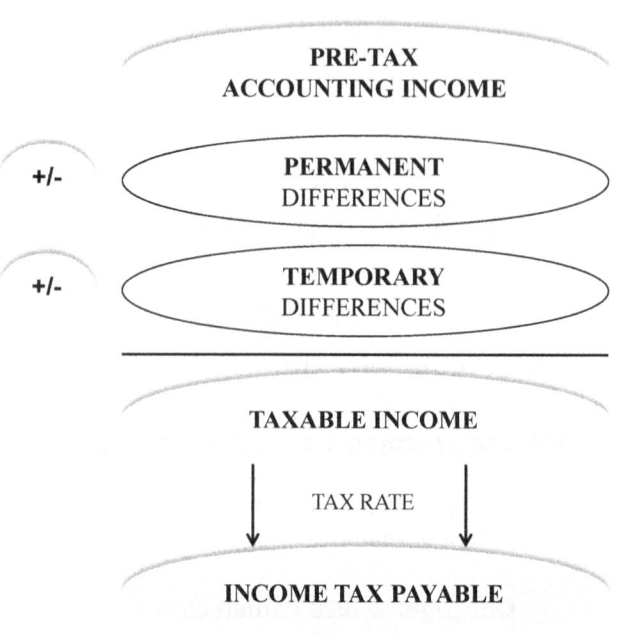

PERMANENT AND TEMPORARY DIFFERENCES
Definitions

A **permanent difference** arises when an income statement element – a revenue, gain, expense, or loss – enters the computation of either taxable income or pre-tax accounting income but never enters into the computation of the other.

Also known as a nonreversing difference.

A **temporary difference** arises when the tax basis of an asset or liability differs from its accounting carrying value.

There are two types of temporary differences: (1) a **taxable temporary difference**, which will result in higher taxable income in the future, and (2) a **deductible temporary difference**, which will result in lower taxable income in the future.

Also known as a reversing difference.

PERMANENT DIFFERENCES
Examples

- Dividends received by Canadian corporations from other taxable Canadian corporations

- 50% of capital gains

- Golf club dues

- 50% of meals and entertainment expenses

- Political contributions

- Equity in earnings from associate companies

Part 4

TEMPORARY DIFFERENCES
Examples

- Depreciation for accounting purposes vs. CCA for tax

- Amortization of capitalized development costs for accounting vs. immediate deduction for tax

- Write-down of inventories, investments, or tangible capital assets for accounting vs. loss recognized only when realized for tax

- Bond discount or premium, amortized for accounting vs. taxable expense or revenue only when the principal is settled at maturity

- Fair value increases for investment properties or biological assets vs. gain taxable only when property is sold

---

Part 4

ACCOUNTING FOR CORPORATE INCOME TAX
Extent of Allocation - Review

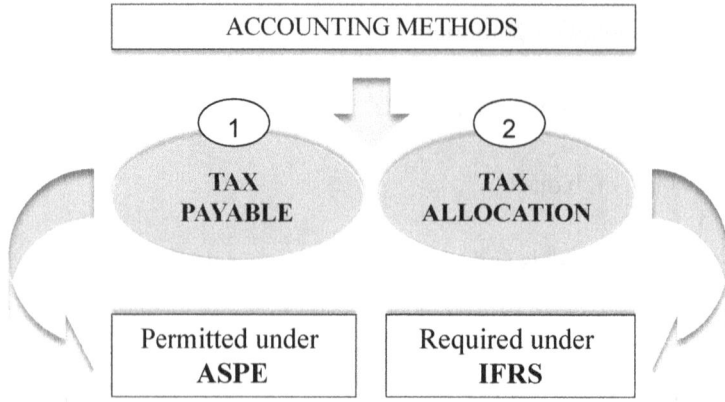

ACCOUNTING FOR CORPORATE INCOME TAX
Tax Payable Method - Review

(1)

Journal Entry

Income Tax Expense	XXX	
Income Tax Payable		XXX

Income Tax Expense = Current Income Tax Payable

ACCOUNTING FOR CORPORATE INCOME TAX
Tax Allocation Method - Review

(2)

Journal Entry

Income Tax Expense	XXX	
Deferred Income Tax	X X	
Income Tax Payable		XXX

Income Tax Expense = Income Tax Payable + Deferred Income Tax
(from temporary differences)

INCOME TAX ALLOCATION RELATED TO BUSINESS COMBINATIONS
Temporay Differences

Part 4

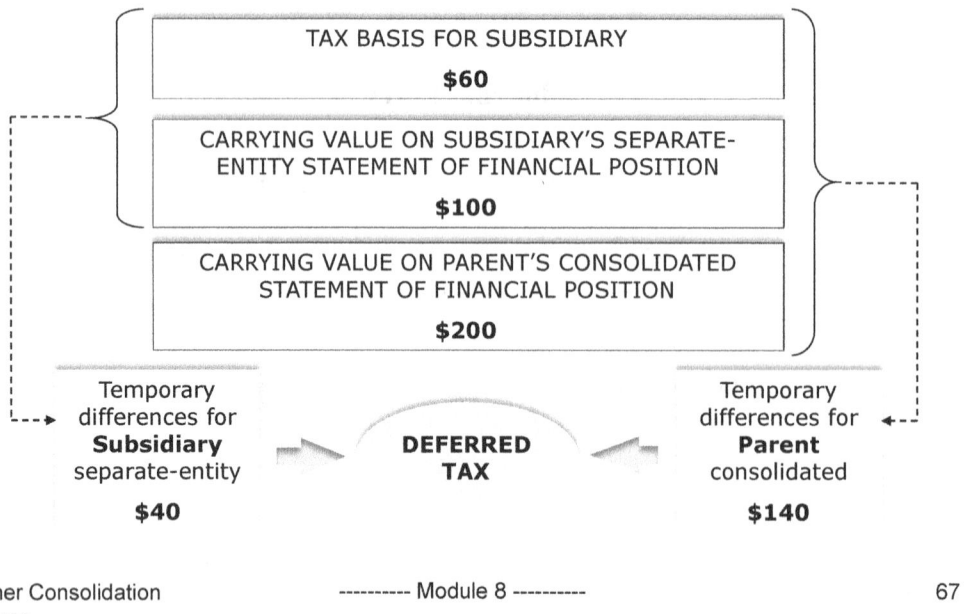

INCOME TAX ALLOCATION RELATED TO BUSINESS COMBINATIONS
If Tax Basis for Subsidiary Equals Carrying Values on Subsidiary's Separate-Entity Statement of Financial Position

Part 4

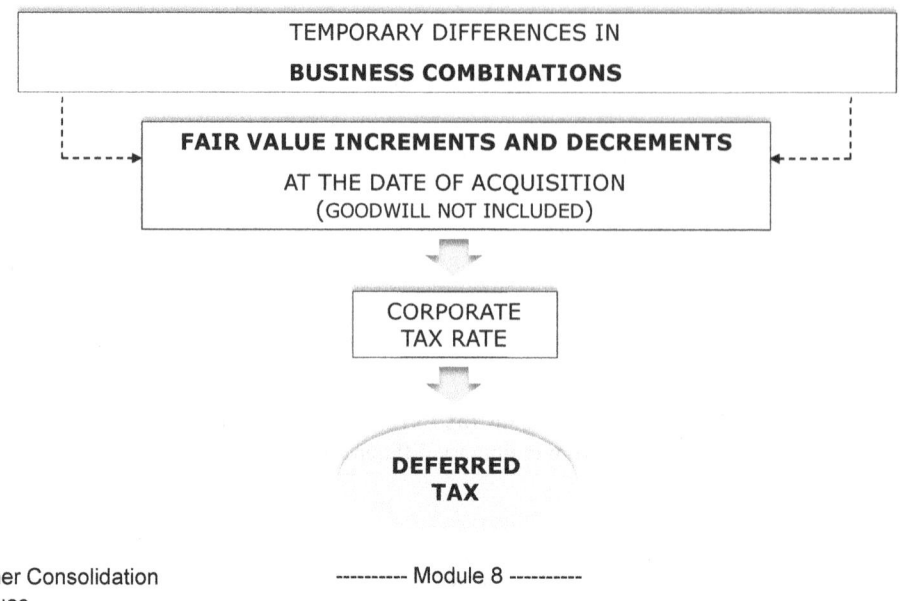

INCOME TAX ALLOCATION RELATED TO BUSINESS COMBINATIONS

Impact on the Consolidation: Date of Acquisition
Allocation of the Purchase Price Excluding Deferred Tax

- Purchase price $1,200,000

- Net book value of Subsidiary:
    - Common shares $200,000
    - Retained earnings   600,000   800,000

- Price differential   400,000

- Fair value increments:
    - Land   100,000
    - Buildings   200,000   (300,000)

- Goodwill $100,000

INCOME TAX ALLOCATION RELATED TO BUSINESS COMBINATIONS

Impact on the Consolidation: Date of Acquisition
Allocation of the Purchase Price, Including Deferred Tax (If Corporate Tax Rate = 20%)

- Purchase price $1,200,000

- Net book value of Subsidiary:
    - Common shares $200,000
    - Retained earnings   600,000   800,000

Price differential   400,000

- Fair value increments:
    - Land   100,000   **Tax rate 20%**
    - Buildings   200,000   (300,000)

Deferred Tax Liability   60,000

Goodwill $160,000

Part 4

INCOME TAX ALLOCATION RELATED TO BUSINESS COMBINATIONS
Impact on the Consolidation: Date of Acquisition
Consolidation Entry

1a — **Double-Counting of $800,000**
- Common Shares (Subsidiary) 200,000
- Retained Earnings (Subsidiary) 600,000
    - Investment in Subsidiary (Parent) 800,000

1b — **Price Differential of $400,000**
- Land (Subsidiary) 100,000
- Buildings (Subsidiary) 200,000
- Goodwill (Subsidiary) 160,000
    - Deferred Tax (Subsidiary) 60,000
    - Investment in Subsidiary (Parent) 400,000

Investment: $1,200,000

To establish the FV of Subsidiary at date of acquisition

Part 4

INCOME TAX ALLOCATION RELATED TO BUSINESS COMBINATIONS
Impact on the Consolidation: Post-Acquisition Periods
Taken from Module 7 (Full Goodwill)

Items	Price Differential Balance at Acquisition	Amortization Prior Years (X2-X4)	Amortization Current Year (X5)	Unamortized Excess at December 31, X5
Land	$100,000	$100,000		-
Buildings	200,000	60,000	20,000	$120,000
Total	$300,000	$160,000	$20,000	$120,000
Deferred Tax (20%)	$60,000	$32,000	$4,000	$24,000

Part 4
INCOME TAX ALLOCATION RELATED TO BUSINESS COMBINATIONS
Impact on the Consolidation: Post-Acquisition Period
Consolidation Adjustment

Amortization/Realization of Price Differential: Effect on Income Tax Allocation

Deferred Tax	36,000	
Income Tax Expense		4,000
Retained Earnings		32,000

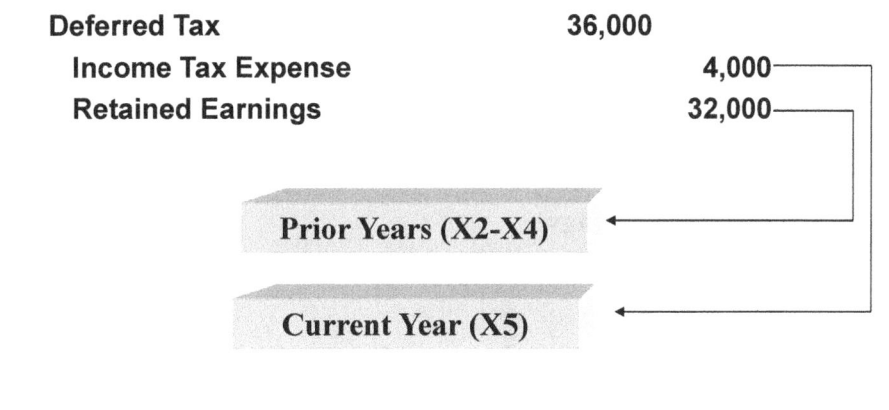

Prior Years (X2-X4)

Current Year (X5)

Other Consolidation Issues — Module 8 — 73

Part 4
INCOME TAX ALLOCATION RELATED TO INTERCOMPANY TRANSFERS
Temporary Differences

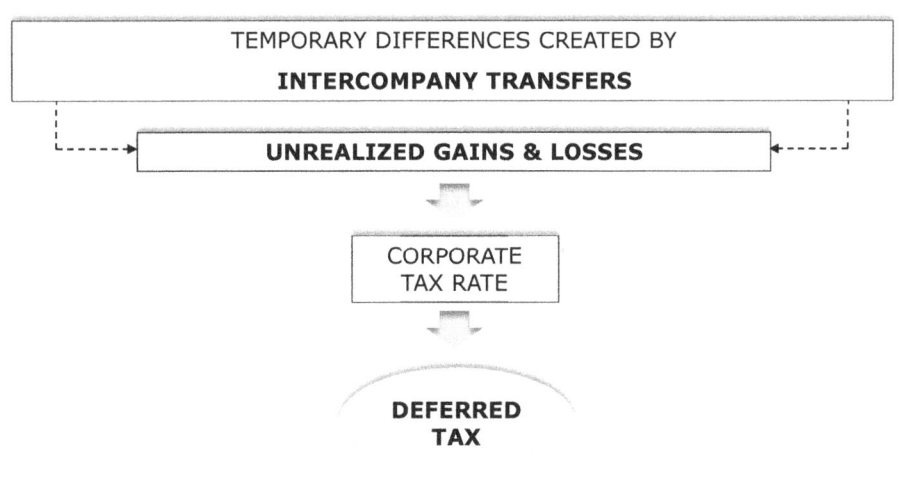

Other Consolidation Issues — Module 8 — 74

Part 4

INCOME TAX ALLOCATION RELATED TO INTERCOMPANY TRANSFERS
Consolidation Entries
Unrealized Gain

YEAR OF TRANSFER

Deferred Tax	XXX	
Income Tax Expense		XXX

YEAR SUBSEQUENT TO YEAR OF TRANSFER

Deferred Tax	XXX	
Retained Earnings		XXX

Part 4

INCOME TAX ALLOCATION RELATED TO INTERCOMPANY TRANSFERS
Consolidation Entries
Unrealized Gain Being Realized

YEAR OF TRANSFER

No adjustment required

YEAR SUBSEQUENT TO YEAR OF TRANSFER

Income Tax Expense	XXX	
Retained Earnings		XXX

Part 4

INCOME TAX ALLOCATION RELATED TO INTERCOMPANY TRANSFERS
Intercompany Sale of Inventory (1)
Taken from Module 7

Current-Year Downstream Sale of Inventory

Sales (Parent)	60,000	
Cost of Goods Sold (Parent)		55,500
Inventory (Subsidiary)		4,500

Tax

Deferred Tax	900	
Income Tax Expense		900

If corporate tax rate is 20%: ($4,500 ×20%) = $900

Part 4

INCOME TAX ALLOCATION RELATED TO INTERCOMPANY TRANSFERS
Intercompany Sale of Inventory (2)
Taken from Module 7

Realization of Prior-Year Profit on Downstream Sale of Inventory

Retained Earnings (Parent)	1,800	
Cost of Goods Sold		1,800

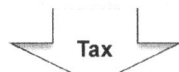
Tax

Income Tax Expense	360	
Retained Earnings		360

If corporate tax rate is 20%: ($1,800 ×20%) = $360

Part 4

INCOME TAX ALLOCATION RELATED TO INTERCOMPANY TRANSFERS
Intercompany Sale of Equipment
Taken from Module 7

Unrealized Portion of the Gain at the Beginning of X5

Retained Earnings (Parent & Sub.)	9,000	
Buildings & Equip. (net) (Parent)		9,000

Tax

Deferred Tax	**1,800**	
Retained Earnings		**1,800**

If corporate tax rate is 20%: ($9,000 ×20%) = $1,800

Part 4

INCOME TAX ALLOCATION RELATED TO INTERCOMPANY TRANSFERS
Intercompany Sale of Equipment
Taken from Module 7

Excess Depreciation of the Current Period

Buildings & Equip. (net) (Parent)	1,000	
Depreciation Expenses (Parent)		1,000

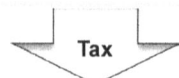
Tax

Income Tax Expense	**200**	
Deferred Tax		**200**

If corporate tax rate is 20%: ($1,000 ×20%) = $200

Part 4

INCOME TAX ALLOCATION RELATED TO INTERCOMPANY TRANSFERS
Impact on the Computation of NCI
Taken from Module 7 (Full Goodwill)

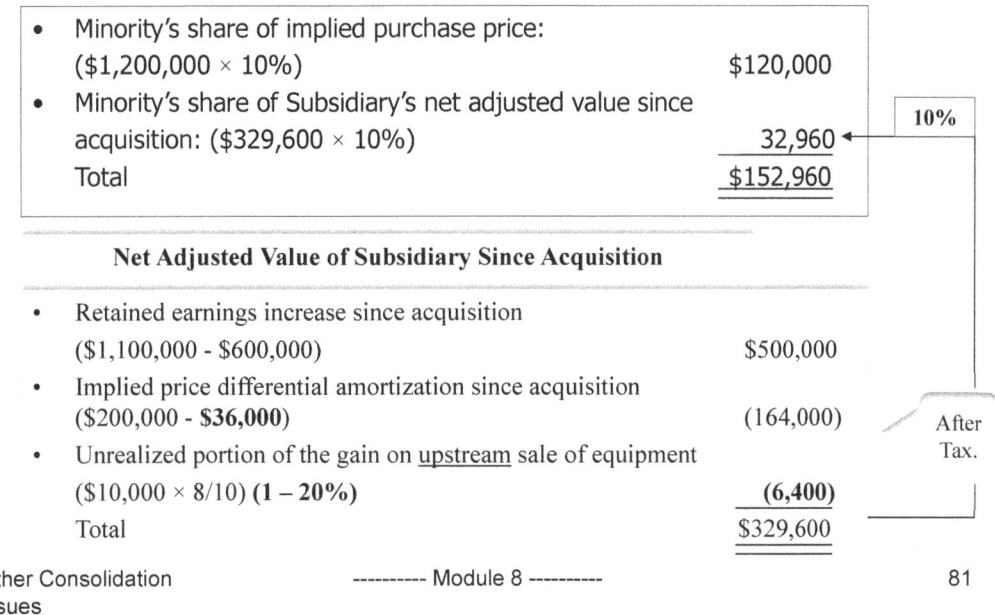

- Minority's share of implied purchase price:
  ($1,200,000 × 10%) $120,000
- Minority's share of Subsidiary's net adjusted value since acquisition: ($329,600 × 10%)   32,960
- Total $152,960

Net Adjusted Value of Subsidiary Since Acquisition

- Retained earnings increase since acquisition
  ($1,100,000 - $600,000) $500,000
- Implied price differential amortization since acquisition
  ($200,000 - **$36,000**)   (164,000)
- Unrealized portion of the gain on <u>upstream</u> sale of equipment
  ($10,000 × 8/10) **(1 – 20%)**   **(6,400)**
- Total $329,600

Part 4

INCOME TAX ALLOCATION RELATED TO INTERCOMPANY TRANSFERS
Impact on the Computation of Retained Earnings
Taken from Module 7

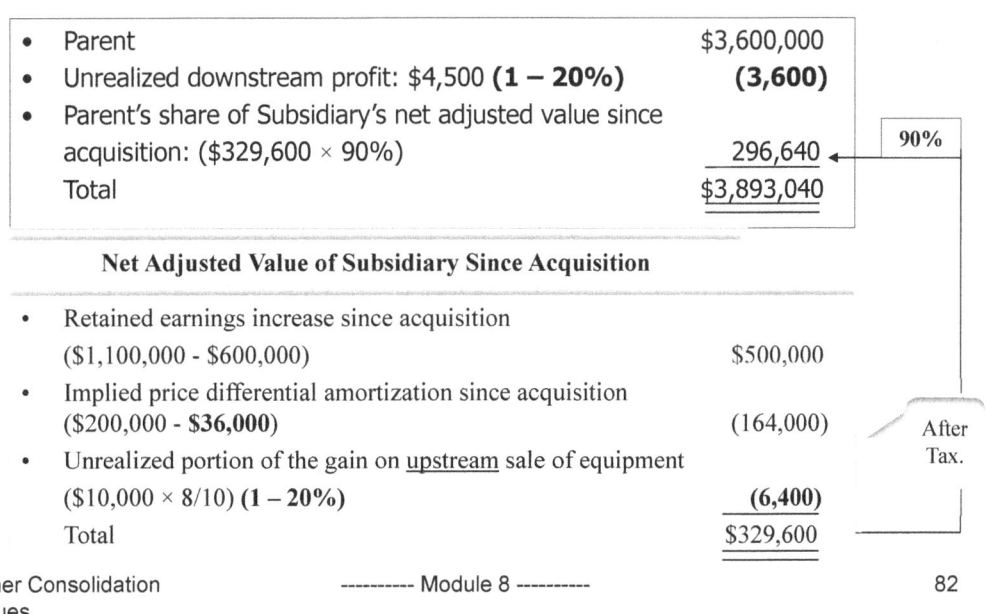

- Parent $3,600,000
- Unrealized downstream profit: $4,500 **(1 – 20%)**   **(3,600)**
- Parent's share of Subsidiary's net adjusted value since acquisition: ($329,600 × 90%)   296,640
- Total $3,893,040

Net Adjusted Value of Subsidiary Since Acquisition

- Retained earnings increase since acquisition
  ($1,100,000 - $600,000) $500,000
- Implied price differential amortization since acquisition
  ($200,000 - **$36,000**)   (164,000)
- Unrealized portion of the gain on <u>upstream</u> sale of equipment
  ($10,000 × 8/10) **(1 – 20%)**   **(6,400)**
- Total $329,600

Part 5

PART 5
PUSH-DOWN ACCOUNTING

This publication is protected by copyright, and permission should be obtained from the publisher prior to any prohibited reproduction, storage in a retrieval system, or transmission in any form or by any means, electronic, mechanical, photocopying, recording, or otherwise.

Copyright © 2020 Parmitech

Part 5

PUSH-DOWN ACCOUNTING
Definition

FAIR VALUES CAN BE 'PUSHED DOWN' TO THE ACQUIREE'S BOOKS IF ALL OR VIRTUALLY ALL OF THE EQUITY INTERESTS (90% AND MORE) HAVE BEEN ACQUIRED.

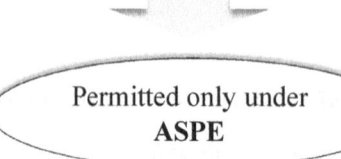

Permitted only under **ASPE**

If the condition above is met (acquisition of 90% and more of the stocks), the acquiree has the choice to report all its assets and liabilities using fair values at the date of acquisition (change from BV to FV on the acquiree's records). Applying push-down accounting will somewhat simplify the consolidation accounting process in post-acquisition periods because no adjustments will be required for price differential.

Other Consolidation Issues ---------- Module 8 ---------- 84

PUSH-DOWN ACCOUNTING
Illustration - Taken from Module 3

Part 5

On December 31, X1, Parent Company acquires all the outstanding voting shares of Subsidiary by issuing 40,000 shares with a market value of $30, or $1,200,000 total, in exchange. At the date of combination, the fair values of Subsidiary's land and buildings exceeded their book values by $100,000 and $200,000, respectively.

The fair values of all of Subsidiary's other assets and liabilities were equal to their book values. Subsidiary had common shares of $200,000 and retained earnings of $600,000 at the date of acquisition. The remaining useful life of the buildings from the date of acquisition is ten years. Subsidiary uses the straight-line method to calculate amortizations.

Particularity:

Subsidiary, a private company, elects to revalue all its assets and liabilities using fair values at the date of acquisition.

PUSH-DOWN ACCOUNTING
Illustration - Allocation of the Purchase Price

Part 5

Purchase price			$1,200,000
Net book value of Subsidiary:			
- Common shares	$200,000		
- Retained earnings	600,000	800,000	
Price differential		400,000	
Fair value increments:			
- Land	100,000		
- Buildings	200,000	(300,000)	
Goodwill		$100,000	

Revaluation Capital. (brace around Common shares and Retained earnings)

Fair value increments and Goodwill: *Pushed down to Subsidiary's books*

Part 5

ILLUSTRATION OF PUSH-DOWN ACCOUNTING
Journal Entry on the Books of Subsidiary

Price Differential of $400,000

Land	100,000	
Buildings	200,000	
Goodwill	100,000	
Revaluation Capital		400,000

Price Differential
Reported in the Equity section of Subsidiary

This journal entry is reported by Subsidiary if the latter elects to apply push-down accounting. Push-down accounting revalues assets to reflect FV at the date of combination. Consequently, Subsidiary will amortize Buildings based on the FV and will consider any goodwill impairment on its own records.

Other Consolidation Issues   ---------- Module 8 ----------

Part 5

ILLUSTRATION OF PUSH-DOWN ACCOUNTING
Consolidation Entry at Date of Acquisition and Subsequent to Date of Acquisition

Elimination of the Investment Account

Common Shares (Subsidiary)	200,000	
Retained Earnings (Subsidiary)	600,000	
☆ Revaluation Capital (Subsidiary)	400,000	
Investment in Subsidiary (Parent)		1,200,000

No additional consolidation entry is necessary to account for price differential amortization/realization in post-acquisition periods since this aspect has been taken care of by Subsidiary on its own records.

Other Consolidation Issues   ---------- Module 8 ----------

Part 6

PART 6
CONTINGENT CONSIDERATION

This publication is protected by copyright, and permission should be obtained from the publisher prior to any prohibited reproduction, storage in a retrieval system, or transmission in any form or by any means, electronic, mechanical, photocopying, recording, or otherwise.

Copyright © 2020 Parmitech

Part 6

TYPES OF CONTINGENT CONSIDERATION

1
BASED ON CONDITIONS

- CONTINGENCIES BASED ON **EARNINGS**.
- CONTINGENCIES BASED ON GUARANTIES OF FUTURE **SECURITY PRICES**.
- CONTINGENCIES BASED ON THE **OUTCOME OF A LAW SUIT**.

2
BASED ON CONSIDERATIONS

- **Contingency classified as a liability**

When the contingent consideration will be paid in the form of cash or another asset.

- **Contingency classified as equity**

When the contingent consideration will be paid by issuing additional shares.

Part 6

CONTINGENCIES BASED ON CONDITIONS
Earnings versus Share Prices

EARNINGS

It is not uncommon for the owners of an acquiree to make the argument that the enterprise is really worth more than is being offered by the acquirer, and that the earnings of some future periods will support this contention. A way of dealing with this possibility is for the acquirer to agree to pay additional consideration should the acquiree's belief about the future earnings prove to be correct.

SECURITY PRICES

When shares are used as consideration in a business combination transaction, the acquirer is likely to be making the argument that the shares being offered are worth more than their current value, and that this view will be supported by some future market price for the stock. In this case, the acquirer may agree to pay additional amounts or issue additional shares if the market value of the shares does not reach a certain price at some future point in time.

Part 6

ACCOUNTING FOR CONTINGENT CONSIDERATION
At the Date of Acquisition

GENERAL APPROACH

IFRS require that contingent consideration be recognized when it is probable that it will be paid and can be reliably measured.

WHEN CONSIDERATION IS RECORDED

Contingency is considered as part of the purchase price.

ACCOUNTING FOR CONTINGENT CONSIDERATION
After the Date of Acquisition

Part 6

CONTINGENCY CLASSIFIED AS LIABILITY

Any consideration issued at some future date is recorded at fair value, and the change in fair value is recognized in net income.

CONTINGENCY CLASSIFIED AS EQUITY

Any consideration issued at some future date is recorded at fair value, and the change in fair value is reported as adjustments to equity (no impact on net income)

CONTINGENT CONSIDERATION CLASSIFIED AS A LIABILITY
Illustration - Taken from Module 3

Part 6

On December 31, X1, Parent Company acquires all the outstanding voting shares of Subsidiary by issuing 40,000 shares with a market value of $30, or $1,200,000 total, in exchange. At the date of combination, the fair values of Subsidiary's land and buildings exceeded their book values by $100,000 and $200,000, respectively.

The fair values of all of Subsidiary's other assets and liabilities were equal to their book values. Subsidiary had common shares of $200,000 and retained earnings of $600,000 at the date of acquisition. The remaining useful life of the buildings from the date of acquisition is ten years. Subsidiary uses the straight-line method to calculate amortizations.

Condition:

Parent also agreed to pay an additional $150,000 to the former shareholders of Subsidiary if the average post-acquisition earnings over the next two years equaled or exceeded $800,000.

At the date of acquisition, assume that the above condition is expected to be met.

CONTINGENT CONSIDERATION CLASSIFIED AS A LIABILITY
Illustration - On the Books of Parent

Part 6

Investment in Subsidiary	1,350,000	
Common Shares		1,200,000
Liability for Contingent Consideration		150,000

The contingency ($150,000) is considered as part of the purchase price because it is probable that it will be paid and can be reliably measured.

Other Consolidation Issues   ---------- Module 8 ----------   95

CONTINGENT CONSIDERATION CLASSIFIED AS A LIABILITY
Illustration - Allocation of the Purchase Price

Part 6

- Purchase price:
  - ① - Purchase price $ 1,200,000
  - ② - Contingent consideration   150,000
  -      1,350,000

  Contingent consideration is added to the purchase price

- Net book value of Subsidiary:
  - Common shares $200,000
  - Retained earnings   600,000   800,000

- Price differential   550,000

- Fair value increments:
  - Land   100,000
  - Buildings   200,000   300,000

- Goodwill $250,000

Increases Goodwill

Other Consolidation Issues   ---------- Module 8 ----------   96

Part 6
CONTINGENT CONSIDERATION CLASSIFIED AS A LIABILITY
Illustration - Consolidation Entry at Acquisition

Double-Counting of $800,000		
Common Shares (Subsidiary)	200,000	
Retained Earnings (Subsidiary)		600,000
Investment in Subsidiary (Parent)		800,000

Price Differential of $400,000		
Land (Subsidiary)	100,000	
Buildings (Subsidiary)	200,000	
Goodwill (Subsidiary)	250,000	
Investment in Subsidiary (Parent)		550,000

Investment: $1,350,000

To establish the FV of Subsidiary at date of acquisition

Part 6
CONTINGENT CONSIDERATION CLASSIFIED AS A LIABILITY
Illustration - On the Books of Parent - If Purchase of Net Assets

Cash and Receivables	200,000	
Inventory	50,000	
Land	400,000	
Buildings	550,000	
Goodwill	250,000	
Accounts Payable		100,000
Common Shares		1,200,000
Liability for Contingent Consideration		150,000

CONTINGENT CONSIDERATION CLASSIFIED AS A LIABILITY
Illustration - Post-Acquisition

Part 6

The Target is met

Liability for Contingent Con.	150,000	
Cash		150,000

The Target is NOT met

Liability for Contingent Con.	150,000	
Other Income		150,000

Change in fair value of contingency is recognized in the profit for the year.

CONTINGENT CONSIDERATION CLASSIFIED AS EQUITY
At the Date of Acquisition

Part 6

At the date of acquisition, no additional entry is required.

The acquisition is recorded based on the current market value of Parent's common stock.

Part 6

CONTINGENT CONSIDERATION CLASSIFIED AS EQUITY
After the Date of Acquisition

The Target is met
No entry required

The Target is NOT met		
Common Shares (old)	XXX	
Common Shares (new shares)		XXX

Change in fair value of contingency has no impact on the profit for the year. New shares are issued to compensate for the loss in value for shares initially issued.

Other Consolidation Issues ---------- Module 8 ---------- 101

Part 7

PART 7
INTERIM ACQUISITIONS

This publication is protected by copyright, and permission should be obtained from the publisher prior to any prohibited reproduction, storage in a retrieval system, or transmission in any form or by any means, electronic, mechanical, photocopying, recording, or otherwise.

Copyright © 2020 Parmitech

Part 7

INTERIM ACQUISITIONS
Presentation of the Subsidiary's revenues and expenses in the consolidated income statement in the year of acquisition

GENERAL APPROACH

Revenues and expenses of the acquired company are included with those of the acquiring company only from the date of acquisition forward.

ALTERNATIVES

Full-year reporting

This approach consists of including the subsidiary's revenues and expenses in the consolidated statement for the entire year. Then, a deduction is needed at the bottom of the consolidated income statement for the applicable pre-acquisition earnings.

Partial-year reporting

This approach consists of including the subsidiary's revenues and expenses in the consolidated statement only from the date of acquisition. To accomplish this, Subsidiary must close the books on the date of acquisition so that pre-acquisition income is closed to retained earnings.

Part 8

PART 8
SUBSIDIARY WITH PREFERRED SHARES

This publication is protected by copyright, and permission should be obtained from the publisher prior to any prohibited reproduction, storage in a retrieval system, or transmission in any form or by any means, electronic, mechanical, photocopying, recording, or otherwise.

Copyright © 2020 Parmitech

SUBSIDIARY WITH PREFERRED SHARES
Illustration - Taken from Module 3

On December 31, X1, Parent Company acquires all the outstanding voting shares of Subsidiary by issuing 40,000 shares with a market value of $30, or $1,200,000 total, in exchange. At the date of combination, the fair values of Subsidiary's land and buildings exceeded their book values by $100,000 and $200,000, respectively.

The fair values of all of Subsidiary's other assets and liabilities were equal to their book values. Subsidiary had common shares of $200,000 and:

1,000 non-cumulative / non-participating preferred shares of $50,000 ($10 dividends).

Retained earnings amount to $600,000 at the date of acquisition. The remaining useful life of the buildings from the date of acquisition is ten years. Subsidiary uses the straight-line method to calculate amortizations.

ALLOCATION OF PURCHASE PRICE
No Dividends in Arrears at the Date of Acquisition

Purchase price		$1,200,000	
Net book value of Subsidiary:			
- Common shares	$200,000		
- Retained earnings	600,000	800,000	
Price differential		400,000	
Fair value increments:			
- Land	100,000		
- Buildings	200,000	300,000	
Goodwill		$100,000	

The BV of preferred shares is not included in the allocation but assigned to NCI instead

Part 8
CONSOLIDATION ENTRY AT THE DATE OF ACQUISITION
No Dividends in Arrears at the Date of Acquisition
Non-Controlling Interest

Book Value of Preferred Shares Assigned to NCI

Preferred Shares (Subsidiary)	50,000	
Non-Controlling Interest		50,000

Part 8
ALLOCATION OF PURCHASE PRICE
If Dividends in Arrears of $20,000 at the Date of Acquisition

Purchase price		$1,200,000
Net book value of Subsidiary:		
- Common shares	$200,000	
- Retained earnings	600,000	
- Dividends in arrears	(20,000)	780,000
Price differential		420,000
Fair value increments:		
- Land	100,000	
- Buildings	200,000	300,000
Goodwill		$120,000

The BV of preferred shares as well as dividends in arrears are assigned to NCI

Part 8

CONSOLIDATION ENTRY AT THE DATE OF ACQUISITION
If Dividends in Arrears of 20,000$ at the Date of Acquisition
Non-Controlling Interest

BV of Preferred Shares ($50,000) and Dividends in Arrears ($20,000) are Assigned to NCI

Preferred Shares (Subsidiary)	70,000	
Non-Controlling Interest		70,000

Foreign Currency Transactions and Hedging Activities

Module 9

What you will find in this section

- How to Walk Through Module 9
- Slides
- Exercises and Solutions

Module 9
Foreign Currency Transactions and Hedging Activities

How to Walk Through Module 9

◇ <u>Readings</u>

1- <u>Student Manual</u> "Advanced Accounting": Module 9
   PART 1: ACCOUNTING FOR FOREIGN CURRENCY TRANSACTIONS
   PART 2: HEDGING ACTIVITIES USING A FORWARD CONTRACT
   PART 3: HEDGE ACCOUNTING

◇ <u>Assignments</u>

2- <u>Student Manual</u>: End-of module quiz questions
3- <u>Student Manual</u>: Exercises 1 to 6

◇ <u>Additional readings</u>

5- <u>IAS</u> 21, <u>IFRS</u> 9, <u>IFRIC</u> 22

When you have successfully completed this module, you will be able to do the following:

- Describe the general approach to accounting for transactions conducted in a foreign currency;

- Describe the general practice of hedging;

- Account for forward contracts;

- Define and describe hedge accounting.

FOREIGN CURRENCY TRANSACTIONS AND HEDGING ACTIVITIES
Module 9

Copyright © 2020 Parmitech

Advanced Accounting: Student Manual

Copyrighted Material

Editor: Parmitech

This publication is protected by copyright, and permission should be obtained from the publisher prior to any prohibited reproduction, storage in a retrieval system, or transmission in any form or by any means, electronic, mechanical, photocopying, recording, or otherwise.

Corresponding Author

Richard Bozec Ph.D., CPA, CGA
bozec@telfer.uottawa.ca

Copyright © Parmitech

TEACHING MATERIAL
Electronic Sources

IFRS

IAS 21 — The Effects of Changes in Foreign Exchange Rates

IFRS 9 — Financial Instruments
Chapter 6: Hedge Accounting

IFRIC 22 — Foreign Currency Transactions and Advance Consideration

---

TEACHING MATERIAL
Exercises

Module 9

- 9.1 Loan in US Dollar
- 9.2 Receivables in Pounds Sterling
- 9.3 Receivables in Pesos
- 9.4 Monetary Balances in Euros
- 9.5 Forward Contract to Hedge a Liability
- 9.6 Forward Contract to Hedge a Receivable

OUTLINE OF THE PRESENTATIOIN

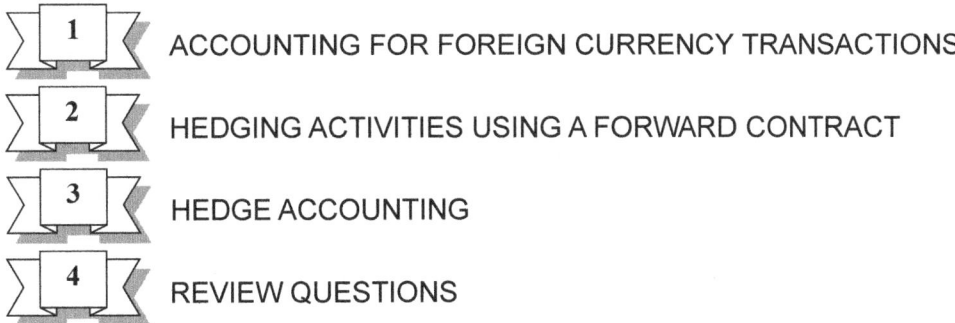

1. ACCOUNTING FOR FOREIGN CURRENCY TRANSACTIONS
2. HEDGING ACTIVITIES USING A FORWARD CONTRACT
3. HEDGE ACCOUNTING
4. REVIEW QUESTIONS

Part 1

PART 1

Accounting for Foreign Currency Transactions

Objectives of this section

Illustrate the general approach to accounting for transactions conducted in a foreign currency.

Illustrate the accounting for exchange gains and losses when balances are translated at different rates at different points in time.

Illustrate the accounting for different types of financial assets: monetary, held to maturity, available for sale, and held for trading.

Key concepts

- Foreign currency transactions
- Exchange gains and losses
- Exchange rate / Spot rate
- Direct exchange rate
- Functional Currency

INTERNATIONAL ACTIVITIES
Continuum

Part 1

TRANSACTIONS
IN FOREIGN CURRENCIES

Module 9

Module 10

FOREIGN-BASED SUBSIDIARIES or BRANCHES

Transborder transactions are very common, accounting for about 40% of Canada's GDP. Over 80% of those transactions are with the US. Indeed, Canada and the US share the longest unprotected border in the world.

FOREIGN CURRENCY TRANSACTIONS
Definition

Part 1

General Definition

TRANSACTIONS DENOMINATED IN A CURRENCY OTHER THAN THE ENTITY'S **FUNCTIONAL CURRENCY**.

Functional Currency

CURRENCY OF THE PRIMARY ECONOMIC ENVIRONMENT IN WHICH THE ENTITY OPERATES, USUALLY THE COUNTRY IN WHICH THE ENTITY IS LOCATED.

The objective of IAS 21 *The Effects of Changes in Foreign Exchange Rates* is to prescribe how to include foreign currency transactions and foreign operations in the financial statements of an entity and how to translate financial statements into a presentation currency. The principal issues are which exchange rate(s) to use and how to report the effects of changes in exchange rates in the financial statements.

Part 1

FUNCTIONAL CURRENCY
Indicators

Primary Indicators

- **SALES AND CASH INFLOWS**
  - Currency in which sales prices for goods and services are denominated and settled.
  - Competitive forces.

- **EXPENSES AND CASH OUTFLOWS**
  - Currency that mainly influences labor, materials and other costs.

Secondary Indicators

- **FINANCING ACTIVITIES**
  - Currency in which funds from financing activities are generated.

- **RETENTION OF OPERATING INCOME**

Part 1

FUNCTIONAL CURRENCY
Additional Indicators for Foreign Operations

1. DEGREE OF AUTONOMY
2. FREQUENCY OF TRANSACTIONS WITH REPORTING ENTITY
3. CASH FLOW IMPACT ON REPORTING ENTITY
4. FINANCING

It is possible for an entity to have two and more foreign operations in a given country and determine different functional currency for those entities.

Part 1

FUNCTIONAL CURRENCY
Illustration 1

A Canadian entity has a subsidiary in the United States. This subsidiary is linked closely with the Canadian parent: its funding comes from the parent, most of its sales are to the parent, and the sales prices are driven by the Canadian dollar. Even though the subsidiary is located in the US and has financial statements denominated in US dollars, its functional currency will be deemed to be the Canadian dollar.

Therefore, the subsidiary will consider that all the transactions it does in US dollars are *foreign currency transactions*. Therefore, when translating them in Canadian dollars (its functional currency), the subsidiary will be in fact translating foreign currency transactions. Conceptually, this translation process will be performed at the subsidiary level, not at the parent's level.

Part 1

FUNCTIONAL CURRENCY
Illustration 2

A real estate entity operates in Russia. It owns several office buildings in Moscow and St Petersburg that are rented to Russian and foreign companies. All lease contracts are denominated in US dollars, but payments can be made either in US dollars or in Russian rubles. However, the majority of the lease payments are settled in rubles. This has been the historical pattern of payment.

On first analysis, the "sales and cash inflows" indicators appear to produce a mixed response, because the currency that mainly influences the pricing of the lease contracts is the US dollar, whereas the cash inflows are in rubles. In addition, cash outflows such as the principal operating costs, management of properties, insurance, taxes and staff costs are likely to be incurred and settled in rubles, which would indicate that the functional currency is the Russian ruble. Although the lease payments are denominated in US dollars, the US dollar is not considered to be significant to the entity's operation.

FUNCTIONAL CURRENCY
Illustration 2 (continued)

It follows that it is the currency of the Russian economy, rather than the currency in which the lease contracts are denominated, that most faithfully represents the economic effects of the real estate activity in Russia.

FUNCTIONAL CURRENCY
Illustration 3

Entity A operates an oil refinery in Saudi Arabia. All of the entity's income is denominated and settled in US dollars. The oil price is subject to the worldwide supply and demand, and crude oil is traded routinely in US dollars around the world. Around 45% of entity A's cash costs are imports or expatriate salaries denominated in US dollars. The remaining 55% of cash expenses are incurred in Saudi Arabia and denominated and settled in riyal. The non-cash costs (depreciation) are US dollar denominated since the initial investment was in US dollars.

In this case, the functional currency of entity A is the US dollar. The crude oil sales prices are influenced by global demand and supply. Crude oil is traded globally in US dollars. The revenue analysis clearly points to the US dollar. The cost analysis is mixed.

FUNCTIONAL CURRENCY
Illustration 3 (continued)

Depreciation (or any other non-cash expenses) is not considered, because the primary economic environment is where the entity generates and expends cash. Operating cash expenses are influenced by the riyal (55%) and the US dollar (45%). Management is able to determine the functional currency as the US dollar, because the revenue is clearly influenced by the US dollar and expenses are mixed.

DETERMINATION OF EXCHANGE RATES

Economic Factors

Exchange rates change because of a number of economic factors affecting the supply and demand of a nation's currency. These economic factors include the following:

- INFLATION
- INTEREST RATE
- INVESTMENT LEVELS
- STABILITY AND PROCESS OF GOVERNANCE
- BALANCE OF PAYMENTS

Direct Exchange Rate

Refers to the number of local currency units needed to acquire one foreign currency unit.

Part 1

ACCOUNTING FOR TRANSACTIONS IN FOREIGN CURRENCIES
If the Functional Currency is the Canadian Dollar

Initial Recognition

CANADIAN FOREIGN CURRENCY TRANSACTIONS MUST BE TRANSLATED INTO THE EQUIVALENT AMOUNT IN CANADIAN DOLLARS AT THE DATE OF THE TRANSACTION.

Subsequent Measurement

- ANY **MONETARY** AND **CURRENT-VALUED** BALANCES REPORTED AT THE END OF THE YEAR MUST BE REPORTED AT CURRENT RATE (SPOT RATE).
- FOREIGN CURRENCY GAINS OR LOSSES ARE RECOGNIZED IN PROFIT OR LOSS.
- EXCEPTION FOR EQUITY INSTRUMENTS USING OCI ELECTION: FOREIGN CURRENCY GAINS OR LOSSES MUST BE TAKEN TO OCI (WITH FAIR VALUE CHANGE)

Part 1

ACCOUNTING FOR TRANSACTIONS IN FOREIGN CURRENCIES
Monetary vs. Non-Monetary Items

The essential feature of a **monetary item** is a right to receive (or an obligation to deliver) a fixed or determinable number of units of currency. Examples include: pensions and other employee benefits to be paid in cash; provisions that are to be settled in cash; and cash dividends that are recognized as a liability.

Conversely, the essential feature of a **non-monetary item** is the absence of a right to receive (or an obligation to deliver) a fixed or determinable number of units of currency. Examples include: intangible assets; inventories; property, plant and equipment; and provisions that are to be settled by the delivery of a non-monetary asset.

Part 1

ACCOUNTING FOR TRANSACTIONS IN FOREIGN CURRENCIES
Use of an Average Rate

The Standard permits the use of an average rate for a period for recording foreign currency transactions as a proxy to the actual rate prevailing at the date of each transaction, provided that there is no significant change in rates during the period.

An average rate is unlikely to be applied by companies undertaking few transactions in a foreign currency. It is also unlikely to be used for translating large, one-off transactions that would be recorded at the actual rate.

The flexibility allowed in IAS 21 is likely to be most beneficial to companies that enter into a large number of transactions in different currencies, or that maintain multi-currency ledgers. However, no guidance is provided in the Standard as to how such a rate should be determined.

Part 1

FINANCIAL ASSETS AND LIABILITIES
Recall - IFRS 9

Financial Instrument - Definition

ANY CONTRACT THAT GIVES RISE TO A FINANCIAL ASSET OF ONE PARTY AND A FINANCIAL LIABILITY OR EQUITY OF ANOTHER PARTY

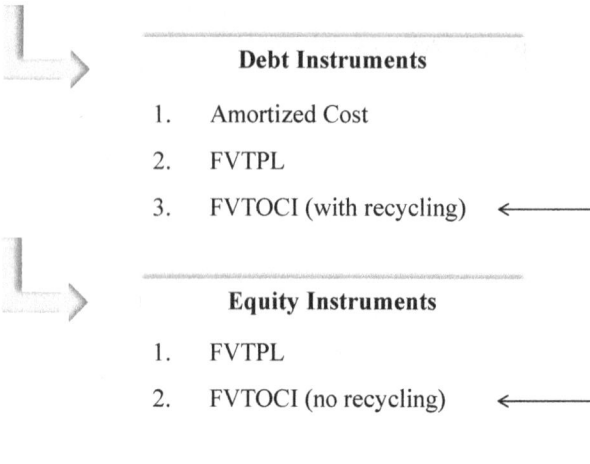

Debt Instruments
1. Amortized Cost
2. FVTPL
3. FVTOCI (with recycling)

Equity Instruments
1. FVTPL
2. FVTOCI (no recycling)

Part 1
ACCOUNTING FOR TRANSACTIONS IN FOREIGN CURRENCIES
Overview of the Illustrations Covered Next

Illustration 1 Foreign Currency-Denominated Receivables

  CASE 1 Collection in the year of transaction
  CASE 2 Collection in the year subsequent to the year of transaction

Illustration 2 Foreign Currency-Denominated Bonds

  CASE 1 Amortized Cost
  CASE 2 Fair Value Through Profit or Loss (FVTPL)
  CASE 3 Fair Value Through OCI (FVTOCI)

Illustration 3 Foreign Currency-Denominated Equity Investment

  CASE 1 Fair Value Through Profit or Loss (FVTPL)
  CASE 2 Fair Value Through OCI (FVTOCI)

Part 1
ACCOUNTING FOR TRANSACTIONS IN FOREIGN CURRENCIES
Illustration 1
Foreign Currency-Denominated Receivables

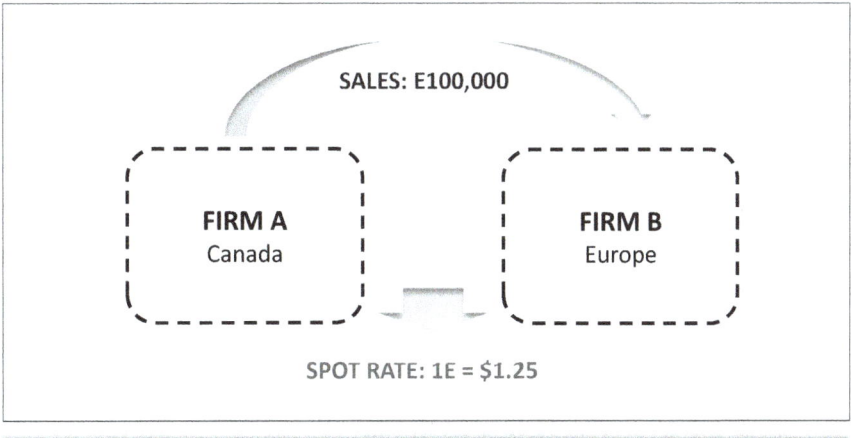

The functional currency for Firm A is the Canadian dollar

Part 1

FOREIGN CURRENCY-DENOMINATED RECEIVABLES
Journal Entry at the Transaction Date

Accounts Receivable	125,000	
Sales		125,000

(E100,000 × 1.25) = $125,000

Accounts Receivable is a monetary balance. Since the settlement is not immediate, and the transaction is stated in Euro, the Canadian firm bears the foreign exchange currency risk. In this case, the risk is for Firm A to receive less than $125,000 at the date of settlement if the Euro decreases in value.

Part 1

FOREIGN CURRENCY-DENOMINATED RECEIVABLES
Case #1: Collection in the Year of Transaction

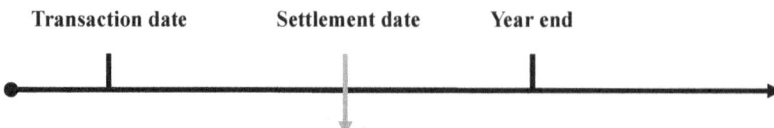

- IF 1E = $1.20

Cash	120,000	
Foreign Currency Exchange Loss	5,000	
Accounts Receivable		125,000

- IF 1E = $1.30

Cash	130,000	
Foreign Currency Exchange Gain		5,000
Accounts Receivable		125,000

Part 1

FOREIGN CURRENCY-DENOMINATED RECEIVABLES
Case #2: Collection in the Year Subsequent to Year of Transaction
Year End

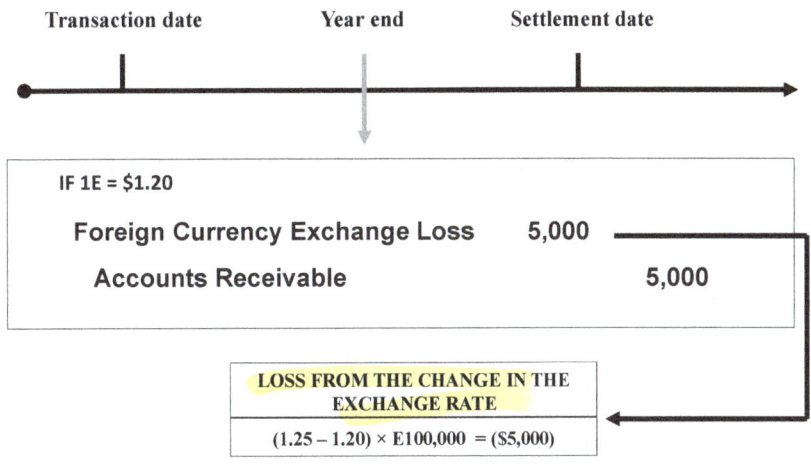

Part 1

FOREIGN CURRENCY-DENOMINATED RECEIVABLES
Case #2: Collection in the Year Subsequent to Year of Transaction
Settlement Date

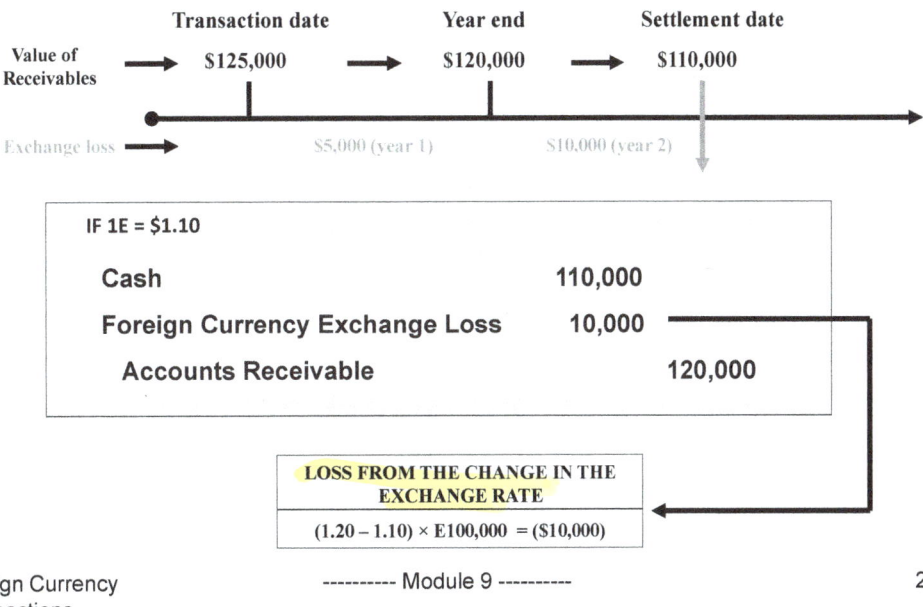

Part 1

ACCOUNTING FOR TRANSACTIONS IN FOREIGN CURRENCIES
Illustration 2
Foreign Currency-Denominated Bonds

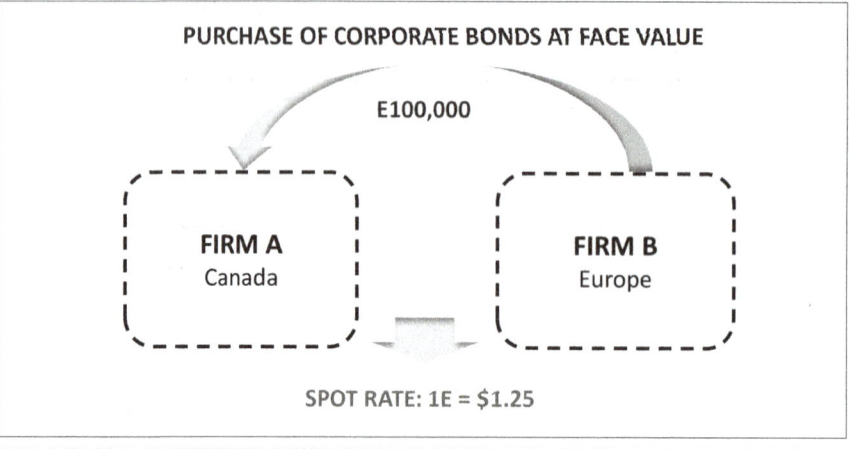

The functional currency for Firm A is the Canadian dollar

Part 1

FOREIGN CURRENCY-DENOMINATED BONDS
Journal Entry at the Transaction Date

Investment in European Bonds	125,000	
Cash		125,000

(E100,000 × 1.25) = $125,000

Potential Designations

1. Amortized Cost
2. FVTPL
3. FVTOCI (with recycling)

FOREIGN CURRENCY-DENOMINATED BONDS
Case #1: Amortized Cost
Year End

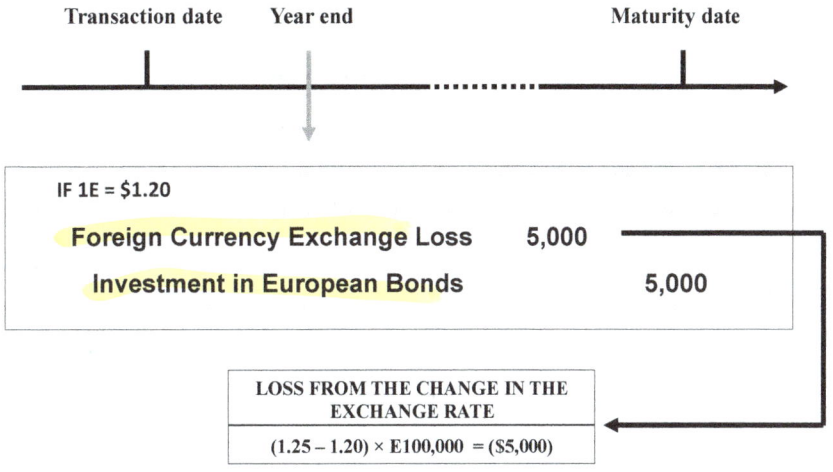

FOREIGN CURRENCY-DENOMINATED BONDS
Case #1: Amortized Cost
Date of Sale

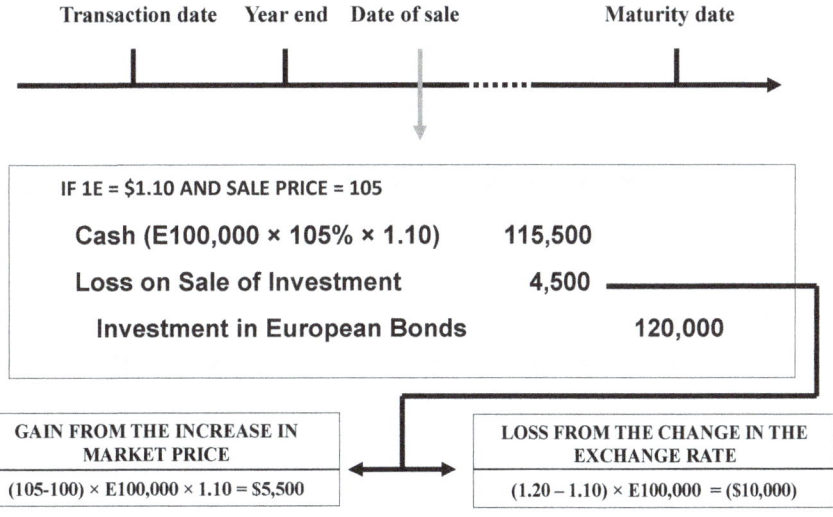

Part 1

FOREIGN CURRENCY-DENOMINATED BONDS
Case #2: The Bonds are Designated at Fair Value Through Profit or Loss
Year End

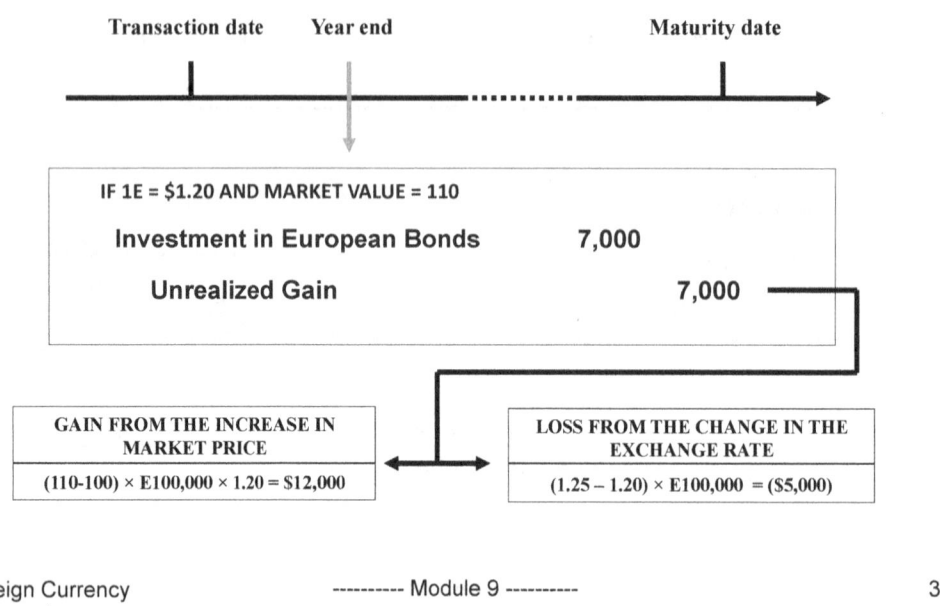

Part 1

FOREIGN CURRENCY-DENOMINATED BONDS
Case #2: The Bonds are Designated at Fair Value Through Profit or Loss
Date of Sale

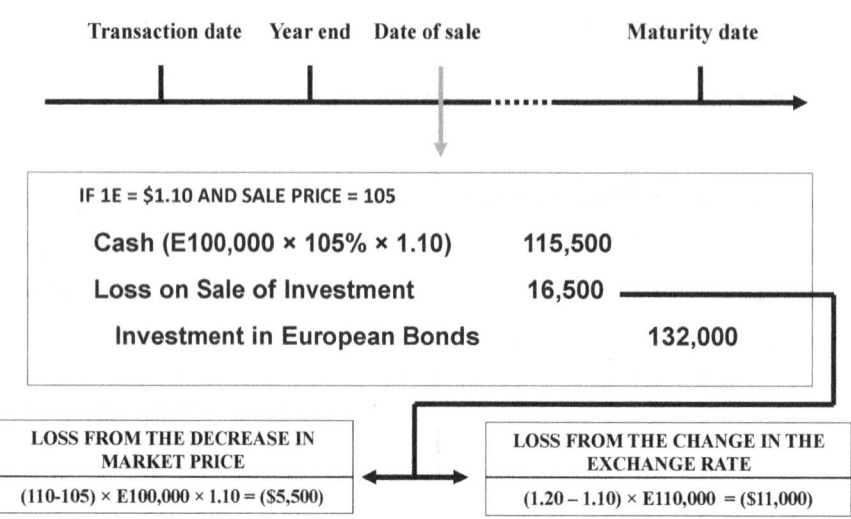

Part 1
FOREIGN CURRENCY-DENOMINATED BONDS
Case #3: The Bonds are Designated at FV Through OCI (with recycling)
Year End

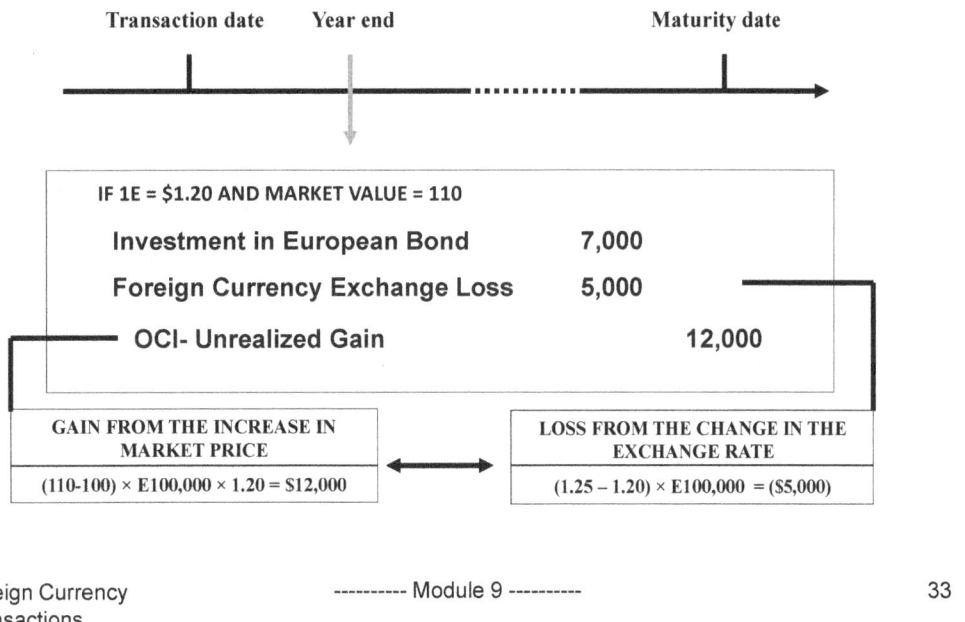

Part 1
FOREIGN CURRENCY-DENOMINATED BONDS
Case #3: The Bonds are Designated at FV Through OCI (with recycling)
Date of Sale

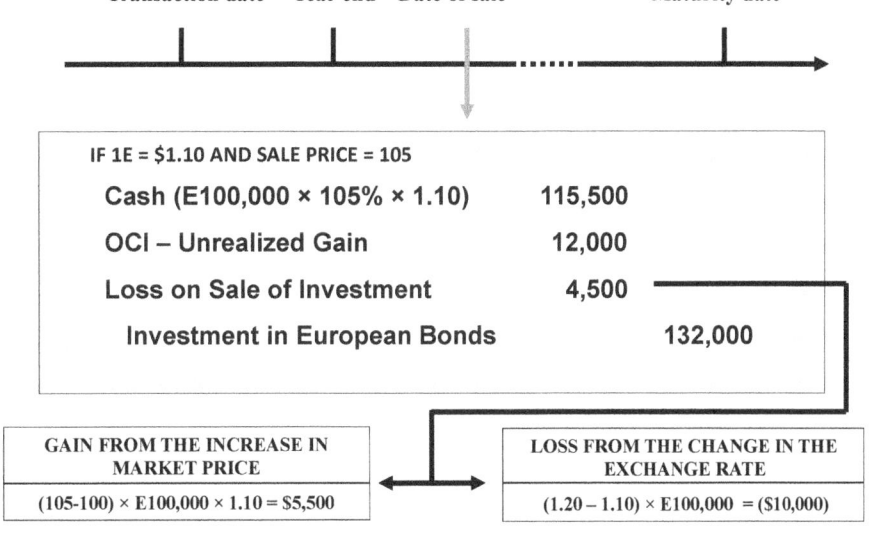

Part 1
ACCOUNTING FOR TRANSACTIONS IN FOREIGN CURRENCIES
Illustration 3
Foreign Currency-Denominated Equity Investment

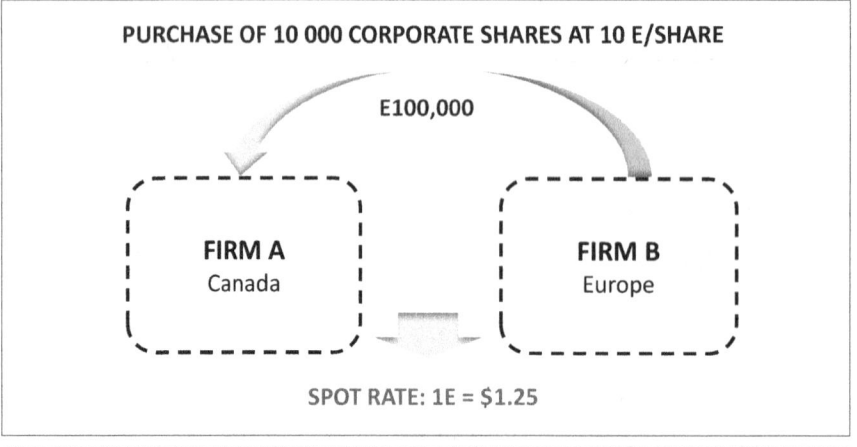

The functional currency for Firm A is the Canadian dollar

Part 1
FOREIGN CURRENCY-DENOMINATED EQUITY INVESTMENT
Journal Entry at the Transaction Date

Portfolio Investment	125,000	
Cash		125,000

(E100,000 × 1.25) = $125,000

Potential Designations

1. FVTPL
2. FVTOCI (with NO recycling)

Part 1

FOREIGN CURRENCY-DENOMINATED EQUITY INVESTMENT
Case #1: The Investment is Designated at FV Through Profit or Loss
Year End

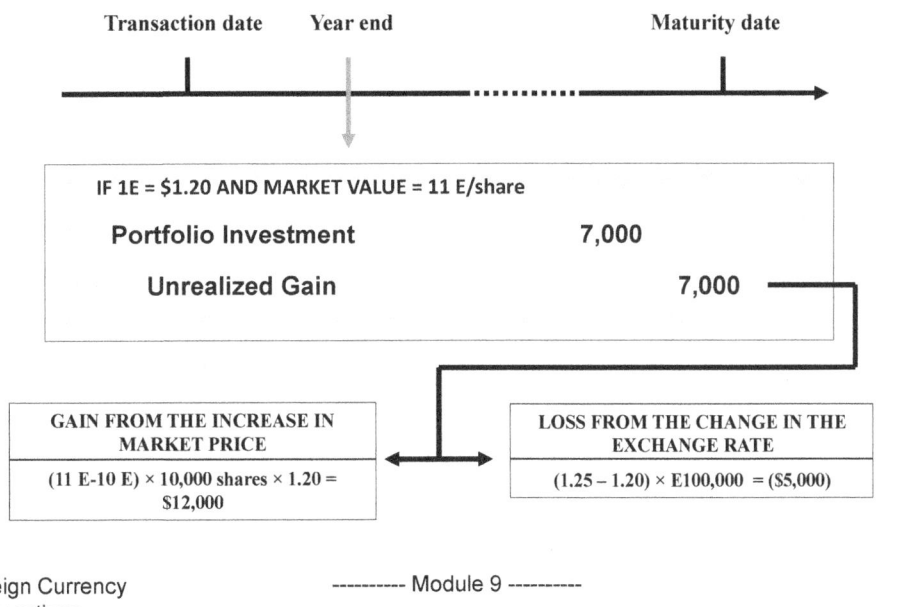

Part 1

FOREIGN CURRENCY-DENOMINATED EQUITY INVESTMENT
Case #1: The Investment is Designated at FV Through Profit or Loss
Date of Sale

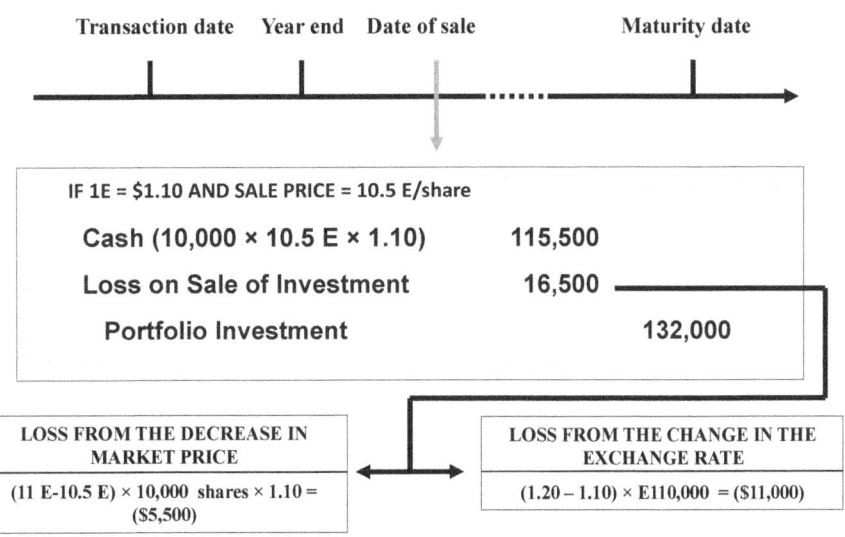

Part 1

FOREIGN CURRENCY-DENOMINATED EQUITY INVESTMENT
Case #2: The Investment is Designated at FV Through OCI (no recycling)
Year End

IF 1E = $1.20 AND MARKET VALUE = 11 E/share

Portfolio Investment	7,000	
OCI- Gain		7,000

GAIN FROM THE INCREASE IN MARKET PRICE
(11 E-10 E) × 10,000 shares × 1.20 = $12,000

LOSS FROM THE CHANGE IN THE EXCHANGE RATE
(1.25 – 1.20) × E100,000 = ($5,000)

Foreign Currency Transactions ---------- Module 9 ---------- 39

Part 1

FOREIGN CURRENCY-DENOMINATED EQUITY INVESTMENT
Case #2: The Investment is Designated at FV Through OCI (no recycling)
Date of Sale

IF 1E = $1.10 AND SALE PRICE = 10.5 E/share

Cash (10,000 × 10.5 E × 1.10)	115,500	
OCI – Loss	16,500	
Portfolio Investment		132,000

LOSS FROM THE DECREASE IN MARKET PRICE
(11 E-10.5 E) × 10,000 shares × 1.10 = ($5,500)

LOSS FROM THE CHANGE IN THE EXCHANGE RATE
(1.20 – 1.10) × E110,000 = ($11,000)

Foreign Currency Transactions ---------- Module 9 ---------- 40

ACCOUNTING FOR CURRENCY-DENOMINATED FINANCIAL ASSETS AND LIABILITIES
Summary

Types of financial assets or liabilities	Carrying value on SFP	Disposition of unrealized gains and losses	Disposition of foreign currency gains and losses
Receivables and other financial liabilities	Historical cost	Not applicable	Profit for the year
Debt instruments at cost	Amortized cost	Not applicable	Profit for the year
FV Through Profit or Loss (FVTPL)	Fair value	Profit for the year	Profit for the year
FV Through OCI (FVTOCI)	Fair value	*With recycling:* OCI *No recycling:* OCI	Profit for the year OCI

ACCOUNTING FOR CURRENCY-DENOMINATED NON FINANCIAL ASSETS AND LIABILITIES
Inventory

If the purchase of inventory is with cash, the transaction must be reported by firm A using the spot rate or current rate at the date of purchase. Moreover, since the inventory in a non-financial asset, there is no further consideration in periods subsequent to the purchase as long as the inventory is not written down. If applicable, the use of the spot rate to the market price stated in foreign currency would be required.

Rule
CURRENT-VALUED BALANCES REPORTED AT THE END OF THE YEAR MUST BE REPORTED AT CURRENT RATE (SPOT RATE).

Part 1

IFRIC 22
Foreign Currency Transactions and Advance Consideration

The interpretation addresses foreign currency transactions or parts of transactions where: (1) there is consideration that is denominated or priced in a foreign currency; (2) the entity recognizes a prepayment asset or a deferred income liability in respect of that consideration, in advance of the recognition of the related asset, expense or income; and (3) the prepayment asset or deferred income liability is non-monetary.

Consensus

The date of the transaction, for the purpose of determining the exchange rate, is the date of initial recognition of the non-monetary prepayment asset or deferred income liability. If there are multiple payments or receipts in advance, a date of transaction is established for each payment or receipt.

Part 1

ACCOUNTING FOR TRANSACTIONS IN FOREIGN CURRENCIES
From Bombardier - 2016 Annual Report, page 142

Transactions denominated in foreign currencies are initially recorded in the functional currency of the related entity using the exchange rates in effect at the date of the transaction. Monetary assets and liabilities denominated in foreign currencies are translated using the closing exchange rates. Any resulting exchange difference is recognized in income except for exchange differences related to retirement benefits asset and liability, as well as financial liabilities designated as hedges of the Corporation's net investments in foreign operations, which are recognized in OCI.

Non-monetary assets and liabilities denominated in foreign currencies and measured at historical cost are translated using historical exchange rates, and those measured at fair value are translated using the exchange rate in effect at the date the fair value is determined.

Revenues and expenses are translated using the average exchange rates for the period or the exchange rate at the date of the transaction for significant items.

Part 2

OUTLINE OF THE PRESENTATIOIN

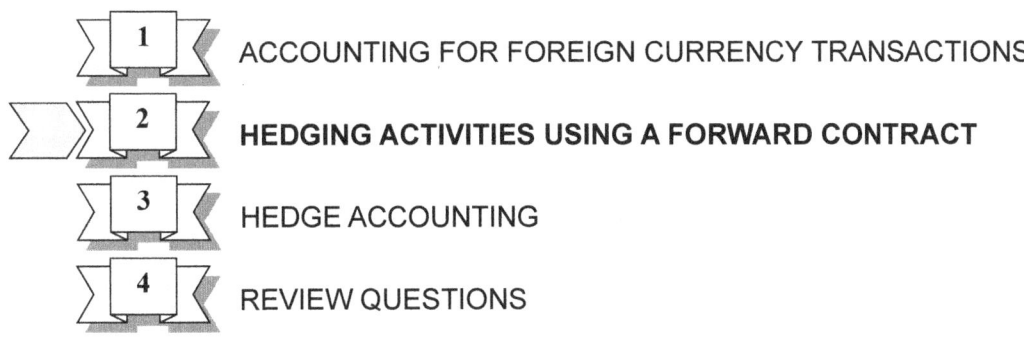

1. ACCOUNTING FOR FOREIGN CURRENCY TRANSACTIONS
2. **HEDGING ACTIVITIES USING A FORWARD CONTRACT**
3. HEDGE ACCOUNTING
4. REVIEW QUESTIONS

Part 2

PART 2
Hedging Activities Using a Forward Contract

Objectives of this section

Present the general nature of hedging.

Illustrate how to hedge an existing financial asset or financial liability using a forward contract.

Key concepts

- Hedging activities
- Hedge relationship; Hedged item; Hedging item
- Fair value hedge; Cash flow hedge
- Forward contract

Part 2

COMPONENTS OF A HEDGE

```
                    HEDGE
          ┌───────────┴───────────┐
          ▼                       ▼
    HEDGED ITEM              HEDGING ITEM
```

Item that exposes the entity to a risk of changes in FV or future cash flows.

Item whose FV or cash flows are expected to offset changes in FV or cash flows of a designated hedged item.

Foreign Currency Transactions ---------- Module 9 ---------- 47

Part 2

TYPES OF RISKS

In general, value changes can be in response to the change in a:

- ❏ Specified interest rate
- ❏ Financial instrument price
- ❏ Commodity price
- ❏ Foreign exchange rate
- ❏ Index of prices or rates
- ❏ Credit rating/index
- ❏ Other….

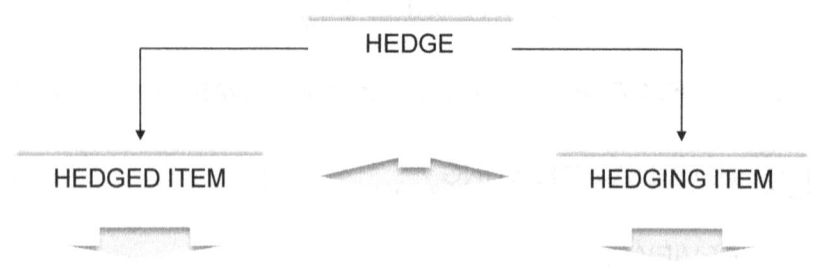
Covered in this Module

Foreign Currency Transactions ---------- Module 9 ---------- 48

Part 2

TYPES OF HEDGED ITEMS

Hedged items can take the following forms:

- Asset/Liability
- Firm commitment — Covered in this Module
- Highly probable forecast transaction
- Net investment in a foreign operation

Foreign Currency Transactions ---------- Module 9 ---------- 49

Part 2

TYPES OF HEDGING ITEMS

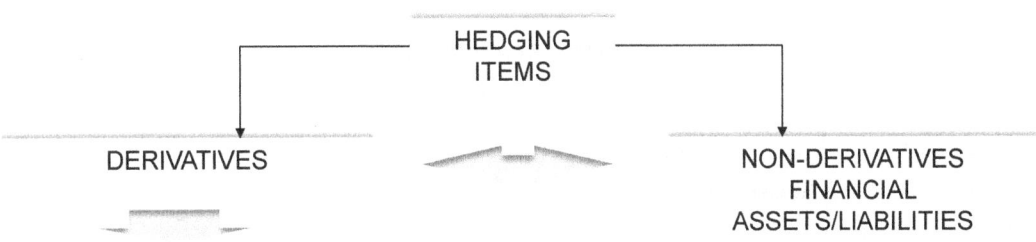

DERIVATIVES

- Financial instruments that derive its value from an underlying price or index
- Require no initial investment
- Settled at a future date

NON-DERIVATIVES FINANCIAL ASSETS/LIABILITIES

Foreign Currency Transactions ---------- Module 9 ---------- 50

Part 2

TYPES OF DERIVATIVES

Hedged items can take the following forms:

- Forward contract — Covered in this Module
- Futures contract
- Swap contract
- Option contract

Foreign Currency Transactions ---------- Module 9 ---------- 51

Part 2

TYPES OF HEDGING RELATIONSHIPS

HEDGING RELATIONSHIPS

FAIR VALUE HEDGE

A hedge of the exposure to changes in FV of a recognised asset or liability or an unrecognised firm commitment.

CASH FLOW HEDGE

A hedge of the exposure to variability in cash flows that is attributable to a particular risk associated to a recognized asset or liability or a highly probable forecast transaction.

Foreign Currency Transactions ---------- Module 9 ---------- 52

WHAT WILL BE COVERED IN THIS MODULE
Summary

Part 2

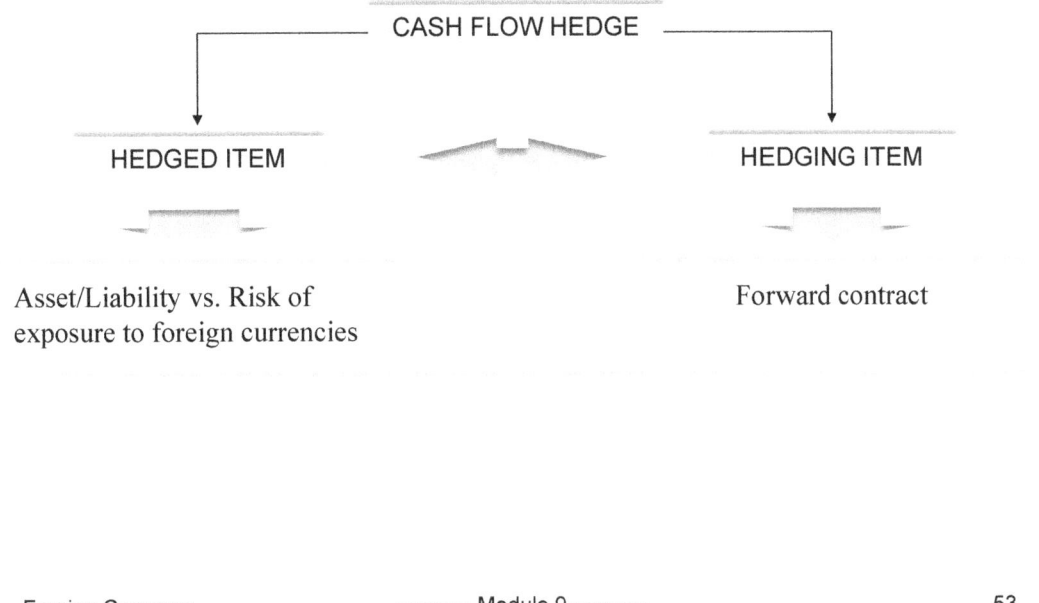

CASH FLOW HEDGE

HEDGED ITEM — Asset/Liability vs. Risk of exposure to foreign currencies

HEDGING ITEM — Forward contract

Foreign Currency Transactions — Module 9 — 53

ASSET/LIABILITY vs. RISK EXPOSURE TO FOREIGN CURRENCIES

Part 2

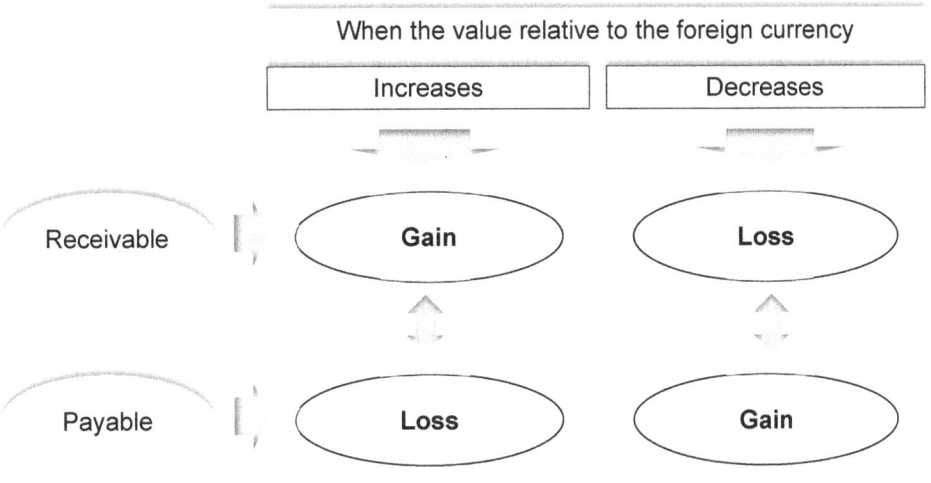

When the value relative to the foreign currency

	Increases	Decreases
Receivable	Gain	Loss
Payable	Loss	Gain

Foreign Currency Transactions — Module 9 — 54

Part 2

HEDGING vs. RISK EXPOSURE TO FOREIGN CURRENCIES

Objective

CREATION OF AN OFFSETTING BALANCE IN THE SAME FOREIGN CURRENCY

Perfect Hedge

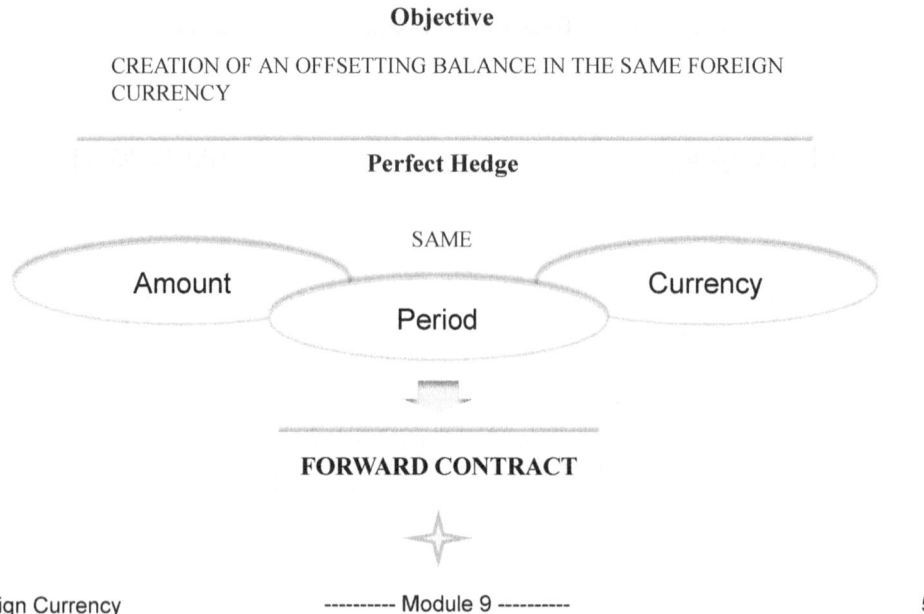

FORWARD CONTRACT

Part 2

FORWARD CONTRACT
Definition

A forward contract is a customized contract between two parties to buy or sell an asset at a specified price on a future date. A forward contract can be used for hedging or speculation, although its non-standardized nature makes it particularly apt for hedging. Unlike standard futures contracts, a forward contract can be customized to any commodity, amount, and delivery date. A forward contract settlement can occur on a cash or delivery basis.

Forward contracts do not trade on a centralized exchange and are therefore regarded as over-the-counter (OTC) instruments.

Investopedia

Part 2

FORWARD CONTRACT
Overview of the Illustrations Covered Next

Illustration 1 Forward Contract to Hedge a Monetary Asset

　　CASE 1 No premium or discount and no intervening year end

　　CASE 2 Discount at inception and no intervening year end

　　CASE 3 Discount at inception and intervening year end

Illustration 2 Forward Contract to Hedge a Liability

Foreign Currency Transactions ---------- Module 9 ---------- 57

Part 2

FORWARD CONTRACT
TO HEDGE A MONETARY ASSET
Illustration

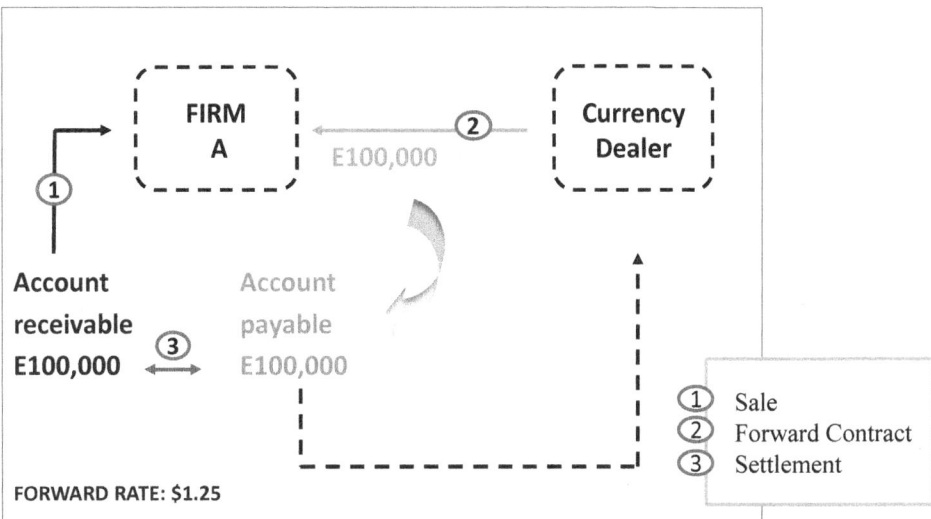

Foreign Currency Transactions ---------- Module 9 ---------- 58

Part 2

FORWARD CONTRACT
TO HEDGE A MONETARY ASSET
Illustration - How It Works

1. Firm A buys a forward contract for an equivalent amount of Euro and receives, on paper, E100,000 from the currency dealer.
2. This way, Firm A creates an account payable of E100,000 with the same settlement date as the account receivable.
3. The commitment to pay E100,000 will offset the commitment to receive E100,000 from Firm B (hedging).
4. The commitment is to transfer back, on paper, the E100,000 to the currency dealer at the time the account receivable is collected from Firm B.
5. Hence, any potential exchange loss incurred on the account receivable will be perfectly offset by the gain incurred on the account payable (and vice versa if a gain is recognized on the account receivable).

Part 2

FORWARD CONTRACT
TO HEDGE A MONETARY ASSET
Case #1: No Premium or Discount and no Intervening Year End
Journal Entries

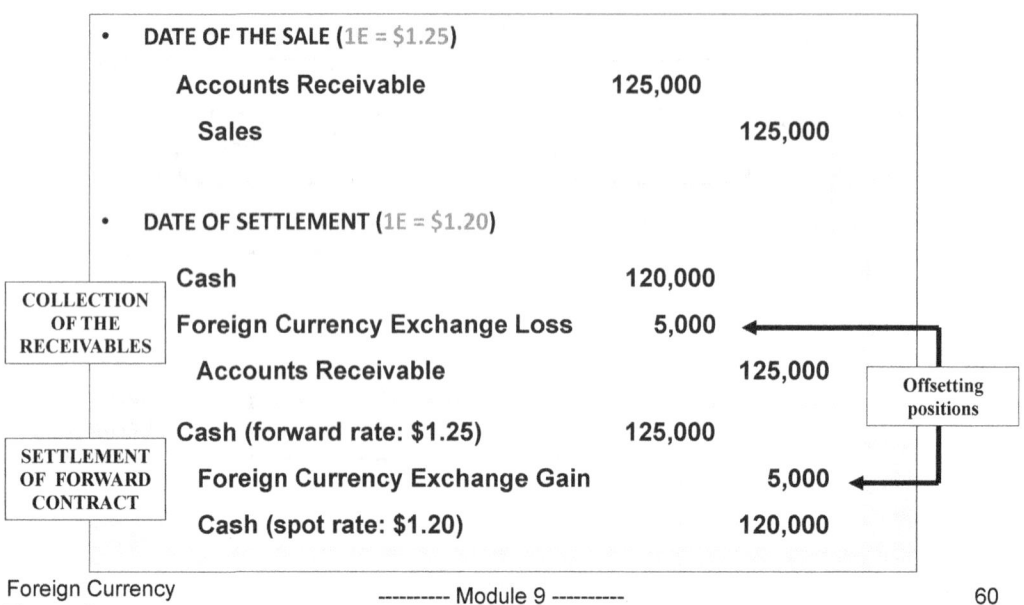

Part 2

FORWARD CONTRACT
TO HEDGE A MONETARY ASSET
Case #1: Alternative Recording Method
Journal Entries

- DATE OF THE SALE (1E = $1.25)

Accounts Receivable	125,000	
Sales		125,000
Forward Contract Receivable	125,000	
Forward Contract Payable		125,000

Foreign Currency Transactions — Module 9 — 61

Part 2

FORWARD CONTRACT
TO HEDGE A MONETARY ASSET
Case #1: Alternative Recording Method
Journal Entries

- DATE OF SETTLEMENT (1E = $1.20)

COLLECTION OF THE RECEIVABLES

Cash	120,000	
Foreign Currency Exchange Loss	5,000	
Accounts Receivable		125,000

SETTLEMENT OF FORWARD CONTRACT

Cash (forward rate: $1.25)	125,000	
Forward Contract Receivable		125,000
Forward Contract Payable	125,000	
Foreign Currency Exchange Gain		5,000
Cash (spot rate: $1.20)		120,000

Foreign Currency Transactions — Module 9 — 62

Part 2

FORWARD CONTRACT
TO HEDGE A MONETARY ASSET
Case #2: Discount at Inception and no Intervening Year End
Journal Entries If 2% Discount

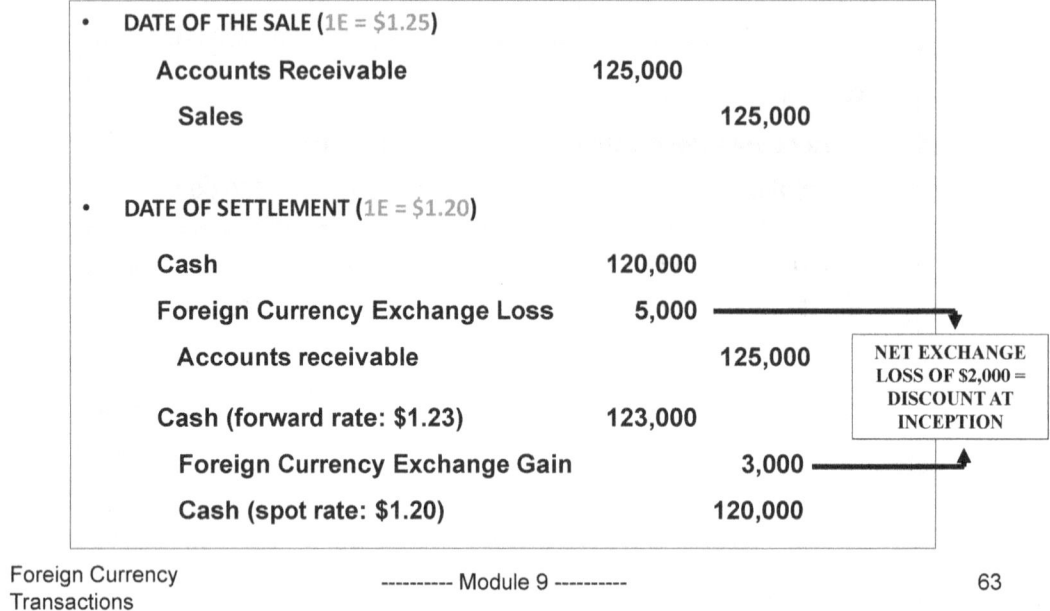

- DATE OF THE SALE (1E = $1.25)

Accounts Receivable	125,000	
Sales		125,000

- DATE OF SETTLEMENT (1E = $1.20)

Cash	120,000	
Foreign Currency Exchange Loss	5,000	
Accounts receivable		125,000
Cash (forward rate: $1.23)	123,000	
Foreign Currency Exchange Gain		3,000
Cash (spot rate: $1.20)		120,000

NET EXCHANGE LOSS OF $2,000 = DISCOUNT AT INCEPTION

Part 2

FORWARD CONTRACT
TO HEDGE A MONETARY ASSET
Case #2: Alternative Recording Method
Journal Entries If 2% Discount

- DATE OF THE SALE (1E = $1.25)

Accounts Receivable	125,000	
Sales		125,000
Forward Contract Receivable	123,000	
Forward Contract Payable		123,000

Part 2

FORWARD CONTRACT
TO HEDGE A MONETARY ASSET
Case #2: Alternative Recording Method
Journal Entries If Discount of 2%

- DATE OF SETTLEMENT (1E = $1.20)

Cash	120,000	
Foreign Currency Exchange Loss	5,000	
Accounts Receivable		125,000
Cash (forward rate: $1.23)	123,000	
Forward Contract Receivable		123,000
Forward Contract Payable	123,000	
Foreign Currency Exchange Gain		3,000
Cash (spot rate: $1.20)		120,000

Part 2

FORWARD CONTRACT
TO HEDGE A MONETARY ASSET
Case #3: Discount at Inception and Intervening Year End
Date of Transaction

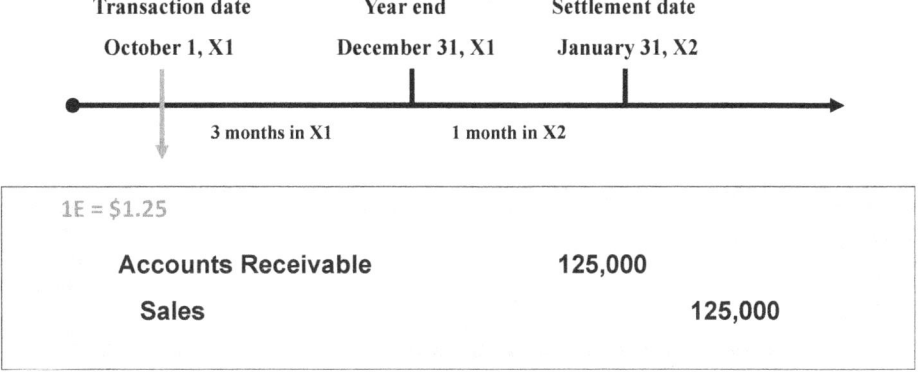

1E = $1.25

Accounts Receivable	125,000	
Sales		125,000

Part 2

FORWARD CONTRACT
TO HEDGE A MONETARY ASSET
Case #3: Discount at Inception and Intervening Year End
Year End

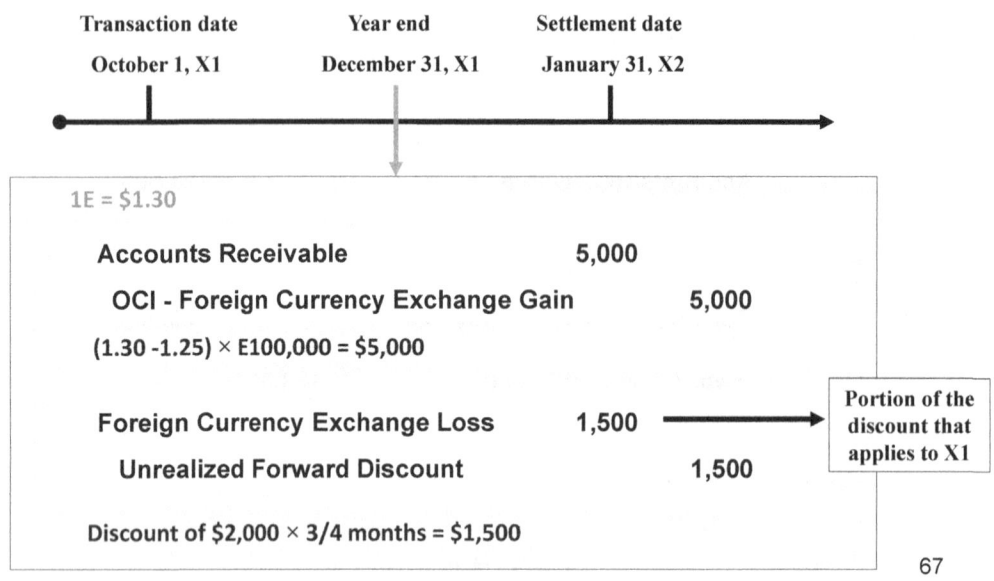

Part 2

FORWARD CONTRACT
TO HEDGE A MONETARY ASSET
Case #3: Discount at Inception and Intervening Year End
Settlement Date

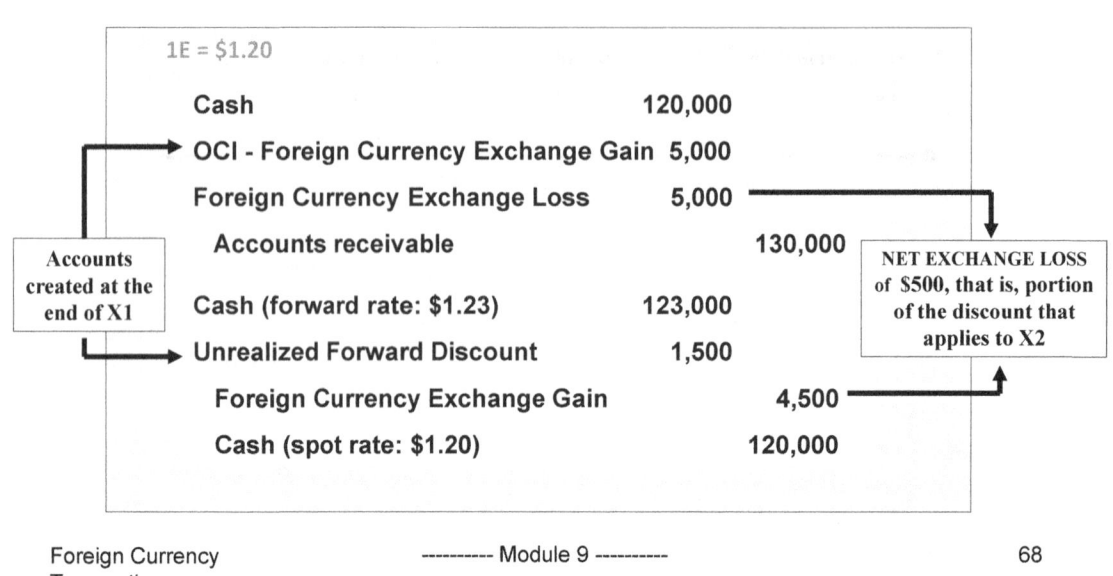

Part 2

FORWARD CONTRACT
TO HEDGE A MONETARY ASSET
Case #3: Alternative Recording Method
Journal Entries

- **DATE OF THE SALE (1E = $1.25)**

Accounts Receivable	125,000	
Sales		125,000
Forward Contract Receivable	123,000	
Forward Contract Payable		123,000

YEAR END (1E = $1.30)

Accounts Receivable	5,000	
Foreign Currency Exchange Gain		5,000
Foreign Currency Exchange Loss	6,500	
Forward Contract Payable		6,500

Part 2

FORWARD CONTRACT
TO HEDGE A MONETARY ASSET
Case #3: Alternative Recording Method
Journal Entries

- **DATE OF SETTLEMENT (1E = $1.20)**

Cash	120,000	
Foreign Currency Exchange Loss	10,000	
Accounts Receivable		130,000
Cash (forward rate: $1.23)	123,000	
Forward Contract Receivable		123,000
Forward Contract Payable	129,500	
Foreign Currency Exchange Gain		9,500
Cash (spot rate: $1.20)		120,000

PURCHASE OF ASSETS
IN A FOREIGN CURRENCY
Illustration

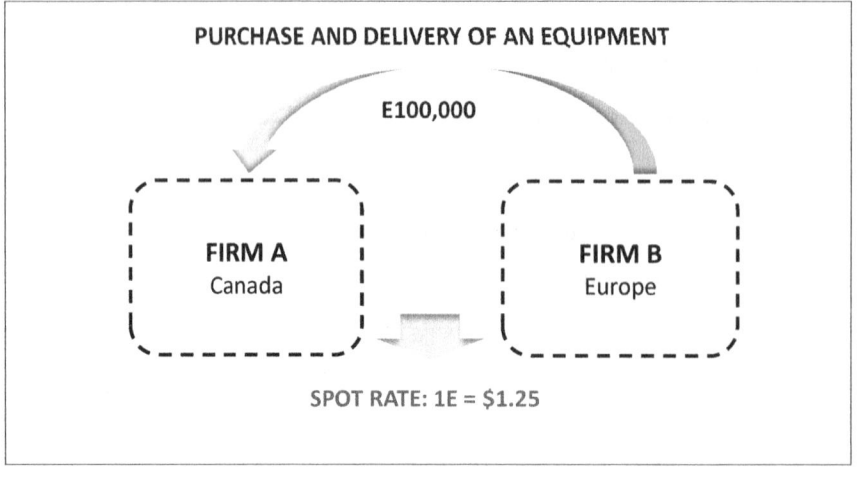

The functional currency for Firm A is the Canadian dollar

FORWARD CONTRACT
TO HEDGE A MONETARY LIABILITY
Illustration

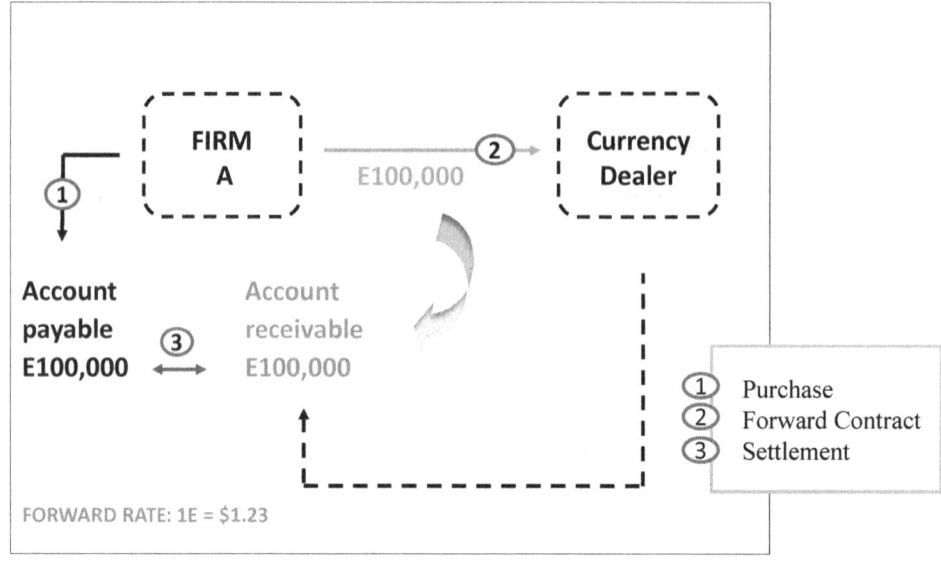

Part 2

FORWARD CONTRACT WITH DISCOUNT TO HEDGE A LIABILITY
Journal Entries

- **DATE OF THE PURCHASE**

Equipment	125,000	
Accounts Payable		125,000

- **DATE OF SETTLEMENT (1E = $1.20)**

PAYMENT OF PAYABLES:

Accounts Payable	125,000	
Foreign Currency Exchange Gain		5,000
Cash		120,000

SETTLEMENT OF FORWARD CONTRACT:

Cash (spot rate: $1.20)	120,000	
Foreign Currency Exchange Loss	3,000	
Cash (forward rate: $1.23)		123,000

Part 2

FORWARD CONTRACT WITH DISCOUNT TO HEDGE A LIABILITY
Alternative Recording Method
Journal Entries

- **DATE OF THE PURCHASE**

Equipment	125,000	
Accounts Payable		125,000
Forward Contract Receivable	123,000	
Forward Contract Payable		123,000

Foreign Currency Transactions — Module 9

Part 2

FORWARD CONTRACT WITH DISCOUNT TO HEDGE A LIABILITY
Alternative Recording Method
Journal Entries

- DATE OF SETTLEMENT (1E = $1.20)

PAYMENT OF PAYABLES

Accounts Payable	125,000	
Foreign Currency Exchange Gain		5,000
Cash		120,000

SETTLEMENT OF FORWARD CONTRACT

Forward Contract Payable	123,000	
Cash (forward rate: $1.23)		123,000
Cash (spot rate: $1.20)	120,000	
Foreign Currency Exchange Loss	3,000	
Forward Contract Receivable		123,000

Part 3

OUTLINE OF THE PRESENTATIOIN

1. ACCOUNTING FOR FOREIGN CURRENCY TRANSACTIONS
2. HEDGING ACTIVITIES USING A FORWARD CONTRACT
3. **HEDGE ACCOUNTING**
4. REVIEW QUESTIONS

PART 3
Hedge Accounting

Part 3

Objectives of this section

Illustrate the overall concept of hedge accounting.

Key concepts

- Hedge accounting
- Imperfect and Implicit Hedges
- Hedge Effectivness

HEDGES
Typology

Part 3

- PERFECT → Forward Contract
- IMPLICIT
- IMPERFECT

Offsetting positions created in the normal course of business (linked to IMPLICIT and IMPERFECT)

In a normal course of business, a company may have receivables and payables in the same foreign currency, which may unintentionally create an offsetting position. However, it is not a perfect hedge since the amount and the period from each position will most likely be different. However, if the hedge is expected to be highly effective, **hedge accounting** could be used.

HEDGE ACCOUNTING
Definition

HEDGE ACCOUNTING IS A METHOD FOR RECOGNIZING THE GAINS, LOSSES, REVENUES, AND EXPENSES ASSOCIATED WITH THE ITEMS IN A HEDGING RELATIONSHIP SUCH THAT THOSE GAINS, LOSSES, REVENUES, AND EXPENSES ARE RECOGNIZED IN THE NET INCOME IN THE SAME PERIOD WHEN THEY WOULD OTHERWISE BE RECOGNIZED IN DIFFERENT PERIODS.

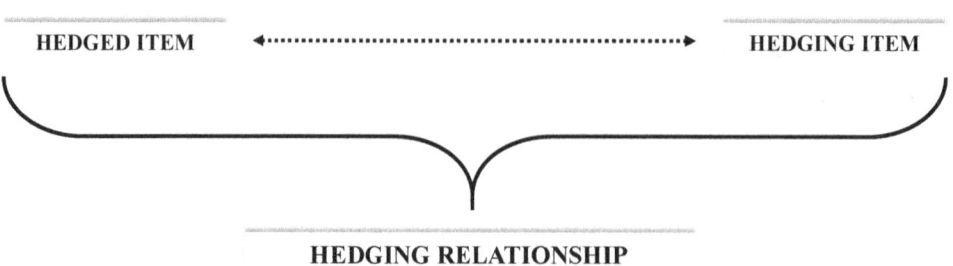

HEDGE ACCOUNTING
Effective Hedges

- Hedge effectiveness is the extent to which changes in the fair value or cash flows of the hedging instrument offset the changes in the fair value or cash flows of the hedged item.

- Hedge effectiveness should be assessed on inception of a hedge relationship and for each reporting date.

- Hedge effectiveness can be assessed through the use of either quantitative or qualitative techniques. However, the mechanics of the different tests are beyond the scope of this module.

HEDGE ACCOUNTING
Cash-Flow Hedge - The process

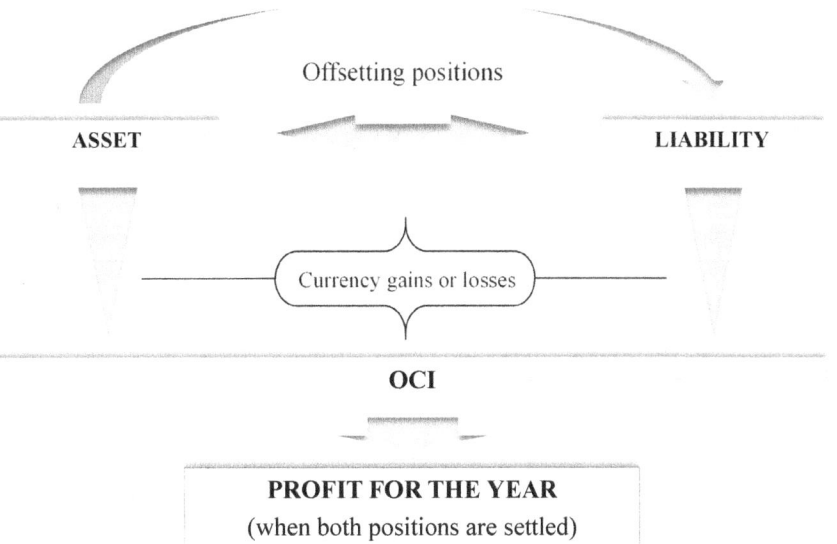

Part 3

HEDGE ACCOUNTING
Fair Value Hedge - The process

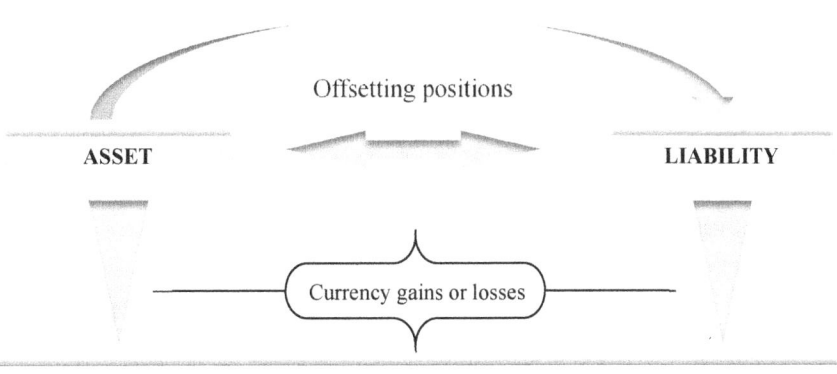

Part 3

Part 3

HEDGE ACCOUNTING
Cash-Flow Hedge - Illustration - Year 1

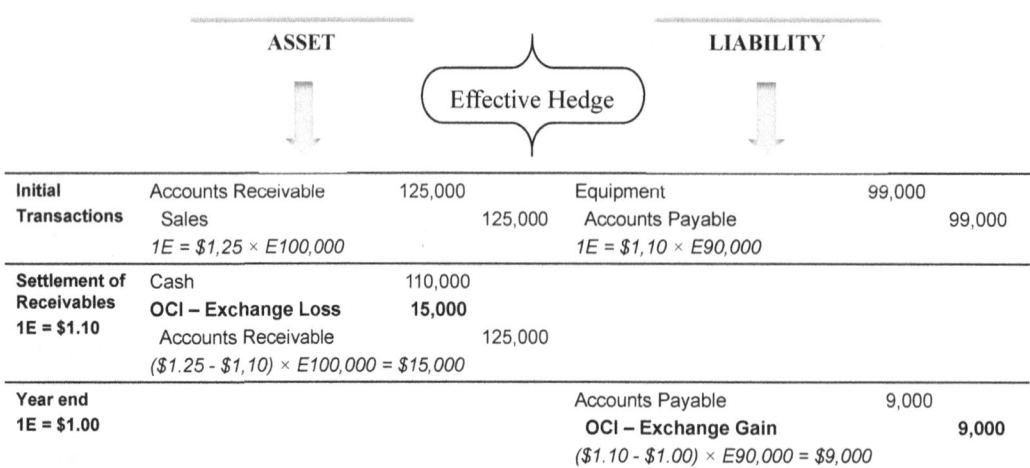

Exchange gain and loss from the monetary balances (Receivables and Payables) are deferred through the OCI until both positions are settled. Hedge accounting has the ability to change the timing of recognition of the hedging instruments.

Part 3

HEDGE ACCOUNTING
Cash-Flow Hedge - Illustration - Year 2

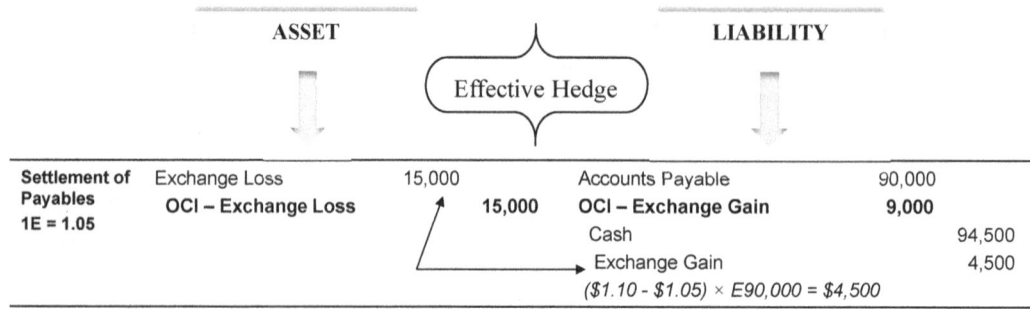

In Year 2, when Payables are settled, the offsetting gain and loss from the hedging instruments is recognized in net income. Net exchange loss: $10,500 = ($15,000 - $4,500). Hedge accounting helped to synchronize the recognition of both positions within the same year.

Part 4

OUTLINE OF THE PRESENTATIOIN

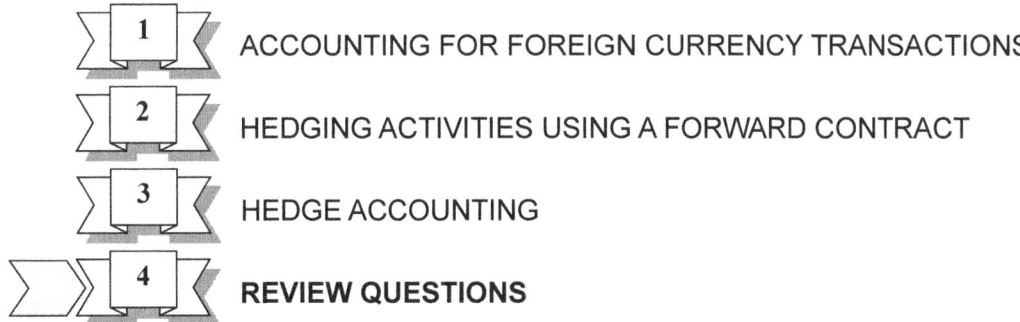

1. ACCOUNTING FOR FOREIGN CURRENCY TRANSACTIONS
2. HEDGING ACTIVITIES USING A FORWARD CONTRACT
3. HEDGE ACCOUNTING
4. **REVIEW QUESTIONS**

Part 4

PART 4
Review Questions

1 Define or explain the following terms:

- Hedging activities
- Forward contract
- Hedge accounting
- Hedge relationship
- Offsetting positions
- Forward contract with premium or discount

- Foreign currency transactions
- Exchange gains and losses
- Exchange rate
- Direct exchange rate
- Spot rate
- Functional currency

2 How is the discount or premium on a forward contract accounted for?

3 What is meant by 'hedge accounting'?

4 Under what circumstances might hedge accounting be applied?

REVIEW QUESTIONS
(continued...)

Part 4

5. How are assets and liabilities denominated in foreign currency measured and recorded at the date of transaction? At year end?

6. Why would someone choose not to hedge a monetary balance denominated in foreign currency?

7. Is there cash payment made to an exchange broker when a forward contract is initiated? Explain.

8. What are the three characteristics for a perfect currency hedge?

9. Can a forward contract be qualified as a perfect hedge? Explain.

10. Why a difference usually exists between a currency's spot rate and forward rate?

11. What types of risk are encountered by a Canadian company when it conducts business with a foreign company?

Exercise 9-1
Loan in US Dollar

On January 1, X7, a Canadian based company, Flower Corporation, borrowed US$200,000 from a bank in New York. Interest of 7% per annum is to be paid on December 31 of each year during the four-year term of the loan. Principal is to be repaid on the maturity date on December 31, X10.

The foreign exchange rates for the first two years were as follows:

- January 1, X7   C$1.38 = US$1.00
- December 31, X7   C$1.41 = US$1.00
- December 31, X8   C$1.35 = US$1.00

Required
Determine the exchange gain or loss on the loan to be disclosed in the financial statement of Flower Corporation for the years ended December 31, X7 and X8.

X7

X8

Exercise 9-2
Receivables in Pounds Sterling

Canado, a Canadian company, sells its products to customers in UK at prices quoted in pounds sterling.

- On November 14, X7, Canado sold and shipped goods that had cost of $160,000 to produce to an English company for 200,000 pounds sterling.
- On December 20, Canado received an international draft for part of the amount due, 80,000 pounds sterling. At December 31, the remaining 120,000 pounds sterling was unpaid.
- On February 12, X8, Canado received payment of the remaining 120,000 pounds sterling.

The foreign exchange rates were as follows:

- November 14, X7   C$1.80 = 1.00 pound sterling
- December 20, X7   C$1.85 = 1.00 pound sterling
- December 31, X7   C$1.87 = 1.00 pound sterling
- February 12, X8   C$1.84 = 1.00 pound sterling

Required
Prepare journal entries to record the above events, and any adjustments necessary at year end.

Nov. 17, X7

Dec. 20, X7

Dec. 31, X7

Feb. 12, X8

Exercise 9-3
Receivables in Pesos

Dec. 31, X7

	Debit	Credit
Exchange loss	2,155.18	
Accounts receivable (Receivable 1)		1,388.89
Accounts receivable (Receivable 2)		766.29

Receivable 1: (2,000,000 / 180) − (2,000,000 / 160) = 11,111.11 − 12,500.00 = (1,388.89)
Receivable 2: (4,000,000 / 180) − (4,000,000 / 174) = 22,222.22 − 22,988.51 = (766.29)

Dec. 1, X8

	Debit	Credit
Cash (2,000,000 / 110)	18,181.82	
Accounts receivable		11,111.11
Exchange gain		7,070.71

Dec. 31, X8

	Debit	Credit
Accounts receivable (Receivable 2)	22,222.22	
Exchange gain		22,222.22

Receivable 2: (4,000,000 / 90) − (4,000,000 / 180) = 44,444.44 − 22,222.22 = 22,222.22

Exercise 9-4
Monetary Balances in Euros

During X7, Spot, a Canadian company, completed two important transactions with companies in Europe:

- On July 1, X7, Spot acquired equipment at a cost of 250,000 Euros from Poire Company. Spot received reasonable terms regarding this purchase acquisition. The 250,000 Euros was in the form of a notes payable to be paid on June 30, X10, at an interest rate of 8% per annum, the interest to be paid semiannually on December 31 and June 30.

- On October 1, X7, Spot sold inventory that cost C$50,000 to another European company, Tartuf, for 87,500 Euros. Payment is due from Tartuf on March 1, X8. Spot uses a perpetual inventory system.

The foreign exchange rates were as follows:

- July 1, X7   C$1.00 = 1.25 E
- October 1, X7   C$1.00 = 1.125 E
- December 31, X7   C$1.00 = 1.00 E
- March 1, X8   C$1.00 = 0.875 E
- Average rate, X7   C$1.00 = 1.20 E
- Average rate, July 1 – Dec. 31, X7 C$1.00 = 1.075 E

Required

a) Prepare journal entries regarding Spot's notes payable and interest-related transactions on July 1, X7, and December 31, X7.
b) Prepare all journal entries regarding Spot's sales, cost of sales, and accounts receivable transactions on October 1, X7, December 31, X7, and March 1, X8.

a)

July 1, X7	

Dec. 31, X7

b)

Oct. 1, X7

Dec. 31, X7

March 1, X8

Exercise 9-5
Forward Contract to Hedge a Liability

On May 5, X7, a Canadian based company, Florence Corporation, purchased inventory from a Japanese supplier, and gave the supplier a 90-day note for 20,000,000 Yens.

On the same date, Florence entered a forward contract with its currency dealer to receive 20,000,000 Yens in 90, days. The spot rate for the Yen was C$0.0095. The forward rate was C$0.0100.

Required
Prepare the journal entries to record the purchase, the hedge, and final settlement of both the note and the hedge, assuming each of the following spot rates at the date of settlement:

a) $0.0095
b) $0.0100
c) $0.0093
d) $0.0102

Purchase

a)

Payment

Hedge

b)

Payment

Hedge

c)

Payment

Hedge

d)

Payment

Hedge

Exercise 9-6
Forward Contract to Hedge a Receivable

On October 15, X7, Gloomy, a Canadian company, sold merchandise to two companies in Portugal.

- In the first transaction, the price was 3,000,000 Escudos and was to be paid in 90 days. Worried about the exposure to the exchange risk, the company hedged the receivable for a 90-day period with a forward contract.

- In the second transaction, the price was 3,600,000 Escudos and the date of payment was November 15, X10. Due to difficulty of getting a forward contract to match the date payment is due, Gloomy decided to remain in an unhedged position on this receivable.

The foreign exchange rates were as follows:

- October 15, X7   C$1.00 = 800 Escudos
- December 31, X7   C$1.00 = 910 Escudos
- January 13, X8   C$1.00 = 945 Escudos
- October 15, X7 (forward 90-day rate)   C$1.00 = 926 Escudos
- December 31, X8   C$1.00 = 775 Escudos

Required

a) In general journal form, prepare all journal entries required for the first sale for X7 and X8.
b) Assuming instead that Gloomy had not hedged the receivable from the first sale, prepare all journal entries required for the first sale for X7 and X8.
c) In general journal form, prepare all journal entries required for the second sale for X7 and X8.

a)

Nov. 14, X7	

Dec. 31, X7

Jan. 13. X8

b)

Oct. 15, X7

Dec. 31, X7

Jan. 13. X8

c)

Oct. 15, X7

Dec. 31, X7

Jan. 13. X8

Copyright © 2020, Parmitech, Ottawa. Parmitech. All rights reserved.

Solutions to Exercises

9-1

a) <u>Exchange loss for X7</u>:
US$200,000 (1,41 − 1,38) = **C$6,000**

b) <u>Exchange gain for X8</u>:
US$200,000 (1,41 − 1,35) = **C$12,000**

9-2

Nov. 14, X7	Accounts Receivable	360,000	
	Sales		360,000
	(PS200,000 × 1,80) = C$360,000		
	Cost of Goods Sold	160,000	
	Inventory		160,000
Dec. 20, X7	Cash (PS80,000 × 1,85)	148,000	
	Accounts Receivable (PS80,000 × 1,80)		144,000
	Exchange Gains and Losses		4,000
Dec. 31, X7	Accounts Receivable	8,400	
	Exchange Gains and Losses		8,400
	PS120,000 × (1,87 − 1,80) = C$8,400		
Feb. 12, X8	Cash (PS120,000 × 1,84)	220,800	
	Exchange Gains and Losses	3,600	
	Accounts Receivable (PS120,000 × 1,87)		224,400

9-3

Dec. 31, X7	Exchange Gains and Losses	1,389	
	Accounts Receivable		1,389
	P2,000,000 × (1/160 − 1/180) = C$1,389		
	Exchange Gains and Losses	767	
	Accounts Receivable		767
	P4,000,000 × (1/174 − 1/180) = C$767		
Dec. 1, X8	Cash (P2,000,000 × 1/110)	18,182	
	Exchange Gains and Losses		7,071
	Accounts Receivable (PS2,000,000 × 1/180)		11,111

Dec. 31, X8	Accounts Receivable	22,222	
	Exchange Gains and Losses		22,222
	P4,000,000 × (1/180 – 1/90) = C$22,222		

9-4

a)

July 1, X7	Equipment	200,000	
	Notes Payable		200,000
	(E250,000/1,25) = C$200,000		
Dec. 31, X7	Interest Expense (E250,000×8%×½)/1,075	9,302	
	Exchange Loss	698	
	Cash (E10,000 × 1)		10,000
	Exchange Loss	50,000	
	Notes Payable		50,000
	(E250,000/1) – C$200,000 = C$50,000		

b)

Oct. 1, X7	Accounts Receivable	77,778	
	Sales		77,778
	(E87,500/1,125) = C$77,778		
	Cost of Goods Sold	50,000	
	Inventory		50,000
Dec. 31, X7	Accounts Receivable	9,722	
	Exchange Gains and Losses		9,722
	(E87,500/1) – C$77,778 = C$9,722		
March 1, X8	Cash (E87,500/0,875)	100,000	
	Exchange Gains and Losses		12,500
	Accounts Receivable (E87,500/1)		87,500

9-5

July 1, X7		Inventory	190,000	
		Accounts Payable		190,000
		(Y20,000,000 × 0,0095) = C$190,000		

a) Spot rate = 0,0095

Cash (Y20,000,000 × 0,0095)	190,000	
Exchange Gains and Losses	10,000	
Cash (Y20,000,000 × 0,0100)		200,000
Accounts Payable	190,000	
Cash (Y20,000,000 × 0,0095)		190,000

b) Spot rate = 0,0100

Cash (Y20,000,000 × 0,0100)	200,000	
Cash (Y20,000,000 × 0,0100)		200,000
Accounts Payable	190,000	
Exchange Gains and Losses	10,000	
Cash (Y20,000,000 × 0,0100)		200,000

c) Spot rate = 0,0093

Cash (Y20,000,000 × 0,0093)	186,000	
Exchange Gains and Losses	14,000	
Cash (Y20,000,000 × 0,0100)		200,000
Accounts Payable	190,000	
Cash (Y20,000,000 × 0,0093)		186,000
Exchange Gains and Losses		4,000

d) Spot rate = 0,0102

Cash (Y20,000,000 × 0,0102)	204,000	
Exchange Gains and Losses		4,000
Cash (Y20,000,000 × 0,0100)		200,000
Accounts Payable	190,000	
Exchange Gains and Losses	14,000	
Cash (Y20,000,000 × 0,0102)		204,000

9-6

a)

Nov. 14, X7	Accounts Receivable	3,750	
	Sales		3,750
	(ES3,000,000/800) = C$3,750		

Dec. 31, X7	OCI - Exchange Gains and Losses	454	
	Accounts Receivable		454
	ES3,000,000 (1/800 – 1/910) = C$454		

	Exchange Gains and Losses	436	
	Unrealized Forward Discount		436
	ES3,000,000 (1/800 – 1/926) × 77/90 = C$436		

Jan. 13, X8	Cash (ES3,000,000/945)	3,174	
	Exchange Gains and Losses	576	
	Accounts Receivable		3,296
	OCI – Exchange Gains and Losses		454

	Cash (ES3,000,000/926)	3,240	
	Unrealized Forward Premium	436	
	Cash (ES3,000,000/945)		3,174
	Exchange Gains and Losses		502

b)

Oct. 15, X7	Accounts Receivable	3,750	
	Sales		3,750

Dec. 31, X7	Exchange Gains and Losses	454	
	Accounts Receivable		454

Jan. 13, X8	Cash	3,174	
	Exchange Gains and Losses	122	
	Accounts Receivable		3,296

c)

Oct. 15, X7	Accounts Receivable	4,500	
	Sales (ES3,600,000/800)		4,500

Dec. 31, X7	Exchange Gains and Losses	544	
	Accounts Receivable		544
	ES3,600,000 (1/800 – 1/910) = C$544		

Dec. 31, X8	Accounts Receivable	690	
	Exchange Gains and Losses		690
	ES3,600,000 (1/910 – 1/775) = C$690		

Reporting Foreign Operations

Module 10

What you will find in this section

- How to Walk Through Module 10
- Slides
- Exercises and Solutions

Module 10
Reporting Foreign Operations

How to Walk Through Module 10

◇ <u>Readings</u>

1- <u>Student Manual</u> "Advanced Accounting": Module 10

PART 1: FUNCTIONAL CURRENCY *versus* PRESENTATION CURRENCY

PART 2: TRANSLATION OF FINANCIAL STATEMENTS OF PARENT FOUNDED FOREIGN SUBSIDIARIES

PART 3: TRANSLATION OF FINANCIAL STATEMENTS OF ACQUIRED FOREIGN SUBSIDIARIES

◇ <u>Assignments</u>

2- <u>Student Manual</u>: End-of module review questions and the exercise in the recap section.
3- <u>Student Manual</u>: Exercises 1 to 4

◇ <u>Additional readings</u>

5- <u>IAS</u> 21, 29

When you have successfully completed this module, you will be able to do the following:

- Differentiate between Functional Currency and Presentation Currency;

- Describe the conceptual alternatives to translate the financial statements of foreign operations;

- Report the translation gain or loss in the financial statements;

- Compute the translation gain or loss when the functional currency is different from that of the reporting entity;

- Proceed with the consolidation of parent-founded foreign subsidiaries (when the investment in the subsidiary is accounted for using the cost method and when there are no intercompany transactions);

- Contrast the translation of financial statements of acquired subsidiaries with that of parent founded subsidiaries.

REPORTING FOREIGN OPERATIONS
Module 10

Copyright © 2020 Parmitech

Advanced Accounting: Student Manual

Copyrighted Material

Editor: Parmitech

This publication is protected by copyright, and permission should be obtained from the publisher prior to any prohibited reproduction, storage in a retrieval system, or transmission in any form or by any means, electronic, mechanical, photocopying, recording, or otherwise.

Corresponding Author

Richard Bozec Ph.D., CPA, CGA
bozec@telfer.uottawa.ca

Copyright © Parmitech

TEACHING MATERIAL
Electronic Sources

IFRS

IAS 21   The Effects of Changes in Foreign Exchange Rates

IAS 29   Financial Reporting in Hyperinflationary Economies

TEACHING MATERIAL
Exercises

Module 10

- **10.1** Translation - Statement of Financial Position
- **10.2** Translation – Income Statement
- **10.3** Translation of Financial Statements and Translation Gain/Loss
- **10.4** Translation of Financial Statements

OUTLINE OF THE PRESENTATION

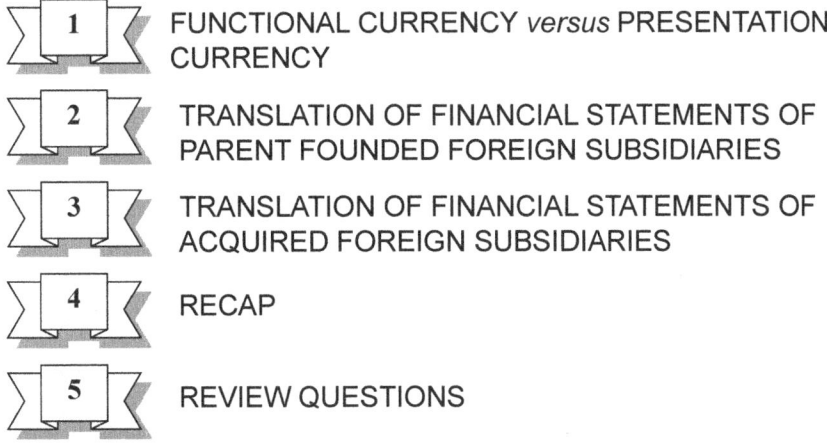

1. FUNCTIONAL CURRENCY *versus* PRESENTATION CURRENCY
2. TRANSLATION OF FINANCIAL STATEMENTS OF PARENT FOUNDED FOREIGN SUBSIDIARIES
3. TRANSLATION OF FINANCIAL STATEMENTS OF ACQUIRED FOREIGN SUBSIDIARIES
4. RECAP
5. REVIEW QUESTIONS

Foreign Operations ---------- Module 10 ----------

Part 1

PART 1
Functional Currency *versus* Presentation Currency

Objective of this section

Differentiate between Functional Currency and Presentation Currency in order to determine the appropriate method of translation.

Key concepts

- Self-sustaining vs. Integrated foreign operation
- Presentation currency
- Current rate method vs. temporal method

Foreign Operations ---------- Module 10 ----------

FORMS OF FOREIGN OPERATIONS

Part 1

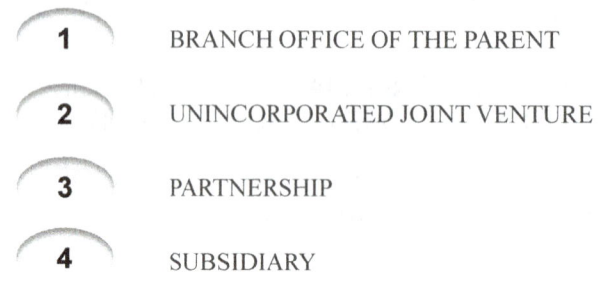

1. BRANCH OFFICE OF THE PARENT
2. UNINCORPORATED JOINT VENTURE
3. PARTNERSHIP
4. SUBSIDIARY

Since the foreign operation is subject to the laws of the host country, including its tax laws, an incorporated subsidiary is often more practical. This form of organization is also more suitable if the foreign operation runs into financial or legal difficulties. It will offer the parent company some protection against these adverse situations that could compromise its core business. Whatever the form of organization, the challenge in accounting for the parent company remains: translating the financial statements of the foreign operation using the same currency as the presentation currency. The objective of this module is to discuss the accounting for foreign operations and illustrate the translation process.

PRESENTATION CURRENCY
Definition

Part 1

PRESENTATION CURRENCY IS THE CURRENCY IN WHICH THE FINANCIAL STATEMENTS ARE PRESENTED. THEREFORE, THE PRESENTATION CURRENCY IS THE **FUNCTIONAL CURRENCY** OF THE REPORTING ENTITY, THE **PARENT COMPANY**.

Functional Currency - Recall

CURRENCY OF THE PRIMARY ECONOMIC ENVIRONMENT IN WHICH THE ENTITY OPERATES.

Part 1

WHEN IS TRANSLATION OF FINANCIAL STATEMENTS REQUIRED
From a Conceptual Standpoint

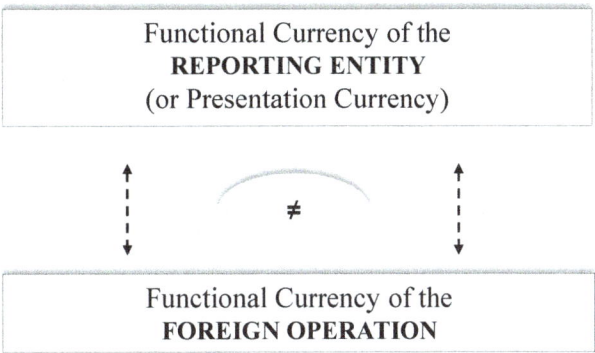

Translation is required when the functional currency of the foreign operation is different from that of the reporting entity, the parent (translation from the functional currency to the presentation currency). Conceptually, when the functional currency of the foreign operation is the same as that of the reporting entity, the translation process is performed at the subsidiary level, not at the parent level. However, in practice, such a translation will be performed at the parent level.

Foreign Operations ---------- Module 10 ---------- 9

Part 1

UNDER ASPE

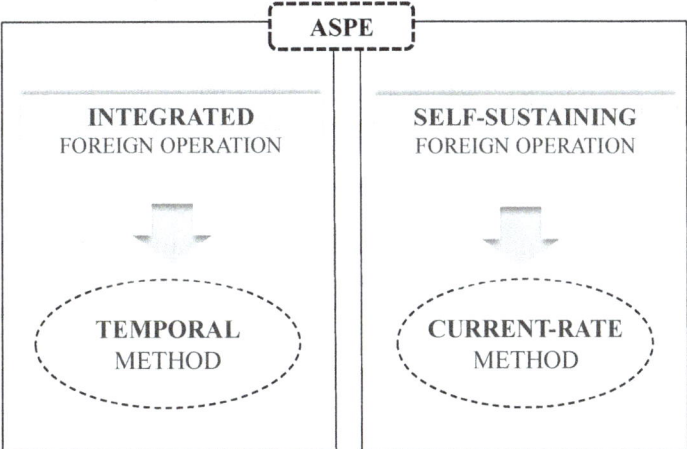

Before IFRS adoption, there were two translation methods namely, the **temporal** method and the **current-rate** method. The choice of either one or the other translation method exclusively depended on whether or not the foreign operation was identified as an **integrated** or **self-sustaining** operation. This terminology is still used today for private enterprises (see ASPE).

Foreign Operations ---------- Module 10 ---------- 10

Part 1

UNDER IFRS
Functional Currency Approach

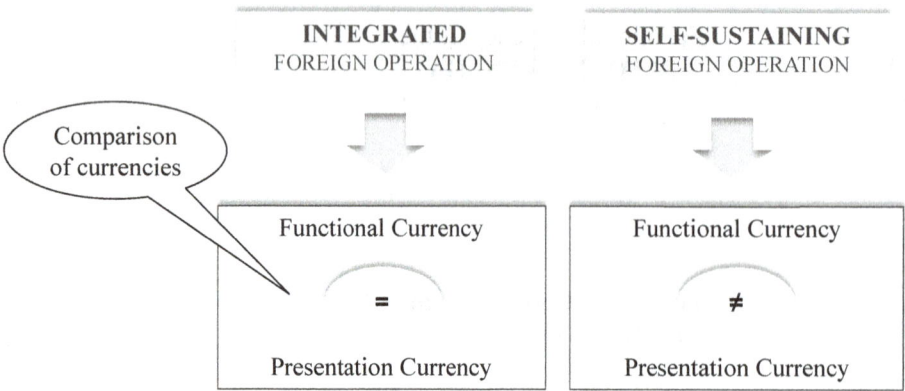

The expressions "Temporal method" and "Current-rate method" are absent in IAS 21. However, the methods used in IAS 21 to translate F/S are the same, even though they are not mentioned by name. To select the appropriate translation method, we need to determine beforehand the functional currencies of the parent company and its foreign operation.

Foreign Operations ---------- Module 10 ---------- 11

Part 1

JUDGING THE LEVEL OF INTERDEPENDENCE
Indicators

- DEGREE OF AUTONOMY
- FREQUENCY OF TRANSACTIONS WITH REPORTING ENTITY
- CASH FLOW IMPACT ON REPORTING ENTITY
- FINANCING

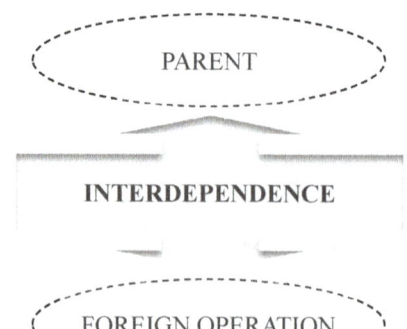

Determining the level of interdependence between the foreign operation and the reporting entity (Parent) is a critical first step in order to select the right translation method. If the parent and the foreign operation are highly interdependent, one can conclude that the functional currency of the foreign operation is the same as that of the reporting entity. Instead, if the two entities are deemed independent from each other, we can assume that their functional currencies are different.

Foreign Operations ---------- Module 10 ---------- 12

Part 2

OUTLINE

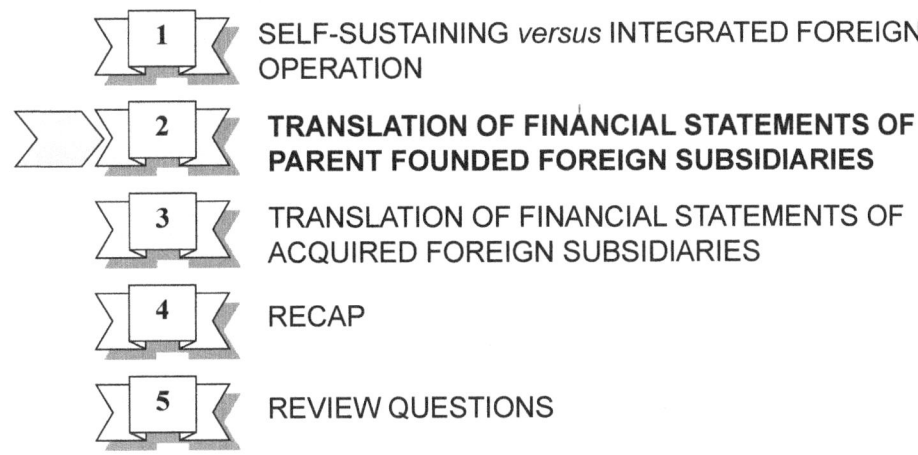

1. SELF-SUSTAINING *versus* INTEGRATED FOREIGN OPERATION
2. **TRANSLATION OF FINANCIAL STATEMENTS OF PARENT FOUNDED FOREIGN SUBSIDIARIES**
3. TRANSLATION OF FINANCIAL STATEMENTS OF ACQUIRED FOREIGN SUBSIDIARIES
4. RECAP
5. REVIEW QUESTIONS

Part 2

PART 2
Translation of Financial Statements of Parent Founded Foreign Subsidiaries

Objectives of this section

Illustrate the translation of financial statements of a parent founded foreign subsidiary.

Present the translation gain or loss in the financial statements.

Compute the translation gain or loss when the functional currency is different from that of the reporting entity.

Illustrate the consolidation process of parent founded subsisiaries located in a foreign country. <u>Particularities</u>: the investment in the subsidiary is accounted for using the cost method and there are no intercompany transactions.

Key concepts

- Accounting exposure
- Translation gain or loss

Part 2

TRANSLATION METHODS
Overview of the Illustrations Covered Next

Illustration 1: First year after creation (X1)

CASE 1 Functional currency ≠ Presentation currency
(Self-sustaining foreign operation)

CASE 2 Functional currency = Presentation currency
(Integrated foreign operation)

Illustration 2: Second year after creation (X2)

CASE 1 Functional currency ≠ Presentation currency
(Self-sustaining foreign operation)

CASE 2 Functional currency = Presentation currency
(Integrated foreign operation)

Part 2

TRANSLATION METHODS
Illustration #1
First Year After Creation

Early X1, Canado Company established a subsidiary in Sunia. The subsidiary was named Small Limited, and Canado's investment was $1,250,000. When the initial investment was translated into Sunian Fraser (SF), the currency of Sunia, the initial capitalization amounted to SF500,000. After being established, Small engaged in a few transactions, including the negotiation of a 3-year bank loan from a Sunian bank and the purchase of capital assets.

Exchange rate information for X1

- Initial investment: SF500,000 (1SF = $2.50)
- 3-year bank loan: SF200,000 (1SF = $2.40)
- Purchase of capital assets: SF600,000 (1SF = $2.30)
- Dividends are declared and paid at the end of the year
- 19X1 average exchange rate (A): $2.20.
- 19X1 year-end exchange rate (C): $2.00.

Part 2

TRANSLATION PROCESS
Illustration #1
When functional and presentation currencies are different

SELF-SUSTAINING FOREIGN OPERATION

STEPS	F/S	RATES
1	I/S	Average rate (A) for all revenues and expenses
2	RE	Average rate (A) for Dividends
3	SFP	Current rate (C) for all assets and liabilities Historical rate (H) for Share Capital
4	PLUG	(Cumulative)

Foreign Operations — Module 10 — 17

Part 2

Case #1: Functional Currency ≠ Presentation Currency
X1

	Local currency	Exchange rate	Canadian $
Revenue	SF220,000	2.20 (A)	$484,000
Depreciation expense	60,000	2.20 (A)	132,000
Interest expense	40,000	2.20 (A)	88,000
Other expenses	80,000	2.20 (A)	176,000
Profit for the year	SF40,000		$88,000
Cash	SF160,000	2.00 (C)	$320,000
Accounts receivable	30,000	2.00 (C)	60,000
Capital assets	600,000	2.00 (C)	1,200,000
Acc. depreciation	(60,000)	2.00 (C)	(120,000)
Total assets	SF730,000		$1,460,000
Accounts payable	SF20,000	2.00 (C)	$40,000
Note payable, long term	200,000	2.00 (C)	400,000
	220,000		440,000
Share capital	500,000	2.50 (H)	1,250,000
Retained earnings	10,000		22,000
Translation Loss	-		(252,000)
Total liabilities and equity	SF730,000		$1,460,000
Profit for the year	SF40,000	(see step #1)	$88,000
Dividends	(30,000)	2.20 (A)	(66,000)
Retained earnings (end)	SF10,000		$22,000

Steps: 1 (I/S), 3 (SFP), 4 (Translation Loss), 2 (RE)

Part 2

TRANSLATION PROCESS
Illustration #2
When functional and presentation currencies are the same

INTEGRATED FOREIGN OPERATION

STEPS	F/S	RATES
1	I/S	**Average** rate (A) for revenues and expenses that accrue evenly **Historical** rate (H) otherwise
2	RE	**Historical** rate (H) for Dividends
3	SFP	**Current** rate (C) for monetary and current valued balances **Historical** rate (H) otherwise
4	PLUG	(Cumulative)

Part 2

TRANSLATION PROCESS
When functional and presentation currencies are the same

Consistent with the concept of interdependence, since Subsidiary typically operates as an extension of the Parent in the foreign country, transactions conducted by Subsidiary can be viewed as transactions conducted by Parent. Therefore, the translation method adopts the basic translation rules described in Module 9. In fact, when the functional and presentation currencies are similar, the translation method should be the same as the method used by Parent for reporting the results of its foreign currency transactions.

Hence, the **current** exchange rate (year-end spot rate or closing rate) is used to translate monetary balances (including non-monetary balances reported at FV), whereas the **historical** exchange rate (exchange rate that existed when the element was first recognized) is used to translate the income statement and non-monetary balances reported at historical cost.

Part 2

Case #2: Functional Currency = Presentation Currency
X1

	Local currency	Exchange rate	Canadian $
Revenue	SF220,000	2.20 (A)	$484,000
Depreciation expense	60,000	2.30 (H)	138,000
Interest expense	40,000	2.20 (A)	88,000
Other expenses	80,000	2.20 (A)	176,000
Profit for the year	SF40,000		$82,000
Cash	SF160,000	2.00 (C)	$320,000
Accounts receivable	30,000	2.00 (C)	60,000
Capital assets	600,000	2.30 (H)	1,380,000
Acc. depreciation	(60,000)	2.30 (H)	(138,000)
Total assets	SF730,000		$1,622,000
Accounts payable	SF20,000	2.00 (C)	$40,000
Note payable, long term	200,000	2.00 (C)	400,000
	220,000		440,000
Share capital	500,000	2.50 (H)	1,250,000
Retained earnings	10,000		22,000
Translation Loss	—		**(90,000)**
Total liabilities and equity	SF730,000		$1,622,000
Profit for the year	SF 40,000	(see step #1)	$82,000
Dividends	(30,000)	2.00 (H)	(60,000)
Retained earnings (end)	SF10,000		$22,000

Sections labelled: 1 (income statement), 3 (balance sheet), 4 (Translation Loss), 2 (retained earnings reconciliation).

Part 2

ACCOUNTING EXPOSURE

ACCOUNTS TRANSLATED AT THE CURRENT EXCHANGE RATE

When functional currencies are the **SAME** → Net balance of monetary & current valued assets & liabilities

When functional currencies are **DIFFERENT** → Net investment

Only balances that are translated at current rate give rise to translation gains or losses since the rate at which they are translated keeps changing. We refer to these balances as the **accounting exposure**.

Foreign Operations ---------- Module 10 ----------

Part 2

TRANSLATION LOSS OF X1
When the Functional Currency is Different from that of the Reporting Entity

BREAKDOWN OF THE TRANSLATION LOSS INTO ITS CORE COMPONENTS

1 NET INVESTMENT AT THE BEGINNING OF X1 : SF500,000
CHANGE IN EXCHANGE RATE FROM 2.50 (H) TO 2.00 (C)

Exchange loss

SF500,000 (2.50 – 2.00) = $250,000

2 CHANGE IN NET INVESTMENT (RETAINED EARNINGS) DURING THE YEAR: SF10,000
CHANGE IN EXCHANGE RATE FROM 2.20 (A) TO 2.00 (C)

Exchange loss

SF10,000 (2.20 – 2.00) = $2,000

Total translation loss: $252,000

Part 2

REPORTING FOR TRANSLATION GAIN (LOSS)
Basic Rules

WHERE THE TRANSLATION GAINS AND LOSSES ARE REPORTED

When functional currencies are the **SAME**	When functional currencies are **DIFFERENT**
Profit for the year	**OCI**

When the functional currencies are different, the net gain or loss that arises from the translation is not recognized in the net income, but reported as OCI. In this context, we assume that the gain or loss has no impact on the parent's cash flows, the accounting exposure being limited to the net investment of the parent in the foreign operation.

Part 2

REPORTING FOR TRANSLATION GAIN (LOSS)
Year X1

Functional Currency = Presentation Currency

Exchange Losses	90,000	
Translation Loss		90,000

Functional Currency ≠ Presentation Currency

Other Comprehensive Income	252,000	
Translation Loss		252,000

Working Paper Entries

Part 2

CONSOLIDATION OF SMALL
Year Ended December X1
Consolidation Entry

Double-Counting

Common Shares (Small)	1,250,000	
Investment in Small (Canado)		1,250,000

Double-counting of $1,250,000 is the amount initially invested by Canado at the establishment of Small. This amount also matches the translated balance of Share Capital (Common Shares) of Small using the historical exchange rate. To simplify, we assume that there are no intercompany transactions. Therefore, the elimination of the double-counting is the only entry required in order to consolidate the F/S of Canado at December 31, X1.

Part 2

ACCOUNTING FOR FOREIGN OPERATIONS
Recap

STEPS	DESCRIPTION
1	**Determine** the functional currencies of the parent and its foreign operation
2	**Select** the translation method
3	**Translate** the F/S of the foreign operation
4	**Compute** the translation gain or loss that arises from the translation
5	**Report** the translation gain or loss in the F/S
6	**Combine** the F/S

Part 2

TRANSLATION METHODS
Illustration #2
Second Year After Creation

Exchange rate information for X2

- Purchase of Land : SF200,000 (1SF = $1.90)
- Dividends are declared and paid at the end of the year
- 19X2 average exchange rate (A): $1.70
- 19X2 year-end exchange rate (C): $1.50

Part 2

Case #1: Functional Currency ≠ Presentation Currency
X2

	Local currency	Exchange rate	Canadian $
1			
Revenue	SF300,000	1.70 (A)	$510,000
Depreciation expense	60,000	1.70 (A)	102,000
Interest expense	40,000	1.70 (A)	68,000
Other expenses	120,000	1.70 (A)	204,000
Profit for the year	SF80,000		$136,000
3			
Cash	SF30,000	1.50 (C)	$45,000
Accounts receivable	40,000	1.50 (C)	60,000
Land	200,000	1.50 (C)	300,000
Capital assets	600,000	1.50 (C)	900,000
Acc. depreciation	(120,000)	1.50 (C)	(180,000)
Total assets	SF750,000		$1,125,000
Accounts payable	SF10,000	1.50 (C)	$15,000
Note payable, long term	200,000	1.50 (C)	300,000
	210,000		315,000
Share capital	500,000	2.50 (H)	1,250,000
Retained earnings	40,000		73,000
4 Translation Loss	—		(513,000)
Total liabilities and equity	SF750,000		$1,125,000
2			
Retained earnings (beg.)	SF10,000	(see Year X1)	$22,000
Profit for the year	80,000	(see step #1)	136,000
Dividends	(50,000)	1.70 (A)	(85,000)
Retained earnings (end)	SF40,000		$73,000

Case #2: Functional Currency = Presentation Currency
X2

	Local currency	Exchange rate	Canadian $
1			
Revenue	SF300,000	1.70 (A)	$510,000
Depreciation expense	60,000	2.30 (H)	138,000
Interest expense	40,000	1.70 (A)	68,000
Other expenses	120,000	1.70 (A)	204,000
Profit for the year	FS80,000		$100,000
3			
Cash	SF30,000	1.50 (C)	$45,000
Accounts receivable	40,000	1.50 (C)	60,000
Land	200,000	1.90 (H)	380,000
Capital assets	600,000	2.30 (H)	1,380,000
Acc. depreciation	(120,000)	2.30 (H)	(276,000)
Total assets	SF750,000		$1,589,000
Accounts payable	SF10,000	1.50 (C)	$15,000
Note payable, long term	200,000	1.50 (C)	300,000
	210,000		315,000
Share capital	500,000	2.50 (H)	1,250,000
Retained earnings	40,000		47,000
4 Translation Loss	—		(23,000)
Total liabilities and equity	SF750,000		$1,589,000
2			
Retained earnings (beg.)	SF10,000	(see Year X1)	$22,000
Profit for the year	80,000	(see step #1)	100,000
Dividends	(50,000)	1.50 (H)	(75,000)
Retained earnings (end)	SF40,000		$47,000

Part 2

TRANSLATION LOSS OF X2
When the Functional Currency is Different from that of the Reporting Entity

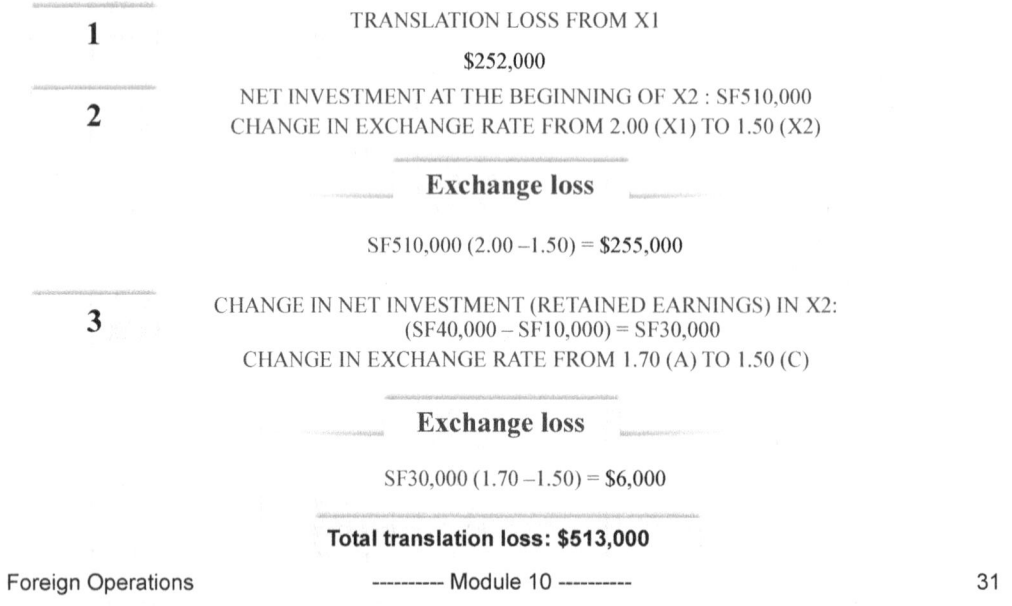

1 — TRANSLATION LOSS FROM X1
$252,000

2 — NET INVESTMENT AT THE BEGINNING OF X2 : SF510,000
CHANGE IN EXCHANGE RATE FROM 2.00 (X1) TO 1.50 (X2)

Exchange loss

SF510,000 (2.00 – 1.50) = $255,000

3 — CHANGE IN NET INVESTMENT (RETAINED EARNINGS) IN X2:
(SF40,000 – SF10,000) = SF30,000
CHANGE IN EXCHANGE RATE FROM 1.70 (A) TO 1.50 (C)

Exchange loss

SF30,000 (1.70 – 1.50) = $6,000

Total translation loss: $513,000

Part 2

REPORTING FOR TRANSLATION GAIN (LOSS)
Year X2

Functional Currency = Presentation Currency

Retained Earnings	90,000
Exchange Gains	67,000
Translation Loss	23,000

Functional Currency ≠ Presentation Currency

Other Comprehensive Income	261,000
Accumulated – OCI	252,000
Translation Loss	513,000

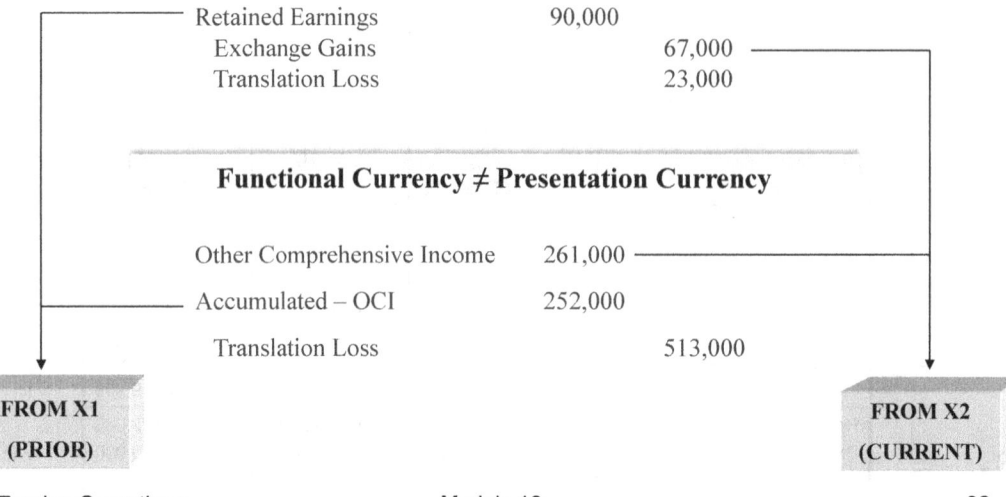

FROM X1 (PRIOR) — FROM X2 (CURRENT)

Part 2

CONSOLIDATION OF SMALL
Year Ended December 31 X2
Consolidation Entry

Double-Counting

Common Shares (Small)	1,250,000	
Investment in Small (Canado)		1,250,000

Recall that double-counting of $1,250,000 is the amount initially invested by Canado at the establishment of Small. Assuming that there are still no intercompany transactions, the recurring elimination of the double-counting is the only entry required in order to consolidate the F/S of Canado at December 31, X2.

Foreign Operations ---------- Module 10 ---------- 33

Part 3

OUTLINE

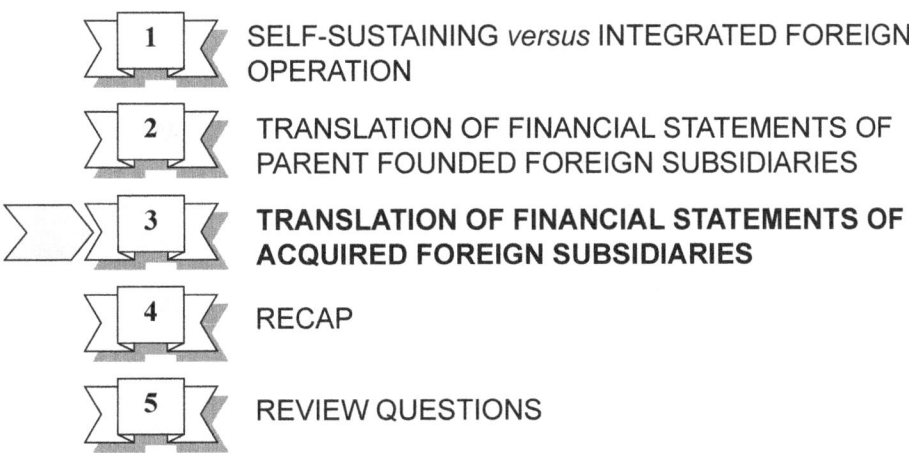

1. SELF-SUSTAINING *versus* INTEGRATED FOREIGN OPERATION
2. TRANSLATION OF FINANCIAL STATEMENTS OF PARENT FOUNDED FOREIGN SUBSIDIARIES
3. **TRANSLATION OF FINANCIAL STATEMENTS OF ACQUIRED FOREIGN SUBSIDIARIES**
4. RECAP
5. REVIEW QUESTIONS

Foreign Operations ---------- Module 10 ---------- 34

PART 3
Translation of Financial Statements of Acquired Foreign Subsidiaries

Objectives of this section

Contrast the translation of financial statements of acquired subsidiaries with that of parent founded subsidiaries.

Illustrate the consolidation process of foreign subsidiaries at the date of acquisition.

ILLUSTRATION

Assume that on January 01, X1, Canado Company, a Canadian based company, acquires all the outstanding voting stocks of Small Limited, a foreign subsidiary located in Sunia. The purchase price is $1,300,000, paid cash.

At date of acquisition, 1 Sunian Fraser (SF) is equal to $2.50, and Small's fair values of identifiable net assets are equal to book values.

Required

Prepare the consolidated statement of financial position of Canado at the date of acquisition.

FINANCIAL STATEMENT TRANSLATION
When Foreign Subsidiaries are Acquired

For assets and liabilities at date of acquisition

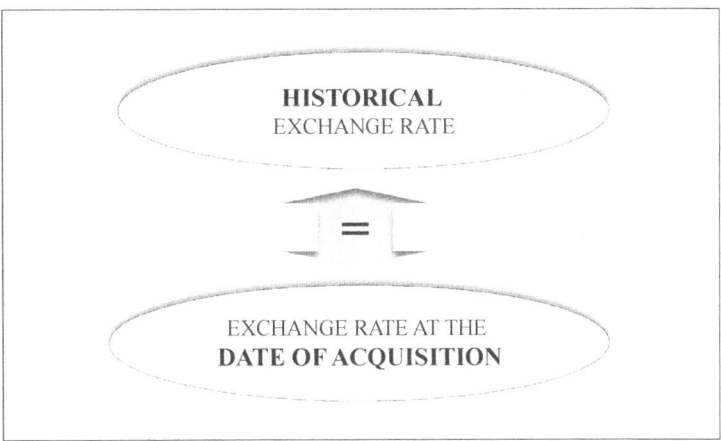

TRANSLATION OF SMALL'S STATEMENT OF FINANCIAL POSITION
At Date of Acquisition

	Local currency	Exchange rate at acquisition	Canadian $
Cash	SF160,000	2.50	$400,000
Accounts receivable	30,000	2.50	75,000
Capital assets	600,000	2.50	1,500,000
Acc. depreciation	(60,000)	2.50	(150,000)
Total assets	SF730,000		$1,825,000
Accounts payable	SF20,000	2.50	$50,000
Note payable, long term	200,000	2.50	500,000
Share capital	500,000	2.50	1,250,000
Retained earnings	10,000	2.50	25,000
Total liabilities and equity	SF730,000		$1,825,000

The translated financial statements of Small at date of acquisition are now used for consolidation, starting with the allocation of the purchase price.

Part 3

PURCHASE PRICE ALLOCATION

Purchase price		$1,300,000
Net book value of Small:		
- Common shares	$1,250,000	
- Retained earnings	25,000	1,275,000
Price differential		25,000
Goodwill		$25,000

The purchase price allocation is based on the translated figures.

Foreign Operations ---------- Module 10 ----------

Part 3

CONSOLIDATION OF SMALL AT THE DATE OF ACQUISITION
Consolidation Entries
Elimination of the Investment Account

1a- Double-Counting of $1,275,000

Common Shares (Small)	1,250,000	
Retained Earnings (Small)	25,000	
Investment in Small (Canado)		1,275,000

1b- Price Differential of $25,000

Goodwill (Small)	25,000	
Investment in Small (Canado)		25,000

Investment: $1,300,000

Foreign Operations ---------- Module 10 ----------

Part 3

ADDITIONAL ASPECTS OF TRANSLATION
Cost of Goods Sold

	Functional currency ≠ Presentation currency	Functional currency = Presentation currency
INVENTORY at the beginning	**AVERAGE** RATE	HISTORICAL RATE
PURCHASE during the year	**AVERAGE** RATE	AVERAGE RATE
INVENTORY at the end	**AVERAGE** RATE	HISTORICAL RATE

Part 4

OUTLINE

1. SELF-SUSTAINING *versus* INTEGRATED FOREIGN OPERATION

2. TRANSLATION OF FINANCIAL STATEMENTS OF PARENT FOUNDED FOREIGN SUBSIDIARIES

3. TRANSLATION OF FINANCIAL STATEMENTS OF ACQUIRED FOREIGN SUBSIDIARIES

4. **RECAP**

5. REVIEW QUESTIONS

PART 4
Recap

On January 1, X8, Power Company, a Canadian based company, purchased a controlling interest in Excel Management Consultants (EMC) located in Ziba. EMC's financial statements for the year ended December 31, X8, stated in Ziba currency (Z), are reported below.

Statement of financial position		Income Statement	
Assets		Revenue	Z 75,000
Cash & Receivables	Z 55,000	Operating expenses	27,000
Net property, plant & Equip. (net)	37,000	Depreciation	3,000
Total assets	Z 92,000	Profit for the year	45,000
Liabilities and Equity		Retained earnings (beginning)	Z 10,000
Accounts payable	Z 32,000		55,000
		Dividends	(15,000)
Share capital	20,000	Retained earnings (end)	Z 40,000
Retained earnings	40,000		
Total liabilities and equity	Z 92,000		

ILLUSTRATION
(continued...)

Exchange rates

- January 1, X8   Z1.00 = C$0.5987
- December 31, X8   Z1.00 = C$0.5321
- Dividend declaration & payment   Z1.00 = C$0.5810
- Average for X8   Z1.00 = C$0.5654

Required

Translate the financial statements of EMC at December 31, X8, into Canadian dollars, assuming:

1) the functional currency is different from that of the reporting entity (EMC is a self-sustaining operation),

2) the functional currency is the same as that of the reporting entity (EMC is an integrated operation).

In each case, treat the translation gain or loss as a single, balancing figure (PLUG).

Part 4

Functional Currency ≠ Presentation Currency
X8

	Local currency	Exchange rate	Canadian $
Revenue	Z 75,000	0.5654 (A)	$ 42,405
Operating exp. & Deprec.	30,000	0.5654 (A)	16,962
Profit for the year	Z 45,000		$ 25,443
Cash & Receivables	Z 55,000	0.5321 (C)	$ 29,266
Capital assets	37,000	0.5321 (C)	19,688
Total assets	Z 92,000		$ 48,954
Accounts payable	Z 32,000	0.5321 (C)	$ 17,027
Share capital	20,000	0.5987 (H)	11,974
Retained earnings	40,000		22,949
Translation Loss			(2,996)
Total liabilities and equity	$ 92,000		$ 48,954
Retained earnings (beg.)	Z 10,000	0.5987 (H)	$ 5,987
Profit for the year	45,000	(see step #1)	25,443
Dividends	(15,000)	0.5654 (A)	(8,481)
Retained earnings (end)	Z 40,000		$ 22,949

Foreign Operations ---------- Module 10 ----------

Part 4

Functional Currency = Presentation Currency
X8

	Local currency	Exchange rate	Canadian $
Revenue	Z 75,000	0.5654 (A)	$ 42,405
Operating expenses	27,000	0.5654 (A)	15,266
Depreciation	3,000	0.5987 (H)	1,796
Profit for the year	Z 45,000		$ 25,343
Cash & Receivables	Z 55,000	0.5321 (C)	$ 29,266
Capital assets	37,000	0.5987 (H)	22,152
Total assets	Z 92,000		$ 51,418
Accounts payable	Z 32,000	0.5321 (C)	$ 17,027
Share capital	20,000	0.5987 (H)	11,974
Retained earnings	40,000		22,615
Translation Loss			(198)
Total liabilities and equity	$ 92,000		$ 51,418
Retained earnings (beg.)	Z 10,000	0.5987 (H)	$ 5,987
Profit for the year	45,000	(see step #1)	25,343
Dividends	(15,000)	0.5810 (H)	(8,715)
Retained earnings (end)	Z 40,000		$ 22,615

Foreign Operations ---------- Module 10 ----------

Part 4

TRANSLATION LOSS OF X8
When the Functional Currency is Different from that of the Reporting Entity

1 — NET INVESTMENT AT THE BEGINNING OF X8 (date of acquisition):
(CS of Z20,000 + RE of Z10,000) = Z30,000
CHANGE IN EXCHANGE RATE FROM 0.5987 (H) TO 0.5321 (C)

Exchange loss

Z30,000 (0.5987 − 0.5321) = $1,997

2 — CHANGE IN NET INVESTMENT (RETAINED EARNINGS) DURING THE YEAR: Z30,000
CHANGE IN EXCHANGE RATE FROM 0.5654 (A) TO 0.5321 (C)

Exchange loss

Z30,000 (0.5654 − 0.5321) = $999

Total translation loss: $2,996

Part 4

REPORTING FOR TRANSLATION GAIN (LOSS)
Year X8

Functional Currency = Presentation Currency

Exchange Losses	198	
Translation Loss		198

Functional Currency ≠ Presentation Currency

Other Comprehensive Income	2,996	
Translation Loss		2,996

Part 5

OUTLINE

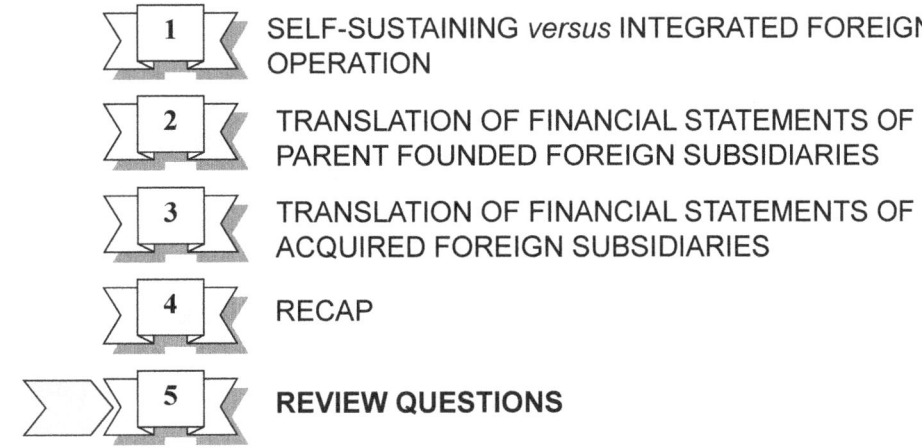

1. SELF-SUSTAINING *versus* INTEGRATED FOREIGN OPERATION
2. TRANSLATION OF FINANCIAL STATEMENTS OF PARENT FOUNDED FOREIGN SUBSIDIARIES
3. TRANSLATION OF FINANCIAL STATEMENTS OF ACQUIRED FOREIGN SUBSIDIARIES
4. RECAP
5. **REVIEW QUESTIONS**

Part 5

PART 5
Review Questions

1. Define or explain the following terms:
   - Self-sustaining foreign operation
   - Integrated foreign operation
   - Presentation currency
   - Accounting exposure ; Translation gain or loss

2. At what exchange rate would the retained earnings account of a foreign subsidiary be translated? Explain.

3. Explain how to determine the amount of translation gain or loss when the functional currency is different from that of the reporting entity?

4. In what general ways will consolidation of a foreign subsidiary differ from consolidation of a Canadian subsidiary at the date of acquisition?

5. How should the translation gain or loss be reported when the functional currency is different from the presentation currency?

REVIEW QUESTIONS
(continued...)

6. Name three factors that could be used to determine if the functional currency is different from that of the reporting entity.

7. What is the rationale underlying the use of the translation method when the functional currency is different from that of the reporting entity?

8. What is the rationale underlying the use of the translation method when the functional currency is the same as that of the reporting entity?

9. Is the amount of gain or loss from the translation of financial statements affected by the translation method used? Explain.

10. What is the accounting exposure under each translation method?

Exercise 10-1
Translation - Statement of Financial Position

Tool Corporation is a foreign subsidiary of a Canadian parent company. Tool is located in the country of Macrale. The statement of financial position of Tool, stated in Macra (M), is presented below.

	Local currency
Cash	M 20,000
Accounts receivable	10,000
Inventory	60,000
Capital assets	200,000
Acc. depreciation	(80,000)
Long-term note receivable	50,000
Total assets	**M 260,000**
Accounts & notes payable	M 40,000
Bonds payable	150,000
Share capital	70,000
Total liabilities and equity	**M 260,000**

Additional information

1. Tool is wholly owned by Canado. Canado established Tool when the Macra was worth C$2.00.
2. The capital assets were purchased when the Macra was worth C$2.40.
3. The bonds payable were issued when the exchange rate for the Macra was worth C$2.30.
4. The long-term note receivable arose when the Macra was worth C$2.60.
5. The inventory was purchased when the Macra was worth C$2.80.
6. The current exchange rate for the Macra is C$3.00.

Required
Translate the statement of financial position of Tool Corporation into Canadian dollars, assuming that:

- The functional currency of Tool is different from that of Canado,
- The functional currency of Tool is the same as that of Canado.

In each case, treat the translation gain or loss as a single, balancing figure (PLUG).

Complete the following chart.

		Functional currencies are	
		different	*the same*
Cash	M 20,000		
Accounts receivable	10,000		
Inventory (at market)	60,000		
Capital assets	200,000		
Accumulated dep.	(80,000)		
Long-term note receiv.	50,000		
Total assets	**M 260,000**		
Accounts and notes payable	M 40,000		
Bonds payable	150,000		
Share capital	70,000		
Translation gain (loss)			
Total equities	**M 260,000**		

Exercise 10-2
Translation – Income Statement

Slam Corporation is a foreign subsidiary of a Canadian parent company. Slam is located in the country of Francis. The income statement of Slam for X7, stated in Franco (F), is presented below.

	Local currency
Sales revenue	F 3,000,000
Cost of goods sold:	
Beginning Inventory	F 200,000
Purchases	1,000,000
Ending Inventory	(400,000)
	F 800,000
Depreciation	300,000
Other operating expenses	900,000
Interest expenses	200,000
Total expenses	F 2,200,000
Profit for the year	**F 800,000**

Additional information

1. Slam is wholly owned by Brown, a company located in Canada.
2. Sales revenue, purchases of inventory, and operating expenses all occurred evenly through the year, but was all paid at the end of the year.
3. The beginning inventory was purchased on October 1, X6, when the exchange rate for the Franco was worth C$0.82. The ending inventory was purchased on November 1, X7, when the Franco was worth C$0.93.
4. The capital assets were acquired when the Franco was worth C$0.70.
5. Exchange rate for December 31, X6, is C$0.85, and December 31, X7, C$0.95. The average exchange rate for X7 is C$0.90.

Required

Translate the income statement of Slam Corporation into Canadian dollars assuming that:

- The functional currency of Slam is different from that of Brown,
- The functional currency of Slam is the same as that of Brown.

Complete the following chart.

		Functional currencies are	
		different	*the same*

Sales   F3,000,000

COGS

- Inventory (beg.)   200,000
- Purchases   1,000,000
- Inventory (end)   (400,000)

                              800,000

Depreciation   300,000

Other expenses   900,000

Interest expense   200,000

Profit for the year   **F 800,000**

Exercise 10-3
Translation of Financial Statements and Translation Gain/Loss

On December 31, X6, Parent Company of Ottawa acquired 100% of the voting stock of Pepper Company of Philipp. On this date, the fair values of Pepper's assets and liabilities were equal to their carrying values.

Pepper's financial statements for the year ended December 31, X7, stated in Philippo (P), are reported below.

Financial Position	X7	X6
Assets		
Cash	P 80,000	P 60,000
Accounts receivable	140,000	80,000
Inventory	110,000	80,000
Plant & Equip. (net)	250,000	280,000
Total assets	**P 580,000**	**P 500,000**
Liabilities and Equity		
Accounts payable	P 150,000	P 115,000
Bonds payable	120,000	120,000
Share capital	140,000	140,000
Retained earnings	170,000	125,000
Total liabilities and equity	**P 580,000**	**P 500,000**

Income Statement	
Sales revenue	P 850,000
Cost of goods sold	500,000
Gross margin	350,000
Depreciation	30,000
Other expenses	245,000
Profit for the year	**P 75,000**
Retained earnings (beg.)	P 125,000
Dividends	(30,000)
Retained earnings (end)	**P 170,000**

Additional information

1. Inventory on hand as at December 31, X6, and December 31, X7, was purchased evenly over the final three months of X6 and X7, respectively, from suppliers in Philipp. Sales and purchases occurred evenly throughout the year.
2. The plant and equipment on hand at December 31, X6, was originally acquired for P450 000 on January 1, X1. No plant and equipment was acquired or sold during X7.
3. Dividends were declared and paid on September 30, X7.
4. The bonds were issued on January 1, X2, and mature on December 31, X11.
5. The foreign exchange trend has little effect on Pepper's sales prices, which are largely determined by local competition.

Exchange rates were as follows:

- January 1, X1   P1.00 = C$0.60
- December 31, X7   P1.00 = C$0.90
- January 1, X2   P1.00 = C$0.70
- Average Oct.-Dec. X6   P1.00 = C$0.78
- December 31, X6/January 1, X7   P1.00 = C$0.80
- Average Oct.-Dec. X7   P1.00 = C$0.89
- July 1, X7   P1.00 = C$0.86
- Average for X7   P1.00 = C$0.85
- September 30, X7   P1.00 = C$0.88

Required

a) Based on the information provided, indicate if Pepper's functional currency is the same as that of Parent. State three facts from the problem to support your conclusion.
b) Translate the financial statements of Pepper for the year ended December 31, X7, first, assuming that Pepper's functional currency is different from that of the reporting entity, second, assuming that the functional currencies are the same.
c) Calculate the cumulative translation adjustment on the December 31, X7, translated statement of financial position.

		Functional currencies are	
		different	*the same*
Cash	P 80,000		
Accounts receivable	140,000		
Inventory	110,000		
Plant and equip. (net)	250,000		
Total assets	**P 580,000**		
Accounts payable	P 150,000		
Bonds payable	120,000		
Share capital	140,000		
Retained earnings	170,000		
Translation gain (loss)			
Total equities	**P 580,000**		
Sales	P 850,000		
COGS			
➢ Inventory (beg.)	80,000		
➢ Purchases	530,000		
➢ Inventory (end)	(110,000)		
	500,000		
Depreciation	30,000		
Other expenses	245,000		
Profit for the year	**P 75,000**		

Exercise 10-4
Translation of Financial Statements

On December 31, X2, Manufacturing Ltd. from Edmonton acquired 100 percent of the outstanding voting shares of Sandora Ltd, a company located in Flint, Michigan.

The price for the acquisition has been set at US 13,000,000. All of Sandora's identifiable assets and liabilities had fair values that were equal to their carrying values except for the capital asset which had a fair value that was US 500,000 higher than its stated value. The capital assets had a remaining useful life of 10 years at the date of acquisition.

The following presents the comparative statements of financial position and the income statement of Sandora for X3.

Sandora Ltd.
Statements of Financial Position
At December 31, X3

	X3	X2
Cash	US 780,000	US 900,000
Account receivable	6,100,000	4,800,000
Inventory	5,700,000	6,300,000
Capital assets (net)	6,600,000	7,200,000
	US 19,180,00	US 19,200,000
Current liabilities	US 1,900,000	US 2,400,000
Bonds payable	4,800,000	4,800,000
Share capital	5,000,000	5,000,000
Retained earnings	7,480,000	7,000,000
	US 19,180,000	US 19,200,000

Income Statement – X3

Sales	US 6,000,000
Cost of goods sold	4,440,000
	1,560,000
Depreciation	600,000
Others expenses	360,000
Profit for the year	**US 600,000**

Additional information

1. Exchange rate:
   - December 31, X2   US 1 = Cdn $ 0.86
   - September 30, X3   US 1 = Cdn $ 0.82
   - December 31, X3   US 1 = Cdn $ 0.80
   - X3 average   US 1 = Cdn $ 0.83

2. On September 30, X3 Sandora paid dividends.
3. The ending inventory has been acquired when the exchange rate was US 1 = Cdn $ 0.81.

Required

Translate the X3 statement of financial position and income statement for Sandora Ltd assuming:

a) Sandora Ltd is a self-sustaining subsidiary (functional currencies are different).
b) Sandora Ltd is an integrated subsidiary (functional currencies are the same).

Complete the following chart.

Copyright © 2020, Parmitech, Ottawa. Parmitech. All rights reserved.

		Functional currencies are	
		different	*the same*
Cash	US 780,000		
Accounts receivable	6,100,000		
Inventory	5,700,000		
Capital assets (net)	6,600,000		
Total assets	**US19,180,000**		
Current liabilities	US1,900,000		
Bonds payable	4,800,000		
Share capital	5,000,000		
Retained earnings	7,480,000		
Translation gain (loss)			
Total equities	**US19,180,000**		
Sales	US6,000,000		
COGS			
➢ Inventory (beg.)			
➢ Purchases			
➢ Inventory (end)			
	4,440,000		
Depreciation	600,000		
Other expenses	360,000		
Profit for the year	**US 600,000**		

Copyright © 2020, Parmitech, Ottawa. Parmitech. All rights reserved.

Solutions to Exercises

10-1

Translated statements of financial position of Tool Corporation:

			Functional currencies *are different*		Functional currencies *are the same*
Cash	M 20,000	@ 3.00	$60,000	@ 3.00	$60,000
Accounts receivable	10,000	@ 3.00	30,000	@ 3.00	30,000
Inventory (at market)	60,000	@ 3.00	180,000	@ 3.00	180,000
Capital assets	200,000	@ 3.00	600,000	@ 2.40	480,000
Accumulated dep.	(80,000)	@ 3.00	(240,000)	@ 2.40	(192,000)
Long-term note Rec.	50,000	@ 3.00	150,000	@ 3.00	150,000
Total assets	**M 260,000**		**$780,000**		**$708,000**
Accounts and notes payable	M 40,000	@ 3.00	$120,000	@ 3.00	$120,000
Bonds payable	150,000	@ 3.00	450,000	@ 3.00	450,000
Share capital	70,000	@ 2.00	140,000	@ 2.00	140,000
Translation gain (loss)	–		70,000		(2,000)
Total equities	**M 260,000**		**$780,000**		**$708,000**

10-2

	Functional currencies *are different*		Functional currencies *are the same*	
	rate @ 0.90			
Sales	$2,700,000		0.90	$2,700,000
Cost of goods sold:				
Beginning inventory	180,000		0.82	164,000
Purchases	900,000		0.90	900,000
Ending inventory	(360,000)		0.93	(372,000)
	720,000			692,000
Depreciation	270,000		0.70	210,000
Other expenses	810,000		0.90	810,000
Interest expense	180,000		0.90	180,000
Total expenses	1,980,000			1,892,000
Profit for the year	**$720,000**			**$808,000**

Note: the interest, like all expenses, is translated at the rate in effect when the expense is incurred, rather than when it is paid.

10-3

a) It appears that Pepper's functional currency is different from that of Parent based on the following:
- Inventory is purchased from suppliers in Philipp.
- Sales prices are largely immune to changes in exchange rates.
- Sales prices are determined largely by local competition.

b) Translation of Pepper's financial statements – X7

			Functional currencies *are different*		Functional currencies *are the same*
Sales	P850,000	@ 0.85	$722,500	@ 0.85	$722,500
Inventory, January 1	80,000	@ 0.85	68,000	@ 0.80	64,000
Purchases (1)	530,000	@ 0.85	450,500	@ 0.85	450,500
Inventory, December 31	(110,000)	@ 0.85	(93,500)	@ 0.89	(97,900)
Amortization expense	30,000	@ 0.85	25,500	@ 0.80	24,000
Other expenses	245,000	@ 0.85	208,250	@ 0.85	208,250
Profit for the year	**P 75,000**		**$ 63,750**		**$ 73,650**
Retained earnings, January 1, X7	P125,000	@ 0.80	$100,000	@ 0.80	$100,000
Dividends paid	(30,000)	@ 0.85	(25,500)	@ 0.88	(26,400)
December 31, X7	**P170,000**		**$138,250**		**$147,250**
Cash	P 80,000	@ 0.90	$72,000	@ 0.90	$72,000
Accounts receivable	140,000	@ 0.90	126,000	@ 0.90	126,000
Inventory (at market)	110,000	@ 0.90	99,000	@ 0.90	99,000
Plant & equip. (net)	250,000	@ 0.90	225,000	@ 0.80	200,000
Total assets	**P580,000**		**$522,000**		**$497,000**
Accounts payable	P150,000	@ 0.90	$135,000	@ 0.90	$135,000
Bonds payable	120,000	@ 0.90	108,000	@ 0.90	108,000
Translation gain (loss)			28,750		(5,250)
Share capital	140,000	@ 0.80	112,000	@ 0.80	112,000
Retained earnings	170,000	As translated	138,250	As translated	147,250
Total equities	**P580,000**		**$522,000**		**$497,000**

(1) Purchases = (500,000 + 110,000 – 80,000) = P530,000

a) Translation gain for X7 (when the functional currencies are different)

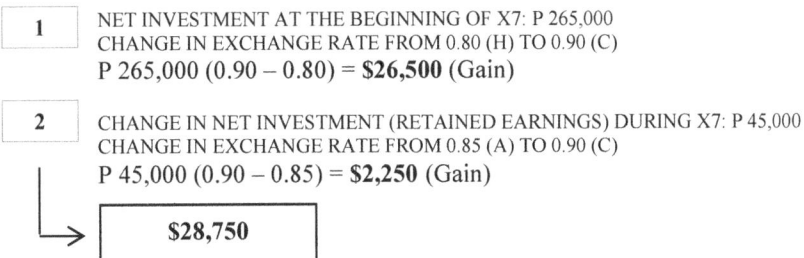

10-4

Translation of Sandora's financial statements – X3

			Functional currencies *are different*		**Functional currencies** *are the same*	
Sales	US6,000,000	@ 0.83	$4,980,000	@ 0.83	$4,980,000	
Inventory, January 1	6,300,000	@ 0.83	5,229,000	@ 0.86	5,418,000	
Purchases	3,840,000	@ 0.83	3,187,200	@ 0.83	3,187,000	
Inventory, Dec. 31	(5,700,000)	@ 0.83	(4,731,000)	@ 0.81	(4,617,000)	
Amortization exp.	600,000	@ 0.83	498,000	@ 0.86	516,000	
Other expenses	360,000	@ 0.83	298,800	@ 0.83	298,800	
Profit for the year	**US600,000**		**$498,000**		**$177,000**	
Retained earnings, January 1, X3	US7,000,000	@ 0.86	$6,020,000	@ 0.86	$6,020,000	
Dividends paid	(120,000)	@ 0.83	(99,600)	@ 0.82	(98,400)	
December 31, X3	**US7,440,000**		**$6,418,400**		**$6,098,600**	
Cash	US780,000	@ 0.80	$624,000	@ 0.80	$624,000	
Accounts receivable	6,100,000	@ 0.80	4,880,000	@ 0.80	4,880,000	
Inventory	5,700,000	@ 0.80	4,560,000	@ 0.81	4,617,000	
Capital assets (net)	6,600,000	@ 0.80	5,280,000	@ 0.86	5,676,000	
Total assets	**US19,180,000**		**$15,344,000**		**$15,797,000**	
Current liabilites	US1,900,000	@ 0.80	$1,520,000	@ 0.80	$1,520,000	
Bonds payable	4,800,000	@ 0.80	3,840,000	@ 0.80	3,840,000	
Translation G. (loss)			(734,400)		38,400	
Share capital	5,000,000	@ 0.86	4,300,000	@ 0.86	4,300,000	
Retained earnings	7,480,000	As translated	6,418,400	As translated	6,098,000	
Total equities	**US19,180,000**		**$15,344,000**		**$15,797,000**	